# Encyclopedic Dictionary of Applied Linguistics

## A Handbook for Language Teaching

*Edited by*
*Keith Johnson and Helen Johnson*

BLACKWELL
*Publishers*

Copyright © Blackwell Publishers Ltd 1998, 1999

First published 1998

Reprinted 1999

Blackwell Publishers Ltd
108 Cowley Road
Oxford OX4 1JF, UK

Blackwell Publishers Inc
350 Main Street
Malden, Massachusetts 02148, USA

*British Library Cataloguing in Publication Data*
A CIP catalogue record for this book is available from the British Library

*Library of Congress Cataloging in Publication Data*
Encyclopedic dictionary of applied linguistics: a handbook for language teaching /
    [edited by] Keith Johnson and Helen Johnson.
        p.   cm.
    Includes bibliographical references and index.
    ISBN  0–631–18089–3 —  ISBN  0–631–21482–8  (pbk)
    1. Applied linguistics—Dictionaries. I. Johnson, Keith, 1958–
II. Johnson, Helen.
    P129.E53    1998
    418'.003—dc21                                97–24551
                                                        CIP

The publishers apologise for any errors or omissions in the acknowledgements to
articles and would be grateful to be notified of any corrections that should be
incorporated in the next edition or reprint of this book.

Typeset in  10 ½ on 11 ½ pt Ehrhardt
by Graphicraft Typesetters Limited, Hong Kong
Printed and bound in Great Britain by MPG Books Ltd, Bodmin, Cornwall

This book is printed on acid-free paper

# Contents

# Figures

# Tables

# Contributors

**R. L. (Dick) Allwright**                                    RLA
Department of Linguistics and Modern English Language
Lancaster University

**Guy Cook**                                                  GC
Languages in Education
University of London Institute of Education

**Vivian Cook**                                               VJC
Department of Language and Linguistics
University of Essex

**Clare Furneaux**                                            CLF
Centre for Applied Language Studies
University of Reading

**Roger Hawkins**                                             RH
Department of Language and Linguistics
University of Essex

**Adam Jaworski**                                             AJ
Centre for Language and Communication Research
University of Wales, Cardiff

**Ewa Jaworska**                                              EJ
Linguistics Department
University of Wales, Bangor

**Keith Johnson**                                             KJ
Department of Linguistics and Modern English Language
Lancaster University

**Jo McDonough**                                              JMCD
EFL Unit
University of Essex

**Steven McDonough**                                          SMCD
Department of Language and Linguistics
University of Essex

**Kristyan Spelman Miller**                                   KSM
Department of Linguistic Science
University of Reading

**John Roberts**                                                    JTR
Department of Language and Linguistics
University of Essex

One entry ('Teaching reading') was provided by **Eddie Williams** (EW), Centre for Applied Language Studies, University of Reading.

# Preface

The *Encyclopedic Dictionary of Applied Linguistics* is, as its subtitle states, *A Handbook for Language Teaching*. It is intended for all those with an interest in the field of applied linguistics as it relates to second and foreign language education. The book will prove an invaluable source of reference for students following any course in the area of language teaching, as well as those professionally engaged in language education.

When the *Dictionary* was in preparation, entries were initially grouped under the three categories of language, language learning and language teaching. The team of contributors was assembled to provide expertise in these three general areas, and they have been allowed a degree of freedom in what they say. The aim has been to provide basic information, but occasional comments which reveal personal positions in regard to the topics considered have not been discouraged.

The entries vary in length, usually in proportion to their importance, but sometimes an important area has a short entry. One example is COMMUNICATIVE LANGUAGE TEACHING. The entry on this large topic is short because a series of larger entries (like COMMUNICATIVE METHODOLOGY and COMMUNICATIVE SYLLABUS) together cover the field. The short entry on COMMUNICATIVE LANGUAGE TEACHING refers readers to these longer entries.

Cross-referencing is achieved in two ways. Within the text, words which have their own alphabetical entries are printed in small capital letters, as in the paragraph above. There is also a comprehensive index to help readers track down topics which do not have entries dedicated to them.

Wherever we have felt it would save the reader a laborious search, we have permitted information to be repeated in more than one entry. Nearly all entries are accompanied by a bibliography. Sometimes items in these are marked with an asterisk, indicating the most important recommendations for further reading.

We wish to thank the contributors for their participation and co-operation in this large venture. Thanks also to Philip Carpenter of Blackwell Publishers for (among other things) the part he played in initiating the project, and to Steve Smith and Alison Dunnett for their support – and patience!

HJ
KJ
*Lancaster*
*May 1997*

# A

**accent** is the component of DIALECT which refers to pronunciation. Regional accents locate speakers geographically, e.g. British, American, Welsh, Scottish (with the exception of the non-localized RECEIVED PRONUNCIATION (RP) in the United Kingdom). Regional accents intersect with social ones which depend on the speaker's class, education, ethnicity and other characteristics.

BIBLIOGRAPHY
Trudgill, P. (1975). *Accent, Dialect and the School.* London: Edward Arnold.
Wells, J. C. (1982). *Accents of English*. Cambridge: Cambridge University Press.

AJ

**acculturation hypothesis** Some researchers have stressed the similarities between Second Language Acquisition and contact situations involving speakers of different languages, such as those in which PIDGINS AND CREOLES are found. The best-known is the acculturation model initially proposed by John Schumann (1978).

The starting-point is the resemblance of pidgin languages to L2 learners' languages, particularly in terms of the overall simplicity of SYNTAX. Schumann and two colleagues (Cancino, Rosansky and Schumann, 1974) originally studied six Spanish learners of different ages learning English in the USA over a period of ten months. Schumann's acculturation work focused on a single 33-year-old speaker of Spanish called Alberto, who showed noticeably less improvement than the others. Alberto's speech exhibited several characteristics of pidgin languages such as the lack of inflectional MORPHOLOGY. While certain morphemes such as plural *-s* (85%) and irregular past *-ed* (65%) were supplied by Alberto fairly consistently, others, such as regular past *-ed* and inversion, were supplied only 7% and 5% of the time respectively. The other five learners in the study proceeded through a sequence of acquisition for the auxiliary that went through *is, am, can, do, does, was, did* and *are*; Alberto only got as far as *is, am, can* and *are*. He used only four auxiliaries by the end of the observation period, having 'acquired' only *is* satisfactorily; the others had acquired from 4 to 18 auxiliaries.

The similarities between Alberto's speech and pidgins are, according to Schumann:

- both use a single negative marker *no* and have a rule that negation can be expressed through a formula of 'no + Verb' as in *I no see*
- both lack inversion of subject and verb, as in *Where the paper is?*; auxiliaries, as in *she crying*; possessive *-s*, as in *The king food*; present and past tense inflections, as in *Yesterday I talk with one friend*; and subject pronouns as in *no have holidays*
- both tend to use unmarked forms of the verb bereft of inflectional morphology

Alberto therefore appears to speak a pidginized English.

Why should the speech of an individual learner resemble the conventional communication language evolved by speakers of two languages? Schumann sees the cause as residing in the functions of language. Pidgin languages are used only for communicating ideas, never for bringing people together through language or for expressing the speaker's deepest emotional wants, since the speaker will always resort to the first language for these. A pidgin is a restricted language that serves only the communicative function (perhaps this is news to advocates of communicative language teaching who see communication as the highest function of language!); speakers of pidgins do not identify themselves primarily with the group who speak the pidgin but go back to their own group apart from purposes of contact. Alberto was of normal intelligence etc. What separated him from other learners was that he did not use English for social purposes, for instance, he did not go to classes or watch television and he listened to Spanish music. The pidginized nature of early L2 language is then due to the social isolation inherent in L2 learning, something which most learners overcome. But not, however, Alberto.

In the original research the concept of acculturation accounted for failure and success in L2 learning, 'acculturation' meaning social and psychological integration with the target group. Social factors are covered by the notion of social distance: if one group dominates the other, if one group isolates itself from the other, if one group is very small, and so on, social distance is high and success is consequently low. Psychological factors come down to psychological distance: if the person feels language shock at not being able to express themselves, or culture shock, or is poorly motivated then distance will be too great for success. Hence the theory largely applies to the relationships between groups in an immigrant situation, not to short-term visits or to foreign language situations. There was indeed a second concept of 'enculturation' that was invoked to describe people who learn an L2 in order to function in their own society; in England or in Russia in the past a 'gentleman' knew French, i.e. some foreign languages acquire status within a society

unrelated to their usefulness outside this group.

Intriguing as the idea was, little research support for it has materialized; an L2 theory cannot be based on the malfunctioning of a single L2 learner, the now notorious Alberto. A theme would appear to be that lack of successful interaction with native speakers is a key factor in failure to learn the L2 (*pace* a learner called Wes who led a fully integrated life in Hawaii but did *not* progress as expected). Roger Andersen (1990) has described a cognitive-interactionist model developing its themes within a broader cognitive perspective. The original links to creole studies have also been taken further in the BioProgram model of Derek Bickerton (1981), and the work of Andersen with nativization and denativization, for example, Andersen (1981).

BIBLIOGRAPHY
Andersen, R. W. (1981). Two perspectives on pidginization as Second Language Acquisition. In R. W. Andersen (ed.), *New Dimensions in Second Language Acquisition Research*. Rowley, MA: Newbury House.
——(1990). Models, processes, principles and strategies: second language acquisition inside and outside the classroom. In B. VanPatten, and J. F. Lee (eds), *Second Language Acquisition/Foreign Language Learning*. Clevedon: Multilingual Matters, 45–68.
Bickerton, D. (1981). *Roots of Language*. Ann Arbor, MI: Karoma.
Cancino, E., Rosansky, E. and Schumann, J. (1974). Testing hypotheses about second language acquisition: the copula and negative in three subjects. *Working Papers on Bilingualism*, 88–96.
Schumann, J. H. (1978). *The Pidginization Process: A Model for Second Language Acquisition*. Rowley, MA: Newbury House.*
——(1986). Research on the acculturation model for second language acquisition. *Journal of Multilingual and Multicultural Education*, 7, 379–92.
——(1990). Extending the scope of the Acculturation/Pidginization Model to include cognition. *TESOL Quarterly*, 24/4, 667–84.

VJC

**accuracy/fluency** Different pedagogic practices have aimed either at accuracy or fluency as the prime targets of students' attainment in L2 proficiency (Brumfit, 1984). For example, other things being equal, explicit GRAMMAR TEACHING and more intense ERROR CORRECTION are accuracy-orientated procedures, whereas COMMUNICATIVE LANGUAGE TEACHING and the relative infrequency of error correction are fluency-oriented (see also CONSCIOUSNESS RAISING, FORM-FOCUS, MESSAGE-FOCUS, PROCESS VS PRODUCT).

The distinction between accuracy and fluency is parallel to that of code and communication in SLA respectively. The emphasis on the former (accuracy/code) deals with the production of structurally correct instances of L2. The latter (fluency/communication) focuses on functional appropriateness and the smooth 'flow' of L2. Oral fluency is associated with the lack of undue pausing and hesitation, and both oral and written fluency has been defined in terms of the natural use of vocabulary, idioms and automatization of grammatical structures (Leeson, 1975).

Practising accuracy relies largely on the type of oral and written exercise which was developed by AUDIOLINGUALISM: the drill. Drills which give students opportunities to produce correct instances of language take a variety of forms. They can be choral or individual, rote or meaningful, based on repetition or substitution, and so on. On the other hand, fluency is fostered by classroom activities which give students opportunities to produce L2 utterances which are more spontaneous and less constrained by strict formalism, e.g. ROLE PLAY AND SIMULATION, real life/personal discussion, guessing activities, games and puzzles, problem-solving activities, open-ended listening, open-ended reading (for a discussion of these techniques see Mitchell, 1988). (See also CONTROLLED PRACTICE TECHNIQUES, 'PRESENTATION – PRACTICE – PRODUCTION' TEACHING SEQUENCE.)

The accuracy/fluency polarity underlies much controversy over the role of formal instruction in SLA. For example, Krashen's MONITOR MODEL rejects extensive grammar instruction in favour of teaching communication. On the other hand, Sharwood Smith sees the teaching of grammar (see CONSCIOUSNESS RAISING) as a 'short cut' to attaining communicative fluency. The inevitable middle-of-the-road position, represented for example by Bialystok (1982), suggests that the decision over formal instruction in the classroom should be based on the analysis of students' goals. Ellis (1985: 244–5) states that

[i]f the goal is to participate in natural conversation, the learner will need to develop his vernacular style by acquiring L2 knowledge that is automatic but unanalysed. This can be achieved directly by means of instruction that emphasizes communication in the classroom [fluency]. It may also be achieved indirectly by teaching that focuses on the code [accuracy], if there are also sufficient practice opportunities to trigger the passage of knowledge from the careful to the vernacular style. If the learner's goal is to participate in discourse that requires careful, conscious planning, he will need to develop a careful style by acquiring L2 knowledge that is automatic and analysed. This can best be accomplished by formal instruction that focuses on the L2 code [accuracy].

Hammerly (1991) takes a programmatically reconciliatory position towards communicative fluency and linguistic accuracy. Being somewhat critical of COMMUNICATIVE METHODOLOGY, he reviews the results of IMMERSION PROGRAMMES in Canada and the United States, and observes that although these programmes were successful in the students' attaining a high level of communicative proficiency (fluency), they failed in the area of linguistic accuracy. Hammerly (1991: 5) cites studies which indicate that 'an error-laden classroom pidgin becomes established as early as Grade 2 or 3 because students are under pressure to communicate and are encouraged to do so regardless of grammar' (see FOSSILIZATION). Therefore, he advocates a 'balanced' approach to language teaching and learning in which the question of accuracy/fluency is perceived not as one of kind but degree. The author is also in favour of greater emphasis on the teaching of accuracy in the beginning and intermediate stages of L2 learning, and fluency at the more advanced levels.

Certainly, the success of L2 learners in attaining near-native proficiency is not only regulated by their exposure to accuracy- or fluency-oriented teaching. There are many individual learner characteristics which to some degree determine the success of L2 mastery by a student. One of the crucial factors is age. It is possible for most people to learn a second language at any time in their lives and achieve a considerable degree of fluency in effective communication. However, it is rare for learners over the age of puberty to be as successful in acquiring all the grammatical properties of L2 as those who start learning L2 below that age (see CRITICAL PERIOD HYPOTHESIS).

BIBLIOGRAPHY
Bialystok, E. (1982). On the relationship between knowing and using forms. *Applied Linguistics*, 3, 181–206.
Brumfit, C. (1984). *Communicative Methodology in Language Teaching*. Cambridge: Cambridge University Press.*
Ellis, R. (1985). *Understanding Second Language Acquisition*. Oxford: Oxford University Press.
Hammerly, H. (1991). *Fluency and Accuracy: Toward balance in language teaching and learning*. Clevedon: Multilingual Matters.
Leeson, R. (1975). *Fluency and Language Teaching*. London: Longman.
Mitchell, R. (1988). *Communicative Language Teaching in Practice*. London: Centre for Information on Language Teaching and Research.
AJ

**achievement strategies**   (See also AVOID-ANCE STRATEGIES, COMMUNICATION STRATEGIES, TEACHING SPEAKING.) Faced with difficulty in meeting an intended communicative goal in the L2, a learner may improvise or expand existing resources by borrowing from L1, using L2 paraphrase, word coinage or generalizing, appealing for help, using mime/gesture, or retrieval strategies.

BIBLIOGRAPHY
Bialystok, E. (1990). *Communication Strategies*. Oxford: Blackwell.
KSM

**achievement tests** measure success in achieving objectives and are directly related to language courses followed. Final achievement tests at the end of a course may be based on the course syllabus and materials or on the objectives of the course. Progress achievement tests measure students' progress towards course objectives. (See also LANGUAGE TESTING.)

BIBLIOGRAPHY
Hughes, A. (1989). *Testing for Language Teachers*. Cambridge: Cambridge University Press.
KSM

**acquisition/learning**   The distinction is associated with the work of Krashen (1982) and his MONITOR MODEL. He characterizes acquisition as a 'natural' process, where there is no 'conscious focusing on linguistic forms'. First and second language acquisition are comparable, and both may be described in terms of CREATIVE CONSTRUCTION THEORY. The minimum condition for acquisition to occur is 'participation in natural communication situations'. Learning is a conscious process, marked for Krashen by two characteristics: the presence of feedback (error correction), and rule isolation – the procedure of dealing with language points one at a time. The distinction is criticized by some, who find the processes insufficiently distinguished.

BIBLIOGRAPHY
Krashen, S. D. (1982). *Principles and Practice in Second Language Acquisition*. Oxford: Pergamon Institute of English.
KJ

**action research** (AR) derives from the work during the 1940s of Kurt Lewin, who used it as a method of research into social issues. In education, it has become closely associated with the broader area of TEACHER RESEARCH AND DEVELOPMENT. Its underlying rationale is to encourage teachers in the reflective and critical investigation of their own practice. AR is characteristically context-specific and collaborative and, most important, oriented to pedagogic change brought about by the participants in a setting. Most models of AR are conceived in terms of a cycle or 'spiral' which offers a sequential set of research steps. See also TEACHER EDUCATION.

BIBLIOGRAPHY
Elliott, J. (1991). *Action Research for Educational Change*. Milton Keynes and Philadelphia: Open University Press.
Hopkins, D. (1993). *A Teacher's Guide to Classroom Research*. 2nd edn. Buckingham and Philadelphia: Open University Press.
Kemmis, S. and McTaggart, R. (eds) (1982). *The Action Research Planner*. Geelong: Deakin University.
Nunan, D. (1990). Action research in the language classroom. In J. C. Richards and D. Nunan (eds) *Second Language Teacher Education*. Cambridge: Cambridge University Press, 62–81.

JMCD

**adjacency pairs** In conversation, certain utterances make a particular response very likely. For example, a greeting is likely to be followed by another greeting. In conversation analysis, the two turns together are called an adjacency pair. Often there are alternative responses; for example, blame may elicit denial or admission. (See also DISCOURSE ANALYSIS, TURN-TAKING.)

BIBLIOGRAPHY
Cook, G. (1989). *Discourse*. Oxford: Oxford University Press, 53–5.

Levinson, S. (1983). *Pragmatics* Cambridge: Cambridge University Press, 303–45.
McCarthy, M. (1991). *Discourse Analysis for Language Teachers*. Cambridge: Cambridge University Press, 119–22.

GC

**affective filter** A term coined by Dulay and Burt and developed by Krashen to refer to a putative mental process whereby a learner's brain would filter available input, letting in to the central acquisition processes only those items that were affectively (i.e. emotionally, attitudinally) acceptable to the learner. (See also INPUT HYPOTHESIS.)

BIBLIOGRAPHY
Dulay, H. and Burt, M. (1977). Remarks on creativity in language acquisition. In M. Burt, H. Dulay and M. Finnochiaro (eds), *Viewpoints on English as a Second Language*. New York: Regents, 95–126.
Dulay, H., Burt, M. and Krashen, S. D. (1982). *Language Two*. New York: Oxford University Press.
Krashen, S. D. (1982). *Principles and Practice in Second Language Acquisition*. Oxford: Pergamon.

RLA

**affective variables** 'Affective' means 'related to feelings'. One of the three areas considered to make up the INDIVIDUAL DIFFERENCES between learners which influence their degree of success in foreign language learning is the affective area, and MOTIVATION and ATTITUDE are generally regarded as the two major affective variables. Both are considered to be of considerable importance to learning success, particularly in certain contexts (many affective variable studies have been undertaken in the bilingual context of Canada). Some commentators use the term more widely than this, to include variables like EXTROVERSION/INTROVERSION, although these are more generally considered under PERSONALITY VARIABLES.

BIBLIOGRAPHY
Gardner, R. C. (1985). *Social Psychology and Second Language Learning: The role of attitudes and motivation.* London: Edward Arnold.*
Gardner, R. C. and Lambert, W. E. (1972). *Attitudes and Motivation in Second Language Learning.* Rowley, MA: Newbury House.
Skehan, P. (1989). *Individual Differences in Second-Language Learning.* London: Edward Arnold.

KJ

**age learning differences**   Cumulative empirical research of the past fifteen years seems to point to the following generalizations about the relationship between age and SLA (see Long, 1990, 1993 for reviews):

• adolescent and young adult L2 learners (as a group) are faster in the initial stages of L2 learning than young children (as a group) on all linguistic measures (SYNTAX MORPHOLOGY, pronunciation, LEXIS);
• with continued exposure, young children (as a group) become more native-like than adolescent and adult learners (as a group) on all linguistic measures;
• individual learners may depart from these generalizations (e.g. some older learners may be slower than young children in the early stages, some older learners may ultimately become as successful as child learners, and so on);
• the process of L2 development appears to be highly similar across child and adult learners;
• deterioration in sensitivity to linguistic material begins as early as age 6 in some individuals (Long, 1993);
• loss of sensitivity to linguistic material is not sudden, but progressively declines with age.

ADOLESCENTS AND YOUNG ADULTS ARE FASTER LEARNERS IN THE INITIAL STAGES OF SLA

Here are three sets of findings representative of studies which show that older L2 learners have an initial advantage over younger learners. Snow and Hoefnagel-Höhle (1978) studied 42 English-speaking initial learners of Dutch in Holland over a 13-month period. They ranged in age from 3 years to adulthood. The measures on which subjects were tested were pronunciation, auditory discrimination, morphology, vocabulary, sentence repetition and translation, and tests were administered at $4\frac{1}{2}$-month intervals. Snow and Hoefnagel-Höhle found that at the first testing the adolescent and adult subjects outperformed the child learners on all measures except auditory discrimination. However, by the time of the final testing there was no significant difference between the subjects. To summarize, over a period of 13 months child L2 learners of Dutch did not outperform adolescent/adult learners, and adolescent/adult learners were actually faster during the initial period of acquisition.

Ervin-Tripp (1974) studied a group of 31 4–9-year-old English-speaking children acquiring French in Switzerland after 9 months of exposure. She tested their development on syntax, morphology and pronunciation, and found that the 7–9-year-olds significantly outperformed the 4–6-year-olds on all three measures.

Swain (1981) has compared L1 English-speaking adolescents in late French IMMERSION PROGRAMMES in Canada with younger children in early immersion programmes, and found that the adolescents performed as well on reading comprehension and a CLOZE test after about 1,400 hours of immersion as the children did after 4,000 hours of immersion (although the early immersion students were better on listening comprehension).

CHILD LEARNERS ARE ULTIMATELY MORE SUCCESSFUL L2 LEARNERS THAN ADOLESCENTS/ADULTS

Here are three representative sets of findings which suggest that child L2 learners are ultimately more successful than older L2 learners. Patkowski (1980) and Johnson and Newport (1989, 1991) have both investigated the effect of the age of first consistent naturalistic exposure to an L2 in subjects who have had considerable lengths of exposure. Patkowski selected 67 L2 English speakers from mixed L1 backgrounds, of various ages, who had all been resident in the USA for at least five years. He recorded their performance in an interview, together with the performance of 15 native speaker controls, transcribed the data to eliminate an accent factor, and asked trained native-speaking raters to rate each sample for nativeness. In analysing the results, Patkowski made an arbitrary division between those who had first arrived in the USA before the age of 15, and those who had arrived after the age of 15. He found that those who had arrived before the age of 15 were strikingly more likely to be rated as native speakers or near-native speakers than those who had arrived after the age of 15. Length of exposure and type of exposure (whether the subjects had formal instruction as well as naturalistic exposure) had no effect on the ratings.

Johnson and Newport (1989, 1991), in a similar kind of study with Chinese- and Korean-speaking learners of English who had also been resident in the USA for at least 5 years, focused on grammatical intuitions rather than production data. They found that subjects who had arrived in the USA prior to the age of 7 performed as well on a grammar test as native-speaking control subjects. Those subjects who had arrived after the age of 7 performed progressively less well – the older the subject, the less native-like was the performance on the grammar test. Decline was gradual rather than sudden.

## L2 DEVELOPMENT APPEARS SIMILAR ACROSS CHILD AND ADULT LEARNERS

Studies which compare child and adult L2 development generally find that children and adults go through the same stages. For example, Bailey, Madden and Krashen (1974) found a similar accuracy order in adult L2 English morphology to that found by Dulay and Burt (1973) with children. Studies of the acquisition of German word order have found that learners go through the same stages whether they are children or adults (Meisel, Clahsen and Pienemann, 1981), and so on.

## EXPLANATIONS FOR AGE DIFFERENCES

Four main types of explanation have been offered for age differences: (a) the language faculty is just as capable of learning L2s in older learners as in child learners, but 'affective' factors like threatened self-esteem, low EGO PERMEABILITY and perceived social distance act as a barrier between L2 data and the language faculty (Krashen, 1982); (b) input to adult learners is less well-tuned than to children, so that older learners do not get the data they require to be fully successful; (c) COGNITIVE DEVELOPMENT (development of advanced thinking processes) somehow inhibits language learning ability (Krashen, 1982); (d) changes in the nature of the brain with age cause a decline in language learning ability (see CRITICAL PERIOD HYPOTHESIS). For a review of these explanations, see Long (1990).

## FUTURE TRENDS

In the past, attempts to formulate generalizations about age-related differences in language learning have been bedevilled by apparently incompatible results: the fact that older learners can appear to achieve native-like pronunciation in reading lists of words after only a few hours' practice conflicts with the generalization that, with exposure, young children (as a group) become more native-like on all linguistic measures than their older counterparts, as does the fact that young children may not appear to be as successful as older learners over the first few months of L2 learning. These apparent conflicts are resolved once mere 'parroting' is teased apart from real acquisition, and development is distinguished from potential ultimate knowledge. Long (1993) suggests a number of ways in which the design of future studies of age differences could be tightened to eliminate such factors. He also hypothesizes that if future studies are more tightly controlled, it will become clear that the 'sensitive period' for language acquisition is up to the age of 6, and beyond that there is progressive deterioration of all linguistic abilities.

BIBLIOGRAPHY
Bailey, N., Madden, C. and Krashen, S. (1974). Is there a 'natural sequence' in adult second language learning? *Language Learning*, 24, 235–43.
Dulay, H. and Burt, M. (1973). Should we teach children syntax? *Language Learning*, 23, 245–58.
Ervin-Tripp, S. A. (1974). Is second language learning like the first? *TESOL Quarterly*, 8, 111–27.
Johnson, J. and Newport, E. (1989). Critical period effects in second language learning: the influence of maturational state on the acquisition of English as a second language. *Cognitive Psychology*, 21, 60–99.*
——(1991). Critical period effects on universal properties of language: the status of subjacency in the acquisition of a second language. *Cognition*, 39, 215–58.
Krashen, S. (1982). Accounting for child-adult differences in second language rate and attainment. In S. Krashen, R. Scarcella, and M. Long (eds).
Krashen, S., Scarcella, R. and Long, M. (eds) (1982). *Child-Adult Differences in Second Language Acquisition*. Rowley, MA: Newbury House.
Long, M. (1990). Maturational constraints on language development. *Studies in Second Language Acquisition*, 12, 251–85.
——(1993). Second language acquisition as a function of age: research findings and methodological issues. In K. Hyltenstam and A. Viberg (eds), *Progress and Regression in Language*. Cambridge: Cambridge University Press.*
Meisel, J., Clahsen, H. and Pienemann, M. (1981). On determining developmental stages in natural second language acquisition. *Studies in Second Language Acquisition*, 3, 109–35.
Patkowski, M. (1980). The sensitive period for the acquisition of syntax in a second language. *Language Learning*, 30, 449–72.
Singleton, D. (1989). *Language Acquisition: The age factor*. Clevedon: Multilingual Matters.*
Snow, C. and Hoefnagel-Höhle, M. (1978). The critical age for language acquisition: evidence from second language learning. *Child Development*, 49, 1114–28.
Swain, M. (1981). Time and timing in bilingual education. *Language Learning*, 31, 1–15.
RH

## analytic/synthetic teaching strategies

Wilkins (1976) distinguishes two strategies for syllabus organization. In a synthetic approach teaching items are presented one by one to the learner, who builds up or 'synthesizes' knowledge incrementally. In analytic teaching the learner does the 'analysis' (i.e. 'works out' the system) from data presented in 'natural chunks' (the phrase is Newmark's, whose views influence Wilkins's arguments). Wilkins associates synthetic teaching with the STRUCTURAL SYLLABUS and analytic with NOTIONAL/FUNCTIONAL SYLLABUSES because in these structures are not presented one by one, in a carefully graded way. Brumfit (1979) and Johnson (1979) argue against Wilkins's association.

BIBLIOGRAPHY
Brumfit, C. J. (1979). 'Communicative' language teaching: an educational perspective. In C. J. Brumfit and K. Johnson (eds), *The Communicative Approach to Language Teaching*. Oxford: Oxford University Press, 183–91.
Johnson, K. (1979). Communicative approaches and communicative processes. In C. J. Brumfit and K. Johnson (eds), *The Communicative Approach to Language Teaching*. Oxford: Oxford University Press, 192–205.

Newmark, L. (1966). How not to interfere with language learning. *International Journal of American Linguistics*, 32/1, 77–83.
Wilkins, D. A. (1976). *Notional Syllabuses*. Oxford: Oxford University Press.

KJ

**anomie** The term Durkheim (1897) used for feelings of dissatisfaction with one's role in society. These may make one open to other cultures and hence facilitate L2 learning. But where the L2 learning experience itself causes anomie, it may lead to negative feelings towards the L2. See AFFECTIVE VARIABLES.

BIBLIOGRAPHY
Durkheim, E. (1897). *Le suicide*. Paris. [(1952). *Suicide*, trans. J. Spalding and G. Simpson. London: Routledge and Kegan Paul.]
Gardner, R. C. (1975). Motivational variables in second language learning. In G. Taggart (ed.), *Attitude and Aptitude in Second Language Learning*. Proceedings of the 5th Symposium of the Canadian Association of Applied Linguistics, Toronto, May 1974.
Lambert, W. (1967). A social psychology of bilingualism. *Journal of Social Issues*, 23, 91–109.

KJ

**ANOVA** ANalysis Of VAriance is a technique (see STATISTICS IN APPLIED LINGUISTICS RESEARCH) which allows a researcher to test the significance of the relationship between one or more dependent VARIABLES and the treatment manipulated by the experimenter, and the strength of the interaction between the variables.

BIBLIOGRAPHY
Woods, A., Fletcher, P. and Hughes, A. (1986). *Statistics in Language Studies*. Cambridge: Cambridge University Press, 194–222.

SMCD

**applied linguistics** The term 'applied linguistics' appears to be of relatively recent currency (the second half of the twentieth century). It was needed in the late 1940s and 1950s in both Britain and the USA to refer to the new academic discipline of the study of the teaching and learning of second or foreign languages. The journal *Language Learning* started in 1948 with the subtitle 'A Quarterly Journal of Applied Linguistics', but, curiously, the first two issues contain no other reference to the term. It became a term used to name not only schemes of academic study but also university institutions themselves (for example, the School of Applied Linguistics at Edinburgh University, Scotland, founded in 1956).

For reasons of historical accident – the considerable growth in the last five decades of English as a world language, and the consequent growth in worldwide demand for academically qualified professionals – 'applied linguistics' has been principally identified with the teaching of English as a foreign or second language.

The term seems never to have been in common usage to refer to its three most obvious apparent implications: first, a restriction in scope to the practical APPLICATION of theory, second, a restriction in scope to the application of specifically LINGUISTIC theory, and, third, a broadening of scope to the application of linguistic theory in *any* language-related *field*.

The term has instead been most commonly used to cover all aspects of the academic study of language teaching and learning second and/or foreign languages (including such psychological rather than linguistic topics as motivation for language learning, for example, and such professional issues as language teacher training). And, until relatively recently, it has been used to refer somewhat exclusively to the field of language teaching and learning, rather than to any field where language is a relevant consideration. Only in the last decade or so (the 1980s) has the term begun to be used to refer more widely to any area of study, beyond 'linguistics' itself, that is language-related.

This change is exemplified in the successive association newsletters and conference programmes of the British Association for Applied Linguistics, which in the 1980s significantly widened the scope of its concerns as an association. However, the authoritative journal *Applied Linguistics*, representing the major international association and two major national associations (see below), maintains the priority given to language teaching and learning by foregrounding 'language education' in its stated aim 'to promote a principled approach to language education and other language-related concerns by encouraging enquiry into the relationship between theoretical and practical studies' (inside the back page of every issue).

THE SCOPE OF APPLIED LINGUISTICS AS
AN ACADEMIC DISCIPLINE IN THE FIELD
OF LANGUAGE TEACHING

The discipline of applied linguistics is free from dependence on linguistics as the sole source discipline, and, for historical reasons, is often strongly professional in orientation, with schemes specifically designed for postgraduates with several years of (usually English) language teaching experience. They are usually year-long schemes, offered under a very wide variety of names, with relatively few institutions in the UK, for example, using the term 'applied linguistics' itself. They are likely to cover a very wide range of topics, beyond the 'standard' linguistic components. SOCIOLINGUISTICS and PSYCHOLINGUISTICS are likely to be strongly featured, with an emphasis on language learning theory. 'Professional' course components are likely to cover language teaching methods, curriculum, syllabus and materials design, and testing and evaluation. Given increasing interest worldwide in pursuing applied linguistic studies at doctoral level, beyond the research-based dissertation usually required at MA level, there are also likely to be course components in appropriate

research methods for applied linguistics. A recent arrival as content for applied linguistics schemes is 'critical language teaching', asking questions about whose interests are being served by what happens in the field of language teaching (for example, asking questions about English as a vehicle for 'linguistic imperialism').

## Associations for applied linguists

The major international body in the field is the International Association of Applied Linguistics (known as AILA, from the French original of the name – Association Internationale de la Linguistique Appliquée). For further information on this and other relevant associations see the separate entry on ORGANIZATIONS FOR APPLIED LINGUISTS.

## Publications in applied linguistics, in the field of language teaching

The first academic journals of international standing to devote themselves explicitly to applied linguistics (although the US-based *Modern Language Journal* – founded in 1916 – had already established an international reputation for its coverage of topics related to language teaching and learning) appear to have been, in North America, the journal *Language Learning* (1948), and, in Europe, the *International Review of Applied Linguistics* (IRAL) (1963). Other internationally recognized journals have since appeared, notably the *TESOL Quarterly* (1966), the official academic publication of the US-based association of Teachers of English to Speakers of Other Languages, and *System* (1973), and, most recently, but probably most authoritatively, *Applied Linguistics* itself (1980), under joint British and North American editorship, sponsored by the British and American associations for Applied Linguistics (BAAL and AAAL), and published in cooperation with the International Association of Applied Linguists (AILA). Since 1981 an *Annual Review of Applied*

*Linguistics* has appeared, published by Cambridge University Press. The major abstracting journal in the field is *Language Teaching*, published quarterly by Cambridge University Press, and carrying a substantial 'state of the art' review in each issue.

BIBLIOGRAPHY
Howatt, A. P. R. (1984). *A History of English Language Teaching.* Oxford: Oxford University Press.
Stern, H. H. (1983). *Fundamental Concepts of Language Teaching.* Oxford: Oxford University Press. [See especially ch. 3, 'Towards a conceptual framework', 35–52.]*

RLA

**approach** as a technical term was first proposed by Anthony in his article 'Approach, method and technique' first published in 1963. He was concerned with two problems: (1) how to relate language teaching theory and practice to each other; (2) how to describe this relationship. His solution is conveyed in his title, the term 'approach' encapsulating the theory underlying practice:

I view an approach ... as a set of correlative assumptions dealing with the nature of language and the nature of language teaching and learning. An approach is axiomatic. It describes the nature of the subject matter to be taught. It states a point of view, a philosophy. (Anthony, 1965: 5)

Approach as a 'set of correlative assumptions' contrasts with method as 'an overall plan for the orderly presentation of language material' (p. 6). Moreover, 'a method is procedural.' A technique, on the other hand, 'is implementational', 'a particular trick, stratagem, or contrivance used to accomplish an immediate objective' (p. 7).

An approach to language teaching and learning represents an outline conception of the way in which these should proceed, a seedbed from which a method springs, but is not yet a strategy specifying details of classroom practice. There must also be a logical fit between approach and method as an 'overall plan ... no part of which contradicts, and all of which is based upon, the selected approach'. However, 'Within one approach, there can be many methods' (p. 6). Exemplifying this, Anthony claims that mim-mem (see GI METHOD) and pattern practice are two methods sharing the aural-oral approach. We might state, conversely, that the approach represented by the REFORM SCHOOL found exponents in the Natural, the Psychological, the Phonetic and the Unit Methods (Mackey, 1965: 151–4) as well as in the DIRECT METHOD, in so far as this is uniquely identifiable. All of these were consonant with oral, inductive, 'natural' principles, and were related to each other, despite procedural differences.

Anthony's perspective is hierarchical: 'The organizational key is that *techniques* carry out a *method* which is consistent with an *approach*' (p. 5). This suggests a logical sequence leading from theory to plan for teaching to procedures for the classroom. While the general concept of approach has proved uncontroversial, Anthony's hierarchical perspective has been contested. His model is also viewed by some as simplistic. Richards and Rodgers (1986: 16), for example, argue (in unfortunate wording, since 'comprehensiveness' is first granted to Anthony but then seemingly rescinded):

Although Anthony's original proposal has the advantage of simplicity and comprehensiveness and serves as a useful way of distinguishing the relationship between the underlying theoretical principles and the practices derived from them, it fails to give sufficient attention to the nature of a method itself. Nothing is said about the roles of teachers and learners ... for example,

**APPROACH**
↓
**METHOD**
↓
**TECHNIQUE**

**Figure 1**  Anthony's sequence.

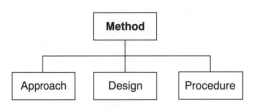

**Figure 2**   Richards and Rodgers's model.

nor about the role of instructional materials or the form they are expected to take. It fails to account for how an approach may be realized in a method ... In order to provide a more comprehensive model for the discussion of approaches and methods, we have revised and extended the original Anthony model.

They subsume Anthony's concepts of method and technique under their concepts of design and procedure and supply (their figure 2.1) a 'summary of elements and subelements that constitute a method', reserving method for the 'output' of a non-hierarchical combination of approach, design and procedure, depicting their conception as in figure 2.

Under 'approach' they place 'a theory of the nature of language' and 'a theory of the nature of language learning', under 'design', 'the general and specific objectives of the method', 'a syllabus model', 'types of learning and teaching activities', 'learner roles', 'teacher roles' and 'the role of instructional materials', and under 'procedure', 'classroom techniques, practices, and behaviours observed when the method is used'. While the concept of 'approach' is similar to Anthony's, it is no longer in splendid isolation at the top of a hierarchy, and Anthony's 'techniques' now fall under the wider concept 'procedure', while 'design' is a new element, incorporating what might be summarized as 'major practical considerations'.

The more detailed Richards and Rodgers analysis allows for the complex interplay of many variables, both theoretical and practical, behind the scenes of a method. None the less, it is uncertain whether their own model is totally non-hierarchical, since it

could be verbalized as follows: 'Subtending "method" are "approach", "design" and "procedure"' or even: 'A method is the "output" of "approach", "design" and "procedure".' But by contrast, Anthony might give the impression that a method springs forth directly from a theory alone.

A good reason for disambiguating the terms 'approach' and 'method' is that there are approaches to language teaching not leading to any 'established method'. Though one talks, for example, of COMMUNICATIVE LANGUAGE TEACHING and the communicative approach, there is no 'communicative method'. In the case of the (British) Communicative Approach the initiative began with Wilkins (1972, 1976), who suggested novel language teaching objectives, but never a novel method or novel techniques. None the less, the pursuit of the novel objectives provoked a language teaching revolution. While certain techniques are associated with the approach, a 'communicative method' has not emerged because the approach itself contains no learning theory. (See Nunan, 1989: 194–5 for a useful overview of the component of various established approaches and methods.)

As noted, there is broad agreement between Anthony and Richards and Rodgers that an approach encompasses 'a theory of the nature of language' and 'a theory of the nature of language learning', though Anthony also includes 'assumptions dealing with the nature of language teaching'. Such a view on either part is, of course, basically 'linguistic', yet there are directions in language teaching subtended less by ideas about language than about psychology – e.g. SILENT WAY – also constituting an 'approach', but stressing learning processes rather than language itself (see, for example, Stern, 1981). In this light, then, an approach is a body of theory drawn from fundamental disciplines considered most pertinent to solving problems involved in language teaching and learning. Even so, the spectrum of meaning contained in 'approach' differs considerably between individuals. For some, it implies only linguistic or psychological stances, but for others it includes, say, an educational philosophy and wide educational goals. Ultimately, no unassailable definition of 'approach' is available, but it may be said grossly to relate to the 'general thinking' behind a language teaching initiative as opposed to a step-by-step 'recipe' for the conduct of language teaching. As for the hierarchical question, sometimes an approach is conceived first, subsequently leading to practices consistent with it, but as Richards and Rodgers remark (p. 29): 'One can, for example, stumble on or invent a set of teaching procedures . . . and then later develop a design and theoretical approach that explain or justify the procedures.'

BIBLIOGRAPHY
Alatis, J. E., Altman, H. B. and Alatis, P. M. (eds) (1981). *The Second Language Classroom: Directions for the 1980s.* Oxford: Oxford University Press.
Allen, H. B. (ed.) (1965). *Teaching English as a Second Language.* New York: McGraw-Hill.
Anthony, E. M. (1965). Approach, method and technique. In H. B. Allen (ed.), *Teaching English as a Second Language.* Originally published in *English Language Teaching*, 17 (January 1963), 63–7.*
Mackey, W. F. (1965). *Language Teaching Analysis.* London and Harlow: Longmans, Green.
Nunan, D. (1989). *Designing Tasks for the Communicative Classroom.* Cambridge: Cambridge University Press.
Richards, J. C. and Rodgers, T. S. (1986). *Approaches and Methods in Language Learning: A description and analysis.* Cambridge: Cambridge University Press.*
Stern, H. H. (1981). Communicative language teaching and learning: toward a synthesis. In Alatis et al. (eds), *The Second Language Classroom.*
Wilkins, D. A. (1972). An investigation into the linguistic and situational content of the common core in a unit/credit system. Council of Europe: Committee for Out-of-School Education and Curriculum Development, Strasbourg (mimeographed).

——(1976). *Notional Syllabuses.* Oxford: Oxford University Press.

JTR

**a priori/a posteriori syllabus**   Most syllabuses are a priori: they are drawn up before teaching begins. An a posteriori or 'retrospective' syllabus is drawn up after the teaching. It provides a record or checklist of items covered. Such a syllabus might be used in relation to the DEEP-END STRATEGY.

BIBLIOGRAPHY
Johnson, K. (1983) Syllabus design: possible future trends. In K. Johnson and D. Porter (eds), *Perspectives in Communicative Language Teaching.* London: Academic Press, 47–68.

KJ

**aptitude**   It is generally held that some people have 'a flair for languages', but it has proved difficult to establish the notion empirically, except in the more prosaic and restricted terms of what characteristics correlate with success in language learning at school, for which whole test batteries were devised in the 1950s and 1960s (MLAT, PLAB). Not surprisingly, aptitude measurement was initially seen as being important where resources are limited and language teaching can in practice be restricted to those most likely to benefit from it (for example, in military training). Governments are, however, typically committed to providing language learning opportunities for all. Interest in aptitude has therefore shifted from focusing on it as a measurable characteristic to be used for predicting learning success or failure towards a more descriptive interest in tracing the relationship between relative progress in first language development and subsequent progress in second or foreign languages. The potential of aptitude measures/descriptions as the basis for tailoring courses to suit learners' needs (rather than for guaranteeing or denying them access to courses) has not yet been adequately explored (Skehan, 1989: 39).

The result of aptitude research in general has tended to confirm the notion of aptitude as a relatively stable and educationally important characteristic of the individual. See also COGNITIVE STYLE, COGNITIVE VARIABLES, INDIVIDUAL DIFFERENCES.

BIBLIOGRAPHY
Carroll, J. B. and Sapon, S. (1959). *Modern Language Aptitude Test – Form A*. New York: Psychological Corporation.
Pimsleur, P. (1966). *The Pimsleur Language Aptitude Battery*. New York: Harcourt Brace Jovanovich.
Skehan, P. (1989). *Individual Differences in Second-Language Learning*. London: Edward Arnold. [See especially ch. 3, 'Language aptitude'.]
RLA

**artificial intelligence** (AI) is concerned with programming computers to perform tasks – including text interpretation – which are usually considered to need human intelligence (McTear, 1987). Whether successful performance would actually imply intelligence has been hotly debated (Born, 1987). Although limited in success, AI has yielded important insights into the relation between world knowledge and language knowledge in discourse (Cook, 1994: 59–122).

BIBLIOGRAPHY
Born, R. (ed.) (1987). *Artificial Intelligence: The case against*. Beckenham: Croom Helm.
Cook, G. (1994). *Discourse and Literature*. Oxford: Oxford University Press.
McTear, M. (1987). *The Articulate Computer*. Oxford: Blackwell.
GC

**attitudes** may be thought of as opinions, beliefs, ways of responding, with respect to some set of problems. They may not be formulated verbally until someone asks; they may not even be immediately available to conscious attention. They may be formed from haphazard experience, or they may be the result of deliberate thought. They may conform to cultural or peer-group norms or not. As such, they are vague, loose and difficult to capture. They may exert considerable control over a learner's behaviour in numerous ways, and therefore may be related directly or indirectly to levels of achievement.

*Language learning* Attitudes that have been explored in relation to language learning range from anxiety about the language and the learning situation, through attitudes to speakers of the L2, the country in which it is spoken, the classroom, the teacher, other learners, the nature of language learning, particular elements in the learning activities, tests and beliefs about learning in general.

*Research methods* Methods of research employed in this exploration have been largely based on questionnaires, but there has also been some more individual interview research, and some use of discourse analysis and diaries (see also RESEARCH METHODOLOGY FOR LANGUAGE LEARNING).

*Attitudes and motivation* This entry should be read in conjunction with that on MOTIVATION since one of the largest and most extensive research projects concerning attitudes makes an explicit link between the two concepts, in Gardner's (1985) Attitude Motivation Index (AMI). Gardner conceives of motivation as a composite of effort, desire to learn the language and attitudes. Not all attitude research in language learning limits itself to the question of motivation.

*Implications for teaching* Attitudinal information has a place in language teaching, but it tends to be restricted to two areas: a) preparing the student to learn, and this may involve both the discovery of the student's own underlying attitudes, and a process of attitude change, and b) preferences for particular kinds of learning activities and the resulting potential for conflict between teachers and student.

*Early work and current questions*   Attitudes and their contribution to motivation were the subject of Gardner's work, first at McGill and later at Western Ontario University. The Good Language Learner study (Naiman, Fröhlich, Stern and Todesco, 1978) investigated attitudes, proficiency and classroom behaviour, using a number of methods including interviews and observation, and psychometric measurement (see GOOD LANGUAGE LEARNER STUDIES). These two traditions have spawned several newer approaches, which have highlighted a number of important issues:

(1)   How can attitudes best be characterized?
(2)   How do attitudes relate to achievement?
(3)   What is the optimum role of attitude information in language course and materials design?
(4)   How can the results of attitude measurement using different procedures be compared?
(5)   How do attitudes interact with motivation?
(6)   How do attitudes affect strategies of learning and language use?
(7)   How do attitudes change?

## RELATION TO LANGUAGE LEARNING

*Anxiety*   Learners may suffer from anxiety in relation to a number of aspects of the teaching–learning process; for example, about the language itself, about speaking in front of other learners, about the language class, about the behaviour of their peers, about their standing in the competition with fellow learners, about taking tests, about the speakers of the language they are learning, etc. Gardner's work on the AMI includes a questionnaire about being in the French class (French class anxiety), and this has proved to be quite strongly related (but negatively) to achievement. In other research (Gardner and MacIntyre, 1993) he also used a questionnaire about using French in other

situations (French use anxiety). This also had quite strong effects on most of their measures of learning achievement. In fact, in their FACTOR ANALYSIS of the results of the study, the second strongest factor was language anxiety, and the major contributions were from the French class anxiety and the use anxiety scales, plus a third one, the Horwitz (1986) foreign language classroom anxiety scale. This third scale was developed by Horwitz as an independent measure of students' worries about their own performance in the language inside and outside class. All three scales correlated strongly together with both the objective measures of proficiency, and even more highly with the students' self-ratings of what they thought they could actually do ('can do statements') in terms of speaking, understanding, writing and reading the language: the more anxious they were, the less well they believed they could perform.

A different approach to anxiety is taken by Bailey (1983) in a review of diaries (see DIARY STUDIES) written by herself and other learners of FL's. She noted her own anxieties, stemming largely from comparisons with other learners in the class, and she found herself seeing them as threats with whom she had to compete. She identified her feelings with Gardner's French class anxiety, but noted that such anxiety, for other diary-writers as well as herself, is linked to competitiveness. Not all the diary-writers she surveys made the same link, but, in general, the link was widespread, and she notes seven important aspects (not all mentioned by all the diarists):

(1)   Overt self-comparison of the language learner;
(2)   Emotive responses to the comparisons;
(3)   A desire to out-do other language learners;
(4)   Emphasis on or concern with tests and grades;
(5)   A desire to gain the teacher's approval;
(6)   Anxiety experienced during the language lesson;
(7)   Withdrawal from the language learning experience (Bailey, 1983: 13–14).

Another study of learner diaries, Howell-Richardson and Parkinson (1988) concentrated on diaries written as an L2 exercise, at the request of the teachers on a general English course. In an analysis of the content of these, Howell-Richardson and Parkinson found three aspects which they then tried to relate statistically to the differences in achievement among the writers: informativity, anxiety and leisure use of the foreign language. Leisure use correlated significantly with general proficiency; informativity was not associated with general proficiency but, curiously, it was with end-of-unit tests; and mentions of anxiety did not correlate at all. They comment that this surprising result might be attributed to failing to distinguish between facilitating (a little anxiety is arousing) and debilitating anxiety. Anxieties, motivation, and achievement clearly affect each other, but the relationship is complex and the evidence incomplete.

*Attitudes to L2 speakers*    Gardner's AMI included two scales concerning attitudes to speakers of the L2, French. Ten questions concerned French Canadians, another ten concerned European French people. They were positively worded statements with which the respondents could mark a level of agreement or disagreement (a so-called Likert scale). These attitudes also proved to be quite strongly associated with motivation and with success in learning the language.

These questionnaires illustrate two general points which are worth raising here. First, attitudes and the focus of attitudes are not generalizable: these two focuses, Canadian and European French speakers, are obviously important for a learner of French in English-speaking Canada, but learners of French elsewhere would have different focuses. A learner of French in the UK may have a collection of attitudes towards continental French speakers, but is unlikely to be troubled by attitudes towards French Canadians or other French speakers – however unfair that might be to users of

French worldwide. There is, of course, no obviously identifiable group of French speakers within the UK with equal language rights (in terms of the public media, employment, etc.) to the English speakers. The second general point illustrated here is that the form of these questions – positive statements for agreement or disagreement – can invite a judgement on the social acceptability of agreement or disagreement; in other words, people may agree with what they think will be approved of. Commentators (e.g. Skehan, 1989) tend to side with Gardner's refutation of this criticism.

*Beliefs about language learning*    Horwitz (1987) presents a Likert scale questionnaire designed to elicit beliefs from language students about a number of issues. Horwitz developed the instrument in order to understand student beliefs, to understand teachers' selection of learning activities and to identify areas of conflict. The 34-item questionnaire, the Beliefs About Language Learning Inventory, asks about five different areas, and exists in a student and a teacher version. Nine questions ask about aptitude, assessing the participants' beliefs about equality of their starting-point in terms of learning skill; six questions about the difficulty of language learning, both comparing different languages and different language skill areas; six questions about opinions about the nature of language learning, how it compares to other kinds of learning, the role of culture and of translation; eight questions about learning strategies and communication strategies; five questions about motivations. While such an instrument is considerably easier and quicker to administer than the AMI, one should remember that it is formally unvalidated, either by comparison with other questionnaires or by triangulation with other kinds of data and, as Horwitz acknowledges, student beliefs do not necessarily translate into action or know-how.

Another attempt to discover language students' beliefs was reported by Wenden

(1987). She used a rather different method, involving semi-structured interviews lasting 90 minutes each, which were then analysed for content using a rather disciplined procedure, identifying salient themes on the following criteria: they were *generalizations*; they functioned as *justifications* or *descriptions* of behaviour; they were either *spontaneous* contributions or *responses* to probing questions; they appeared in certain verbal *frames*; they *recurred* several times in an interview; and they carried *conviction* and *detail*. Wenden focused on prescriptive beliefs about language learning, and gave examples of student statements under the following headings:

Use the language
    Learn the natural way
    Practice
    Think in your second language
    Live in an L2 environment
    Don't worry about mistakes
Learn about the language
    Learn grammar and vocabulary
    Take a formal course
    Learn from mistakes
    Be mentally active
Personal factors are important
    Emotional aspect is important
    Self-concept
    Aptitude for learning

Clearly these are the beliefs of students in the middle of the experience of language learning, and one cannot know (a) to what extent the beliefs about good learning embodied in the course arrangements, materials and the teacher's strategies have influenced the students' revealed opinions, nor (b) whether and how these beliefs actually translated into action.

*Learning preferences and COGNITIVE STYLE*
Willing (1985) investigated attitudes to processes and activities in language classrooms in a large-scale questionnaire among the clients of the Australian Migrant English Programme, asking them, among other things, to rate preference statements from 'best' downwards. He analysed the results in a number

of interesting ways: by sex, length of residence, ethnic group, etc., and also simply by volume of preferences overall. For example, 62% of the sample marked 'I like to practise the sounds and pronunciation' as 'best', 39% 'I like to study grammar' and 10% 'In class I like to learn by games.' Bottom was 'I like to study English by myself (alone)' with only 3%. Because this was a large sample, he was able to apply statistics to find learner types, on the basis of the clustering of the preference statements, which gives a different perspective on cognitive style: he discovered four prevalent types within his sample, 'communicative', 'concrete', 'authority-oriented' and 'analytical'.

Another piece of research with a similar intent, though in a quite different learning situation, was conducted using ESL students in the USA by Reid (1986). Reid investigated preconceived styles rather than activity and mode of learning preferences: visual, auditory, kinaesthetic, tactile, group and individual learning. Her results showed that such preferences were reflected in cultural differences and subject choices of the students.

*Attitudes to teaching styles* Considerable interest has been shown in attitudes to teaching styles across cultures. The volume on *Socio-cultural Issues in English for Academic Purposes* (Adams et al., 1991) contains a number of papers exploring the effects of different cultural attitudes on the language performance of overseas students learning English for academic study in the UK, particularly in respect of writing and a seminar distinction. MacLennan (1987) used a questionnaire to investigate her Hong Kong students' reactions to features of teaching methodology – what they thought made a 'good teacher'. To some extent the attitudes they manifested could be seen as attitudes towards an 'imported' notion of good teaching, and they compared interestingly with attitudes displayed by Chinese students in the People's Republic. For example, the mainland students tended to consider a good teacher to be one who was good at the language whereas in Hong Kong they rated being trained to teach more highly. With regard to participating in class, this Hong Kong population put 'listening to the teacher' firmly ahead of 'communicating with the teacher alone in the class', and that firmly ahead of 'talking to my other students', in turn ahead of 'working with a partner'.

*Group attitudes*    Schumann's acculturation model of language learning (see ACCULTURATION HYPOTHESIS) highlighted the effect of group attitudes. Some of his components of social and psychological distance can be seen as attitudinal concepts. Schumann posited 10 components:

*Social*

| | |
|---|---|
| Cultural, economic dominance | as between L1 and L2 group |
| Integration pattern | of either group |
| Cultural congruence | of the two groups |
| Cohesion | of either group |
| Size | of learning group |
| Enclosure | of learning group |

*Psychological*
Language shock
CULTURE SHOCK
EGO PERMEABILITY
Orientation (integrative vs instrumental)

Dominance is as much a matter of perceptions as it is fact; integration pattern is a question of characteristic cultural attitudes to foreign influences. Congruence, cohesion, size and enclosure are different factual aspects of the speech communities involved. Language shock may sound a little fanciful nowadays, but it referred to learners' perceptions of alienation from the language they were intending to learn. Culture shock is all too real for many migrant learners, whether intending to stay long-term in a new community or short-term to gain qualifications or experience or to do business. Surveys of attitudes among so-called 'guest-workers' from outside the European Community

– Turkish and Yugoslav workers in Germany and Holland – have shown how strong this shock can be. Case studies of individuals (McDonough and McDonough, 1992), also reveal the effects of culture shock – sometimes reducing highly educated and intelligent people to silence and confusion because they can find no appropriate means of operating within a culture for which they may be quite unprepared. Ego permeability and orientation referred to PERSONALITY and MOTIVATION factors respectively.

## THE ROLE OF ATTITUDE INFORMATION IN LANGUAGE COURSE DESIGN

Finally, it is important to consider how many aspects of language learning aggregated under the term 'attitudes' can be recognized and catered for in instructional materials, course design, teacher training, etc. Dubin and Olshtain (1986) propose that an important part of the preparation for writing a new course has to be the gathering of data on group and individual attitudes prevalent within the group of people who are going to be using the materials, along with qualitative and quantitative data about societal needs and demographic facts. They are writing particularly in the context of preparing courses for learning 'languages of wider communication', where a language – usually English – is required as a means of establishing access to knowledge, markets, influence, aid, etc., but the same principle must also be true of preparing courses for learning minority languages. In general, there are three means of incorporating attitudinal information:

(a)   writing attractive materials;
(b)   allowing several ways of reaching the same goal;
(c)   LEARNER TRAINING.

(a) Writing attractive materials means discovering what the learners respond positively to and incorporating that in the materials.

There are difficulties with an extreme learner-centred approach, since the attractiveness of the materials must be strong enough to outweigh any threat to the learners' self-esteem or receptiveness from the challenge of the linguistic difficulties, rather than denying the difficulties.

(b) Allowing several ways of reaching the same goal means catering for possible conflicts between individual student attitudes and learning group attitude, and also between student and teacher attitudes. Examples of such conflicts are the realization of the necessity or desirability of the language of wider communication against negative feelings towards it from colonial history or even war; and the kind of mismatch between attitudes to learning within a community and attitudes embodied in an 'imported' methodology.

(c) Learner training usually involves two kinds of processes: (1) help for learners to gradually become aware of their own beliefs and attitudes to the language, learning, the L2 community, classroom activities, individual work, etc., which is itself based on the contentious belief that being aware of one's own personal ways of perceiving and processing input is the first step towards becoming an independent learner, and (2) ways of inducing attitude change, which might refer to easing people out of culture shock by explanation and confidence-inducing activities, or convincing people that particular learning activities which are negatively rated are in fact both painless and beneficial, and even fun.

## SUMMARY

From the description above, it will be apparent that the concept of attitude, its development and measurement, the description of particular attitudes, their nature and effect, the validity of particular descriptions, the reliability of various statements elicited, and the role and utility of attitudinal information in practical teaching and course design are all surrounded by controversy. This article has attempted (a) to indicate some of the problems of description and measurement through questionnaires, diaries and interviews; (b) to give some actual examples of different recent investigations; and (c) to discuss the ways in which information of this sort can be utilized in practical teaching, and course and materials design.

It should be clear that attitudes interact with a number of other concepts such as MOTIVATION, LEARNER TRAINING, PERSONALITY, ACCULTURATION, for which the relevant entries should also be read. Future research in attitudes will probably concentrate on (a) establishing better validity for the description of attitudes, both by more sophisticated statistical treatment and by comparison with data from different methods, for example, comparisons between questionnaire and interview data; (b) clarifying the puzzles discovered in existing work, for example, the confusing relationship between anxiety and achievement, the local nature of attitudes to L2 speakers, the status and power of attitudes in the classroom; (c) establishing, via formative evaluation of language teaching projects, how to optimize the use of attitude information and select appropriate means of recognizing and catering for those existing attitudes among learners and teachers. Attitudes may be interesting in themselves, but developments in utilization are crucial in any application of the knowledge gained.

BIBLIOGRAPHY

Adams, P., Heaton, B. and Howarth, P. (eds) (1991). *Socio-cultural Issues in English for Academic Purposes*, London: Macmillan.

Bailey, K. M. (1983). Competitiveness and anxiety in adult second language learning: looking *at* and *through* the diary studies. In H. Seliger and M. Long (eds), *Classroom Oriented Research in Second Language Acquisition*, Rowley, MA: Newbury House.

Dubin, F. and Olshtain, E. (1986). *Course Design*. Cambridge: Cambridge University Press.

Gardner, R. C. (1985). *Social Psychology and Second Language Learning: The role of attitudes and motivation*. London: Edward Arnold.*

Gardner R. C. and MacIntyre, P. (1993). On the measurement of affective variables in second language learning. *Language Learning*, 43/2, 157–94.

Horwitz, E. (1986). Preliminary evidence for the reliability and validity of a foreign language anxiety scale. *TESOL Quarterly*, 20, 559–62.

——(1987). Surveying student beliefs about language learning. In A. Wenden and J. Rubin (eds), *Learner Strategies in Language Learning*. New York: Prentice-Hall, 119–32.

Howell-Richardson, C. and Parkinson, B. (1988). Learner diaries: possibilities and pitfalls. In P. Grunwell (ed.), *Applied Linguistics and Society*. London: Centre for Information on Language Teaching and Research, 74–80.

McDonough, J. E. and McDonough, S. H. (1993). From EAP to chemistry: risking the anecdotal. In G. M. Blue (ed.), *Language, Learning and Success: Studying through English*. London: Macmillan, 132–40.

MacLennan, C. (1987). An investigation of the criteria which a group of Hong Kong students of English list as those which make a good teacher. *Proceedings of the Institute of Language in Education 3rd International Seminar*, December, 61–74.

Reid, J. (1986). Learning style preferences of ESL students. *TESOL Quarterly*, 20, 87–111.

Schumann, J. H. (1976). Social distance as a factor in second language acquisition. *Language Learning*, 26/1, 135–43.

Skehan, P. (1989). *Individual Differences in Second Language Learning*. London: Edward Arnold.*

Wenden, A. (1987). How to be a successful learner: insights and prescriptions from L2 learners. In A. Wenden and J. Rubin (eds), *Learner Strategies in Language Learning*. New York: Prentice-Hall, 103–18.

Willing, K. (1985). *Learning Styles in Adult Migrant Education*. Sydney: New South Wales Adult Migrant Education Service.

SMCD

**audiolingualism** This term derives from the adjective *audiolingual*, proposed by Brooks (1960: 201) to replace the phonetically ambiguous description *aural-oral* as applied to foreign language teaching methodology, but both epithets highlight *listening* and *speaking*. Strictly, audiolingualism is an APPROACH rather than a method, since it does not of itself prescribe one fixed set of classroom procedures. In practice, however, it has become synonymous with the *audiolingual method*. This was launched in the United States in the years following the Second World War in a crusading spirit, but soon attracted criticism leading to its abandonment by many who had at first embraced it.

The roots of audiolingualism lie in the early years of this century, when developments were taking place which were to exert a significant influence on language teaching theory. Among these were: (1) the entrenchment of positivistic pragmatism; (2) the blossoming of American structural linguistics (see STRUCTURALISM) and behaviourist psychology (see BEHAVIOURISM); (3) the expression of 'scientific thought' through formalisms, with the resultant exclusion from debate of the uninitiated. These developments, however, only came to bear upon language teaching once opportune historical circumstances had presented themselves: the Second World War and its aftermath.

In the Second World War the Americans discovered the need for mastery of foreign languages by service personnel. Help was sought from the structuralist linguists, the pioneers of field linguistics. These elaborated, in the context of the Army Specialized Training Program, and essentially as a hurried pragmatic measure, the *mimicry-memorization method* (see GI METHOD). The operation was deemed a success.

After the war it was judged politic to train all young Americans to mastery level in one foreign language (on the basis that one breaks the ice for all others), and recourse was again made to structuralist linguists. But now the latitude afforded by peace-time enabled these, in conjunction with behaviourist psychologists, to bring the whole of their theoretical armoury to bear upon the creation of a method for school use. Dogma in theory became axiom in practice. Teachers were told that their students were to be presented with the first 'scientific' language teaching method. The core was mimicry-memorization in the form of programmed learning and with formal explanation (allowed for in mimicry-memorization) largely withdrawn in favour of inductive principles. Historically, the audiolingual method deserves to be noted as an attempt at a language teaching *technology* in so far as practice flowed logically from theory.

To characterize the theoretical background, the structuralist linguists were as much imbued in positivistic-pragmatism as the behaviourists; the phenomena of the world were to be interpreted through the senses, and this applied to language also. There was no real search for underlying systems. The structuralists consequently worked on surface data, concentrating on classificatory or 'taxonomic' activities. Their *modus operandi*, though appropriate for the purposes of field linguistics, therefore promoted a 'repertoire view' of language.

The behaviourists drew inspiration from Pavlov's *conditioning* experiments, which promoted an account of behaviour in terms of *stimulus* and *response* and suggested that these could be expanded into an ever-widening network through *association*, newly learnt responses being strengthened through *reinforcement*. The stance on language was that it was *verbal behaviour* and that its development could be explained in similar fashion. This position is consistent with the idea that, complex as languages may be, they are ultimately finite entities and may be learnt through *imitation* and *practice*, which allow for increments in the network of stimuli and responses through association. Further, it should be noted that behaviourist psychologists believed that behaviour, or behaviours, were shaped (see SHAPING), that is, determined or 'engineered', by reinforcement

of appropriate responses to stimuli (and non-reinforcement or 'negative reinforcement' of inappropriate responses). In the natural environment, the 'shaping' of behaviours required very complex explanation, but psychologists such as B. F. Skinner claimed to be able to deliberately and straightforwardly 'shape' the behaviour of certain 'organisms' (typically rats and pigeons) under laboratory conditions, i.e. to cultivate given habitual behaviours. By extension, at the time of audiolingualism a parallel was drawn between the behaviourist experimenter and the language instructor, such that the latter was held to be responsible for 'shaping' the verbal behaviour of language learners.

Applied to language teaching, the views of the structuralists and behaviourists emerge, according to Rivers (1964), in four assumptions:

(1) Foreign language learning is basically a mechanical process of habit formation;
(2) Language skills are learnt more effectively if items of the foreign language are presented in spoken form before written form;
(3) Analogy provides a better foundation for foreign language learning than analysis;
(4) The meanings which the words of a language have for the native speaker can be learnt only in a matrix of allusions to the culture of the people who speak that language.

Concretized into a language teaching methodology – and Rivers (1964) is again used as a source – the above assumptions, or approach, translate into the following major sub-principles and steps of the audiolingual method:

The aim is to teach *listening, speaking, reading, writing*, in that order, with the emphasis in early years on the language of everyday situations. At first, learning is based on dialogues using frequent items of everyday vocabulary and structure. Dialogues are learnt by mimicry-memorization and attention is paid to pronunciation and intonation. When the whole class is word-perfect in the dialogues, it is divided, and dialogues are performed as though they were 'real-life' ones, with questions and answers exchanged between divisions and with role reversal. Dialogues are then adapted to the situation of individual students and further practice ensues. The structures of the dialogues are consolidated and expanded by pattern drill, done first in groups and then by individuals, or in the LANGUAGE LABORATORY. Later, there is introduction to written texts, though writing is at first imitative and consists in copying exercises. In the earlier stages, verbal transactions are limited to vocabulary and syntax already rehearsed. Errors are corrected immediately. Erring students must repeat what they were 'supposed to say' lest mistakes become part of their speech habits. Emphasis on reading increases with time.

The method did not live up to the claims made for it, at least, at school level. The disappointment of the 'duped' teachers may be witnessed in, for example, the *Modern Language Journal* for the late fifties and the sixties – 'Never trust "the experts" again.' Experiments designed to 'prove' its superiority over traditional methods came to nought (see Scherer and Wertheimer, 1964 and METHOD COMPARISONS). The theoretical claims for audiolingualism were in any case demolished, indirectly, in the work of Chomsky, not least by his insistence that language cannot be regarded as a repertoire and that its acquisition is not a mechanistic process (see CHOMSKYAN LINGUISTICS).

BIBLIOGRAPHY

Brooks, N. (1960). *Language and Language Learning: Theory and practice*. New York: Harcourt, Brace.
Rivers, W. M. (1964). *The Psychologist and the Foreign Language Teacher*. Chicago: University of Chicago Press.\*
Scherer, G. A. C. and Wertheimer, M. (1964). *A Psycholinguistic Experiment in Foreign Language Teaching*. New York: McGraw-Hill.

JTR

**audiovisualism**   As Rivers (1968: 174–5) states: 'The term "audiovisual" . . . cannot be identified with one specific method.' This is because all sorts of methods can be supported by an audiovisual element in the form of objects, pictures, wall charts, flash cards, cartoons, gestures and mime, slides, film-strips, loop-films, films, overhead projector transparencies and videos. The blackboard and whiteboard can also serve as audiovisual aids if a teacher is adept at drawing. However, these last two media are ephemeral and require repeated effort on the part of the teacher. Though images produced through them have the advantage of being changed easily, they may mislead learners when teachers are not so good at drawing as they suppose, whereas other types of audiovisual media offer possibilities of the reuse of professionally produced materials.

Any materials to be strictly described as 'audiovisual' *must combine an auditory signal with a visual image*; thus a 'general interest picture' in a course book included to convey an aspect of the target society may be a visual but is not an audiovisual aid, while the showing of a pictorial representation of a hippopotamus accompanied by the utterance 'hippopotamus' is an instance of audiovisualism. Illustrated language texts date back to the Middle Ages, but the systematic use of visual aids intended to heighten the interest and attention of the learner, or to 'fix' an association between an image and a word in *written form* seems to date from the *Orbis pictus* of Comenius in the seventeenth century. The linking of object or image with *sound* for the purpose of teaching vocabulary and structure, on the other hand, has its roots in the DIRECT METHOD, and practitioners of this method were often expected to possess drawing skills.

While it is commonly assumed that visual and audiovisual aids and materials maintain motivation and increase the impact of teaching, Wright (1974) points out that deciding on appropriate aids is a complex matter, involving considerations such as the age of the learners and their cultural background.

Moreover, though 'highly realistic' aids, e.g. feature films and recorded television programmes, can have dramatic effects, they carry dangers of ambiguity and distraction from linguistic points.

To the above must be added the qualification that a particular method calling itself explicitly 'audiovisual' arose during the 1950s – *La méthode audio-visuelle structuro-globale de Saint-Cloud*. The account given under ST CLOUD is elaborated on here, as the founders of the method made strong claims not just for the efficacy but for the indispensability of an audiovisual approach. The principles of the Audio-Visual Global and Structural Method were initially formulated by Rivenc in 1954, but he was subsequently joined by Guberina, who helped him refine the method over the next two years. The first course produced was *Voix et Images de France*, but this underwent further development between 1956 and 1960. A second course, *Bonjour Line*, appeared in 1963.

As in AUDIOLINGUALISM, speech was considered the prime channel of language, but it was held that effective learning of a foreign language was based 'on a permanent connection between a situation – context – picture – and a group of words and meaning, "globally" organized and functioning in a "structural" manner' (Guberina, 1964). Again as in audiolingualism, there was an assumption that the best way to learn a further language is in the manner in which the child is presumed to do so:

When a child learns his mother tongue, he primarily relies on the presence of a reality. The acoustic signal for the objects is only a supplementary representation of these same objects. In the first phase of searching for a name for an object, the quickest way is to see the object (i.e. the reality), and to refer to it by its name. The beginner does not know the words of a foreign language. It would therefore be useless for him to hear them, unless there is a visual stronghold. (ibid.)

This view was accompanied by the belief that 'traditional' methods of teaching foreign languages proceeded in the wrong order, presenting learners first with words to which meaning then had to be assigned. By contrast, the Audio-Visual Global and Structural Method set out to transmit 'meanings' via visual images and then to provide words designating these 'meanings' or 'realities'. Guberina maintains that 'This method works on the principles of physio-acoustics and brain stimulation' (ibid.).

Theory was transferred to practice by playing a spoken text dealing with everyday situations on a tape-recorder and simultaneously projecting pictures representing the development of the situations onto a screen. Each picture was intended to link with grammatical structures and vocabulary in the text. Much was made of creating 'reality' or 'realities' for the learner in this way. Moreover, it was supposed that: 'The reality makes an efficient use of the ear and the eye, and through this combination, the signals of language are memorized easily' (ibid.). It was also an axiom, as it must be with all methods, that transfer of learning to 'similar structural situations' would occur.

Howatt (1984: 225) notes that a British attempt 'to emulate [the French audiovisual courses] came too late since, by that time, a simpler adaptation . . . had been popularized by L. G. Alexander in . . . *First Things First*.' Here, cartoons accompanied new structural patterns for oral practice. But another sense in which any attempt to emulate the French courses would have come too late was that by the end of the 1960s the implications of CHOMSKYAN LINGUISTICS were making themselves felt, and the Audio-Visual Global and Structural Method suddenly looked very 'behaviouristic'. Moreover, the 'communicative revolution' of the early 1970s militated against exclusive use of situational and structural courses. This did not lead to the abandonment of audiovisual materials and aids. On the contrary, the concern with 'AUTHENTICITY' has promoted the use of audiovisual aids offering 'high realism'. Currently, it looks as though the computer, which is developing more and more into a multimedia device, will assume an increasingly important role in this domain, especially as CD Rom disks with audiovisual elements are becoming easily available. (See MEDIA RESOURCES.)

BIBLIOGRAPHY
Guberina, P. (1964). The audio-visual global and structural method. In B. Libbish (ed.), *Advances in the Teaching of Modern Languages*, vol. 1. Oxford: Pergamon Press, 1–17.*
Howatt, A. P. R. (1984). *A History of English Language Teaching*. London: Oxford University Press.
Rivers, W. (1968). *Teaching Foreign Language Skills*. Chicago: University of Chicago Press.
Wright, A. (1974). Audio-visual materials in language teaching. In J. P. B. Allen and S. P. Corder (eds), *The Edinburgh Course in Applied Linguistics*, vol. 3. London: Oxford University Press, 255–78.

JTR

**authenticity**    Texts are said to be authentic if they are genuine instances of language use as opposed to exemplars devised specifically for language teaching purposes. The question of authenticity emerged as an important issue within COMMUNICATIVE LANGUAGE TEACHING and in relation to NOTIONAL/FUNCTIONAL SYLLABUSES, where emphasis was placed on ensuring that the classroom contained natural language behaviour, with content identified as relevant to the learner through the process of NEEDS ANALYSIS. There are various other reasons why authenticity may be regarded as important. One is that it presents learners with language exposure similar to that enjoyed by native speakers, including all the characteristics of natural language which may be necessary for the learner properly to interpret texts. In addition, there is motivational attraction for insisting on authentic texts, created as a means of communicating content and not for some pedagogic purpose.

Breen (1985: 61) extends the common notion of authenticity and identifies four types:

(1)  Authenticity of the texts which we may use as input data for our students;
(2)  Authenticity of the learners' own interpretations of such texts;
(3)  Authenticity of tasks conducive to language learning;
(4)  Authenticity of the actual social situation of the classroom language.

By identifying a category of task authenticity, Breen is able to recognize that a classroom activity may be valid, natural and 'authentic' to the language learning process, while the instances of language use that it entails may be inauthentic in the established sense of the word. Widdowson (1990: 46) argues that to generalize the meaning of authenticity in this way is to rob the term of true significance. He himself views authenticity as a relation between the learner and a text, and he speaks (1980: 218) of the necessity for learners to be able to 'authenticate' texts as pieces of communication. Elsewhere (1979, chapter 12) he distinguishes between *authenticity* (a process, characterized as above), and *genuine*, used to refer to attested instances of language use (a product – see PROCESS VS PRODUCT).

Widdowson (1980) also points out that 'the pedagogic presentation of language . . . necessarily involves methodological contrivance which isolates essential features from their natural surroundings.' This captures the common argument against the necessity for authenticity, and opens the way for the simplification, and other doctoring of texts for reasons of pedagogic presentation – clarifying and giving salience to selected language points, for example.

BIBLIOGRAPHY
Breen, M. P. (1985). Authenticity in the language classroom. *Applied Linguistics*, 6/1, 60–70.*
Widdowson, H. G. (1979). *Explorations in Applied Linguistics*. Oxford: Oxford University Press.

——(1984). Teaching language as and for communication. In *Explorations in Applied Linguistics 2*. Oxford: Oxford University Press, 215–28.
——(1990). *Aspects of Language Teaching*. Oxford: Oxford University Press.

KJ

**autonomous learning** is based on the principle that learners should take maximum responsibility for, and control of, their own learning styles and stages outside the constraints of the traditional classroom. In practice a number of large- and small-scale frameworks have been designed. (See INDIVIDUALIZATION, LEARNER TRAINING, STUDENT AUTONOMY.)

JMCD

**avoidance strategies** are one type of communication strategy (see ACHIEVEMENT STRATEGIES, COMMUNICATION STRATEGIES, TEACHING SPEAKING). A learner with limited L2 resources may choose to alter or reduce his/her communicative goal to avoid problems of form or function. This may involve topic avoidance or message abandonment, restricting communication to safe choices.

BIBLIOGRAPHY
Bialystok, E. (1990). *Communication Strategies*. Oxford: Blackwell.
Tarone, E. (1977). Conscious communication strategies in Interlanguage. In H. D. Brown, C. A. Yorio and R. C. Crymes (eds), *On TESOL '77*. Washington, DC: TESOL.

KSM

# B

**behavioural objectives** stated in a syllabus or as the goals of a language course are best understood in contrast with *linguistic objectives*. The latter might take a form such as: 'By the end of the third year, learners will have mastered the conditional in English.' This would be an objective typical of the STRUCTURAL SYLLABUS, in that it designates an aspect of the English linguistic system which learners must acquire. However, it does not specify how they might *use* knowledge of this part of the system, or, in other words, what (linguistic) behaviours it will facilitate. A behavioural objective, on the other hand, might be expressed as follows: 'By the end of the third year, learners will be able to participate in debates on non-technical subjects, evaluating the arguments of others, expressing an opinion on them in either approving or disapproving but tactful terms, and offering their own viewpoint articulately and persuasively.' This now clarifies what they will (in theory) be able to *do* or *how* they will actually be able to *behave* through language as opposed to describing the systemic knowledge they will possess. A change of focus is therefore involved.

This shift of focus is often associated with NOTIONAL/FUNCTIONAL SYLLABUSES and the development of COMMUNICATIVE METHODOLOGY and ENGLISH (or other languages) FOR SPECIFIC PURPOSES. The major theoretical precursor here was Hymes (1971), who maintained that *linguistic competence* (in the Chomskyan sense – see, for example, Chomsky 1965: 3f. and COMPETENCE/PERFORMANCE) should be seen as an element of COMMUNICATIVE COMPETENCE and, in contradistinction to

Chomsky, insisted that *performance*, that is, instances of the use of language and the using of language itself, was central to the understanding of language in the 'real world', in which it serves as a social tool. The crux of his argument was that though systemic knowledge is essential for pursuing transactional goals through language, such knowledge cannot be utilized for behavioural purposes unless accompanied by a 'theory of speech acts' (see SPEECH ACT THEORY), or sociocultural knowledge. In short, knowledge of a language is not in itself knowledge of how to behave in and through that language.

Where the British Communicative Approach is concerned, it was through the pioneering work of Wilkins (1972), in which behavioural categories (named by him 'CATEGORIES OF COMMUNICATIVE FUNCTION' and usually known since as 'functions') were proposed, that the inspiration was provided to stress behavioural rather than linguistic objectives. Though he himself does not employ the term 'behavioural', it is perhaps Munby (1978), following in the footsteps of Wilkins, who furnishes one of the clearest examples of the pursuit of behavioural objectives within syllabus design. He claims (1978: 218) to supply a 'sociolinguistic model for specifying communicative competence'. In his chapter 'The Instrument Applied' (pp. 190–216), he does, it is true, supply lists of 'linguistic forms', but these are only *possible* realizations of the language appropriate to 'communicative activities' such as: 'Attending to customers' arrival'; 'Attending to customers' order'; 'Serving the order';

'Attending to customers' complaints and well-being' (activities to be participated in here by a hypothetical Spanish head-waiter). Munby's initiative, then, in keeping with communicative initiatives in general, is to start out from the behavioural categories and, by the same token, objectives, pertinent to particular learners, and then to derive samples of linguistic exponents associated with the relevant behaviours, for instance: 'Please follow me/Will you sit here, please.' In terms of Wilkins's (1972: 18) taxonomy of categories of communicative function, these two potential utterances would represent *suasion*, and would plainly be intended to have behavioural consequences.

The centrality of behavioural objectives within communicative methodology notwithstanding, their history commences earlier. They might, indeed, be traced back at least to Erasmus, who aimed *inter alia* at teaching students to produce the 'well-turned insult' (Kelly, 1969: 121). In the heyday of audiolingualism, it was fashionable to talk of 'terminal behaviour', this (somewhat unfortunate) phrase referring precisely to what learners would be able to 'do in the language' once learnt. In so far as behavioural objectives are also to be equated with *performance objectives* and '*linguistic performance abilities*', there was much interest in them during the 1960s in connection with the specification of language proficiency (Stern, 1983: 347ff.), and they are foreshadowed in the American Foreign Service Institute proficiency ratings. The interest was immediately generated and then followed up, particularly in the United States, by the seminal work of Benjamin S. Bloom and a team of collaborators which resulted in *Taxonomy of Educational Objectives: The classification of educational goals* (1956). Here the concern is with cognitive, affective and psychomotor objectives, behavioural objectives as such not being mentioned (though there is a hint of them in the much later *Handbook on Formative and Summative Evaluation of Student Learning* (1971: Section 14), also produced

by Bloom and colleagues), but a methodology for specifying objectives of any sort is clearly demonstrated. Specific concern with behavioural objectives is attributed by Stern (1983: 449, note 31) to Valette, mentioned below in conjunction with Disick.

Valette and Disick, discussing performance objectives in the context of individualization, state (1972: 10): 'Goals that specify the observable outcomes of instruction are called performance objectives. Performance objectives are also frequently referred to as behavioural or instructional objectives.' Their orientation is pedagogically rather than sociolinguistically determined, their concern being that objectives should be stated in terms which learners readily comprehend, and for them a performance objective comprises four elements: (1) purpose; (2) student behaviour; (3) conditions (under which performance is to be demonstrated); (4) criterion (for assessment of performance). This type of objective differs from 'communicative' objectives in that it relates to what can be expected of students in class, whereas the latter are referenced to the 'authentic' use of language in the 'outside world'. None the less, it is common to the two types of objective that they place the emphasis on 'doing' rather than simply 'knowing'.

A problem besetting behavioural objectives of the 'communicative' sort is that, in so far as these are related to language functions, there are no direct mappings between functions and linguistic EXPONENTS. Thus, to return to Munby, he is only able to give *plausible examples* of the language involved in 'Attending to customers' arrival' ('Please follow me/Will you sit here, please'). Phrases of such illocutionary force may be predictable, but not the precise words or structures – cf. 'There's a table in the corner, if you'd like it,' 'If you wouldn't mind waiting five minutes, there are some customers about to leave.' In other words, starting with behavioural categories militates against specification and systematization of language content. The debate is essentially the following: does one set up as objectives the learning of linguistic structures which perhaps can be 'filled with meaning' only later, or does one identify behavioural objectives which are 'meaningful', yet supply only partial and unsystematic exemplification, accessing the linguistic system randomly?

BIBLIOGRAPHY
Bloom, B. S. et al. (eds) (1956). *Taxonomy of Educational Objectives: The Classification of Educational Goals.* 2 vols. London: Longman.*
Bloom, B. S., Hastings, J. T. and Madaus, G. F. (eds), (1971). *Handbook on Formative and Summative Evaluation of Student Learning.* New York: McGraw-Hill.
Chomsky, N. (1965). *Aspects of the Theory of Syntax.* Cambridge, MA: MIT Press.
Hymes, D. H. (1972). On communicative competence. In J. B. Pride and J. Holmes (eds), *Sociolinguistics.*
Kelly, L. G. (1969). *25 Centuries of Language Teaching.* Rowley, MA: Newbury House.
Munby, J. (1978). *Communicative Syllabus Design.* Cambridge: Cambridge University Press.
Pride, J. B. and Holmes, J. (eds.) (1972). *Sociolinguistics.* Harmondsworth: Penguin Books.
Stern, H. H. (1983). *Fundamental Concepts of Language Teaching.* Oxford: Oxford University Press.
Valette, R. M. and Disick, R. S. (1972). *Modern Language Performance Objectives and Individualization.* New York: Harcourt Brace Jovanovich.
Wilkins, D. A. (1972). *An Investigation into the Linguistic and Situational Content of the Common Core in a Unit/Credit System.* Council of Europe, Committee for Out-of-School Education and Curriculum Development, Strasbourg (mimeograph).

JTR

**behaviourism**   A predominantly American learning theory developed earlier this century and associated with psychologists like Thorndike and Skinner. Learning is viewed as the development of stimulus-response associations through habit formation, habits being developed by practice and reinforcement. Complex behaviours are broken down into parts; see SHAPING. Behaviourism had a strong effect on both linguistics (particularly STRUCTURALISM) and language teaching, with AUDIOLINGUALISM attempting to apply its tenets. McDonough (1981) argues that language teaching based itself on a partial and soon outdated account of behaviourism. Chomsky (1959) bitterly attacked Skinner's (1957) application of behaviourism to language; see CHOMSKYAN LINGUISTICS.

BIBLIOGRAPHY
Chomsky, N. (1959). Review of *Verbal Behavior* by B. F. Skinner. *Language,* 35, 26–58.
McDonough, S. H. (1981). *Psychology in Foreign Language Teaching* London: Allen and Unwin.*
Skinner, B. F. (1957). *Verbal Behavior.* New York: Appleton Century-Crofts.

KJ

**Berlitz** is associated with language schools of that name in many countries of the world, specializing in courses for beginners; the first one was opened by Maximilian Berlitz in Providence, Rhode Island, in 1878. A secondary association is with the method developed by Berlitz, which he insisted on calling the 'Berlitz method', though one could view it as a variant of the DIRECT METHOD. The major principle is to use only the target language in class. Oral work is emphasized, initial teaching is through object-lessons and question-and-answer techniques form the core of teaching. The schools employ only NATIVE SPEAKERS of the languages taught.

BIBLIOGRAPHY
Howatt, A. P. R. (1984). *A History of English Language Teaching.* Oxford: Oxford University Press, 203–8.

JTR

**BICS/CALP**   One of those who challenged Oller's UNITARY COMPETENCE HYPOTHESIS was Cummins (1980), who distinguishes 'basic interpersonal communicative skills' and 'cognitive/academic language proficiency'. The latter are the skills which many tests tap, and are 'strongly related to general cognitive skills . . . and to academic achievement' (1980: 176). BICS is a quite separate dimension, to do with communicative capacity especially in interpersonal oral communication. A similar distinction is found in earlier studies like Genesee's (1976) on the role of intelligence in language learning. Cummins (1981) later related the distinction to 'context-reduced' (CALP associated) and 'context-embedded' communication (BICS associated).

BIBLIOGRAPHY

Cummins, J. (1980). The cross-lingual dimension of language proficiency: implications for bilingual education and the optimal age issue. *TESOL Quarterly*, 14, 175–87.
——(1981). The role of primary language development in promoting educational success for language minority students. Sacramento, CA: California State Department of Education, Office of Bilingual Bicultural Education.
Genesee, F. (1978). The role of intelligence in second language learning. *Language Learning*, 26/2, 267–80.

KJ

**bilingualism** The starting-point is the meaning of the term *bilingual* and its derivatives. In popular speech a bilingual is undoubtedly seen as a person who speaks two languages equally well; *so-and-so is bilingual in French and English* means that they use the two languages with equal ease. Nevertheless, even in non-technical usage, *bilingual* is sometimes more restricted. Advertisements for bilingual secretaries seem to require an ability to use the second language for professional purposes alone; those for bilingual teachers often require the ability to teach non-English-speaking children rather than knowledge of a second language.

One group of academic definitions of *bilingual* echoes this ideal of equal knowledge or 'balanced' bilingualism, for example, Bloomfield's definition of bilingualism as 'nativelike control of two languages', perhaps less ambiguously christened *ambilingualism* by Halliday, MacIntosh and Strevens (1964). These bilinguals have as extensive control of their second language as of their first. This is often called a 'maximal' definition of bilingualism.

The opposing group of definitions is based on the idea of use; Haugen claims that bilingualism starts at 'the point where a speaker can first produce complete meaningful utterances in the other language'. A tourist who successfully gets a cup of coffee in Germany by saying *Ein Kaffee* is bilingual, as is a schoolchild saying *Guten Morgen* in their first ever German lesson. This is often called the 'minimal' definition of bilingualism.

These types of definitions then oppose 'complete' knowledge of a second language versus any ability to use the second language at all; the difference comes from how much of the L2 it takes to be termed bilingual. The controversies over bilingualism have often been soured by an inability to see that the definitions in fact cover very different things. It is perfectly proper to investigate people who know two languages equally well; it is just as proper to look at people's ability to use a second language for everyday purposes to whatever degree. But they should not be confused.

The ambilingual with perfect control of two languages is in fact a rarity; most L2 users control a different range of REGISTERS and styles in the two languages; most research has shown subtle differences between the two languages in otherwise ambilingual people, with the dominant language having faster reaction times, more word associations, slightly different grammaticality judgements, and so on. A danger is that this definition sets an impossible ideal, dismissing everybody who does not achieve it as defective; the study of second language learning is a matter of accounting for people's failure to achieve this ideal. Language teaching becomes a history of failure since only a minute number of students succeed. While we do not expect schoolchildren to 'speak physics' like professional physicists, we expect them to leave school speaking French like Frenchmen! In this ambilingual type of definition bilingualism is also related solely to the knowledge of the native speaker, which the bilingual is *not* by definition; bilingual knowledge of language is not accepted as different from that of a monolingual. Mostly the field of Second Language Acquisition research has adopted this type of definition and talks of its learners in terms of failure and deficiency. Typically the people who speak the second language are referred to as L2 *learners*, rarely as L2 *speakers* or L2 *users* – L2 learning apparently never stops!

On the other hand, the anything-goes definition, perhaps, more frequent in bilingualism research, can trivialize language learning. Language is not just a matter of obtaining coffee in restaurants, even if this is the goal of some language teaching methods. It seems wrong to ascribe bilingualism to people who have not internalized language to the extent that they can use it for a variety of functions, both external interpersonal relationships and internal cognitive functions. Studying L2 users who only know how to say *Bonjour* diminishes the achievement and complexity of second language use.

Of course, most L2 users come somewhere in between, neither having knowledge of an L2 equivalent to their L1 for all their daily purposes nor being restricted to a single situation of language use. To avoid this dichotomized use of *bilingualism*, the neutral term *multi-competence* has been introduced to refer to knowledge of a second language, however extensive, and the person who knows a second language is a multi-competent speaker (Cook, 1992).

Many other factors have been seen as relevant to bilingualism by different writers: whether the individual identifies with both languages rather than one; the type of

learning situation encountered, say the one-person-one-language method often advocated for bilingual children in the home or the home/school split often found in later years; the age of the learner, whether 'early' child bilingualism or 'late' bilingualism.

In particular, the relationship between the two languages in the mind has figured in the discussion. The terms COMPOUND/COORDINATE BILINGUALISM derive from Weinreich (1953) (who in fact called them 'compound' and 'coordinative' bilingualism). In coordinate bilingualism the words of the two languages are kept separate in the mind so that a Russian/English bilingual has an English concept *book* pronounced /buk/, and a Russian concept *kniga* pronounced /knɪːgə/, with no connection between them; in compound bilingualism the words of the two languages refer to a common concept so that the single concept *book-kniga* is associated with both the English word /buk/ and the Russian word /knɪːgə/. Weinreich also employed a third term, *subordinative* bilingualism, which has fallen out of favour; this refers to the situation when the word in one language depends on the word in the other so that the concept *book* is linked to the English /buk/ which is linked in turn to the Russian word /knɪːgə/. While the compound/coordinate division became almost a household term, it fell into disrepute among psychologists, who found it difficult to establish experimentally, particularly when based on the manner in which the second language was acquired rather than on Weinreich's concept of language knowledge.

## BILINGUALISM IN SOCIETY

It is crucial to distinguish societal from individual bilingualism. Whether or not a country is officially bilingual has little to do with whether an individual is bilingual or whether that country has many bilingual individuals. That is to say, a bilingual country is a political concept recognizing the use of two languages within that country; but they may not be used in the same place, for example Canada with French and English in geographically separate areas, or Belgium with Walloon (French) and Flemish (Dutch) separated by a line on the map, apart from the city of Brussels. A bilingual individual may or may not live in an officially bilingual country and may not be bilingual in the official languages of that country – many bilinguals in Toronto probably speak English alongside Chinese, Japanese or Italian rather than French. Nor is the official language necessarily spoken as a first language by many of its inhabitants; Singapore has English as the official L1, Mandarin Chinese, Bahasa Malaysia and Tamil as the mother tongues of its citizens; Tanzania uses Swahili although only 10% of the population are native speakers. The choice of bilingualism at an official level reflects the aspirations of that society, its trading goals in the world and the attitudes of its ruling group, not necessarily the reality of bilingualism among its citizens. (See LANGUAGE PLANNING.)

Probably bilingualism in society usually means bilingualism of use in certain specified contexts rather than ambilingualism. Such bilingualism shades into DIGLOSSIA – the use of two codes, a Higher and a Lower in different circumstances, for example Swiss German versus High German in Switzerland or Classical Arabic versus local varieties in countries such as Morocco and Syria. Indeed, there seems to be a continuum between the ability to use both languages, the ability to use two dialects of the same language, and the ability to switch styles and registers within only one language. As Bailey (1973) has put it, 'competence is polylectal.'

Groupings of bilinguals are present in many countries, if not in all; national borders correspond poorly with linguistic borders. It is indeed rare to find a country where only a single language is spoken. France, for example, might seem to be associated only with French, but it has an estimated 9 million

people who are bilingual in other indigenous languages, as well as 2 million migrant workers.

One possibility is so-called 'internal colonies' – a minority language effectively surrounded by a majority language, like Welsh in Wales (or possibly in Patagonia), Basque in Spain, Sorbian in the east of Germany, Dyirbal in Australia or Ainu in Japan. In this case the minority language is not associated with another country outside its borders but exists within an enclave.

A second possibility is languages that stretch across several countries. One subgroup has no official status in any country, for example, the dialects of Romany spoken by gipsies across Europe, Yiddish, formerly spoken by Jews across Eastern Europe, or Same spoken by Lapps across Scandinavia. A second subgroup consists of languages spoken officially in one country but used by large minorities outside this, for instance, Swedish in Finland and Korean in Japan; folk myths insist that Melbourne is the largest Maltese-speaking city in the world and the Bronx the biggest Gujerati-speaking city outside the Indian subcontinent. Indeed, many of the political problems of Eastern Europe seem to result from borders that are linguistically arbitrary, such as the recent separations of Czechs from Slovaks, Ukrainians from Russians, and so on.

Thirdly there are the languages of groups that have moved to another country for political or economic reasons. To take an example from the seemingly monolingual country of England, almost any Londoner will be able to identify areas where other languages can be found: Gujerati in Southall, Polish in Ealing, Bengali in Whitechapel, German in Swiss Cottage, Greek in Finsbury Park, Turkish in Stoke Newington, Chinese in Soho, etc.

This multilingualism is in part the consequence of political domination of one country by another at some historical period, say the Korean speakers in Japan or the Algerians in France. The streets and restaurants of the capitals of the old colonial empires still reflect the mix of languages spoken in their former colonies, whether London, Amsterdam or Paris. Such people often had the right to immigrate from former colonies, at least until immigration laws were tightened. Many immigrants to the UK came from ex-British colonies such as India or Cyprus, where English already played some role; some in fact already spoke other regional varieties of English, whether West Indian or Australian (again readily associated by Londoners with Earls Court and Notting Hill). Most had some right of residence; many were actively recruited by British business as a source of labour. Alternatively, some countries have a 'right of return' for people who belong ethnically to the group but do not have the language, for example, Jews moving to Israel from Russia, or Germans to Germany from Poland.

This category overlaps with 'migrant' workers from countries with no political ties; Moroccans, Turks and Kurds arrived in Germany to earn money to send home and later brought families, and so on. Such migrant workers did not have previous contact with the language or the culture and, initially at any rate, there was no presumption that they would be staying.

A third possibility is political, ethnic, or religious refugees from some particular regime. Again to take London as an example, people stranded by the history of the twentieth century include: Jews from 1930s Austria, Poles from 1940s Poland, Indians from 1960s Uganda, Vietnamese from 1970s Vietnam, Bosnians from 1990s ex-Yugoslavia, and many more.

Fourthly there are so-called 'elite' bilinguals whose parents decided to bring them up speaking two languages, usually the language of one of the parents, sometimes not, as in the case of George Saunders (1982) bringing up his children to speak German in Australia. This upbringing may either be via the home situation or through the various schools that use more than the majority language of the country, whether the 'bilingual' schools in Canada where English-speaking children were taught through French (see IMMERSION PROGRAMMES), or 'international schools' where, for example, English is found in Kenya, India or Chile. Many case histories of this type of bilingualism have appeared, and also many guides to parents hoping to bring up their children in this way. Usually such parents belong to the middle or upper classes, sometimes to particular ethnic groups; for example, English is apparently widely used in Chinese homes in Malaysia.

The speakers of the majority language in a country may take very different attitudes to bilingualism in these groups of newcomers. This can be exemplified by the British progression from 'English for immigrants' which took it for granted that the newcomer had to learn the majority language, to 'multicultural English' which assumed that people could keep their L1 provided they learnt English alongside it, to 'bilingual English' which asserted that people had the right to keep both alive. English for immigrants often took the children out of the usual classroom in order to prepare them for life within it; bilingual English keeps the child within the normal classroom by providing ancillary help rather than by actively developing the child's bilingualism across both languages; this is partly a consequence of the Calderdale report (Commission for Racial Equality, 1987), which decided that any separate treatment of non-English-speaking children amounted to racial discrimination. In the US almost the opposite route has been followed, with decisions that the child has to be given access to his or her own language and that the child has the right to have specialist attention, though this has had some backlash in the form of the *English First* movement.

BILINGUALISM IN THE INDIVIDUAL

There may be many different reasons for an individual to become bilingual. Some are determined by the educational system. On the one hand languages are taught for local reasons internal to the country: children are required to learn the majority language because it is necessary to its effective functioning; they learn a foreign language because it has traditionally been seen as a mark of education. On the other hand there are international reasons for language teaching: students' jobs or careers may make use of another language; English is essential for many scientific careers because of its use in international science. There are also individual reasons for acquiring another language. It might be that people admire a particular country and so learn its language; it might be that they belong to a religion that requires a particular language for its devotions, such as Islam using Arabic, the Jewish religion Hebrew and, until recently, Roman Catholicism Latin. Or it may be that the educational system sets individual goals that the students will achieve through language teaching – understanding of foreign cultures, extra cognitive skills, understanding of the nature of language or even good citizenship.

The main question people ask about individual bilingualism is: is it a good thing? In one sense this is an odd question since it already presupposes that there is a problem. No one bothers to ask the equally sensible question: is monolingualism a good thing? At one time it was held that bilingualism was a disadvantage; for example, Thompson claimed in 1952 'There can be no doubt that the child reared in a bilingual environment is handicapped in his language growth.' Later research has mostly pointed to the advantages of bilingualism: children who know a second language are better at separating semantic from phonetic aspects of words, at classification tasks, and at creativity tests, and have better metalinguistic awareness. Diaz (1985) expressed a typical modern view: 'growing up with two languages is, indeed, an asset to children's intellectual development.' The multi-competent mind is more than the sum of its parts; multi-competent speakers score over monolinguals in areas other than the possession of a second language.

Nevertheless some warnings have been expressed. Lambert made a useful distinction between *additive* bilingualism in which speakers saw the L2 as an addition to their repertoire because it did not threaten their L1 identity and *subtractive* bilingualism in which the L2 takes away from their identity by undermining their L1. Cummins (1984) has seen a threshold in L2 learning; when the child gets through the threshold, the L2 is an advantage; until then it is a disadvantage. The moral for teaching is to make the L2 non-threatening and to allow the learner to persevere long enough to feel the benefits.

The second question asked about individuals is: how do the two languages relate in the mind of the individual? The alternatives seen by Grosjean (1989) are either *wholism* in which the two languages are inter-related or *separatism* in which they form separate systems. Experiments with adults, chiefly in the area of vocabulary, suggest that the two language systems are closely related: reaction times for a word are sensitive to the frequency of its cognate in a second language; morphemically unrelated translations do not influence performance while morphemically related words do; bilinguals have access to the meaning of a word in both languages rather than just the language being used. However, research with children suggests that, after an initial semantically organized phase, children keep the systems of the two languages distinct; they do not mix the words of the two languages or confuse their syntax. Research with physical location of languages in the brain used to claim that L2 users put greater emphasis on the right hemisphere; more recent research has been unable to find clear differences in location of the two languages in the brain (Zatorre, 1989).

The final issue concerns CODE-SWITCHING. This is the phenomenon unique to L2 learning in which speakers alternate two languages in a single discourse. In the context of discussion of bilingualism the issue is whether this is a good thing. Again, earlier work saw it as carelessness or lack of skill in the L2 when two languages were mixed together; later work has emphasized the complexity of code-switching in terms of the rules for its use, etc.

BIBLIOGRAPHY
Bailey, C.-Y. (1973). *Variation and Linguistic Theory*. Arlington, VA: Center for Applied Linguistics.
Commission for Racial Equality (1986). *Teaching English as a Second Language: Report of a formal investigation in Calderdale Education Authority*.
Cummins, J. (1979). Linguistic interdependence and the educational development of bilingual children. *Review of Educational Research*, 49, 222–51.
Diaz, R. M. (1985). The intellectual power of bilingualism. *Quarterly Newsletter of the Laboratory of Comparative Human Cognition*, 7/1, 16–22.
Grosjean, F. (1982). *Life with Two Languages*. Cambridge, MA: Harvard University Press.*
——(1989). Neurolinguists, beware! The bilingual is not two monolinguals in one person. *Brain and Language*, 36, 3–15.
Halliday, M. A. K., McIntosh, A. and Strevens, P. (1964). *The Linguistic Sciences and Language Teaching*. London: Longman.
Lambert, W. E. (1981). Bilingualism and language acquisition. In H. Winitz (ed.), *Native and Foreign Language Acquisition*. New York: New York Academy of Sciences.
Ludi, G., Milroy, L. and Muyskens, P. (1995). *One Speaker, Two Languages*. Cambridge: Cambridge University Press.
Romaine, S. (1994). *Bilingualism*, Oxford, Blackwell.*
Saunders, G. (1982). *Bilingual Children: Guidance for the family*. Clevedon: Multilingual Matters.
Skutnabb-Kangas, T. (1981). *Bilingualism or Not: The education of minorities*. Clevedon: Multilingual Matters.
Weinreich, U. (1953). *Languages in Contact*. The Hague: Mouton.
Zatorre, R. J. (1989). On the representation of multiple languages in the brain: old problems and new solutions. *Brain and Language*, 36, 127–47.

VJC

**bilingual syntax measure**   Devised by Burt, Dulay and Hernandez-Chavez (1975), this language elicitation procedure involves a series of cartoon drawings and associated questions (originally in English and Spanish). For example, subjects are presented with a cartoon of a large man and asked 'Why is he so fat?' It was designed to elicit data for MORPHEME ACQUISITION STUDIES.

BIBLIOGRAPHY
Burt, M., Dulay, H. and Hernandez-Chavez, E. (1975). *Bilingual syntax measure*. New York: Harcourt Brace Jovanovich.
Dulay, H. and Burt, M. (1973). Should we teach children syntax? *Language Learning*, 23, 245–58.

RH

**bottom-up processing**   In this type of processing the reader/listener attends to individual words and structures in the text itself, using these to build up an interpretation of the whole. Traditional linguistic analysis has involved bottom-up procedures, but recently the importance of TOP-DOWN PROCESSING has become recognized.

BIBLIOGRAPHY
Brown, G. and Yule, G. (1983). *Discourse Analysis*. Cambridge: Cambridge University Press.

KJ

# C

**case grammar** A grammatical framework developed within GENERATIVE GRAMMAR by Charles Fillmore (1968, 1977) and others as an alternative to the mainstream TRANSFORMATIONAL grammar. Sentence STRUCTURE is analysed here in terms of modality and proposition with 'semantic cases' Agent, Patient, Source, Goal, etc. functioning as arguments of the predicates.

BIBLIOGRAPHY
Fillmore, C. J. (1968). The case for case. In E. Bach and R. T. Harms (eds), *Universals in Linguistic Theory*. New York: Holt, Rinehart and Winston, 1–88.
——(1977). The case for case reopened. In P. Cole and J. Sadock (eds), *Syntax and Semantics*, 8. New York: Academic Press, 59–81.

EJ

**case studies** These involve the study of individual learners longitudinally. Some examples are Hakuta's (1976) description of the language development over 13 months of a 5-year-old Japanese-speaking girl learning English, Schumann's (1978) 10-month study of a Spanish-speaking adult learning English, and Huebner's (1985) year-long study of an adult Hmong speaker learning English. Typically case studies look at the development of a range of linguistic phenomena. They may be observational (e.g. Hakuta, 1976) or observational and interventionist (e.g. Schumann, 1978) who both observed and instructed his subject). Some case studies take the form of 'diaries', where researchers report their own L2 development (e.g. Schumann and Schumann, 1977). (See DIARY STUDIES, RESEARCH METHODOLOGY.)

BIBLIOGRAPHY
Hakuta, K. (1976). A case study of a Japanese child learning English as a second language. *Language Learning*, 26, 321–51.
Huebner, T. (1985). System and variability in interlanguage syntax. *Language Learning*, 35, 141–63.
Schumann, J. (1978). *The Pidginization Process: A model for second language acquisition*. Rowley, MA: Newbury House.
Schumann, F. and Schumann, J. (1977). Diary of a language learner: an introspective study of second language learning. In H. Brown, C. Yorio and R. Crymes (eds), *On TESOL '77*. Washington, DC: TESOL.

RH

**categories of communicative function** One of three category types in Wilkins's notional syllabus (see NOTIONAL/FUNCTIONAL SYLLABUSES). Commonly called 'functions', these categories express uses of language. Wilkins (1976) considers his functions under six headings. Two are: *Judgement and Evaluation* (functions like *expressing approval*) and *Emotional Relations* (e.g. *greeting*).

BIBLIOGRAPHY
Wilkins, D. A. (1973). An investigation into the linguistic and situational common core in a unit/credit system. In J. L. M. Trim, R. Richterich, J. A. van Ek, and D. A. Wilkins, *Systems Developments in Adult Language Learning*. Oxford: Pergamon Institute of English, 129–46.

——(1976). *Notional Syllabuses*. Oxford: Oxford University Press.

KJ

**chi-square** estimates the significance (see STATISTICS IN APPLIED LINGUISTICS RESEARCH) of an association between two variables expressed as frequencies. It compares the observed frequencies with those expected assuming no real difference. It is used to analyse questionnaires, coding tallies from observations, error occurrences and experiments.

BIBLIOGRAPHY
Woods, A., Fletcher, P. and Hughes, A. (1986). *Statistics in Language Studies*. Cambridge: Cambridge University Press, 132–53.

SMCD

**Chomskyan linguistics**    Since the mid-1950s linguistics has fed off the work of Noam Chomsky. Whether linguists sympathize with it or not, they have defined themselves by reacting to his models, not only in terms of general concepts of language and acquisition, but also in terms of the actual forms of linguistic description, whether syntax or phonology. This article first gives a brief historical sketch of the main periods in Chomskyan thinking, then looks at some of the main ideas, chiefly from the point of view of the present.

## HISTORICAL ERAS IN CHOMSKYAN LINGUISTICS

This section provides a brief historical outline for the reader who encounters Chomskyan linguistics through writings in other disciplines that have latched on to different phases of the theory for their own ends without noticing that it has moved on, for instance, that the concept of a 'rule', once vital, is now seen as peripheral, if not misleading.

## Syntactic Structures

Chomsky's first book *Syntactic Structures* (1957) gave its name to the first wave of thinking, which was chiefly concerned with grammatical description. Its contribution was to show that mentalistic grammar could be made scientific by the use of explicit and rigorous forms of statement, known as GENERATIVE GRAMMAR. Hierarchical phrase structure was described through 'rewrite rules' of the S→ NP VP type that expand one element into others, yielding eventually 'kernel sentences' of the language. But such rules were incapable of describing the whole of human language and needed to be amplified by 'transformations' that could modify the structure of the kernel sentence into passives, questions, etc. A key example sentence was *Colourless green ideas sleep furiously*, held to show the difference between grammaticality and meaningfulness. At more or less the same time Chomsky (1959) was savaging Skinner's behaviourist theory of language acquisition on the grounds *inter alia* that it ignored the crucial creative aspect of language through which we produce and understand sentences that are completely new to us.

*Key terms*: rewrite rule, phrase structure rule, transformation, kernel sentence.

## Aspects

The next wave again took its name from a book, *Aspects of the Theory of Syntax* (Chomsky, 1965). The major innovation was the recognition that all sentences had 'deep' structures that were transformed into the final 'surface' structures. Vocabulary became important in terms of the subcategorization possibilities of lexical items that permitted words to occur only in certain structural environments. The theory of generative phonology also started, which emphasized the underlying phonological form related to the phonetic representation by complex rules. Aspects theory recognized the difference between *linguistic competence* (the knowledge of language present in the individual mind) and *performance* (both examples of language that have been produced and the process through which speech is produced and comprehended (see COMPETENCE/PERFORMANCE); it also started to talk positively about language acquisition in terms of the Language Acquisition Device (LAD) which enables children to acquire language and argued that crucial aspects of language knowledge are built-in to LAD, that is to say innate. Key example sentences were *John is easy to please* and *John is eager to please*, demonstrating that two sentences with the same surface structure had different deep structures according to whether *John* was the object or subject of *please*. As this model developed, it became known first as the *Standard* Model, then as the *Extended Standard* Model, which refined the types of rules that were employed, in particular restricting the use of transformations.

*Key terms*: competence, performance, deep and surface structure, LAD.

## Government/binding theory

Again the book published as *Lectures on Government and Binding* (Chomsky, 1981) gave the name to this generation of thinking. The grammar now consisted of abstract principles that do not vary between languages and parameters that capture the variation between them (see examples below). The main levels were *D-structure*, that gave the 'pure' grammatical form, and *S-structure* linked to D-structure via movement, the only type of transformation now allowed; S-structure then connected to *Logical Form* (LF) on the one hand, and through *surface structure* to *Phonological Form* (PF); syntax was handled through X-bar syntax (see GENERATIVE GRAMMAR). Acquisition was now integrated with description; competence was always seen in the context of how it was acquired, i.e. how the parameters were

'triggered' by the language input. As it developed, this model became known as 'principles and parameters theory'; Chomsky's 1986 book *Barriers* revised X-bar syntax and so gave rise to *Barrier's syntax*, which gave the same abstract phrase structure to functional phrases such as the inflection phrase as to lexical phrases such as the noun phrase based on lexical heads. In this phase the theory started expanding from English, first to the Romance languages, then to Japanese, Chinese, and Arabic in particular.

*Key terms*: principles, parameters, movement, functional categories.

## The minimalist program

The current version, still in its early unsettled days, builds on developments in phase 3 (Chomsky, 1989, 1992, 1994): by establishing even more general properties of language, such as the *Principle of Economy*; by seeing language acquisition as a process of acquisition of lexical entries with parameter settings; and by abandoning the internal levels of D- and S-structure in favour of a complex relationship between the LF and PF components.

*Key terms*: economy, full interpretation, minimalism.

## LANGUAGE AS PART OF THE MIND

Chomskyan theory has always emphasized language as a property of the mind rather than as social behaviour. The first goal of linguistics is to establish what an individual human mind knows – *linguistic competence*. Hence the term 'grammar' is more fundamental than the term 'language'; language is an artificial generalization to do with society, an epiphenomenon; what the individual mind knows is a grammar.

Language knowledge takes the form of universal principles common to all languages and parameters with values specific to a particular language. These elements have quite different properties from other cognitive systems and do not develop out of them. Hence language is claimed to be a separate mental faculty of its own, quite distinct from other faculties of the mind. Furthermore animal communication systems do not have the same properties; nor have animals been clearly shown to be capable of acquiring them. So the language faculty is held to be the unique genetic endowment of the human species. Studying the bases of human language knowledge can bring about understanding of the unique qualities of the human mind. In principle, not only is language part of the psychology of the mind but it is also part of the study of the brain: in due course the actual physical existence of UNIVERSAL GRAMMAR (UG) will be established.

What you know about language (linguistic competence) is distinct from what you do with language (PRAGMATIC COMPETENCE). On the one hand you know the structure and meaning of *Can you close the door?*; on the other you know whether it is being used to ask a question or make a request. Chomsky does not deny that language has functions, nor that it is legitimate to study them, but insists that this is a separate goal of linguistics, subsequent to answering what language *is*. He does, however, question whether communication is the chief function of language, pointing out the many internal functions that language has for individuals in organizing their cognitive lives. Similarly the psychological processes for producing and comprehending sentences are secondary to the study of competence; while they make use of competence, they are limited by many psychological elements such as working memory that are irrelevant to competence.

The evidence for what we know could be of many kinds. The form of evidence that comes easiest to hand is sample sentences of the language such as *John ate an apple*. Any theory will have to explain how this fits into English grammar – unless, of course, someone denies that the sentence is English. Once this easy source of evidence is exhausted we

could go on to examining experiments, language disorders, children's grammars etc.

The topic of study is then *Universal Grammar* (UG), the part of the mind common to all human beings that enables them to know and acquire languages. The important things are the general properties that languages have in common rather than the idiosyncratic ways in which they differ. Knowledge of language is forced into a particular mould by the human mind. Languages are basically very similar, differing largely in the actual lexical items and their behaviour.

## DETAILS OF PRINCIPLES AND PARAMETERS

Throughout all its phases Chomskyan linguistics has been based on precise claims about the description of language. It is all too easy to fall into the trap of seeing the theory as simply a set of general ideas divorced from the 'facts' of language. Principles and parameters theory uses an apparatus of fearsome complexity to interrelate a small handful of principles and parameters, such as the following:

- the *Principle of Structure-dependency*: the movement of elements of the sentence to form questions, etc., invariably takes account of the structural relationships of the sentence rather than the sheer order of the words;
- the *Projection Principle*: the properties of lexical items project onto the syntax of the sentence, that is to say, much of the structure of the sentence depends upon the idiosyncratic properties of the vocabulary it contains; for example, the verb *pay* projects onto the sentence the requirement for a subject, a direct object and an indirect object, as in *He paid the money to a middleman*;
- the *Binding Principles*: whether or not pronouns can relate to particular antecedents is controlled by universal principles that state the 'domain' within which this relationship can take place with some parametric variation between languages; for instance, *him* in *Peter said John would feed him* must not

relate to *John*, and *herself* in *Jane wondered if Helen had faith in herself* must not relate to *Jane*;

- *Full Interpretation*: there are no redundant elements in the structure of language, so that every element that appears in a structure must play some role in its interpretation;
- *the Principle of Economy*: language structures must be as economical as possible: the only elements that can appear in a sentence are those that have to;
- *the Opacity Parameter*: languages like English have an opaque AGRP (Agreement Phrase) so that the verb cannot move across it to get *\*John likes not Mary*; languages like French have non-opaque AGRP permitting *Jean n'aime pas Marie*;
- *the Pro-drop (Null Subject) Parameter*: some languages like Italian permit sentences without subjects as in *Sono di Torino*; others like English do not, as in *\*Am from Turin*.

## GENERAL IDEAS OF LANGUAGE ACQUISITION

How does the human mind come effortlessly to acquire knowledge of such complexity in a matter of a few years? Only because the task is extremely circumscribed; the mind automatically presumes that the language has certain properties and varies within narrow limits; hence it does not have to bother with exploring all the possibilities for language, but can exclude most of them in advance. Language acquisition then builds on the pre-existing properties of the human language faculty. The principles are imposed upon the grammar; the parameter settings are derived from the child's language experience (see INNATENESS HYPOTHESIS).

The crucial relationship is that between the language evidence that children hear and the grammar that they come to know. The type of knowledge that forms linguistic competence could not be acquired from the actual sentences they hear. This is called the 'poverty-of-the-stimulus argument'. It is claimed that language acquisition must take place on the basis of positive evidence

of sentences that the child hears rather than from negative evidence of parents' corrections or from forms that do *not* occur or from social interaction, imitation, etc. This is partly because such negative evidence is not found to occur on any large scale with children, partly because children do not make the right mistakes or adults know the right information to supply them with, partly because the type of information used in principles and parameters theory could not be extracted from the language evidence they hear.

The child's mind starts in a particular state; language evidence comes from outside, partly to show how principles are instantiated, partly to trigger particular parameter settings, above all to provide the vocabulary in all its complexity. All the child needs to acquire language is exposure to a sample of sentences that provide the data on which knowledge of language can be built. Nothing else is in principle necessary for acquisition. Thus the prime evidence for the linguist that something has been acquired is that it forms part of competence; there is no requirement to follow the actual stages of acquisition by a child if clearly something is known. A crucial early insight spelled out by David McNeil (1966) was the independent grammars assumption that children should be treated in their own right, not as deficient adult speakers.

## RECENT RESEARCH QUESTIONS IN LANGUAGE ACQUISITION

While earlier versions of Chomskyan linguistics emphasized the 'logical problem' of language acquisition distinct from any study of actual children, the 1980s saw a large amount of research work into the application of this model with data from children or L2 learners. Typical questions were:

- *how does the child set parameters in the L1?* Hyams's classic work (1986) first established that English children appear to go through a stage where they produce sentences without subjects, as if they were speaking Spanish; the other setting for the parameter needs to be triggered by positive evidence of sentences with *there* and *it* subjects. Modern thinking has redefined the description of pro-drop and relates it to the possession of 'morphological uniformity' – whether a language has uniform morphology in the present tense (all forms inflected or none) or has non-uniform morphology (some forms inflected but not all); the child has to spot which is the case;

- *is all of UG present at birth?* Two possibilities exist; one is the *continuity hypothesis* that the whole set of UG principles and parameters is present in the mind from birth, like the heart, their presence not being obvious because of the restrictions on the child's performance, etc.; the other is the *maturational hypothesis* that the principles and parameters emerge in a fixed order, like the teeth;
- *do L2 learners have access to UG?* L2 learners might have *direct access* to UG and so be uninfluenced by the L1. Or they might have *indirect access* to UG via the L1. Or they might have *no access* to UG and learn the L2 without its help. Considerable discussion took place over this with strong positions being taken for each possibility; many found that, while L2 learners could be demonstrated to know UG to some extent, they did not know it as well as in the L1. Others have argued that the metaphor of access is misguided as UG *is* itself the process of learning and *is* itself the product of learning rather than being a separate object;
- *how do learners acquire functional categories?* As the theory moved towards depending on functional categories such as the Inflection Phrase, so it began to ask how children acquired them. The most radical approach is that of Radford (1990) who claims that children lack functional phrases till around the age of 20 months; this means that they are unable in English to use tense inflections, determiners, etc. and that in languages like German they are unable to move the verb from its underlying position to its surface verb second position (as there is nowhere in the structure for it to land).

## APPLICATIONS TO LANGUAGE TEACHING

Direct applications to language teaching are rather few. Undoubtedly Chomsky's strong attack on Skinner (Chomsky, 1959) was one of the factors contributing to the decline of AUDIOLINGUALISM, which depended on similar learning ideas, and hence to the rise of COMMUNICATIVE LANGUAGE TEACHING. Frequently, however, Chomsky's idea of linguistic competence has been used as a bogey-man to convince people of the rightness of Hymes's concept of COMMUNICATIVE COMPETENCE – without any mention of the Chomskyan concept of pragmatic competence. Otherwise the independent grammars assumption came into Second Language Acquisition research as the concept of INTERLANGUAGE – L2 learners have grammars of their own which they build upon for themselves. Again this liberated the teacher from being the only source of knowledge and thus was one element that provided an academic justification for the groupwork and pairwork of the communicative approach as well as its communicative ends.

Direct attempts to apply Chomskyan linguistics have mostly been based on misconceptions. So-called transformation drills changed one sentence into another, failing to realize that transformations worked on structures not on sentences. COGNITIVE CODE teaching claimed explicit explanation aided L2 learning, quite unsupported by the theory which has never claimed that native speakers have conscious understanding of the components of linguistic competence. Krashen's NATURAL APPROACH was based on a model that had a language acquisition device at its core, even if it heretically assigned more importance to the properties of the input (see COMPREHENSIBLE INPUT) than to those of the learner's mind. More recent research has examined whether provision of negative evidence helps in the acquisition of certain syntactic structures, not the most central problem in language teaching. Overall implications of principles and parameters theory would seem to be: UG is concerned only with the core area of language acquisition, which automatically takes care of itself, and so does not have much to say for teachers; teaching should provide input for learners to set parameters and adequate vocabulary in context to promote the acquisition of the idiosyncratic aspects of the syntax; language teaching should remember that language is knowledge in the mind, not just social interaction with other people. (See also FIRST AND SECOND LANGUAGE ACQUISITION, LINGUISTICS IN LANGUAGE TEACHING, MONITOR MODEL.)

BIBLIOGRAPHY

Chomsky, N. (1957). *Syntactic Structures*. The Hague: Mouton.
——(1959). Review of B. F. Skinner *Verbal Behavior*. *Language*, 35, 26–58.
——(1965). *Aspects of the Theory of Syntax*. Cambridge, MA: MIT Press.
——(1981). *Lectures on Government and Binding*. Dordrecht: Foris.
——(1986). *Barriers*. Cambridge, MA: MIT Press.
——(1989). Some notes on economy of derivation and representation. *MIT Working Papers in Linguistics*, 10, 43–74.
——(1992). A minimalist program for linguistic theory. *MIT Occasional Papers in Linguistics*, no. 1.
——(1994). Bare phrase structure. *MIT Occasional Papers in Linguistics*, no. 1.
——(1995). *The Minimalist Program*. Cambridge, MA: MIT Press.
Cook, V. J. and Newson, M. (1995). *Chomsky's Universal Grammar*. 2nd edn. Oxford: Blackwell.*
Goodluck, H. (1991). *Language Acquisition: A linguistic introduction*. Oxford: Blackwell.
Haegeman, L. (1991). *Introduction to Government and Binding Theory*. Oxford: Blackwell.
Hyams, N. (1986). *Language Acquisition and the Theory of Parameters*. Dordrecht: Reidel.
McNeill, D. (1966). Developmental psycholinguistics. In F. Smith and G. A. Miller (eds), *The Genesis of Language: A psycholinguistic approach*. Cambridge, MA: MIT Press.
Radford, A. (1990). *Syntactic Theory and the Acquisition of English Syntax*. Oxford: Blackwell.
Roca, I. (1994). *Generative Phonology*. London: Routledge.

VJC

**classroom management** Richards (1990: 10) has the following definition: 'classroom management refers to the ways in which student behaviour, movement and interaction during a lesson are organized and controlled by the teacher.' Various possible organizational structures (e.g. whole class, groups, pairs) have attracted much discussion; see McDonough and Shaw (1993: 229) for a useful diagrammatic representation of these possible organizational structures. The effect of such structures on interaction patterns has also been the subject of much debate (see Long, 1975, for example), while Wright (1987) *inter alia* views them in terms of a wider socialization process. There is also a large literature on the problem of large classes; see Nolasco and Arthur (1988).

BIBLIOGRAPHY

Long, M. H. (1975). Group work and communicative competence in the ESOL classroom. In M. K. Burt and H. C. Dulay (eds), *On TESOL '75: New Directions in Second Language Learning, Teaching and Bilingual Education*. Washington, DC: TESOL, 211–23.
McDonough, J. and Shaw, C. (1993). *Materials and Methods in ELT*. Oxford: Blackwell.*
Nolasco, R. and Arthur, L. (1988). *Large Classes*. Basingstoke: Macmillan.
Richards, J. C. (1990). The dilemma of teacher education in second language teaching. In J. C. Richards and D. Nunan (eds), *Second Language Teacher Education*. Cambridge: Cambridge University Press, 3–15.
Wright, T. (1987). *Roles of Teachers and Learners*. Oxford: Oxford University Press.

KJ

**classroom observation** (CO) is a means of undertaking research into what occurs in classrooms by attempting systematically to observe and keep records of classroom events. CO has its roots in the general field of education, and it is only in recent decades that systems intended specifically for second language classrooms have been developed. According to Chaudron (1988), four research traditions are evident in the development of CO: the psychometric tradition, interaction analysis, DISCOURSE ANALYSIS and ethnographic or ethnomethodological (see ETHNOMETHODOLOGY). Across these traditions are found a variety of observational modes; in some cases it may be enough for the observer to work with a pre-prepared matrix, filling it in as the lesson occurs. In other cases full transcriptions from tape may be required, with lengthy and complex analysis. CO has been used as a technique in the study of many aspects of language teaching activity. Learner behaviour has been intensively studied, with attention given to issues like what learners do to generate input, and what strategies good (and bad) learners employ. Teacher behaviour has similarly been covered, with particular attention focused on strategies of error correction and on questioning techniques. It is natural that CO should also have been used to attempt to discern cause/effect relationships between types of learner or teacher behaviour and instances of successful learning. One common use of CO is in the field of teacher education, where trainee teachers are led to an awareness of aspects of classroom behaviour which might otherwise escape attention by means of observation. Although CO clearly has an important role to play in the study of language learning and teaching, its limits need to be recognized. It is by definition concerned with observable and overt behaviour; since so many learning processes are covert, they will not be easily discernible simply by observation, and other research techniques, like INTROSPECTION, will need to be employed. For general discussions of CO in relation to language learning and teaching, see Chaudron (1988), Allwright (1988) and Mitchell (1985).

## THE FOUR RESEARCH TRADITIONS

An early tradition in the history of CO is the psychometric one. The term psychometry refers to the measurement of psychological characteristics, and, for Taylor and others (1970): 'the essence of psychological measurement is the assigning of numerical values to behavioural events such that differences in behaviour are represented by differences in score.' A large number of the psychometric CO studies involved attempts in the 1950s and 1960s at METHOD COMPARISONS, a celebrated one being the Pennsylvania project (Smith, 1971), which involved a version of CO, largely to explore the extent to which the teaching methods being used were in fact being adhered to. The failure of method comparisons to reach acceptable conclusions is partly the reason for a move towards the second CO tradition, that of interaction analysis. Flanders (1970) was a pioneer in this tradition and, as Moskovitz (1968) notes, 'the Flanders categories were used first to determine normative patterns of classroom interaction between teachers and pupils and later in the inservice and preservice training of teachers as a tool for self-analysis and self-improvement.' Moskovitz herself began by using Flanders's categories, but she later adapted them into her own system, known as FLint (for details see Moskovitz, 1971). Although FLint was the most popular system in this tradition, Mitchell (1985) mentions several other competing models. The basis of the discourse analysis tradition lies in the interest developed in the 1970s in SPEECH ACT THEORY. In the general educational field, Bellack and others (1966) introduced the MOVE as a unit of analysis. Sinclair and Coulthard (1975) built on this by developing a system of units intended to characterize the functions of pieces of discourse. Their units are 'lesson', 'transaction', 'exchange', 'move', 'act'. Fanselow (1977) developed another system specifically for the language learning field, and he called it FOCUS, for Foci for Observing Communications Used in Settings. He speaks of the need to develop a technical language to speak about classrooms: 'we have,' he says, 'phonemes and morphemes but no teachemes.' Fanselow's categories are: 'who speaks'; 'pedagogic purpose'; 'medium used'; 'area of content'; 'how mediums are used to communicate content areas'. Others in this tradition are Long and others (1976 – an experiment in Mexico comparing lockstep and pairwork interaction) and Naiman and others (1978 – one of the GOOD LANGUAGE LEARNER STUDIES). The final research tradition is the ethnographic or ethnomethodological one. The basis of the ethnomethodology tradition is that it studies the 'rules of the game' with central concepts being that of the 'participant observer' and of contextual features. Chaudron (1988: 46) notes that 'the result of [ethnographic CO] investigation is usually a detailed description of the research site, and an account of the principles or rules of interaction that guide the participants to produce their actions and meanings and to interpret the actions and utterances of others.' Van Lier (1984) provides a full example of ethnomethodological CO; see particularly his chapter on REPAIR.

## MODES OF OBSERVATION

It is apparent from the above that the types of categories used in the analysis of classroom events have differed according to the aims of the observer, as well as to prevailing patterns of linguistic analysis. Similar variation has occurred over the mode of recording events. In some models, like Moskovitz's (1968) FLint, the observer has an empty matrix specifying the categories for analysis. Entries are made in the matrix during class at regular intervals (every ten seconds, for example) so that by the end of a lesson a graphic record of events is available. This mode of recording is inevitably somewhat

crude, but for many purposes this may not matter, since what is required may only be a rough indication of classroom events. The mode has distinct advantages, requiring neither technology (tape-recorders, which may break down) to record, nor vast expense of time to make transcriptions. But, as Moskovitz's FLint exemplifies, these observational modes may involve a large amount of observer training before the observation can be handled competently. Where the purpose of the CO requires it, lessons may be transcribed (at great expense of time) and a more thorough analysis undertaken. It is important to link method of analysis to purpose. It is not automatically the case that the most detailed analysis will be the best. The kind of detail a phonetician may require of samples of learner language would simply be unnecessary for what is required by a teacher trainer who wishes to indicate to trainees what proportion of a lesson is filled with teacher talk.

There are many other problems which modes of analysis raise, particularly where some form of quantification is required. Hence even an apparently simple issue such as quantifying the proportion of teacher talk introduces the question of what units one counts in. An obvious unit is the word; alternatives such as Bellack and others' (1966) move have also been mentioned, and there are others such as the T-UNIT.

CO has been used by educationalists and applied linguists for a variety of purposes. The following consideration of these is based on Chaudron (1988).

## OBSERVING LEARNER BEHAVIOUR

A good deal of CO research has been directed at observing learner behaviour in classrooms. Some of this has been concerned to identify characteristics associated with good learners. The major GOOD LANGUAGE LEARNER STUDY, Naiman and others (1978), involves a large-scale CO component in which they use their own class observation schedule. Part of the aim of this study was to identify overt behaviours of good learners, but in this the researchers were only partially successful. Hence they manage to correlate proficiency scores with hand-raising for the purposes of asking questions, but they are forced to conclude that it is other research techniques (particularly the interview) which provide most information. This part of the Naiman study is essentially concerned with LEARNING STRATEGIES. Chaudron (1988: 110) lists studies in learner strategies, most (though not all) of which employ CO.

Studies of learner interactions form another considerable research area where CO has been shown to have a role. In these studies the concept of NEGOTIATION OF MEANING has central importance. Many feel that this form of negotiation contributes to language learning in various ways, and as a result there are studies which attempt to identify its presence in different forms of interaction. Varonis and Gass (1985), for example, show that non-native speaker interactions involve more meaning-negotiated exchanges than native to non-native interactions. Other such studies include Long and others (1976), Doughty and Pica (1986), and Gaies (1983).

Two other important areas are the study of input and output. The role of input in language learning has attracted strong opinions over the decades, and the concept of the HIGH/LOW INPUT GENERATOR has been explored by Seliger (1977) using a type of CO. (See also INPUT HYPOTHESIS.) The role of output is similarly open to exploration through CO; see Swain (1985).

## OBSERVING TEACHER BEHAVIOUR

As much attention has been paid to teachers' classroom behaviour as to that of learners, with some studies concerned with amount of teacher talk, others with its functional distribution, and still others with the modifications to normal speech which teachers employ in second language classrooms. For discussion of these issues, see TEACHER TALK. Two specific issues which are given detailed treatment in the literature are how learners are given feedback on performance, and what questioning techniques teachers use. For the first of these, see ERROR CORRECTION. Studies on teachers' questioning behaviour typically consider the different QUESTION TYPES, the display/referential differentiation being a much used one in such studies – see Long and Sato (1983). The general finding, confirmed over a number of studies, is that language teachers use significantly more display and fewer referential questions with non-native speakers, although there is some evidence to suggest that this is not so much the case in less form-focused classrooms.

Chaudron (1988: 127) considers various studies that have looked at question modifications used by L2 teachers. These involve such things as an increase in repetitions of questions, plus longer 'wait-times', with teachers being prepared to wait longer for an answer. Long (1981) considers another parameter, the rephrasing of questions with an 'or-choice' alternative. Chaudron's example is substitution of 'what would you like to drink?' with 'would you like coffee, tea, beer?' Other studies are concerned with the role different questions play in interactions, and in this respect the distinctions between 'comprehension checks', 'confirmation checks' and 'clarification requests' are relevant. The first of these check that the listener has understood, while in the second and third the speaker is checking the speaker's comprehension of the listener – the second asks for a yes/no type of response, while the third is more open-ended. There is an assumption that modes like these will lead to increased negotiation of meaning and hence (it may be hypothesized) to more learning.

## DISCERNING CAUSE/EFFECT RELATIONSHIPS

CO is one of a number of techniques associated with work which tries to establish cause/effect relationships between pedagogic practices and success in learning. It is natural that applied linguistics should be particularly interested in such relationships. But a number of research problems are involved. Where there is evidence of success occurring, it is often difficult to isolate one particular variable in the experimental situation which may be said to have caused it. A further difficulty is to establish what constitutes success; one common procedure is to administer a test immediately after the pedagogic practice under consideration. But to be sure that true learning (as opposed to memorization, for example) is what has been occurring would involve investigation over a longer time-span.

Lightbown (1983) provides an example of another common research area where CO is used – attempts to relate frequency of occurrence of a form in teacher talk with its occurrence in learner talk. She quantified the input to and output from different groups of learners and her study suggests the conclusion that frequency in input may influence learners' production over the short but not the long term. Hence learners may reproduce a structure frequently occurring in class during a particular week (say), but the same structure may dramatically decrease in output a month later. This is clearly an area where longitudinal data would be useful.

Mitchell and others (1981: 10) summarize well the problems associated with these kinds of research thus: 'at present hardly any variable identified by any researcher among the multifarious events of the FL teaching/learning process has been empirically demonstrated to be "effective" in the sense of having a causal link with the acquisition of the target FL by pupils.' The model they develop for their research is particularly geared to studying the effects of pedagogic procedures on FL teaching, and it examines such variables as the type of language activity, topics of discourse, the mode of teacher involvement (instructing, watching, interacting etc.). They attempt to correlate such aspects of lessons with learner achievement on tests, and find positive ones between achievement and teachers' use of metalanguage, as well as the degree of learner talk. Among the variables which have attracted research interest in other studies are the degree of form focus, the amount of explicit grammar instruction and the amount of learner initiation of interactions.

## CO AS A TOOL IN TEACHER EDUCATION

One of the major uses to which CO has been put is in the training of language teachers. For details of this use, see Allwright (1988), particularly chapter 2, and Allwright and Lenzuen (1997). The work of Moskovitz (1968) exemplifies it. She is concerned with the use of observational systems 'to increase [teachers'] sensitivity to their own classroom behaviour and its effects and influence on students' (p. 76). She reports various experiments where different systems, based on that of Flanders, were taught to different teacher groups, some pre-service and some in-service. The teachers were then asked to analyse their own lessons, and to suggest changes they would make in their own teaching based on their analysis. Moskovitz reports highly positive findings, with a good deal of enthusiasm on the part of the trainees for this mode of instruction.

In a more recent study, Peck (1988) advocates the use of CO as the basis for ACTION RESEARCH. He notes (p. 203)

that some groups of teachers are already collaborating in order to help each other improve their results. In one school, for instance, a department of three language teachers has agreed to use a mixture of reciprocal observation and recording of lessons using a simple domestic radio-cassette recorder in order, first of all, to establish their existing method of teaching and the differences between themselves as individuals, and then jointly to plan principled changes to their teaching practice, in order to seek improvement in their students' performance.

## ADVANTAGES AND LIMITATIONS OF CO

The literature is full of warnings for those tempted to think that CO is the definitive research tool in applied linguistic research. Here is one from Naiman and others (1978: 99) whose substantial CO study is mentioned above:

Strict observation in language learning classrooms does not reveal language learning strategies or specific techniques other than fairly obvious indicators; for example, participation or non-participation in classroom activities. In other words, on the basis of mere observation neither teachers nor trained observers can be expected to identify whether or not these students are successfully learning, and whether or not they are employing useful learning techniques.

At the same time, CO is able to offer a degree of concrete evidence for assertions about learning and teaching. Often it finds a use alongside other techniques, supporting but not supplanting them. Such is the conclusion of Wall and Alderson (1993), who studied the effect of changes in the Sri Lankan examination system on teaching practice. Their study makes a methodological claim for the value of combining techniques such as interview with CO, with the latter giving support to the findings of the former, but not in itself being a powerful enough research tool to provide sufficient evidence alone.

BIBLIOGRAPHY

Allwright, R. L. (1988). *Observation in the Language Classroom*. London: Longman.*

Allwright, R. L. and Lenzuen, R. (1997). Exploratory practice: work at the Cultura Inglesa, Rio de Janeiro, Brazil. *Language Teaching Research*, 1/1, 73–9.

Bellack, A. A., Kliebard, H. M., Hymen, R. T. and Smith, F. L. (1966). *The Language of the Classroom*. New York: Teachers' College Press.

Chaudron, C. (1988). *Second Language Classrooms*. Cambridge: Cambridge University Press.*

Doughty, C. and Pica, T. (1986). Information gap tasks: do they facilitate second language acquisition? *TESOL Quarterly*, 20, 305–25.

Fanselow, J. F. (1977). Beyond 'Rashomon' – conceptualizing and describing the teaching act. *TESOL Quarterly*, 11, 15–39.

Flanders, N. A. (1970). *Analyzing Teaching Behavior*. New York: Addison-Wesley.

Gaies, S. J. (1983). Learner feedback: an exploratory study of its role in the second language classroom. In H. W. Seliger and M. H. Long (eds), *Classroom Oriented Research in Second Language Acquisition*. Rowley, MA: Newbury House, 190–212.

Lightbown, P. A. (1983). Exploring relationships between developmental and instructional sequences in L2 acquisition. In H. W. Seliger and M. H. Long (eds), *Classroom Oriented Research in Second Language Acquisition*. Rowley, MA: Newbury House, 217–43.

Long, M. H. (1981). Questions in foreigner talk discourse. *Language Learning*, 31, 135–57.

Long, M. H., Adams, L., McLean, M. and Castanos, F. (1976). Doing things with words: verbal interaction in lockstep and small group classroom situations. In J. F. Fanselow and R. Crymes (eds), *On TESOL '76*. Washington, DC: TESOL, 137–53.

Long, M. H. and Sato, C. J. (1983). Classroom foreigner talk discourse: forms and functions of teachers' questions. In H. W. Seliger and M. H. Long (eds), *Classroom Oriented Research in Second Language Acquisition*. Rowley, MA: Newbury House, 268–83.

Mitchell, R. (1985). Process research in second-language classrooms. *Language Teaching*, 18, 330–52.

Mitchell, R., Parkinson, B. and Johnstone, R. (1981). *The Foreign Language Classroom: An observational study*. Stirling Educational Monographs no. 9. Stirling: Department of Education, University of Stirling.

Moskovitz, G. (1968). The effects of training foreign language teachers in interaction analysis. *Foreign Language Annals*, 1, 218–35.

——(1971). Interaction analysis – a new modern language for supervisors. *Foreign Language Annals*, 5, 211–21.

Naiman, N., Fröhlich, M., Stern, H. H. and Todesco, A. (1978). *The Good Language Learner.* Toronto: Ontario Institute for Studies in Education.

Peck, A. (1988). *Language Teachers at Work: A description of methods.* London: Prentice Hall.

Seliger, H. W. (1977). Does practice make perfect? A study of interaction patterns and L2 competence. *Language Learning,* 27, 263–78.

Sinclair, J. McH. and Coulthard, M. (1975). *Towards an Analysis of Discourse.* Oxford: Oxford University Press.

Smith, P. D. (1971). A comparison of the cognitive and audiolingual approaches to foreign language instruction: the Pennsylvania foreign language project. Philadelphia: Center for Curriculum Development.

Swain, M. (1985). Communicative competence: some roles of comprehensible input and comprehensible output in its development. In S. M. Gass and C. G. Madden (eds), *Input in Second Language Acquisition.* Rowley, MA: Newbury House, 235–53.

Taylor, A., Sluckin, W., Davies, D. R., Reason, J. T., Thomson, R. and Colman, A. M. (1970). *Introducing Psychology.* Harmondsworth: Penguin Books.

Van Lier, L. (1988). *The Classroom and the Language Learner.* London: Longman.

Varonis, E. M. and Gass, S. (1985). Native/ nonnative conversations: a model for negotiation of meaning. *Applied Linguistics,* 6, 71–90.

Wall, D. and Alderson, J. C. (1993). Examining washback: the Sri Lankan impact study. *Language Testing,* 10/1, 11–39.

KJ

**classroom studies in SLA** Language learning in classrooms can be viewed from three perspectives: (a) from the perspective of interaction (between teacher and learners, and learners with each other) and the effects this has on development; (b) from the perspective of the effects of instruction on language development (as opposed to noninstructed development); (c) from the perspective of whether different methods of instruction have different effects on development (see also METHOD COMPARISONS). The second and third perspectives will be the subject of this entry. (For the first see CLASSROOM OBSERVATION.)

It is important to be clear, in considering classroom studies, that the term 'classroom' can refer to a range of different practices. In this discussion, we shall assume three cardinal reference points usefully defined by Lightbown and Spada (1993): naturalistic acquisition, acquisition in a traditional instructional environment and acquisition in a communicative instructional environment.

## DEFINITIONS OF NATURALISTIC AND CLASSROOM ENVIRONMENTS

In naturalistic acquisition learners are surrounded by the L2 for many hours a day, encounter varied, unselective and random input, encounter different native speakers and have to use the L2 for a variety of real-life purposes (getting information, getting meaning across). Furthermore, learners are rarely corrected.

In traditional instructional environments learners are exposed to the L2 for only a few hours each week, encounter few native speakers, encounter carefully selected L2 data (which progressively introduces the structures of the L2) and encounter a limited variety of discourse types. The focus is on the form of the L2, learners are frequently corrected, and learners are motivated to be correct in order to pass exams.

In communicative instructional environments, although learners are also exposed to the L2 for only a few hours each week, encounter few native speakers, and may also want to pass exams, the focus is on conveying meaning through the L2 (rather than on the L2 itself). ERROR CORRECTION is limited, a variety of discourse types are encountered (through communicative activities like storytelling, role playing, using realia (newspapers, menus, tickets, etc.)), and the language used is selective only in order to be comprehensible, not for the purpose of introducing structures progressively.

## GRAMMATICAL PROFICIENCY IN TRADITIONAL CLASSROOM AND NATURALISTIC LEARNERS

Given these broad definitions, one group of classroom studies of SLA has looked at whether L2 learners in traditional instructional environments develop grammatical proficiency differently from naturalistic learners. Results seem to suggest that the route of development is broadly similar under both conditions, although the rate may be accelerated by traditional instruction (see RATE/ROUTE IN SLA).

For example, Pica (1983) established three groups of adult L1 Spanish-speaking learners of English: an instruction-only group, a naturalistic group and a mixed (instruction/naturalistic) group. She examined their accuracy on nine grammatical morphemes in a one-hour interview in English and found a high correlation not only between the three groups, but also with accuracy orders found in previous studies of child instructed/mixed subjects (Dulay and Burt, 1973). The only real difference between Pica's instructed and mixed subjects and the naturalistic subjects was a tendency for the classroom learners to *oversupply* morphemes (i.e. using them in contexts where they are not required: *she went-ed, four children-s*). This kind of study suggests that the route that learners follow in acquiring grammatical morphology is not broadly affected by classroom instruction.

Pienemann (1989) suggests that although classroom instruction cannot alter the route of L2 development, classroom learners may benefit from instruction if they are ready to acquire the particular property being taught. He found that instructing L2 learners of German on a word-order stage just beyond their current one accelerates the acquisition of that stage (see TEACHABILITY HYPOTHESIS).

One has to be careful, however, in interpreting such findings because other studies have found that such accelerating effects of instruction may only be temporary. For example, White (1991) taught English adverb placement (as in *My mother sometimes bakes cakes*) and English question formation to two groups of L1 French-speaking English learners. Although both groups appeared to have acquired these phenomena up to six weeks after testing (compared with control groups who had not), a year later the subjects' performance on adverb placement had regressed, while six months later the performance on question formation was still as good as immediately after instruction. Thus, while instruction may speed up the rate of acquisition, its effect may not be long-lasting on all properties.

## COMPARATIVE BENEFITS OF TRADITIONAL AND COMMUNICATIVE ENVIRONMENTS

A second group of classroom studies has investigated the comparative benefits of traditional instructional environments and communicative instructional environments. For example, Savignon (1972) compared three groups of American college students learning French, all of whom had the same number of hours of traditional instruction. One group had an additional 'communicative hour', however, a second group had an extra 'cultural hour' in English, but about French culture, and a third group had an additional instructed hour in the language laboratory. When subjects were tested on grammatical proficiency, Savignon found that there were no differences between the three groups. But when they were tested on communicative proficiency, the 'communicative group' significantly outperformed the other two. This might suggest that to develop communicative ability in the L2, learners need to engage in communicative tasks.

Lightbown (1992) describes a radical approach to teaching English to young L1 French-speaking learners in elementary schools in Canada, which does not require the learner to engage in communicative tasks. From the age of 8 onwards pupils listen only to English tapes and read English books during their thirty-minute daily English classes. There is no oral practice or instruction. The children choose the tapes they want to listen to and the books they want to read, and these are not graded beyond being selected intuitively by course planners as appropriate to the age group in question. Lightbown has compared hundreds of these children with those of a similar age learning English in a standard classroom environment. She has found that 'learners in the comprehension-based programme learn English as well as (and in some cases better than) learners in the regular programme' (Lightbown and Spada, 1993: 89) not only in comprehension *but also in the development of speaking skills*. It is not clear, however, whether such an approach has the same benefits at more advanced levels of acquisition, where students in regular classrooms begin to outperform the comprehension-only groups (Lightbown, personal communication).

### GENERAL TRENDS

Results from classroom studies of SLA seem to suggest that L2 instruction may have a general accelerating effect on the rate at which properties of the L2 are acquired as opposed to pure naturalistic exposure. Learners who are restricted to exposure to the L2 in the classroom may be able to acquire listening and speaking skills in the early stages on the basis of comprehension activities only (and without the need for instruction), although there may be a ceiling to this effect. Learners who are restricted to exposure to the L2 in the classroom may benefit from programmes which involve both communicative activities and some focusing on the linguistic properties of the L2.

BIBLIOGRAPHY
Dulay, H. and Burt, M. (1973). Should we teach children syntax? *Language Learning*, 23, 245–58.
Ellis, R. (1990). *Instructed Second Language Acquisition*. Oxford: Blackwell.*

Lightbown, P. (1992). Can they do it themselves? A comprehension-based ESL course for young children. In R. Courchêne, J. Glidden, J. St John and C. Thérien (eds), *Comprehension-based Second Language Teaching*. Ottawa: University of Ottawa Press.
Lightbown, P. and Spada, N. (1993). *How Languages are Learned*. Oxford: Oxford University Press.*
Pica, T. (1983). Adult acquisition of English as a second language under different conditions of exposure. *Language Learning*, 33, 465–97.
Pienemann, M. (1989). Is language teachable? *Applied Linguistics*, 10, 52–79.
Savignon, S. (1972). *Communicative Competence: An experiment in foreign language teaching*. Philadelphia: Center for Curriculum Development.
White, L. (1991). Adverb placement in second language acquisition: some effects of positive and negative evidence in the classroom. *Second Language Research*, 7, 133–61.

RH

**cloze** is a testing technique whereby a complete text is gapped with a consistent number of words (from five to eleven) between gaps after a few sentences of introduction. Learners try to fill each gap with a word that fits the context. Marking can be either for the exact word (which is more reliable) or an equivalent. Cloze is often used as a test of reading comprehension, though there are questions as to what reading skills it reveals (see Weir, 1990). The term was coined in 1953 from the gestalt notion of 'closure', referring to the human tendency to complete patterns once grasped. (See LANGUAGE TESTING.)

BIBLIOGRAPHY
Hughes, A. (1989). *Testing for Language Teachers*. Cambridge: Cambridge University Press.
Weir, C. J. (1990). *Communicative Language Testing*. Hemel Hempstead: Prentice Hall.

CLF

**code-switching** The alternate use of two languages in the same discourse, for example, Spanish/English *Todos los Mexicanos* *were riled up*. Sociolinguists investigate pragmatic causes like reporting other people's speech, discussing certain topics and emphasizing particular social roles (see PRAGMATICS). Linguists examine switch-points: the 'free MORPHEME constraint' (the speaker may not switch language between a word and its endings unless the word is pronounced as if it were in the language of the ending) and the 'equivalence constraint' (the switch can come at a point in the sentence where it does not violate the grammar of either language); the government model (the switch cannot come within a maximal phrase); and the Matrix Language Framework Model (the sentence has a matrix language structure into which open class content morphemes are inserted). Psychologists stress the bilingual's unique ability to use two languages simultaneously. See BILINGUALISM.

BIBLIOGRAPHY
DiSciullo, A.-M., Muysken, P. and Singh, R. (1986). Code-mixing and government. *Journal of Linguistics*, 22, 1–24.
Grosjean, F. and Soares, C. (1986). Processing mixed language, some preliminary findings. In J. Vaid (ed.), *Language Processing in Bilinguals: Psycholinguistic and neuropsychological perspectives*. Hillsdale, NJ: Erlbaum, 145–79.
Ludi, G., Milroy, L. and Muyskens, P. (eds) (1995). *One Speaker, Two Languages*. Cambridge: Cambridge University Press.*
Myers-Scotton, C. (1993). *Social Motivations for Code-switching*. Oxford: Clarendon Press.
Poplack, S. (1980). Sometimes I'll start a sentence in English y termino en español. *Linguistics*, 18, 581–616.

VJC

**cognitive anti-method**   Sometimes called *nativism*, this was a method (the term *anti-method* stemming from detractors) advocated in Newmark and Reibel (1968) and based on the assumption that foreign language teaching was overlarded with complicated techniques, whereas all that was required was for learners to gain exposure to the target language in 'meaningful chunks'. The proposals developed Newmark's earlier assertions that learning would occur if natural heuristics were not interfered with. The authors claim to take a 'common-sense' viewpoint, yet the influence of the theory of innate ideas in its modern form (Chomsky) is evident, as is a reaction against AUDIO-LINGUALISM. See also GRAMMAR TEACHING.

BIBLIOGRAPHY
Newmark, L. (1966). How not to interfere with language learning. *International Journal of American Linguistics*, 32/1, Part II, 77–83. (Reprinted in M. Lester (ed.) (1970). *Readings in Applied Transformational Grammar*. New York: Holt, Rinehart and Winston, 219–27.)*
——(1971). A minimal language-teaching program. In P. Pimsleur and T. Quinn (eds), *The Psychology of Second Language Learning*. Cambridge: Cambridge University Press, 11–18.
Newmark, L. and Reibel, D. (1968). Necessity and sufficiency in language learning. *IRAL*, 6/2, 145–64. (Reprinted in M. Lester (ed.) (1970). *Readings in Applied Transformational Grammar*. New York: Holt, Rinehart and Winston, 228–52.)

JTR

**cognitive code**   Sometimes referred to disparagingly in terms such as 'a jazzed-up version of GRAMMAR-TRANSLATION', cognitive code-learning theory was a foreign language teaching method based on gestalt psychology and transformational linguistics. It aimed to foster competence (in the Chomskyan sense – see COMPETENCE/PERFORMANCE). The gestalt assumption was that learning must be holistic but accompanied by understanding. The linguistics of the day, which depicted syntactic relationships in terms of transformations commencing from *kernel sentences* or other basic structures, seemed to offer the key to both 'whole learnings' and cognitive awareness, so that teaching concentrated upon 'transforms'. See Carroll (1966) for further details of psychological aspects. See also GRAMMAR TEACHING.

BIBLIOGRAPHY
Carroll, J. B. (1966). The contributions of psychological theory and educational research to the teaching of foreign languages. In A. Valdman (ed.), *Trends in Language Teaching*. New York: McGraw-Hill, 93–106.
Mueller, T. H. (1971). The effectiveness of two learning models: the audio-lingual habit theory and the cognitive code-learning theory. In P. Pimsleur and T. Quinn (eds), *The Psychology of Second Language Learning*. Cambridge: Cambridge University Press, 113–22.

JTR

**cognitive development**  Cognitive development refers to the growth of complex representational and decontextualized thought as a human being grows from infancy to adulthood. For example, the ability to understand the concepts involved in a sentence like 'Had John been here he would have been able to answer the question,' which describes a person who is not present at the time of speaking providing a hypothetical answer to a question, appears to be an ability which may not be present at birth, but has to develop over time, given experience of the world.

Psychologists and linguists have had different views about the interaction of cognitive development with language acquisition. Some have viewed the establishment of nonlinguistic cognitive knowledge as a prerequisite for language to develop at all. Others have seen cognitive development as an entirely separate matter from language development.

The work of Jean Piaget (see Boden, 1979, for an overview) assumes that cognitive development is a prerequisite for linguistic development. According to Piaget, cognitive development takes place in a series of stages where the acquisition of each stage is a necessary requirement for the acquisition of a subsequent stage (see PIAGETIAN DEVELOPMENTAL STAGES). For example, the *sensorimotor* period in a child's development, which lasts from birth to about the age of 2, begins with the child making simple physical movements in response to the environment, which become repetitive habits, then coordinated actions to produce effects on the environment, and finally lead to the child discovering 'object permanence' (the belief that an object still exists even when it is no longer in view (i.e. is covered by a blanket or otherwise hidden)). In Piaget's view, the development of decontextualized concepts like 'object permanence' is required before language can develop – hence the fact that children do not start to produce grammatically structured sentences until around the age of 2 years, the stage at which they are capable of conceptualizing objects not present in the immediate environment.

Various properties of later stages of cognitive development are also held to be necessary before the linguistic means to express them can be acquired. For example, during the *pre-operational* period (about 2 to 7 years) children develop the ability to recognize that a substance remains the same when it takes on different shapes. Piaget calls this the ability to recognize 'conservation of matter'. For example, if water in a short, fat beaker is poured into a tall, thin one, it is still the same water. Before the pre-operational period, however, children will say that there is more water in the tall, thin beaker, because the level is higher. It has been claimed by some researchers that knowledge of conservation is a prerequisite for acquiring comparative constructions involving 'more than', 'less than', 'the same as', or passives like 'the truck pushed the tractor' and 'the tractor was pushed by the truck', where the semantic roles of 'the truck' (agent) and 'the tractor' (patient) are conserved in different syntactic environments (Sinclair-de Zwart, 1979).

Another, different version of the view that language development is dependent on cognitive development can be found in the work of Vygotsky (see Lantolf and Appel, 1994, for applications to second language acquisition). Vygotsky argued that linguistic knowledge is the internalization and decontextualization of behaviour which is learned in social interaction. Children are first exposed to samples of language in its social use, and they learn that it can be used to regulate social interaction. Progressively, they internalize the external regulative function of language to enable them to regulate their own cognitive activity. The acquisition of language is therefore bound up with the development of regulated cognitive activity.

A consequence of the view that language acquisition is dependent on cognitive development is that first language acquisition must be qualitatively different from second language acquisition in older learners, for the simple reason that older learners are cognitively more mature. And this is indeed a view that some researchers have taken. Dulay and Burt (1973), for example, suggested that while there would be sequences in the acquisition of syntax common to first language learners, and sequences common to second language learners, the order would not be the same in the two cases because the older learners 'are more sophisticated with respect to cognitive and conceptual development' (p. 252).

Others have attempted to explain the observed differences between first and second language acquisition (the stopping short of full success in second language acquisition, the typically greater effort required in development, the greater variability across learners) as an effect of cognitive maturity. Dulay, Burt and Krashen (1982: 92) cite a study by Elkind (1970) in which it is proposed that when people reach Piaget's stage of formal operational thinking (between 11 and 15, roughly – see PIAGETIAN DEVELOPMENTAL STAGES), they become afflicted by affective inhibitions like self-consciousness, ego impermeability (see EGO PERMEABILITY) and so on, which inhibit normal language acquisition.

The view that cognitive development is a prerequisite for linguistic development is not held by all researchers. There is strong evidence that complex linguistic ability can develop in the absence of normal cognitive abilities (see Hatch, 1983, and Smith and Tsimpli, 1994, for discussion), and also that linguistic knowledge develops prior to the cognitive stages which are supposed to be prerequisites for that knowledge (see Goodluck, 1991: 165–7). This leads many linguists to doubt that there is a causal relation between cognitive development and linguistic development.

BIBLIOGRAPHY
Boden, M. (1979). *Piaget*. Glasgow: Fontana.*
Dulay, H. and Burt, M. (1973). Should we teach children syntax? *Language Learning*, 23, 245–58.
Dulay, H., Burt, M. and Krashen, S. (1982). *Language Two*. Oxford: Oxford University Press.
Elkind, D. (1970). *Children and Adolescents: Interpretative essays on Jean Piaget*. Oxford: Oxford University Press.
Goodluck, H. (1991). *Language Acquisition: A linguistic introduction*. Oxford: Blackwell.
Hatch, E. (1983). *Psycholinguistics: A second language perspective*. Cambridge, MA: Newbury House.
Lantolf, J. and Appel, G. (eds) (1994). *Vygotskian Approaches to Second Language Research*. Norwood, NJ: Ablex.*
Sinclair-de Zwart, H. (1979). Language acquisition and cognitive development. In V. Lee (ed.), *Language Development*. London: Croom Helm.
Smith, N. and Tsimpli, I. (1994). *The Mind of a Savant*. Oxford: Blackwell.

RH

**cognitive style** refers to people's preferred modes of processing information, and hence to preferred ways of learning. A person's cognitive style may be dependent on task and topic, and is not thought to be immutable. There may be an interaction, therefore, between the kind of thinker a person is and the kind of teaching methodology they favour. There might also be an interaction between cognitive style and topic: some styles might suit learning a language more than others. Both of these questions have been researched extensively in the last twenty years.

One interpretation of cognitive style is modality preference, e.g. preferring visual (eye-mindedness) or aural (ear-minded) presentation. Such preferences are certainly real, but it is not so obvious that the preference relates significantly to success in language learning (Reid, 1986). Most work in cognitive style has concerned psychometric assessment of certain traits of individual difference, such as:

field dependence – independence;
broad – narrow categorizing;
reflectivity – impulsivity;
levelling – sharpening in memory;
belief congruence vs contradiction.

Assessment of the educational importance of these has been undertaken by measuring people on the appropriate test and then correlating (see CORRELATION) their scores with learning achievement. It is assumed that these measures are independent of general intelligence, and the traits constitute as it were different routes to the same goal, but in fact there is often a close link between intelligence and one pole of the continua in question. The different measures might even be tapping the same underlying trait.

The bulk of work in this field concerning cognitive style in language learning has been conducted on field independence vs dependence, sometimes called analytic vs global thinking. This trait is assessed using the timed embedded figures test. *The Good Language Learner* study (Naiman et al., 1975) in Canada (see GOOD LANGUAGE LEARNER STUDIES) found that this trait did distinguish learners both in terms of success and in terms of characteristic errors, whereas other measures did not. Field independent learners were more successful overall in Toronto schools learning French, and in a repeating back task, they would typically recover more of a sentence in which they had made a

mistake than the field dependent learners. Following this result, Hansen and Stansfield (1981) showed that field independence was associated with grammatical tests and field dependence with communicative tests, so they confirmed the interaction between the preferred mode and topic. In later research (1983) they demonstrated that field independent learners performed better on CLOZE tests, confirming the interaction between mode of thinking and task. However, this result also demonstrates that cloze tests are contaminated by the non-linguistic factor of cognitive style: if particular kinds of thinkers do better on them, they are not purely language tests. Later research by Hansen (1984) showed that there is considerable variation across cultures in the association between field independence and cloze tests, which indicates that neither the psychological trait nor the language test format has universality.

Hawkey (1987) observed learners with measured field independence/dependence in actual classes, in order to assess how their cognitive style affected their patterns of interaction, conduct of an independent group learning task and overall success in a reading comprehension test. Whereas the previous research had used mainly statistical analysis, Hawkey was concerned to describe any consistency between the psychometric assessment of his learners (of English at a London teaching institute) and their interaction and problem-solving behaviour. His results were not clear-cut, but there were several interesting trends. The F/I learners, of which there were two groups, actually scored higher overall on the reading comprehension measure – but this was a cloze test. In the group reading task, moreover, it was clear that the F/I groups were better organized and more efficient than the F/D group or the mixed control group. However, the two F/I groups did not behave entirely similarly; both were decisive, but one made a strange decision – to fragment discussion and report writing on the reading task – which cost them some effectiveness.

Clearly some other factors were at play here. The F/D group did not score so well, and transcripts of their group discussion revealed that much of their discussion was personal reaction to the topics and not focused deliberation about the meaning of the actual text. Furthermore, they were unable to reconstruct the relationship of the individual parts of the text read by individuals to the whole.

Hawkey's aim in this research was to explore the role of individual differences in cognitive style in the context of communicative learning activities, and he used observation transcripts, written reports from the groups' activities and cloze measures of reading comprehension.

Field independence and dependence have been associated with wider areas of individual difference, such as social awareness, constancy in specialism preference, inner- and outer-directedness, convergent and divergent thinking, etc. However, it is unwarranted to use a single measure – the time it takes to locate a shape in a more complex geometric figure – as an index of preferences in such a wide variety of human behaviour. For this reason, and for reasons of doubt about validity, other researchers in the area of INDIVIDUAL DIFFERENCES have used different methods, like questionnaires. Willing (1985) discusses this cognitive style at length, explaining why his own research into learning preferences among the learners enrolled in the Australian Migrant English Programme used a questionnaire in preference to the embedded figures test.

The status of cognitive style in language learning thus remains controversial. There is a relationship between scores on the embedded figures test and various learning product measures, indicating that certain intellectual characteristics give an advantage. There may well be significant differences in the behaviour of individuals differing in cognitive style in interactive and cooperative learning situations. There may, however, be other factors independent of the psychometric traits considered which govern what learners like to do, how they respond to learning tasks and what they can learn from different activities, which can only be tapped in more detailed research. (See also COGNITIVE VARIABLES.)

BIBLIOGRAPHY
Hansen, J. and Stansfield, C. (1981). The relationship of field dependent-independent cognitive styles to foreign language achievement. *Language Learning*, 31/2, 349–67.
Hansen, L. (1984). Field dependence-independence and language testing. Evidence from six Pacific Island cultures. *TESOL Quarterly*, 18/2, 311–24.
Hawkey, R. (1987). Language learner characteristics and classroom interaction: an experiment and its implications. In B. K. Das (ed.), *Communication and Learning in the Classroom Community*. Singapore: Regional Language Centre Anthology Series, 9, 130–59.
Naiman, N., Fröhlich, M. and Stern, H. (1975). *The Good Language Learner*. Modern Language Centre, Department of Curriculum, Ontario Institute for Studies in Education.
Reid, J. M. (1986). Learning style preferences of ESL students. *TESOL Quarterly*, 20, 87–111.*
Stansfield, C. and Hansen, J. (1983). Field dependence-independence as a variable in second language Cloze test performance. *TESOL Quarterly*, 17/1, 29–38.
Willing, K. (1985). *Learning Styles in Adult Migrant Education*. Sydney: New South Wales Adult Migrant Education Service.

SMCD

**cognitive variables**   One of the three areas considered to make up the INDIVIDUAL DIFFERENCES between learners which influence the degree of success in foreign language learning is the cognitive area. The main cognitive variables are INTELLIGENCE and APTITUDE, but MEMORY is often also included, as is the ability to utilize general learning mechanisms. (See also COGNITIVE STYLE.) An issue in this research area is how learner characteristics interact with teaching methods. It may not be, for example, that the intelligent learn languages better, but that they can benefit more from types of tuition which assume use of intelligence.

BIBLIOGRAPHY
McDonough, S. H. (1981). *Psychology in Foreign Language Teaching*. London: Allen and Unwin.
Skehan, P. (1989). *Individual Differences in Second-language Learning*. London: Edward Arnold.
KJ

**coherence** is the quality of meaning unity and purpose perceived in discourse. It is not a property of the linguistic forms in the text and their denotations (though these will contribute to it), but of these forms and meanings interpreted by a receiver through knowledge and reasoning. As such, coherence is not an absolute quality of a text, but always relative to a particular receiver and context. A description of coherence is usually concerned with the links inferred between sentences or utterances. It is often contrasted with COHESION, which is the linguistic realization of such links (Halliday and Hasan, 1976).

BIBLIOGRAPHY
Brown, G. and Yule, G. (1983). *Discourse Analysis*. Cambridge: Cambridge University Press, 191–9.
Cook, G. (1989). *Discourse*. Oxford: Oxford University Press, 1–43.
Halliday, M. A. K. and Hasan, R. (1976). *Cohesion in English*. London: Longman.
Widdowson, H. G. (1984). *Explorations in Applied Linguistics*. Vol. 2. Oxford: Oxford University Press, 95–136.
GC

**cohesion**   In investigating the COHERENCE of a text (see SPOKEN AND WRITTEN DISCOURSE) an analyst examines a range of phenomena that contribute to its cohesion – the linguistic marking of the links between a sequence of grammatically distinct sentences that make these sentences hang together, giving a text its *texture*. The term established its currency in the fields of DISCOURSE ANALYSIS, STYLISTICS and GRAMMAR with the development of the concept in Halliday and Hasan (1976).

Cohesion is a semantic notion referring to relations of meaning between elements of a text. For example, the two sentences in (1) constitute a (fragment of a) text due to the semantic relation between *them* and *six cooking apples*.

(1)   Wash and core *six cooking apples*. Put *them* into a fireproof dish.

In this context, the interpretation of the pronoun *them* presupposes the meaning 'six cooking apples'. Thus there is a cohesive *tie* between the *presupposing* and the *presupposed* elements. Given the standard linguistic terminology, this (anaphoric) relation holds between the pronoun and its *antecedent*.

According to Halliday and Hasan (1976: 13), cohesive ties exist only where the interpretation of an expression can be recovered from some other verbally explicit element within the text. Thus the exchange in (2), for example, is not cohesive.

(2)   A:   Will you be at the meeting?
      B:   Pavarotti is in performance tonight.

Yet it is coherent due to other semantic and pragmatic properties: B's reply is a (negative) answer to A's question. Conversely, (3) illustrates that a text which *is* marked by cohesive ties does not have to be coherent.

(3)   I bought a Ford. A car in which President Wilson rode down the Champs Élysées was black. Black English has been widely discussed. The discussion between the presidents ended last week. A week has seven days. Every day I feed my cat. Cats have four legs. The cat is on the mat. Mat has three letters. (from Brown and Yule, 1983: 197)

Thus cohesion is neither necessary nor sufficient for a text to be coherent, a point discussed at some length in Brown and Yule (1983: 194–9).

Since cohesion typically (though not necessarily) involves relations between sentences, an analysis of the cohesion of a text is, in principle, independent of the grammatical framework assumed for the description of sentence STRUCTURE. In practice, however, work on cohesion is grounded in SYSTEMIC GRAMMAR, or rather its descendant, the systemic-functional grammar developed by M. A. K. Halliday (1994).

The following linguistic devices constitute the set of Halliday and Hasan's *cohesive relations*: reference, substitution, ellipsis, conjunction and lexical relations. In a recent reiteration of the concept of cohesion, Halliday (1994) preserves this classification.

*Reference* is a relation between linguistic expressions where one determines the interpretation of the other. The latter may be a personal pronoun, a demonstrative or a comparative expression. The following examples illustrate it:

(4)    *Three blind mice*, three blind mice.
       See how *they* run! See how they run!

Here there is a cohesive tie of reference between the pronoun *they* and the expression *three blind mice*.

(5)    Doctor Foster went to *Gloucester* in a shower of rain.
       He stepped in a puddle right up to his middle and never went *there* again.

The demonstrative *there* refers to the expression *Gloucester*.

(6)    *Henry* can't play today. We'll have to find *someone else*.

The expression *someone else* (= 'someone other than Henry') refers to *Henry*.

If a presupposing element follows the presupposed, as in (4)–(6), the reference relation is *anaphoric*. The opposite order marks a *cataphoric* relation, exemplified in (7).

(7)    (a)    Before *he* wrote the letter, *Peter* had a drink.
       (b)    This is *the* house *that Jack built*.
       (c)    He ate *more than the Carpenter* [ate], though.

It is worth noting that the use of the terms 'reference' and 'anaphora' here differs from their use in mainstream linguistics. There, 'reference' is a direct relation between a linguistic expression and its situational referent, and 'anaphora' is the relation between co-referential expressions regardless of their relative order.

*Ellipsis* is a lexico-grammatical device involving the omission of part of a sentence whose meaning will be retrievable from the preceding text. (8) is one example, with the 'elliptic' material indicated.

(8)    John used to like Mary and Bill Sue. [used to like]

Sometimes, the elliptic material is marked by some other lexical material – substituted as a 'placeholder':

(9)    I quite like this picture but I prefer the other (one). [picture]

Thus *substitution* is a special case of ellipsis, with the elliptic element indirectly represented, usually by a pro-form like *one*, *do* or *so*.

*Conjunction* is a cohesive relation marking logical-semantic relations between linguistic expressions and linking paragraphs. *Conjunctive expressions* are classified (and subclassified) into three broad categories on the basis of their function in the text:

(10)   (a)    *Elaboration*
              in other words, I mean (to say); for example, thus . . .
       (b)    *Extension*
              and, also, nor; but, on the other hand, however; instead, except for that; alternatively . . .
       (c)    *Enhancement*
              behind, then, finally, an hour later; likewise, thus; therefore, with this in view; in this respect . . .

*Lexical cohesion* depends on the choice by the speaker/writer of particular lexical items, which are related to the relevant preceding expressions through some recognizable semantic relation. Some examples are given in (11):

(11) (a) Algy met a *bear*. The *bear* was bulgy. (repetition)

(b) *Henry*'s thinking of rowing the Atlantic. Go and talk to *the wretched fool*. (synonymy)

(c) Why does this little *boy* wriggle all the time? *Girls* don't wriggle. (antonymy)

Cohesion is also marked at the phonological level, as in poetry, for example. Features like rhythm and alliteration are repetitions reminiscent of some cohesive relations described above.

Different GENRES and REGISTERS make different uses of the cohesion devices. For example, conjunction of a certain type will be prominent in argumentative essays, and certain literary pieces will be highly marked by lexical cohesion features.

Cohesion and the associated ideas about text analysis are popular among applied linguists and language teachers. Discourse-based EFL SYLLABUSes and materials, and EDUCATIONAL LINGUISTICS materials for the teaching of English as a mother tongue draw widely on Halliday and Hasan and related work (see Carter, 1990: 3; McCarthy and Carter, 1994: 89ff.). See also TEXT GRAMMAR.

BIBLIOGRAPHY

Brown, G. and Yule, G. (1983). *Discourse Analysis* (Cambridge Textbooks in Linguistics). Cambridge: Cambridge University Press. [A textbook exposition and critique of Halliday and Hasan, 1976.]

Carter, R. (1990). Introduction. In R. Carter (ed.), *Knowledge about Language and the Curriculum: The LINC reader*. London: Hodder and Stoughton, 1–20.

Halliday, M. A. K. (1994). *An Introduction to Functional Grammar*. 2nd edn. London: Edward Arnold.*

Halliday, M. A. K. and Hasan, R. (1976). *Cohesion in English*. London: Longman.*

Hoey, M. (1983). *On the Surface of Discourse*. London: Allen and Unwin.

Leech, G., Deuchar, M. and Hoogenrad, R. (1982). *English Grammar for Today*. Harmondsworth: Penguin Books.

McCarthy, M. and Carter, R. (1994). *Language as Discourse: Perspectives for language teaching*. London: Longman.

Quirk, R., Greenbaum, S., Leech, G. and Svartvik, J. (1985). *A Comprehensive Grammar of the English Language*. London: Longman.

EJ

**collocation** is one of the binding forces in language, organizing LEXIS according to which words typically occur together and showing networks of word association. Learners experience difficulty where collocation is language-specific (e.g. 'blue blood') and not determined by universal semantic constraints (e.g. 'green grass'). See also VOCABULARY TEACHING.

BIBLIOGRAPHY

Carter, R. and McCarthy, M. (eds) (1988). *Vocabulary and Language Teaching*. Harlow: Longman.*

McCarthy, M. (1990). *Vocabulary*. Oxford: Oxford University Press.

CLF

**common core** is a concept specifically coined within the COUNCIL OF EUROPE Unit/Credit Scheme for language learning. It refers to those aspects of language use (notions and functions) common to all students, independent of particular topics, situations, individual learning needs and specializations (see also THRESHOLD LEVEL).

BIBLIOGRAPHY

Johnson, K. (1981). Introduction: some background, some key terms and some definitions. In K. Johnson and K. Morrow (eds), *Communication in the Classroom*. Harlow: Longman.

JMCD

**communication strategies** are 'techniques of coping with difficulties in communicating in an imperfectly known second language' (Stern, 1983: 411). Three characteristics associated by many with such strategies are that they are problem-based (being used when communication problems arise), conscious and intentional. Tarone's (1977) typology of communication strategies was an influential early one, subsequent important ones including Faerch and Kasper's (1983a) and Bialystok's (1990). Most studies have been concerned with lexical strategies, and various ones have attempted to relate communication strategy use to variables such as learner proficiency, task type and learner personality, while there have been attempts (notably in Bialystok, 1990) to draw parallels with the use of L1 strategies, particularly by children. A few writers have considered the role communication strategies play in the learning process, but clear conclusions are not yet available. There are also differences of opinion as to the value of training learners in strategy use. For a succinct discussion of communication strategies, see Ellis (1994: 396–403); for lengthier treatment, see Bialystok (1990), and Faerch and Kasper (1983b).

There have been various attempts to define communication strategies (CSs hereafter); Bialystok (1990: 3) lists four such definitions, the most general and accessible of which is perhaps Stern's, cited above. Bialystok begins her study with an example from her own experience, of how a friend wanted to buy some real silk but not knowing the proper Spanish word to use (nor the words for 'silkworm' and 'cocoon'), paraphrased in Spanish with 'it's made by little animals, for their house, and then turned into material.' This example illustrates what many commentators have noted, namely that CS studies have tended to concentrate on the lexical level.

Ellis (1994) suggests that there are two general approaches to CSs, the *interactional* and the *psycholinguistic* approaches. In the former, CSs are seen as discourse strategies in learner interactions, attempts to achieve 'conversational maintenance'. In relation to

this approach he cites Larsen-Freeman and Long (1991). More common is the approach that looks at CSs as cognitive processes, exemplified by the work of Faerch & Kasper (1983b).

According to Bialystok (1990) there are three characteristics common among the varying definitions and approaches to CSs. The first of these is *problematicity* (problem-orientedness in Faerch and Kasper) and the 'idea that strategies are used only when a speaker perceives that there is a problem which may interrupt communication (p. 3). The second is the notion of *consciousness*, that 'speakers who employ them are aware (to some extent, in some undefined way) of having done so' (p. 4). The third characteristic presupposes consciousness and is *intentionality*: 'the assumption that the speaker has control over the strategy that is selected and that the choice is responsive to the perceived problem' (p. 5).

Having identified these characteristics, Bialystok then questions all three of them. Thus she notes that CSs can occur in the absence of problematicity, where, for example, an explanation might legitimately involve the kind of description of silk exemplified earlier – as a deliberate means of expression rather than as a resource in the absence of the *mots justes*. The criterion of consciousness is even more problematical. Faerch and Kasper (1983a: 35) discuss this matter at length and conclude with a definition which clarifies that CSs need not on all occasions be conscious: 'potentially conscious plans for solving what to an individual presents itself as a problem in reaching a particular communicative goal'. Regarding intentionality, Bialystok (p. 5) observes that if this characteristic were definitional, then one would expect the systematic selection of given strategies in recurring communicative conditions. The research to date, she notes, does not testify to this; 'accordingly,' she concludes, 'the intentionality of communication strategies is questionable' (p. 5). Bialystok's overall response to these difficulties in identifying definitional characteristics is to state that 'communication strategies are continuous with "ordinary" language processing and cannot be severed from it by virtue of distinctive features.' A similar conclusion results from her look at general problem-solving strategies in L1 children: the same sorts of characteristics as outlined above are discussed, but there is a similar lack of 'unequivocally strategic' characteristics.

Among the various taxonomies of CSs, the following are particularly important: Tarone's (1977), Varadi's (1980), Faerch and Kasper's (1983a), that associated with the Nijmegen project to be described below (Bongaerts et al., 1987), and Bialystok's (1990). Tarone's typology was developed out of a study which included looking at nine intermediate level subjects who were asked to describe various drawings and illustrations both in their own language and in English. This experiment has two characteristics common in CS studies: it hopes to identify problematicity by comparing L1 and L2 production (the L1 production characterizing what the speaker says where there are no linguistic barriers), and secondly that it is referential, namely focusing on the description of objects (at the lexical level, that is). Since the resulting typology has been used as a basis for various subsequent ones, it is given in full below (table 1) (the categories are Tarone's own; short descriptive statements have been added).

Varadi's taxonomy appears to have been developed at about the same time as Tarone's but is more restricted, his strategies being confined (as Bialystok, 1990: 42 notes) to Tarone's 'paraphrase' category. Central to his system is the notion of *message adjustment* whereby an intended message is changed to make it expressible by means of available resources. In Faerch and Kasper's (1983a) model, the central distinction is between avoidance or REDUCTION STRATEGIES and ACHIEVEMENT STRATEGIES. These relate to the two approaches which, according to them, are open to learners facing communication

problems. One approach is to change the speaker intention by the use of message adjustment strategies. Alternatively, some other way of expressing the original meaning may be sought by use of an achievement strategy. Faerch and Kasper's reduction strategies are divided into two: in *formal reduction* strategies the 'learner communicates by means of a "reduced" system, in order to avoid producing nonfluent or incorrect utterances by realizing insufficiently automatized or hypothetical rules/items' (p. 52). With *functional reduction* strategies, on the other hand, the learner 'reduces his communicative goal in order to avoid a problem'. Various types of *achievement* strategy are listed; these include compensatory strategies like 'code-switching', 'transfer', and 'paraphrase'.

In a large-scale study undertaken in Nijmegen (and hence known as the Nijmegen project) fifteen Dutch learners of English at different proficiency levels were given four tasks of varying difficulty, involving lexical referential operations. The taxonomy derived from analysis of the data makes a main distinction between 'conceptual' and 'linguistic' strategies; as Kellerman (1991, cited in Ellis, 1994) notes: 'learners can either manipulate the concept so that it becomes expressible through their available linguistic (or mimetic) resources, or they can manipulate the language so as to come as close as possible to expressing their original intention.'

Ellis (1994) notes that Faerch and Kasper's strategies, unlike Tarone's, are located within a theory of L2 production. He makes the same point about Bialystok's; she uses her own 'analysis/control' distinction (see, for example, Bialystok, 1982) to identify 'knowledge-based' and 'control-based' CSs. The difference between these strategy types clearly touches on others described above. Knowledge-based strategies involve adjustment to message content, while 'control-based' ones involve some alternative mode of expressing the desired content. It is important for Bialystok herself that she should be able to relate

**Table 1**   Tarone's (1977) typology of communication strategies (with added descriptive statements).

| Communication strategy | Description of strategy |
|---|---|
| **1   Avoidance** | |
| (a)   Topic avoidance | Avoiding reference to a salient object for which learner does not have necessary vocabulary |
| (b)   Message abandonment | The learner begins to refer to an object but gives up because it is too difficult |
| **2   Paraphrase** | |
| (a)   Approximation | The learner uses an item known to be incorrect but which shares some semantic features in common with the correct item (e.g. 'worm' for 'silkworm') |
| (b)   Word coinage | The learner makes up a new word (e.g. 'person worm' to describe a picture of an animated caterpillar) |
| (c)   Circumlocution | The learner describes the characteristics of the object instead of using the appropriate TL item(s) |
| **3   Conscious transfer** | |
| (a)   Literal translation | The learner translates word for word from the native language (e.g. 'He invites him to drink' in place of 'They toast one another') |
| (b)   Language switch | The learner inserts words from another language (e.g. 'balon' for 'balloon') |
| **4   Appeal for assistance** | The learner consults some authority – a native speaker, a dictionary |
| **5   Mime** | The learner uses a non-verbal device to refer to an object or event (e.g. clapping hands to indicate 'applause') |

CSs to some general model: 'an explanation of communication strategies for second-language learners must build on existing frameworks developed to address related problems in other areas' (1990: 2).

One of the issues addressed in the CS literature is how L2 strategies relate to those used in the first language, and indeed in other areas of human 'problem-solving' activity. Though conceding that L1/L2 strategies will be different in some ways, Bialystok's view is that 'it would seem odd if the cognitive mechanisms that produced communication strategies in the second language were fundamentally different from those responsible for the strategic use of a first language' (1990: 2). In order to seek out common cognitive mechanisms, Bialystok considers what is known about the way L1 children compensate for gaps in their knowledge of language and manage to function as effective communicators. She cites Clark's (1983) three main child strategies for filling lexical gaps. The first is *overgeneralization* (for example using 'dog' for all four-legged animals). Second is the use of *all-purpose terms* like 'that', 'thing', 'do' to stand for unknown lexical items. Third is the process of *word-creation*; e.g. 'he's keying the door' (these examples are Clark's, cited in Bialystok). Bialystok's claim is that these processes will 'provide a model' for the way L2 learners develop CSs, and indeed there are clear similarities between the strategies listed above and those identified in Tarone (1977).

Bialystok also discusses the work of Snow and others (1989), who look at children's ability to provide definitions of common nouns in both the L1 and the L2. 'It is striking from these findings,' they conclude (p. 24), 'that non-native speakers can score as high as native speakers on various components of skill in giving definitions.' For Bialystok this again suggests (p. 109) that 'descriptions of what adults are doing to solve communication problems could be profitably built out of a more detailed description of how children learn to define words.' The Nijmegen study finds similar parallels between L1 and L2 strategy use.

Based on the various taxonomies available, a number of CS studies have attempted to relate strategy use to different variables. These include learner proficiency, and the Nijmegen project found more CSs used at a lower level of proficiency, as well as some other level-related differences. Bialystok and Fröhlich (1980), among others, look at the effect of elicitation task type, while Kellerman (1978) considers L1 influence, and Tarone (1977) personality variables.

A further issue touched on in the literature (though not, as Ellis laments, given extensive coverage) is the extent to which CSs may contribute to the acquisition process. Corder (1978) characterizes strategies as 'risk-avoiding' and 'risk-taking' (a distinction echoed in Faerch and Kasper's reduction and achievement strategies, and elsewhere). He identifies risk-taking as likely to benefit acquisition, and notes that 'if one wishes at this stage of the art to consider the pedagogical implications of studying communicative strategies, then clearly it is part of good language teaching to encourage resource expansion strategies and, as we have seen, successful strategies of communication

may eventually lead to language learning' (1983: 17). The risk-avoiding strategies are more problematical, and others (including Faerch and Kasper, 1983a) share with him the worry that the development of such strategies may lead to a lack of linguistic forward movement. In this context, Ellis (1994: 403) reminds us of the finding of Schmidt (1983) that a learner who develops STRATEGIC COMPETENCE may do so at the expense of the development of linguistic competence. Tarone (1980) on the other hand makes the point that CSs of all categories do at least keep communication channels open and hence make reception of comprehensible input possible.

There are similar differences of perspective regarding the value of teaching CS use to learners. Bialystok cites Kellerman's (1991) distinction between *strong* and *moderate* positions regarding the teaching of CSs. According to the strong view, there is benefit to the direct teaching of specific strategies. But according to Bialystok (1990: 142), 'training studies have frequently been unsuccessful where training was based on specific techniques rather than on general operating solutions.' This is also suggested, she claims, by studies on teaching children effective CSs in the L1; there is 'little point in teaching strategies per se' (p. 143). The moderate view is that we can draw attention to CSs in teaching: 'what instruction can hope to achieve is to enhance the processing skills that are responsible for the effective use of strategies' (Bialystok 1990: 145). Kellerman (1991: 158) appears to reach a similar conclusion: 'there is no justification for providing training in compensatory strategies . . .' he argues. 'Teach the learners more language and let the strategies look after themselves.'

BIBLIOGRAPHY
Bialystok, E. (1982). On the relationship between knowing and using forms. *Applied Linguistics*, 3, 181–206.
——(1990). *Communication Strategies: A psycholinguistic analysis of second-language use*. Oxford: Blackwell.\*

Bialystok, E. and Fröhlich, M. (1980). Oral communication strategies for lexical difficulties. *Interlanguage Studies Bulletin*, 5, 3–30.

Bongaerts, T., Kellerman, E. and Bentlage, A. (1987). Perspective and proficiency in L2 referential communication. *Studies in Second Language Acquisition*, 9, 171–200.

Clark, E. V. (1983). Meanings and concepts. In J. H. Flavell and E. M. Markman (eds), *Handbook of Child Psychology*. Vol. III: *Cognitive Development*. New York: John Wiley.

Corder, S. P. (1978). Language-learner language. In J. Richards (ed.), *Understanding Second and Foreign Language Learning: Issues and approaches*, Rowley, MA: Newbury House.

——(1983). Strategies of communication. In C. Faerch and G. Kasper (eds), *Strategies in Interlanguage Communication*. London: Longman, 15–19.

Ellis, R. (1994). *The Study of Second Language Acquisition*. Oxford: Oxford University Press.

Faerch, C. and Kasper, G. (1983a). Plans and strategies in foreign language communication. In C. Faerch and G. Kasper (eds), *Strategies in Interlanguage Communication*. London: Longman, 20–60.*

Faerch, C. and Kasper, G. (eds) (1983b). *Strategies in Interlanguage Communication*. London: Longman.

Kellerman, E. (1978). Giving learners a break: native language intuition, a source of predictions about transferability. *Working Papers in Bilingualism*, 15, 59–89.

——(1991). Compensatory strategies in second language research: a critique, a revision, and some (non-)implications for the classroom. In R. Phillipson, E. Kellerman, L. Selinker, M. Sharwood Smith and M. Swain (eds), *Foreign/Second Language Pedagogy Research*. Clevedon: Multilingual Matters.

Larsen-Freeman, D. and Long, M. (1991). *An Introduction to Second Language Acquisition Research*. London: Longman.

Schmidt, R. (1983). Interaction, acculturation and the acquisition of communicative competence. In N. Wolfson and E. Judd (eds), *Sociolinguistics and Second Language Acquisition*. Rowley, MA: Newbury House.

Snow, C. E., Cacino, H., Gonzalez, P. and Shriberg, E. (1989). Second language learners' formal definitions: an oral language correlate of school literacy. In D. Bloome (ed.), *Literacy in Functional Settings*. Norwood, NJ: Ablex.

Stern, H. H. (1983). *Fundamental Concepts of Language Teaching*. Oxford: Oxford University Press.

Tarone, E. (1977) Conscious communication strategies in interlanguage. In H. D. Brown, A. Yorio and R. C. Crymes (ed.), *On TESOL '77*. Washington, DC: TESOL.

——(1980). Communication strategies, foreigner talk, and repair in interlanguage. *Language Learning*, 30, 417–31.

Varadi, T. (1980). Strategies of target language learner communication: message adjustment. *International Review of Applied Linguistics*, 18, 59–71.

KJ

## communicative competence

**communicative competence** (CC) is the knowledge which enables someone to use a language effectively and their ability actually to use this knowledge for communication. The term is most usually attributed to Dell Hymes's paper 'On communicative competence' (Hymes, 1970). Hymes distinguishes four sectors of CC: knowledge of what is possible, feasible, appropriate and actually done. In an important reinterpretation, Canale and Swain (1980) alternatively propose three sub-competences: grammatical, sociolinguistic (comprising sociocultural and DISCOURSE COMPETENCE), and STRATEGIC COMPETENCE. Since Hymes, the term 'communicative competence' has been widely used in SOCIOLINGUISTICS and language teaching, often in rather vague and conflicting ways. Current confusion over the term is attributable partly to the many developments and interpretations of the original notion, partly to misunderstanding and simplifications of it, partly to its fashionable status – but also to some considerable conceptual confusion in Hymes's original formulation.

### HYMES'S MODEL OF COMMUNICATIVE COMPETENCE

*Hymes's attack on Chomsky*   Hymes begins his advocacy of CC by drawing attention to the narrowness of CHOMSKYAN LINGUISTICS, and its inability to account for many aspects of language use. Chomsky (1965: 4) had distinguished between

*competence* (the speaker-hearer's knowledge of his language) and *performance* (the actual use of language in concrete situations) (see COMPETENCE/PERFORMANCE).

Chomsky argues that only the former (conceived as an idealized static knowledge of phonological and syntactic rules) is the proper subject-matter of linguistics. Hymes's main point is that there must be other kinds of knowledge, 'rules of use', which enable actual speakers to use the language effectively. Hymes's argument becomes confused when he not only rejects Chomsky's programme for linguistics, but also suggests that it is internally inconsistent. This leads him into some misrepresentation, as Chomsky (1965) neither claims to deal with the competence of actual users (but only of an idealized speaker-hearer) nor denies that actual individuals may also possess other knowledge which enables them to make use of their linguistic competence. In addition, by adopting Chomsky's own term 'competence', Hymes seems in part to accept it. Perhaps for this reason, many people have interpreted the possibility sector of CC as equivalent to competence in Chomsky's sense, and the other three sectors merely as additions to this. This common interpretation, however, does not fit with Hymes's claim that 'one must transcend the dichotomy of competence: performance' (p. 281) nor with his phrase of 'competence for use' (p. 279) which, by suggesting a necessary link between static knowledge and the processes of performance, is fundamentally at odds with the Chomskyan definition. Given the widespread acceptance of Chomsky's definition, Hymes's use of the same term in an argument rejecting Chomsky's programme is unfortunate. He would have been better advised to reject both Chomsky's narrow conception of linguistics and his terminology as well.

*Hymes's rationale for CC*   Although Hymes's critique of Chomsky is confused, the more positive part of his paper, the proposal of CC, has provided a rich theoretical framework for the study and teaching of language. Having pointed to a number of aspects of language with which Chomskyan linguistics cannot deal, Hymes stresses the need for:

a theory that can deal with a heterogeneous speech community, differential competence [i.e. variation between individuals], the constitutive role of sociocultural features, . . . socio-economic differences, multilingual mastery, relativity of competence in 'Arabic', 'English' etc., expressive values, socially determined perception, contextual styles and shared norms for the evaluation of variables. (p. 277)

The theory of CC is proposed to answer this need.

Hymes distinguishes two very different conceptions of performance. One is the 'actual data of speech', seen as rule-less *in contrast to* the rule-bound nature of linguistic competence; another is behaviour governed by underlying rules of use which, *in addition to* the rules of linguistic competence, allow the language user to communicate effectively. His concern is with the second of these interpretations. Such additional rules, he argues, must of necessity exist, for a person whose linguistic behaviour was governed only by 'the ability to produce and understand (in principle) any and all of the grammatical sentences of a language' (p. 277) would be regarded as mad, and in addition would not produce many appropriate but ungrammatical utterances which occur in language use. What is needed for effective communication is 'competence for use' (p. 279), which comprises the knowledge that is 'communicative competence'.

Hymes (p. 281) proposes four questions which this additional knowledge must be able to answer:

(1)   Whether (and to what degree) something is formally possible;

(2) Whether (and to what degree) something is feasible in virtue of the means of implementation available;

(3) Whether (and to what degree) something is appropriate (adequate, happy, successful) in relation to a context in which it is used and evaluated;

(4) Whether (and to what degree) something is in fact done, actually performed, and what its doing entails.

In a loose use of the word 'parameter', Hymes refers to the knowledge which enables these questions to be answered as the four 'parameters' of CC. An actual (as opposed to idealized) speaker-hearer who can answer these four questions will be able to use that language and other means of communication effectively in a given culture.

### HYMES'S FOUR SECTORS OF CC

*Whether (and to what degree) something is formally possible*   This has often been interpreted as linguistic competence in Chomsky's sense. There are, however, important differences. First, Hymes's criterion of possibility encompasses not only linguistic grammaticality but also non-verbal and cultural 'grammaticality' (i.e. conformity to meaningful rules of behaviour). Second, this aspect of competence (like the others) is not an idealized state, a tacit knowledge which, as in Chomsky's theory, might in principle exist independent of performance. It is rather 'dependent both upon (tacit) knowledge and (ability for) use'. It cannot be separated from 'what persons can do' (p. 282).

*Whether (and to what degree) something is feasible*   This refers to psycholinguistic factors such as 'memory limitation, perceptual device(s), effects of properties such as nesting, embedding, branching and the like' (p. 285). Canale and Swain (1980) illustrate this with the following sentence:

the cheese the rat the cat the dog saw chased ate was green

This is grammatical in that it follows the rules for embedding clauses, but cannot be feasibly processed automatically. (The main clause is 'the cheese was green'; within it are multiply embedded relative clauses. The cheese is 'the cheese the rat ate'; the rat is 'the rat the cat chased'; the cat is 'the cat the dog saw'.) Understandably, this sector of CC has received least attention in language teaching, as users will almost by definition neither produce nor encounter language use which is not feasible. Canale and Swain argue for excluding it from a model of CC altogether 'since perceptual strategies, memory constraints, and the like would seem to impose themselves in a natural and universal manner' (p. 16).

*Whether (and to what degree) something is appropriate*   Appropriateness concerns the relation of language to context. Further theoretical support and information for the notion has been provided by PRAGMATICS and DISCOURSE ANALYSIS. Attention has concentrated particularly on cultural appropriateness, on the way in which an utterance or sequence of utterances may be grammatical and feasible but inappropriate in a given context. This inappropriateness may be linguistic (e.g. in Britain, addressing one's new bank manager as 'comrade') or, in line with Hymes's broad interpretation of the term 'grammar', non-linguistic (e.g. kissing the new bank manager on being introduced).

This is the sector of CC which has received most attention, especially in language teaching. This is hardly surprising when one considers the interpretation of possibility as grammaticality; the practical irrelevance of feasibility (see above); and – until recently – the lack of evidence about whether something is done (see below). In language teaching this parameter of CC has often been interpreted simplistically to imply that the successful language learner must of necessity conform to the norms of the culture whose language he or she is learning. This misrepresents, however, Hymes's notion of

CC as knowledge which enables someone to interpret or produce meaningful behaviour (linguistic or otherwise) within a given culture, because meaning may result as much from deliberate divergence from the norm as from conformity to it. Thus the person who addresses the bank manager as comrade but knows (and is known to know!) that this is unusual, is behaving as meaningfully as the person who adopts less startling choices. In interpretations of Hymes's concept of 'appropriateness', as in interpretations of the other three sectors, there is neglect of an important phrase in Hymes's original formulation 'and to what degree'. Significantly, this phrase is often omitted from summaries. The phrase implies that behaviour is not to be assessed as conforming or not conforming to the norm, but on a continuum from the most possible/feasible/appropriate/done to the least. This crucial omission and misunderstanding has led to a good deal of chauvinism in COMMUNICATIVE LANGUAGE TEACHING, where it is sometimes suggested that language learners must conform to the new culture rather than choose to preserve their own patterns of behaviour. Little heed is paid to the possibility that learners may be fully aware that their patterns of behaviour are different, and yet consciously seek to preserve them; nor to the fact that within the community where the language is spoken, this different behaviour of outsiders may be perceived to be both consciously preserved and significant.

*Whether (and to what degree) something is done*   As Hymes observes (p. 286): 'something may be possible, feasible, appropriate and not occur.' Language users, it may be assumed, have some knowledge of which forms actually occur, and of the probability of that occurrence. At the time of Hymes's writing, and during the initial period in which CC caught the imagination of language teachers and sociolinguists, this particular claim was speculative, necessary to the theory, but incapable of any large-scale demonstration. The recent rapid growth of CORPUS LINGUISTICS, using computers to search very large corpora of actually occurring language, has not only borne out this claim, but also identified particular forms of high probability and possible forms of low probability. Native-like performance depends upon memorized chunks of language, whether fully or partly lexicalized, and native-like CC includes knowledge of the probabilities of occurrence (Pawley and Syder, 1983). Language learners (assuming their goal is to appear native-like) will need to acquire such knowledge in addition to rules of possibility and appropriateness. Again it would be wrong to suppose that possession of this aspect of CC entails necessary conformity. There are many occasions of language use, such as creative or humorous discourse, in which speakers and writers deliberately seek out the unusual.

This last point reflects a crucial but frequently neglected issue: the way the four proposed components of CC relate to each other, and the circumstances in which the demands of one may outweigh the demands of another. There are times, for example, when it is appropriate to use a form which is not formally possible or which has never occurred. Any worthwhile theory of CC or application of such a theory to language teaching must address the principles which govern such interactions, rather than treat the four sectors as modular and separate. In language teaching, in reaction against an earlier over-emphasis on grammar, there has been a tendency to over-emphasize appropriateness at the expense of the other three sectors. There is now a similar disproportionate emphasis on whether something is actually done (i.e. authentic) which can be at the expense of developing knowledge of what is possible and appropriate.

## SUBSEQUENT DEVELOPMENTS

CC rapidly became a fashionable notion, especially in language teaching. In many circles the communicative approach became a new orthodoxy. In the consequent proliferation of theoretical writings and language teaching materials, there is often considerable vagueness, confusion and simplification, reflecting more the commercial advantages of invoking the term than any serious attempt to develop a rigorous model. Among notable exceptions to this general razzmatazz are theoretical discussions of CC by Canale and Swain (1980), Canale (1983), Taylor (1988) and Widdowson (1989).

*Canale and Swain (1980)*   In an outstanding and influential paper re-examining CC, Canale and Swain offer a critique of Hymes; a discussion of the relationship of the notion to other socially oriented theories; a balanced discussion of the implications of the notion for language teaching and testing; and a new model of CC. Having discounted any psycholinguistic component (see above) they present a three-part competence (see figure 1) consisting of grammatical competence, sociolinguistic competence and strategic competence, with sociolinguistic competence further broken down into sociocultural competence and DISCOURSE COMPETENCE. Each of these components includes knowledge of probability of occurrence.

Grammatical competence is knowledge of the language code and includes 'knowledge

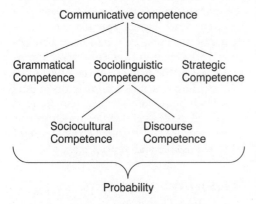

**Figure 1**   Diagrammatic representation of Canale and Swain's (1980) components of CC.

of lexical items and of rules of morphology, syntax, sentence-grammar semantics, and phonology'. Sociocultural competence is knowledge of the relation of language use to its non-linguistic context. Discourse competence is knowledge of rules for 'the combination of utterances and communicative functions' which may be conceived as knowledge of factors governing the creation of COHESION and COHERENCE. In these respects, the taxonomy may be viewed as a clarification and improvement of Hymes. Knowledge of formal possibility is elucidated; knowledge of feasibility is eliminated; knowledge of appropriateness broken down and clarified; and knowledge of what is done distributed among the other components. Canale and Swain substantially depart from Hymes, however, in the suggestion of a strategic competence. This is defined (with a somewhat circular use of the words 'competence' and 'strategies' to define themselves) as

verbal and non-verbal communication strategies that may be called into action to compensate for breakdowns in communication due to performance variables or to insufficient competence. (p. 30)

This notion introduces some confusion into their classification, for elsewhere in the discussion they have confined the notion of competence to knowledge rather than ability for use. Yet just as Hymes's term 'competence for use' seems to imply interpersonal performance rather than static intrapersonal knowledge, so it is hard to conceive of a knowledge of a strategy which is not related to some particular context of use. Like Hymes himself, in other words, Canale and Swain seem unable to free themselves from the Chomskyan connotations of the word competence. As Taylor (1988: 158–9), in a discerning critique of varying uses of the term 'competence', comments: 'on the one hand they fail to distinguish between knowledge and ability, or rather they incorporate both, and on the other hand they do not distinguish between those strategies which all speakers have, both native and non-native, and those which are peculiar to non-native speakers.' This comment also draws attention to a further weakness in most theories of CC: the failure to specify how much of a given speaker's CC is language-specific or culture-specific and how much is universal.

*Further developments* In a slight reformulation of Canale and Swain (1980), Canale (1983) alters the original scheme by separating discourse competence from sociolinguistic competence, to make it an autonomous fourth sub-competence. He also expands the definition of strategic competence to include 'efforts to enhance the effectiveness of communication'. Though his summary is clear and insightful, Canale (1983) makes no substantial changes.

The notion of strategic competence has generated considerable subsequent research into strategies: for communication (see, for example, Bialystok, 1990), for learning (see, for example, O'Malley and Chamot, 1990) and for teaching (see Stern, 1992: 279–349). (See COMMUNICATION STRATEGIES and LEARNING STRATEGIES.)

Some progress towards clarifying the confusion engendered by the term CC is achieved by Widdowson (1983: 7–31, 1989). In general, Widdowson's work on CC maintains and develops the strengths of Hymes's original formulation, while also pointing out and clarifying its many internal contradictions. Widdowson (1989) suggests that each of the four sectors of Hymes's CC should be regarded as having both a competence aspect and a performance aspect (respectively knowledge and ability for use). This expands Hymes's four sectors to eight, but thereby avoids the constant confusion as to whether we are talking about static intrapersonal knowledge or dynamic interpersonal skill.

*Communicative competence and proficiency* Although Hymes's original paper was not concerned with language teaching, but with

providing a theoretical framework which could describe the knowledge and capabilities of the successful language user, his model has exerted a considerable influence on all aspects of language teaching and assessment, including overall approach (Widdowson, 1978; Brumfit and Johnson, 1979), syllabus design (Johnson, 1982), methodology (Johnson and Morrow, 1981) and testing (Spolsky, 1989; Bachman, 1990). CC is often conflated with proficiency and equated with the knowledge of the NATIVE SPEAKER presented as the final (if usually unattainable) goal of language learning (for further discussion see Davies, 1996). Models for LANGUAGE TESTING are often close to models of CC, and exhibit the same theoretical problems concerning taxonomies of components: a danger of an open-ended proliferation of terms, difficulty in distinguishing knowledge from ability for use, and a need to specify relations between one component and another.

BIBLIOGRAPHY
Bachman, L. F. (1990). *Fundamental Considerations in Language Testing*. Oxford: Oxford University Press.
Bialystok, E. (1990). *Communication Strategies*. Oxford: Blackwell.
Brumfit, C. J. and Johnson, K. (1979). *The Communicative Approach to Language Teaching*. Oxford: Oxford University Press.
Canale, M. (1983). From communicative competence to communicative language pedagogy. In J. C. Richards and R. W. Schmidt (eds), *Language and Communication*. Harlow: Longman, 2–27.*
Canale, M. and Swain, M. (1980). Theoretical bases of communicative approaches to second language teaching and testing. *Applied Linguistics*, 1/1, 1–47.*
Chomsky, N. (1965). *Aspects of the Theory of Syntax*. Cambridge, MA: MIT Press.
Davies, A. (1996). Proficiency or the native speaker: what are we trying to achieve in ELT? In G. Cook and B. Seidlhofer (eds), *Principle and Practice in Applied Linguistics*. Oxford: Oxford University Press.
Hymes, D. (1970). On communicative competence. In J. J. Gumperz and D. Hymes (eds),

*Directions in Sociolinguistics*. New York: Holt, Rinehart and Winston. [Page references are to the reprint in J. B. Pride and J. Holmes (eds), (1972), *Sociolinguistics*. Harmondsworth: Penguin Books, 269–93. The original paper was presented at the Research Planning Conference on Language Development in Disadvantaged Children, New York City, June 1966.]*

Johnson, K. (1982). *Communicative Syllabus Design and Methodology*. Oxford: Pergamon Institute of English.

Johnson, K. and Morrow, K. (1981). *Communication in the Classroom*. Harlow: Longman.

O'Malley, J. M. and Chamot, A. V. (1990). *Learning Strategies in Second Language Acquisition*. Cambridge: Cambridge University Press.

Pawley, A. and Syder, F. H. (1983). Two puzzles for linguistic theory: nativelike selection and nativelike fluency. In J. C. Richards and R. W. Schmidt (eds), *Language and Communication*. Harlow: Longman, 191–227.

Spolsky, B. (1989). Communicative competence, language proficiency and beyond. *Applied Linguistics*, 10/2, 138–56.

Stern, H. H. (1992). *Issues and Options in Language Teaching*. Oxford: Oxford University Press.

Taylor, D. (1988). The meaning and use of the term 'competence' in linguistics and applied linguistics. *Applied Linguistics*, 9/2, 148–68.*

Widdowson, H. G. (1978). *Teaching Language as Communication*. Oxford: Oxford University Press.

——(1983). *Learning Purpose and Language Use*. Oxford: Oxford University Press.

——(1989). Knowledge of language and ability for use. *Applied Linguistics*, 10/2, 128–37.*

GC

## communicative language teaching

Regarded by many (e.g. Richards and Rodgers, 1986) as an APPROACH rather than a method, CLT grew up during the 1970s and is mainly associated with British applied linguistics. Its roots lie in the emphasis given at that time to sociolinguistics (see SOCIO-LINGUISTICS IN LANGUAGE TEACHING) and PRAGMATICS. In terms of syllabus, CLT is associated with the COUNCIL OF EUROPE's work, and with attempts to list language

concepts and uses (see NOTIONAL/FUNCTIONAL SYLLABUSES). In terms of methodology, the emphasis is placed on MESSAGE-FOCUS, on the ability to understand and convey messages. See also COMMUNICATIVE METHODOLOGY, LINGUISTICS IN LANGUAGE TEACHING.

BIBLIOGRAPHY

Brumfit, C. J. and Johnson, K. (1979). *The Communicative Approach to Language Teaching*. Oxford: Oxford University Press.*

Littlewood, W. (1981). *Communicative Language Teaching: An introduction*. Cambridge: Cambridge University Press.

Richards, J. C. and Rodgers, T. S. (1986). *Approaches and Methods in Language Teaching*. Cambridge: Cambridge University Press.

KJ

## communicative methodology (CM)

is the term used to describe teaching procedures which have developed in relation to COMMUNICATIVE LANGUAGE TEACHING. There are many versions of CM, but one is so widespread as to be regarded as the 'standard' model. This British model is associated with techniques such as the INFORMATION/OPINION GAP and INFORMATION TRANSFER types of exercise. Much importance is given in the model to achieving MESSAGE-FOCUS, and attempts are made to develop class activities that simulate the conditions of real communication. For descriptions of this model, see Richards and Rodgers (1986: chapter 5), Littlewood (1981) and Johnson (1982). The theoretical framework of standard CM is associated with American sociolinguists like Hymes, and British linguists like Halliday; see Brumfit and Johnson (1979) for the background to CM. Other versions of CM find their roots not in linguistics but in insights about learning, and give importance to providing meaningful and personal language practice. For a general discussion of CM, see Brumfit (1984) and Widdowson (1978a).

Because the term *communicative* has been invested with so many meanings, there are many versions of CM. One widespread model is the one developed largely in Britain, and at least in its early history closely associated with the NOTIONAL/FUNCTIONAL SYLLABUS. It is now found widely throughout the world, particularly where British applied linguistics has some influence.

## THEORETICAL BASIS OF THE 'STANDARD MODEL'

The roots of this standard model lie partly in the reconceptualization of language behaviour which occurred in the early 1970s with the work of sociolinguists like Hymes, ethnographers of speaking, ethnomethodologists, speech act theorists and others. The work of British linguists, particularly Halliday, who place emphasis on language as an instrument for conveying meanings in social settings, has also been highly influential in the development of CM. While what such people say is by no means irrelevant to the study of language learning, it is not their primary focus. Because standard CM derives from these sources, it may be characterized as inspired by a view of language rather than by a view of language learning. For those who insist that a methodology should have roots in learning theory, this is undoubtedly a shortcoming.

Hymes (1970) calls CHOMSKYAN LINGUISTICS a 'Garden of Eden' view, suggesting that it is too reductionist for those who would study language as used in society. Hymes accordingly provides what might be characterized as an 'enriched' model: one which is prepared to extend its purview beyond Chomsky's study of language structure. The difference between CM and its precedents might similarly be characterized in terms of enrichment. Whereas before, much of the methodologist's attention was given to the skill of producing correct language (in structural, phonological and semantic terms), CM recognizes that successful language use involves many more skills, previously ignored. It may be said

that standard CM derives its inspiration from a revised view of the nature of language and results in an enriched conception of what skills need to be practised in the classroom.

## FIVE CHARACTERISTICS OF 'STANDARD' CM

There are five areas in which the new, enriched conception made itself felt in CM. The first relates to the teaching of appropriateness. One of the major parameters which Hymesian, but not Chomskyan, linguistics encompasses is the study of 'the appropriate'. Hymes's (1970) dictum that 'there are rules of use without which the rules of grammar would be useless' has had a great impact on language teaching. The largest impact has been in the field of syllabus design (Wilkins's notional/functional syllabus indirectly owes much to this view). It is undoubtedly the case that, although CM now leads a life of its own outside that of the notional/functional syllabus, many methodological departures called communicative were first developed within that framework. Exercises intended to teach appropriateness are a case in point. If, as in notional/functional, the syllabus designer decrees that areas such as *making plans* or *inviting* are to be covered, this pushes the methodologist in certain directions. It forces him into a world of pretence, into rubrics which begin '*Pretend that you meet a friend in the street . . .*' and into techniques (much used in CM) of ROLE PLAY AND SIMULATION. Speech acts come to the methodologist via the syllabus designer, and the attempt to teach them has given shape to many of the techniques associated with CM.

The second area concerns the centrality of MESSAGE-FOCUS. For many this is the defining characteristic of CM, and the existence of different varieties of it is largely due to the different views on how this centrality may best be achieved. The attempt to produce message-focus pervades standard CM. In the most general terms, the emphasis is placed on what Widdowson in a seminal paper (1978b) calls *use* as opposed to *usage* (see USE/USAGE); that is, pieces of language are treated in the class as carriers of message, rather than simply as exemplars of grammatical structure. On the level of receptive practice the quest for message-focus leads to the ubiquitous information transfer exercises. In these, students typically extract information from a passage and use it to fill in a table, mark a route on a map, or perform some other task. An important characteristic of such exercises is that they treat language input as use rather than usage, in the sense described above.

In terms of productive practice, the desire for message-focus has led some to follow a general strategy whereby students are placed in positions where they will want to say something; then, if necessary, provided with the means to say it. The starting-point for practice is thus a desire to communicate, and the teacher's task is to help provide the means for messages to be encoded. This procedure is well exemplified by a strategy which Brumfit (1978) outlines. He suggests that a lasting impact of communicative language teaching may involve modification of the traditional 'PRESENTATION – PRACTICE – PRODUCTION' SEQUENCE to the following: *students communicate with available resources – teacher presents items shown to be necessary – drill if necessary*. Johnson (1982) refers to this as the DEEP-END STRATEGY. Once again, here one finds production of messages as the starting-point for language teaching.

Desire for message-focus is also partly responsible for the popularity of another ubiquitous technique – the information gap exercise. In this, students convey information that the others do not already have (for example, Student 1 is given information withheld from Student 2, the latter's task being to request that information, the former's to convey it). Because information is conveyed in such exercises, the prediction is that learners will concentrate on getting the message across; that is, there will be a degree of message-focus. This is in contrast to traditional non-information gap exercises where the learners tell each other things they already know, and hence may be forgiven for regarding the exercises as having no point except for practising structures (with, that is, FORM-FOCUS).

CM utilizes other means to encourage message-focus. It is seen to be important, for example, that learners should know that they are being judged on whether messages are conveyed effectively. Thus, at least at some point in the operation, feedback should be given on the communicative effectiveness of interactions (whether the message has been successfully conveyed) rather than solely on their grammatical correctness. For similar reasons, much standard CM attempts to create what Johnson (1982) calls 'task dependency'; tasks are created which utilize information gained in some preceding task; for example, students may have to read descriptions of holiday resorts in order to decide with their friends (classmates) where to go on holiday. The reading task is likely to be regarded as message-focus because it requires information extraction for some further end. The JIGSAW PRINCIPLE, developed by Geddes and Sturtridge (1979), exemplifies the principle of task dependency well. In general terms, CM makes attempts to ensure that learners are made accountable for the language they produce.

The third sense in which CM may be seen as an enrichment of traditional methodology lies in the fact that this methodology makes a real attempt to simulate psycholinguistic processes. For many, the justification of techniques like the information gap is motivational: the tedium of non-information gap practice, where learners constantly tell each other things that they already know, is replaced by at least a degree of genuine information exchange. But an equally persuasive justification relates to processing.

The overwhelming importance for CM of message-focus lies in the fact that real language use is itself message-focused, and all the psycholinguistic processes used in communication begin with the user's desire to convey a message. This is a view of communication that owes much to Halliday. Much justification for the use of information-gap techniques is made in these terms; where there is no information gap it is difficult to see how communicative processes can be practised. Similarly, an important characteristic of information transfer exercises is that they simulate the selective top-down nature of listening and reading (see TOP-DOWN PROCESSING). Psycholinguistics provides us with the insight that listeners process selectively, not attending equally to every word of a message. Unlike traditional listening comprehension exercises in which the learner is made to focus on each word, information transfer requires the learner to attend only to those parts of the message relevant to the task set. Other characteristics of CM discussed above may be regarded in the same light, as an attempt to base practice on what psycholinguistics has to say about communicative processes.

The fourth characteristic of 'standard' CM is the importance it places on risk-taking skills. These were ignored in the past, partly because of the emphasis given to thoroughness in teaching and partly through the prevailing desire to avoid errors (a notion derived from behaviourist learning theory). The desire for thoroughness in teaching is responsible for the way in which students were characteristically taught to read text, word by word. CM recognizes that this procedure not only fails to help, but also positively hinders, development of an important communicative skill – that of understanding message in a linguistic context which is only partially understood. Learners, particularly when they visit a country where the target language is spoken, will constantly be in situations where they need to use this skill: they need to be able to comprehend messages in contexts where they do not understand all that is said. If they have been taught to understand messages only when each word of the message is completely understood they will be constantly at a loss. In this context, information transfer exercises are again useful, since they require only partial understanding of language input (see STRATEGIC COMPETENCE).

The desire to avoid error informs the traditional teaching sequence of presentation – practice – production, and an important characteristic of the so-called deep-end strategy (described above) is that it helps to develop risk-taking skills. The student is being asked at the first stage to say things which may not have been taught yet – another situation likely to occur when he is engaged in real conversation outside the classroom. The strategy might be expected to develop great confidence in learners. There are, of course, concomitant dangers associated with this approach; one criticism worth mentioning (because it is often levelled at CM in general) is that it may lead the learner to overdevelop certain COMMUNICATION STRATEGIES (such as avoidance strategies) so that further progress in learning is inhibited.

The development of free practice techniques is the fifth area in which CM has enriched traditional methodology. The importance of holistic practice has been pointed out by many skill psychologists, particularly where the skill being learned involves the simultaneous execution of sub-skills. Language is just such a skill. When we speak, for example, our utterances must conform along many parameters (the grammatical, phonological, semantic, discourse, interpersonal and so on) simultaneously; we have to get it right on many levels at the same time. The ability to operate along all these parameters at the same time is crucial in the development of many skills; in language it is generally referred to as fluency. Johnson (1982) uses the term 'combinatorial practice' to refer to holistic practice which aims to practise sub-skills in combination.

Earlier language teaching placed the emphasis on part practice, often indeed completely ignoring the free production stage (new language was presented, drilled and nothing more). In CM the balance has been redressed with something of a vengeance, and much of CM's creative energy has gone into the development of free practice techniques. Indeed, for some it is the drilling or practice stage which needs to justify its presence in a communicative approach. Some would argue that the notions of CM and of drilling are essentially incompatible.

It was noted earlier that the pedigree of standard CM lies in a view of language rather than language learning. However, Richards and Rodgers (1986: 72) cite various attempts to locate CM within a learning theory, specifically within the model sometimes referred to as the 'information processing' or 'cognitive' model. In such models, importance is given to the concept of automatization, the procedure whereby learned material comes to be used 'automatically'. It can be argued that the techniques of CM may be regarded as automatizing procedures and hence may justify themselves in terms of the information processing learning theory.

## OTHER VERSIONS OF CM

It has been noted that, of the five characteristics described here, the one which has been subject to the most debate is the centrality of message-focus. In the standard model it is because the provision of messages is seen as a prerequisite for the simulation of processes that so much importance is placed on it. Little attention is given to the actual nature of the messages; students may be asked, for example, to convey the contents of a bus timetable or describe a route through a fictitious town; tasks which, it may be argued, have little meaning or motivational value for them. Indeed, it is criticisms such as this that led Prabhu (1987) to eschew the word 'communicative' altogether, and to coin

the term 'communicational' to describe his own approach (see PROCEDURAL SYLLABUS). His concern is to produce true message-focus ('preoccupation with meaning'); for him many of the techniques of CM produce only sham message-focus, where the learner is asked to do tasks so meaningless that, despite the presence of information gaps and the like, they cannot but be regarded as anything other than form-focused language practice.

It is possible to view message-focus, not as a prerequisite for communicative processes to occur, but as important for learning to take place, and many proponents of CM would place much more attention than the standard model does on developing meaningful tasks by tapping students' own situations, experiences, opinions, feelings and preferences. Indeed, for many teachers the term CM would simply refer to a methodology in which the exercises were made as meaningful and as personal as possible. Note that placing emphasis on meaningful and personal practice finds justification in terms which relate to learning theory, and at this point CM finds common cause with the humanistic school, where meaningfulness is seen as essential for learning to take place (in the work of Stevick, for example: see HUMANISTIC APPROACHES).

Another strand of CM has it that free practice is the vehicle by which acquisition takes place: learners acquire through use, or what Prabhu (1987) calls 'deployment'. This leads some to speak in terms of an INTERACTION HYPOTHESIS whereby classroom interaction and learning process become one; claiming, that is, that linguistic development is the direct outcome of the interaction itself (see, for example, Long, 1983). Similar views are held by proponents of CM such as Savignon. Brumfit's (1984) position is slightly different. It rests on a distinction between accuracy and fluency practice, there being a place in language teaching for both. For Brumfit, fluency practice can occur in all the four language skills of listening, speaking, reading and writing; its role is not to activate or automatize already internalized language, but rather to provide an opportunity for acquisition processes to work. A similar position is developed in Ellis (1984). Allwright, Brumfit and Ellis all draw on the second language acquisition literature in their work, and it is clear that their versions of CM find justification in terms of a learning theory. In this, their approach has similarities to that of Krashen, and indeed Richards and Rogers (1986: 72) argue that Krashen's NATURAL APPROACH is 'compatible with the principles of CLT'.

Although it is often convenient to treat methodology and syllabus design as separate entities, they do of course interact. Prabhu (1987) argues that we cannot achieve true 'preoccupation with meaning' within the bounds of a linguistic syllabus; if learners are to interact in a natural way, they cannot be constrained by a linguistic programme. Hence he avoids a linguistic syllabus and has instead a syllabus of tasks (his 'procedural syllabus'). Similar arguments are followed by Breen and Candlin (1979). For them, communication cannot be taught through what Breen refers to as a 'content syllabus', which specifies content in discrete items. The PROCESS SYLLABUS which Breen and Candlin develop aims to exemplify and encourage true communication as students and teacher 'negotiate' the content of lessons and procedures for learning.

THE FUTURE

Many would regard CM as having had its day. Whether this is so or not rather depends on what one is prepared to consider as CM. Much creative energy is at present expended in the direction of TASK-BASED LANGUAGE TEACHING, which one might wish to regard as a form of CM; certainly some versions of task-based teaching seem very similar to the function-based teaching which arguably gave birth to CM. Further, it may be that viewing CM's techniques within an information-processing model, as procedures for automatizing, will provide a different perspective which will give new life to this methodology.

BIBLIOGRAPHY

Allwright, R. L. (1984). The importance of interaction in classroom language learning. *Applied Linguistics*, 5, 156–71.

Breen, M. P. and Candlin, C. N. (1979). Communicative materials design: some basic principles. University of Lancaster, Institute of English Language Education (mimeograph).

Brumfit, C. J. (1978). 'Communicative' language teaching: an assessment. In P. Strevens (ed.), *In Honour of A. S. Hornby*. Oxford: Oxford University Press, 33–44.

——(1984). *Communicative Methodology in Language Teaching*. Cambridge: Cambridge University Press.*

Brumfit, C. J. and Johnson, K. (1979). *The Communicative Approach to Language Teaching*. Oxford: Oxford University Press.*

Ellis, R. (1984). *Classroom Second Language Development*. Oxford: Pergamon Institute of English.

Geddes, M. and Sturtridge, G. (1979). *Listening Links*. London: Heinemann.

Halliday, M. A. K. (1970). Language structure and language function. In J. Lyons (ed.), *New Horizons in Linguistics*. Harmondsworth: Penguin Books.*

Hymes, D. (1970). On communicative competence. In J. J. Gumperz and D. Hymes (eds), *Directions in Sociolinguistics*. New York: Holt, Rinehart and Winston. [Reprinted in 1972 in J. B. Pride and J. Holmes (eds), *Sociolinguistics*. Harmondsworth: Penguin Books, 269–93.]

Johnson, K. (1982). *Communicative Syllabus Design and Methodology*. Oxford: Pergamon Institute of English.*

——(1996). *Language Teaching and Skill Learning*. Oxford: Blackwell.

Johnson, K. and Morrow, K. (1981). *Communication in the Classroom*. Harlow: Longman.*

Littlewood, W. (1981). *Communicative Language Teaching: An introduction*. Cambridge: Cambridge University Press.*

Long, M. (1983). Native speaker/nonnative speaker conversation in the second language classroom. In M. Clarke and J. Handscombe (eds), *On Tesol '82: Pacific perspectives on language learning and teaching*. Washington, DC: TESOL, 207–25.

Prabhu, N. S. (1987). *Second Language Pedagogy*. Oxford: Oxford University Press.

Richards, J. C. and Rodgers, T. C. (1986). *Approaches and Methods in Language Teaching*. Cambridge: Cambridge University Press.

Widdowson, H. G. (1978a). *Teaching Language as Communication*. Oxford: Oxford University Press.*

——(1978b). The teaching of English as communication. *English Language Teaching*, 27/1, 15–19.

KJ

and word meaning; the examinee may have some choice of what to communicate or what level of proficiency to be tested on in certain skills; texts used tend to be up to date and representative of the testee's intended use of the language. (See also COMMUNICATIVE COMPETENCE, COMMUNICATIVE LANGUAGE TEACHING, LANGUAGE TESTING.)

BIBLIOGRAPHY
Hughes, A. (1989). *Testing for Language Teachers*. Cambridge: Cambridge University Press, 19–20.

SMCD

**communicative syllabus**  Though some prefer to reserve the term 'communicative' for an approach and a methodology (see Widdowson, 1984) many use it to refer to syllabuses, usually NOTIONAL/FUNCTIONAL SYLLABUSES, which list conceptual and use categories. These would normally be based on a THRESHOLD LEVEL type of inventory, possibly following a NEEDS ANALYSIS.

BIBLIOGRAPHY
Munby, J. (1978). *Communicative Syllabus Design*. Cambridge: Cambridge University Press.

Widdowson, H. (1984). Educational and pedagogic factors in syllabus design. In *General English Syllabus Design*, ELT Documents 118. Oxford: Pergamon Press and the British Council.

Yalden, J. (1983). *The Communicative Syllabus: Evolution, design and implementation*. Oxford: Pergamon Institute of English.

KJ

**communicative testing** refers to testing communicative proficiency and to using communicative events as test items. Thus items usually relate directly to language use; tasks in the test are as authentic as possible; knowledge of language function and appropriateness of expression to social situation are tested as well as knowledge of structure

**community language learning**, or **counselling learning**, is a foreign language teaching method inspired by Carl Rogers's work but developed by Curran. Learners or *clients* form a 'community', sitting round a tape-recorder. The *counsellor* remains outside the community, but, where necessary, supplies target-language equivalents of utterances produced by the clients in their mother tongue. The day's recordings are transcribed and presented to the clients, with errors hinted at, for analysis. Conventional teaching is available upon request, but in principle the clients must solve their own problems. Materials are generated by the community. Techniques include translation, group-work, conversation and reflection upon learning.

BIBLIOGRAPHY
Curran, C. (1976). *Counseling-Learning in Second Languages*. Apple River, IL: Apple River Press.

La Forge, P. G. (1983). *Counseling and Culture in Second Language Acquisition*. Oxford: Pergamon.

JTR

**competence/performance** is one of the fundamental dichotomies within CHOMSKYAN LINGUISTICS, concerned with the difference between the NATIVE SPEAKER'S (or the speaker-hearer's) UNCONSCIOUS or implicit knowledge (see EXPLICIT/IMPLICIT KNOWLEDGE) of language on the one hand and the use of language on the other. The distinction was originally drawn by Chomsky (1964) and elaborated in Chomsky (1965) and subsequent work.

Within linguistic theory, competence is the system of phonological, syntactic and lexical rules – a formal grammar – acquired, or internalized, by a native speaker during the language acquisition process in early childhood. It underlies his or her ability to produce and understand the sentences of a given language, and identify ambiguous and deviant sentences. A characterization of this system, labelled *linguistic* or *grammatical* competence, is the main focus of GENERATIVE GRAMMAR. Competence in this sense is only one factor involved in performance.

Performance – the production of utterances in specific situations – depends additionally on memory limitations, as in the case of the production and the comprehension of extremely long sentences, social conventions, as in the case of the use of formal and informal linguistic expressions, personality, interests, tiredness, sobriety and other diverse non-linguistic factors. Thus competence is an idealization of, or an abstraction from, linguistic performance.

The distinction partly reflects the Saussurean LANGUE/PAROLE distinction. Both share an explicit commitment to the view that any human language can be seen as a realization in utterances of the associated abstract linguistic system and that it is the latter that is the core object of linguistic inquiry (see STRUCTURALISM). The fundamental difference between the two is that whereas *langue* is a social object in the collective mind of a given speech community, competence is a psychological object, located in the mind of the individual native speaker-hearer. *Parole* is, then, an imperfect realization of *langue*. It is 'imperfect' because no single individual has total access to the whole of the linguistic system. In contrast, given the competence/performance model, every individual has access to a complete linguistic system, as represented in his or her mind and – allowing for the non-linguistic considerations referred to above – this is manifested in performance. The other source of insights into the mental grammar of an individual, regarded by theoretical linguists as the primary source of linguistic data, is INTROSPECTION – native speakers' intuitive judgements about the acceptability, ambiguities, usage (see USE/USAGE) and other formal features of sentences and other linguistic expressions of a given language.

The difference between the Saussurean and the Chomskyan views about the locus of *langue* and competence has a bearing on the question, 'What is a language?' Within the Saussurean approach, a language (French, English, Swahili, etc.) – or, more precisely, an underlying linguistic system – is associated with a given speech community, it is a shared social object, definable in social and geopolitical terms. Within the Chomskyan approach, a linguistic system is associated with individual speakers and manifested through their idiolects. It is a psychological object. Given this view, there are as many languages as there are native speakers, each with their own linguistic competence. One of the advantages of this approach is that it permits one to account for individual variation in linguistic performance and competence between speakers. Collections of speakers with sufficiently similar idiolects constitute speech communities and speakers of specific languages in the conventional sense. However, given the vagueness of the notion of 'sufficiently similar' idiolects, the identification of speech communities depends on non-linguistic factors and therefore has no privileged status in Chomskyan linguistics.

Since Chomsky (1986), the terms *I-language* and *E-language* have gained prominence over 'competence' and 'performance'. I-language is an abstract linguistic system which develops during language acquisition, grounded in the human, genetically determined capacity for language in the form of UNIVERSAL GRAMMAR. Universal grammar is a blueprint for the acquisition of any I-language. I-language, then, is essentially the same as 'competence': a body of unconscious knowledge which, together with other kinds of knowledge, is relevant to the production of utterances.

E-language, on the other hand, is a collection of some kind – of sentences, UTTER-ANCES, SPEECH ACTS, etc. – the output, or *external manifestations*, of the individual internalized grammars (I-languages).

The original view that a speaker-hearer's linguistic competence (knowledge of language) is characterized by a system of rules of the formal grammar of a given language has changed with the shift of emphasis to I-language. I-language is not a rule system but a system of the *principles* of universal grammar whose *parameters* have been fixed on the basis of the linguistic input to a child acquiring language. This 'principles and parameters' model of grammar has been adopted in many studies of FIRST AND SEC-OND LANGUAGE ACQUISITION.

Chomsky's original notion of grammatical competence as fundamental to linguistic performance encountered many criticisms, some of which were constructive.

The most influential counter-idea was that of COMMUNICATIVE COMPETENCE (Hymes, 1971), which includes both Chomskyan linguistic competence and other unconscious and conscious knowledge and skill necessary for the production of utterances appropriate in a given situation and for the comprehension of utterances. Some authors, however, especially within APPLIED LINGUISTICS, have posited both grammatical and communicative competence, thus narrowing down the scope of the latter (see Newmeyer, 1982: 37–8). In response to the criticism of the narrow scope of linguistic competence, Chomsky (1980) has suggested the complementary concept of PRAGMATIC COMPETENCE, which

accounts for the speaker-hearer's knowledge of the conditions of appropriate and effective use of the formal system. Several other types of competence have been identified, notably, in connection with language learning and teaching (see DISCOURSE COMPETENCE, STRATEGIC COMPETENCE) and the interpretation of literature – literary competence (Culler, 1975). (See also COGNITIVE DEVELOPMENT, CRITICAL PERIOD HYPOTHESIS, INNATENESS HYPOTHESIS, MENTALISM.)

BIBLIOGRAPHY
Botha, R. P. (1992). *Twentieth Century Conceptions of Language: Mastering the metaphysics market*. Oxford: Blackwell* [particularly Section 3.1].
Chomsky, N. (1964). *Current Issues in Linguistic Theory*. The Hague: Mouton.
——(1965). *Aspects of the Theory of Syntax*. Cambridge, MA: MIT Press.
——(1980). *Rules and Representations*. New York: Columbia University Press.
——(1986). *Knowledge of Language: Its nature, origin and use*. New York: Praeger* [particularly chapter 1].
Culler, J. (1975). *Structuralist Poetics: Structuralism, linguistics and the study of literature*. London: Routledge and Kegan Paul.
Hymes, D. (1971). Competence and performance in linguistic theory. In R. Huxley and E. Ingram (eds), *Language Acquisition: Models and methods*. New York: Academic Press, 3–24.*
Newmeyer, F. J. (1983). *Grammatical Theory: Its limits and its possibilities*. Chicago: University of Chicago Press [particularly Section 1.5.1].

EJ

## compound/coordinate bilingualism

These terms refer to the degree of semantic equivalence between two codes in a bilingual person. Compound bilingualism occurs when both codes are fused and neither dominates the other. Coordinate bilingualism is frequently encountered in a foreign language learner whose use of L2 is 'mediated' through the dominant L1. See BILINGUALISM.

BIBLIOGRAPHY
Diller, K. C. (1970). 'Compound' and 'coordinate' bilingualism: a conceptual artifact. *Word*, 26, 254–61.
Fishman, J. (1971). *Sociolinguistics: A brief introduction*. Rowley, MA: Newbury House.

AJ

**comprehensible input**   The concept of comprehensible input is that second language acquisition depends upon the learners' attempts to extract meaning from the language input. This must include new forms beyond their existing competence, called i + 1, otherwise they will never advance. To be comprehensible, the gap between what they hear (i + 1) and their existing knowledge (i) must be bridged through their own deductive powers, the teacher's gestures, or any other means to hand. Comprehensible input is believed to be the key element in the success of all language teaching methods. This controversial notion is specific to the Input Hypothesis Model, alias the MONITOR MODEL, put forward by Steven Krashen. See also INPUT HYPOTHESIS. For an interesting critique of the notion of comprehensible input, see Prabhu (1987: 66).

BIBLIOGRAPHY
Gregg, K. W. (1984). Krashen's Monitor and Occam's razor. *Applied Linguistics*, 5, 79–100.
Krashen, S. (1982). *Principles and Practice in Second Language Acquisition*. Oxford: Pergamon.
——(1985). *The Input Hypothesis: Issues and implications*. Harlow: Longman.*
——(1994). The Input Hypothesis and its rivals. In N. Ellis (ed.), *Implicit and Explicit Learning of Languages*. London: Academic Press.
Prabhu, N. S. (1987). *Second Language Pedagogy*. Oxford: Oxford University Press.
Swain, M. (1985). Communicative competence: some roles of comprehensible input and comprehensible output in its development. In S. Gass and C. Madden (eds), *Input in Second Language Acquisition*. Rowley, MA: Newbury House, 235–45.

White, L. (1987). Against comprehensible input: the Input Hypothesis and the development of L2 competence. *Applied Linguistics*, 8, 95–110.

VJC

**comprehension processes**   Models of comprehension processing recognize a role for linguistic analysis of a text (including procedures like parsing), as well as for background knowledge which greatly assists the listener/reader with interpretation. The psycholinguistic literature abounds with a variety of models for comprehension: Garman (1990) provides a useful survey. The special comprehension problems which the L2 learner faces have similarly been well covered in the literature. Different models of second language acquisition postulate dramatically different roles for the comprehension of input; for some it is central and for others no more than peripheral. For a consideration of these roles, see Faerch and Kasper (1986). The strategies which L2 learners use for listening and reading have also received much recent attention, with different strategy uses being associated with effective and ineffective learners. For a consideration of such strategies, see O'Malley and Chamot (1990).

Garman (1990: 305) notes that a number of terms are used in the literature in association with comprehension, and that because of our present lack of knowledge there is no agreed usage for the terms. These include *perception* (usually reserved for the initial processing of input), *understanding* (the end product), *recognition*, which implies a stored memory element, and *interpretation*, which suggests a creative process going beyond the strict properties of the signal.

Two broad processing types have generally been discussed in the literature. These are TOP-DOWN PROCESSING and BOTTOM-UP PROCESSING. In the latter the starting-point is the text itself; the reader/listener attends to individual words and structures in the text itself, using these to build up an interpretation of the whole. The emphasis in psycholinguistics before the 1970s tended to be on bottom-up processing and the attempt to identify the stages involved in decoding messages, as well as the order in which they occur. Two central concepts in any such discussion are that of *lexical access*, and *parsing*. The former involves retrieving word meanings from wherever they are stored; the latter the 'processing' or 'computing' of relationships between the lexical items (Garman, 1990: 312). In bottom-up models both these processes would occur before any *interpretation* took place. Models specifying the temporal relations between these two processes are called *serial* where they involve one occurring before the other. Possibly the simplest model, involving a 'lexical access ——▶ parsing' sequence may on occasion occur, but it has obvious limitations, as illustrated by Lewis Carroll's Jabberwocky poem (' 'twas brillig and the slithy toves . . .') where readers show the capability to process strings including non-words. Other modified serial approaches include Berwick and Weinberg's (1984) and that of Carroll and others (1978). The second, contrasting type of model which Garman identifies involves *parallel processing*; in this model type the processing elements, including lexical access and parsing, occur together as the input unfolds; so the listener/reader will bring various comprehension processes to bear from the first word, and will gradually build up an interpretative picture until (roughly) the end of the text, by which time the analysis will be complete. Marslen-Wilson and others' (1978) 'on-line interactive' model is a parallel processing model of this sort.

In recent years more emphasis has been placed on the top-down, interpretative aspects of processing, and on the listener/reader's own contribution to this. In Anderson and Lynch's (1988: 6) words: 'the listener has a crucial part to play . . . by activating various types of knowledge, and by applying what he knows to what he hears and trying to understand what the speaker means.' It is recognized that listeners/readers possess types of information and knowledge other than strictly linguistic, and that these play an important role in the comprehension of a text. Hedge (1985) divides this background knowledge into general knowledge, subject-specific knowledge and cultural knowledge. Discussion of the interpretative aspects of comprehension owes much to cognitive psychology, and three structures in particular have been used in the description of prior knowledge. These are schemata, frames and scripts (see SCHEMA THEORY). It is clear that schemata, as data structures representing our knowledge about concepts, are brought into play in the comprehension process, sometimes at an early stage. Thus our knowledge of a given topic will be activated by its mention in a text, and that knowledge will play a significant role in how we interpret the text. Similar comments may be made about the roles of frames and scripts; for full discussion of these concepts, and the way they affect processing, see Brown and Yule (1983).

One effect of recognizing the importance of these concepts is to emphasize the role of prediction, 'guessing' or what Faerch and Kasper (1986: 265) call 'inferencing procedures' in the comprehension process. Sometimes inferencing is necessary to bridge actual gaps in textual information, but it is important to note that such procedures come into play even when they are not strictly required. It is emphatically not the case that comprehension follows a totally bottom-up pathway, logically working through all possible interpretations before deciding on the most appropriate. We characteristically short-cut a lengthy interpretative process by using background knowledge to select the most likely interpretation, without perhaps even being aware that other interpretations are available. Studies of ambiguity clearly exemplify this procedure at work. Hence, faced with a sentence like Clark and

Clark's (1977) *The farmer put the straw on a pile beside his threshing machine*, we are likely to interpret 'straw' to mean 'grain stalk' without even being aware of the alternative possible meaning of 'drinking tube'. As Faerch and Kasper (1986: 265) point out: 'the principle that "all input must be accounted for" applies to computational but not to human information processing.'

As often pointed out in the literature, a further effect of top-down interpretative processes is the loss of awareness of what information has been supplied by a given utterance and what information already existed in background knowledge. Hence (to modify an example from Anderson and Bower, 1973), subjects who know that George Washington was the first president of the Unites States, and who read the sentence *George Washington had good health* are likely to report that what they in fact read was the sentence *The first president of the United States had good health*, thereby incorporating world knowledge into what has been read.

Other factors which play an important part in comprehension are the maxims that Grice (1975) identifies as holding in conversational discourse. According to Sperber and Wilson (1982) *relevance* is the most important of these maxims, meaning that a reader/listener will carry through comprehension processes under the assumption that utterances in a discourse are relevant to it, and will favour interpretations of utterances which give them the most relevance.

A further effect of the top-down nature of comprehension is that it leads to the assumption that different reader/listeners will arrive at different interpretations of the same text, according to their different states of background knowledge. This view is in sharp contrast to one which has meaning residing in the message itself, as an encoding of the speaker/writer's intention. In this latter view, the comprehension process is seen as an attempt to reconstruct the speaker/writer's intention: a view which has long held sway in the area of literary criticism,

for example. Common sense suggests that a plausible view of comprehension needs to allow for different listener/reader interpretations while at the same time requiring these interpretations to bear some resemblance to a speaker/writer's intention. It may be suggested that Brown's (1986) view captures these elements by stressing the importance of the interaction of listener, text and context in arriving at a 'reasonable interpretation' of the message.

There have been various models which attempt to capture both bottom-up and top-down aspects of processing. One which has had some influence on second language learning comprehension studies is that of the cognitive psychologist Anderson (1983, 1985). The model has three stages – perceptual processing, parsing and utilization. The first involves focusing on input and retaining elements of it in echoic memory. The second involves parsing and thereby generating a meaningful representation. The final stage relates this representation to existing knowledge, and involves interpretation. Rost's (1990) characterization recognizes what he calls low-level and high-level inferences. The former are inferences 'about the actual verbal indices that a speaker is using' (p. 56), and include items like 'identifying a sequence of phonetic units in a stream of speech' and 'identifying possible functions for tone contours over utterances: for example, to indicate "shared information" vs. "new information" or to indicate "question" vs. "statement" '. Consistent with a view of meaning 'as active knowledge construction, rather than passive reception of information', Rost also has higher-level inferences such as 'constructing propositional meaning through supplying case-relational links' and 'assuming a plausible intention for the speaker's utterances'.

Although comprehension models need to recognize both top-down and bottom-up dimensions of processing, Faerch and Kasper (1986: 264) make the point that there will be situations where one or other of these processing directions will be favoured. In highly predictable contexts, for example, top-down may prevail, while in situations where little context is provided bottom-up will be useful.

In their important paper, Faerch and Kasper also consider factors that come into play specifically in the L2 (as opposed to the L1) situation. The L2 user, they note, is likely to encounter special problems, partly due in some cases to lower relevant knowledge (associated with the L2 culture and world) and perhaps also to higher comprehension expectations inculcated by teaching procedures that place emphasis on word-by-word understanding. In addition, the L2 learner has to battle with L1 transfer, in effect having not just one but two systems to work with.

Faerch and Kasper also review the role comprehension plays in various approaches to second language acquisition. Two pole positions are represented by the transformational grammar view and by that of Krashen's Input Hypothesis. In the well-known Chomskyan characterization, the L1 child receives 'degenerate and deficient data'; she or he manages to acquire almost *despite* rather than *because of* the nature of the input received. TG models, even the less extreme versions, fail according to Faerch and Kasper adequately to explain comprehension processes. As its name suggests, the Input Hypothesis gives central importance to input, describing it (Krashen, 1981: 57) as 'the only causative variable in second language acquisition'. Krashen's notion of i + 1 is characterized by Faerch and Kasper thus: 'the learning process is assumed to be triggered when there is a gap between a structure or form in the input and the learner's current level of competence' (p. 260). See Krashen (1982, chapter 3) for a defence of the crucial role of input. Faerch and Kasper argue that Krashen's view, like that of the transformational grammarians, is vague in its characterization of comprehension processes.

At a later point in their paper (p. 267), Faerch and Kasper note that it is no longer useful to regard second language acquisition as a 'monolithic process' explicable in terms of a single hypothesis. They identify various situations where comprehensible input will not have a role of the sort Krashen envisages it playing in acquisition/learning. One involves types of learning which (for example) relate to knowledge and its accessibility – so automatization and CONSCIOUS-NESS RAISING will occur in second language acquisition, and these will not place central importance on comprehensible input. They also speak of learning based on input but not on comprehension of communication, which may occur in vocabulary explanation, for example.

In the past decade a considerable literature on the topic of listening/reading strategies has been developed. O'Malley and others (1989) use the Anderson model described earlier and identify listening strategies at each of the three stages. Like others, they also find strategy differences between effective and ineffective listeners; among other findings are that effective listeners engage in more self-monitoring (being more aware, for example, of periods of inattentiveness) and in more inferencing. Various researchers have found that ineffective listeners tend to rely on bottom-up processes to an extent which may severely affect their efficiency.

The teaching of comprehension skills has developed in accordance with views as to what the various skills entail. Much traditional training focuses on bottom-up processing and places emphasis on word-by-word understanding; comprehension questions test whether this has occurred. In more recent times recognition has been given to the importance of top-down as well as bottom-up processing. INFORMATION TRANSFER exercises require learners to extract information from a text for some stated purpose, thereby helping to develop selective comprehension strategies which involve differential attention given to different parts of a text. CLOZE and similar techniques may be said to develop inferencing procedures (see also TEACHING LISTENING SKILLS and TEACHING READING SKILLS). Given recent emphasis on top-down processes, it is important not to forget the bottom-up ones; Paran (1996) argues that we have been guilty of doing just this.

At the end of their 1986 paper, Faerch and Kasper consider some pedagogic implications arising from their survey. They observe (p. 270) that 'if input is to function as intake to the learning of higher-level L2 material, learners need to experience comprehension problems; such problems have to be perceived as deficits in their knowledge structure'; and, in the same vein: 'if learners wish to improve their formal correctness, one way of de-stabilising their fossilized rules may be to provide them with reception tasks aiming at the identification of formal L2 features rather than on the reconstruction of the message.' See Johnson (1992) and Skehan (1992) for practical suggestions related to this issue.

BIBLIOGRAPHY

Anderson, A. and Lynch, T. (1988). *Listening*. Oxford: Oxford University Press.

Anderson, J. R. (1983). *The Architecture of Cognition*. Cambridge, MA: Harvard University Press.

——(1985). *Cognitive Psychology and Its Implications*. New York: Freeman.

Berwick, R. and Weinberg, A. (1984). *The Grammatical Basis of Linguistic Performance*. Cambridge, MA: MIT Press.

Brown, G. (1986). Investigating listening comprehension in context. *Applied Linguistics*, 3, 284–302.

Brown, G. and Yule, G. (1983). *Discourse Analysis*. Cambridge: Cambridge University Press.

Carroll, J. M., Tanenhaus, M. K. and Bever, T. G. (1978). The perception of relations: the interaction of structural, functional and contextual factors in the segmentation of sentences. In W. J. M. Levelt and Flores D'Arcais (eds), *Studies in the Perception of Language*. Chichester: John Wiley.

Clark, H. H. and Clark, E. V. (1977). *Psychology and Language*. New York: Harcourt Brace Jovanovich.

Faerch, C. and Kasper, G. (1986). The role of comprehension in second-language learning. *Applied Linguistics*, 7/3, 257–74.*

Garman, M. (1990). *Psycholinguistics*. Cambridge: Cambridge University Press.

Grice, P. (1975). Logic and conversation. In P. Cole and J. L. Morgan (eds), *Studies in Syntax*. Vol. III. *Speech Acts*. New York: Academic Press.

Hedge, T. (1985). *Using Readers in Language Teaching*. London: Macmillan.

Johnson, H. (1992). Defossilizing. *ELT Journal*, 46/2, 180–9.

Krashen, S. D. (1981). *Second Language Acquisition and Second Language Learning*. Oxford: Pergamon.

——(1982). *Principles and Practice in Second Language Acquisition*. Oxford: Pergamon.

Marslen-Wilson, W. D., Tyler, L. K. and Seidenberg, M. (1978). Sentence processing and the clause boundary. In W. J. M. Levelt and Flores D'Arcais (eds), *Studies in the Perception of Language*. Chichester: John Wiley.

O'Malley, J. M. and Chamot, A. U. (1990). *Learning Strategies in Second Language Acquisition*. Cambridge: Cambridge University Press.

O'Malley, J., Chamot, A. U. and Kupper, L. (1989). Listening strategies in second language comprehension. *Applied Linguistics*, 10/4, 418–37.*

Paran, A. (1996). Reading in EFL: facts and fictions. *English Language Teaching Journal*, 50/1, 25–34.

Rost, M. (1990). *Listening in Language Learning*. Harlow: Longman.

Skehan, P. (1992). Second language acquisition strategies and task-based learning. In P. Skehan and C. Wallace (eds), *Thames Valley University Working Papers in English Language Teaching*. Vol. 1. Department of English Language Teaching, Thames Valley University.

Sperber, D. and Wilson, D. (1982). Mutual knowledge and relevance in theories of comprehension. In N. V. Smith (ed.), *Mutual Knowledge*. London: Academic Press.

KJ

**computational linguistics** can be seen as a branch of APPLIED LINGUISTICS, dealing with computer processing of human language. Automatic translation between natural languages, text processing and communication between people and computers are among its central concerns. Speech recognition and understanding and speech synthesis allow people to communicate with computers using spoken language. Computational GRAMMARS with TOP-DOWN and BOTTOM-UP PROCESSING capabilities have been developed in this connection. COMPUTER-ASSISTED LANGUAGE LEARNING programmes are among numerous applications of the new technology. Computerized corpora of written and spoken texts facilitate research on USAGE using CONCORDANCES. (See also CORPUS LINGUISTICS.)

BIBLIOGRAPHY
Butler, C. S. (1992). *Computers and Written Texts.* Oxford: Blackwell.*
Fromkin, V. and Rodman, R. (1993). *An Introduction to Language.* 5th edn. Fort Worth, TX: Harcourt Brace Jovanovich [Chapter 3].
Garside, R., Leech G. and Sampson, G. (1987). *The Computational Analysis of English.* London: Longman.
Gazdar, G. and Mellish, C. (1987). Computational linguistics. In J. Lyons, R. Coates, M. Deuchar and G. Gazdar (eds), *New Horizons in Linguistics 2: An introduction to contemporary linguistic research.* London: Penguin Books, 225–48.
Grishman, R. (1986). *Computational Linguistics: An introduction.* Cambridge: Cambridge University Press.*

EJ

## computer-assisted language learning (CALL)

For several decades the computer appeared to hold great promise for language teaching. In particular, a spurt in the 1980s followed the availability of the microcomputer, during which much investment of time and money took place. Since then the field has lost some of its impetus, becoming more of a specialist developmental area with its own concerns rather than part of the mainstream of language teaching. General surveys can be found in Jones and Fortescue (1987), Leech and Candlin (1986) and Hardisty and Windeatt (1989).

The earliest phase reflected the fact that computers were large mainframe machines kept in research institutions. Large-scale schemes were developed for teaching, such as the PLATO (Programmed Logic for Automated Teaching Operations) at the University of Illinois. The teaching methodology was often in the conventional traditions either of grammatical explanation, in which the learner saw a screen display explaining a point and then had practice material on it, or of AUDIOLINGUALISM in which language points were drilled over and over (though only in written form); the mode was normally self-instruction with one student per computer, sometimes gathered together into a computer laboratory parallel to a LANGUAGE LABORATORY. Programs were stored on large mainframe computers and could only be accessed from terminals on certain university sites; they were mostly ambitious large-scale operations in which language teaching played only a small part.

In the second phase the advent of small computers costing no more than a tape-recorder made a new generation of programs possible. In England, they were chiefly written for the BBC computer that was widely used in schools; programs could be stored on tapes or floppy disks; the whole system was then eminently portable. Most of these were devised by teachers who had taught themselves computing rather than by the psychologists or computer experts who had dominated the earlier phases. Hence they were eclectic, pragmatic and student-oriented, rather than assuming massive models of language or theories of teaching. The most celebrated program was *Storyboard*, available under several names; this reduced a text to a series of asterisks; the student had to guess words which were supplied anywhere they occurred in the text until eventually the whole text was restored. While it was unclear in learning terms what this type of program was doing, it has remained extremely popular with students. It became clear with this type of program that the learning was not so much supplied by the language of the text itself as by the cognitive problem-solving techniques and the interaction between students in the group. Other programs exploited this aspect by using the computer as a trigger for interaction between the students. So rather than the computer being an individual resource for each student, it came to be seen as the focal point for group work, thus allowing some activities that could be termed 'communicative', such as role-play inter-action. The typical teaching format was then either several students interacting around a single computer or a single computer acting as a resource for a whole class.

As the BBC computer died away, so did the enthusiasm of many of the original pro-grammers. While the IBMs and Macintoshes that replaced it were superior in many ways, they did not offer either as easy control of the screen or as effective a version of the BASIC programming language; nor did many BBC programs adapt successfully to other formats. British language teaching publishers, who had been quick to publish the first programs, in particular the set produced by the British Council, have of late hardly produced any novel material at all. Much of the development has retreated to universities and those private language schools that invested heavily in networks of computers.

It has also become concerned with exploiting the services a computer already provides rather than with writing specific programs for language teaching. Word-processing – the one outstanding successful use of the personal computer – adapts to language teaching by enabling students to compose and try out their writings in a non-permanent form. E-mail correspondence between schools in different countries is a motivating use. Concordancing of texts (finding all the contexts of a word in some collection of texts – see CONCORDANCE) lends itself to a range of classroom activities

(Tribble, 1990), particularly as large-scale corpora become generally available, together with the techniques for analysing them made available through CORPUS LINGUISTICS. Again these developments are largely unrelated to contemporary ideas about language, language learning or language teaching, but they use pragmatically whatever actually works in a teaching context.

At the more academic end, experiments have started with the use of multimedia technology to enable a variety of information types to be simultaneously available on the computer so that it is no longer restricted to presenting written sentences on a screen but can also produce spoken language and mov-ing video (Fox et al., 1990). In the Teesside project the student watches a video with the usual fast forward, etc. facilities but with the additional possibilities of alternative soundtracks in the target or first language, subtitles giving the original soundtrack or a translation, with grammar overlays on the screen to explain any points the student wants, an 'oral' dictionary to give both sounds and meanings of words, and so on. As such technology becomes a household necessity, language teaching using such means will doubtless become more widespread. Some work has taken place on integrating CALL with the more orthodox ideas of learning in the field of COMPUTATIONAL LINGUISTICS, leading to ICALL (Intelligent CALL), thus bringing the wheel full circle back to cur-rent views of language in the cognitive sci-ence tradition rather than those of linguistics.

BIBLIOGRAPHY

Fox, J., et al. (1990). *Education and Technology in Modern Language Learning*. Norwich: University of East Anglia.
Hardisty, D. and Windeatt, S. (1989). *CALL*. Oxford: Oxford University Press.
Jones, C. and Fortescue, S. (1987). *Using Computers in the Classroom*. Harlow: Longman.
Leech, G. and Candlin, C. N. (1986). *Computers in English Language Teaching and Research*. Harlow: Longman.

Tribble, C. (1990). *Concordances in the Class-room*. Harlow: Longman.*

VJC

**concordance** A list, today usually de-rived from a CORPUS, showing all instances of a chosen lexical item and indicating its immediate context (before and after). This allows statements to be made about the item's COLLOCATION (the importance of which was emphasized in Firth's work on lexical context). Concordances may be used as a tool in language teaching, to assist learners (or trainee teachers) to become aware of how chosen items behave; see Goodale (1995) for an example. (See also COMPUTATIONAL LINGUISTICS.)

BIBLIOGRAPHY
Goodale, M. (1995). *Concordance Samplers 2: Phrasal Verbs*. London: HarperCollins.

KJ

**consciousness raising** Various types of knowledge about language may be seen as important to second language learning. A broad distinction may be drawn between *explicit* and *implicit* knowledge (see EXPLICIT/IMPLICIT KNOWLEDGE and also CONSCIOUS/UNCONSCIOUS KNOWLEDGE). Explicit teaching about the language is referred to as con-sciousness raising (CR), defined by Ruther-ford and Sharwood Smith (1985: 274) as a 'deliberate attempt to draw the learner's attention specifically to the formal proper-ties of the target language'.

Language teaching methods vary consid-erably in terms of their belief in how much the learner's attention should be specifically directed towards formal properties of the language. In this respect, two dimensions may be distinguished: explicitness and elab-oration. At one end of the scale of the for-mer dimension are approaches such as the DIRECT METHOD, with no explicit grammar teaching. At the other end, with an extreme

form of explicit teaching about structure, is the GRAMMAR TRANSLATION method, where complex metalanguage is employed in the classroom. CR can also be achieved in less overt ways by means of implicit clues, or simply by drawing attention to items with-out providing any glossing comment. The elaboration of a CR activity can be minimal (as in some forms of error correction, for example) or lengthy, with much class time devoted to it (Sharwood Smith, 1991).

The usefulness of CR is thrown into ques-tion by certain findings from SLA research (see FIRST AND SECOND LANGUAGE ACQUISI-TION), for example, the existence of a nat-ural order of acquisition (see NATURAL ORDER HYPOTHESIS). However, while there are many who now feel that CR activities do not affect the 'route' of acquisition, there are those who believe that they can affect the 'rate' (see RATE/ROUTE IN SLA). Rutherford and Sharwood Smith (1985: 275) propose a Ped-agogic Grammar Hypothesis which states that: 'instructional strategies which draw the attention of the learner to specifically struc-tural regularities of the language, as distinct from the message content, will under cer-tain conditions significantly increase the rate of acquisition over and above the rate ex-pected from learners acquiring that language under natural circumstances where atten-tion to form may be minimal and sporadic.'

Gass (1989) cites supporting evidence for this hypothesis and for the use of explicit grammar explanation from three studies dealing with the acquisition of relative clauses. She does not claim that explicit explanation of grammatical structures is absolutely essen-tial for their acquisition, but argues that focused instruction provides a short cut. See NOTICING for the view associated with Schmidt (1990) that when a learner's atten-tion is directed (by whatever means) to an item, this will facilitate its acquisition. Fotos (1993) reports an experiment in which a CR activity is shown to lead to the learner's noticing specific structures in subsequent input, with this noticing in turn facilitating retention of the structures. (Incidentally, an interesting trend can be discerned in some recent EFL textbooks: the replacement of practice activities with CR ones.)

Many writers use the terms consciousness raising and language awareness (LA) interchangeably, though others use the latter term more widely to refer to knowledge about language not simply in the L2 learning context, but with reference to L1 learning, in mother tongue education, TEACHER EDUCATION, and in relation to issues associated with LANGUAGE PLANNING and intergroup relations. For discussion of LA, see James and Garrett (1991).

BIBLIOGRAPHY
Fotos, S. S. (1993). Consciousness raising and noticing through focus on form: grammar task performance versus formal instruction. *Applied Linguistics*, 14/4, 385–407.
Gass, S. (1989). Grammar instruction, selective attention and learning process. In R. Phillipson, E. Kellerman, L. Selinker, M. Sharwood Smith and M. Swain (eds), *Foreign/Second Language Pedagogy Research*. Clevedon: Multilingual Matters, 134–41.
James, C. and Garrett, P. (eds) (1991). *Language Awareness in the Classroom*. London: Longman.*
Rutherford, W. and Sharwood Smith, M. (1985). Consciousness raising and universal grammar. *Applied Linguistics*, 6/3, 274–82.
Schmidt, R. (1990). The role of consciousness in second language learning. *Applied Linguistics*, 11/2, 129–58.*
Sharwood Smith, M. (1991). Speaking to many minds: on the relevance of different types of language information for the L2 learner. *Second Language Research*, 7/2, 118–32.

AJ

**conscious/unconscious knowledge** Some parts of language knowledge, learning and processing (e.g. of PHONOLOGY or GRAMMAR) cannot easily be made explicit in a speaker's mind. This is subconscious knowledge. Other conscious knowledge (e.g. of LEXIS or GENRE) is more readily accessible. The terms 'subconscious' and 'unconscious' are often used interchangeably and confused with the Freudian unconscious: a hypothetical mental repository of suppressed desires. (See also EXPLICIT/IMPLICIT KNOWLEDGE.)

BIBLIOGRAPHY
Schmidt, R. (1990). The role of consciousness in second language learning. *Applied Linguistics*, 11/2, 129–58.

GC

**contrastive analysis** A contrastive analysis describes the structural differences and similarities of two or more languages. As an area of enquiry, contrastive analysis (CA) is concerned with the principles and uses of such descriptions. It implies a belief in language universals; as in any contrast, if there were no features in common, there would be no basis for comparison. (A cuckoo and a crow can be compared more easily than a cuckoo and a cough.) Broadly defined, CA has been used as a tool in historical linguistics to establish language genealogies, in comparative linguistics to create language taxonomies and in translation theory to investigate problems of equivalence. In language teaching it has been influential through the Contrastive Analysis Hypothesis (CAH) which claims that difficulties in language learning derive from the differences between the new language and the learner's first language, that errors in these areas of difference derive from first language interference and that these errors can be predicted and remedied by the use of CA. The CAH was widely influential in the 1950s and 1960s, but from the 1970s its influence dramatically declined. This was due in part to the supplanting of structuralist linguistics, with which it was closely associated. The CAH was also at odds with the views in SLA and INTERLANGUAGE theory that only a small proportion of errors derived from first language interference. In recent years the reputation of CA has revived. This is due in part to a reappraisal of the role of interference and also to the extension of CA to PRAGMATICS and DISCOURSE ANALYSIS.

In a broad sense, CA has always been practised in linguistics and is implicit in many language teaching materials. However, it was the structuralist linguists of the 1940s and 1950s (see STRUCTURALISM) who promoted the term and drew explicit attention to the relevance for language teaching of linguistic description in general and of contrastive descriptions in particular. Fries (1945), for example, summarized the CAH by writing that:

The most efficient materials are those that are based upon a scientific description of the language to be learned carefully compared with a parallel description of the native language of the learner.

The first systematic and extensive formulation of the CAH was by Lado (1957) in *Linguistics across Cultures: Applied linguistics for teachers*, a book which is widely regarded as having launched the CA 'movement' in language teaching. Using structuralist linguistic methods, Lado set out procedures for the comparison of PHONOLOGY, GRAMMAR and vocabulary, and discussed ways in which such analyses might be relevant to syllabus and materials design, methodology and testing. He also embarked upon a simplistic contrastive analysis of cultures. His methods are most successful in the area of pronunciation (where interference is evident, extensive and easily described), rather less successful in the description of grammar and lexis, and least successful of all in the analysis of culture. The book inspired an eruption of activity in contrastive analysis and the 1960s saw numerous research projects and publications. The same period saw parallel work using CA in lexicology and in translation (Catford, 1965). Another active area at this time was the empirical study of language universals (Greenberg, 1963) using CA to categorize languages by structural similarities and differences.

The growing challenge to structuralist linguistics mounted by CHOMSKYAN LINGUISTICS from the late 1950s onwards initially contributed to the decline of the CA. There was also disenchantment with the over-confidence of the structuralists that insights from linguistics would lead automatically to improvements in language learning and teaching. (In contrast, Chomsky wisely disclaimed any direct relevance of his theories to language teaching.) A rejection of CA does not follow from the abandoning of structural linguistics, however, for its principles may stand independently of any particular school of linguistic description, and indeed di Pietro (1971) produced an influential approach to CA based on TRANSFORMATIONAL GENERATIVE GRAMMAR.

A more fatal blow to the CAH was the widespread acceptance of the MORPHEME ACQUISITION STUDIES claiming that foreign language errors derived more from a natural order of acquisition (see NATURAL ORDER HYPOTHESIS) than from first language interference. These studies received theoretical backing from the writings of Krashen. In addition, the theory of INTERLANGUAGE listed a number of sources of error of which first language interference was only one. ERROR ANALYSIS, the examination of attested learner errors, began to replace the error prediction of CA. Although the morpheme studies were soon discredited and the importance of interference re-established, the fashion for contrastive analysis had passed. Its rapid decline was furthered by a growing Anglo-centricity in English language teaching. The promotion of NATIVE-SPEAKER monolinguals as teachers is at odds with CA, as such teachers often do not have the necessary knowledge of their students' languages to use CA. In addition, a systematic application of CA was impossible in classes of a type very common in the English-speaking countries, with students from several language backgrounds.

Recent years have seen some revival of interest in CA under new names. In

Chomskyan linguistics the growing interest in parameter setting contributed to some revival, as has the study of TRANSFER analysis in SLA.

Although CA of linguistic systems for language teaching has never been revived on the scale of the 1960s, an interest has developed in contrastive PRAGMATICS and DISCOURSE ANALYSIS, based on a premise very similar to that of the CAH: that descriptions of areas of difference can be used to predict areas of difficulty for learners (James, 1980). As in linguistic CA, contrastive pragmatics (Thomas, 1983) has relied upon statements of universal principles in order to elucidate different realizations. The Contrastive Rhetoric Hypothesis has developed the notion that 'different speech communities have different ways of organising ideas in writing, which reflect their cultural thought patterns' (Kachru, 1995) and that such differences may cause failure of communication for learners. Both contrastive rhetoric and CP encounter the problem that there is no one-to-one relationship between language and culture or between culture and nation, and that there is far less homogeneity in the discourse and pragmatic behaviour among members of a given culture than there is in their language. Yet despite theoretical and descriptive problems, many interesting insights have been achieved, and both areas are undoubtedly important to an understanding of the ability to communicate in a foreign language.

BIBLIOGRAPHY
Catford, J. C. (1965). *A Linguistic Theory of Translation*. London: Oxford University Press.
Di Pietro, R. (1971). *Language Structures in Contrast*. Rowley, MA: Newbury House.
Fisiak, J. (ed.) (1981). *Contrastive Linguistics and the Language Teacher*. Oxford: Pergamon.
Fries, C. C. (1945). *Teaching and Learning English as a Foreign Language*. Ann Arbor: University of Michigan Press.
Greenberg, J. (ed.) (1963). *Universals of Language*. Cambridge, MA: MIT Press.
James, C. (1980). *Contrastive Analysis*. London: Longman.*
Kachru, Y. (1995). Cultural meaning and rhetorical styles: toward a framework for Contrastive Rhetoric. In G. Cook and B. Seidlhofer (eds), *Principle and Practice in Applied Linguistics*. Oxford: Oxford University Press. 171–85.
Lado, R. (1957). *Linguistics across Cultures: Applied linguistics for teachers*. Ann Arbor: University of Michigan Press.
Thomas, J. (1983). Cross-cultural pragmatic failure. *Applied Linguistics*, 4, 91–112.
Stern H. H. (1983). *Fundamental Concepts of Language Teaching*. Oxford: Oxford University Press, 152–86.*

GC

**controlled practice techniques** The practice ('drilling' or 'manipulation') stage is the second in the traditional 'PRESENTATION – PRACTICE – PRODUCTION' SEQUENCE. Some important characteristics of this middle stage are that it relies on repetition for its effect; that, given this repetitive element, a degree of meaninglessness in the exercises is inevitable (though steps may be taken to minimize this – see below); that it is almost always 'part practice' in which one or more elements of the language are isolated for the practice; that it is relatively controlled practice, often with the learner having very little choice as to the response given. Some have used the word 'scales' to refer to this sort of practice, thereby indicating that it occurs in a variety of skill-learning situations, including learning to play a musical instrument.

The most cogent justification for drilling this century has been in terms of AUDIOLINGUALISM, with its theoretical basis in BEHAVIOURISM, and the view that language learning is a question of habit formation. It was believed that habits are formed by practice, which is why the repetitive element of drilling is important. Practice should be controlled because 'practice makes permanent,' and errors repeated (= 'practised') will become ingrained. By practising small elements at a time, errors would be avoided. See SHAPING and also Rivers (1964) for a comprehensive consideration of drilling, behaviourism and audiolingualism.

CHOMSKYAN LINGUISTICS set out to demonstrate the relatively unimportant role of practice in L1 acquisition, showing, for example, how L1 children will repeat (practise) ill-formed structures which rather than becoming permanent will eventually disappear. There is no doubt that such a stance did much to curb the excesses of audiolingualism and dampen the L2 teacher's faith in the effectiveness of drilling. Nevertheless, language teaching has continued to retain a role for controlled practice.

Mackey (1965) divides traditional ('repetition') drills into rote; incremental; variational; and operational. *Rote* involves the repetition of the same unchanging forms over and over again, while in *incremental* drills words are successively added to a given sentence. In *variational* drills the teacher gives a sentence and asks for one word to be substituted. *Operational* drills are not quite so repetitive, but they involve practising language the teacher knows the students have learned. An example would be warm-up exercises where the teacher-learner engage in rapid question and answer sequences going over known language. Mackey's (1965) Appendix A contains a broader taxonomy of drill types, classified according to the FOUR SKILLS. The LANGUAGE LABORATORY is often much used in controlled practice, with a tape supplying cues and answers. In a common laboratory drill sequence, the tape gives a cue, the learner responds; the tape then provides the correct response, which the learner repeats. It is easy to identify behaviourist elements in this sequence: stimulus – response – reinforcement (hearing the tape repeat the answer the learner correctly gave) – practice (the learner repeating the correct response).

Byrne (1976) likens the teacher's role at the practice stage to that of the orchestral conductor, controlling events and indicating who is to perform when. In traditional drilling the teacher stands at the front of the class, sometimes requesting responses from the whole class, sometimes from individuals. Nowadays group and pair work often replace the teacher-in-front configuration. Traditionally a high degree of accuracy is expected at this stage, with the teacher correcting errors as and when they occur.

Dakin (1973) makes a distinction between meaningless and meaningful drilling. He notes that many traditional drills may be done mechanically, without requiring any comprehension. For him, meaningful implies 'related to a context' – the learner has to refer to some given situation (context) to identify what should be said – for example, looking at a picture to determine the appropriate answer to a question. In recent years, meaningfulness has in general been given importance in language teaching, and elaborate efforts are often made to ensure that even the most small-scale practice is made as meaningful as possible. This may be done by placing it within a context which relates to the learner's life and interests, as well as introducing some problem-solving element to engage the learner cognitively.

A further issue of recent interest concerns the role of drilling in a communicative approach. For some, the existence of an information gap (see INFORMATION/OPINION GAP) is an important element in making language practice communicative. It is possible to introduce information gaps into controlled practice and hence, Johnson (1980) argues, to speak of a 'communicative drill'. Information gap drills are now commonplace. One ingenious way of introducing them is to have two textbooks containing different information available for a class. Students work in pairs; one student in each pair has 'Book A' and the other 'Book B'. For an example (including various sorts of practice, not just the controlled type), see Watcyn-Jones (1981).

For others, the essence of communicative practice is that it should involve learners in expressing what it is they themselves want to say. If this formulation is closely followed, it is difficult to see any place for the notion of a communicative drill (see Harmer, 1982).

In the days of audiolingualism, controlled practice was fundamental to the teaching sequence. In more communicative days, emphasis has tended to shift to the free production stage. Indeed, some teaching models, particularly those which look towards first and second ('naturalistic') language acquisition for inspiration (e.g. Prabhu's; see PROCEDURAL SYLLABUS) avoid controlled practice altogether. But another recent trend, for language teaching with an information processing perspective, appears to see a place for a practice stage, at which language is routinized; see McLaughlin (1987) and Johnson (1996).

Another recent issue concerns the relative values of (controlled) practice and CONSCIOUSNESS RAISING. See Ellis (1994: 643) for a summary of his argument that research into the role of practice (or more generally, of learner participation in classes) is not encouraging, and that consciousness raising offers an alternative.

BIBLIOGRAPHY
Byrne, D. (1976). *Teaching Oral English*. Harlow: Longman.*
Dakin, J. (1973). *The Language Laboratory and Language Learning*. Harlow: Longman.
Ellis, R. (1994). *The Study of Second Language Acquisition*. Oxford: Oxford University Press.
Harmer, J. (1982). What is communicative? *English Language Teaching Journal*, 36/3, 164–8.
Johnson, K. (1980). Making drills communicative. Reprinted in K. Johnson, *Communicative Syllabus Design and Methodology*. Oxford: Pergamon Institute of English.
——(1996). *Language Teaching and Skill Learning*. Oxford: Blackwell.
Mackey, W. F. (1965). *Language Teaching Analysis*. London: Longman.
McLaughlin, B. (1987). *Theories of Second-Language Learning*. London: Edward Arnold.
Rivers, W. (1964). *The Psychologist and the Foreign Language Teacher*. Chicago: University of Chicago Press.*

Watcyn-Jones, P. (1981). *Penguin Functional English: Pairwork, Student A*, and *Pairwork, Student B*. London: Penguin Books.

KJ

**conversational analysis** is an approach to discourse dealing with the linguistic analysis of conversation, and strongly associated with ETHNOMETHODOLOGY. It is concerned with the structure of conversations, dealing with such matters as TURN-TAKING (using the ADJACENCY PAIRS concept), topic change and conversational structure – rules governing the opening and closing of conversations (e.g. on the phone) have been studied in detail. Conversational analysis has been used as a tool in SLA research to study the different types of interaction relevant to language acquisition, including issues related to discourse management, like topic nomination (Long, 1983) and communication breakdown (see Schiffrin, 1994, and Coulthard, 1985).

BIBLIOGRAPHY
Coulthard, M. (1997). *An Introduction to Discourse Analysis*. London: Longman.
Long, M. (1983). Native speaker/non-native speaker conversation and the negotiation of comprehensible input. *Applied Linguistics*, 4, 126–41.
Schiffrin, D. (1994). *Approaches to Discourse*. Oxford: Blackwell.

KJ

**corpus linguistics**   A corpus (plural 'corpora') is a large computer-held collection of texts (spoken, written, or both) collected together to stand as a representative sample of a language or some part of it. Corpora provide easily accessible and accurate data, useful to descriptive and theoretical linguists. They may also be used to calculate the frequency of occurrence of items and, as repositories of actual instances of language use, they have a place in language teaching textbook design. Corpora rely for their effect on size. Two of the best known are the British National Corpus (100 million words) and the Longman/Lancaster Corpus (30 million words). Some corpora are tagged so that parts of speech, for example, may be identified. Parallel corpora holding comparable texts in two languages also exist, as do corpora of learner language (see Thomas and Short, 1996, and Leech, 1993). (See also LINGUISTICS IN LANGUAGE TEACHING.)

BIBLIOGRAPHY
Leech, G. (1993). 100 million words of English. *English Today*, 9, 9–15.
Thomas, J. and Short, M. (1996). *Using Corpora for Language Research*. London: Longman.
                                                    KJ

**correlation** refers to the strength and direction of the relationship between two sets of scores produced by the same group of people. People can score similarly on both tests (positive correlation) or very differently (negative correlation). It is used to determine the VALIDITY and RELIABILITY of TESTS IN LANGUAGE TEACHING. (See also STATISTICS IN APPLIED LINGUISTICS RESEARCH.)

BIBLIOGRAPHY
Woods, A., Fletcher, P. and Hughes, A. (1986). *Statistics in Language Studies*. Cambridge: Cambridge University Press, 154–74.
                                                    SMCD

**Council of Europe** An association of European states, established in 1949. Following the 1971 Rüschlikon symposium, it set up a group of experts to establish a language teaching system for use in all member countries. To provide flexibility the team developed a unit/credit model, with learners following different pathways and receiving credits for teaching units taken. The system has COMMON CORE units, as well as specialized ones. The Council's work has been highly influential, and within the unit/credit framework a model of NEEDS ANALYSIS was developed, the THRESHOLD LEVEL syllabus inventory was produced, and NOTIONAL/FUNCTIONAL SYLLABUSES originated.

BIBLIOGRAPHY
Trim, J. L. M. (1973). Draft outline of a European unit/credit system for modern language learning by adults. In J. L. M. Trim, R. Richterich, J. A. van Ek and D. A. Wilkins, *Systems Development in Adult Language Learning*. Strasbourg: Council of Europe.
                                                    KJ

**creative construction theory** Proposed by Dulay and Burt (1973), it asserts that L2 learners do not merely imitate the language they are exposed to, but subconsciously construct mental grammars which allow them to produce and understand words, phrases and sentences they have not heard before.

BIBLIOGRAPHY
Dulay, H. and Burt, M. (1973). Should we teach children syntax? *Language Learning*, 23, 245–58.
Flynn, S. (1989). Contrast and construction in a parameter-setting model of L2 acquisition. *Language Learning*, 37, 19–62.
                                                    RH

**critical linguistics** A movement associated originally with linguists working at the University of East Anglia (see particularly Fowler et al., 1979). It attempts to explore relationships between language use and the social conditions of that use. The word critical is associated with 'critique', and the idea, in Fairclough's (1985) terms, of 'making visible the connectedness of things', particularly exploring (more than traditional descriptive linguistics would do) the wider social connotations of language use. The critical linguist views the world as social structures manifesting different ideologies, and studies the way language use reflects these. The movement is closely associated with Halliday's functional linguistics and the belief that a language's grammatical system is closely related to the social and personal needs that language serves. Critical linguistics deals with all levels of linguistic analysis, but the branch most commonly referred to is perhaps critical discourse analysis, the aims of which are described in Fairclough (1985). (See also LINGUISTICS IN LANGUAGE TEACHING.)

BIBLIOGRAPHY
Fairclough, N. L. (1985). Critical and descriptive goals in discourse analysis. *Journal of Pragmatics*, 9, 739–63.
Fowler, R., Hodge, R., Kress, G. and Trew, T. (1979). *Language and Control*. London: Routledge and Kegan Paul.
Kress, G. (1985). *Linguistic Processes in Sociocultural Practice*. Victoria: Deakin University Press.
KJ

## Critical Period Hypothesis

**Critical Period Hypothesis** The Critical Period Hypothesis claims that there is a stage in the maturation of a human being during which language acquisition is possible in a natural fashion; before and after this period true language acquisition cannot take place. This agrees with the popular notion that children are able to learn L2s successfully while adults are not. Evidence from L1 acquisition necessarily concerns children with various types of deficiency who, for one reason or another, learn a first language late. The L2 evidence, though extensive, is far from conclusive. Explanations have ranged from biological to social to cognitive ones.

In the first language the claim is that there is a maturational 'window' during which language acquisition is possible, by analogy to similar stages of development in other areas. For example, the young of several species must bond to their caretakers within a certain period – often cited in arguments about whether mothers should go out to work. The existence of such a period can only be substantiated by showing that first languages are effectively not learnt before or after a

certain age. It is evident that children do not usually start to speak before, say, 15 months. But many factors, such as control of the speaking apparatus or cognitive development, might prevent the ability to learn language early being manifested. Experiments with Voice Onset Time have shown, for example, that children are fully capable of distinguishing voiced from voiceless plosives at the age of 2 months, even if their ability to comprehend words comes much later.

One possible source of evidence is from brain injuries; it was claimed that children who suffered trauma under a particular age relearned their first language undetectably; older children were unable to regain it (Lenneberg, 1967); the crucial age ranges from 5 to the early teens in different research. An alternative source is to look at children who have been deprived of language until their teens. On the one hand, 'wolf children' found living in the wild, such as the Wild Boy of Aveyron found in the woods in France in 1797 (see Lane, 1976, on which the Truffaut film was based), seem incapable of full language; on the other the infamous case of Genie, who was locked in a shed strapped to a chair till she was discovered at the age of 13, showed that full language acquisition did not take place despite a promising start (Rymer, 1993). A contrary note is struck by research showing that deaf people without language exposed to signing in their thirties nevertheless become proficient users. These are necessarily extreme cases of physical harm, deprivation or handicap, which are hard to interpret as evidence for normal acquisition. Each individual case of language deprivation is open to the objection that the treatment given to the child involved did not reflect adequate teaching of language; clearly, for example, Genie was treated as a special case rather than being given the approaches normally offered to children with special needs; an alternative treatment for the Wild Boy has indeed been suggested by a modern psychologist, Harlan Lane.

Second language acquisition has been used as evidence for a critical period. The popular belief among both laypeople and linguists has been that children are far superior to adults at L2 learning. Much of the SLA research is more concerned with the progressive effects of age rather than with the cut-off point implied by the Critical Period Hypothesis. A typical summary of the research claims that there is a distinction between long- and short-term learning: children are better over a period of many years, adults over periods of up to a year, shown, for instance, by superior results from several pieces of research for younger immigrants to the USA and by studies of the short-term superiority of adults at learning Dutch in Holland (Krashen, Scarcella and Long, 1982).

The evidence is largely contradictory. Studies by Eckstrand (1978), for example, using all the children currently studying Swedish as a second language in Sweden, showed a clear *improvement* with age. Studies by Johnson and Newport (1989), however, showed a progressive *decline* with age for L2 learners of English in the US. Neither of these show the sudden cut-off expected by the Critical Period Hypothesis. Indeed, research with undergraduate learners of German in England found that, while success indeed declined with an age of starting in the early teens, it improved in the later teens (Gomes-da-Costa, Smith and Whitely, 1975).

Even if one accepted that the critical period existed, one would still be left with a choice between possible explanations. Physiological explanations vary from the loss of 'plasticity' in the brain, to the specialization of the brain into hemispheres, to the growth of gyrus granule cells in the brain. Social explanations talk of the different situations and input for child and adult. Affective explanations talk of the affective barrier that gets raised in the teens between the learner and the input. Cognitive explanations talk of the difficulties of learning language for those in the later Piagetian stages of devel-

opment and of the formation of a 'language ego' that is hard to 'permeate'. Linguistic explanations talk of the lack of access to UNIVERSAL GRAMMAR in L2 learning. There seem rather more explanations than there are facts to explain; with so much changing in human development, almost any of these might be the cause of the putative decline. (See also AGE LEARNING DIFFERENCES, FIRST AND SECOND LANGUAGE ACQUISITION, NUFFIELD PRIMARY FRENCH PROJECT, TEACHING YOUNG LEARNERS.)

BIBLIOGRAPHY
Cook, V. J. (ed.) (1986). *Experimental Approaches to Second Language Learning*. Oxford: Pergamon. [Chapter 2.]
Eckstrand, L. (1978). Age and length of residence as variables related to the adjustment of migrant children with special reference to second language learning. In G. Nickel (ed.), *Proceedings of the Fourth International Congress of Applied Linguistics*. Stuttgart: Hochschulverlag, 3, 179–97.
Gomes-da-Costa, B., Smith, T. M. F. and Whitely, D. (1975). *German Language Attainment*. Heidelberg: Julius Groos.
Harley, B. (1986). *Age in Second Language Acquisition*. Clevedon: Multilingual Matters.
Johnson, J. S. and Newport, E. L. (1989). Critical period effects in second language learning: the influence of maturational state on the acquisition of English as a Second Language. *Cognitive Psychology*, 21, 60–99.
Krashen, S., Scarcella, R. and Long, M. (eds) (1982). *Child-Adult Differences in Second Language Acquisition*. Rowley, MA: Newbury House.*
Lane, H. (1976). *The Wild Boy of Aveyron*. Cambridge, MA: Harvard University Press.
Lenneberg, E. H. (1967). *Biological Foundations of Language*. New York: John Wiley.
Rymer, R. (1993). *Genie: A Scientific Tragedy*. London: Penguin Books.
Singleton, D. (1989). *Language Acquisition: The age factor*. Clevedon: Multilingual Matters.
                                        VJC

**cross-linguistic studies** examine the second language acquisition of specific phenomena *either* across a range of target L2s *or* across speakers of different L1s learning the same L2. Studies of the former kind are important for determining how easy or difficult phenomena are for L2 learners in general. Studies of the latter kind are important for determining the weight to be given to first language influence in SLA. Some cross-linguistic studies have also considered the effect of learning an L2 on subsequent learning of an L3, L4, etc. (Kellerman, 1983) and the influence of learning L2, L3, etc. on an individual's L1 (Cook, 1992).

BIBLIOGRAPHY
Cook, V. (1992). Evidence for multi-competence. *Language Learning*, 42, 557–91.
Kellerman, E. (1983). Now you see it, now you don't. In S. Gass and L. Selinker (eds), *Language Transfer in Language Learning*. Rowley, MA: Newbury House.
Kellerman, E. and Sharwood Smith, M. (1986). *Crosslinguistic Influence in Second Language Acquisition*. Oxford: Pergamon.

RH

**cross-sectional/longitudinal studies**
Cross-sectional studies examine the language behaviour of a group or groups of language learners at a single point in their development. Longitudinal studies examine the language behaviour of one or more subjects as that behaviour develops over time. Comparison of cross-sectional studies of learners at different developmental stages yields a 'pseudo-longitudinal' effect.

RH

**culture shock**   An individual experiences culture shock when contact with a culture different from his or her own results in anxiety, fear, disorientation and inability to cope with the communicative and environmental conditions of life in a non-native context. See ACCULTURATION HYPOTHESIS.

BIBLIOGRAPHY
Smith, E. C. and Luce, L. F. (eds) (1972). *Toward Internationalism: Readings in cross-cultural communication*. Rowley, MA: Newbury House. [See especially the papers by Oberg on 'Culture shock' and Hanvey on 'Cross-cultural awareness'.]

AJ

**curriculum**   For many, this is a wider term than SYLLABUS and refers (White, 1988: 4) to 'the totality of content to be taught and aims to be realized within one school or educational system', with syllabus referring to content in just one subject area. For some, a curriculum specifies just aims and content, while others would also expect statements regarding methods and evaluation. Some prefer the term curriculum over syllabus because it views language content within a wider context of educational aims. In the United States curriculum is often synonymous with syllabus. See White (1988) for discussion of both terms.

BIBLIOGRAPHY
White, R. V. (1988). *The ELT Curriculum*. Oxford: Blackwell.

KJ

**cyclical/linear syllabus**   A linear syllabus covers its teaching items once only, a cyclical or spiral syllabus more than once, enabling them to be treated at different levels of complexity. Basics may be introduced on the first cycle, with later cycles providing revision and coverage of more difficult points.

BIBLIOGRAPHY
White, R. V. (1988). *The ELT Curriculum*. Oxford: Blackwell.

KJ

# D

**declarative/procedural** is a distinction between 'knowing that' and 'knowing how'. In Anderson's model, declarative memory (static cognitive units) differs from procedural memory (dynamic processes or 'procedures'). It is applied occasionally to L2 research in COMMUNICATION STRATEGIES and LEARNING STRATEGIES. Procedural computer languages such as BASIC consist of commands; declarative languages such as PROLOG of statements. (See also INFORMATION PROCESSING MODELS.)

BIBLIOGRAPHY
Anderson, J. R. (1983). *The Architecture of Cognition*. Cambridge, MA: Harvard University Press.
Faerch, C. and Kasper, G. (1983). Plans and strategies in foreign language communication. In C. Faerch and G. Kasper (eds), *Strategies in Interlanguage Communication*. London: Longman, 20–60.
O'Malley, J. M. and Chamot, A. U. (1990). *Learning Strategies in Second Language Acquisition*. Cambridge: Cambridge University Press.
VJC

**deep-end strategy** Brumfit (1978) suggests that the communicative movement involves a shift from the traditional 'PRESENTATION – PRACTICE – PRODUCTION' SEQUENCE to one where the learner first communicates with available resources. Presentation and practice follow if found necessary. For Brumfit this sequence's major advantage is that teaching content becomes 'student-determined' – based on learners' needs revealed at the first stage. The sequence also practises important risk-taking skills because the learner attempts to communicate at the first stage, perhaps using inadequate resources. For this reason, Johnson (1980) calls it the 'deep-end strategy' – the learner is 'thrown in at the deep end'.

BIBLIOGRAPHY
Brumfit, C. J. (1978). 'Communicative' language teaching: an assessment. In P. Strevens (ed.), *In Honour of A. S. Hornby*. Oxford: Oxford University Press, 33–44.
Johnson, K. (1980). The 'deep-end' strategy in communicative language teaching. In K. Johnson, *Communicative Syllabus Design and Methodology*. Oxford: Pergamon Institute of English, 192–200.
KJ

**dependency grammar** A model of GRAMMAR developed in the 1950s in which sentence STRUCTURE is a system of dependencies between words – governors and dependents – rather than phrasal constituents. In *John saw a spider*, the verb *see* governs *John* and *spider*, which are its dependents, and *spider* governs the article *a*, which is its dependent.

BIBLIOGRAPHY
Hudson, R. (1990). *English Word Grammar*. Oxford: Blackwell. [A recent application of dependency grammar principles within a GENERATIVE GRAMMAR framework.]
Matthews, P. H. (1981). *Syntax*. Cambridge: Cambridge University Press. [See particularly chapter 4.]
EJ

**diagnostic tests** provide information about students' strengths and weaknesses which may be useful in determining future teaching needs. Analysis of samples of performance may help build profiles of students' ability, but because sampling (for example, of grammatical structures) will not be comprehensive, the information provided is likely to be sketchy. (See LANGUAGE TESTING.)

BIBLIOGRAPHY
Hughes, A. (1989). *Testing for Language Teachers.* Cambridge: Cambridge University Press.

KSM

**dialect** is a language variety which is associated with a geographical area and/or the social background of the speaker. For example, a British speaker from the south of England may say *I haven't seen him* while her counterpart from the north may say *I've not seen him*. Dialects are usually mutually intelligible despite variation in ACCENT, GRAMMAR and LEXIS. The 'standard' is a dialect which has gained the most prestige in an area and has come to be associated with the nation's *language* (in the case of nation-states). English has several standard dialects, e.g. Standard British English and Standard American English (see STANDARD ENGLISH).

BIBLIOGRAPHY
Chambers, J. K. and Trudgill, P. (1980). *Dialectology.* Cambridge: Cambridge University Press.
Trudgill, P. (1994). *Dialects.* London: Routledge.
Wolfram, W. and Fasold, R. W. (1974). *The Study of Social Dialects in American English.* Englewood Cliffs, NJ: Prentice-Hall.

AJ

**diary studies** The writing of diaries is an established research technique in social science within the naturalistic and ethnographic paradigm, and has a long tradition in anthropology. In education, diaries may be written by learners or teachers; they have been used in a variety of ways for both pedagogic and research purposes, as well as their more 'private' use in personal professional development as a route to greater self-awareness. (See also TEACHER RESEARCH AND DEVELOPMENT and RESEARCH METHODOLOGY.) The common denominator for the genre is that diaries – referred to by Walker (1985) as 'intraviews' – contain accounts of reactions, thoughts, reflections, assumptions, feelings and so on that are not accessible by external observation. They are thus based on a view of writing as an exploratory process. The terms 'log' and 'journal' are also found in the literature, each with slightly different connotations, but 'diary' will be retained here as the umbrella term.

LEARNERS' DIARIES

The two principal strands to the writing of diaries by learners of a language are, first, their classroom-based pedagogic use, and second, research by individuals into their own language learning experiences. (Diaries may also be used as contributory data in other kinds of research projects, such as case studies of individuals or the investigation of learning styles and strategies.)

Language teachers have for some time seen the multiple advantages of setting up routine diary-writing habits with their learners. Typically class members are asked to make regular entries in a designated notebook, with guidelines as to useful data to record. This may include comments on classes, teachers and other learners, feelings about useful ways of learning, out-of-class learning activities, or simply narrative on recent events (McDonough and Shaw, 1993: 255–7). The teacher receives valuable feedback on, for instance, individual needs, perceptions, reactions to lessons, and even on the role of the wider learning environment.

Although personal diaries are not the optimum forum for assessing learners' control of language, the exploration of personal views in writing may automatically lead to a development in proficiency. Learner diaries should be a confidential matter between teacher and student. They can also develop into a 'dialogue journal', where teachers write queries and observations on specific entries which learners address in subsequent entries.

A number of researchers, linguists and experienced teachers have kept diaries, often with the explicit objective of charting their own language learning strategies and experiences. A well-known study is that of Bailey (1983), who, after examining data from her own diary and those of a number of other people, concluded that there appears to be a direct relationship between anxiety levels and competitive attitudes in the classroom learning context. Other studies have used introspective self-report data of this kind to look at a range of cognitive, interpersonal and affective factors in language learning.

TEACHERS' DIARIES

The most frequently reported application of diary-writing techniques from the teacher perspective is in the area of teacher training, both pre- and in-service. This kind of teacher diary may well serve a dual function. On the one hand, trainees are invited to reflect on their experience in the classroom; on the other, they may be asked to write about aspects of the training course itself, and in this latter sense are engaging in an activity akin to the learner-diary paradigm outlined earlier. In most documented instances of novice-teacher writing, trainers provide clear (and sometimes prescriptive) guidelines and checklists of points to be addressed, which in turn may be fed into other aspects of the training programme.

The literature on trainee diaries is rich in examples of themes that such writers tend to address. They include time management, control of classes, lesson planning and preparation, perceptions of self and adjusting to one's role, learner responses, and development in the understanding of methodology or 'craft knowledge'. Where comment is explicitly invited on the training course itself, there are reports on such preoccupations as the variable value of learnt 'theory' to practice, anxiety about relative achievements compared with other trainees, or conversely possibilities for peer cooperation. (See particularly Bailey, 1990; Jarvis, 1992; Porter et al., 1990; Thornbury, 1991.)

There are rather fewer accessible published reports on diary data from experienced teachers, although that there is considerable 'private' activity in this area is well attested. McDonough (1994) identifies a number of themes that recur in 'expert' diaries. Some of them, such as methods, materials and the personal role, are comparable to trainee diaries, but with quite different emphases; others, such as an interest in the learning development of individuals and their effect on the whole class, appear much more frequently for the experienced teacher.

DIARIES AND DIARY STUDIES

A useful and important distinction is to be made between the keeping of a diary for the purpose of personal reflection and development, and the systematic analysis of diary data leading to a more formal and public study. Bailey and Ochsner (1983: 190), for example, offer a flow chart for the process of moving from the purely personal account through systematic analysis to the final public (even published) outcome. The pivotal stage is clearly that of the search for patterns and recurring themes in the accumulated mass of recorded data, which may be subjected to quantitative as well as qualitative analysis. Bailey (1990: 225) quotes Butler-Wall's rather striking point that 'a diary is more than the sum of its parts; although I was the one who recorded every single item, I did not realize what I had recorded until I had recorded many items.'

A diary, then, may be used through retrospective analysis to identify issues, and in this sense is hypothesis-generating, to be followed by further research or by formulating a solution to a teaching problem. Conversely, a diary may be a possible research tool once an issue has been identified, selected for its appropriateness to the question under consideration. A diary study in particular, by going public professionally, helps to disseminate knowledge on many aspects of teaching and learning.

BIBLIOGRAPHY
Bailey, K. M. (1983). Competitiveness and anxiety in adult second language acquisition: looking *at* and *through* the diary studies. In H. W. Seliger and M. H. Long (eds), *Classroom-oriented Research in Second Language Acquisition*. Rowley, MA: Newbury House, 67–103.
——(1990). The use of diary studies in teacher education programs. In J. C. Richards and D. Nunan (eds), *Second Language Teacher Education*. Oxford: Oxford University Press, 215–26.*
Bailey, K. M. and Ochsner, R. (1983). A methodological review of the diary studies: windmill tilting or social science? In K. M. Bailey, M. H. Long and S. Peck (eds), *Second Language Acquisition Studies*. Rowley, MA: Newbury House, 188–98.*
Jarvis, J. (1992). Using diaries for teaching reflection on in-service courses. *ELT Journal*, 46/2, 133–43.
McDonough, J. (1994). A teacher looks at teachers' diaries. *ELT Journal*, 48/1, 57–65.
McDonough, J. and Shaw, C. (1993). *Materials and Methods in ELT*. Oxford: Blackwell.
Porter, P. A., Goldstein, L. M., Leatherman, J. and Conrad, C. (1990). An ongoing dialogue: learning logs for teacher preparation. In J. C. Richards and D. Nunan (eds), *Second Language Teacher Education*. Oxford: Oxford University Press, 227–40.
Richards, J. C. and Nunan, D. (eds) (1990). *Second Language Teacher Education*. Oxford: Oxford University Press.
Thornbury, S. (1991). Watching the whites of their eyes: the use of teaching practice logs. *ELT Journal*, 45/2, 140–6.*
Walker, R. (1985). *Doing Research*. London: Methuen.

JMCD

**dictation** was a technique associated with traditional, accuracy-focused methodology: the teacher read a text aloud right through and then with pauses, while students wrote down exactly what was said. Used primarily as a FORM-FOCUSed testing device, with marks deducted for errors, it was abandoned by COMMUNICATIVE METHODOLOGY. However, in the late 1980s it re-emerged as a means of promoting necessary accuracy while integrating skills. Variations include dictogloss (the text is read at normal speed, then learners piece together what they heard – see Wajnryb, 1990), CLOZE dictation (completion of gapped texts) and picture dictation (students draw as the teacher describes).

BIBLIOGRAPHY
Davis, P. and Rinvolucri, M. (1988). *Dictation: New methods, new possibilities*. Cambridge: Cambridge University Press.
Wajnryb, R. (1990). *Grammar Dictation*. Oxford: Oxford University Press.

CLF

**diglossia**    Ferguson (1959) used the term to refer to the use of two different varieties of the same language by the same speaker in separate socially-determined contexts. For example, in Haiti, French is used in most written and formal spoken situations (government, education, national news broadcasts, etc.); Haitian Creole is used in conversation, selling things, political propaganda, soap operas, etc.). In diglossic situations more generally, one variety is prestigious, codified (with dictionaries, academic grammars) and taught at school (Ferguson's 'High' variety), the other, the 'Low' variety, is none of these things. Fishman (1971) extends the term 'diglossia' to situations involving unrelated languages (e.g. the case of Spanish and Guarani in Paraguay). (See also BILINGUALISM, LANGUAGE PLANNING.)

BIBLIOGRAPHY
Ferguson, C. (1959). Diglossia. *Word*, 15, 325–40. [Reprinted in P. Giglioli (ed.) (1972).

*Language and Social Context: Selected readings*. Harmondsworth: Penguin Books.]

Fishman, J. (1971). *Sociolinguistics: A brief introduction*. Rowley, MA: Newbury House.

Wardhaugh, R. (1986). *An Introduction to Sociolinguistics*. Oxford: Blackwell.

RH

**Direct Method**   It is debatable whether the Direct Method was, on the one hand, a distinct method or, on the other, a generic concept, a shorthand for various 'treatments', some of which were designated by their designers as methods in themselves, e.g. the Phonetic Method. The position taken here is the latter one, i.e. that because these 'treatments' and associated methods share more common features than differences, and are based on the same general APPROACH, it is convenient to refer to them collectively as 'the Direct Method'. Reference here and elsewhere in this *Dictionary* to the Direct Method should therefore be interpreted thus, and not as implying that the Direct Method is well-defined and invariant in its application.

Admittedly, it is confusing that some scholars – e.g. Kelly and Mackey – talk of the Direct Method as though it is easily definable and clearly distinguishable from other similar methods of the same era (the late nineteenth century), when it is not certain where the term 'Direct Method' came from in the first place, nor how its use spread. One source might be Passy's 1899 publication *De la méthode directe dans l'enseignement des langues vivantes*. However, the designation seems to have become popularized not during the heyday of the Direct Method, but afterwards, to refer to methods placing the stress on oral ability and teaching the language 'directly' rather than 'about it'.

Mackey (1965: 151f.) presents his perception of the Direct Method *per se* as follows:

Its main characteristics are: 1. The use of everyday vocabulary and structure. 2. Grammar taught by situation. 3. Use of many new items in the same lesson to make the language sound natural and to encourage normal conversation. 4. Oral teaching of grammar and vocabulary. 5. Concrete meanings through object lessons; abstract ones through the association of ideas. 6. Grammar illustrated through visual presentation. 7. Extensive listening and imitation until forms become automatic. 8. Most of the work done in class; more class hours needed for the method. 9. The first few weeks devoted to pronunciation. 10. All reading matter first presented orally.

He claims as closely associated to the above method: (1) the Natural Method, which progresses more cautiously than the Direct Method, new words being explained through known words, and in which there is more reliance on written materials; (2) the Psychological Method, which places emphasis on mental visualization; (3) the Phonetic Method, which begins with extensive ear-training and uses phonetic notation rather than normal orthography in texts.

Kelly (1969: 312) maintains that the 'theories of education and learning' of the German educationalist J. F. Herbart 'were the basis of the teaching practice of the Direct Method'. Further: 'The five steps of the Herbartian lesson can be seen in every treatment of the Direct Method' (ibid.). These five steps were, according to Kelly: (1) preparation (revision of old material); (2) presentation (imparting new facts); (3) association (of the new with the old); (4) systematization (recapitulation of the new work in its context); (5) application (practice).

Kelly's analysis plainly provides a framework for the linking of practices or methods different at the level of detail but united in their broad sweep. What needs further emphasis is that any 'treatments' or methods subsumable under the title 'Direct Method': (1) emerged in the last quarter of the nineteenth century as an alternative, or riposte, to the GRAMMAR-TRANSLATION Method (see also GRAMMAR TEACHING); (2) placed the aural/oral aspect, as opposed to the reading/writing component, in the foreground; (3)

sought to teach learners to progress from recognition of the sounds of a foreign language to oral production (and only later how to read and write in it) in a fully systematic way, i.e. through organized imitation and practice rather than through a less disciplined 'conversational' approach; (4) saw language learning mainly as a process of habit formation rather than cognition.

Those who pioneered the Direct Method are cited under the entry REFORM SCHOOL. What is to be noted is that they were *phoneticians*, the same people who founded the Phonetic Teachers' Association in 1886 and the International Phonetic Association in 1897. They differed from the average school language teacher of the day in that they: (1) did not see language as residing principally in books, but as being connected with sounds produced in the mouth; (2) were interested in languages for the purposes of communication rather than as tools of access to 'great literature'; (3) consequently, were sceptical of the view that one turned to the 'great writers' rather than the native speaker in the street for insights into use of the language; (4) realized (unlike the 'schoolmen') that there were many languages in the world not conforming to the European model, and concluded that each language had its own 'genius'; (5) knew that many speech communities in the world did not possess a written form of their language, which led them to regard speech as the prime channel of language; (6) observed that speech was also prime in the sense that children learnt the mother tongue through speech, and only later, in given societes, acquired reading and writing; (7) noted that native speakers learnt their languages through imitation and practice, not by reading grammar books; (8) perceived interest in and sympathy with the target society as necessary to efficient learning.

The approach represented in the eight points above was not in every detail new in its own time, connecting, for example, with the 'learning-by-doing' view going back at least to Hoole in the seventeenth century. But it was perhaps better and more 'scientifically' articulated than in earlier times, and promised much. The problems for the Direct Method were partly practical, e.g. teachers competent in the spoken form of foreign languages were rare, and the method demanded more time than those based on reading and writing. There was also a dead weight of old-fashioned pedantry to combat in academic institutions. If the Direct Method had its successes, it was primarily in private institutions, training those who needed to speak languages at a practical level for the purposes of trade and commerce.

BIBLIOGRAPHY
Kelly, L. G. (1969). *25 Centuries of Language Teaching*. Rowley, MA: Newbury House.
Mackey, W. F. (1965). *Language Teaching Analysis*. London and Harlow: Longmans, Green.*
Passy, P. (1899). *De la méthode directe dans l'enseignement des langues vivantes* [On the Direct Method of Teaching Living Languages]. Paris: Colin.

JTR

**discourse analysis** is the study of how stretches of language used in communication assume meaning, purpose and unity for their users: the quality of COHERENCE. There is now a general consensus that coherence does not derive solely from the linguistic forms and propositional content of a text, though these may contribute to it. Coherence derives from an interaction of text with given participants, and is thus not an absolute property, but relative to context. Context includes participants' knowledge and perception of paralanguage, other texts, the situation, the culture, the world in general and the role, intentions and relationships of participants. Early attempts to find linguistic rules operating across sentence boundaries, or to create TEXT GRAMMARS specifying rules for generating possible sequences of propositions, have generally been replaced or supplemented by theories and techniques allowing the examination of text in context. Prominent among such theories and techniques are functional analysis, pragmatic theories of speech acts (see SPEECH ACT THEORY) and conversational principles, conversation analysis, SCHEMA THEORY, GENRE theory and critical discourse analysis.

The study of cohesive devices – the overt textual signals of semantic and pragmatic links between clauses – is usually considered an element of discourse analysis (see COHESION). Cohesive devices include such features as pronouns, ellipsis and conjunctions. Taxonomies of cohesive devices and discussion of their role in creating cohesion can be found in Quirk and others (1985: 1423) and Halliday (1985: 287–314). Knowing how cohesive devices function in a given language, and being able both to understand and to use them appropriately, is an important but until recently neglected element in language learning.

However, the fundamental insight of PRAGMATICS that the meaning and function of an utterance may not be explicit but need to be inferred suggests that many links are also inferred rather than present in the text. Widdowson (1979: 138) gives the following invented, readily comprehensible but non-cohesive example.

> That's the telephone
> I'm in the bath
> OK

Functionally the three utterances relate coherently to each other as request, refusal, acceptance. This principle may be extended to longer stretches of coherent discourse. Sequences of functions and larger functional units have been proposed for particular types of discourse.

In the analysis of interactive spoken discourse, CONVERSATIONAL ANALYSIS has been influential in suggesting that management of TURN-TAKING is a major factor (Levinson, 1983: 296–364). Participants in conversation are seen as orienting towards particular types and sequences of turn, which they signal by

a variety of linguistic and non-linguistic means. Again, some understanding and practice of how conversation is typically managed in the target language is an important element in language learning.

Interpretation of meanings and implicit links depends upon the shared knowledge of participants in discourse, and each participant's assessment of what is known and unknown to the others. This is true even at the grammatical level, where choices among possible clause structures are influenced by prediction of what is given information or new information (Halliday, 1985: 278–81; Quirk et al., 1985: 1360). Even monologues and extended writing are structured by the sender's assumptions about the knowledge of the addressees (Cook, 1989: 64–7). Schema theory, developed in ARTIFICIAL INTELLIGENCE (AI) research in the 1970s, provides an account of how such knowledge is organized, and explains the basis for the omission of information in discourse on the assumption that it can be reinstated by the receiver where necessary (Cook, 1994).

Schema theory, however, is often only concerned with knowledge of the non-linguistic world. Also important is knowledge of larger rhetorical structures, and of how the same information or the same functions may be differently realized in different genres (Swales, 1990). Genre theory attempts to describe how participants orient towards recognizable types of discourse which may be signalled by one or a combination of features including paralanguage, linguistic choices, functional structure, situation, role and relations of participants.

There are a number of different approaches to discourse analysis and there is often some disagreement and confusion about the meaning of both the terms 'discourse' and 'discourse analysis' (Schiffrin, 1993). The approach described above may be characterized as the British-American school (Pennycook, 1994), and has been the most significant in applied linguistics and in language teaching. It is, broadly speaking, an approach which has emerged from detailed study of language. Confronted with the absence of linguistic or semantic explanations for coherence, it has sought help from other disciplines. Historically, it has moved from consideration of the most local textual phenomena, such as cohesion, towards more global concepts such as schemata and genres.

An approach which may be characterized as moving in the opposite direction derives its theoretical base from the work of the French philosopher Michel Foucault, who intuitively identifies orders of discourse (medicine, law, natural history, etc.) defined as the textual expression of ideology and social relationships (Foucault, 1970). Starting from this general overview, Foucault points the way towards textual analysis as a means of understanding social practices.

A third approach is critical discourse analysis (see CRITICAL LINGUISTICS). While making use of insights from both the Anglo-American and the Foucauldian traditions of discourse analysis, it draws particularly upon the Hallidayan view of language as a social semiotic (Halliday, 1973). Its analyses concentrate on how linguistic choices in texts reflect the power relations between senders and receivers, and how texts are used to maintain or create social inequalities through manipulation (Fairclough, 1989). (See LANGUAGE AND POWER.)

Discourse analysis has been influential in COMMUNICATIVE LANGUAGE TEACHING as a source of principles for the detailed description of the resources other than language knowledge which are needed in communication (Widdowson, 1979, 1984; Cook, 1989; McCarthy, 1991). Although DISCOURSE COMPETENCE is sometimes regarded as discrete and separate from other components of COMMUNICATIVE COMPETENCE, it may also be regarded as a superordinate term which embraces all factors in communication, both linguistic and non-linguistic. However, despite the broad scope of the discipline and its descriptive and theoretical importance,

it does not follow that all aspects of discourse competence can or should be taught. Some, such as inferencing procedures, may be universal; others, such as some paralinguistic signals (see PARALINGUISTIC FEATURES), may be acquired – if at all – without tuition; others, such as relevant knowledge, may be gained by learners acting autonomously, as a result of learning the language code rather than as a prerequisite of it.

BIBLIOGRAPHY

Brown, G. and Yule, G. (1983). *Discourse Analysis*. Cambridge: Cambridge University Press.

Cook, G. (1989). *Discourse*. Oxford: Oxford University Press.*

——(1994). *Discourse and Literature*. Oxford: Oxford University Press.

Coulthard, M. (1985). *An Introduction to Discourse Analysis*. London: Longman.*

Fairclough, N. (1989). *Language and Power*. London: Longman.

Foucault, M. (1970). *The Order of Things*. London and New York: Tavistock and Routledge.

Halliday, M. A. K. (1973). *Explorations in the Function of Language*. London: Edward Arnold.

——(1985). *An Introduction to Functional Grammar*. London: Edward Arnold.

Levinson, S. C. (1983). *Pragmatics*. Cambridge: Cambridge University Press.

McCarthy, M. (1991). *Discourse Analysis and the Language Teacher*. Cambridge: Cambridge University Press.*

McCarthy, M. and Carter, R. (1994). *Language as Discourse*. London: Longman.

Pennycook, A. (1994). Incommensurable discourses. *Applied Linguistics*, 15/2, 115–38.

Quirk, R., Greenbaum, S., Leech, G. N. and Svartvik, J. (1985). *A Comprehensive Grammar of the English Language*. London: Longman.

Schiffrin, D. (1993). *Approaches in Discourse*. Oxford: Blackwell.

Swales, J. (1990). *Genre Analysis*. Cambridge: Cambridge University Press.

Widdowson, H. G. (1979). *Explorations in Applied Linguistics*. Oxford: Oxford University Press [Sections 4 and 5].

——(1984). *Explorations in Applied Linguistics 2*. Oxford: Oxford University Press [Sections 2 and 3].

GC

**discourse competence** is a term coined by Canale and Swain (1980) to refer to a speaker's knowledge of rules governing 'the combination of utterances and communicative functions' in discourse. It is a component of sociolinguistic competence which is, in turn, a part of COMMUNICATIVE COMPETENCE. (See also DISCOURSE ANALYSIS.)

BIBLIOGRAPHY
Canale, M. (1983). From communicative competence to communicative language pedagogy. In J. C. Richards and R. W. Schmidt (eds), *Language and Communication*. Harlow: Longman, 2–27.
Canale, M. and Swain, M. (1980). Theoretical bases of communicative approaches to second language teaching and testing. *Applied Linguistics*, 1/1, 1–47.

GC

**discourse intonation** is the study of INTONATION in relation to its contribution to those areas of language use associated with DISCOURSE ANALYSIS. Discourse intonation is concerned with topics such as the contribution of intonation to the expression of speech acts (see SPEECH ACT THEORY); the relationship between units of discourse (like the MOVE) and intonation patterns; how, in general, intonation plays a part in the expression of use rather than usage (see USE/USAGE; see Coulthard, 1977; Brazil et al., 1980).

BIBLIOGRAPHY
Brazil, D. C., Coulthard, R. M. and Johns, C. M. (1980). *Discourse Intonation and Language Teaching*. London: Longman.
Coulthard, R. M. (1977). *Introduction to Discourse Analysis*. London: Longman.

KJ

**discrete-point vs integrative testing**
Following Lado (1961), discrete-point testing assumes that language knowledge can be divided into a number of independent facts: elements of grammar, vocabulary, spelling and punctuation, pronunciation, intonation and stress. These can be tested by pure items (usually multiple-choice recognition tasks). Integrative testing argues that any realistic language use requires the coordination of many kinds of knowledge in one linguistic event, and so uses items which combine those kinds of knowledge, like comprehension tasks, dictation, speaking and listening. Discrete-point testing risks ignoring the systematic relationship between language elements; integrative testing risks ignoring accuracy of linguistic detail. (See also LANGUAGE TESTING.)

BIBLIOGRAPHY
Hughes, A. (1989). *Testing for Language Teachers*. Cambridge: Cambridge University Press, 16–17.
Lado, R. (1961). *Language Testing*. Harlow: Longman.

SMCD

**distribution** refers to the variation in scores obtained by people on a test. Distributions may be symmetrical or skewed, unimodal or bimodal. A distribution of scores that is symmetrical about its mid-point or 'mean' may approximate the mathematical 'normal' or 'bell-shaped' distribution, which has advantages in applying tests of statistical significance.

BIBLIOGRAPHY
Woods, A., Fletcher, P. and Hughes, A. (1986). *Statistics in Language Studies*. Cambridge: Cambridge University Press, 86–93.

SMCD

**drama** is 'a supplementary technique of COMMUNICATIVE LANGUAGE TEACHING' (Wessels, 1987: 5). Its uses range from improvement of spoken language (from the level of pronunciation to that of communication skills in general) to literature teaching. Drama techniques allow scope for the imagination and provide learners with opportunities for language practice in contexts not otherwise possible in the classroom. The adoption of character roles can free learners from cultural or personality constraints. Mime activities allow a TOTAL PHYSICAL RESPONSE. Drama serves to increase learner confidence, and, hence, MOTIVATION. Activities include drama games, ROLE PLAY AND SIMULATION.

BIBLIOGRAPHY
Holden, S. (1981). Drama. In K. Johnson and K. Morrow (eds), *Communication in the Classroom*. Harlow: Longman, 131–6.
Maley, A. and Duff, A. (1982). *Drama Techniques in Language Learning*. Cambridge: Cambridge University Press.*
Wessels, C. (1987). *Drama*. Oxford: Oxford University Press.

CLF

# E

eclecticism in language teaching was a reaction against the profusion of rival approaches and methodologies, and their frequent dogmatism. It holds that no single one is adequate, but many contain valuable insights; the practitioner should therefore select the best from each. Eclecticism's strength is a recognition of diversity, its weakness a tendency to vagueness and lack of principle.

BIBLIOGRAPHY
Grittner, F. M. (1977). *Teaching Foreign Languages*. New York: Harper and Row.
Rivers, W. (1981). *Teaching Foreign-language Skills*. Chicago: University of Chicago Press.
Widdowson, H. G. (1984). The role of theory in practice. In H. G. Widdowson, *Explorations in Applied Linguistics 2*. Oxford: Oxford University Press, 28–36.

GC

educational linguistics is a relatively new linguistics sub-discipline concerning the full range of questions of the relation between language and education. Language is recognized as an essential ingredient of the education process in the classroom and society at large. Thus, educationalists' explicit knowledge about specific aspects of language such as FIRST AND SECOND LANGUAGE ACQUISITION, STRUCTURE, historical development and usage (see USE/USAGE) is advantageous in teaching, from early literacy skills to LANGUAGE PLANNING in multilingual communities. In England and Wales, with the introduction of the schools' National Curriculum in 1989, educational linguistics research focuses on mother tongue and second language teaching.

See also LANGUAGE ACROSS THE CURRICULUM, LINGUISTICS AND LANGUAGE TEACHING, QUALIFICATIONS IN ENGLISH LANGUAGE TEACHING, SOCIO-EDUCATIONAL MODEL, TEACHER EDUCATION.

BIBLIOGRAPHY
Brumfit, C. (ed.) (1995). *Language Education in the National Curriculum*. Oxford: Basil Blackwell.* [Language in education.]
Carter, R. (1995). *Keywords in Language and Literacy*. London: Routledge.
Carter, R. (ed.) (1982). *Linguistics and the Teacher*. London: Routledge and Kegan Paul. [Language, education and society.]
——(1990). *Knowledge about Language and the Curriculum: The LINC reader*. London: Hodder & Stoughton.*
Stubbs, M. (1990). Language in education. In N. E. Collinge (ed.), *An Encyclopaedia of Language*. London: Routledge, 551–89.*

EJ

ego permeability refers to the ease with which new experiences, cultural features or perceptions of other people may pass the defences of one's personality (see PERSONALITY VARIABLES). The term was borrowed from clinical psychology, and used by language researchers to explain learners' openness or otherwise to a foreign language or culture. See also INDIVIDUAL DIFFERENCES.

SMCD

elicited imitation is a research technique aiming at revealing learners' grammatical competence (see COMPETENCE/PERFORMANCE) by requiring them to repeat sentences, the argument being that, when their capacity is strained, their mistakes will reveal their underlying rule system. It was used in L1 acquisition around the early 1970s and has been found sporadically in L2 research since.

BIBLIOGRAPHY
Cook, V. J. (1973). The comparison of language development in native children and foreign adults. *IRAL*, 11/1, 13–28.
Flynn, S. (1987). *A Parameter-setting Model of L2 Acquisition*. Dordrecht: Reidel.
Slobin, D. I. and Welsh, C. (1973). Elicited imitation as a research tool in developmental psycholinguistics. In C. Ferguson, and D. Slobin (eds), *Studies of Child Language*. New York: Holt, Rinehart and Winston.
VJC

# English for specific purposes (ESP)

is a broad and diverse field of English language teaching. In its earlier manifestations in the 1960s, it was particularly associated with the notion of a special language or register, and with the important sub-field of English for science and technology (EST). Later developments have included a communicative view of language as applied to ESP, a recognition of the importance of needs analysis procedures, and an increasing focus on appropriate perspectives on language learning and language skills. Current research and practice are equally broad, comprising the 'narrow and deep' analysis of genres as well as exploration of the links with other areas of education. The place of materials, and the role and training of the ESP teacher, remain important concerns. In its most straightforward definition, the term 'ESP' describes language programmes designed for groups or individuals who are learning with an identifiable purpose and clearly specifiable needs. This statement provides a useful starting-point, but the picture is inevitably a more complex one.

## DEFINITIONS

There are a number of issues relating to possible ways of defining and delineating ESP as a recognizable activity within the broader professional framework of English language teaching, with implications for the design of syllabuses and materials as well as for the specification of areas of research. One of these concerns the much quoted distinction between ESP and EGP, 'English for general purposes' (see GENERAL PURPOSE ENGLISH). This is an unhelpful polarization, particularly because the meaning of 'general purpose' is typically left vague; a more useful view is suggested by Strevens (cited in Robinson, 1991), who prefers the term 'English for educational purposes' (EEP) to account for the school-based learning of a language as a subject element within the overall school curriculum. A related problem concerns the multiplicity of terms used to characterize the various sub-branches of ESP: English for business, banking, botany, pilots, computing, economics, secretaries, medicine, science and many more. Seen from this perspective, ESP becomes synonymous with a large number of separate activities defined according to a subject or a profession or job, and underlying features – of programme and materials design, classroom management, or test construction, for instance – tend to be relegated to a position of less importance than they should have. The common trends, and the links between ESP and ELT in general, are commented on further in subsequent sections.

An accepted solution to such difficulties of definition has been to classify ESP initially into two main sub-branches: *English for academic purposes* (EAP), dealing with the use of English in study settings (particularly but not exclusively in higher education) where the main goal of language learning is the ability to cope in the student's chosen academic specialism; and *English for occupational purposes* (EOP), where the language is needed in the workplace environment of a job or profession. Each of these main divisions can then be further sub-classified into specific disciplines or professions. There are obvious overlaps and grey areas in this kind of dividing up of the world of ESP, where one branch merges into another (the use of business English in academic and working contexts, for example), but the categorization has a common-sense usefulness.

Finally under this heading, reference should be made to Robinson's (1991: 2–4) overview of ESP as consisting of, on the one hand, *criterial* features common to virtually all ESP programmes, as well as, on the other, characteristics that in quantitative terms are likely to occur. Her two criterial features are that ESP is

● goal-directed, i.e. a means rather than an end in itself. This perspective is fundamental to a view that sees language as a 'service' rather than a subject studied for its own sake, and has been a powerful influence on most areas of ESP research and practice;
● based on an analysis of learners' needs (see NEEDS ANALYSIS).

Typical characteristics include

● learners are frequently adults;
● the time period available for learning is often limited;
● homogeneity (of subject background or profession) *may* exist.

Ways in which such views have developed and influenced the practical pedagogy of ESP are charted directly or indirectly in the following sections.

BACKGROUND AND THEORETICAL BASES

It must be stressed here that ESP cannot be seen as a totally separate enterprise, but rather as embedded in and contributing to many traditions and developments in language teaching and applied linguistics. Hutchinson and Waters (1987: 17) use the organic image of a tree, with the roots planted deeply in learning and communication, and rising up through the various divisions and subdivisions of language teaching already outlined. Ways in which this has happened, however, have obviously changed over time. The following potted history of ESP also points to a number of loose parallels between theories and 'movements' in language teaching and particular time periods, not so much as a series of rejections as growth and modification based on reflection and experience. These stages are explored in detail in Swales's *Episodes in ESP* (1985), a collection of seminal papers by different writers set out chronologically and annotated by the editor.

*Register analysis*　It is difficult, and not particularly productive, to put a precise date on the origins of theories or movements. ESP as a recognizable concept can nevertheless be traced back about thirty years or so to its 'early days' in the 1960s, when a reaction against the dominant literary tradition in language teaching gradually set in. Strevens's landmark paper, with the self-explanatory title 'Alternatives to Daffodils' (published in 1971), was clearly conceived in the spirit of the times, arguing for a more pragmatic view of course design and methodology rooted in learners' own goals and realities. Among the principal exponents of this essentially 'service' perspective were Ewer and Latorre and their colleagues, working in Chile at the University of Santiago. In order to develop language materials that would be appropriate for undergraduates with a range of different specialisms, they analysed a very large corpus of texts from a variety of subjects (physics, chemistry, biology and medicine, for instance), eventually producing *A Course in Basic Scientific English* (1969). The significant outcomes of their analysis were the establishment of the *frequency* and *range* (across subjects) of (a) sentence patterns and (b) lexis within the corpus. This was then taken to constitute the 'register' or 'common core' of scientific and technological English (EST), and was duly converted into a syllabus for teaching.

The analysis and description of language according to the frequency of sentence-based and lexical features – common at the time, not only in ESP – have now been broadened to become a necessary but not sufficient basis for devising language programmes. There are, however, many more recent echoes, for example in continental Europe, where terminological analysis continues to be an important research tradition and to underpin methodology.

*Needs analysis*   Needs analysis is the subject of a separate entry in this volume. Nevertheless brief mention must be made of it at this point because of its significance in the chronology of ESP. As a concept, it became most fully discussed and explored from the mid-1970s onwards. It evolved partly within the framework of the communicative approach (see COMMUNICATIVE LANGUAGE TEACHING), as evidenced, for example, by the title of Munby's important if controversial proposal for a model of ESP needs analysis (*Communicative Syllabus Design*, 1978). Furthermore, it triggered an explicit awareness of the large number of variables that might make up a learner's 'needs profile', thus moving on from the rather close (even narrow) relationship between needs and linguistic data characterized by the analysis of (scientific) REGISTER.

*ESP and the communicative approach*   Communicative theory has obviously had far-reaching consequences for the whole of language teaching, not only for ESP. At the same time there are a number of key areas where ESP took up and developed communicative principles in directions considered to be appropriate to its own terms of reference.

Most generally, the argument that register analysis is by itself an inadequate basis for learning and for generating language programmes became a prevalent one during the 1970s. Widdowson (1978, for example) referred to the formal, structural properties of language as *usage*, and polarized this with *use* (see USE/USAGE), a self-explanatory term for a view of language that focuses on its communicative and functional purposes in a real-world context. Such a perspective was felt to be particularly important for adult learners who may well have been exposed for several school years to a grammatical syllabus and who would not be helped or motivated by re-exposure to the same kind of material.

More specifically, Widdowson set out a number of significant arguments that eventually led to the publication of the first course book in the *Focus* series, *English in Physical Science* (1978). (Note that EST was still a dominant area of attention.) He proposed that science has a 'communicative deep structure', independent of its realizations in different languages and akin to the methodologies and procedures used in all kinds of scientific investigation. This methodology includes (for example) description, measurement, and hypothesis formation, as well as the use of non-verbal representation, and the formal linguistic exponents of each of these categories may then be taught in the pragmatic framework of use in scientific discourse and not just as grammatical manipulation. Although the idea of universal categories has been controversial, these views have had concrete and lasting implications for teaching and materials design, particularly in EAP. A further corollary of the communicative approach has been the analysis of language beyond the boundaries of the grammatical sentence in terms of the properties of whole texts, under the headings of the COHESION of text and the COHERENCE of discourse. (See DISCOURSE ANALYSIS.)

This discoursal view of language, where grammatical description is embedded in a wider context of meaning and use, has been paralleled in the USA in terms of 'rhetorical analysis', particularly by Trimble (1985) and his colleagues in Washington. Their research has been particularly concerned with the form-function relationship inherent in EST, exploring, for instance, the links between tense choice and argument structure. More recently, this orientation to language analysis has been phased into a focus on 'GENRE', which considers not only texts in themselves, but the sociolinguistic role that texts play in particular environments and whole discourse communities: in other words, their communicative *purpose* as well as their linguistic-communicative properties (Swales, 1990).

*Skills in ESP*   It can be argued that the developments described in the preceding sections have been primarily significant in offering increasingly rich ways of analysing language – in terms of register, communicative context of use, text, discourse, rhetoric, genre. Whereas earlier register-based approaches tended to deal with text as an amalgam of items of language (grammar, lexis), the 1980s saw increasing attention being given, not only to the text (written or spoken) as a product to be understood, but to the human processor or producer of that text (see PROCESS VS PRODUCT). This has led to a concern with both STUDY SKILLS and language skills, the latter in common with language teaching more generally.

An initial and indeed continuing focus in ESP has been the skill of reading, for the practical and international reason that, in a great number of study contexts throughout the world, English is primarily required as the 'library language' of textbooks and research reporting where otherwise teaching takes place in the student's mother tongue. Subsequent ESP research and practice has been concerned with the remaining three of the so-called FOUR SKILLS, looking for instance at lecture comprehension (listening), writing in academic contexts, and the speaking skills required in both EAP (such as seminar participation) and EOP (such as many of the oral skills required in business communication).

A direct effect of the nature of ESP and the requirements of ESP teaching programmes has been the need to redefine the boundaries between the traditional four skills in relation to the learners' target situations. Thus, for example, the lecture situation typically involves the skill of listening, but also the rather specialized writing associated with condensing information and reducing it to note form. There is, in other words, a *composite* skill derived from the target activity. Candlin and others (1978: 199) see this activity or 'mode' as a kind of filter for the subsequent specification of a range of micro-skills. A further significant consequence of this perspective has been the possibility of using these micro-skills to sequence and grade pedagogic materials in terms of learning tasks, as well as linguistic items. Skills converted into tasks then become a series of enabling steps leading to successful target performance – the overall goal of learning.

An issue in ESP that also deals with the nature of the learning process concerns the hypothesis that there are different kinds of COGNITIVE STYLE which may condition the way in which an individual perceives the world and therefore his or her choice of academic discipline (or perhaps even profession). It may be, for example, that so-called 'divergent' thinkers tend to choose arts-based subjects, whereas the 'convergent' prefer the kind of logico-deductive reasoning associated with the methodology of science (Flowerdew, 1986). This remains a controversial research issue as yet rather than a basis for the design of language programmes, but it is a further illustration of the possibilities inherent in the exploration of language processing and strategies for learning alongside analysis of the properties of language.

## PRINCIPLES IN PRACTICE

The preceding discussion of the chronological development of ESP has been largely concerned with what Richards and Rodgers

(1986) call APPROACH, in other words with the theoretical foundations of practice rather than the detailed and more contextualized aspects of course design and implementation. These approaches, together with basic issues of ESP definition, have multifarious implications for ESP practitioners, just three of which from many are enumerated here.

First of all, aspects of the design of teaching materials have been of primary importance; indeed, for many years the writing of materials was perceived to be virtually a *sine qua non* for involvement in ESP. In a branch of language teaching associated with different kinds of specificity, the question of the relevance of published materials versus the supposed virtues of home-produced ones has been a very pertinent one (see, for example, Swales, 1980). Furthermore, definitions and principles impinge directly on specific design features of materials, such as the breadth of ESP topic area (the 'wide-angle' vs 'narrow-angle' debate); sources of language data, including the question of AUTHENTICITY of text; the role of subject-specific lexis; and coverage of skills and tasks in both 'enabling' and 'target' terms.

Second, although developments and trends in ESP have been presented chronologically here, it must be stressed that context is of crucial importance in determining the nature of an ESP programme and the design choices that are made. By 'context' is meant both the immediate learning situation, but also the wider educational and sociopolitical environment, and attitudes to change and innovation. Developments thus take place at different times in different countries; and the worldwide geographical spread of ESP shows clearly the enormous range of possibilities of interpretation, practice and cross-fertilization. (The ESP literature reports regularly on work in – to name just a few places – Australia, the Middle East, the UK, the USA, SE Asia, Eastern Europe, Latin America.)

Third and finally, the nature of the ESP teacher's role has been, and continues to be, a central concern. Two issues in particular have preoccupied the profession. One of these is the breadth of role of many ESP teachers who are typically involved in all aspects of course planning, even management and administration, in addition to their more traditional classroom role. This clearly derives in part from the characteristics of ESP courses outlined at the beginning of this entry. However, the question that has arguably been the single most prominent one – over time and worldwide – is that of the extent to which ESP teachers should specialize in the subjects or professions of their learners, or even be practitioners in those areas and only subsequently trained in ELT or ESP. There is, of course, no single answer to this, and it is influenced in no small degree by prevailing educational philosophies, as well as by the 'narrow-angle vs wide-angle' debate applied to the ESP teacher's function and training.

RESEARCH AND DEVELOPMENT

It is difficult, if not impossible, to generalize about or circumscribe current ESP research or developments in ESP practice, because so much depends on context, history, and individual experience and interpretations of theory and principle. Some trends are nevertheless discernible, albeit too diverse to categorize neatly.

In the period of ESP outlined here, there has continued to be active redefinition of established terms of reference (needs analysis, the role of the teacher, course evaluation, design features of materials, for example). At the same time, there have been two parallel but rather different developments. One of these is the trend to what Swales (1990: 7) calls 'narrower and deeper' analyses, particularly characterized by the micro-investigation of genres or specific areas of discourse. There are many instances of this kind of work in *English for Specific Purposes*, the major journal in the field. The other is the exploration of the boundaries of ESP, and of the breadth of possibilities for growth at its interface with (for example) management studies, the teaching of the mother tongue, and research paradigms (such as ACTION RESEARCH) in general education.

Finally, it is particularly characteristic of work in ESP that research and practice have always been tightly interwoven: just as in any applied field, the former has infiltrated the latter, so reflection on and awareness of practice have frequently been a stimulus for research.

BIBLIOGRAPHY

Allen, J. P. B. and Widdowson, H. G. (1978). *English in Focus: Physical science*. Oxford: Oxford University Press.

Candlin, C. N., Kirkwood, J. M. and Moore, H. M. (1978). Study skills in English: theoretical issues and practical problems. In R. Mackay and A. Mountford (eds), *English for Specific Purposes*. London: Longman, 190–219.

Ewer, J. R. and Latorre, G. (1969). *A Course in Basic Scientific English*. London: Longman.

Flowerdew, J. (1986). Cognitive style and specific-purpose course design. *English for Specific Purposes*, 5/2, 121–9.

Hutchinson, T. and Waters, A. (1987). *English for Specific Purposes*. Cambridge: Cambridge University Press.*

Munby, J. (1978). *Communicative Syllabus Design*. Cambridge: Cambridge University Press.

Richards, J. C. and Rodgers, T. C. (1986). *Approaches and Methods in Language Teaching*. Cambridge: Cambridge University Press.

Robinson, P. (1991). *ESP Today: A practitioner's guide*. New York and London: Prentice Hall International.*

Strevens, P. (1971). Alternatives to Daffodils. *CILT Reports and Papers*, 7, 7–11.

Swales, J. (1980). ESP: the textbook problem. *ESP Journal*, 1/1, 11–23.

——(1985). *Episodes in ESP*. Hemel Hempstead: Prentice-Hall.*

——(1990). *Genre Analysis*. Cambridge: Cambridge University Press.

Trimble, L. (1985). *English for Science and Technology: A discourse approach*. Cambridge: Cambridge University Press.

Widdowson, H. G. (1978). *Teaching Language as Communication*. Oxford: Oxford University Press.

JMCD

**error analysis** (EA) saw its heyday in the 1970s. It is an approach to understanding second language acquisition (SLA) which consists of compiling a corpus of L2 learner deviations from the target second language norms – the 'errors' learners make – classifying these errors by type and hypothesizing possible sources for the errors.

In the history of SLA research, error analysis was a phase of enquiry which followed on from CONTRASTIVE ANALYSIS. Contrastive analysis had been interested in comparing two linguistic systems – the learner's L1 and the target L2 – with a view to determining structural similarities and differences. The view of SLA which underpinned contrastive analysis was that L2 learners *transfer the habits of their L1 into the L2*. Where the L1 and the L2 were the same, the learner would transfer appropriate properties and be successful: a case of *positive transfer*. Where the L1 and the L2 differed, the learner would transfer inappropriate properties and learner errors would result: a case of *negative transfer*. This was the Contrastive Analysis Hypothesis. Errors on this account were predicted to occur entirely at points of divergence between the L1 and the L2.

The Contrastive Analysis Hypothesis lost favour with many researchers during the 1960s as the result of (a) a growing scepticism about the plausibility of a behaviourist (i.e. habit formation) account of language acquisition; and (b) the accumulation of empirical studies of SLA which indicated that the Contrastive Analysis Hypothesis made the wrong predictions.

The awareness that some of the errors which L2 learners make are not the result of negative transfer led to researchers focusing on errors themselves, rather than on comparing the source and target languages. This shift of interest was captured in a well-known article by Corder (1967) dealing with the significance of learners' errors. Errors came to be viewed as a reflection of L2 learners' mental knowledge of the second language: their INTERLANGUAGE grammars (Selinker, 1972). Researchers therefore began to analyse corpora of second language errors in order to understand better the nature of interlanguage grammars.

The starting-point for error analysis was to construct a corpus of errors produced by L2 learners. An important methodological consideration at the outset was to set aside those errors which were transient 'lapses' or 'mistakes' (Corder, 1974) from those which were systematic differences between the linguistic knowledge of the L2 learner and the native speaker. For example, an L2 learner may inadvertently use a wrong verbal agreement as in *He have been there* on one occasion as the result of inattention, tiredness, drunkenness, etc., where ordinarily that same speaker would systematically make the appropriate verbal agreements. This would be a simple performance lapse, not corresponding to the L2 learner's underlying knowledge. If, however, it is clear that a speaker regularly fails to make subject–verb agreements, this would be a systematic divergence between the L2 learner and the native speaker, and such errors would merit being included in the corpus for error analysis.

Once a corpus had been compiled, the researcher would begin to classify the errors into types. The result of grouping together and labelling subgroups within a corpus is known generally as a *taxonomy*. Various taxonomies for L2 learner errors have been used. For example, Richards (1971), in one of the earliest error taxonomies, classifies errors by their *linguistic* type. He compiled a corpus of L2 English errors produced by speakers from eleven different L1 backgrounds. The errors in this corpus are classified as:

- errors in the production of the verb group, e.g. *He was died last year* (*be* is not a possible auxiliary for *die* in English);
- errors in the distribution of verb groups, e.g. *I am having my hair cut on Thursdays* (the progressive *-ing* is incompatible with a habitual interpretation);
- errors in the use of prepositions, e.g. *entered in the room*;
- errors in the use of articles, e.g. *She goes to bazaar every day*;
- errors in the use of questions, e.g. *Why this man is cold?*
- a dustbin category of miscellaneous errors, e.g. *I am very lazy to stay at home; this is not fit to drink it.*

Dulay, Burt and Krashen (1982: 138–99), in a lengthy consideration of errors, describe three other major types of taxonomy. First, a *surface strategy taxonomy* which classifies errors not by specific linguistic type, but by the structural deformations the utterance undergoes. For example, *omission* of items in the L2 learner's utterances which would be present in those of a native speaker (e.g. *I bought φ in Japan, φ is very hard for me to learn English right*); *addition* of items not present in the target language (e.g. *The fishes do*es*n't live in the water*); the *double marking* of properties which are singly marked in the target language (e.g. *She* **did**n't **went**, *That's the man* **who** *I saw* **him**); the *over-regularizing* of target-language properties (e.g. *I falled*, where the regular past tense *-ed* has been extended to a verb which in native English is an irregular verb); *over-generalizing* (e.g. *that dog, that dogs*, where the demonstrative *that* is being used by the L2 learner for both singular and plural nouns – what Dulay, Burt and Krashen refer to as an 'archiform') and finally *misordering* of target-language word orders (e.g. *What daddy is doing? He is all the time late*).

Second, a *comparative taxonomy* where second-language learner errors are classified by similarity with children's first-language learner deviations from target-language norms and/or by similarity with the errors made by L2 speakers from different L1 back-grounds. For example, both second-language learners and child L1 learners produce sentence types like the following: *apple come down* (no determiner *the*, no auxiliary verb *have*); *Did I did it?* (double-marking of past tense).

Third, a *communicative effect taxonomy*. Here errors are classified by the effect they have on native speakers, whether in terms of comprehension or in terms of the way that non-native speakers are perceived by native speakers. For example, Burt and Kiparsky (1972) used sentences like:

(1)   The English language use much people
(2)   English language use many people
(3)   Much people use English language

to ask native speakers of English for judge-ments of comprehensibility. Sentence (3) was judged as more comprehensible than sen-tences (1)–(2), suggesting that word-order errors are a greater hindrance to compre-hension than the correct use of determiners or quantifiers (Dulay, Burt and Krashen, 1982: 190).

Up to this point the task has been essen-tially one of labelling subgroups within a corpus. And some error analyses stopped there (for example, Richards, 1971). Others, however, went on to suggest possible causes for error types. For example, Selinker (1972: 216–21) proposes five 'processes' involved in the production of errors: *language* TRANS-FER, *transfer of training, strategies of second-language learning, strategies of second-language communication* and *over-generalization of target-language linguistic material*.

Language transfer is the notion familiar from the Contrastive Analysis Hypothesis, but it is now just one of a set of potential sources for L2 error, rather than the over-riding source. To illustrate transfer of training, Selinker cites the difficulty that Serbo-Croatian learners have in their L2 English with the gender distinction in the third person singular pronouns *he/she*, pre-ferring to use *he* everywhere. According to

Selinker (1972: 218), at the time he was writing, 'textbooks and teachers . . . almost always present drills with *he* and never with *she*.' This would be a case where learners have apparently transferred their training in the use of *he* into their interlanguage gram-mars. An example of a strategy of second-language learning is 'simplification': the tendency to reduce the target language to a small set of general properties. For example, the cases of over-regularization mentioned above might be considered to be the effect of a learning strategy: once a learner has noticed a regular pattern, that pattern is used everywhere. The strategy of second-language communication is not all that well defined by Selinker. He suggests that one type of communication strategy is for learners to produce utterances which they know them-selves to be marked by transfer, simplifica-tion and other errors, but which are fluent. They do this, rather than 'think about' (p. 220) the grammatical processes involved in their utterances, in order to avoid a break-down in communication and in order to avoid native speakers becoming impatient with them. As an example of over-generalization, Selinker cites a learner who extends the verb *drive* to include bicycles: *drive a bicycle*. (See COMMUNICATION STRATEGIES.)

## EVALUATION OF ERROR ANALYSIS

A number of problems arose with the use of error taxonomies as an approach to the study of SLA; they have been well documented in the literature (see Dulay, Burt and Krashen, (1982: 141–6) and Larsen-Freeman and Long (1991: 61–2) for some discussion).

First, error taxonomies often confuse description with explanation. Consider the following example involving progressive *-ing*. Suppose that an L2 learner inflects every verb he or she utters with *-ing*, as in:

(4)   (a)   I having dinner.
        (b)   I having my hair cut.

(c)  I knowing the answer.
(d)  I having my hair cut on Thursdays.

Error analyses would treat the status of (4a–b) differently from (4c–d). In (4a–b) the error would be the simple omission of a required form of the copula: *am*. In (4c–d) the error would not only be the omission of *am*, but also the inappropriate use of the progressive -*ing* with a stative verb (*know*) and a habitual event (*on Thursdays*). But these separate sub-classifications would miss the point that the L2 speaker has an underlying misrepresentation of all verbs as inflected for -*ing*. The description of the errors involved is not the same thing as an explanation for them.

Second, for a taxonomy to be effective it should be easy to classify items uniquely under one category or another. But in the case of error taxonomies it has often been difficult to determine why an error should be classified in one way rather than another. For example, to classify an error like *Lily no have money* made by a Spanish speaker as a 'transfer' error (example from Dulay, Burt and Krashen, 1982: 142) may appear to be appropriate in view of the fact that Spanish has an equivalent construction *Lily no tiene dinero*. However, when it is discovered that other L2 learners from different L1 backgrounds without an equivalent construction also make the same error, it becomes unclear whether such an error should be classified as a transfer error or an omission error for the Spanish speaker (omission of *do*). As another example, Dulay, Burt and Krashen classify *falled* (where the regular past -*ed* has been extended to a verb which is irregular in the target language) as an error of over-regularization, but they classify *that* used with both singular and plural nouns (*that dog, that dogs*) as an over-generalization of the use of *that*. But if the reason why -*ed* is classed as an 'over-regularization' is that it is a single form used for marking all cases of simple past tense, it is just as easy to say that *that* is a single

form marking all cases of non-proximate deixis, i.e. is also an 'over-regularization'.

Third, it was noted above that in compiling error corpora it is necessary to separate transient 'lapses' which do not reflect underlying incompetence from 'errors' which do. However, it is not always easy to make such decisions. How many tokens does one need to come across before one can be certain of an error rather than a lapse? In Richards's (1971) taxonomy there are errors under the 'miscellaneous errors' category like *I am very lazy to study at home* (where the native speaker would use *too lazy*). Such examples are likely to be fairly infrequent in an L2 learner's utterances, and it is not clear why one is justified in classing them as errors rather than lapses.

Fourth, Schachter (1974) has argued that one of the influences that an L1 can have on L2 acquisition is to make the learner *avoid* difficult constructions. For example, she suggests that Chinese and Japanese learners of English make fewer errors on relative clauses than Spanish and Farsi speakers. But the reason they do so is because they produce fewer relative clauses. According to Schachter, Chinese and Japanese speakers avoid producing relative clauses because they know they are very different in English from Chinese and Japanese. An error taxonomy would not reveal this fact.

## THE DEMISE OF ERROR ANALYSIS

Error analysis was an inductive phase of enquiry in SLA research. That is, it worked from corpora of collected samples of error and tried to draw generalizations about patterns in those samples. While the observation of such patterns is an important step in moving towards an understanding of SLA, work since the 1980s has on the whole been deductive. Researchers start with a theory about SLA which generates hypotheses, which are themselves then tested against error patterns. Deductive approaches are potentially much richer sources of explanation than inductive approaches, and for that reason few researchers nowadays conduct error analyses of the type described above. (See also ERROR CORRECTION, ERROR EVALUATION, ERROR/MISTAKE/LAPSE.)

BIBLIOGRAPHY
Burt, M. and Kiparsky, C. (1972). *The Gooficon: A repair manual for English*. Rowley, MA: Newbury House.
Corder, S. P. (1967). The significance of learners' errors. *International Review of Applied Linguistics*, 5, 161–70.
——(1974). Error analysis. In J. Allen and S. P. Corder (eds), *The Edinburgh Course in Applied Linguistics*. Vol. 3. Oxford: Oxford University Press.
Dulay, H., Burt, M. and Krashen, S. (1982). *Language Two*. Oxford: Oxford University Press.* [Chapter 7.]
Ellis, R. (1994). *The Study of Second Language Acquisition*. Oxford: Oxford University Press.* [Chapter 2.]
Larsen-Freeman, D. and Long, M. (1991). *An Introduction to Second Language Acquisition Research*. London: Longman.
Richards, J. (1971). A non-contrastive approach to error analysis. *English Language Teaching*, 25, 204–19.
Schachter, J. (1974). An error in error analysis. *Language Learning*, 24, 205–14.
Selinker, L. (1972). Interlanguage. *International Review of Applied Linguistics*, 10, 209–31.
RH

**error correction**    Attitudes towards learner errors have changed considerably in recent decades. Approaches based on behaviourist principles (particularly AUDIOLINGUALISM) advocate the initial avoidance of errors, and their diligent correction should they occur. More recent attitudes have displayed more tolerance; advocates of COMMUNICATIVE LANGUAGE TEACHING, for example, recognize the need for fluency practice, and this may lead to occasions when errors are allowed to pass uncorrected, though perhaps only temporarily. Others point out that in L1 acquisition mistakes often go uncorrected, yet are eventually eradicated; error correction in this situation appears to be unnecessary, and to have little effect.

Error correction is a form of feedback, and there is a wide literature on the general topic of feedback (see Annett, 1969, for example). In recent decades the topic has attracted much attention in the language teaching field. Questions regarding the effectiveness of error correction techniques, particularly entailing comparisons of various techniques, involve great difficulties of research methodology, and the result is that in this area there tend to be more expressions of opinion than of fact.

Chaudron (1988) identifies a series of questions that research has addressed: should errors be corrected? If so, when? Which errors? How should they be corrected, and by whom? Learner and teacher attitudes towards errors are further areas of research. On the issue of whether error correction has any value, it has already been noted that for L1 acquisition there is little effect of correction, and Krashen (1982) among others assumes that this will also be the case for L2 acquisition (as opposed to learning; see ACQUISITION/LEARNING). Chaudron (1986) reports a study in which only 39 per cent of corrections in an immersion class led to subsequent observable avoidance of the corrected errors; but the research methodology problems involved in ascertaining the results of error correction over time are indeed substantial.

Chaudron (1988) contains a summary of research into the issue of when teachers tend to correct errors. The main (unsurprising) finding is that teachers tend to correct more errors on occasions when there is greater form-focus in the class. Regarding the question of 'which errors?' Chaudron (1988) again provides a useful summary of research, showing that in a number of studies lexical, discourse and content errors receive more attention than errors in phonology and grammar. However, studies on ERROR EVALUATION indicate the necessity to consider exactly who is doing the correction; considerable differences exist between native speaker and non-native speaker teachers as regards the focus of corrections.

On the issue of how best to treat errors, there have been various taxonomies of error modes, all indicating the rich set of possibilities open to the teacher. Allwright's taxonomy (1988: 207) lists as many as sixteen types of error treatment by the teacher. The first six are expressed in terms of options such as 'to treat or to ignore completely' and 'to treat immediately or delay'. The remaining ones are classified as possible features of error treatments, such as 'blame indicated', 'location indicated'. See Chaudron (1988: 146–7) for a further list; also REFORMULA-TION for one particular correction mode. Johnson (1988) follows Corder in distinguishing *errors* (caused generally by a lack of knowledge) from *mistakes* (caused by a failure to put what is known into practice); he argues that both need very different treatments; in particular, to treat a mistake as if it were an error is unlikely to meet with any success.

As Chaudron (1988: 150) points out, possible answers to the question of who should correct are the teacher, the learner making the error and other learners. There is research to indicate that all these three occur in various situations. This is of interest in itself because one might question the occurrence of much peer correction; in fact, Hendrickson (1978) shows that peers may be effective correctors of one another's writing. Once again, it is an area where there are more views than facts, doubtless again due to the difficulties of establishing through research the relative effects of different correction modes.

Learner opinions on error correction have been studied in some detail. Chaudron (1988) cites a study by Cathcart and Olsen (1976) indicating that although students say that they want to be corrected a lot, they find that when this happens communication is hampered. Chenoweth and others (1983) find a similar desire for correction. The language teaching and teacher training literature is full of suggestions on how error correction may be accomplished. Brumfit (1977), for example, suggests stages whereby the teacher can move students towards the desirable state of self-correction (see also McDonough and Shaw, 1993).

BIBLIOGRAPHY
Allwright, R. L. (1988). *Observation in the Language Classroom*. London: Longman.*
Annett, J. (1969). *Feedback and Human Learning*. Harmondsworth: Penguin Books.
Brumfit, C. J. (1977). Correcting written work. *Modern English Teacher*, 5/3, 22–3.
Cathcart, R. and Olsen, J. (1976). Teachers' and students' preferences for correction of classroom errors. In J. Fanselow and R. Crymes (eds), *On TESOL '76*. Washington, DC: TESOL, 41–53.
Chaudron, C. (1986). Teachers' priorities in correcting learning errors in French immersion classes. In R. Day (ed.), *Talking to Learn: Conversation in Second Language Acquisition*. Rowley, MA: Newbury House, 64–84.
——(1988). *Second Language Classrooms: Research on teaching and learning*. Cambridge: Cambridge University Press.
Chenoweth, N. A., Day, R. R., Chun, A. E. and Luppescu, S. (1983). Attitudes and preferences of nonnative speakers to corrective feedback. *Studies in Second Language Acquisition*, 6, 79–87.
Hendrickson, J. M. (1978). Error correction in foreign language teaching: recent theory, research, and practice. *Modern Language Journal*, 62, 387–98.*
Johnson, K. (1988). Mistake correction. *English Language Teaching Journal*, 42, 89–96.
Krashen, S. D. (1982). *Principles and Practice in Second Language Acquisition*. Oxford: Pergamon Institute of English.
McDonough. J. and Shaw, C. (1993). *Materials and Methods in ELT*. Oxford: Blackwell.

AJ/KJ

**error evaluation** studies look at the effect of errors on addressees, rather than primarily on what role they play for the learner. Ludwig (1982) surveys twelve such studies undertaken in the 1970s and early 1980s, and Ellis (1994: 64) contains a useful table summarizing selected papers. The term 'error gravity studies' is used to describe papers focusing on addressee judgements about error seriousness.

One common concern of error evaluation studies is the nature of the criteria used to evaluate errors. Chief among criteria traditionally used is what Ludwig (1982: 277) calls 'acceptability', defined as 'the degree to which a given L2 violates language norms'. Hughes and Lascaratou (1982) mention a related criterion which they call 'basicness', involving judgements that particular rules are somehow 'more fundamental' than others. This criterion is often likely (as Johansson, 1973, notes) to relate to syllabus concerns; teachers understandably regard as serious errors in areas which have been taught rather than in those that have not. Frequency of error occurrence is a further criterion traditionally used.

Many error evaluation studies may be seen as a reaction to the use of such traditional criteria, born of a growing desire evident in all areas of language teaching in the 1970s to give increasing attention to comprehensibility as opposed to formal correctness. Johansson's (1973) early study well illustrates this reaction and desire. He notes that 'the principles of evaluation [traditionally followed in Sweden for examination marking] seem to be based on the idea that conformity, rather than comprehensibility, should be the primary goal in foreign language teaching' (p. 105). Comprehensibility should, he argues, be given greater importance as a criterion, along with a further one which he calls 'degree of irritation', characterized by Ludwig (p. 275) as 'a function of the speaker/writer's erroneous use of a language measured against the characteristics and expectations of the interlocutor'.

Error evaluation studies commonly contain a comparative element, looking at differences in error judgements between native speakers (NSs) and non-native speakers (NNSs), and in some cases between teachers (Ts) and non-teachers (NTs). James (1977) showed fifty selected errors to twenty NS teachers and twenty NNS teachers, asking them to identify mistakes and to indicate their seriousness on a scale from 0 to 5. Hughes and Lascaratou's (1982) study develops this procedure, adding a group of NSNTs (native-speaker non-teachers), and asking the subjects to explain the error gravity judgements they make. The results of these and similar studies are broadly comparable, with differences of detail. In general, NNSs are stricter in their evaluations, though at the same time (as Ervin's 1977 study concludes) NNS teachers are the most 'accepting of efforts' made by lower proficiency learners, being most 'tolerant of interlanguages'.

The criteria the different addressee groups used also differ. Galloway (1980: 431) concludes that 'overall, the native speaker did . . . seem to be listening for the message, while the non-native teachers appeared to be focusing more on grammatical accuracy.' He also notes the NNS's lack of attention to PARALINGUISTIC FEATURES (even though, potentially, paralinguistics may contribute significantly to message intelligibility. Similarly, 'basicness' is identified by Hughes and Lascaratou (1982) as one of the main criteria used by NNS teachers. In their study, the NSNT group were at the opposite extreme, placing most importance on intelligibility. The NST group came between the two extremes (NSNT and NNST).

Error evaluation studies also provide information on which error types are felt to be important by different addressee groups. If it is indeed the case that NSs as opposed to NNSs are more concerned with intelligibility, then this information will also suggest what errors have greatest effect on intelligibility. In the Hughes and Lascaratou study, spelling errors are sometimes felt to have the greatest effect on intelligibility. Lexical errors are also high on the list – though, strangely, James's NS subjects do not give importance to lexical errors. Burt (1975) distinguishes between 'local' errors (affecting single elements of sentences) and 'global' ones affecting overall organization (her example, p. 56, being 'missing, wrong or misplaced connectors'). Burt's conclusion is that global errors cause more irritation to the NS. Albrechtsen and others (1980) make a further point, that pauses, self-corrections and general disruptions to fluency can also have a serious effect on comprehension.

Given findings of this sort, it is tempting to try and draw up a typology of errors using a criterion of intelligibility. Johansson (1973) does in fact move in this direction, suggesting hard and fast criteria which might provide marking schedules giving due importance to his two main criteria of comprehensibility and degree of irritation. But he makes his attempts in the recognition, shared by other commentators, that no rigid classification of errors along these lines will be possible. Albrechtsen and others (1980: 394) are particularly sceptical about such attempts. They found that the number of wrong content words as a proportion of the total number of words in an interlanguage text did not seriously affect communication. This leads them to the conclusion that 'all errors are equally irritating.'

Although generally stopping short of rigid classifications, most error evaluation studies make pedagogic suggestions. Among Ludwig's are that more attention should be given to vocabulary and discourse errors, that learners should be made aware of paralinguistic devices, and the more general one that teachers need to regard errors selectively, giving attention not just to acceptability but also to effect on communication. Many early studies highlight the last of these, which may again be seen as part of communicative language teaching's emphasis on message conveyance rather than formal correctness. A further interesting conclusion is reached by Albrechtsen and colleagues. They note (p. 395) that NSs are able to distinguish

message and messenger: 'the interlocutors evaluated personality and content independently of the evaluation of language and comprehension.' An implication they draw from this is that NNSs will not improve the attitude they provoke in NSs by improving their grammar.

BIBLIOGRAPHY
Albrechtsen, D., Henriksen, B. and Faerch, C. (1980). Native speaker reactions to learners' spoken interlanguage. *Language Learning*, 30, 394.
Burt, M. (1975). Error analysis in the adult EFL classroom. *TESOL Quarterly*, 9, 53–63.
Ellis, R. (1994). *The Study of Second Language Acquisition*. Oxford: Oxford University Press.
Ervin, G. (1977). A study of the use and acceptability of target language communication strategies employed by American students of Russian. Unpublished Ph.D. dissertation, Ohio State University.
Galloway, V. (1980). Perceptions of the communicative efforts of American students of Spanish. *Modern Language Journal*, 64, 430.
Hughes, A. and Lascaratou, C. (1982). Competing criteria for error gravity. *English Language Teaching Journal*, 36/3, 175–82.*
James, C. (1977). Judgements of error gravities. *English Language Teaching Journal*, 31/2, 116–24.*
Johansson, S. (1973). The identification and evaluation of errors in foreign languages: a functional approach. In J. Svartvik (ed.), *Errata: Papers in error analysis*. Lund: CWK Gleerup, 102–14.
Ludwig, J. (1982). Native-speaker judgements of second-language learners' efforts at communication: a review. *Modern Language Journal*, 66. 274–83.

KJ

**error/mistake/lapse**   These terms are associated with Corder. In various papers (e.g. 1967) the distinction is drawn between errors on the one hand and mistakes or lapses on the other. An error is a breach of the language's code, resulting in an unacceptable utterance; with L2 learners this might occur because 'the learners have not yet internalized the formation rules of the code' (1973: 259). Mistakes or lapses are 'the result of some failure of performance' (1967: 18). They occur when the language user (who might be a native speaker) makes a slip such as a false start or a confusion of structure. Corder's (1973) example is 'that's a question which, if you were to press me, I wouldn't know how to answer it.' (See COMPETENCE/PERFORMANCE.)

The above use of these terms is the generally accepted one, though Corder (1973) draws the distinctions differently. There he uses 'error' as above, but distinguishes between 'lapses' (the performance failures above) and 'mistakes' which are seen as the result of inappropriate usage; in a naval context, for example, a 'ship' might be referred to mistakenly as a 'boat'. This usage has not become common.

Johnson (1988) regards it important to distinguish L2 mistakes from errors, suggesting that different remedial action will be appropriate for each; to treat mistakes as if they were errors is, he argues, unhelpful (see ERROR ANALYSIS).

BIBLIOGRAPHY
Corder, S. P. (1967). The significance of learners' errors. Reprinted in 1981 in S. P. Corder, *Error Analysis and Interlanguage*. Oxford: Oxford University Press, 5–13.
Corder, S. P. (1973). *Introducing Applied Linguistics*. Harmondsworth: Penguin Books.
Johnson, K. (1988). Mistake correction. *English Language Teaching Journal*, 42/2, 89–96.

KJ

**ethnocentrism**   An individual's attraction to his or her own group. Ethnocentrism is a universal attitude. It is manifested in the feelings of superiority of one's language and culture over others and it depends on the in-group members' perceptions of their prototypicality in comparison to the members of other groups, and on the strength of the in-group members' shared values and identity.

BIBLIOGRAPHY
Apte, M. L. (1994). Linguistic ethnocentrism. In R. E. Asher (ed.), *The Encyclopedia of Language and Linguistics*. Vol. 4. Oxford: Pergamon, 2222–3.
Turner, J. C. (1987). *Rediscovering the Social Group: A self-categorization theory*. Oxford: Blackwell, 57–65.

AJ

**ethnography of communication**   This discipline is often viewed as a branch of SOCIOLINGUISTICS and is closely related to ETHNOMETHODOLOGY. It aims at describing the forms and functions of verbal and non-verbal communicative behaviour in particular cultural or social settings. Formal descriptions in the ethnography of communication focus on linguistic units above the sentence: speech situations (e.g. ceremonies, fights, hunts), speech events (e.g. parties, medical consultations) and speech acts (jokes, greetings, compliments). Functional explanations refer to larger social and cultural contexts. In relation to SLA the ethnography of communication has provided input to COMMUNICATIVE LANGUAGE TEACHING, especially through Hymes's formulation of the notion of COMMUNICATIVE COMPETENCE.

BIBLIOGRAPHY
Hymes, D. (ed.) (1964). *Language, Culture and Society: A reader in linguistics and anthropology*. New York: Harper and Row.
——(1974). *Foundations in Sociolinguistics*. Philadelphia: University of Pennsylvania Press.
Saville-Troike, M. (1989). *The Ethnography of Communication: An introduction*. 2nd edn. Oxford: Blackwell.

AJ

**ethnomethodology**   A branch of sociology which deals with the questions of social order, organization and (inter)action.

Since most of these processes are mediated through language, ethnomethodologists use transcripts of naturally occurring conversations to arrive at descriptions of the interactants' knowledge about the social structure in which they operate. While DISCOURSE ANALYSIS is largely interested in the structure of conversation (e.g. the organization of TURN-TAKING), in its inductive, data-driven approach, ethnomethodology is primarily concerned with the question of how individuals constitute their shared knowledge about the world through talk.

BIBLIOGRAPHY
Benson, D. and Hughes, E. C. (1983). *The Perspective on Ethnomethodology*. Harlow: Longman.
Button, G. (ed.) (1991). *Ethnomethodology and the Human Sciences*. Cambridge: Cambridge University Press.
Heritage, J. C. (1984). *Garfinkel and Ethnomethodology*. Cambridge: Polity Press.
Sharrock, W. W. and Anderson, R. J. (1986). *The Ethnomethodologists*. Chichester: Ellis Harwood.
Turner, R. (ed.) (1974). *Ethnomethodology*. Harmondsworth: Penguin Books.\*

AJ

# evaluation of course books or materials evaluation

**evaluation of course books** or **materials evaluation**, as it will be more broadly referred to here, is a field supported until now by only a relatively small specialist literature. The concept of evaluating materials in order to select for class use a particular set from among those available is not, of course, a new one. However, in recent years the term *materials evaluation* has taken on a more formal connotation in response to attempts to *systematize* it, most saliently through the introduction of the *checklist* (see below). The motivation for systematization has been the proliferation of materials, notably in connection with English as a foreign language. It is one thing for one evaluator to compare two or three course books and to be satisfied that the final choice made is justifiable. It is a different situation when even in 1987, as Goodman and Takahashi

(1987) report, 28 United States publishers were offering a total of 1623 ESL textbooks. Of course, many among 1623 textbooks could quickly be deemed inappropriate for given purposes, perhaps on the strength of the publishers' descriptions, but the evaluator might still be faced with a residue of 50 contenders. Moreover, the task of evaluating 50 textbooks would almost certainly indicate the desirability of a team of evaluators. The problem here, then, either for the lone evaluator faced with comparing 50 books, or the team of evaluators confronted with the same task, would be how to maintain *consistency* of judgement, in the first case within one individual, and in the second case both within and between different individuals. Attempts at systematization, therefore, are largely driven by the imperative of consistency.

As to the question: 'Who acts as an evaluator and with what freedom to choose?' all depends upon specific contexts. Sometimes, classroom teachers, either individually or collectively, are empowered to select any text available from anywhere for their learners. Sometimes teachers can choose, but only from among materials commissioned by a Ministry of Education. Sometimes there is a Ministry of Education evaluator who selects above the level of the school. Sometimes there is no choice at all: the Ministry prescribes just one text, and teachers must use it. In the private sector, arrangements depend upon the management.

## THE 'IDEAL' MODEL FOR MATERIALS EVALUATION

The model in figure 1 addresses most directly the situation in which institutions or teachers depend mainly or exclusively upon commercially produced materials, typically in the form of 'the textbook for the course'. The ethos underlying this situation and the role accorded in it to materials have not gone unchallenged – see, for example,

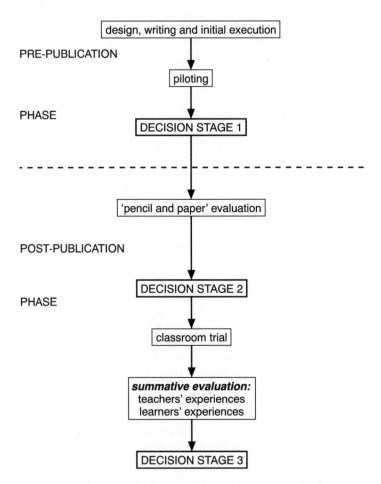

**Figure 1** The schema proposed as an 'ideal' model for the materials evaluation process.

Allwright (1981). However, the perspective offered by O'Neill (1982) and McDonough and Shaw (1993: 63–5) undoubtedly mirrors what continues to be 'orthodox' thinking and practice; as McDonough and Shaw put it (p. 64), 'the reality for many is that the book [i.e. the commercially produced textbook] may be the only choice open to them.' See also Matthews (1985: 202) and Sheldon (1988: 237–8).

In the model, it is assumed that preliminary decisions made by materials designers to compile them, by commissioning bodies to order them or by publishers to issue contracts, come at the stage of design, writing and initial execution. It is also assumed that the beginnings of the evaluative process, though perhaps not formally conducted, will be implicit in the acceptance or refusal of a proposal or a manuscript by publishers, and with the designer's reflection upon whether correct options are being pursued at each point in the design – in this latter context, see Low (1989). When ready in draft form, the materials are piloted on a sample of the target population, and the results of the pilot lead to DECISION STAGE 1, at which the materials are declared acceptable or in need of modification or are rejected. The materials then pass into the public domain and are subjected first to a 'paper and pencil' evaluation, that is, evaluators assess them by inspecting them, but without trying them out on the sub-population, or a sample of it, with which they are directly concerned – the learners in their own school, for instance. At DECISION STAGE 2 the evaluators decide which materials to select for further consideration and which to reject on the basis of the evidence thus far. The classroom trial of the materials passing the 'paper and pencil' evaluation leads into the summative evaluation, in which all the information gathered, including the reactions to the materials of teachers and learners (and possibly published review findings), is assembled. At DECISION STAGE 3 certain materials are adopted and others declared unsuitable.

Of course, the model represents an ideal far removed, for most, from everyday experience: not all materials are piloted before release, classroom trials are rarely feasible and not all teaching authorities consult learners, or even teachers, on their opinions of materials. A particular problem with classroom trials is the expense involved in purchasing sufficient sets of materials to test on an adequate sample without any commitment to using them beyond the duration of the trials. For this reason and others, the checklist is accorded importance, since it is precisely a recipe for the 'pencil and paper' evaluation.

THE CHECKLIST

Early examples of checklists are given in Tucker (1975) and Messih Daoud (1977). The latter's system, applying to 'the pupil's textbook' and 'the teacher's manual', has two phases: (1) recording the data and (2) evaluating them. Recording falls into two parts: *survey* (skimming to gain a general impression); *analysis* (listing the contents of the pupil's textbook and the teacher's manual). Evaluation or *judgement* requires the completion of the checklist proper (one version for the pupil's textbook, another for the teacher's manual) and the writing of 'comments and suggestions for improvement'. There is a 28-question checklist for the textbook divided between five rubrics, and the 20 questions on the checklist for the teacher's manual are equally grouped under five headings. The rating system, borrowed from Tucker, requires responses on a merit scale of 0 to 4. Though suggesting that consistency of judgement might be facilitated if evaluators concerned with the same teaching context asked the same questions, the questions here (e.g. 'Do the sentences gradually increase in length to suit the growing reading ability of the pupils?, 'Do illustrations create a favourable atmosphere for reading and speech by showing realism and action?') nicely point up the need for rigour in choosing relevant questions and formulating them unambiguously. There is also the oddity of using yes/no questions to elicit graded responses.

Tucker's system is an original and sophisticated attempt at producing an algorithmic method of evaluation. The checklist does not contain questions, but *criteria* on which judgement is sought, e.g. 'Adequacy of drill model and pattern display', grouped under four headings: 'pronunciation criteria', 'grammar criteria', 'content criteria' and 'general criteria'. In the text accompanying the checklist, the way each criterion should be interpreted is explained; so is 'good practice' associated with that criterion, as conceived at the time of publication. Unfortunately, Tucker's checklist is so firmly anchored in the theory of audiolingualism that it has long since been unusable in its initial form. However, it includes a useful feature, increasing the flexibility of the checklist, which can be abstracted from the immediate context: *weighting*. Recognizing that the importance of individual criteria varies from one teaching situation to the other, Tucker allows each of these to be assigned a 'value' from 0 to 5, e.g. under 'general criteria', 'adequate guidance for non-native teachers' might be irrelevant, because the materials are to be taught exclusively by native teachers, and the value assigned would therefore be 0. If the complete converse applied, i.e. teaching to be done only by non-native teachers, not highly competent in the language, then the value assigned would probably be 5. If some non-native teachers were to be involved in teaching, but not many, the value might be 2. For the treatment of the criterion in question, there is also a 'merit scale' from 0 to 4, the score awarded reflecting the adequacy or otherwise of treatment. The next column in the checklist provides for a 'value merit product', calculated by multiplying the weighting by the merit score. Thus, if for 'quality of editing and publishing' the weight assigned is 2 and the merit score is 3, the 'value merit product' is 6. If the value assigned is 1 and the merit score is 3, the product is 3. No departure from normal arithmetic is required: any criterion assigned a value of 0 will lead to a product of 0, since a value of 0 means irrelevancy, and one is, in effect, wasting one's time in awarding a merit score in such an instance. The idea of weighting is taken up in the proposals of, for example, D. Williams (1983) and Cunningsworth (1984). One further subtlety of Tucker's system is that it allows for 'the graphic display of an evaluation', using the type of form he illustrates, on which the profile of the materials ideally required can be plotted together with the profiles of those examined. The profiles can be used to highlight differences of opinion between different evaluators and to establish the evaluative mean, as well as to show at a glance how materials compare.

While Tucker's system, though not his criteria, still arguably has potential application, not all embrace algorithmic or purely *quantitative* methods of evaluation. Matthews (1985), for example, proposes that 'to discover which textbook fits [the teacher's] situation most exactly', an analysis is required

(1) of the specific teaching situation and (2) of the competing textbooks. He suggests questions grouped under 7 headings in relation to the first, and questions under 18 headings together with a summary of 19 'main criteria for assessing the pros and cons of textbooks' in relation to the second. However, he does not offer a scoring system; rather, the implication is that the suggested questions are intended to focus the mind on the relevant parameters. A similar stance is taken by McDonough and Shaw (1993: 66–79). They propose a two-stage model: the 'external or macro-evaluation' and the 'internal or micro-evaluation'. The first stage includes the examination of publishers' claims or, in Cunningsworth's words (1989: 2) 'what the coursebooks say about themselves', reading the introduction and table of contents and gaining a general impression of the suitability of the materials for the intended audience. If the materials look promising, they are next subjected to the second stage, the 'in-depth investigation'. The questions and/or criteria put forward are more economical than those of Matthews, particularly as the intention is to supply a 'model ... flexible enough to be used in ELT contexts worldwide', and no scoring system is proposed. Indeed, 'long checklists of data' are eschewed. However, McDonough and Shaw conclude that 'materials once selected can only be judged successful after classroom implementation and feedback'; in other words, they foresee a process similar to the 'classroom trial' included in the 'ideal' model, figure 1, above.

Cunningsworth (1989) and Sheldon (1988) occupy a mid-way position where numerical scoring is concerned. The former emphasizes (p. 64) that quantitative should be tempered with *qualitative* evaluation: 'I suggested earlier that the process of evaluation could not be a purely mechanical one and that professional judgement was involved at every stage.' Thus, his summarizing checklist (pp. 74–9) contains both questions eliciting a numerical response and others which 'require an evaluative or descriptive comment'. Sheldon, whose criteria represent a 'summary of common-core factors that reviewers, administrators, teachers, learners and educational advisers most frequently use in deciding whether or not a textbook is chosen' also provides a mixture of ratings and comments, his ratings being expressed in terms of *Poor, **Fair, ***Good, ****Excellent.

An inventory of questions with an orientation different from that of most checklists by virtue of its outspoken learner-centredness is offered by Breen and Candlin (1987). This inventory might be better described as a 'pre-checklist' than a checklist as such, since the hope (p. 13) is that 'from the questions teachers can derive criteria to help them explore what we can use materials for, especially in the classroom.' The evaluation process has two phases, the first focusing upon the materials, their aims and content, the demands they make upon teachers and learners and their function as a classroom resource, the second upon 'criteria for the choice and use of materials in ways which are sensitive to classroom language learning' (ibid.). Sample questions for eliciting learners' views of and reactions to materials are provided. The approach is essentially qualitative, but since the questions constitute a guide rather than a prescription, they could conceivably lead to the design of checklists with some quantitative aspects.

A checklist using + or – judgements and page counts developed for use in conjunction with the relatively neglected realm of *teach-yourself materials*, in this case for *ab initio* English-speaking learners, and details of its development and inter-rater reliability score are furnished by Jones (1993).

## PROBLEMS

Whether to settle on *qualitative* or *quantitative* evaluation of materials is a question basically unanswerable in the abstract, though there are evidently differing views here. Much will depend upon the complexity of a particular evaluation task, and what can be demanded of evaluators. The advantages of the qualitative approach are that evaluators enjoy free expression and may volunteer information of a type not predicted by the designer of an evaluation instrument; the disadvantages, that potential respondents may feel that the writing involved is likely to be inordinately time-consuming and that, where several evaluators are involved, it may prove impossible to locate comparative opinions expressed in prose by different individuals. The advantages of the quantitative approach are that checklists answered numerically are often quickly dealt with and allow easy comparison of the answers of different evaluators; the disadvantages, that they may stifle unpredicted but valuable reactions, that it is not, in the end, clear that one evaluator's '3' is to be interpreted as significantly divergent from another's '4', and that they can all too easily convey a spurious 'objectivity'. Furthermore, the margins between the qualitative and the quantitative are blurred. It is not clear whether an evaluator who writes: 'This book is exactly right for my students' has in fact taken time to consider the issues, neither is it clear that someone who gives a rating of '5' to a textbook has not spent hours brooding over this response. What is clear, by contrast, is the consensus that evaluation is about *judgement*, however elicited. Any compiler of a checklist, qualitative or quantitative, exercises judgement in selecting the parameters to ask about (and not to ask about), and the checklists referred to above demonstrate sometimes wide divergencies in this respect. Whatever the means of elicitation adopted, judgement is again being invited.

Perhaps because 'judgement' sometimes appears synonymous with 'subjectivity' or even 'arcaneness', a point on which the literature does not always supply reassurance,

Low (1989: 153) remarks: 'The assessment of language teaching materials, even when supplemented, as it should be, by empirical studies, remains . . . something of a "black art".' It is true that it is not an exact science, because the variables it must encompass involve human values. However, this is far from saying it is impossible or uninformative, providing its purpose, scope and limitations are not misconstrued.

One step which might be helpful would be to abandon anxiety about *universals*: cf. Sheldon (1988: 246): 'we need to discover whether or not a *de facto* evaluative consensus exists at all, and whether there is any foundation upon which universal criteria could be erected.' Possibly, the only true universal criteria which can figure in any checklist are theoretically trivial, e.g. the cost, availability and durability of materials. More interesting criteria, such as *cultural bias*, will obviously have different exponents, depending upon the setting in which given materials might be employed. Thus, starting out from the setting or 'local' context is likely to be the most productive solution, since designers of evaluation instruments and evaluators working together can arrive through dialogue at consensual judgements, can establish that they 'speak the same language' and can ensure that when criteria are enshrined within a checklist, all concerned share an understanding of what those criteria mean. A possible model for the dialogue or 'brainstorming' which might precede the production of a definitive checklist is offered (albeit with reference to teacher training) by R. Williams (1981). Consequently, checklists and other proposed evaluative procedures appearing in the literature are unlikely to be suitable for wholesale adoption, but serve best in an illustrative and suggestive capacity.

Notwithstanding the above remarks, any evaluation procedure will need to relate materials to at least the criteria listed below, though the weight and value placed on these individually will vary:

*Learners*: age, stage in learning, enabling and disabling factors, interests and motivation, preferred learning styles;

*Teachers*: teaching competence and experience, competence in the language, preferred teaching styles;

*Aims*: of the course and of the learners;

*Syllabus and (if any) prescribed methods*: constraints imposed;

*Examinations and/or tests*: constraints imposed and WASHBACK EFFECT;

*Cultural and related factors*: acceptability or non-acceptability of the values conveyed in materials in given cultural and social contexts;

*Practical factors*: time available for teaching, presence or absence of homework, size of classes, availability of hardware to implement materials, the teaching and learning environment, etc.

Two final points: (1) In the interests of efficiency, computer technology has an increasing role to play in materials evaluation. For example, databases of 'master' checklists can be generated, subsections of which can be extracted for particular purposes. (2) It is a question of relevance within educational philosophy, with obvious consequences for materials evaluation, to what extent materials should always be selected as compatible with the classroom *status quo*, and to what extent and in what circumstances they might be viewed as 'political' tools, such that the selection of this or that set of materials might influence change.

BIBLIOGRAPHY

Allwright, R. L. (1981). What do we want teaching materials for? *English Language Teaching Journal*, 36/1, 5–17.

Breen, M. and Candlin, C. (1987). Which materials? A consumer's and designer's guide. *English Language Teaching Documents*, 126, 13–28.

Cunningsworth, A. (1989). *Evaluating and Selecting EFL Teaching Materials*. London: Heinemann.

Goodman, P. and Takahashi, S. (1987). The ESL textbooks explosion: a publisher profile. *TESOL Newsletter*, 4, 49–51.

Jones, F. R. (1993). Beyond the fringe: a framework for assessing teach-yourself materials for *ab initio* English-speaking learners. *System*, 21/4, 453–69.

Low, G. (1989). Appropriate design: the internal organisation of course units. In R. K. Johnson (ed.), *The Second Language Curriculum*. Cambridge: Cambridge University Press, 136–54.

McDonough, J. and Shaw, C. (1993). *Materials and Methods in ELT: A teacher's guide*. Oxford: Blackwell.*

Matthews, A. (1985). Choosing the best available textbook. In A. Matthews, M. Spratt and L. Dangerfield (eds), *At the Chalkface*. London: Edward Arnold, 202–6.

Messih Daoud, A. (1977). Evaluating an English language textbook. *Workpapers in Teaching English as a Second Language*, 11, 113–17.

O'Neill, R. (1982). Why use textbooks? *English Language Teaching Journal*, 36/2, 104–11.

Sheldon, L. (1988). Evaluating ELT textbooks and materials. *English Language Teaching Journal*, 42/4, 237–46.

Tucker, C. A. (1975). Evaluating beginning coursebooks. *English Language Teaching Forum*, 13/3–4, 355–61.

Williams, D. (1983). Developing criteria for textbook evaluation. *English Language Teaching Journal*, 37/3, 251–5.

Williams, R. (1981). A procedure for ESP textbook analysis and evaluation on teacher education courses. *ESP Journal*, 1/2, 155–62.

JTR

**evaluation of curricula** Even when restricted, as here, to refer to whole programmes, 'evaluation' is a very broad term with a number of different dimensions, and consequently is difficult to delineate. A CUR-RICULUM cannot be evaluated in a vacuum without reference to its context, aims and objectives, designers, managers, teachers and its resource base, which leads to some complex permutations. Related but narrower terms are 'assessment', 'appraisal' and 'testing'. Evaluation has long been of major importance in general education (e.g. Norris, 1990) and now has particular currency in a climate of public accountability and quality control.

DEFINITIONS AND FRAMEWORK

Brown (1989: 223) offers the following definition: '*evaluation* is the systematic collection and analysis of all relevant information necessary to promote the improvement of a curriculum, and assess its effectiveness and efficiency, as well as the participants' attitudes within the context of the particular institutions involved.' This is a useful but of course global definition, which triggers more specific questions and categories:

*What* is to be evaluated? Teachers, learners, programme design, delivery materials?
*When* is the evaluation to take place? At the end of the course, in the middle, several times?
*Who* is/are the evaluators? Sponsors, teachers, Ministry of Education officials, senior staff, external consultants?
*Why* is evaluation necessary in this situation? Is it for development, accountability, assessment purposes?
*How* is the evaluation to be carried out? What is its methodology?

A number of writers have proposed frameworks that attempt to systematize the evaluation process: see, for example, Weir and Roberts (1994: 11ff.); White (1988: 151); Rea (1983). Rea-Dickins and Germaine (1992: 74) also add questions to do with contextual constraints in carrying out evaluations – such as access, funding and so on – and raise the useful meta-issue of how the worth of the evaluation itself is to be assessed.

KEY PARAMETERS

In most contexts there will be multiple rather than single-strand responses to framework questions, as when, for example, it is necessary to evaluate individual elements (management, staff, resources) for differing purposes on an ongoing basis, as well as overall outcomes. In the theory and practice of educational evaluation, a number of related distinctions have been made in an attempt to classify goals and procedures. By far the most frequently cited of these dichotomies is that between *summative* and *formative* evaluation. Briefly, the first of these is typically carried out retrospectively at the end of a programme or project, focuses on the final *product* or outcome and is concerned with accountability. Formative evaluation, on the other hand, deals with the details of the ongoing *process* of programme delivery and may take place at regular intervals; its primary purpose is curriculum improvement and development (Rea-Dickins and Germaine; Weir and Roberts). Like most opposing terms, however, these are not really polarizations and as Mackay (1994) points out, the summative/formative distinction is sometimes more apparent than real: even summative evaluations are fed back into programme decisions, both positively (for development and change) and negatively (even cessation of a course or project).

In addition to these formative/summative, process/product, development/accountability paradigms, the literature on evaluation also discusses the further dimension of *extrinsic/intrinsic*, which distinguishes between an externally imposed and controlled evaluation and one which is generated and 'owned' by the people directly involved in the curriculum. This is in turn related to a *bureaucratic* (sometimes autocratic) or *democratic* distinction, which itself indicates that the concept of evaluation has an obvious political dimension. Finally, Norris (1990: 133–4) discriminates between 'two kinds of generalization: those about a programme and those from the experiences of a programme', i.e. its transferability of judgements and experience.

In many ways the above distinctions can be seen as offering two separate perspectives on educational evaluation. However, a comprehensive approach would be able to take in both dimensions simultaneously: Weir and Roberts (1994: 8–9) suggest ways in which this might be done from the point of view of both goal specification and the personnel involved. White (1988) likewise cautions that evaluation is best seen as an integrated and collaborative endeavour, not just as an add-on which sets objectives and then asks whether they have been achieved; and Mackay (1994: 145) makes a strong case for the proactive initiation of evaluation by internal staff and the consequent down-playing of bureaucratic procedures.

## METHODOLOGY AND SELECTED EXAMPLES

The methodology of data collection for evaluative purposes is clearly heavily dependent on the framework questions set out earlier: the criteria established for an extrinsic purpose will lead to the use of differing techniques from those available and appropriate for an internally motivated undertaking. A general distinction is often made between *quantitative* and *qualitiative* types of data. The first of these is self-explanatory, and covers any kind of information which can be expressed numerically and statistically. It may include test scores, student data of various kinds, success rates, tabulation of institutional data, analysis of questionnaire responses and so on. The second, on the other hand, covers information that is systematically collected but not readily quantifiable, such as observations, interviews, reports, records and minutes, diary keeping and the like. Brown (1989: 231–3) argues 'for gathering as much information as possible from as many perspectives as reasonable in order to make the evaluation and the resulting decisions as accurate and useful as humanly possible', and then goes on to cross-refer these categories and procedures with the role of the evaluator.

In the published literature on evaluation, there is a common distinction between ongoing, regular programmes and educational 'projects' which, even though renewable, usually run for a specified time span.

Many examples of project evaluation viewed both extrinsically and intrinsically are to be found in Rea (Tanzania); Mackay (Indonesia); Williams and Burden (Switzerland); Weir and Roberts (Nepal); Rea-Dickins and Germaine (India-Bangalore). A different kind of 'quality control' evaluation is operated in the inspection of British ELT, both of language schools and state colleges (British Council Accreditation Unit) and universities (British Association of Lecturers in English for Academic Purposes – BALEAP).

BIBLIOGRAPHY
Brown, J. D. (1989). Language program evaluation: a synthesis of existing possibilities. In R. K. Johnson (ed.), *The Second Language Curriculum*. Cambridge: Cambridge University Press, 222–41.
Mackay, R. (1994). Undertaking ESL/EFL programme review for accountability and improvement. In *ELT Journal*, 48/2, 142–9.
Norris, N. (1990). *Understanding Educational Evaluation*. London: Kogan Page.
Rea, P. (1983). Evaluation of educational projects, with special reference to English language education. In *Language Teaching Projects for the Third World*. ELT Documents 116. Oxford and New York: Pergamon Press with the British Council.
Rea-Dickins, P. and Germaine, K. (1992). *Evaluation*. Oxford: Oxford University Press.*
Weir, C. and Roberts, J. (1994). *Evaluation in ELT*. Oxford and Cambridge, MA: Blackwell.*
White, R. V. (1988). *The ELT Curriculum*. Oxford: Blackwell.*
Williams, M. and Burden, R. (1994). The role of evaluation in ELT project design. *ELT Journal*, 48/1, 22–7.

JMCD

**expectancy grammar** features in Oller's conception of language proficiency as unitary, i.e. not differential as between diverse skills and competences. For him, reception involves matching messages with expectancies, grammatical and pragmatic, about their nature; production entails expectancies about decoding. Pragmatic, but not grammatical, expectancies are transferred to foreign language learning. (See also UNITARY COMPETENCE HYPOTHESIS.)

BIBLIOGRAPHY
Oller, J. W. Jr (1976). Evidence for a general proficiency factor: an expectancy grammar. *Die Neueren Sprachen*, 2, 165–74.

JTR

**explicit/implicit knowledge** This is a distinction particularly associated with the work of Bialystok (1982, for example). For Bialystok, when linguistic knowledge is implicit it is unanalysed, i.e. consists of formulas of single words representing whole utterances (see FORMULAIC SPEECH). When linguistic knowledge is explicit, it consists of analysed grammatical and lexical units which can be productively combined to produce novel utterances. Some writers (see, for example, Ellis, 1994: 355) have equated 'implicit' with 'subconscious' knowledge of language (equivalent to Krashen's notion of 'acquisition') and 'explicit' with 'conscious' knowledge of language (equivalent to Krashen's notion of 'learning' – see MONITOR MODEL). However, in Bialystok's approach explicit linguistic knowledge need not be conscious knowledge. The defining characteristic of 'explicit' is that language is represented as analysed components, and these may be stored in areas of the brain not accessible to conscious awareness. (See CONSCIOUS/UNCONSCIOUS KNOWLEDGE.)

BIBLIOGRAPHY
Bialystok, E. (1982). On the relationship between knowing and using forms. *Applied Linguistics*, 3, 181–206.
Ellis, R. (1994). *The Study of Second Language Acquisition*. Oxford: Oxford University Press.
Karmiloff-Smith, A. (1986). From meta-process to conscious access: evidence from children's metalinguistic and repair data. *Cognition*, 23, 95–147.

RH

**exponent** is a term associated with the development of NOTIONAL/FUNCTIONAL SYLLABUSES. With a language programme organized on this basis, the actual language practised derives from the particular notions and functions selected. The *exponents* are thus the explicit language forms most commonly associated with these notions/functions in appropriate situations. For example, exponents such as 'you ought to . . .' or 'I think you'd better . . .' express the functional category of advice; 'be careful' or 'don't do that' or 'if you do that, then . . .' are exponents of warning.

BIBLIOGRAPHY
Van Ek, J. A. (1977). *The Threshold Level for Modern Language Learning in Schools*. London: Longman, 15–16.

JMcD

**extroversion – introversion** is a personality trait measured by the Eysenck Personality Inventory. Extroversion perhaps explains the degree of active participation in class and therefore may relate to language learning success, but less active, introverted class members may benefit more by observing their more active peers. (See INDIVIDUAL DIFFERENCES, PERSONALITY VARIABLES.)

BIBLIOGRAPHY
Skehan, P. (1989). *Individual Differences in Second Language Learning*. London: Edward Arnold, 100–6.

SMCD

# F

**factor analysis** refers to a number of techniques for discovering the underlying systematicity present in a set of CORRELATIONS. It reduces the data to a small number of underlying factors and estimates the strength of each factor in each original score. Its use is controversial since different techniques produce different factors. (See also STATISTICS IN APPLIED LINGUISTICS RESEARCH.)

BIBLIOGRAPHY
Woods, A., Fletcher, P. and Hughes, A. (1986). *Statistics in Language Studies*. Cambridge: Cambridge University Press, 273–95.

SMCD

**first and second language acquisition** First language acquisition displays a number of general characteristics which are common to all normal children who have reasonable exposure to the language:

- acquisition is rapid;
- there are systematic stages of development;
- acquisition results from simple contact with naturally occurring tokens of the target language, and not through correction, reward or reinforcement;
- the mental grammars that children develop go beyond the information available in the input they get;
- acquisition is inevitable and successful.

There have been at least two approaches to explaining these characteristics. The *nativist* approach argues that children are born with a language faculty which is already equipped with considerable knowledge about the form that human language takes, and have only to be exposed to particular human languages for their mental grammars to be fixed in appropriate ways. The *interactionist* approach argues that language development is parasitic on more general human cognitive capacities for memorizing, learning and generalizing. On this view, linguistic knowledge grows as the result of children interacting with the world, and with their caretakers, in progressively more complex interactions. This leads to the growth of both knowledge of the world and knowledge of language.

Second language acquisition (SLA) has a number of characteristics in common with first language acquisition, but also displays some differences:

- there are systematic stages of development;
- correction, reward and reinforcement do not appear to be *directly* influential in SLA, although some kinds of metalinguistic awareness may be;
- the knowledge that L2 learners develop goes beyond what they were exposed to in the input;
- SLA is not inevitable (learners may fossilize at different stages of development) and rarely fully successful.

There have been at least two major approaches to explanation in SLA: the *nativist* approach (which assumes that the innate language faculty involved in first language acquisition is also involved in second language acquisition) and the *cognitivist* 'perceptual strategies' approach (which argues that second language linguistic knowledge develops as the result of learners applying general learning mechanisms to the specific case of second language acquisition).

## FIRST LANGUAGE ACQUISITION

First language (L1) acquisition is character-istically rapid. Most structures of the target language are acquired within the first five years of life (Fry, 1977) (although vocabu-lary acquisition and the acquisition of some structures may continue into later years). L1 acquisition is successful: children end up having the same grammatical knowledge (more or less) as the speakers around them. L1 acquisition is inevitable: children cannot choose *not* to learn the language spoken around them (as they can choose not to learn to play football, or not to learn to ride a bike). L1 acquisition proceeds in stages. First there are broad developmental stages: cry-ing in the first few months of life gives way to babbling (the stringing together of system-atic, but meaningless, sequences of sounds like *angangang, bababa, dududu*, etc.). After about a year the first recognizable words appear (e.g. *ball, dog, give, more*, etc.). Six to eight months later combinations of essen-tially lexical (content) words appear (e.g. *mummy book* (asking mummy to read a story), *daddy kick* (telling daddy to kick the ball), etc.). Four to six months after that combina-tions of both lexical and functional words (determiners, auxiliaries, tense markers, etc.) start appearing, and from then on the length of the child's utterances increases until by around 5 years of age the child is using language as complex as that of mature nat-ive speakers. The age at which these stages emerge varies from child to child, but the chronology is the same in all cases. (For a collection of papers concerning the general course of L1 development see Fletcher and Garman, 1986).

Then, within these broad stages, there are developmental stages specific to particu-lar types of linguistic knowledge. One area of considerable interest is the systematicity that children display in acquiring grammat-ical knowledge. To take an example, children acquiring English information questions (those involving *wh*-phrases like *what, who, which book*, etc.) invariably begin by putting the *wh*-phrase at the front of the sentence without subject-verb inversion: *Who he bite?* When they acquire subject-verb inversion, they first allow it only in affirmative, but not negative sentences. Thus they can be saying at one period of development: *Who did he bite? Who he not bite?* Finally, when they allow subject inversion in both affirm-ative and negative information questions, they overextend the pattern to embedded clauses, saying *Who did he bite? Who didn't he bite? I wonder who did he bite.* Only later do they restrict inversion appropriately to main clauses.

Last, but not least, children acquire their language without the benefit of correction (so-called 'negative evidence') reward or reinforcement (feedback). Children who are systematically corrected do not respond to that correction in any direct way (Brown and Hanlon, 1970), and children who have limited input nevertheless develop normal knowledge of language (see Sachs et al., 1981). Furthermore, the knowledge they acquire goes beyond the input they have received. For example, all native speakers of English know that the sentence *Who do you think that he likes?* is grammatical, while *\*Who do you think that likes him?* is much less so. The only difference between them is that in the first case *who* is understood as the object of *likes*, while *who* in the second one is understood as the subject of *likes*. It seems that sequences of *that + empty subject* are not possible in English (instead you have to delete *that*: *Who do you think likes him?*). This kind of knowledge is not evident in any input children receive, nor is it ever taught to most native speakers, and yet they know it in some sense.

An important task for L1 acquisition re-searchers is to develop a theory which will explain why it is that language develops this way in first language acquisition. One power-ful theory which has provided important insights is the nativist theory of UNIVERSAL

GRAMMAR. This holds that children are born with an innately endowed language faculty. The language faculty consists of a set of general principles which determine the form that human languages can take. For example, one of the principles determines the way in which structure is built up from individual lexical items (the Projection Principle); another principle (the Empty Category Principle) determines the possible distribution of null (but meaningful) elements in sentences, as in the case of the grammatical missing object in *Who do you think that he likes e?*, and the ungrammatical missing subject in *\*Who do you think that e likes him?* described above. The principles determine that human languages can only be of a certain kind, and infants will know from the beginning that languages fall into this class because they know the principles innately.

However, individual languages do differ one from another in a number of respects, suggesting that the principles can be realized in different ways. These are *parameters* along which principles can be realized. A child learning a particular language will have to fix the appropriate values of parameters associated with principles. Parameter settings are fixed by contact with examples of the language being learned. For example, while the Empty Category Principle determines, invariantly, the conditions necessary for an empty category to be allowed in a human language, languages may vary in whether they make use of all the types of empty category allowed. English allows empty categories after prepositions in sentences like *Who did she leave with e?* By contrast, French does not, *\*Qui est-elle partie avec e?* although it does allow empty categories after transitive verbs: *Qui a-t-elle accompagné e?* 'Who did she accompany?' Whether empty categories can appear after prepositions or not is a parameter of variation. (For a general introduction to principles and parameters theory in the context of first language acquisition

see Atkinson, 1992. See also CHOMSKYAN LINGUISTICS.)

Given that what the child L1 learner expects to find in human languages is already considerably constrained by innate knowledge of the principles, the fixing of the parameters should be deterministic: triggered by exposure to appropriate examples. On this view the core of the grammar of a language is not 'learned' but 'grows'. As plants grow in response to nutrients and light, so the first language grammar grows in response to samples of the language spoken around the child (Chomsky, 1975).

Various researchers have explored the explanatory value of a theory of this sort with respect to the characteristics of first language acquisition described above (see, for example, Radford, 1990).

Another type of theory about the development of the L1 is that it is parasitic on more general COGNITIVE DEVELOPMENT. On this view there is no innately predetermined language faculty. Instead, knowledge of language is just one of the results of more general mental abilities which enable humans to construct mental representations of the world. Knowledge of language grows as the child's mental abilities grow, this being the effect of the child interacting with his or her environment (O'Grady, 1987).

## SECOND LANGUAGE ACQUISITION

Second language acquisition (SLA), like L1 acquisition, also proceeds in broadly systematic stages. A lot of evidence has accumulated to show that learners develop knowledge of phenomena like grammatical MORPHOLOGY, negation, question formation, relative clauses, clausal word order, pronominal reference and so on in ways which are independent of the input, independent of the circumstances in which the L2 is being learned (classroom versus naturalistic) and which are common to L2 learners as a group (for general overview discussions of developmental systematicity or 'natural orders' see Dulay, Burt and Krashen, 1982; Larsen-Freeman and Long, 1991; Ellis, 1994). (See also NATURAL ORDER HYPOTHESIS.)

Second, studies which have looked specifically at the effect of tutored environments on SLA have generally found that the effect of correction, reward and reinforcement is not directly evident in the way L2 learners develop. Instructed environments appear to enhance the *rate* at which learning proceeds, but the *route* of development is not directly affected by correction, reward or reinforcement (see Ellis, 1990, for discussion and RATE/ROUTE IN SLA).

Third, the knowledge that L2 learners acquire appears to go beyond what they were exposed to in the input, just as in the case of L1 learners; it is *generative*, in the sense that L2 learners are able to produce novel utterances which they have not encountered in the input on the basis of the linguistic knowledge they have acquired. Moreover, some studies seem to show that L2 learners are sensitive to properties of the L2 which are not instantiated in their L1, and which are not obviously given by the input they receive (Bley-Vroman et al., 1988).

However, L2 acquisition is not inevitable. There are considerable differences between individuals in success in acquiring L2s (Skehan, 1989). And, as a group, L2 learners are rarely as successful as native speakers, even given considerable exposure. There appears to be a critical period for acquiring languages: beyond the age of 6 or 7 it seems to be progressively more difficult for the majority of L2 learners to acquire the same mental representations for the target language as native speakers (see AGE LEARNING DIFFERENCES and CRITICAL PERIOD HYPOTHESIS).

An important task for SLA researchers is to develop a theory which will explain these properties of SLA. In the development of such a theory some researchers have been struck by the similarities between SLA and first language acquisition: the systematicity of development, the lack of direct effect of instruction and feedback on development,

the generativity of L2 knowledge. These researchers have then explored the possibility that a theory appropriate to first language acquisition may also be appropriate to SLA. For example, a number of researchers have hypothesized that L2 learners have access to principles and parameters of universal grammar in the construction of L2 grammars. (For general discussion of this topic see White, 1989; Towell and Hawkins, 1994). It is access to these properties of the subconscious language faculty which produces the observed systematicity, the ineffectiveness of correction and feedback on the route of development, and generativity of L2 grammars.

One of the problems for this approach is to explain why there should be *differences* between first and second language acquisition; in particular, why there appears to be a critical period after which acquisition becomes less successful. Such explanations range from suggesting that factors external to the language faculty are responsible for inhibiting its operation (for example, affective factors, motivational factors (see MOTIVATION), attitudinal factors (see ATTITUDES), differences in the kind of input addressed to young children and older learners, differences in the availability of learning mechanisms) to factors internal to the language faculty (maturation, the influence of the first language).

By contrast, other researchers have been struck by the dissimilarity between SLA and first language acquisition, and have argued for the Fundamental Difference Hypothesis (Bley-Vroman, 1989). From this perspective, the mechanisms which underlie L2 development are radically different from those involved in first language acquisition. The learning of second languages is an inductive procedure, where the learner constructs hypotheses on the basis of samples of the L2 encountered, and then tests those hypotheses against further samples of the L2. This idea is usually coupled with some notion of the perceptual saliency of certain types of data over others. For example, in one influential account of the acquisition of German word order (Meisel, Clahsen and Pienemann, 1981) it is claimed that learners start by acquiring the 'canonical' word order subject–verb–object, because this is the most salient in the samples of language learners encounter, then acquire a property which places non-finite verb forms at the ends of sentences, because operations involving the beginnings and ends of sentences are the most salient next to canonical word order, and then subsequently acquire an operation which involves categories internal to the sentence.

The debate between these two approaches has been one of the major features of SLA research during the late eighties and nineties.

## FUTURE TRENDS

In research into both first language acquisition and SLA it looks likely that the controversy over whether language development is the effect of a 'dedicated' language faculty or of more general cognitive abilities used by humans to acquire knowledge about the environment they live in will continue into the foreseeable future. There is, however, a clear imbalance at present in the relative sophistication of theory construction in the two camps. While linguists, over the past forty years, have been developing a rich theory of the properties of the language faculty which makes specific and testable claims, theories of general cognition which have been applied to language acquisition appear to be still at a very elementary stage. One possible future trend is that proponents of this approach will develop a more articulated and specific account.

BIBLIOGRAPHY

Atkinson, R. M. (1992). *Children's Syntax.* Oxford: Blackwell.*

Bley-Vroman, R. (1989). What is the logical problem of foreign language learning? In S. Gass and J. Schachter (eds), *Linguistic Perspectives on Second Language Acquisition.* Cambridge: Cambridge University Press.

Bley-Vroman, R., Felix, S. and Ioup, G. (1988). The accessibility of universal grammar in adult language learning. *Second Language Research,* 4, 1–32.

Brown, R. and Hanlon, C. (1970). Derivational complexity and the order of acquisition in child speech. In J. Hayes (ed.), *Cognition and the Development of Language.* New York: John Wiley.

Chomsky, N. (1975). *Reflections on Language.* New York: Pantheon.

Dulay, H., Burt, M. and Krashen, S. (1982). *Language Two.* Oxford: Oxford University Press.*

Ellis, R. (1990). *Instructed Second Language Acquisition.* Oxford: Blackwell.

——(1994). *The Study of Second Language Acquisition.* Oxford: Oxford University Press.

Fletcher, P. and Garman, M. (eds) (1986). *Language Acquisition.* Cambridge: Cambridge University Press.

Fry, D. (1977). *Homo loquens.* Cambridge: Cambridge University Press.

Larsen-Freeman, D. and Long, M. (1991). *An Introduction to Second Language Acquisition Research.* London: Longman.

Meisel, J., Clahsen, H. and Pienemann, M. (1981). On determining developmental stages in natural second language acquisition. *Studies in Second Language Acquisition,* 3, 109–35.

O'Grady, W. (1987). *Principles of Grammar and Learning.* Chicago: University of Chicago Press.

Radford, A. (1990). *Syntactic Theory and the Acquisition of English Syntax: The nature of early child grammars in English.* Oxford: Blackwell. *

Sachs, J., Bard, B. and Johnson, M. (1981). Language learning with restricted input: case studies of two hearing children of deaf parents. *Applied Psycholinguistics,* 2, 33–54.

Skehan, P. (1989). *Individual Differences in Second Language Learning.* London: Edward Arnold.

Towell, R. and Hawkins, R. (1994). *Approaches to Second Language Acquisition.* Clevedon: Multilingual Matters.

White, L. (1989). *Universal Grammar and Second Language Acquisition.* Amsterdam: John Benjamins.

RH

## foreign vs second language learning

The basis for this distinction is the geographical context in which a language is spoken. An ESL situation is one where English is widely used in commerce, administration and education. It is a foreign language (EFL) in a country where English plays no such role. When English is taught to non-native speakers in an English-speaking country, ESL usually refers to people who are long-stay or permanent residents, whereas EFL is taught to those who return after a period of time to their own country.

BIBLIOGRAPHY
Broughton, G., Brumfit, C., Flavell, R., Hill, P. and Pincas, A. (1978). *Teaching English as a Foreign Language*. London: Routledge and Kegan Paul, 4–6.
Stern, H. H. (1983). *Fundamental Concepts of Language Teaching*. Oxford: Oxford University Press, 15–17.*

JMCD

**formal and naturalistic learning environments**   In formal ('tutored') environments L2 learners are encouraged to focus on the form of the L2 and are often corrected. Input is selective, and time for learning usually limited. In naturalistic environments learners are simply exposed, in their everyday lives, to the L2 as it is spoken by native speakers. (See also CLASSROOM STUDIES IN SLA.)

BIBLIOGRAPHY
Ellis, R. (1990). *Instructed Second Language Acquisition*. Oxford: Blackwell.
Long, M. (1988). Instructed interlanguage development. In L. Beebe (ed.), *Issues in Second Language Acquisition: Multiple Perspectives*. Rowley, MA: Newbury House, 115–41.

RH

**form-focus**   A task may be said to have form- as opposed to MESSAGE-FOCUS, if it allows learners to think about the form rather than the content of their output. Gap-filling exercises involving grammatical items are form-focused. The form/message-focus distinction plays an important role in VARIABILITY

IN SLA studies, where greater accuracy is sometimes achieved in more formal 'styles' permitting form-focus; see Tarone (1988). 'Monitoring' (see MONITOR MODEL) clearly entails form-focus. Recent interest in CONSCIOUSNESS RAISING partly derives from research findings that attention to form may help learning. See Schmidt and Frota (1986), and NOTICING.

BIBLIOGRAPHY
Schmidt, R. and Frota, S. (1986). Developing basic conversational ability in a second language: a case study of an adult learner of Portuguese. In R. Day (ed.), *'Talking to Learn': Conversation in second language acquisition*. Rowley, MA: Newbury House, 237–326.
Tarone, E. (1988). *Variation in Interlanguage*. London: Edward Arnold.

KJ

**formulaic speech**   Formulas are stretches of speech acquired as unanalysed wholes by L2 learners, but which for native speakers consist of smaller constituent parts. For example, Wong-Fillmore (1979) cites a learner (Nora) who used *How-do-you-do-dese?* as a generalized question form: *How-do-you-do-dese flower power?* (What is flower power?), *How-do-you-do-dese in English?* (What's this in English?) Formulas can be of two types: 'patterns' are partially productive, as in the Nora example; 'routines' are free-standing formulas: e.g. *have-a-nice-day*. Wong-Fillmore (1979) argues that formulas are the source for later analysed L2 knowledge. Krashen and Scarcella (1978) argue that they are independent of analysed knowledge.

BIBLIOGRAPHY
Krashen, S. and Scarcella, R. (1978). On routines and patterns in language acquisition and performance. *Language Learning*, 28, 283–300.
Wong-Fillmore, L. (1979). Individual differences in second language acquisition. In C. Fillmore, D. Kempler and W. Wang, (eds), *Individual Differences in Language Ability and Language Behaviour*. New York: Academic Press.

RH

**fossilization** is the phenomenon whereby linguistic items (particularly erroneous ones) become permanent in a learner's INTERLANGUAGE. The term is used by Selinker (1972) in relation to the processes of 'levelling' (lack of forward movement) or 'regression' ('backsliding', where a learner's language reverts to an earlier stage). Fossilization may occur in relation to any linguistic level, a 'foreign accent' being the result of one form of fossilization.

The phenomenon is well attested in both FORMAL AND NATURALISTIC LEARNING ENVIRONMENTS, and various explanations for it have been put forward. Selinker (1972) relates it to the presence of tension or extreme relaxation. Vigil and Oller (1976) associate it with the feedback a learner receives from interlocutors. If a learner produces erroneous forms, but interlocutors signal comprehension ('I understand') then the learner has no motive to abandon the erroneous (which might occur if the reaction were 'I don't understand'). Selinker and Lamendella (1978) counter-argue that the linguistic items L1 children use do not become fossilized even though they receive 'I understand' reactions from parents. Their explanations are: low motivation (no desire to move forward); age (neurological mechanisms making change difficult with age); limited input. Schumann's (1978) explanation relates to the first of these; he argues that fossilization occurs when communicative needs are met; if a learner has a desire to acculturate to the L2 culture, then the motivation to eradicate fossilized forms will exist (see ACCULTURATION HYPOTHESIS).

Canale and Swain (1980) point out that fossilization will occur if insufficient attention is given to linguistic form in teaching. Some have observed that language teaching approaches which advocate a concentration on MESSAGE-FOCUS may have the positive result of developing the learner's ability to convey messages, but also the negative one of inducing early fossilization. Johnson (1992), among others, discusses ways in which teaching procedures might avoid this by building in a degree of FORM-FOCUS.

BIBLIOGRAPHY
Canale, M. and Swain, M. (1980). Theoretical bases of communicative approaches to second language teaching and testing. *Applied Linguistics*, 1, 1–47.
Johnson, H. (1992). Defossilizing. *ELT Journal*, 46/2, 180–9.
Schumann, J. (1978). *The Pidginization Process: A model for second language acquisition*. Rowley, MA: Newbury House.*
Selinker, L. (1972). Interlanguage. *International Review of Applied Linguistics*, 10, 209–31.
Selinker, L. and Lamendella, J. (1978). Two perspectives on fossilization in interlanguage learning. *Interlanguage Studies Bulletin*, 3, 143–91.*
Vigil, N. A. and Oller, J. W. (1976). Rule fossilization: a tentative model. *Language Learning*, 26/2, 281–95.

KJ

**four skills** of reading and listening (receptive skills), speaking and writing (productive skills) have traditionally formed the foundation for the planning of language teaching programmes and the design of materials. Earlier emphasis on the manipulation of language forms, using the four skills as a vehicle, has diversified into an understanding of the processing strategies involved in the skills themselves, and a concomitant development in teaching materials. In particular, more communicative views of language use suggest that the traditional division into discrete skills is not always valid and realistic (see also COMMUNICATIVE METHODOLOGY, TEACHING INTEGRATED SKILLS).

BIBLIOGRAPHY
Johnson, K. and Morrow, K. (eds) (1981). *Communication in the Classroom*. Harlow: Longman.

JMCD

**français fondamental** represented the first systematic attempt to specify a basic vocabulary of *spoken* French for foreign learners, derived from tape-recordings of 163 conversations involving 275 participants and lists made by 900 schoolchildren. *Frequency* was the main criterion for selection, but the study also identified *disponibilité* ('availability') as crucial.

BIBLIOGRAPHY
Gougenheim, G., Michea, R., Rivenc, P. and Sauvageot, A. (1964). *L'élaboration du français fondamental (1er degré): Etude sur l'établissement d'un vocabulaire et d'une grammaire de base.* New edn. [*The elaboration of fundamental French (first degree): A study directed at the establishment of a basic vocabulary and grammar.*] Paris: Didier. [First published in 1956 under the title *L'élaboration du français élémentaire.*]
Halliday, M. A. K., McIntosh, A. and Strevens, P. (1964). *The Linguistic Sciences and Language Teaching.* London: Longman, 190–8.
JTR

**free practice techniques** The production, or free practice, stage is the last in the traditional 'PRESENTATION – PRACTICE – PRODUCTION' SEQUENCE. Some important characteristics of this final stage are: it usually allows learners some freedom over what they say and how they say it; the practice does not rely on repetition for its effect; emphasis is placed on achieving meaningfulness; and attempts are made to simulate the conditions of actual communication (as far as is possible in the classroom situation).

In many language teaching approaches, like AUDIOLINGUALISM, the free practice stage tends to be de-emphasized, but in recent years its importance has been increasingly realized, particularly within the COMMUNICATIVE LANGUAGE TEACHING movement. Three main reasons for this are recognized, one being that learners are given freedom – necessary so that (among other things) risk-taking skills can be brought into play. Second, meaningfulness is valued because only through practice where the starting-point is a 'desire to mean' can the process of encoding meanings linguistically be developed. Third, free practice is fluency practice, where the skill of combining various learned elements together to form actual discourse is brought into play. The free practice stage also provides both learners and teachers with feedback on the learning and teaching that has so far taken place. For discussion of the production stage and techniques associated with it, see Byrne (1976), and Part B of Johnson and Morrow (1981).

Recent views of this stage recognize the need for free practice throughout the teaching operation, not just at the end (which tended to be the case in earlier approaches). Because of the stage's aims, where learners are often encouraged to express personal opinions and a degree of personal commitment is involved, particular importance is given to creating a good atmosphere in the class. The teacher tends to take a back seat, the roles of 'guide' and 'adviser' being those which Byrne (1976) associates with this stage. Error correction does not characteristically take place in mid interaction, so that constant interruptions for correction do not impair fluency, and a relaxed atmosphere is maintained.

Free practice techniques involve different configurations of participants, but although work with the class as a whole is not excluded, the emphasis tends to be on GROUP WORK/PAIR WORK, or on what Spratt (1985) calls 'mingles' (where learners move around class, perhaps joining different groups or interviewing other students). As Byrne (1976) points out, group work in which the interaction is with peers is likely to create an atmosphere which is more conducive to the interaction which free practice techniques aim to foster. A number of studies (Long et al., 1976, for example) suggest such beneficial characteristics of group work.

The main general areas of free practice techniques are ROLE PLAY AND SIMULATION, DRAMA, communication games and discussions (although there are others, like Byrne's 'oral composition' – e.g. telling stories back from picture sets – which do not fit easily into this categorization). The prominence given to role play, simulation and drama is related to the element of pretence in them; learners can pretend they are in various situations in order to be able to practise areas of language use which go well beyond the speech act areas normally occurring in class-rooms – *pretending* to make holiday plans, *pretending* to be in a supermarket, etc. One of the important variables at the free production stage is the degree of control exerted over learner output. Role play exercises of the sort sometimes referred to as 'discourse chains' clearly lay out the form an interaction will have, and tell the participants at each point what should be said, though not usually how it should be said. Freer role plays may be based on dialogues, texts or visuals; but at their most free learners are simply given general instructions on the situation they are to act out, perhaps with some broad indication of the roles they have to play. No linguistic guidance is given, and learners are left to develop the actual interactions as they see fit. Clearly the actual wording of rubrics plays an important part in exerting variable degrees of control, and the writing of suitable instructions is an important part of creating good free practice exercises.

It is possible to see drama or dramatization as a special type of role play, and a number of books for language teachers concentrate on providing techniques for this. See particularly Maley and Duff (1978) and Holden (1981).

Wright and others (1979) is one of a number of texts providing taxonomies of communication games. The variables these writers recognize as important are degree of guidance, linguistic level and participant pattern (whole class, group work, pair work, individual practice). Byrne (1976) subdivides his games into those which practise one structure, those covering a small number of identified structures and open-ended games where no specific linguistic expectations are identified. Rinvolucri (1984) is one of a number of texts which concentrate on the first two of these categories. Many games involve an INFORMATION/OPINION GAP, with communication occurring as this is bridged, and it is to be noted how natural such gaps are to the nature of many games (the traditional 'Blind Man's Buff' being a case in point, where the blindfold in effect creates an information gap). The JIGSAW PRINCIPLE also commonly features in games of this sort.

Discussions have long been part of the language teacher's repertoire, but in recent years recognition has been given to the degree of preparation (not just linguistic, but also psychological and cognitive) necessary for discussions to succeed. Ur (1981) provides general consideration of the issues involved in setting up discussions so that high degrees of participation and motivation are achieved. Her book contains many examples for actual discussion classes.

Byrne (1976) illustrates well the importance given to preparation for all free activities, not just discussions. His treatment contains many valuable and detailed proposals for the use of both visuals and texts as stimuli for discussion, dialogue production, role play and dramatization.

BIBLIOGRAPHY

Byrne, D. (1976). *Teaching Oral English*. Harlow: Longman.\*

Holden, S. (1981). Drama. In K. Johnson and K. Morrow (eds), *Communication in the Classroom*. Harlow: Longman, 131–6.

Johnson, K. and Morrow, K. (eds) (1981). *Communication in the Classroom*. Harlow: Longman.\*

Long, M. H., Adams, L., McLean, M. and Castaños, F. (1976). Doing things with words: verbal interaction in lockstep and small groups classroom situations. In R. Crymes and J. Fanselow (eds), *On TESOL '76*. Washington, DC: TESOL.

Maley, A. and Duff, A. (1978). *Drama Techniques in Language Teaching*. Cambridge: Cambridge University Press.

Rinvolucri, M. (1984). *Grammar Games*. Cambridge: Cambridge University Press.

Spratt, M. (1985). The production stage. In A. Matthews, M. Spratt and L. Dangerfield (eds), *At the Chalkface*. London: Edward Arnold, 12–16.

Ur, P. (1981). *Discussions that Work*. Cambridge: Cambridge University Press.\*

Wright, A. D., Betteridge, D. and Buckby, M. (1979). *Games for Language Learning*. Cambridge: Cambridge University Press.

KJ

# G

**general purpose English** (EGP) is polarized with ESP (see ENGLISH FOR SPECIFIC PURPOSES) to refer to contexts such as the school where needs cannot readily be specified. This view is misleading, since purpose is always inherent. EGP is more usefully considered as providing a broad foundation rather than a detailed and selective specification of goals.

BIBLIOGRAPHY
Hutchinson, T. and Waters, A. (1987). *English for Specific Purposes*. Cambridge: Cambridge University Press, 53–4.

JMCD

**generative grammar**   The term 'generative' means that the grammar is formal and explicit; 'when we speak of the linguist's grammar as a "generative grammar" we mean only that it is sufficiently explicit to determine how sentences of the language are in fact characterized by the grammar' (Chomsky, 1980). Hence generative grammars contrast with traditional grammars, which left many rules of the grammar to the interpretation of the reader; such grammars dealt primarily with the idiosyncratic forms that were not 'obvious' and thus left it to the reader to know what a 'noun' was or what the basic word order of the sentence was. A generative grammar therefore tried to specify everything that is necessary on the printed page rather than leaving it to the imagination.

This approach, pioneered by Chomsky in 1957, made the form of the rules explicit so that nothing needed to be read into them. This was achieved through a formal way of expressing rules as 'rewrite rules', seen in:

$$S \rightarrow NP\ VP$$

In a rewrite rule such as this, the arrow symbolizes the relation 'consists of'; the rule therefore states that an S (sentence) consists of an NP (noun phrase) and a VP (verb phrase). The reader needs nothing more to interpret this than the rule itself. But what are the symbols NP and VP? Again these are specified through further rewrite rules rather than being left to the reader's intuition:

$$NP \rightarrow Det\ N$$

saying that an NP consists of a Det (determiner) and an N (noun), and:

$$VP \rightarrow V\ NP$$

saying that a VP consists of a V (verb) and another NP. But we still do not know what V, N, and Det consist of. So there is a lexicon consisting of entries that expand each into appropriate words:

Det → the, a
V → likes, sees, chews
N → woman, dog, book

This now enables us to generate the structures of actual English sentences:

The woman sees a dog.
A dog chews the book.
The dog likes a woman.

And several others. All these sentences (S) consist of an NP and VP; in each of them the first NP consists of a determiner (Det) and an N; in each of them the verb phrase

(VP) consists of a V (verb) and an NP. The short set of rules then generates the structures of the sentences and the lexical items in them, without involving the reader's interpretation. The reader never needs to ask what a sentence is or what a noun is; the rules define this for us – a sentence is any possible rewriting of S down to the final words consequent on the first rule; a noun is all the possible words that can fit in the last rule, and so on.

This handful of rules is a partial attempt at describing English explicitly, that is to say, at a generative grammar. On the one hand the lexicon needs refining to avoid:

*The book likes the dog.

On the other the VP rule needs to allow for intransitive sentences without objects such as:

The dog barks.

In principle, though, bigger and better grammars could be written to encompass the facts of English.

This type of rewrite rule which expands one symbol into others is a way of capturing the insight that language has phrase structure, that is to say that the elements fit together into structures rather than having simply a linear order. Chomsky (1957), however, claimed phrase structure was inadequate for human languages without transformational rules – operations that can be performed on the elements in the sentence other than expansion, such as moving elements about and adding them to get questions etc. as in

John likes what?

becoming

What does John like?

by moving *What* to the beginning and adding *does*.

But the set of rules could in principle be expanded enormously to generate all the sentences of English, that is to say, to handle their description. The description would,

however, still be totally explicit. The grammar goes beyond the sentences that we have given; the grammar must not deal only with sentences such as 'John ate an apple' that have been said in the past; it must also handle sentences that might be produced tomorrow, to decide whether any sentence is possible in English or not. The grammar uses a finite set of rules to describe a potentially infinite set of sentences.

'Generative' in this sense is thus a technical term applied to any grammar that states the rules explicitly. It is a methodological requirement for an adequate linguistic description; it does not mirror how native speakers process language in their minds. The ability to produce new sentences that have not been heard before is indeed crucial, but it is nothing to do with the methodological term 'generative'. These two are frequently confused in popularizations of grammar, a mistake called by Botha (1989) *the Generative Gaffe*. Applied linguists in particular have spoken of the need for the syllabus to be 'generative' in the sense that the learner must be able to go beyond what is specified. Worthy as this sentiment may be, they are using the term 'generative' in its everyday 'productive' sense since they are not proposing that the grammar syllabus should be spelled out explicitly.

In principle there is no one way of doing generative grammar; any grammar is generative if its form of statement is sufficiently explicit. The above examples of rewrite rules were drawn from the early Chomskyan tradition of generative grammar, perhaps the best-known form of generative grammar. This has been vastly changed over the past forty years and concentrates on general principles and parameters of which such rules are artefacts. In so far as rewrite rules are used nowadays in the Chomskyan tradition, they are found at a more abstract level called X-bar syntax. This has two central rules:

$$X'' \rightarrow \text{(specifier) } X'$$
$$X' \rightarrow X \text{ (complement(s))}$$

All top-level (two-bar, i.e. X″ or XP) phrases consist of a compulsory expansion into a mid-level phrase X′ and a possible specifier; thus a V″ (verb phrase or VP) consists of a specifier (usually the underlying subject) and V′, an NP of a specifier and an N′, and so on. The NP *his fear of the dark* is therefore an N″ (*his* + N′); *fear of the dark* is an N′ (N + *of the dark*). All mid-level phrases (X′) consist of a head (X) with a lexical entry and possible complements; thus a V′ consists of a verb and its possible complements, a P′ of a P and an NP complement, etc.

However, other schools of grammar such as lexical functional grammar (LFG) and generalized phrase structure grammar (GPSG) also lay claim to the generative label and are particularly fond of versions of X-bar syntax (Gazdar et al., 1985; Horrocks, 1987; Sells, 1985). Indeed Gazdar (1987) attacked current Chomskyan grammar for not being generative since principles and parameters are not as explicit and clearly testable as the earlier rewrite 'rules' and transformations.

GPSG rejects transformational rules, claiming that phrase structure rules are perfectly adequate when expanded in various ways (Gazdar et al., 1985). The above VP rule for example

$$VP \rightarrow V\ NP$$

appears as an *Immediate Dominance* (ID) rule:

$$VP \rightarrow H[2],\ NP$$

This means that a verb phrase consists of a head (H) of type 2, and a noun phrase, but not necessarily in that order. This is accompanied by the *linear precedence* (LP) statement:

$$[SUBCAT] < \_[SUBCAT]$$

that in English a lexical category is followed by a phrase; LP rules describe the order of categories, ID rules their structural relations. (See CHOMSKYAN LINGUISTICS, GRAMMAR, TRANSFORMATIONAL GENERATIVE GRAMMAR, UNIVERSAL GRAMMAR.)

BIBLIOGRAPHY

Botha, R. P. (1989). *Challenging Chomsky: The generative garden game*. Oxford: Blackwell.

Brown, E. K. and Miller, J. E. (1982). *Syntax: Generative grammar*. London: Hutchinson.*

Chomsky, N. (1957). *Syntactic Structures*. The Hague: Mouton.*

——(1980). *Rules and Representations*. Oxford: Blackwell.

Gazdar, G. (1987). Generative grammar. In J. Lyons, R. Coates, M. Deuchar and G. Gazdar (eds), *New Horizons in Linguistics 2*. London: Penguin Books.

Gazdar, G., Klein, E., Pullum, G. and Sag, I. (1985). *Generalized Phrase Structure Grammar*. Oxford: Blackwell.

Horrocks, G. (1987). *Generative Grammar*. Harlow: Longman.

Sells, P. (1985). *Lectures on Contemporary Syntactic Theories*. Stanford, CA: CSLI.

VJC

**genre**   Genres are types of SPOKEN AND WRITTEN DISCOURSE recognized by a discourse community. Examples are lectures, conversations, speeches, notices, advertisements, novels, diaries, shopping lists. Each genre has typical features. Some may be linguistic (particular grammatical or lexical choices), some paralinguistic (e.g. print size, gesture) and some contextual and pragmatic (e.g. setting, purpose). Some genres overlap (a joke may also be a story) and one can contain another (a joke can be a part of a story). Genre identification is essential for communication, yet despite detailed work on particular genres, and considerable interest, no satisfactory classification has yet emerged. (See also DISCOURSE ANALYSIS, TEXT GRAMMAR.)

BIBLIOGRAPHY

Bhatia, V. K. (1993). *Analysing Genre*. London: Longman.

Cook, G. (1992). *The Discourse of Advertising*. London: Routledge. [Chapter 1.]

Swales, J. (1990). *Genre Analysis*. Cambridge: Cambridge University Press.*

GC

**GI method**   Also known as *mimicry-memorization* or the *informant-drill* method, it was pioneered within the Army Specialized Training Programme for American service personnel in World War II. Using imitation and practice based on dialogues and drills rehearsed by a native-speaking 'drill-master', it may be regarded as the precursor of AUDIOLINGUALISM.

BIBLIOGRAPHY

Howatt, A. P. R. (1984). *A History of English Language Teaching*. Oxford: Oxford University Press, 266–7.

Mackey, W. F. (1965). *Language Teaching Analysis*. London: Longmans, Green. [Chapter 5.]
JTR

**good language learner studies**   The good language learner (GLL) studies represent an early approach to learner strategies (see LEARNING STRATEGIES). A logical basis for studying L2 learning should be learners who are good at L2 learning rather than those that are failures, such as Alberto, the learner studied by Schumann (see ACCULTURATION HYPOTHESIS). The research paradigm established a number of strategies claimed to be used by good learners. After the initial batch of studies, the overall approach was submerged under the tidal wave of studies of various forms of strategies of the 1980s.

The first steps were taken by Joan Rubin and David Stern in programmatic articles that laid out the logic of examining what good learners do and seeing what this tells us about L2 learning and how to improve learners who are not so good. Stern's first list, published in 1975, contained ten language learning strategies similar to Rubin's list, which was also published that year:

(i)   *Planning strategy I (cognitive): a personal learning style or positive learning strategies.* Good learners have sufficient self-knowledge to know what style they should adopt to be successful.

(ii)   *Planning strategy II (affective): an active approach to the learning task.* Good learners are not passive but take an active independent role in learning.

(iii)   *Empathic strategy: a tolerant and outgoing approach to the target language and empathy with its speakers.* Integrative motivation is crucial, as is lack of inhibition about learning a new language.

(iv)   *Formal strategy: technical know-how about how to tackle a language.* Good learners are aware of the form of language and consciously try to get to know the second language.

(v)   *Experimental strategy: strategies of experimentation and planning with the object of developing the new language into an ordered system, and revising this system progressively.* The learner has to make guesses about the second language systematically and be prepared to change them.

(vi)   *Semantic strategy: constantly searching for meaning.* Good learners look for meaning in what they hear.

(vii)   *Practice strategy: willingness to practise.* Good learners seize every opportunity for practice.

(viii)   *Communication strategy: willingness to use the language in real communication.* Good learners seek out occasions to use the language in real-life situations.

(ix)   *Monitoring strategy: self-monitoring and critical sensitivity to language use.* Good learners check their output continuously and learn from their mistakes.

(x)   *Internalization strategy: developing the second language more and more as a separate reference system and learning to think in it.* Good learners deliberately cut themselves off from their first language.

On the basis of this a large-scale research study was carried out at OISE (Ontario Institute for Studies in Education). It started by interviewing 34 avowedly good language learners of an academic type about their strategies: this yielded a set of six main strategies, mostly variations on the ten above:

(1)   *GLLs find an appropriate style of learning.* For example, one learner accepted rote

teaching as this was the method by which he learnt.

(2) *GLLs involve themselves in the language learning process.* For instance, one learner listened to the news in both L1 and L2.

(3) *GLLs develop an awareness of language as both system and communication.* While one learner would memorize new vocabulary, another would read the *Reader's Digest* in the target language.

(4) *GLLs pay constant attention to expanding their language knowledge.* One learner wrote new words down in a notebook.

(5) *GLLs develop the L2 as a separate system.* One learner gave monologues to herself in the second language.

(6) *GLLs take into account the demands that L2 learning imposes.* For example, learners talked of the need for a sense of humour and the need to realize that L2 learning is hard work.

The main body of the GLL research investigated classroom behaviour. The aim was to correlate measures of success at learning French and personality measures with specially constructed measures of classroom behaviour in three grades of classroom learners of French in Toronto, totalling 72 children. Conclusions were that good learners could not be identified on the basis of observable classroom behaviour, while personality factors played a role. Nor did teachers tend to treat good learners differently from poor learners; nevertheless the teachers were able to spot good learners.

In some ways this research was disappointing, compared, for example, to later strategies research by O'Malley and Chamot; it confirmed the type of strategy that had been described previously but it did not provide observable classroom correlates. Most work with good language learners has not remained as a separate strand of research but plays some role in mainstream strategies research, coming into language teaching through various attempts to make learners aware of the potential strategies they might use (see LEARNER TRAINING).

BIBLIOGRAPHY
Naiman, N., Fröhlich, M., Stern, H. H. and Todesco, A. (1978). *The Good Language Learner.* Toronto: OISE.*
O'Malley, J. and Chamot, A. (1989). *Learning Strategies in Second Language Acquisition.* Cambridge: Cambridge University Press.
Rubin, J. (1975). What the 'Good Language Learner' can teach us. *TESOL Quarterly,* 9/1, 41–51.*
Skehan, P. (1989). *Individual Differences in Second-Language Learning.* London: Edward Arnold.
Stern, H. H. (1975). What can we learn from the good language learner? *Canadian Modern Language Review,* 31, 304–18.

VJC

**government and binding**   Two of a small number of sub-theories constituting the government–binding framework – a version of TRANSFORMATIONAL GENERATIVE GRAMMAR developed by Noam Chomsky and his associates in the USA and Europe in the 1980s. Government is a relation between a lexical category and phrasal categories. Binding is a relation between phrasal categories. (See also CHOMSKYAN LINGUISTICS and GENERATIVE GRAMMAR.)

BIBLIOGRAPHY
Haegeman, L. (1994). *Introduction to Government and Binding Theory.* 2nd edn. Oxford: Blackwell.*
Chomsky, N. (1981). *Lectures on Government and Binding.* Dordrecht: Foris.

EJ

**grading/sequencing**   Various criteria are used to order items on a STRUCTURAL SYLLABUS, the most common being the simplicity criterion (moving from simple to complex). Efforts to define simplicity in any rigorous way have failed, though contrastive information clearly needs to be taken into account (what is similar and therefore possibly easy for one language group may be different and possibly difficult for another

– see CONTRASTIVE ANALYSIS). Frequency of occurrence and utility are further common criteria. Different types of utility may be recognized – patterns like *what's this?* may be taught early because of their utility in class work (rather than necessarily outside class). Much sequencing is based on the grouping together of structures with common elements; for example, many textbooks move from teaching *be* to the present continuous tense, which utilizes these forms. The various possible criteria may point to conflicting conclusions; e.g. simplicity may demand one ordering while frequency suggests another.

Pienemann (1985) among others notes the lack of a theoretical basis for grading and sequencing procedures in syllabus design. He attempts to utilize information about acquisition orders (see NATURAL ORDER HYPOTHESIS) as the basis for syllabus ordering.

Grading and sequencing in materials not based on structural progression (e.g. in NOTIONAL/FUNCTIONAL SYLLABUSES) is a more complex issue because often a simplicity criterion cannot easily be used, though frequency and utility may remain possible criteria. See Johnson (1982) for discussion.

BIBLIOGRAPHY
Johnson, K. (1982). Unit ordering and handling different proficiency levels. Paper 5 of K. Johnson, *Communicative Syllabus Design and Methodology*. Oxford: Pergamon, 70–6.
Pienemann, M. (1985). Learnability and syllabus construction. In K. Hyltenstam and M. Pienemann (eds), *Modelling and Assessing Second Language Acquisition*. Clevedon: Multilingual Matters, 23–75.

KJ

**grammar** The Greek philosophers first turned their attention to grammar in the fifth century BC. The Indian grammatical tradition predates the Greek, but was not known in the West until the eighteenth century, by which time the Greek tradition, though modified over the ages, and perhaps now more readily thought of as the Latin tradition, had been entrenched for over 2000 years, exerting an inexorable influence over the description of diverse languages and supplying the framework for teaching grammar, whether in connection with classical or modern foreign languages or the mother tongue.

The Greek model spread beyond its immediate domain when borrowed by the Romans for application to Latin. The structure of classical Greek and Latin being related, the fit between the Greek model and Latin was perhaps not too uncomfortable. Later, Latin grammar was investigated independently of that of Greek, and this led to descriptive refinement. Yet the foundations remained Greek, so that in some sense Latin was taught on the basis of Greek grammar. Again, this might not have been altogether injurious, but when the teaching of modern languages entered the curriculum, those teaching them, being imbued in the classical languages, also attempted to squeeze them into the Graeco-Latin mould, this time creating a less comfortable fit. Thus, for example, even in a modern German grammar book (Durrell, 1991: 426) the word *zuliebe* is classified as a preposition, though it is in fact a 'postposition': *Meinem Freund zuliebe* (for the sake of my friend). While it has the same *function* as a preposition, it is nevertheless a distortion, perpetrated because the Graeco-Latin model adopted in the book does not offer a category of 'postpositions', to identify it with words described in terms of their position *before* the noun when in these very terms it behaves otherwise.

THE MEANINGS OF 'GRAMMAR'

'Grammar' is a protean term, meaning different things to different people, but often also used with varying references by the same speaker. To summarize from Lyons (1968), for the Ancient Greeks it was a branch of philosophy. The earliest debates centred on whether it was a *natural phenomenon* beyond human control, or whether it was a *convention* with which humans could meddle. The focus shifted over several centuries to the question as to whether language was principally *regular* or *irregular*. Furthermore, grammar was associated preeminently with the written language, the word originating from the Greek for the 'art of writing'. This association was reinforced when Greek scholars discovered in Alexandria the manuscripts of earlier Greek poets and sought to establish 'correct' versions of them; the link between grammar, writing and literature continued throughout the Middle Ages and the Renaissance, and is still present today in studies which are 'philological' rather than 'linguistic'. One excursus meriting attention is *grammatica speculativa*, 'speculative grammar'. The origins go back, again, to the Ancient Greeks, but it flourished in the Middle Ages and later among the Port Royal grammarians in France. Its object was to establish the relationship between words as 'signs', what they 'signified' and human reason, the Port Royal grammarians in particular being intent on proving that languages were rational constructs and subject to universal principles of logic.

Today, the word *grammar* may be assigned at least the following interpretations:

(1)   Among linguists (i.e. linguisticians), *grammar* as an object of study is usually synonymous with *inflection* and SYNTAX, which together determine how words combine into sentences. Syntax has to do with the sequence and occurrence of words in sentences, and inflection with the 'shape' that words take as determined by grammatical rules. English is not highly inflected, but there are instances in which the concept becomes evident. For example, *I go, you go, we go, they go* contrast with: *he/she/it goes*. In some other languages, this sort of inflection is more complex, for instance, in French. Inflection cannot be ignored when determining the grammaticality of a sentence. For example, (standard) English requires 'agreement' between subject and verb, so that a sentence like *\*She go to work by train*, though well-formed in sequence, is ungrammatical because of the absence of inflection showing that the subject, *she*, and the verb, *go*, 'belong together', or agree. In certain other languages, inflection is also more crucial for meaning than in English, e.g. presented with the ungrammatical German sentence *\*Ich nenne ihm einem Lügner*, one would wonder whether it was supposed to mean 'I call him a liar', 'I am giving him the name of a liar' or 'I am giving his name to a liar.'

Grammar, as a combination of inflection and syntax, is seen more narrowly by today's linguists than in the past, and is separated from questions of style or rhetoric. Moreover, while a grammatical model (see 6 below) such as TRANSFORMATIONAL GENERATIVE GRAMMAR derives basic concepts, for example, *subject* and *verb*, from the Graeco-Latin tradition, this century has seen the introduction of greater formality and complexity. Finally, the approach to grammar as discussed here is *descriptive*, not *prescriptive* (see 3 below), that is, concerned with what native speakers actually say and unconcerned with what one might think they ought to say.

(2)   The grammar typically presented in the context of language teaching and learning, though occasionally tempered with fragments of more modern grammars, is still ultimately of Graeco-Latin provenance. Known as *traditional grammar*, it focuses upon the *'parts of speech'*: the *article*, the *noun*, the *adjective*, the *pronoun*, the *verb*, the *participle*, the *adverb*, the *preposition*, the *conjunction* and the *interjection*. It covers MORPHOLOGY and *syntax* rather than inflection and syntax, morphology subsuming inflection but including also 'word shapes' determined by the rules applying to words,

not sentences. Further, it incorporates features of significance in particular languages; in German, *case* and *modal particles*, for instance, or in French, *adjective–noun agreement*. It may also be felt to be part of grammar teaching to give rules of pronunciation and rules of 'good style' in writing. The teaching of traditional grammar has, of course, for many centuries gone hand-in-hand with translation between the mother tongue and the target language.

(3)   It is where traditional grammarians assert what people *ought* or *ought not* to say and write that traditional grammar intersects with *prescriptive grammar*. Here value systems and conflicts between dialects become involved. None the less, there is an argument, where foreign language learning is concerned, if not for prescriptive, at least for *normative* grammar, since before learners are fully aware of the impression which their phraseology makes upon native speakers of the target language, they are perhaps best advised to use widely acceptable forms representing the *norm*. Prescriptivism exercised by native speakers upon the grammar of other native speakers, however, often causes offence and is frequently misinformed, being of the sort: *'Don't say, "It's me," say, "It is I."'* Preoccupation with prescriptivism can also lead to hypercorrectness which is arguably incorrectness, e.g. *'Between you and I'*. Moreover, identification of what is or is not part of grammar may be vague. Someone who says, *'Regrettably, I did it'*, when they appear to mean, *'Regretfully, I did it,'* might be accused of speaking 'ungrammatically', when in fact the grammar is unassailable, but they have made a wrong lexical choice. Reading prescriptive grammar books for native speakers often reveals how these actually speak, since rules such as *'Don't say x, say y'* are included only because many people do say *x*.

(4)   The word *grammar* is sometimes used to refer to grammar books, many of which are so entitled: *Hammer's German Grammar and Usage*; *Grammaire pratique du français d'aujourd'hui*, etc.

(5)   It is a common supposition, not just among the linguistically unsophisticated, that languages themselves 'contain' a grammar 'which must be learnt'. This is akin to the ancient Greek view of grammar as a natural phenomenon. As will be apparent from paragraph 7 below, this conception is rejected here.

(6)   A novel use for the word *grammar* was introduced by Chomsky (1965: 25):

Clearly, a child who has learned a language has developed an internal representation of a system of rules that determine how sentences are to be formed, used and understood. Using the term 'grammar' with a systematic ambiguity (to refer, first, to the native speaker's internally represented 'theory of his language' and, second, to the linguist's account of this), we can say that the child has developed and internally represented a generative grammar.

Thus, grammar, or a grammar, is not a property of language, but a property of mind –tacit knowledge about what constitutes the native language and 'how it works'. The task of the linguist, for Chomsky, is to try to capture or model the grammar within the mind of the native speaker, and the output on paper of the linguist's deliberations will be a grammar in the more usual sense of a description of the language, but one in principle derived directly from the intuitions of the native speaker. (See CHOMSKYAN LINGUISTICS and GENERATIVE GRAMMAR.)

(7)   This paragraph on the meaning of *grammar* is really a footnote to the first, which was intended to convey a broad spectrum upon which linguists agree. However, in matters of detail they disagree considerably, and for this reason one hears of Chomskyan grammar, Hallidayan grammar, Montague grammar, DEPENDENCY GRAMMAR, phrase-structure grammar, slot-and-filler grammar, and so on. The reason why grammars in the sense of systems of grammar or grammatical models abound is that language itself does not possess some self-evident

organization which the linguist merely has to note down. Grammars, as part of descriptions of language or languages, are ordered interpretations imposed upon them. While certain grammars (in the immediately relevant meaning) are more 'powerful' than others in that they capture the same facts and more, it is impossible, and perhaps always will be, to state absolutely that this or that grammar is 'better' than another, since language has many facets, and linguists tend individually to give emphasis to one or a few facets at the expense of others. Again, much depends on what consumers of grammars want them for. For example, it is arguable that traditional grammar, despite imputed shortcomings, is more appropriate in the context of foreign language teaching than a more 'powerful' grammar which is far less accessible.

For further information, see Crystal (1980: s.v. grammar), Cook (1991: 9–29). (See also CASE GRAMMAR, SYSTEMIC GRAMMAR, TEXT GRAMMAR, UNIVERSAL GRAMMAR.)

BIBLIOGRAPHY
Chomsky, N. (1965). *Aspects of the Theory of Syntax*. Cambridge, MA: MIT Press.
Cook, V. (1991). *Second Language Learning and Second Language Teaching*. London: Edward Arnold.
Crystal, D. (1980). *A First Dictionary of Linguistics and Phonetics*. London: André Deutsch.
Durrell, M. (ed.) (1991). *Hammer's German Grammar and Usage*. 2nd edn. London: Edward Arnold.
Lyons, J. (1968). *Introduction to Theoretical Linguistics*. Cambridge: Cambridge University Press.

JTR

**grammar teaching**   Here the teaching of grammar will be considered in two contexts: that of the foreign language and that of the mother tongue, but precedence will be given to the former. This is not to imply that the latter is unimportant. However, it is simply a fact that there has been more debate, on an international scale, about grammar in foreign language teaching than about the teaching of grammar in the mother tongue setting, in regard to which there is room for many more contributions.

## GRAMMAR TEACHING IN THE FOREIGN LANGUAGE CONTEXT

While grammar in its more technical senses (see GRAMMAR, *meanings* 1 and 6) may nowadays be studied as part of linguistics courses at university, it is *traditional grammar* (*meaning* 2) which has predominated in the language classroom. However, it has rarely, if ever, served as an object of study for its own sake; rather, it has been used as a tool intended to facilitate practical but accurate mastery of the mother tongue and of foreign languages, and in this respect it has attracted controversy in both spheres, though perhaps arguments have been more vehement in the context of foreign language teaching.

In this latter context, the main focus here, the major issue historically has been whether grammar should be taught *deductively* or *inductively*. The deductive approach holds it essential that learners should possess an *explicit* knowledge of grammar, such that they can consciously learn the 'rules' of these. It is also felt useful that they should be able to compare and contrast the system of the foreign language with that of the mother tongue. Moreover, *accuracy* and *valued speech* are in contention, since while the supporters of the deductive approach have probably never denied that people may 'pick up' foreign languages, they have been concerned that they should speak them 'well' and 'correctly'. Those favouring the inductive approach, on the other hand, while agreeing that the 'rules' of foreign languages must be acquired, have argued that such rules may be 'induced' by learners if language input is organized appropriately. This position has often been backed up by the observations that people acquire their mother

**Table 1** Main trends in thought and practice of grammar teaching (from Kelly, 1969: 59).

| Era | Teaching | | Language analysis |
|---|---|---|---|
| | *Inductive* | *Deductive* | |
| Classical | X | X | Grammar |
| Medieval | | X | Grammar, *grammatica speculativa* |
| Renaissance | X | X | Grammar |
| 18/19 C | | X | General grammar |
| 19/20 C | X | X | Linguistics, grammar |

tongue 'naturally', without explicitly learning the 'rules', and that a similar process can apply in the case of the foreign learner; young children and less gifted learners have difficulty with formal grammar and its metalanguage; overt reference to contrasts between the foreign language and the mother tongue causes rather than prevents confusion: learners will not be confounded by *connaître* and *savoir* until it is pointed out to them that both items of the pair 'equate' to the English *know*.

The deductive and inductive approaches have not always been violently opposed; in the Renaissance, particularly, some teachers combined the two, though mindful that the ultimate goal was to teach rhetoric, which required grammatical study. However, even during this period, there were those who argued for the total abandonment of overt reference to grammar. Kelly (1969: 59) represents the 'main trends in thought and practice' as in table 1.

As the table illustrates, the deductive approach, and therefore explicit grammar teaching, have enjoyed an unbroken history since the earliest times, whereas the inductive approach disappeared during the two periods in which the emphasis was almost exclusively on literature and writing. With regard to the modern era of language teaching (beginning with the spread of universal education), the controversy between the approaches resumed upon the emergence of

the REFORM SCHOOL and the DIRECT METHOD. This time, listening and speaking, on the one hand, and reading and writing, on the other, became sharply polarized. It was not that the supporters of an inductive approach rejected reading and writing; they saw these skills as developing late in the learning process, as with native-speaking children. They also deprecated the fact that in the traditional classroom, the native language was used as the means of instruction, thus depriving learners of exposure to the target language. However, no great revolution ensued, even if some enthusiastic teachers embraced reform methods. The sniping between the two camps involved, which may be characterized as grammar-translation and direct method respectively, continued in the literature until the Second World War, but it is noteworthy that there was little discussion of aims, much more of the 'best way to teach'. Yet it is plain, in retrospect, that the reformers viewed languages as tools of communication, whereas those espousing grammar-translation saw in their learning intellectual exercise and a passport to 'great literatures'. The inductive approach met with more spectacular, though short-lived, success in the form of AUDIOLINGUALISM, which forbade the giving of 'grammatical explanations', and which sharpened the assumption underlying the inductive approach that a language was learnt through imitation, practice and habit formation by drawing, for its theoretical underpinnings, on the work of the behaviourist psychologists and, ultimately, their conditioning experiments (see BEHAVIOURISM). Indeed, overt articulation was given to the idea that language learning was 'mechanistic', an idea which, since the theoretical, if not total practical, rejection of audiolingualism, has not been further advocated in the same terms.

To the above must be added that those favouring an inductive approach did not usually believe in exposing learners to the target language at random. The notion that language learning should proceed from the simple to the complex, in terms of both lexis and grammar, is a very old one. Thus, while teachers using inductive methods did not, on the whole, offer explanations, or else, in the manner of Marcel and Gouin, for example, believed that analysis (inductive learning) should precede synthesis (explicit ordering of what had been learnt), they had available to themselves some graded and sequenced inventory of the grammatical points to be contained in the teaching materials, these points constituting a STRUCTURAL SYLLABUS. Again, grading and sequencing became greatly formalized during the era of audiolingualism, though it was this time influenced by the then prevailing orthodoxy that the greatest difficulties for learners would occur at the points of greatest divergence between the native and target languages (an axiom contested in, for example, Corder, 1973), so that the 'divergent' structures of the latter would require the most intensive practice (see CONTRASTIVE ANALYSIS). Thus the view was not that grammar could not be taught, since it was possible, in the interests of efficient learning, to systematize the presentation of it, or rather, to orchestrate the occurrence of structural points within the teaching materials, but that it was either unnecessary or even harmful to teach it explicitly, at least in the first instance. Imitation and practice would lead to the assimilation and retention of structural generalities. As a final but speculative

note here, it may be that those favouring the inductive principle have tended to regard grammar as a 'natural phenomenon' (*meaning* 5) whereas those embracing the deductive approach may betray through their not infrequent prescriptivism the belief that grammar can be imposed upon a language from outside. For further information on the *deductive* versus *inductive* approaches, see Mackey (1965: 141–51); Rivers (1981: 25–7), who uses the terms 'formalism' and 'activism', though to the same effect; Stern (1983: 75–80), who urges caution in interpreting language teaching history, and Titone (1968).

The work of Chomsky opened up a new perspective on the meaning of 'grammar' (*meaning* 6), while developing and formalizing the idea, going back at least to the Port Royal philosopher grammarians and to Humboldt, that children come into the world equipped with a 'theory' of the form of human languages, or a blueprint of those characteristics of languages shared universally, and with natural heuristics enabling them to acquire a particular language by homing in on its specific features as a sub-set of universal features. This idea, the Language Acquisition Device hypothesis, as it became known, constituted a strong rebuttal of 'mechanistic' views of language learning, and, indeed, widely established the term 'acquisition' (rather than 'learning') for the process engaged in by the child assimilating the mother tongue (see ACQUISITION/ LEARNING). Controversy arose among applied linguistics as to whether the innate heuristics continued to function indefinitely or whether there came a cut-off point (at first pinpointed as puberty) at which their functioning ceased, so that further languages had to be learnt rather than acquired, that is, through effort and with the help of adult cognitive capacities (see CRITICAL PERIOD HYPOTHESIS, INNATENESS HYPOTHESIS).

Arguing the case that innate heuristics persisted into adulthood, if allowed to work for themselves, the linguists Newmark and

Reibel (the founders of the COGNITIVE ANTI-METHOD) published in 1968 the paper 'Necessity and sufficiency in language learning', elaborating upon Newmark's earlier article 'How not to interfere with language learning'. In their joint paper, they claim (Lester, 1970: 235–6) that:

the necessary and sufficient conditions for a human being to learn a language are already known: a language will be learned by a normal human being if and only if particular, whole instances of language use are modeled for him and if his own particular acts using the language are selectively reinforced.

They wish to see the focus taken off 'mastery of language structure' and transferred to 'mastery of language use', but while it is their purpose to establish the overriding importance of the latter in devising materials, the crux of their thesis is that the grammar of the target language will be acquired naturally, so that they 'abandon the notion of structural grading and structural ordering of exercise material in favor of situational ordering' (p. 239). Provided the focus is on use, grammar will take care of itself, even though, as they say with reference to the child learner, this grammar will be 'far more complex than any yet formulated by any linguist' (p. 236), and here they use the word 'grammar' in two senses, first, as an internalized grammar in the Chomskyan sense, and second, as the linguist's account of it. Thus, though they do in fact speak of the *induction* of 'a grammar' (p. 236), they are plainly not thinking of induction of the 'grammar of the language' through imitation and practice, but of the mentalistic process of arriving at a personal grammar through creative construction, and are not at all opposed to the idea of random exposure to the target language. While it is not stated expressly, the implication is that grammar in this sense, that is, the learner's grammar, cannot be taught, though conditions can be provided in which it can unfold. Newmark and Reibel further attempted to translate

their ideas into practice through a 'minimal language-teaching programme', but the account of it (Newmark, 1969) leaves many questions unanswered.

A different direction was inspired, at least in part, by another strand of Chomsky's work: his division between competence, as the native speaker's tacit knowledge of the mother tongue, and performance, as instances of language in use (see COMPETENCE/ PERFORMANCE), and this direction is referred to under COGNITIVE CODE. In stark contrast to Newmark and Reibel's position, however, it is assumed in cognitive code learning theory, as the name suggests, that learners should be consciously aware of the relationships between varying structures. It rests plainly on the view that grammar can be taught, and is to be learnt deductively.

Not unrelated to the position of Newmark and Reibel is that of Krashen, who, together with Terrell, developed the NATURAL APPROACH (Krashen and Terrell, 1988), the theoretical beginnings of which were summarized by Krashen in 1981. Two points of prime relevance for this discussion emerge from Krashen's writings: (1) Learners of a foreign language may both *acquire* and *learn*. By *acquiring* is meant inducing or 'picking up' the language through exposure to it, and by *learning* is meant gaining formal 'encyclopedic' knowledge of it, such that a learner can express the fact, for example, that in a given language the subject and verb must agree in number and person. Acquisition, then, implies the building up of a grammar through creative construction (see CREATIVE CONSTRUCTION THEORY) and learning, the conscious amassing of knowledge 'about the language'. The former process can be assisted – as in the view of Newmark and Reibel, through supplying the necessary and sufficient conditions – but is not one which can be 'taught', whereas learning can be assisted through teaching. However, according to Krashen, if there is to be spontaneous language use, this will spring from the acquired system, though the learnt system may, in certain specified circumstances, intervene before an utterance from the acquired system leaves the mouth (and presumably can intervene afterwards where the medium of communication is writing) and 'monitor' it, that is, check it for accuracy, and, if necessary, correct it. Thus the learning of formal grammar does not assist in spontaneous production, but can to some extent modify what is produced (see MONITOR MODEL). In Krashen's conception of acquisition and learning, there is no 'interface' between the two in the sense that what has been learnt cannot pass into the acquired system for spontaneous use. (2) Krashen concludes, on the basis of a number of 'MORPHEME ACQUISITION STUDIES' (sources cited in Krashen, 1981, and Krashen and Terrell, 1988), that is, studies examining the acquisition of morphemes such as 'person', 'number', 'present' and 'past' and their exponents in a particular language, that there is *grossly speaking* a 'natural order' for their acquisition applying across all learners and all languages (see NATURAL ORDER HYPOTHESIS). Pienemann (1985), together with various other writers, has noted that there are different possible responses to the suggestion that there is a universal natural order. One is to abandon any attempt to present language input in any systematic order, since learners will apply their 'built-in syllabuses' to whatever language is presented. A second possible response is for teachers to attempt to follow the 'natural order' in the classroom. Pienemann himself explores this second suggestion, and considers in some detail what it would mean for syllabus designers and teachers to present input in a way which, at the very least, does not deliberately violate what is known about the natural order (see TEACHABILITY HYPOTHESIS).

A methodology such as Prabhu's PROCEDURAL SYLLABUS (see also TASK-BASED TEACHING) is again not unrelated in its underpinnings to those of Newmark and Reibel, on the one hand, and those of Krashen and Terrell on the other, but draws less conspicuously, or perhaps less *technically*, on the idea of grammar as a property of mind associated with natural heuristics permitting the construction of grammars. Yet for Prabhu also, grammar will 'grow' in the mind in the course of prosecuting tasks through the medium of the foreign language. What he seems to wish to cultivate in learners is what Leibniz categorized as *cognitio clara distincta inadequata* (roughly glossed: 'knowledge sufficient to perform a task, but without understanding the principles') – not, as the *inadequata* might suggest – an inadequate knowledge, but the sort of knowledge which a technician needs, in contrast to *cognitio clara distincta adequata* (again, roughly glossed: 'knowledge of the principles underlying a task'), the sort of theoretical knowledge pursued by a scientist. To this extent he makes a distinction between a user of language and a linguistician. The former does not need to possess a fully conscious knowledge of the way in which a language works, whereas the latter strives for this. Thus, for the purposes of practical language learning and use, Prabhu would appear to take the view that teaching formal grammar, or teaching grammar formally, is neither necessary nor useful.

There is a midway position between the 'interventionist' ('teach them formal grammar') and the 'non-interventionist' ('teaching them grammar is a waste of time') schools, which sees the teaching of formal grammar not necessarily as corresponding to direct 'input material', but as a 'CONSCIOUSNESS RAISING' activity which can help learners to focus on the *form* of what they produce, and not simply the content. An initial discussion of this position is to be found in Cook (1991: 28–9). (See also RATE/ROUTE IN SLA.)

A myth of recent years is that the communicative approach to language teaching (see COMMUNICATIVE METHODOLOGY) 'has no place for grammar' in the formal sense. This was never proposed by Wilkins (1973, 1976), the instigator of NOTIONAL/FUNCTIONAL

SYLLABUSES. In fact, he was concerned from the outset (1973), in considering how Europeans might learn each other's languages, with the definition of a 'common grammatical core' that they would have to acquire. While his focus was not grammar as such, but 'expressive needs' divided between, on the one hand, the SEMANTICO-GRAMMATICAL CATEGORIES (including: time, quantity, space, matter, case, deixis) and, on the other, CATEGORIES OF COMMUNICATIVE FUNCTION (including: modality, moral discipline and evaluation, suasion, argument, rational enquiry and exposition, personal emotions, emotional relations, interpersonal relations), he made it very clear that the former categories, at least, 'interact significantly with grammatical categories. This is why they contribute to the definition of the grammatical content of learning.' This 'grammatical content' would appear to mean grammar in the more formal sense. None the less, as indicated above, this part of the message seems to have been largely ignored in some quarters for a considerable time, the emphasis being placed on the sending and receiving of communicatively 'authentic messages' between teacher and learners and learners and learners. With the realization, however, that effective communication cannot take place unless 'messages' are not just phrased appropriately but also accurately, there has been in certain quarters a noticeable return to the teaching of formal grammar in the foreign language class. This points up the current debate, which is almost a replication of the earlier one between inductive and deductive teaching. Yet there is a difference. This lies in the fact that no one can now seriously deny the importance of natural heuristics in the acquisition of grammar. The dividing line is between those who say that natural heuristics account for practically all, on the one hand, and those who say, on the other, that natural heuristics account for much, but that there is a close interface between the acquired and the learnt systems, and that learning can greatly assist acquisition, or is even necessary to perfect it. Inasmuch as the communicative approach to language teaching still exists, it may be said to be characterized by the latter position. See Roberts (1982) and, for an incisive discussion of the role of grammar in communication, Widdowson (1990: chapter 6: 'Grammar, and nonsense, and learning'). (See also 'PRESENTATION – PRACTICE – PRODUCTION' SEQUENCE.)

While the extent to which grammar is taught explicitly in the foreign language classroom today is not quantifiable, in many countries and situations language teaching is still based on a traditional grammatical analysis, and explicit teaching of grammar continues. There is no wish to suggest here that this in itself is unproductive; indeed, for the right sort of students, and at the right stage in learning, formal acquaintance with grammar provides a framework for organizing new knowledge and undoubtedly promotes accuracy; at least, this observation, though open to challenge, is in line with the trend noted in the last paragraph. However, over the centuries, the teaching and learning of grammar have often been slavish, with learning done by rote, about which there is little that is 'deductive'. It should also be noted that though the phrase 'grammatical explanation' is deeply ingrained, teachers do not in fact offer *explanations*, because there are as yet no explanations of such a phenomenon available. What they do is offer *descriptive statements*, and they need to ensure that their descriptions correspond with reality and are not drawn from some outdated, prescriptive grammar book. Again, if grammar, particularly when taught in the mother tongue, is accorded undue time, the natural heuristics of learners will have little chance to function. For further wide-ranging discussion, see Rutherford and Sharwood Smith (1988) and Bygate and others (1994).

For techniques of teaching grammar, see Kelly (1969), Cook (1991), Rutherford (1987) and Batstone (1994).

## GRAMMAR AND THE MOTHER TONGUE

While it was once usual for pupils in secondary education to be taught the (traditional) grammar of their own language, albeit through the dull mechanics of 'clause analysis' and 'parsing', the emphasis in education at least in the English-speaking countries over the last few decades has been on 'creativity' in the mother tongue, a trend accompanied by the abandonment of formal grammar. Some feel that this has led to deterioration in literacy, and so, for example, the relatively new National Curriculum for England and Wales prescribes attention to formalities, though some of these, such as punctuation, may be argued to pertain only tenuously to grammar. See Kingman (1988) and Hudson (1992).

In relation to both foreign language and mother tongue, one still ends up with the question as to whether grammar can be taught or whether one can only facilitate its learning. Much depends, as should be evident from the above, on how the term 'grammar' is interpreted.

## BIBLIOGRAPHY

Batstone, R. (1994). *Grammar*. Oxford: Oxford University Press.*

Bygate, M., Tonkyn, A. and Williams, E. (eds) (1994). *Grammar and the Language Teacher*. New York: Prentice Hall.*

Cook, V. (1991). *Second Language Learning and Language Teaching*. London: Edward Arnold.

Corder, S. P. (1973). *Introducing Applied Linguistics*. Harmondsworth: Penguin Books.

Gouin, F. (1880). *L'art d'enseigner et d'étudier les langues*. Paris: Librairie Sandoz et Fischbacher.

——(1882). *The Art of Studying and Teaching Languages*, trans. H. Swan and V. Bétis. London: George Philip.

Hudson, R. A. (1992). *Teaching Grammar: A guide for the national curriculum*. Oxford: Blackwell.

Humboldt, Wilhelm von (1836). *Über die Verschiedenheit des menschlichen Sprachbaues und ihren Einfluß auf die geistige Entwicklung des Menschengeschlechts*. Berlin: Druckerei der Königlichen Akademie der Wirtschaften. [On the variation of the structure of human language and its influence on the mental development of the human race.]

Kelly, L. G. (1969). *25 Centuries of Language Teaching*. Rowley, MA: Newbury House.

Kingman, J. (1988). *Report of the Commission of Enquiry into the teaching of English language appointed by the Secretary of State under the chairmanship of Sir John Kingman FRS*. London: HMSO.

Krashen, S. D. (1981). *Second Language Acquisition and Second Language Learning*. Oxford: Pergamon.

Krashen, S. and Terrell, T. D. (1988). *The Natural Approach: Language acquisition in the classroom*. London: Prentice Hall.

Leibniz, G. W. (1965). Meditationes de cognitione, veritate et ideis. In G. W. Leibniz, *Kleinere Schriften zur Metaphysik*. Darmstadt: Wissenschaftliche Buchgesellschaft, 32–65. [Meditations on knowledge, truth and ideas.]

Lester, M. (ed.) (1970). *Readings in Applied Transformational Grammar*. New York: Holt, Rinehart and Winston.

Mackey, W. F. (1965). *Language Teaching Analysis*. London: Longman.

Marcel, C. (1853). *Language as a Means of Culture and International Communication or Manual of the Teacher and Learner of Languages*. 2 vols. London: Chapman and Hall.

Newmark, L. (1966). How not to interfere with language learning. *International Journal of American Linguistics*, 32/1, Part II, 77–83. [Reprinted in 1970 in M. Lester (ed.), *Readings in Applied Transformational Grammar*. New York: Holt, Rinehart and Winston, 219–27.]

——(1971). A minimal language-teaching program. In P. Pimsleur and T. Quinn (eds), *The Psychology of Second Language Learning*. Cambridge: Cambridge University Press, 11–18.

Newmark, L. and Reibel, D. (1968). Necessity and sufficiency in language learning. *International Review of Applied Linguistics*, 6/2, 145–64. [Reprinted in 1970 in M. Lester (ed.), *Readings in Applied Transformational Grammar*. New York: Holt, Rinehart and Winston, 228–52.]

Pienemann, M. (1985). Learnability and syllabus construction. In K. Hyltenstam and M. Pienemann (eds), *Modelling and Assessing*

*Second Language Acquisition*. Clevedon: Multilingual Matters, 23–75.

Pimsleur, P. and Quinn T. (eds) (1971). *The Psychology of Second Language Learning*. Cambridge: Cambridge University Press.

Prabhu, N. S. (1987). *Second Language Pedagogy*. Oxford: Oxford University Press.

Rivers, W. M. (1981). *Teaching foreign language skills*. 2nd edn. Chicago: University of Chicago Press.

Roberts, J. T. (1982). Recent developments in ELT, Part I. In *Language Teaching*, 15/2, 94–110. [Reprinted with Part II in 1982 in V. Kinsella (ed.), *Surveys 2: Eight state-of-the-art articles on key areas in language teaching*. Cambridge: Cambridge University Press, 96–141.]

Rutherford, W. and Sharwood Smith, M. (eds) (1988). *Grammar and Second Language Teaching*. New York: Newbury House.

Rutherford, W. E. (1987). *Second Language Grammar: Learning and teaching*. London: Longman.

Stern, H. H. (1983). *Fundamental Concepts of Language Teaching*. Oxford: Oxford University Press.

Titone, R. (1968). *Teaching Foreign Languages: An historical sketch*. Washington, DC: Georgetown University Press.

Widdowson, H. G. (1990). *Aspects of Language Teaching*. Oxford: Oxford University Press.

Wilkins, D. A. (1973). The linguistic and situational content of the common core in a Unit/credit system. In *Systems Development in Adult Language Learning*. Strasbourg: Council of Europe.

——(1976). *Notional Syllabuses*. Oxford: Oxford University Press.

JTR

**grammar-translation** Introduced in the mid-nineteenth century, grammar-translation is still used widely in foreign language teaching today. It is for monolingual classes, and concentrates upon the written language, presenting the language under instruction through explicit statement of rules in the students' L1, then practising and testing these rules through the translation of sentences. In English language teaching, from the end of the nineteenth century onwards, it has come under fierce attack from advocates of various types of DIRECT METHOD, and despite its continued use, has in the twentieth century been ridiculed and ignored.

In grammar-translation language teaching, the structures of the language being taught are graded and presented in units (often equivalent to a lesson or the chapter of a textbook). (See also GRAMMATICAL SYLLABUS.) In each unit a list of new vocabulary items is presented together with translation equivalents; grammar rules are explained in the L1; there are sentences for translation, both into and out of the L2, employing only the vocabulary and grammar encountered in the current and earlier units. These exercises are regarded as a means of instruction, practice and assessment; L2 competence is measured by the accuracy of the lexical and grammatical equivalence attained in translation.

Introduced in the gymnasia of Prussia in the mid-nineteenth century, the grammar-translation method spread rapidly, and it is still used widely today (Howatt, 1984: 131–8). Under its influence written translation exercises became the central feature of language teaching syllabuses: in textbooks for self-study, in schools and in universities. Grammar-translation soon came under attack, however, and at the turn of the century, the self-styled 'Reform Movement' criticized it for ignoring the spoken language, for encouraging false notions of equivalence and for presenting isolated sentences rather than connected texts (Howatt, 1984: 173) (see REFORM SCHOOL). The influential phonetician and language-teaching theorist Henry Sweet ([1899], 1964: 101) ridiculed the kind of sentence found in a typical translation exercise as 'a bag into which is crammed as much grammatical and lexical information as possible', and he produced parodies in illustration such as: 'The merchant is swimming with the gardener's son, but the Dutchman has the fine gun' (Sweet

[1899], 1964: 74). Such sentences, as many have observed, are highly artificial: divorced from purpose, context and actual use. Other attacks on grammar-translation have cited the demotivating difficulty of translating from L1 to L2, the reinforcement of reliance on processing via the L1, strengthening of L1 interference and a detrimental effect on the acquisition of native-like processing skill and speed (for a summary of such arguments see Stern, 1992: 282–7).

Such criticisms have been devastatingly effective in influencing academic opinion against the use of TRANSLATION IN LANGUAGE TEACHING and it has not yet been reinstated as a theoretically justified activity. Opposition to the use of translation has led to its replacement by the direct method: the teaching of an L2 using that language (and only that language) as a means of instruction. Attitudes to translation have varied from a total ban (as in the Berlitz schools) to an indulgent if reluctant admission of it as a necessary last resort ('a refuge for the incompetent', as Kelly (1969) describes it). Almost all twentieth-century methodologies are species of the direct method (for descriptions and discussion see, *inter alia*, Richards and Rodgers, 1986; Stern, 1992).

Meanwhile grammar-translation has continued to be used especially in secondary schools in many parts of the world; it is one of the few methods which is possible in very large classes, and, being structured and predictable, it can give students a sense of confidence and attainment. It is also suited to teachers whose own command of the L2 may be limited. The teacher of grammar-translation must know both the language being taught and the students' L1. Such teachers have the advantage of understanding the language-specific problems of their students, but have recently been undervalued in favour of NATIVE SPEAKER teachers who do not know their students' L1. Changing circumstances and fashions in ELT have contributed to the decline of grammar-

translation, as the numbers of teachers who do not know both L1 and L2, and the number of classes where students have many different first languages, have grown. A shift of focus from writing to speech, and new theories of second language acquisition which downplay first language interference and conscious knowledge of translation equivalence, have also contributed to the decline.

BIBLIOGRAPHY
Howatt, A. P. R. (1984). *A History of English Language Teaching*. Oxford: Oxford University Press.*
Kelly, L. G. (1969). *25 Centuries of Language Teaching*. Rowley, MA: Newbury House.
Richards, J. C. and Rodgers, T. S. (1986). *Approaches and Methods in Language Teaching*. Cambridge: Cambridge University Press.*
Stern, H. H. (1992). *Issues and Options in Language Teaching*, ed. P. Allen and B. Harley. Oxford: Oxford University Press.* [Chapter 10.]
Sweet, H. (1964). *The Practical Study of Languages: A guide for teachers and learners*, ed. R. Mackin. Oxford: Oxford University Press. [First published in 1899.]

GC

**grammatical syllabus** This is the oldest type of syllabus used in foreign language teaching. It was not until the grammar-translation method became firmly established in the nineteenth century and supplanted the 'classical method', which set out to teach style and rhetoric as well as grammar, that structure came to be seen, until the early 1970s and the proposal of the notional/functional syllabus (see NOTIONAL/FUNCTIONAL SYLLABUSES), as the *major* obstacle facing the language learner, and mastery of structure as the key to understanding and using the target language.

A grammatical syllabus is assembled first by producing a taxonomy of the structures present in the foreign language, usually identified on the basis of 'traditional grammar' (see GRAMMAR). Here 'structures' must be understood in a broad sense, and not simply as pertaining to syntax. From among these structures, a *selection* will next be made as appropriate to the level, duration and purpose of the language course (see Mackey, 1965: 161ff.). The structures selected are then *graded*, that is, assigned comparative values in terms of learning difficulty. This is done according to a 'simplicity metric', which, however, is essentially intuitive, though informed by contrastive knowledge of the learners' mother tongue and the foreign language as well as by experience of teaching the latter. For example, it seems to be universally presumed that 'simple' tenses are more easily learnt than 'compound' tenses, that (in case languages) the nominative is somehow 'primordial' and the oblique cases 'more complex', and that structures which are contrastively 'quite different', as is, reputedly, the French subjunctive for English speakers, must be considered 'difficult' (see CONTRASTIVE ANALYSIS). Finally, the structures are *sequenced*, or put into a certain order in the teaching programme, again largely in accordance with intuitions about how increments in knowledge can be most efficiently procured. For instance, though both the perfect and the pluperfect tense in French are formed with the auxiliary *avoir* or *être* plus the past participle, it might be deemed that the perfect can be taught after the present, since the auxiliaries in this case take the present form (*ai, suis*, etc.), whereas the pluperfect cannot be taught until the imperfect is known, since here the auxiliaries have the imperfect form (*avais, étais*, etc.). It might also be held that the perfect can be taught together with a few time adverbs, such as *hier, l'année dernière, tout à l'heure*, whereas the pluperfect, marking anteriority, cannot be operated without further adverbs, such as *auparavant*, but especially not without conjunctions such as *quand, lorsque, après que*. In addition to prescribing structures to be learnt, a grammatical syllabus, in common with all others, will be accompanied by a list of vocabulary to be memorized. This can again be graded and sequenced (Mackey, 1965: 217ff.).

White's perspective on the grammatical syllabus is that it is to be viewed as 'interventionist', that is, 'external to the learner' and 'determined by authority' (1988: 44ff.). In this light, it may be seen as proceeding from the features of a given language rather than being informed by the path along which people learn languages through 'natural heuristics', and to this extent it conflicts with ideas about the learner's 'internal syllabus' as these are represented in, say, the work of Newmark and Reibel, Krashen and Prabhu (see GRAMMAR TEACHING).

Though holding sway for countless years, the grammatical syllabus has attracted strong criticism, particularly in the present century. Not all the faults ascribed to it are necessarily inherent; some arise from its implementation and have come to be viewed as endemic. Among the criticisms are the following:

(1)   The grammatical syllabus as associated with the grammar-translation method has encouraged the explicit teaching of grammar, given the complexities involved, through the mother tongue, thereby reducing the time available for exposure to the target language. For further discussion of such issues, see GRAMMAR TEACHING.

(2)   Since the grammatical syllabus has often been realized through techniques involving translation between the mother tongue and the foreign language, learners are tempted to cultivate a misguided view of literal translational equivalence.

(3)   The grammatical syllabus has frequently drawn on written rather than spoken language, and sometimes restricted, elevated registers, preparing learners to read and perhaps write in certain fields, but not to speak naturally. Even where inductive methods aimed principally at listening and speaking

have been used, the language presented in the classroom has been 'idealized' and inauthentic.

(4) The teaching of structure, combined with translation and literary lexis, led in the past to what may be termed 'la plume de ma tante' language in the classroom – 'Translate into French: "That is the pen of my gardener's friend's uncle's second cousin." '

(5) Although one would expect the structural syllabus to encourage the learning of syntax above all, Wilkins (1976: 10) makes the observation that 'the inventories found in grammatical syllabuses give insufficient attention to syntax.' The example he gives relates to the teaching of the comparative in English:

the learner will learn such facts as that **older** is in contrast with **old** and **oldest** . . . He will also learn that a comparative adjective co-occurs with **than** and he will probably practise the comparative through syntactic structures like **John is older than Peter**. What the syllabus or the course will never do . . . is make it clear that the comparative occurs in sentences like **the ruins were older to a considerable degree than had originally been thought** or **older than the discovery of electricity was the invention of the steam-engine**.

(6) There is a danger that grammatical and functional categories will be equated. Thus, a teacher might say: 'The imperative is used to give orders.' This is true, but only in part, and might lead to the total misinterpretation 'to give orders, use the imperative.' For further discussion, see Widdowson (1971: 38ff.) and Wilkins (1976: 10f.).

(7) Wilkins (1976: 69ff.), in claiming that courses based on a notional/functional syllabus have 'high SURRENDER VALUE', strongly implies that those based on a grammatical syllabus do not, because whereas the former are attractive to learners 'who may need to cash their investment immediately', having learnt certain rudiments of *communication*, the latter 'are regarded as an investment for the future', that is, have to be followed through to the end before learning, particularly learning how to *communicate*, can be put to use.

Notwithstanding the criticisms, Brumfit has argued (in several places, but here we cite Brumfit 1980 and 1981 as startingpoints) in the context of the grammatical versus the notional/functional syllabus, that (1) it is the teacher's task to systematize knowledge, and that only the grammatical syllabus represents systematization; (2) an optimal syllabus would be based on a grammatical core surrounded by a 'spiral' of fluency, or communicative activities. However, few empirical studies subtend the debates here.

BIBLIOGRAPHY

Brumfit, C. J. (1980). From defining to designing: communicative specifications versus communicative methodology in foreign language teaching. In K. E. Müller (ed.), *The Foreign Language Syllabus*, 1–9.

——(1981). Teaching the 'general' student. In K. Johnson and K. Morrow (eds), *Communication in the Classroom*. Harlow: Longman, 46–51.

CILT (Centre for Information on Language Teaching and Research) (1971). *Science and Technology in a Second Language*. London: CILT.

Johnson, K. and Morrow, K. (eds) (1981). *Communication in the Classroom*. Harlow: Longman.

Mackey, W. F. (1965). *Language Teaching Analysis*. London: Longman.

Müller, K. E. (ed.) (1980). *The Foreign Language Syllabus and Communicative Approaches to Teaching: Proceedings of a European-American Seminar*. Special issue of *Studies in Second Language Acquisition*, 3/1.

White, R. V. (1988). *The ELT Curriculum: Design, innovation and management*. Oxford: Blackwell.

Widdowson, H. G. (1971). The teaching of rhetoric to students of science and technology. In CILT, *Science and Technology in a Second Language*, 38–9.

Wilkins, D. A. (1976). *Notional Syllabuses*. Oxford: Oxford University Press.

JTR

**grammaticality judgements** A special type of acceptability judgement, whereby native speakers of a language identify sentences conforming to grammatical rules, which they know unconsciously. Grammatical sentences may be unacceptable if, for example, they are too long or too complex. Grammaticality judgements have nothing to do with prescriptivism.

BIBLIOGRAPHY
Fromkin, V. and Rodman, R. (1993). *An Introduction to Language*. 5th edn. Fort Worth, TX: Harcourt Brace Jovanovich. [Chapter 3.]

EJ

**group work/pair work** is an integral part of COMMUNICATIVE METHODOLOGY (see Brumfit, 1984). They are often based on an INFORMATION/OPINION GAP. The size of groups usually ranges from three to eight students. They reduce the traditional student-teacher polarity, providing greater opportunity for the NEGOTIATION OF MEANING and language acquisition during student–student interaction. Concern has been expressed that the exposure to inaccurate INTERLANGUAGE talk produced in these contexts can lead to FOSSILIZATION. See Ellis (1994) and Chaudron (1988) for discussion of the research perspective, which has also compared interaction in dyads and groups with teacher-centred lessons according to variables such as sex and proficiency. (See also INTERACTION HYPOTHESIS.)

BIBLIOGRAPHY
Brumfit, C. (1984). *Communicative Methodology in Language Teaching*. Cambridge: Cambridge University Press.
Chaudron, C. (1988). *Second Language Classrooms*. Cambridge: Cambridge University Press.
Ellis, R. (1994). *The Study of Second Language Acquisition*. Oxford: Oxford University Press.

CLF

# H

**here-and-now principle** The content of speech addressed to young L1 learners is oriented to what they know: topics concern the immediate environment (the 'here') and current events (the 'now'). Since L1 acquisition is rapid and successful, the assumption is that the here-and-now helps learners decode the linguistic input they receive. By extension, the here-and-now principle in L2 learning proposes that input which makes use of the immediate context will enable L2 learners to identify rapidly the linguistic properties of the L2. (See MONITOR MODEL.)

BIBLIOGRAPHY
Krashen, S. (1981). *Second Language Acquisition and Second Language Learning.* Oxford: Pergamon.
RH

**high/low input generator** A distinction made in the context of an empirical study by Seliger (1977) to refer to learners at the extremes of participation in a classroom setting, it being understood that active participation was of value because of its capacity to generate input for the learners involved, input (see also INPUT HYPOTHESIS) itself being held to be the key to linguistic progress. Seliger found a positive relationship between high input generation and proficiency, a finding challenged in later research by Day.

BIBLIOGRAPHY
Day, R. R. (1984). Student participation in the ESL classroom or some imperfections in practice. *Language Learning*, 34, 69–101.

Seliger, H. W. (1977). Does practice make perfect? A study of interaction patterns and L2 competence. *Language Learning*, 27, 263–78.
RLA

**humanistic approaches** The meaning of *humanistic* as used in the literature of language teaching, especially in the United States, is only tenuously connected with the usual understandings of that word. Indeed, the terms *humanism, humanist* and *humanistic* are applied subjectively in the literature, but those employing them convey by *humanism* and *humanistic approaches* language teaching respecting the integrity of learners, allowing for personal growth and responsibility, taking psychological and affective factors into account and representing 'whole-person learning'. Difficulties with the term 'humanism' itself are attested to even by one of its best-known supporters, Stevick (1982: 7ff.).

'Humanism' is also a reaction against teaching not perceived to entertain similar priorities, and use of the term in this context may have come about to mark opposition to 'dehumanizing' influences. Moskowitz (1978), for example, quotes the following from 'psychologist Arthur W. Combs':

Teachers have long been expert in providing information . . . Our major failures do not arise from lack of information. They come from . . . our inability to help students discover the personal meaning of the information we so extravagantly provide them . . . Our preoccupation with . . . information . . . has dehumanized our schools, alienated our youth, and produced a system irrelevant for most students.

'Humanistic' approaches are not confined to language teaching, but if they loom large in this connection, this is because language is regarded as primordial in human development and interaction. Possibly the precursors of the 'humanistic' movement in language teaching were Jakobovits and Gordon (1974), who, after outlining the contents of C. A. Reich's book *The Greening of America*, discuss *The Greening of the FL Classroom* and the non-violent evolution allegedly needed to turn it into a place in which there is freedom to teach and to learn, but their book was relatively unsuccessful compared with those of Curran (1976), Moskowitz (1978) and Stevick (1980). A major inspiration for all such sources, however, appears to have been found in Rogers (1951, 1970, 1979).

The polemics associated with 'humanism' in language teaching preclude definitive categorization of approaches into *humanistic* versus *non-humanistic*, but as a generalization, the representatives of 'humanism' view 'traditional methods', or any other methods informed more by linguistics than psychology, as 'non-humanistic'. Stevick (1980) sees 'humanistic' qualities in SILENT WAY, COMMUNITY LANGUAGE LEARNING and SUGGESTOPAEDIA.

Given the lack of objectivity, an analysis of 'humanism' perhaps starts best with initiatives explicitly designating themselves 'humanistic', and here the writings of Moskovitz on *humanistic techniques* are illustrative. Her seminal work, *Caring and Sharing in the Foreign Language Class* (1978), contains a collection of techniques aimed at 'humanizing' the classroom, the teacher and the learners. She endorses the dismal picture of school painted by Combs (see above) but claims that:

Today there is an area of education receiving attention, and its spread seems related to concern for personal development, self-acceptance, and acceptance by others, in other words, making students more human . . . Humanistic education is concerned with educating the whole person – the intellectual and the emotional dimensions. It . . . is most directly related to what is referred to as the 'third force', or humanistic psychology, and the human potential movement.

Among the premises underlying 'humanistic' education, Moskovitz enumerates these:

(1) A principal purpose of education is to provide learning and an environment that facilitate the achievement of the full potential of students.
(2) Personal growth as well as cognitive growth is a responsibility of the school. Therefore education should deal with both dimensions of humans – the cognitive or intellectual and the affective or emotional.
(3) For learning to be significant, feelings must be recognized and put to use.
(4) Significant learning is discovered for oneself.
(5) Human beings want to actualize their potential.
(6) Having healthy relationships with other classmates is more conducive to learning.
(7) Learning about oneself is a motivating factor in learning.
(8) Increasing one's self-esteem is a motivating factor in learning.

There are a number of caveats on classroom activities, among which are:

(1) Accentuate the positive and avoid a negative focus.
(2) Low-risk, i.e. non-personally threatening activities, should be used. High risk ones would include:
Something I wish had never happened.
What I dislike about myself.
My saddest memory . . .

The reverse of the above would represent low-risk activities:

Something I'm glad happened.
What I like about myself.
My happiest memory . . .

Some would question how far the practical suggestions are consistent with the philosophy expressed, and how far they do not in fact threaten the ego. An example (1978: 94–6) would be the activity:

**I'M ATTRACTIVE, YOU'RE ATTRACTIVE**
Purposes:
*Affective –*
To give students the opportunity to verbalize before others something they like about themselves, since customarily we are meant to keep this to ourselves.
To encourage students to really look at their peers and focus on seeing the beauty of others.
*Linguistic –*
To give practice in using the expression 'I like'.
To practice the vocabulary of parts of the body.
Levels: *All levels.*

A suggested preface to the activity includes the following:

Today we're going to share some things we don't often share. We all like some things about our physical appearance and often want to change others. What I'd like you to do is to think of something about your physical appearance that you especially like . . . You're also going to take a few moments now to look at each member in your group, noticing one thing that you really like about the physical appearance of each person. When you decide what it is, write it down, including the person's name. It might be that you like one person's hair . . . someone else's slim waistline or smile . . . Since we're not accustomed to saying these things about ourselves and others, it might feel a little embarrassing at first, but that will soon pass when you see how nice it feels to hear these things said.

Practitioners must decide for themselves on the value, linguistic or educational, of such an exercise. Some will also question the extent to which language teachers should act as 'behavioural engineers' or 'therapists', and ask themselves about the extent to which some matters fall within the public, whereas others fall within the private domain. Such issues are discussed provocatively by Brumfit (1982), who says: ' "Humanistic" is a good thing to be . . . [but] . . . Any movement which over-emphasizes experience risks degenerating towards moral chaos, for there are no shared safeguards.'

It is no doubt true that the classroom can give rise to anxiety, and be boring and demoralizing, and that it is the task of the caring teacher to cultivate a good atmosphere. Yet 'humanism' which arrogates to itself this designation rests upon gross assumptions, and while some will see in the classroom dark forces to combat, others, with more positive experiences, even at the hands of grammar-translation teachers, may wonder what sort of windmills self-styled 'humanism' tilts at. It is at least arguable that 'humanism' resides, in the end, more in human relationships in the classroom, including that between teacher and learners, than in methods and techniques. In this light, 'humanism' is not quite so new as some might think, the following passage, for example, being found in Marcel (1853: 182):

. . . a man may be an accomplished scholar or an adept in science, and, yet, be an indifferent teacher. To stoop from the pride of superior attainment; to conceive even the embarrassments that entangle the beginner; to become identified with the feelings and faculties of children; to anticipate and remove the obstacles in their way to knowledge; to curb and regulate their tempers, and, what is still more difficult, one's own; to awaken and sustain attention, and know when to stop, so as to avoid fatigue; to lead by easy steps, through a path which is to them a rugged one, and strewing it with flowers instead of thorns; to slacken one's own steps, in order to keep pace with the pupil, instead of expecting or insisting on gigantic strides; all this is the result of long and careful training; it demands a rare assemblage of qualities.

Stevick (1980) and La Forge (1983) will provide further insights into the subject of 'humanism'. A well-balanced debate on the subject is presented in *ELT Documents*, no. 113.

BIBLIOGRAPHY
Brumfit, C. (1982). Some humanistic doubts about humanistic language teaching. In *Humanistic Approaches: An empirical view*. ELT Documents 113. London: British Council, 11–19.

Curran, C. A. (1976). *Counseling-learning in Second Languages*. Apple River, IL: Apple River Press.

Jakobovits, L. A. and Gordon, B. (1974). *The Context of Foreign Language Teaching*. Rowley, MA: Newbury House.

La Forge, P. G. (1983). *Counseling and Culture in Second Language Acquisition*. Oxford: Pergamon.

Marcel, C. (1853). *Language as a Means of Culture and International Communication or Manual of the Teacher and Learner of Languages*. 2 vols. London: Chapman and Hall.

Moskovitz, G. (1978). *Caring and Sharing in the Foreign Language Class*. Rowley, MA: Newbury House.*

Rogers, C. (1951). *Client-centered Therapy*. Boston: Houghton Mifflin.

——(1970). *On Becoming a Person*. New edn. Boston: Houghton Mifflin.

——(1979). *Freedom to Learn: A view of what education might become*. New edn. Columbus, OH: Merrill.

Stevick, E. W. (1980). *Teaching Languages: A way and ways*. Rowley, MA: Newbury House.

——(1982). Humanism. In *Humanistic Approaches: An empirical view*. ELT Documents 113. London: British Council, 7–10.*

JTR

**hypothesis** Classically a prediction derived from a theory, such that if the prediction itself proves false then the theory must be questioned. For example, if a learning theory predicts that language learners will benefit more from uncontrolled practice than from controlled practice with grammatical explanations, we can therefore hypothesize, for the sake of an experiment, that a given group of learners will make significantly more practical linguistic progress engaging in uncontrolled practice than a parallel group engaging in controlled practice with grammatical explanations. If this result is not obtained, then the original learning theory will need to be re-examined.

The term is often more loosely used, in the field of research on language teaching and learning, to refer to any expected finding, regardless of its logical relationship to a given theory, and sometimes to any general attempt to 'explain' language development (e.g. Krashen's INPUT HYPOTHESIS). (See also RESEARCH METHODOLOGY FOR LANGUAGE LEARNING.)

BIBLIOGRAPHY:
Larsen-Freeman, D. and Long, M. H. (1991). *An Introduction to Second Language Acquisition Research*. London: Longman. [See especially chapter 7 on 'Theories in second language acquisition'.]

RLA

**hypothesis formation and testing in SLA** This is one view of how learners acquire L2s. They encounter samples of L2 data, make a generalization on the basis of the samples, then test the generalization against further data. For example, a learner encountering *Is Mary here?* might form the hypothesis that English yes/no questions are formed by fronting a verb. This would lead to over-generalizations like: *\*Lives Mary here?* The learner tests such cases against other samples of English data for correctness. Hypothesis formation and testing accounts of SLA are incompatible with UNIVERSAL GRAMMAR accounts, which see acquisition as deterministic: samples of data trigger a limited set of predetermined mental options, and hypothesis formation is unnecessary.

RH

# I

**i + 1 (i plus one)** is a concept associated with the NATURAL APPROACH, which rests on the premise that there is a 'natural order' for language acquisition and that learners will acquire a structure when 'ready for it'. In the classroom, learners are supplied with 'comprehensible input' corresponding to their current level of competence (*i*) but also containing new language data relating to the next stage (*+1*) towards which they are moving 'along some natural order'. See Krashen and Terrell (1988: 32ff.). (See also MONITOR MODEL and COMPREHENSIBLE INPUT.)

BIBLIOGRAPHY
Krashen, S. D. and Terrell, T. D. (1988). *The Natural Approach: Language acquisition in the classroom*. New York: Prentice Hall.

JTR

**immersion programmes**   An immersion programme is one in which school pupils are taught the normal school curriculum through the medium of a language which is not their native one. The classic case can be found in Canada, where immersion programmes appear to have originated. Here the parents of native English-speaking children can opt to have their children attend schools where the medium of instruction is French. More generally, the defining property of immersion programmes is that children speaking one language natively are taught *as a group* by teachers who speak a second language. This is to be distinguished from language *submersion*, where a single child who is a native speaker of one language is placed in a school where not only the teachers but also the other pupils are speakers of the second language. This would be the case where, say, a Persian-speaking child from Iran arriving with his or her parents in Britain is placed in an ordinary primary school classroom with English-speaking children.

The impetus for most immersion programmes appears to be cultural rather than linguistic. There is a perception on the part of one group within a community that it would benefit their children to acquire the language and learn about the culture of another group within the same community. In the Canadian case it appears that, initially, a group of middle-class English-speaking parents persuaded educators to set up an experimental immersion programme to enable their children 'to appreciate the traditions and culture of French-speaking Canadians as well as English-speaking Canadians' (Baker, 1993: 158).

Various types of immersion programme are usually distinguished, depending upon the age at which learners are immersed and the extent of the immersion. *Early immersion* involves children in an immersion programme from the beginning of schooling, at the age of 5 or 6. *Middle immersion* typically involves children starting in the middle years of primary or junior school education at around the age of 9–10. *Late immersion* concerns children who enter the programme early in secondary schooling, usually between the ages of 11 and 13. The extent of the immersion may be *total* (i.e. all of the curriculum is taught through the second language) or *partial* (with usually around 50%

of the curriculum taught through the second language). Even with total immersion, the proportion of the curriculum taught through the second language usually decreases after the first few years, with certain subjects coming to be dealt with in the native language. Moreover, in most total immersion programmes children continue to use their native language outside the classroom, i.e. in the playground, in the dining hall, etc. In Canada, according to the Canadian Education Association, early total immersion is the most popular form of immersion, followed by late total immersion (cited in Baker, 1993: 158).

It is generally held that the first recognized immersion programme took place as an experiment in Montreal in 1965, and involved English speakers taught through the medium of French (Lambert and Tucker, 1972). Since then, Canadian programmes have expanded to involve over 250,000 English-speaking pupils in French schools, and other parts of the world have adopted the strategy (for example, immersion in Catalan and Basque for L1 Spanish-speaking children, and immersion in Welsh and Irish for L1 English-speaking children: see Baker, 1993, chapter 11).

Canada has not only seen a considerable growth in immersion programmes themselves, but it is also probably the country in which the effects of immersion on children's linguistic and general intellectual development have been the most intensively studied (with over 1,000 such studies according to Baker, 1993: 162). A number of general observations have emerged from these studies (see for example, Swain and Lapkin, 1982; Lapkin, Swain and Shapson, 1990; Harley, 1991; and Baker, 1993) which are summarized below.

First, early immersion students lag behind their monolingual peers in *literacy* skills (reading, spelling, punctuation) *in the native language* for the first few years. (This is hardly surprising, given that for most of the time they are not concerned with literacy

in the native language.) However, after the first few years they catch up with their peers, and then perform as well as, and on some measures better than, those peers. The lag in literacy skills is much shorter for late immersion students (but then presumably they will already have spent a number of years in primary school developing native language literacy skills). Immersion programmes have no detrimental effect whatsoever on spoken skills in the native language.

Second, children who undergo early total immersion attain near-native proficiency in listening and reading comprehension of the second language by the end of the programme (around the age of 11). In production, however, they do not achieve the same grammatical accuracy as comparable children who are native speakers of the L2. Early partial immersion and late immersion students are less successful than early total immersion students.

Third, immersion programmes have no detrimental effects on the general intellectual development of children. In terms of success in the school curriculum, early total immersion children perform as well as monolingual peers in all areas. However, early partial immersion and late immersion students appear to have more difficulty than comparable monolingual peers with subjects like mathematics and science, at least in the initial stages of immersion.

BIBLIOGRAPHY
Baker, C. (1993). *Foundations of Bilingual Education and Bilingualism.* Clevedon: Multilingual Matters.*
Harley, B. (1991). Directions in immersion research. *Journal of Multilingual and Multicultural Development*, 12, 9–19.
Lambert, W. and Tucker, R. (1972). *Bilingual Education of Children: The St Lambert experiment.* Rowley, MA: Newbury House.
Lapkin, S., Swain, M. and Shapson, S. (1990). French immersion research agenda for the 90s. *Canadian Modern Language Review*, 46, 638–74.

Swain, M. and Lapkin, S. (1982). *Evaluating Bilingual Education: A Canadian case study.* Clevedon: Multilingual Matters.*

RH

**individual differences** Many SLA theories assume all learners are similar, but there is now a good body of research concerned with learner differences. These are often categorized into COGNITIVE VARIABLES, AFFECTIVE VARIABLES, and PERSONALITY VARIABLES. Although much of the research seeks straight correlations between learning success and chosen variables, the need is increasingly felt for models relating these variables to each other, and to other relevant ones (e.g. instructional variables). In this respect Skehan (1989) mentions the work of Carroll (1965) and Spolsky (1989). He also acknowledges the importance of the GOOD LANGUAGE LEARNER STUDIES research model in this area.

BIBLIOGRAPHY
Carroll, J. B. (1965). The prediction of success in foreign language training. In R. Glaser (ed.), *Training, Research, and Education.* New York: John Wiley.
Skehan, P. (1989). *Individual Differences in Second-language Learning.* London: Edward Arnold.
Spolsky, B. (1989). *Conditions for Second Language Learning.* Oxford: Oxford University Press.

KJ

**individualization** as a notion is an inevitable offshoot of the increasing preoccupation with learner-centred education over the last two decades or so. It is related both directly and tangentially to NEEDS ANALYSIS, STUDENT AUTONOMY and LEARNER TRAINING. It offers a broad spectrum of pedagogic possibilities adaptable to conventional classroom structures, one-to-one instruction and self-directed learning modes. It may be teacher-directed or learner-driven. The concept has undergone a considerable metamorphosis since its origins in programmed instruction in the 1950s.

DEFINITION

The term *individualization* is potentially a confusing one because of its diversity of interpretation. (Dickinson (1978) goes so far as to decree that it is 'useless' for precisely this reason, though his position is not a common one.) Blue (1981: 61) quotes Chaix and others' definition, taking it to refer to 'a learning process which, as regards goals, content, methodology and pacing, is adapted to a particular individual, taking this individual's characteristics into consideration'. Such a general definition is, of course, nonspecific in terms of implementation in context, but it does emphasize the need to take into account variables of different kinds.

THE CLASSROOM CONTEXT

The great majority of language teaching and learning takes place in classrooms and, not unusually, in quite large groups. This traditional whole-class environment is often predicated – explicitly or otherwise – on an assumption that a predetermined syllabus can be offered to learners who will be expected to assimilate it more or less at the pace at which it is presented. This is the conventional teacher-fronted 'lockstep' model. If, however, it is considered desirable to modify this in order to address individual differences, the question then is, in Bowers's (1980: 72) words, 'that of ensuring that the place of the individual in planning and participating in the learning process is not suppressed by the predetermination of a "syllabus" or goal-oriented approach, or by the built-in constraints of the group context'. One simple and self-evident point is often overlooked, namely the fact that all classes are by definition comprised of disparate individuals in terms of personality, interest, motivation, attitude, learning style and even proficiency (see INDIVIDUAL DIFFERENCES). Allwright (1988: 37) argues that ordinary classrooms can give space to learners from some of these perspectives, for example, by allowing errors to be viewed as positive contributions to language development and by encouraging learners to ask questions: as he puts it, individualization is 'indigenous' to the classroom anyway and does not automatically require radical solutions.

It is important to stress that individualization is not a particular method, but a principle and a tactical approach that can be expressed in a great variety of ways. The organizational, attitudinal and indeed resource implications of individualization do not need to be large-scale, and attention to this aspect of learning can be achieved very modestly. Even with a tight, externally imposed, syllabus specification, a large class and few if any resources, it is in principle possible, for example, for the teacher to adopt different presentation styles to allow for uptake by individuals; arrange a modicum of pair and group work; provide different kinds of reading materials for personal choice; or set up multi-skill possibilities in the class. Sturtridge (1982) uses the image of offering different 'menus' that permit learners to use tactics that tap into their preferred learning styles. Even small-scale changes, of course, mean that the traditional teacher's directive role of imparter of knowledge is diversified, so that she or he also becomes a facilitator, a helper and a flexible classroom manager.

## VARIATIONS

Nowadays a very common way of addressing the needs and interests of individual learners is in the provision of self-access facilities, which offer a modicum of student choice over learning materials. Sometimes this may simply mean an easily portable box of differentiated reading passages on card,

as, for instance, in the long-established format of the reading laboratory (McDonough and Shaw, 1993), or a mini-library in a cupboard which is accessed by a class in the company of a teacher. Some institutions are able to provide a quite extensive bank of such resources, which may include print material, audio and video equipment and software, and computer facilities (CALL), which will typically be housed in a separate room. The availability of space and resources, however great or small, is not of itself sufficient, and the human resource implications are equally significant. Teachers and institutions need to understand and appreciate their own roles in promoting individualization and in providing the practical frameworks, worksheets and learning pathways that make it a viable goal. (For a detailed discussion of self-access, see Sheerin, 1989.)

From the discussion so far it can be seen that the individualization of instruction varies along at least two different dimensions. First of all, there are varying degrees to which individualized work is overt and explicit, from a situation where learners are given their own material to work on alone, to one where teachers acknowledge as it were implicitly that students adopt a range of learning strategies. Second, individualization implies very varying degrees of independence, autonomy, and the ability to accept responsibility for one's own learning.

There are many other and disparate manifestations of the provision of individualization. A common format is one-to-one tuition, either for limited periods – for remediation, for instance – or for full-scale individualized programmes, perhaps for a business person requiring a maximally focused course in a short time. Such programmes are inevitably expensive for the customer and involve a whole package of social activities as well as tuition. Ideally they derive from a careful NEEDS ANALYSIS and require a style of teaching that is not textbook-driven, but that can respond to these needs with an appropriate choice of methods and materials. The field

of ENGLISH FOR SPECIFIC PURPOSES is particularly rich in examples of individualized modes of tuition; see also self-directed
learning (SDL) under STUDENT AUTONOMY.
Yet another way of paying attention to the
individual learner is through the writing of
diaries (see DIARY STUDIES).

BIBLIOGRAPHY
Allwright, D. (1988). Autonomy and indi-
vidualization in whole-class instruction. In
A. Brookes and P. Grundy (eds), *Individual-
ization and Autonomy in Language Learning*.
London: Modern English Publications with
the British Council, 35–44.*
Blue, G. (1981). Self-directed learning systems
and the role of the ESP teacher. In *The ESP
Teacher: Role, development and prospects*. ELT
Documents 112. London: British Council, 58–
64.
Bowers, R. (1980). The individual learner in the
general class. In H. Altman and C. James (eds),
*Foreign Language Teaching: Meeting individual
needs*. Oxford: Pergamon, 66–80.
Dickinson, L. (1978). Autonomy, self-directed
learning and individualization. In *Individualization in Language Learning*. ELT Documents
103. London: British Council, 7–28.
McDonough, J. and Shaw, C. (1993). *Materials
and Methods in ELT*. Oxford: Blackwell.
Sheerin, S. (1989). *Self-access*. Oxford: Oxford
University Press.*
Sturtridge, G. (1982). Individualized learning:
what are the options for the classroom teacher?
In M. Geddes and G. Sturtridge (eds), *Individualization*. London: Modern English Publications, 8–14.

JMCD

**information/opinion gap**   One of the
principles underlying COMMUNICATIVE METH-
ODOLOGY is MESSAGE-FOCUS. This has given
rise to activities which simulate real communication by involving the exchange of
information or opinion between participants.
In a typical information/opinion gap activity each learner in a pair or group holds
information which is partial, or different from
that of their partner(s). The task involves

conveying information/opinions not already
known to the other participant(s). Such
tasks may vary in linguistic control over
the intended message (e.g. communicative
drills, 'describe and draw', problem-solving)
and type of exchange (one-way/two-way,
optional/obligatory exchange).

BIBLIOGRAPHY
Johnson, K. (1982). *Communicative Syllabus
Design and Methodology*. Oxford: Pergamon.
Littlewood, W. T. (1981). *Communicative Lan-
guage Teaching: An introduction*. Cambridge:
Cambridge University Press.

KSM

**information-processing models**   Information processing mostly refers to a class
of models of second language acquisition
that emphasize the functional processing of
language as the source of language learning.
Hence they tend to be advanced by psychologists rather than by linguists, to integrate language with the other faculties of the
mind and to rely for their evidence on certain paradigms of psychological rather than
linguistic evidence.

Strictly speaking, the name of information
processing has been claimed by the approach
associated with Barry McLaughlin in the 1980s
(McLaughlin, 1987; McLaughlin, Rossman
and McLeod, 1983). This claims a separation of controlled from automatic processes.
A controlled process demands attention and
is therefore limited in capacity; try going
downstairs by consciously taking each step
to see how slow a controlled process can be.
Automatic processes are quick and need
little attention; they have been acquired
through long practice and take up very little
mental capacity; try walking downstairs without thinking and see how little demand it
makes. As a controlled process is practised
it gradually becomes automatic; compare the
first few hours of learning to drive a car,
which utilize controlled processes, with the
smooth unthinking driving of an experienced

driver, which utilizes automatic processes. Unlike Krashen's refusal to allow learnt knowledge to be converted into acquired knowledge, this model insists that the normal course of acquisition is from material that is learnt consciously through practice to automatic unthinking knowledge. (See ACQUISITION LEARNING)

The support for this model is usually taken from experiments that show increasing speed or skill as L2 learners improve. Reaction time experiments have long been used as a test of dominant language; response time is faster in the dominant language; it may take five to eight years of residence in a country for the L2 to have as fast a response time. Slowness of response is also found in timed tests of grammaticality, of reading and of syntactic comprehension. Tasks such as mental arithmetic, counting the flashes from a light bulb and counting backwards and forwards all take longer or are less accurate than in the L1. Similarly, retrieving and remembering information from lectures or written texts is less efficient in an L2. As the L2 processes are practised over time so they improve. The paradigm example of such improvement is the Havana cigar-roller who was still improving her performance after eighteen years!

The most powerful information-processing model in cognitive psychology is that of John Anderson (1983), called ACT* (Adaptive Control of Thought, 'final' version). This depends on three types of memory: *declarative memory* which stores individual facts, *procedural memory* which stores processes, and *working memory* which brings the other two together in carrying out a task (see DE-CLARATIVE/PROCEDURAL). Declarative memory is then 'knowledge that' – knowledge, say, that in England cars drive on the left or that the English past tense *-ed* has three main forms. Procedural memory is 'knowledge how' – knowing how to drive a car round Marble Arch or how to make *look* into a past tense. Learning starts with the declarative stage: we learn the three regular forms

for past tense *-ed*, /t/, /d/ and /id/. But, as there is no procedure for producing past tenses, we have to adapt whatever other procedures are available to our working memory. As this is unwieldy, we proceed to the knowledge compilation stage at which we evoke a new procedure to handle the declarative facts, perhaps by adapting a general procedure or collapsing two existing procedures into one. But this new procedure will still be clumsy; we enter the tuning production stage during which the procedure gets smoother through practice; we gradually produce past tenses more and more efficiently.

ACT* then makes no distinctions between language and other systems of the mind, or between L1 and L2 learning; the stages of learning are exactly the same. The difference between procedural and declarative memory has been invoked in several byways of SLA research. One area is the temporal variables research of the Kassel School in which the learners' productions are studied for pauses, rate of speech, size of uninterrupted 'run' of speech and so on (Dechert, 1984). Results are held to support the sequence of learning from declarative to procedural for German and English learners of French. A second area of application has been the LEARNING STRATEGIES research of O'Malley and Chamot (1990), who claim learning strategies as procedures that are compiled and fine-tuned. They also see L2 learning as going from a conscious knowledge of declarative facts through the process of proceduralization to automatic native-like processing.

A further model that can be linked to information processing is MacWhinney's Competition Model, which has exhaustively researched the transfer of cues to the subject of the sentence from L1 to L2 (MacWhinney and Bates, 1989).

The usefulness of these models so far is limited by the small quantity of attention they give to language, unless of course one believes that any evidence for any kind of learning is also evidence for L2 learning, i.e. that learning is learning. Potentially they nevertheless pose a powerful alternative to the usual language-based theories and one that may be more in tune both with current models of cognitive psychology such as connectionism (Broeder and Plunkett, 1994), and with teachers' ideas of L2 learning.

BIBLIOGRAPHY

Anderson, J. (1983). *The Architecture of Cognition*. Cambridge, MA: Harvard University Press.

Broeder, P. and Plunkett, P. (1994). Connectionism and second language acquisition. In N. Ellis (ed.), *Implicit and Explicit Learning of Languages*. London: Academic Press, 421–53.

Dechert, H. (1984). Second language production: six hypotheses. In H. Dechert, D. Mohle and M. Raupach (eds), *Second Language Productions*. Tübingen: Gunter Narr, 211–30.

McLaughlin, B. (1987). *Theories of Second-Language Learning*. London: Edward Arnold.*

McLaughlin, B., Rossman, R. and McLeod, B. (1983). Second language learning: an information-processing perspective. *Language Learning*, 33, 135–58.*

MacWhinney, B. and Anderson, J. (1986). The acquisition of grammar. In I. Gopnik and M. Gopnik (eds), *From Models to Modules*. Norwood, NJ: Ablex, 3–23.

MacWhinney, B. and Bates, E. (eds) (1989). *The Crosslinguistic Study of Sentence Processing*. Cambridge: Cambridge University Press.

O'Malley, J. M. and Chamot, A. U. (1990). *Learning Strategies in Second Language Acquisition*. Cambridge: Cambridge University Press.

VJC

**information structure**    Various sets of distinctions are relevant to a language user's decision on how to distribute information in a message. A main one concerns given and new information – what pieces of information the user expects the listener/reader already to know. There are various ways of signalling new information. Placing stress on the relevant word is a common one, but various syntactic means may also be used. In answer to the question *Who wrote the letter?* the answer might be *John wrote the letter* with *John* (the new information for the questioner) being given stress. The answer *It was John who wrote the letter* would be another means of conveying the same information. Had the question been *What did John do?* the 'old' information for the questioner would be that John did something; the new information sought would be what it was that John did. In this context the response *It was John who wrote the letter* would be distinctly odd (though not perhaps entirely impossible).

Other distinctions relate to the given/new information one, but are separable. The subject/predicate distinction is a case in point. Generally a sentence's 'topic' is expressed by the subject, with the predicate saying something about that topic. Hence the sentence *John wrote the letter* is likely to be perceived of as a sentence 'about' *John*, while *The letter was written by John* is a sentence 'about' *the letter*. In many (but not nearly all) circumstances, the subject will convey given information, the predicate new. For an accessible discussion of these and other distinctions, see Clark and Clark (1977). See also Halliday (1970).

BIBLIOGRAPHY

Clark, H. H. and Clark. E. V. (1977). *Psychology and Language*. New York: Harcourt Brace Jovanovich.

Halliday, M. A. K. (1970). Language structure and language function. In J. Lyons (ed.), *New Horizons in Linguistics*. Harmondsworth: Penguin Books.

KJ

**information transfer** is a commonly used type of communicative exercise (see COMMUNICATIVE METHODOLOGY), which gives priority to MESSAGE-FOCUS, that is, to language *use* rather than *usage* or form practice (see USE/USAGE). Such activities involve the transfer of information typically from one medium to another (e.g. from a listening or reading text to a form, table, diagram, etc.)

or from one task to another. Communicative processes are supported through a focus on the selection of relevant information in the message for transfer to the other task (see TOP-DOWN PROCESSING) and on the development of real-time processing skills.

BIBLIOGRAPHY
Johnson, K. (1982). *Communicative Syllabus Design and Methodology*. Oxford: Pergamon.
KSM

**innateness hypothesis**    In linguistics, the innateness hypothesis is almost exclusively associated with Chomskyan theories of language acquisition. It is claimed that much of the knowledge of language is built in to the human mind rather than acquired. Recently such innate ideas have been seen in terms of the principles and parameters version of the UG (see UNIVERSAL GRAMMAR) theory of language (Chomsky, 1990; Cook and Newson, 1996).

The original claim for innateness was based on a 'what else' argument: if we can show people know aspects of language that they could not have learnt from the types of language evidence demonstrably available to them, what else could this knowledge be but innate? This became formalized as the poverty-of-the-stimulus argument or 'Plato's problem' (Chomsky, 1986); the complexity of the knowledge we possess compared to the thinness of the evidence we have encountered necessitates postulating that it was already present in our minds.

This could be seen as one interpretation of Chomsky's influential LAD (Language Acquisition Device) metaphor, in which language acquisition is represented in terms of a black box into which the primary linguistic data go and out of which a generative grammar comes.

primary linguistic data → ⃞LAD⃞ → generative grammar

Originally it was claimed that the ultimate goal of linguistic theory was explanatory adequacy – explaining how a particular grammar could be derived from the linguistic data. During the 1970s and 1980s this became an everyday goal rather than something to be shelved till later. *Any* grammar had to show, not just that it was an accurate description of competence (see COMPETENCE/PERFORMANCE) but that it also fitted in with the system for language acquisition.

Until the 1980s it was possible for critics to claim that there was no meat on these bones; however convincing as an argument, it fell down for lack of clear instances of innate ideas. But couching universal grammar in terms of principles and parameters promised to make innateness checkable (Lightfoot, 1982). Principles are the abstract constraints that the human mind places on language; parameters reflect the limited variation possible between human languages. If one could find a principle of language in the competence of a native speaker that could not be decided from the evidence of actual sentences of a language, then such a principle must be innate. If one found that people's minds unerringly chose one or the other setting for a parameter despite the variability of the input, the parameter must be innate.

A familiar example of such a principle is structure-dependency, which claims that syntactic movement in all languages depends upon the structure of the sentence rather than the sequences of words in it. Take the pair of sentences

(a)    *Is Sam is the cat that black?*

and

(b)    *Is Sam the cat that is black?*

Any speaker of English knows that (a) is impossible and (b) is possible. Yet they appear to have been formed in very similar ways by moving an *is* to the beginning of the sentence namely:

(a)   *Is Sam is the cat that black?*

and

(b)   *Is Sam the cat that is black?*

The rule for making questions in English does not therefore merely state that an *is* moves to the beginning; it has to state that only the *is* that is inside the main clause can move. The rule depends upon the structure of the sentence; it is structure-dependent. Sentences such as (a) are impossible because the wrong element in the structure of the sentence has been moved. Since speakers do not naturally produce such sentences, since moreover parents do not correct or explain them, how do native speakers know instantaneously that (a) is ungrammatical rather than being simply a novel sentence they have not heard before?

As an example of a parameter, we can take the null subject (pro-drop) parameter. Some languages called pro-drop languages permit a pronoun subject to be absent from the surface of the sentence, for example, in Japanese, Arabic and Italian. Other non-pro-drop languages do not permit it to be absent, for example, English and French. But in pro-drop languages such as Italian it is possible to hear sentences both with and without subjects; even in non-pro-drop languages such as English it is possible to drop subjects in certain styles and registers, for example, *Can't buy me love*. How can children unerringly come to the conclusion that they are learning a pro-drop or a non-pro-drop language when the evidence is so confusing? Only if the choice is limited by their actual minds; any language they encounter will set the pro-drop 'switch' one way or the other.

In addition to grammar, Chomsky also claimed that certain aspects of PHONOLOGY and of SYNTAX must be innate. But the main concrete claim is that the principles and parameters of universal grammar are in fact an innate component in the human language faculty. This does not mean that they are necessarily present from birth. Recent controversy has divided those who support a growth model in which aspects of UG reveal themselves in the mind over time, like the development of the teeth, from those who support a non-growth model in which all the constituents of UG are present from the start, but may not be apparent in the child's actual speech because of other cognitive or physical constraints on the child's speech (Borer and Wexler, 1987).

Finally, Chomsky has always claimed that there is no real dispute over innateness. Any theory of language acquisition has to attribute certain built-in properties to the mind, whether the ability to associate stimulus and response, or the knowledge of principles and parameters. The dispute is over how much and what aspects of language are innate, as Chomsky has often pointed out, rather than whether anything is innate. (See also CHOMSKYAN LINGUISTICS, FIRST AND SECOND LANGUAGE ACQUISITION.)

BIBLIOGRAPHY

Borer, H. and Wexler, K. (1987). The maturation of syntax. In T. Roeper and E. Williams (eds), *Parameter Setting*. Dordrecht: Reidel, 123–72.

Chomsky, N. (1986). *Knowledge of Language: Its nature, origin and use*. New York: Praeger.

——(1990). Language and Mind. In D. H. Mellor (ed.), *Ways of Communicating*. Cambridge: Cambridge University Press, 56–80.

Cook, V. J. and Newson, M. (1996). *Chomsky's Universal Grammar: An introduction*. Oxford: Blackwell.*

Lane, H. (1976). *The Wild Boy of Aveyron*. Cambridge, MA: Harvard University Press.

Lightfoot, D. (1982). *The Language Lottery: Toward a biology of grammars*. Cambridge, MA: MIT Press.

VJC

**innovation management in language teaching**   This is a new area of study in applied linguistics which draws heavily on models and theories from education. It is important that innovation (which here refers to planned change within a language teaching system) should be understood and well managed to ensure its implementation and continuation. This should lead to more appropriate and productive use of human, financial and material resources.

Innovation has been common in ELT for the last twenty years, with major changes in SYLLABUS design and methodology following the move from traditional, structural approaches in language teaching to a COMMUNICATIVE METHODOLOGY. Major changes have been made to language teaching systems – on a macro level, as in the introduction of a communicative syllabus in Malaysian secondary schools in the 1970s, or at a micro level with, for example, the introduction of self-access centres in language schools as part of programmes to develop STUDENT AUTONOMY. Such changes have resulted from and added to areas of research in linguistics and language learning, but very little attention has been paid until recently to the management implications of such innovations.

Other disciplines, such as education and language planning, have a well developed research methodology and literature in this field. Fullan (1991) identifies four phases in the study of educational innovation in North America:

(i) adoption (1960s), when exciting new ideas in education were enthusiastically introduced;
(ii) implementation failure (1970–7), when innovation became unfashionable through its widespread, often unprincipled, overuse, with inadequate support or follow-up;
(iii) implementation success (1978–82) saw the lessons of the second phase being learned and some successes;
(iv) intensification vs restructuring (1983–90): the former focusing on intensifying course content and pedagogy and the latter on management issues, such as systems organization and the training of personnel (see also MANAGEMENT IN LANGUAGE TEACHING).

Interest in innovation in ELT grew in the late 1980s with retrospective discussion of innovations: the introduction of a PROCEDURAL SYLLABUS in the Bangalore project and the failure of AUDIOLINGUALISM in Japan (Henrichsen, 1989). White (1988, 1991) gave ELT audiences an overview of the education literature in this field, providing a benchmark against which to compare language teaching innovations.

Problems with educational innovations arise because they require changes in teachers' attitudes and practices and lead to increased workloads. They can be costly in terms of time and money and they require evaluation, yet outputs are difficult to measure as they develop over time. There are three main elements in the innovation process (see White, 1988): the change agent, who initiates the innovation and promotes its adoption, the innovation itself and the user, who receives and (it is to be hoped) adopts it. It is crucial that the change agent and receiver communicate at all stages in order to understand each other's perspective and to negotiate on implementation.

White describes three basic models of innovation: (i) research, development and diffusion/dissemination, which tend to be large-scale, top-down projects; (ii) problem-solving – this is the basis of ACTION RESEARCH and tends to be bottom-up; (iii) social interaction, which sees the user/adapter as part of a network of influential social relations and stresses the role of opinion leaders.

All change in education is systemic. Kennedy (1989: 331) considers 'social, political and cultural systems as crucial determinants', which are interconnected. He illustrates this point in figure 1, with outer rings being more powerful and influencing those within.

Strategies of innovation mentioned in the literature (Chin and Benne, 1976, in White, 1988) include: (i) power-coercive, often linked to an autocratic management style; (ii) empirical-rational, which assumes people will be rational and passively accept input; (iii) normative-re-educative, which sees

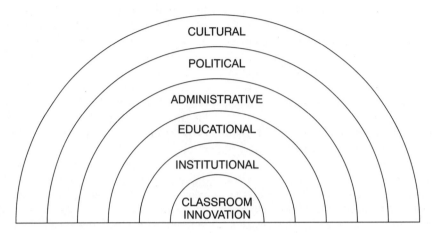

**Figure 1** The hierarchy of interrelating systems in which an innovation has to operate (from Kennedy, 1989: 332).

people as self-activating and not passive in their own re-education. This will involve normative changes (to attitudes, values, skills) as well as cognitive and perceptual change.

The following factors (White, 1988: 91) affect the success of an innovation: (i) antecedent conditions (e.g. pedagogic traditions); (ii) features of the innovation (its complexity, the advantages it offers, its practicality); (iii) the resource system from which the innovation proceeds (its status, receptiveness to feedback); (iv) the intended user system (its capacity to implement the change, the working relationships between people involved).

Key questions must be asked about the above factors. Markee (1993: 230) quotes Cooper's composite question about innovation: 'Who adopts what, where, when, why and how?' In addressing the issue of innovation management, his 1997 book concludes with the following ten governing principles:

(1)  innovation is a complex activity;
(2)  it always takes longer to make a change happen than originally anticipated;
(3)  good communication among project participants is a key to a successful innovation;
(4)  the likelihood that the change agents' proposals will be misunderstood is high;

(5)  the successful implementation of innovations is based on an eight-step process: identify problem, devise potential solution, inform adopters, consult users, modify proposal, arrange support, trial solution, evaluate and redesign if necessary;
(6)  innovation is an inherently messy, unpredictable business;
(7)  it is important for implementers to have a stake in the innovations which they are expected to implement;
(8)  it is important for change agents to work through opinion leaders who can influence their peers;
(9)  in order to promote innovation, it is important for change agents to encourage experimentation by teachers;
(10) innovation involves a mix of professional and administrative change.

Innovation management is important because the adoption of an innovation does not necessarily mean that it has been implemented; innovations fail for a variety of reasons and what is successful in one place may not work elsewhere. Studies in ELT in this field will certainly increase in attempts to ensure that time, energy and money are not wasted. Most ELT practitioners would support Markee's (1997) call for the development of an autonomous tradition of innovation research and practice, borrowing ideas from other disciplines.

BIBLIOGRAPHY

Fullan, M. G. and Stiegelbauer, S. (1991). *The New Meaning of Educational Change*. London: Cassell.

Kennedy, C. (1989). Evaluation of the management of change in ELT projects. *Applied Linguistics*, 9, 329–42.

Henrichsen, L. E. (1989). *Diffusion of Innovations in English Language Teaching: The ELEC effort in Japan, 1956–1968*. New York: Greenwood Press.

Markee, N. (1993). The diffusion of innovation in language teaching. *Annual Review of Applied Linguistics*, 13, 229–43.*

——(1997). *Managing Curricular Innovation*. New York: Cambridge University Press.

Nicholls, A. (1983). *Managing Educational Innovations*. London: Allen and Unwin.

Stoller, F. L. (1994). The diffusion of innovations in intensive ESL programs. *Applied Linguistics*, 15, 300–27.

White, R. V. (1988). *The ELT Curriculum: Design, innovation and management*. Oxford: Blackwell.

White, R., Martin, M., Stimson, M. and Hodge, R. (1991). *Management in English Language Teaching*. Cambridge: Cambridge University Press.* [Chapter 6.]

CLF

**input hypothesis** An influential but controversial (see McLaughlin, 1987) position put forward by Krashen, proposing that the most important factor in the development of second (or foreign) language proficiency is the learner's exposure to the target language (the 'input'). Krashen proposed optimal characteristics for such input (see I + 1), and also hypothesized the existence of an AFFECTIVE FILTER to control the intake of input. (See also MONITOR MODEL.)

BIBLIOGRAPHY

Krashen, S. D. (1985). *The Input Hypothesis: Issues and implications*. New York: Longman.

McLaughlin, B. (1987). *Theories of Second Language Learning*. London: Edward Arnold.

RLA

**instrumental motivation** (or sometimes 'instrumental orientation') refers to a wish by a learner to benefit practically (usually in some material way) from language learning, for example, by being more successful in business dealings with native speakers of the target language. It is contrasted with INTEGRATIVE MOTIVATION. (See also INTRINSIC/EXTRINSIC MOTIVATION and MOTIVATION.)

BIBLIOGRAPHY

Gardner, R. C. and Lambert, W. E. (1972). *Attitudes and Motivation in Second-language Learning*. Rowley, MA: Newbury House.

RLA

**intake** That part of input which the learner accommodates to or utilizes as part of the process of internalizing new language. It is possible to view second language acquisition in terms of the three variables – input, intake and output; see Ellis (1994: 349) for a more complex statement of this. In this formulation, a major issue is how parts of input are converted into intake. See Ellis (1994), Chaudron (1985), Gass (1988); also INPUT HYPOTHESIS, NOTICING, OUTPUT HYPOTHESIS.

BIBLIOGRAPHY

Chaudron, C. (1985). A method for examining the input/intake distinction. In S. Gass and C. Madden (eds), *Input in Second Language Acquisition*. Rowley, MA: Newbury House.

Ellis, R. (1994). *The Study of Second Language Acquisition*. Oxford: Oxford University Press.

Gass, S. (1988). Integrating research areas: a framework for second language studies. *Applied Linguistics*, 9, 198–217.

KJ

**integrative motivation** (sometimes 'integrative orientation') refers to a wish, by a learner, to integrate into, become an accepted member of, the community whose language that person is learning. It is contrasted with

INSTRUMENTAL MOTIVATION. (See also INTRINSIC/EXTRINSIC MOTIVATION and MOTIVATION.)

BIBLIOGRAPHY
Gardner, R. C. and Lambert, W. E. (1972). *Attitudes and Motivation in Second-language Learning*. Rowley, MA: Newbury House.

RLA

**intelligence**   Mental age or the intelligence quotient (IQ) refer to general scholastic ability, so it is to be expected that intelligent students will have a somewhat better chance of learning languages more easily in school situations. However, Genesee (1978) found that this was true only for language skills like reading and structural expression, not for communicative skills in conversation with native speakers. Other measures, such as COGNITIVE STYLE and APTITUDE for languages, also have a high correlation with intelligence, as do several native language indicators like vocabulary size, so it is not clear exactly how intelligence affects language learning. (See also COGNITIVE VARIABLES.)

BIBLIOGRAPHY
Genesee, F. (1978). The role of intelligence in second language learning. *Language Learning*, 26/2, 267–80.
Skehan, P. (1989). *Individual Differences in Second-language Learning*. London: Edward Arnold, 109–11.

SMCD

**interaction hypothesis**   The position that what promotes the development of second (or foreign) language proficiency is the process of face-to-face linguistic interaction, not merely the encountering of 'input' (see INPUT HYPOTHESIS). The 'strong' form of the interaction hypothesis proposes that it is in the interaction process itself that linguistic development occurs. The 'weak' form of the hypothesis proposes that interaction, though important, is better seen simply as the process whereby learning opportunities are made available to learners, who may or may not make productive use of them. (See also OUTPUT HYPOTHESIS.)

BIBLIOGRAPHY
Allwright, D. (1984). Why don't learners learn what teachers teach? The interaction hypothesis. In D. M. Singleton and D. G. Little (eds), *Language Learning in Formal and Informal Contexts*. Dublin: IRAAL, 3–18.

RLA

**interface/non-interface positions in SLA**   This distinction concerns the role that conscious learning about an L2 plays in the development of subconscious, acquired, automatic L2 knowledge. Some researchers (e.g. Krashen, 1985: 39–42) maintain a strong non-interface position: only 'comprehensible input' and not consciously learned knowledge can lead to acquisition (see INPUT HYPOTHESIS, MONITOR MODEL). Krashen distinguishes three possible interface positions: under a 'strong interface position' acquisition can only result from prior conscious learning and practising of L2 patterns. A 'weak interface position' holds that acquisition can result both from conscious learning and from comprehensible input. A 'weaker interface position' holds that conscious learning aids the learner to decipher comprehensible input.

BIBLIOGRAPHY
Krashen, S. (1985). *The Input Hypothesis: Issues and implications*. London: Longman.

RH

**interlanguage**   The concept of interlanguage has been highly influential in second language acquisition research since the 1960s. The term itself comes from an eponymous paper by Larry Selinker in 1972, perhaps the most cited paper in applied linguistics. The concept, however, had been around for some time under various guises. One source was the 'independent grammars assumption', derived from Chomsky's work of the early 1960s by L1 researchers such as David McNeill (1966). This insisted that at a particular moment a child had a grammar that was not just an imitation of the adult grammar but had a system of its own. Hence this assumption enabled researchers such as Martin Braine (1963) to write grammars for children's language rather than treating them as defective adult grammars. Language learners then create grammars of their own, rather than mastering the target grammar imperfectly; at any moment their grammar is an independent system.

In second language acquisition research this concept led to several slightly variant conclusions. In general the L2 learner could be treated as having a language of his or her own, not just as a poor speaker of the target language, and as creating this system for themselves from their experience and internal resources rather than having it thrust down their throats by teachers. This almost by itself led to the liberation of the COMMUNICATIVE LANGUAGE TEACHING method from the teacher's control: it was the learners who had the responsibility of taking in language and building up their own grammar, not the teacher; hence they did not need to be corrected whenever they did things wrong and could learn by doing things themselves rather than being spoon-fed by the teacher. The L2 learning theorists coined several terms for this with slightly different emphases. Nemser (1971) captured this insight through the term 'approximative system': 'Learner speech at a given time is the patterned product of a linguistic system, $L_a$ [approximative language], distinct from $L_s$ [source language] and $L_t$ [target language] and internally structured,' that is to say, emphasizing the growth towards the target language. Corder (1977) used the term 'transitional competence', which he called 'a dynamic goal-oriented language system

of increasing complexity'. Selinker's 'interlanguage' was, however, the term that took the world by storm, creating journals such as *Interlanguage Studies Bulletin* and a flood of papers. Selinker was interested *inter alia* in five central processes of interlanguage:

- *language transfer*, in which features of the L1 are projected onto the L2 (see TRANSFER);
- *over-generalization of L2 rules*, in which L2 rules are applied too widely;
- *transfer of training*, in which language teaching itself creates language rules that are not part of the L2;
- *strategies of L2 learning*, the means through which the learner builds up the L2, such as repetition (see LEARNING STRATEGIES);
- COMMUNICATION STRATEGIES, the ways in which the learner tries to communicate in the L2.

Interlanguage theory did not then cut itself off from contributions from the L1; Selinker (1992) indeed calls language transfer its quintessential notion. But it was how the learner's own system was created through transfer that counted, not the inefficiency with which the learner was mastering a target system.

One slight difficulty is that it is not always clear whether these processes are true of the interlanguage itself or are the means through which the interlanguage came into being. By and large the independent grammars assumption is not so much a theory as an assumption; it depends on your point of view whether you think of learners' grammars as independent or not, with Smith (1973) arguing that children's L1 PHONOLOGY is indeed a version of adult phonology plus 'deformation rules'.

Interlanguage nowadays chiefly exists as a background concept that everyone takes for granted, on a par with description and prescription or the primacy of speech; Selinker (1992) points out that the concept of a 'between language' has been present from Lado onwards. Sharwood Smith (1994), for example, starts from the concept of interlanguage as 'systematic linguistic behaviour of second language learners', restricting it to the performance side, i.e. 'behaviour' rather than competence, i.e. knowledge. It is not then a challengeable proposition that learners have languages of their own but an axiom of the field. The more far-reaching implication that interlanguage should not be judged by native standards has not been taken as seriously by researchers as it might be. Most SLA research methodology, perhaps inevitably, assumes that learner language should be compared with natives, not treated as an independent system of its own, as pointed out by Bley-Vroman (1983), whether the ERROR ANALYSIS of corpora for 'errors' and 'mistakes' (see ERROR/MISTAKE/LAPSE), or the use of grammaticality judgements where the native speaker judgements are taken to be correct. The methodology of the research question 'Do L2 learners have access to UG?' (see UNIVERSAL GRAMMAR) has been based on testing whether or not L2 learners behave like monolingual speakers rather than whether they have systems of their own subject to UG. It is revealing that Sharwood Smith (1992), who has always been linked to interlanguage, puts asterisks in front of learner sentences 'to indicate non-native forms', as if this in itself made them ungrammatical. In other words the interlanguage concept, despite its attractiveness, has still led researchers to see knowledge of one language as being the norm against which other forms of language knowledge are measured, rather than crediting L2 users with a different type of language knowledge in their own right. (See also FIRST AND SECOND LANGUAGE ACQUISITION.)

BIBLIOGRAPHY
Bley-Vroman, R. W. (1983). The comparative fallacy in interlanguage studies: the case of systematicity. *Language Learning*, 33, 1–17.
Braine, M. (1963). The ontogeny of English phrase structure: the first phase. *Language*, 39, 1–13.
Corder, S. P. (1977). Language continua and the interlanguage hypothesis. In S. P. Corder, and E. Roulet (eds), *The Notions of Simplification, Interlanguage, and Pidgins and their Relation to Second Language Pedagogy*. Geneva: Droz.
McNeill, D. (1966). Developmental psycholinguistics. In F. Smith and G. A. Miller (eds), *The Genesis of Language: A psycholinguistic approach*. Cambridge, MA: MIT Press.
Nemser, W. (1971). Approximative systems of foreign language learners. *International Review of Applied Linguistics*, 9, 115–23.
Selinker, L. (1972). Interlanguage. *International Review of Applied Linguistics*, 10, 209–30.*
——(1992). *Rediscovering Interlanguage*. London: Longman.*
Sharwood Smith, M. (1994). *Second Language Learning: Theoretical foundations*. Harlow: Longman.
Smith, N. (1973). *The Acquisition of Phonology: A case study*. Cambridge: Cambridge University Press.

VJC

**intonation** refers to the meaningful changes in pitch of the voice in speech. Such meanings may be grammatical (English types of relative clauses), contrastive (I saw *him*), pragmatic (English statements turned into questions by rising intonation), discourse (pitch range lowering to signal end of topic), attitudinal (anger, friendliness, etc.) or lexical (tone languages such as Yoruba distinguish words by different pitches). Systems to describe intonation commonly use a set of tones (rise, fall, etc.) or a set of levels (high, mid, etc.). It is mostly ignored in language teaching, apart from the obligatory aside in NOTIONAL/FUNCTIONAL SYLLABUSES that functions are related to intonation. See also DISCOURSE INTONATION.

BIBLIOGRAPHY
Brazil, D., Coulthard, M. and Johns, C. (1980). *Discourse Intonation and Language Teaching*. Harlow: Longman.
Halliday, M. A. K. (1970). *A Course in Spoken English: Intonation*. Oxford: Oxford University Press.
Ladd, R. (1980). *The Structure of Intonational Meaning*. Bloomington: Indiana University Press.

O'Connor, J. D. and Arnold, G. J. (1973). *Intonation of Colloquial English*. Harlow: Longman.

VJC

**intrinsic/extrinsic motivation**   Motivation is 'intrinsic' where it is free of any ulterior purpose, 'extrinsic' where an ulterior purpose is involved. For example, 'intrinsically' motivated people will want to learn a language 'for its own sake' (because it is somehow interesting as an object of study), rather than for the 'extrinsic' reason that they wish to integrate (see INTEGRATIVE MOTIVATION) into any community which speaks that language, or wish to benefit materially (see INSTRUMENTAL MOTIVATION) from contact with such a community. (See also MOTIVATION.)

BIBLIOGRAPHY

Gardner, R. C. and Lambert, W. E. (1972). *Attitudes and Motivation in Second-Language Learning*. Rowley, MA: Newbury House.
Skehan, P. (1989). *Individual Differences in Second-Language Learning*. London: Edward Arnold.

RLA

# J

**jigsaw principle** refers to a methodological procedure whereby subgroups of learners in a class are asked to read or listen to different information concerning a particular topic or situation. The full picture is then pieced together, like a jigsaw, when the groups combine in discussion to complete the task. (See also INFORMATION GAP.)

BIBLIOGRAPHY
Geddes, M. (1981). Listening. In K. Johnson and K. Morrow (eds), *Communication in the Classroom*. Harlow: Longman, 78–86.
Geddes, M. and Sturtridge, G. (1979). *Listening Links*. London: Heinemann.
——(1982). *Reading Links*. London: Heinemann.
JMCD

# K

**knowledge/control** This dichotomy in SLA derives from Chomsky's COMPETENCE/ PERFORMANCE distinction. Knowledge is the representation of the language system in the learner's mind; control is the processing system handling this knowledge during performance (Bialystok and Sharwood-Smith, 1985). Learner error may derive from inadequate knowledge, control, or both. (See ERROR ANALYSIS, ERROR/MISTAKE/LAPSE.)

BIBLIOGRAPHY

Bialystok, E. (1982). On the relationship between knowing and using linguistic forms. *Applied Linguistics*, 3, 181–206.

Bialystok, E. and Sharwood Smith, M. (1985). Interlanguage is not a state of mind: an evaluation of the construct for second language acquisition. *Applied Linguistics*, 6, 101–7.

Ellis, R. (1994). *Instructed Second Language Acquisition*. Oxford: Oxford University Press, 182–7.

GC

# L

**language across the curriculum** has emerged in the context of the secondary school curriculum, and mainly in relation to mother tongue teaching. It explores the role of language operationally, beyond its traditional, often literary boundaries, in terms of the communicative and linguistic demands of a broad range of other subjects.

BIBLIOGRAPHY
Bullock Committee Report (1975). *A Language for Life*. London: HMSO.
Marland, M. (ed.) (1977). *Language across the Curriculum*. London: Heinemann.*

JMCD

**language and power** Since the publication of the influential paper by Brown and Gilman (1960 [1972]), the terms *power* and *solidarity* have provided SOCIOLINGUISTICS with one of the most dominant, analytic perspectives for the study of language. Solidarity is concerned with the degree of distance between interactants, which may range from intimacy (solidary relationship) to casual acquaintance to detachment (non-solidary relationship). Solidarity is a symmetrical (reciprocal) dimension having the same 'value' for both interacting parties. Power, on the other hand, is concerned with asymmetry and inequality. Other things being equal, when one party is older, richer, stronger, superior in status, rank or professional standing, he or she holds power over the other party.

The execution and display of power through language has been studied with respect to many interrelated areas, e.g. terms of address (Brown and Gilman, 1960 [1972]; Brown and Ford 1961 [1964]), control and domination (Lakoff, 1975; Henley and Kramarae, 1991; Fowler et al., 1979; Fairclough, 1989), 'unequal' encounters (Thomas, 1985; Clark et al., 1990) and linguistic imperialism (Wolfson and Manes, 1985; Eastman, 1993) among many others.

When solidarity is an overriding aspect of two persons' relationship, they exchange reciprocal pronouns of address, names and titles. However, if their relationship is unequal, the power imbalance will result in a non-reciprocal address pattern. The powerful speaker (the superior) will address the powerless one (the inferior) with an informal or familiar term of address, e.g. the pronoun *tu* in French or the first name in English (e.g. *Robin*), and will be addressed by the inferior with the formal or distant pronoun *vous*, or the title and last name (e.g. *Professor Williams*) (Brown and Gilman, 1960 [1972]; Brown and Ford, 1961 [1964]).

Many other linguistic means of signalling and exerting power have been identified with respect to SPOKEN and WRITTEN DISCOURSE. Different linguistic rights and obligations characterize speakers in unequal encounters. For example, the powerful speakers can choose whether they want to speak or remain silent. If a powerless speaker exerts a similar right contrary to expectation, for example, when a pupil refuses to answer the teacher's question, this is perceived as a sign of defiance. Similarly, powerful speakers are more likely to select conversational topics, control the TURN-TAKING mechanisms, and interrupt others. However, it has also been argued that many of these features (e.g. interruption) may have the facilitative function of showing agreement with the other speakers rather than trying to dominate them (e.g. see Tannen, 1993).

Unequal encounters (Thomas, 1985) which occur in schools, police stations, the law courts, etc. are characterized by the dominant participant limiting the conversational options of the subordinate participant. This can be achieved by meta-pragmatic strategies, i.e. strategies which are manipulative of talk itself. For example, Thomas discusses the following two meta-strategies: 'illocutionary force indicating devices' which are used to add force to an utterance (compare: *Be quiet!* and *I order you to be quiet*) and meta-pragmatic comments, which allow the dominant speaker to 'call a spade a spade' (e.g. headmaster to schoolgirl who has been playing truant: *I warned you, I always find out*; both examples after Thomas, 1985).

Language and gender is one major research area which has been inseparably related to the issues of power, control and dominance. Women have been shown to be linguistically dominated by men in the ways mentioned above (Henley and Kramarae, 1991), as well as socialized into an unassertive speaking style marked by, for example, the use of hedges (*It's sort of hot in here; I'd kind of like to go*), hesitations and tag questions expressing uncertainty (*John is here, isn't he?* instead of *Is John here?*), superpolite, deferential forms (*I'd really appreciate it if . . . ; Would you please open the door, if you don't mind?*) and question intonation in declarative sentences (*Dinner will be ready around 6 o'clock?*) (Lakoff, 1975; examples after O'Barr and Atkins, 1980). However, O'Barr and Atkins (1980) have argued that these features of speech are not limited only to 'women's' speech but all 'powerless' speech, regardless of the speaker's gender. Furthermore, in a recent article, Tannen (1993) has postulated that different discourse strategies do not uniformly create dominance

or powerlessness, that one has to look at their 'meaning' in relation to context, the conversational styles of participants and the interaction between different speakers' styles and strategies.

A view of language as constitutive, rather than merely reflective of social relations has led critical linguistics to identify the mechanisms of reproducing social order through existing language patterns. Critical linguists (e.g. Fowler et al., 1979; Fairclough, 1989; see CRITICAL LINGUISTICS) have examined the structure of spoken and written texts in search of politically and ideologically salient features, which are often not evident to participants.

Some of the linguistic features discussed in the critical linguistic framework include nominalization, passivity and sequencing. They are used for ideological control as 'masking devices' (Ng and Bradac, 1993) as they allow the withholding of the identity of the actors and the causality of events. For example, nominalization: *Failure to display this notice will result in prosecution*, and passivization: *John was murdered* (Fowler, 1985: 71) remove the element of agency and, consequently, responsibility (compare *John was murdered by the police*). Exploitation of sequencing as in: *Fords I find particularly reliable* (Fowler, 1985: 72), is a rhetorical device serving the purpose of manipulating the addressee's attention, and the seemingly semantically equivalent sentences: *Employers always quarrel with unions* and *Unions always quarrel with employers* (Ng and Bradac, 1993: 156) give varying impressions of importance as to who quarrels the most.

The above examples of power-related language use have dealt mainly with microlinguistic contexts (see MACRO/MICROLINGUISTICS). In macrolinguistics, the issues which face language planners (see LANGUAGE PLANNING) are those of power and domination of one language over another and linguistic imperialism (Wolfson and Manes, 1985; Eastman, 1993). In a multilingual community, for example, one language may replace another due to the political, economic and military power enjoyed by its speakers, which has been a common phenomenon in colonial and post-colonial contexts. The domination of one language and the submission of another often results in DIGLOSSIA.

The special status of a linguistic hegemony is sometimes attributed to WORLD ENGLISH, the tremendous spread of which as a dominant second language has been seen as an imposition of Anglo-American ideology and culture on the rest of the world (Phillipson, 1992).

BIBLIOGRAPHY
Brown, R. and Ford, M. (1961). Address in American English. *Journal of Abnormal and Social Psychology*, 62, 454–62. [Reprinted in 1964 in D. Hymes (ed.), *Language in Culture and Society*. New York: Harper and Row, 234–44.]
Brown, R. and Gilman, A. (1960). The pronouns of power and solidarity. In T. A. Sebeok (ed.), *Style in Language*. Cambridge, MA: MIT Press, 253–76. [Reprinted in 1972 in P. P. Giglioli (ed.), *Language in Social Context*. Harmondsworth: Penguin Books, 252–82.]
Clark, R., Fairclough, N., Ivanic, R., McLeod, N., Thomas, J. and Meara, P. (eds) (1990). *Language and Power: Papers from the twenty-second annual meeting of the British Association for Applied Linguistics held at Lancaster University, September 1989*. London: Centre for Information on Language Teaching and Research. [Includes a section on language and power in educational settings.]
Eastman, C. M. (ed.) (1993). *Power in Language*. Special issue of the *International Journal of the Sociology of Language*, 103. Berlin: Mouton de Gruyter.
Fairclough, N. (1989). *Language and Power*. London: Longman.*
Fowler, R. (1985). Power. In T. A. van Dijk (ed.), *Handbook of Discourse Analysis*. Vol. 4. London: Academic Press, 61–82.
Fowler, R., Hodge, R., Kress, G. R. and Trew, T. (1979). *Language and Control*. London: Routledge and Kegan Paul.*
Henley, N. and Kramarae, C. (1991). Miscommunication, gender, and power. In N. Coupland, J. M. Wiemann and H. Giles (eds), *'Miscommunication' and Problematic Talk*. Newbury Park, CA: Sage, 18–43.
Lakoff, R. (1975). *Language and Woman's Place*. New York: Harper and Row.
Ng, S. H. and Bradac, J. (1993). *Power in Language: Verbal communication and social influence*. Newbury Park, CA: Sage.
O'Barr, W. and Atkins, B. K. (1980). 'Women's language' or 'powerless language'? In S. McConnell-Ginet, R. Borker and N. Furman (eds), *Women and Language in Literature and Society*. New York: Praeger, 93–110.
Phillipson, R. (1992). *Linguistic Imperialism*. Oxford: Oxford University Press.
Tannen, D. (1993). The relativity of linguistic strategies: rethinking power and solidarity in gender and dominance. In D. Tannen (ed.), *Gender and Conversational Interaction*. New York: Oxford University Press, 165–88.
Thomas, J. (1985). The language of power: towards a dynamic pragmatics. *Journal of Pragmatics*, 9, 765–83.
Wolfson, N. and Manes, J. (eds) (1985). *Language of Inequality*. Berlin: Mouton de Gruyter.

AJ

**language laboratory**    The designation *language laboratory* may seem a misnomer in so far as it is a teaching aid rather than a research facility. However, Châlon and others (1968) see it as a research centre to the extent that it can be used to gain knowledge *about* as well as *of* spoken language. The language laboratory dates from at least 1906, when the Yale professor Charles C. Clarke, followed closely by J. P. Rousselot in France, started employing 'talking machines', mainly to teach pronunciation. Various universities and academies instituted 'listening rooms' early in the century so that the recorded voices of native speakers could be heard. The direct ancestor of today's laboratories was created in 1930 by Ralph H. Waltz at Ohio State University.

The development of the laboratory has accompanied advances in technical innovation. The earliest versions allowed for listening only, the materials not containing pauses for repetition. The next generation permitted repetition, but with students working in chorus, only one phonograph between them. Waltz's Ohio State laboratory first incorporated individual 'listening posts', affording some soundproofing, and, after improvements by G. Oscar Russell, the possibility of individual recordings. Sound quality was initially abysmal, written texts being needed to follow the recordings. Waltz originally used wax cylinders, which deteriorated rapidly. It was only when electrical recording superseded mechanical means that acoustic quality became reliable. The technology was created in 1926, but Waltz first availed himself of it in 1931. Changing from mechanical to electrical recording increased the frequencies perceived from a range of 350–3000 cycles to one of 30–5500.

Contemporary *audio-active-comparative* teaching laboratories extend Waltz's 'listening-post' conception. Typically, they consist of ten or more soundproofed *booths* or cabins, though booths are not indispensable, since padded headphones and directional microphones limit interference from neighbours. Each position is equipped with a dual-track cassette-recorder, over which the student has complete control except during the broadcasting of materials, and is linked to a central *console*. At this the teacher sits, monitoring and correcting the performance of individual students via intercom. More advanced laboratories have *group* or *conference* facilities for inter-student communication. The idea of including a visual element (via film) in language laboratory work dates at least from Rousselot in 1911, and in the 1970s one of the University of Cambridge laboratories already provided video monitors in each booth. The combining of audio and visual sources is nowadays often routine. All modern laboratories offer a *library* facility, so that students may work independently, and many institutions possess *self-access* laboratories, without a console, for private study (see STUDENT AUTONOMY).

In 1918 Clarke articulated four principles connected with the language laboratory which have not been radically questioned since: (1) the machine always offers the same model (by contrast with a teacher, who may be inconsistent); (2) the machine is indefatigable; (3) the laboratory assists but does not replace the teacher; (4) recordings must be made by native speakers. (Only point 3 might today be controversial, since there now exist many 'home-study' courses which can be used in self-access laboratories, yet even here the consensus would be that it is better to work under a teacher if possible, not least because, though students can record their own responses and compare them with the master recording, they still do not always hear their errors before these are explicitly pointed out.)

The history of the language laboratory dispels the myth that it was invented as a tool specific to AUDIOLINGUALISM, though it naturally went hand-in-hand with an aural-oral approach. It did of course have an immediate application in audiolingualism by reason of its indefatigability, since the audiolingual method, while theoretically utilizable without a laboratory, demands presentation of target language items in such quantity as to exhaust a human model. It also had the advantage over a shared tape-recorder or other broadcasting source of permitting students to work at their own pace. However, what made laboratory technology particularly suitable for audiolingualism was the simple but significant adaptation in *materials* represented by the insertion of pauses. Waltz saw the benefit of pauses as threefold – to allow: (1) repetition after the model; (2) responses to questions on the recorded materials; (3) testing. While for the pioneers the primary function of the laboratory was the teaching of pronunciation, 'pause technology' facilitated its development into a machine for teaching syntax also, and again, though not indispensable, this responded usefully to the exigencies of audiolingualism.

The inserting of pauses into materials, especially in combination with facilities to record student responses in them, enabled the *drill* to become a much-used technique. The most basic drills involve repetition only, and consist of a stem and a gap. For example, *C'est ici qu'habite Jean-Pierre* could be a stem, followed by a pause for repetition, and could serve the purpose of teaching pronunciation, intonation or cleft-sentence structure. Audiolingualism, however, added a refinement, *reinforcement*, through provision of the correct response after the student's attempt in the pause, but preferred *substitution, mutation* and *manipulation* drills to repetition where teaching structure was concerned. (Examples: *substitution*: structural point: *I've been X-ing (living) here for some time*: drill: substitute for 'living' *eating, studying, standing, waiting . . .* ); *mutation*: structural point: infinitive to preterite: *I X-ed (see → saw) that*: drill: *eat: I ate that/drive: I drove that/ feel: I felt that . . .* ); *manipulation*: structural point: replies to tag questions: cue: *You saw him yesterday, didn't you?* response: *No, I didn't see him yesterday*; cue: *You didn't go there this morning, did you?* response: *No, I didn't go there this morning (Yes, I did go there this morning).*)

Because the language laboratory was popularly seen as the instrument of audiolingualism, it fell into disrepute for some time along with the audiolingual method. It was given new life with the appearance in 1973 of Dakin's posthumous work *The Language Laboratory and Language Learning*, in which he proposed imaginative 'meaningful' drills to replace the 'meaningless' audiolingual drills with their 'tum-te-tum effect', but drills which none the less still practised structural aspects of language. Examples include: *application drills*: a picture-prompt is provided to facilitate meaningful interpretation – a picture of a girl eating a fish is accompanied by the structure 'Felicity is eating a fish,' and the next, in which her plate is empty, by 'Felicity has just eaten her fish,' and so on (present progressive aspect/present perfect); *general knowledge drills*: stem: Rod Laver – response: 'Rod Laver plays tennis,' stem: Paul McCartney – response: 'Paul McCartney plays the guitar' (presence or absence of the definite article depending on whether the object is a sport or a musical instrument); *sound effect drills*: stem: (woof, woof) – response: 'I can hear a dog barking,' stem: (tweet, tweet) – response: 'I can hear a bird singing,' etc. (use of participle after a verb of perception).

Nowadays, while still used to some extent to teach aspects of grammar and morphology, the laboratory has mainly reverted to what it was in the first place: an aid in teaching pronunciation (see PRONUNCIATION TEACHING), INTONATION, listening comprehension and transcription. However, there is emphasis on 'communicative' tasks such as jigsaw listening (see JIGSAW PRINCIPLE) and extracting information and replying to 'content questions' in accordance with instructions on a work-sheet. Video materials including feature films are particularly popular with students, and 'off-air' materials such as news bulletins assist not only in exercising comprehension but also with acquisition of cultural knowledge. Self-access facilities enable learners to prepare for classes at their own speed, or to follow up on classes. Where such facilities exist, many teachers now prefer learners to listen or listen and view outside class hours, so that classes can be devoted to interactive tasks and group activities. In its modern form the laboratory is also invaluable in training interpreters.

BIBLIOGRAPHY

Châlon, Y., Bouillon, C., Holec, H., Kuhn, M. and Zoppis, C. (1968). *The Language Laboratory in Higher Education: An experiment*. Strasbourg: AIDELA.

Dakin, J. (1973). *The Language Laboratory and Language Learning*. London: Longman.*

Léon, P. R. (1962). *Laboratoire de langues et correction phonétique* [The language laboratory and phonetic correction]. Paris: Librairie Marcel Didier.

Stack, E. M. (1966). *The Language Laboratory and Modern Language Teaching*. Rev. edn. New York: Oxford University Press.

JTR

**language planning** is the branch of macro(socio)linguistics (see MACRO/MICRO-LINGUISTICS) which is concerned with the selection and implementation of standard languages. Crucial to the work of language planners are such concepts as speech community, ACCENT, DIALECT, BILINGUALISM and DIGLOSSIA.

Language planning is carried out by various formal and informal groups, institutions and individuals. In some countries language planning is the task of specialized academies (e.g. in France, Sweden, Italy, Spain), governmental commissions (e.g. in China), nongovernmental agencies, dictionary makers, printers, educators, missionaries, writers, journalists and so on.

## HAUGEN'S MODEL

Haugen (1972 [1966]) suggested a framework for discussing language planning in four stages:

(1) norm selection;
(2) codification;
(3) acceptance;
(4) elaboration of function.

*Selection* Norm selection is a sociopolitical act of choosing a language or a variety (standard) which will have the most prestige and/or acceptance within a nation (speech community). The choice of a national language (language determination) serves the purpose of unification and separation from others. For example, Hebrew was chosen to be revived in Israel as a symbol of the newly founded country's identity, and Swahili served the same purpose in Tanzania after the country gained independence from the British.

*Codification* Codification is concerned with specifying the form of the chosen standard. Both norm selection and codification depend largely on standardization *ideology* which states that there exists only one standard variety of a language, e.g. that there is only one standard or 'good' variety of English (although, of course, WORLD ENGLISH has many standards). This ideology reinforces the 'complaint tradition' about *bad* usage (Milroy and Milroy, 1985), which in the case of English has been present since the Middle Ages, when complaints were made about the relatively low status of English in comparison to French and Latin. In the fifteenth century STANDARD ENGLISH emerged (London dialect) and William Caxton complained about the great dialectal variation of English which led him to his work on codification of spelling.

Caxton's work was one form of early implementation of standardization. Other contemporary examples include education, the media promotion of a consciousness of the standard, favouring speakers of certain languages in the civil service, etc.

*Acceptance* As Haugen (1972: 252) aptly put it, 'a standard language, if it is not to be dismissed as dead, must have a body of users.' Therefore, the acceptance of the norm by a small but necessarily influential group is a prerequisite for the success of a language planning operation. The acceptance of a norm is weighted on the cost-benefit scale. If the new language or variety is perceived by its potential users as a source of authority, power, prestige, identity, religious affiliation, and so on, it will be likely to replace any other competing variant.

*Elaboration* The complaint tradition about English continued into the sixteenth century after the standard had been selected, codified and accepted. The new complaints dealt with the inadequacy of English in comparison to Latin, Greek, French and Italian in such areas as scholarship, administration, law and the arts. It was then that English developed a rich vocabulary, and continued to develop in new areas of use until the eighteenth century when it started to enjoy the status of a fully developed, autonomous and official language (Milroy and Milroy, 1985).

EVALUATION OF LANGUAGE PLANNING

The success of language planning processes depends on all of the stages mentioned above. Certainly, the results of different language planning programmes vary across the world. For example, the results of the planning efforts in Tanzania and Ireland were very different from each other (Fasold, 1984).

*Tanzania*   In the 1960s, after gaining independence, Tanzania adopted Swahili as its national and subsequently the official language.

Tanganyika in 1961 was a 'triglossic' country where about 135 vernacular languages were spoken, offering their speakers local identity and solidarity. Swahili was the first language of trade, and later the medium of national communication, and English was the post-colonial language of high prestige and national government.

Swahili was chosen and accepted as a national language (with English) because it was an indigenous language without the associations of colonial hegemony and any single sociocultural group struggling for power. It was widely known as a second language. As a Bantu language it was related to the first language of the majority of citizens, and historically it was the language of initial education and local administration.

The Kiunguja dialect was selected as the new standard and the written standard closely matched the spoken standard dialect.

The adoption of Swahili as a standard national language in Tanzania was very successful. It became widely used in administration and primary education, it is accepted as a Tanzanian symbol of national identity, and it was accepted as a means of communication by a vast majority of speakers for whom it remains a second language.

*Ireland*   Irish Gaelic was replaced by English in the seventeenth century. A small fraction (about 3%) of the population of the Irish Republic speaks Irish as a native language today, although the Irish constitution recognizes Irish as the first and English as the second official language. The language planning efforts which have continued from the 1950s to the present have had little success. Official and communicative functions are practically all performed in English. Irish has only a symbolic role in Ireland as a nationalist language. However, on a more formal level of codification, Irish language planning has succeeded in developing a uniform orthographic system, expanding vocabulary and standardization.

CONCLUSION

Language planning is concerned with a more general question of language choice. Such choices need not always be global and involve speakers' national identities, but can be quite local. For example, the choice of a Finnish-British couple to raise their daughter bilingually in Britain will be an act of creating and reasserting their identity as a bicultural family.

Language choice also involves second and foreign languages. Different factors can be responsible for a national policy on which second/foreign language should dominate in the state's educational system. For example, due to the political hegemony of the Soviet Union in Eastern Europe between 1945 and 1989, Russian was officially but largely unsuccessfully taught as the main foreign language in this part of the world. Since 1989 it has been almost entirely replaced by English, although now, due to new economic links between East European countries, it is interesting that Russian (alongside English and German) is gaining in importance as a trade lingua franca.

BIBLIOGRAPHY

Cobarrubias, J. and Fishman, J. A. (eds) (1983). *Progress in Language Planning: International perspectives*. Berlin: Mouton.

Fasold, R. (1984). *The Sociolinguistics of Society*. Oxford: Blackwell. [Particularly chapters 9 and 10.]

Haugen, E. (1972 [1966]). Dialect, language, nation. In A. S. Dil (ed.), *The Ecology of Language: Essays by Einar Haugen.* Stanford, CA: Stanford University Press, 237–54.

Jernudd, B. H. and Shapiro, M. J. (eds) (1989). *The Politics of Language Purism.* Berlin: Mouton de Gruyter.

Milroy, J. and Milroy, L. (1985). *Authority in Language.* London: Routledge.

AJ

**language testing** involves many technologies and developments which are different from language teaching, and yet it interacts closely with most aspects of language teaching. Traditionally, a distinction between proficiency and achievement testing has been drawn: achievement tests assess how successful a learner has been in a course of study, proficiency tests assess a learner's level of language in relation to some absolute scale, or to the specifications of some job which has a language requirement. Both kinds of testing draw on measurement theory to assess VALIDITY and RELIABILITY, use statistics to monitor the performance of the tests as tests and individual items within the tests, and employ applied linguistics and linguistic research to specify language items and test tasks. Both kinds of testing also interact with course design specifications in different ways to establish validity and congruence with the aims of related courses; with teaching methodology to ensure reasonable parity between test tasks and classroom tasks; with needs analysis to ensure reasonable relations between the target language use situation, the course and the test; and both proficiency and achievement tests may have a strong effect – known as washback – on teaching methodology in certain circumstances (see WASHBACK EFFECT).

Testing English as a Foreign Language has developed in particular in proficiency testing, with achievement testing following on behind, perhaps due to the different institutional constraints compared with modern languages in English-speaking countries;

Weir (1993) makes a strong prediction that the next big area of development will be achievement testing. Most of the developments discussed below stem from the world of published, standardized and commercial tests. Most of these are proficiency tests, although many are also used as achievement tests because courses have been designed to teach students how to gain the certification involved.

Development in public standardized testing has been driven by the need to respond:

• to market demands, as in the provision of tests of communicative effectiveness, and of tests with patent relevance to particular situations like business and international commerce;

• to questions in measurement theory as to how to establish what a test is measuring, how accurately it does it, and how to evaluate the proposed items themselves;

• to growth in variety of methods, materials and modes of organization in the classrooms.

CHARACTERISTICS OF A GOOD TEST

*Validity* Traditionally, the characteristics of a good test have been seen to be VALIDITY, RELIABILITY, discrimination and feasibility. A valid test is one in which an individual's score gives a true reflection of that individual's ability on the trait claimed to be measured. Typically, testers have used a mixture of descriptive and statistical means to check this. If proficiency may be described in terms of a list of language items to be known, then a content analysis can determine if those language items, or some representative sample, occur in the test. If proficiency is described in terms of aspects of skill, like reading speed or the variety of text types considered important at a particular level, then similarly a content analysis can be used. In some circumstances validity might be a function of language knowledge, skill in using the language and ability to negotiate certain language activities associated with a particular target use, so task authenticity may be important. Testers use statistics (see STATISTICS IN APPLIED LINGUISTICS RESEARCH) to determine the degree of difference or agreement (using CORRELATION) between sets of scores by the same people on different tests to see if one test is tapping the same language proficiency as another. Recently researchers have also begun to look at what testees say about the experience of answering particular test items in order to try and separate the measurement of relevant aspects of language skill use, e.g. in using reading strategies, from the use of test-taking strategies. This may be seen as a way of opening up construct validity, or the accuracy of measurement of the theoretical essentials of a given skill or area of knowledge.

*Reliability*   Testers attempt to establish the reliability of tests by measures of internal consistency, wide sampling within skill areas, comparison across repeated administrations and measures of agreement between examiners. All these ways of estimating reliability are intended to establish the degree of uncertainty, called the spread of error, around the score obtained by the candidate. Reliability may be increased (the spread of error reduced) by weeding out inconsistent items, increasing the sample of language items, vocabulary and tasks used, training examiners in the use of rating scales, using marking methods employing analytic headings, allowing markers to use only an optimum number of categories. Ultimately, the purpose of increasing reliability of a test is to make the test fair to the candidates; the purpose of estimating reliability is to know its limits. Reliability is essential in a test, because without it one cannot believe the results (and results are not always credible); but it is useless unless the test is valid as well, for without validity one does not know what has been tested.

*Discrimination*   A test has to have the power to discriminate between the candidates. With tests for learners at much the same level, as with most class achievement tests, this is not a serious problem; it is not always possible to design a test which will discriminate reliably at all levels of candidate ability unless the test is going to be fairly long. Even with large-scale tests for all comers such as the IELTS or TOEFL, criticism may be raised on the grounds that discrimination is not equally good across the range. With smaller-scale tests a solution sometimes adopted is to require the candidates who score highly on the test given to the majority to take a further extension, to separate them out. The disadvantage of this system is that the basic test has to be marked first in order to select those who need the extension, thus negating the advantage of a short test where time is at a premium – as when a test is used to place students in ability groups on a course.

Discrimination is also a property of individual items in a test, and one important stage in test development is the analysis of how each item contributes to the discriminative power of the test as a whole. Various techniques for *item analysis* have been proposed which make this comparison. Items should show a reasonably good record of agreeing with the overall score given by the rest of the items. If an item is answered correctly reasonably often by candidates who answer most of the rest of the items right, and reasonably infrequently by candidates who answer most of the others wrong, it has good discrimination. Of course, if everybody – good and poor candidates alike – answers it correctly, it is simply too easy and does not have good discrimination. Items sometimes work the other way round and are answered correctly by poor candidates and incorrectly by good ones, and consequently those items have to be replaced.

These techniques have recently been augmented by a more sophisticated mathematical technique known as Item Response Theory, which models the responses to items on more powerful assumptions: that each item has a level of difficulty associated with it, that the items can be ordered with respect to each other, as in a 'power' or 'ladder' test, and that candidates' responses can be expected to be inconsistent within the limits of their ability levels. With these more powerful techniques comes a more sophisticated approach to test design and pre-administration vetting. The usual examples of these item analysis techniques concern multiple-choice questions (see MULTIPLE-CHOICE TESTING), but in principle all types of item, including scales for rating oral performance, can be subjected to such a rigorous analysis.

One should note that in language tests, it is rarely the case that each item can be assumed to be ordered in difficulty with respect to the others. If there are sections on grammatical knowledge, it may be arguable that some questions are more difficult than others (e.g. one on remote conditions compared to one on the present tense), but equally reasonable to assume that others are of equal difficulty and equally necessary. Similarly, one can question the assumption of a linear order of difficulty in different sections of an oral interview test. It is not obvious that requiring the candidate to talk about their own career prospects and asking the candidates to ask questions of the examiner based on an information card, as happens in the 'speculation and attitudes' and the 'elicitation' phase of the IELTS speaking test, are more or less difficult than each other. In fact, there is very little research as yet on what elements of speaking tests contribute most to the examiners' judgements.

*Feasibility* The fourth requirement has naturally produced a number of technological advances, such as computer marking for large-scale tests, in which the candidate marks the answer on a special computer readable sheet; tests run on PCs, tests using video presentation such as the BBC English Video Test; prerecorded oral tests such as the Simulated Oral Proficiency Interview

and the Test of Spoken English. In general, however, tests remain conservative and still predominantly require modest resources and administration such as pencil and paper.

## DEVELOPMENTS IN TEST ITEM WRITING

Skehan (1988) makes the point that, some fifteen years ago, most testing questions seemed to be answerable, and technology confidently pointed to multiple-choice indirect testing for most purposes. Now, developments are happening in all directions, and confidence in the use of only one kind of objective testing has evaporated. The motive for this diversity is mainly the hunt for valid and reliable tests of communicative proficiency. Several important relationships are in play here: between test activity and target language use; between test activity and teaching activity; and between test and language construct. The importance of the redefinition of what it means to know a language wrought by the notion of COMMUNICATIVE COMPETENCE was clearly chronicled by Morrow (1979).

*Direct tests* Many authorities regard communicativeness as implying direct testing of success in communicative events, just as communicative teaching implies using communication in the classroom as a learning activity rather than only as an aim. Thus, experimentation has produced published tests using monitored group discussion, authentic materials in reading and listening tests, and activities which students will need to be able to complete successfully in real life. The Test of English for Educational Purposes (AEB; CALS, Reading) contains a number of language activities whose importance was attested in doctoral research in UK universities (Weir, 1988). This concern for AUTHENTICITY can have the disadvantage of poor sampling, if a wide enough range of activities is not included.

Another disadvantage is that in some skill areas, the demand characteristics of the test as a test may prevent the task being convincing as an authentic one. This is particularly evident in structured oral interviews, where the true roles of examiner and examinee, with their inherent power and social asymmetry, conspire to negate the pretence of conversation between equals. Van Lier (1989) has shown devastatingly how this can distort the discourse that is produced. Coleman (1991) also raised doubts about equating a short timed writing task with the production of an essay in ordinary self-governed academic conditions.

*Testing follows teaching*    Many tests are also designed to follow current teaching ideas, so where communicative information gap (see INFORMATION/OPINION GAP) exercises have been used, authentic materials employed and open-ended discussions practised, tests have tried to include similar ingredients. Authentic materials – or at least look-alike authentic materials – are employed in the general test of English from the Oxford Delegacy of Local Examinations, and in the business and commerce tests from ODLE, Cambridge and the London Chamber of Commerce and Industry. Information gap exercises based on visuals are employed by the Cambridge Advanced English test and by the Certificates in Communicative Skills in English oral component. Another communicative idea taken up in testing has been the thematic test, in which the items test different aspects of proficiency as related to a single theme, much as a unit of teaching usually is. This approach is currently adopted by the TEEP test and the University of London Certificate of Attainment in English, and is embedded in several business and commerce tests.

*Language knowledge*    A third influence of communicative thought is in respect of the nature of the knowledge interrogated in the test. Appropriate use of the language implies knowledge of setting, participants, level of formality, etc., all of which can be made the subject of test items, as discussed by Morrow (1977).

ACHIEVEMENT TESTING

Weir (1993) makes the point that most of the advances in test construction in recent years have been in published, standardized, proficiency tests, and that the area now needing development is the testing of achievement. However, as Weir discussed, there are more issues at stake here than technical questions about test design: testing achievement implies summative and formative evaluation, and attitudes of teachers and learners to evaluation and assessment, and to the questions of who needs the information, what purpose it is being collected for and what effects it has, are varied, cautious and often suspicious. The politics of proficiency testing usually involve the use of a test as some kind of gate which may close on some, or a ticket for opportunities for others; the politics of achievement testing are bound up with educational appraisal, management and administration – and in some countries, league tables of schools. Nevertheless, teachers are entitled to ask what can be learned from these advances in standardized testing for teacher-made classroom tests and examinations, and how collaborative developments between testers and teachers for fairer and more efficient local testing arrangements may be implemented.

RESEARCH AND DEVELOPMENT IN TESTING

Research in test design is continuing and expanding in many centres. The long tradition of publishing research reports about the TOEFL test established by the Educational Testing Service has recently been adopted by the University of Cambridge Local Examinations Syndicate for the IELTS test, beginning with the reports of the ELTS review, and gradually more information about the performance of this test is becoming available. The same is unfortunately not true about many of the other published tests, perhaps because a conflict lurks here between commercial and scientific interests. However, dissemination of research is healthier than previously, through the journal *Language Testing* (Edward Arnold) and *Language Testing Update* (Centre for Research in Language Education, Lancaster). UCLES publish an occasional series of research reports.

*Comparability*   One issue that has attracted some attention for its practical utility has been that of comparability of tests. An international comparison between TOEFL and FCE was undertaken by Davidson and Bachman (1992). Carroll and West (1989) attempted to devise a method of relating a range of tests produced in the UK to a common scale of descriptors of proficiency levels like the nine bands of the IELTS test called the English Speaking Union Framework. This involved a specially selected number of speech and writing samples being given ratings on the framework scale by independent judges and by different test producers on their own criteria, thus allowing an equation between scores on published tests and the Framework. Currently a different approach is being piloted by Cambridge which involves the validation of a set of 'can do' statements – what a person scoring n on a particular test can do in the language, and presumably by implication cannot do.

*Associations and quality control*   Cambridge's approach to the validation of test comparability is being conducted in the context of an international association, the Association of Language Testers in Europe (ALTE), which links producers of tests of proficiency in their national languages, and which aims to establish a common scale of proficiency which can be used for each of the eleven languages involved.

ALTE has also published a code of practice to which the members promise to adhere to ensure standards of validity, reliability and therefore fairness in terms of content, and of trading. Individual test writers, researchers and producers may join the International Language Testers' Association, which aims to promote test development, information about test design and research into testing theory and practice. The official Newsletter of the ILTA is *Language Testing Update*.

In the UK a number of test producers have joined together in the Association of British ESOL Examining Boards, or ABEEB. This organization has also produced a code of practice for ESOL examinations which the member boards undertake to honour, covering information to users; standardization – question setting; standardization – marking; awarding; appeals; and administration. Since the major market for the tests produced by this group is overseas, it is not surprising that the British Council gives administrative support. These moves underline both the commercial, competitive aspect of proficiency testing and certification, and the need to promote and maintain public standards of performance which has affected all other areas of education.

*Washback*   One major role in language teaching programmes that has been claimed for tests is their assumed ability to control teaching. This is normally called 'washback'. It is reasonable that teachers will want to familiarize their students with test formats and therefore will use teaching time to practise item types – indeed, it contributes to the reliability of the test by reducing the unfairness of surprise. It is also reasonable that teachers will not devote teaching time to skills that are not rewarded in tests: there is little point in organizing conversation practice if there is no oral proficiency component in the test for which the students need preparation. Thus, washback may be a mechanism for conservatism. On the other hand, simply changing the test format does not necessarily bring about changes in teaching styles. Alderson and Wall (1993) raised doubts about the sufficiency of washback as an agent for change in a study of curriculum development in Sri Lanka. They concluded that the introduction of new classroom methodology requires concurrent developments in teacher education, materials and tests: changing only the tests does not give the teachers the means to re-orient their classroom methods for preparing students for the new tests. Thus, washback may not be as powerful an agent for innovation as it is for conservatism.

See also MEASUREMENTS OF SECOND LANGUAGE PROFICIENCY, TESTS IN ENGLISH LANGUAGE TEACHING.

BIBLIOGRAPHY
Alderson, J. C. and Wall, D. (1993). Does washback exist? *Applied Linguistics*, 14/2, 115–29.
Carroll, B. J. and West, R. (1989). *ESU Framework*. Harlow: Longman.
Coleman, H. (1991). The testing of 'appropriate behaviour' in an academic context. In P. Adams, B. Heaton, and P. Howarth (eds), *Socio-cultural issues in English for academic purposes*. London: Macmillan, 14–24.
Davidson F. and Bachman, L. (1990). The Cambridge-TOEFL comparability study: an example of the cross-national comparison of language tests. *AILA Review, 7, Standardization in Language Testing*, 24–45.
Hughes, A. (1989). *Testing for Language Teachers*. Cambridge: Cambridge University Press.
Morrow, K. E. (1977). *Techniques of Evaluation for a Notional Syllabus*. University of Reading, Centre for Applied Language Studies.
——(1979). Communicative language testing: revolution or evolution? in C. Brumfit and K. Johnson (eds), *The Communicative Approach to Language Teaching*. Oxford: Oxford University Press.
Skehan, P. (1988). Language testing: survey article, part 1. *Language Teaching Abstracts*, 21/4, 211–21.

Van Lier, L. (1989). Reeling, writhing, drawling, stretching, and fainting in coils: oral proficiency interviews and conversation. *TESOL Quarterly*, 23/3, 489–508.
Weir, C. J. (1988). The specification, realization, and validation of an English language proficiency test. In A. Hughes (ed.), *Testing English for University Study*. ELT Documents 127. Oxford: Modern English Press, 45–110.
——(1993). *Understanding and Developing Language Tests*. London: Prentice Hall.*
                                          SMCD

**langue/parole**   A distinction made by the Swiss linguist Ferdinand de Saussure (1857–1913) between the abstract language system and its physical manifestations in the production of utterances. No individual NATIVE SPEAKER of a language possesses the full tacit knowledge of a complete *langue* – this exists only in the collective mind of a given speech community. Individuals possess only part of that knowledge. *Langue*, not *parole*, is the main object of linguistic study. It is studied synchronically (see SYNCHRONIC/DIACHRONIC), that is, with reference to its properties at a given time (cf. present-day English, early Modern English). The *langue/parole* dichotomy is present in the COMPETENCE/PERFORMANCE distinction made in CHOMSKYAN LINGUISTICS. However, while *langue* is a social concept, competence is a psychological concept.

See also STRUCTURALISM.

BIBLIOGRAPHY
Lyons, J. (1968). *Introduction to Theoretical Linguistics*. Cambridge: Cambridge University Press, 51–2.
Robins, R. H. (1990). *A Short History of Linguistics*. London: Longman, 220–1.*
                                            EJ

**learnability**   The desire to develop a 'psychologically real' theory of grammar has led linguists to hypothesize that grammars proposed for particular languages must be 'learnable' by the child L1 learner on the basis only of the language it hears around it (positive evidence). 'Learnability theory' investigates the formal properties of grammars which are 'learnable' in this sense.

BIBLIOGRAPHY

Wexler, K. (1981). Some issues in the theory of learnability. In C. Baker and J. McCarthy (eds), *The Logical Problem of Language Acquisition*. Cambridge, MA: MIT Press.
White, L. (1989). *Universal Grammar and Second Language Acquisition*. Amsterdam: John Benjamins.* [Chapter 2.]

RH

## learner/learning/teacher-centred

Instruction is typically said to be 'learner-centred' if pedagogic decisions are taken, by the teacher, with the idiosyncratic interests and needs of each particular group of learners (even each individual learner) given top priority (made 'central'). It is said to be 'learning-centred' (following Prabhu (1984)) if the principal consideration in decision-making is the nature of the learning process envisaged for the learners. It is 'teacher-centred' (often used with pejorative intention) if, by contrast, the decision-making centres on the concerns of the teacher (for example, if teachers are held to be using a particular method because that is how they have been trained to teach, rather than because it is appropriate to their immediate situation). (See also AUTONOMOUS LEARNING.)

BIBLIOGRAPHY

Nunan, D. (1988). *The Learner-Centred Curriculum*. Cambridge: Cambridge University Press.
Prabhu, N. S. (1984). Coping with the unknown in language pedagogy. Paper presented at British Council 50th Anniversary Seminar.

RLA

**learner training** is a relatively new dimension in the application of research outcomes to language teaching programmes, at least in an explicit sense. It has its parentage in learner strategy research (see LEARNING STRATEGIES) which itself developed from the earlier GOOD LANGUAGE LEARNER STUDIES (GLL). Learner training is also closely related to the theory and practice of STUDENT AUTONOMY and self-directed learning.

### DEFINITIONS AND RESEARCH BACKGROUND

In simple terms, *learner training* refers to the awareness-raising of an individual's understanding both of language and of him- or herself as a learner. It is concerned with training *in* what have come to be regarded as effective learning strategies (the research base), and training *for* independence and personal autonomy (both a philosophical and a tactical perspective). In other words, it uses the currently available descriptive studies for a broadly interventionist – 'training' – purpose (McDonough, 1995: chapter 5). It focuses on the 'how' more than on the 'what' aspect of learning. Dickinson (1988: 48) claims that learner training has three necessary components:

● training in processes, strategies and activities;
● instruction designed to heighten awareness of the nature of the target language;
● instruction in aspects of the theory of language learning;

all of which are designed to help learners understand how to learn.

Growing out of the GLL studies and subsequent learner strategy research, there is now a large body of empirical work that has been able to identify the kinds of learning strategies adopted by people who appear to be effective language learners. (Controversies in research assumptions and procedures are not appropriate for discussion here.) The characteristics of such learners include:

● setting personal goals;
● taking 'risks' in the target language; being willing to try things out and make errors;

- trying different learning strategies and choosing the most suitable;
- organizing time and resources;
- actively rehearsing new material;
- using initiative outside the classroom.

(See, for example, Wenden and Rubin, 1987; Wesche, 1979, quoted in Dickinson, 1987; Wenden, 1991; McDonough, 1995.)

The list above represents very broad categories; different researchers have studied specific areas and have identified a wide range of strategies and sub-strategies associated, for example, with different skills, such as listening comprehension or vocabulary acquisition. There are also a number of taxonomies of such strategies, the best-known being that of O'Malley and Chamot (e.g. 1990) who divide them into (a) metacognitive (b) cognitive and (c) social-affective strategies, concerned respectively with thinking about how to approach the learning process itself, dealing with actual learning material and identifying effective interactive contexts of use.

## APPLICATIONS AND TECHNIQUES

The body of research described in the previous section has been harnessed to serve two overlapping yet distinct instructional goals: the promotion of effective learning procedures, including those within the framework of the conventional classroom, where only modest goals may be realizable, and the development of learners' independence and responsibility for their own successful learning. For the purposes of the present discussion, the two are conflated here.

The best-known example of the application of learner strategy research underpinned by an autonomous philosophy is the learner training course devised by Ellis and Sinclair (1989). Starting from the twin assumptions that individuals use a wide variety of different ways to learn, and that effective self-management of learning is fed by knowledge about learning and language, they argue for the need to provide learners with the foundations for making their own informed choices. They then offer what is effectively a self-training manual: Stage 1 sensitizes learners to think about their own characteristics, attitudes, needs and priorities, and Stage 2 takes them through a process of skills training, covering the four skills plus vocabulary and grammar acquisition.

From a comparable perspective, Dickinson (1988) proposes a three-tier system for methodological implementation (originally designed by Nisbet and Shucksmith). The first level is concerned with overall approaches to learning, the second with 'superordinate' and generalized procedures formulated as abilities (for example, to determine task objectives, undertake self-assessment and work cooperatively with others) and the third with the sub-strategies required for acquiring specific skill areas (such as listening for gist and the like). The loose parallels with the O'Malley and Chamot typology are readily discernible here. Nakhoul (1993) incorporated a learner training perspective into a first-year university course in Hong Kong, focusing on self-access learning facilities and with the primary aim of promoting independent learning. A number of course-book writers are also beginning to deal explicitly with learning strategies as well as with skills and language content: Phillips and Sheerin (1990), for instance, include activities based on the notion of the 'good language learner', such as efficient dictionary use and vocabulary acquisition, willingness to ask questions and to take risks. The learner independence/training paradigm is one of a number of outcomes from a growing commitment to learner-centred education. The corollary is the unavoidable implication for the broadening of the teacher's role, both in creating an environment in which 'learning how to learn' can be fostered, and also him- or herself understanding the learning strategy background. There are many contexts in which teachers themselves may not feel this to be appropriate, as when their traditional status places them in a position of authority and control and their learners expect this role to be fulfilled. In other situations, learners may reject the ethos of autonomy and negotiation introduced by the teacher who believes in it.

There are a number of other unresolved issues to do with the application of learner strategy research to learner training. In particular, it is not clear that strategies are sufficiently generalizable to be used with a range of learners who will themselves be affected by factors of context, cultural background, type of problem and proficiency level. Nor is there yet much hard evidence that strategy training leads to improvement in language learning outcomes. As McDonough (1995: 172–3) points out, 'although learning strategies . . . and strategy training are very important elements in the teaching-learning process, great care has to be exercised in moving from a descriptive and taxonomic position to an interventionist one.'

BIBLIOGRAPHY
Dickinson, L. (1987). *Self-Instruction in Language Learning*. Cambridge: Cambridge University Press.
——(1988). Learner training. In A. Brookes and P. Grundy (eds), *Individualization and Autonomy in Language Learning*. ELT Documents 131. Oxford: Modern English Publications with the British Council, 45–53.
Ellis, G. and Sinclair, B. (1989). *Learning to Learn English*. Cambridge: Cambridge University Press.
McDonough, S. H. (1995). *Strategy, Process and Skill in Language Learning*. London: Edward Arnold.
Nakhoul, L. (1993). Letting go: preparing teachers and students for learner independence. In J. Edge and K. Richards (eds), *Teachers Develop Teachers Research*. Oxford: Heinemann, 147–60.
O'Malley, J. M. and Chamot, A.-U. (1990). *Learning Strategies in Second Language Acquisition*. Cambridge: Cambridge University Press.*
Phillips, D. and Sheerin, S. (1990). *Signature*. London: Nelson.
Wenden, A. (1991). *Learner Strategies for Learner Autonomy*. Englefield Cliffs, NJ, and London: Prentice-Hall.*
Wenden, A. and Rubin, J. (eds) (1987). *Learner Strategies in Language Learning*. Englefield Cliffs, NJ, and London: Prentice-Hall.
JMCD

**learning strategies** These are techniques used by second language learners for remembering and organizing samples of the L2. Some researchers claim that learning strategies contribute to L2 development. An example of a learning strategy is the 'keyword' approach to acquiring vocabulary, in which a vocabulary item to be learned is associated with an unusual mental image. A classic example is learning the German word for 'egg' – *Ei* – by imagining an egg with an 'eye' in the middle of it.

In principle, learning strategies should be distinguished from another kind of strategy: COMMUNICATION STRATEGIES. Communication strategies are techniques for maintaining or repairing a dialogue with an interlocutor when it is in danger of breaking down. For example, if an L2 learner does not know the expression for 'ironing-board', and yet wishes to ask for such an object, she or he may resort to paraphrase ('table for doing the ironing on') or risk using the L1 expression in the hope that it may sound like the L2 item, or revert to mime. Such strategies have a good probability of ensuring successful communication. In practice it is not always easy to distinguish learning strategies from communication strategies. If an L2 speaker hears a word that she or he does not know, and asks the interlocutor for an explanation, is this a strategy to make sure the communication is successful, or is it a learning strategy (because as the result of adopting it the learner learns a new word)?

Interest in learning strategies appears to have first emerged from a desire to understand the characteristics of the 'good language learner' (Naiman et al., 1978) (see GOOD LANGUAGE LEARNER STUDIES). For example, Rubin (1975) tried to determine the sorts of learning strategies used by good learners in a classroom setting. Through observation of those learners deemed to be good, she suggested a number of strategies that they used:

- preparedness to guess about the L2;
- attention to the formal properties of the L2;
- a willingness to appear foolish in using the L2;
- an active desire to initiate conversations in the L2;

and so on. This is essentially a speculative list of characteristics putatively associated with successful second language learning. Other early studies also made speculative inventories of learning strategies (see Ellis, 1994: 547 for a summary of strategies found in such studies).

However, there are a number of problems with simple lists of proposed strategies. (See Ellis, 1994: 530–3 for some discussion of the problems.) First, do strategies guide behaviour or are they mental states? If strategies are behavioural then they will prompt the learner to act in certain ways (to start conversations with strangers, to seek out L2 learning situations, etc.). If strategies are mental states they will determine how the learner's mind interacts with L2 data (for example, focusing attention on form, mentally rehearsing newly encountered data, etc.). Or are they both, and does it matter anyway?

Second, if (at least some) learning strategies relate to mental states, are they conscious or unconscious? For example, can a learner *decide* to focus on form, or is focusing on form beyond conscious control and dependent on the context in which language is encountered or the innate disposition of the learner? This issue is of considerable importance if one wishes to teach L2 learners learning strategies (see, for example, Wenden and Rubin, 1987). If learning strategies are not under conscious control, it is debatable whether trying to teach them to learners will have any success.

Third, if some learning strategies seem to be common to all good language learners, how are they related to acquisition? Are they the cause of successful language learning, or are they instead types of behaviour which successful language learners happen to display, independent of success in language learning?

Recent work on learning strategies has attempted to address these issues, but without any clear answers emerging. Some research has subdivided learning strategies to distinguish between the behavioural and the mental or cognitive. Skehan (1989), for example, suggests that there are three broad domains covered by learning strategies:

- those which determine the learner's personal involvement in the learning process (these are behavioural strategies: seeking learning opportunities, setting aside regular practice times, etc.);
- those which enable the learner to sort and organize the L2 data (these are cognitive strategies: searching for patterns, mentally recalling and rehearsing L2 patterns, etc.);
- those which cause the learner to monitor his or her progress (these are meta-cognitive strategies: for example, checking performance against that of native speakers).

Seliger (1984) focused on the conscious/unconscious distinction and suggested that consciously deployed techniques are 'tactics' (e.g. seeking out learning opportunities, conscious rehearsing of L2 patterns) whereas unconscious modes of sorting and organizing L2 data are strategies proper (e.g. the unconscious over-regularizing of regular past tense forms in cases like *She goed there, I didn't bought it* would be examples of an unconscious strategy at work).

O'Malley and Chamot (1990) have divided strategies into meta-cognitive and cognitive (corresponding to mental states, but not distinguishing conscious and unconscious) and social/affective (corresponding to behaviour).

Oxford (1990) distinguishes direct strategies (which engage the L2 directly) and indirect strategies (where the learner seeks out situations which will enable him or her to engage with the L2 directly).

While these various subdivisions are clearly attempts to refine our understanding of the nature of learning strategies, several problems still remain. First, as Ellis notes (1994: 540) many of the strategies proposed in the literature require considerable 'interpretation': that is, they are not fully explicit. Take a strategy like 'attention to form'. Good language learners are supposedly those who attend to form. But how much attention do they give? Is attention conscious or not? Do levels of attention vary across individuals and across tasks in the same individual? Factors like these are just not explicit in the label applied to the strategy. Second, there seem to be no constraints on the potential for proposing new strategies, many of which might be quite ludicrous. For example, one might claim that learners who eat fudge at the weekend are better language learners than those who do not. While this is absurd, there is as yet no theoretical base for filtering out plausible strategies from implausible ones, and this is a serious weakness in any enterprise to isolate good language learning strategies. Finally, the strategy taxonomies which have been proposed often classify the same strategy under different categories (for example, a tactic in Seliger's (1984) sense might be classed as a social/affective strategy in O'Malley and Chamot (1990) and as an indirect strategy in Oxford (1990)).

Some of the more robust findings of strategy research are summarized in Ellis (1994: 555–6):

- strategies appear to change as learners become more advanced;
- successful language learners appear to use more strategies than less successful ones;
- successful language learners pay attention both to meaning and form;
- different strategies may contribute to different aspects of L2 proficiency;
- learning strategies used by adults and children appear to differ: children use more socially oriented strategies, adults use more cognitive strategies.

(See also LEARNER TRAINING.)

BIBLIOGRAPHY
Ellis, R. (1994). *The Study of Second Language Acquisition.* Oxford: Oxford University Press.* [Chapter 12.]
Naiman, N., Fröhlich, M., Stern, H. and Todesco, A. (1978). *The Good Language Learner.* Research in Education Series no. 7. Toronto: OISE.
O'Malley, J. and Chamot, A. (1990). *Learning Strategies in Second Language Acquisition.* Cambridge: Cambridge University Press.*
Oxford, R. (1990). *Language Learning Strategies: What every teacher should know.* Rowley, MA: Newbury House.
Rubin, J. (1975). What the 'good language learner' can teach us. *TESOL Quarterly*, 9, 41–51.
Seliger, H. (1984). Processing universals in second language acquisition. In F. Eckman, L. Bell and D. Nelson (eds), *Universals of Second Language Acquisition.* Rowley, MA: Newbury House.
Wenden, A. and Rubin, J. (eds) (1987). *Learner Strategies in Language Learning.* Englewood Cliffs, NJ: Prentice-Hall.*

RH

**lesson planning** is the process of deciding, in advance, what and how to teach according to the aims of a particular lesson. Taking into account syllabus and learner characteristics, good lesson planning promotes a clear progression of interrelated activities. Lesson plans range from detailed notes, with specified aims and descriptions of each stage (e.g. language/skill focus, material, class management), to a short outline of activities. A plan is a teaching guide, not a blueprint to be followed slavishly; plans are often adapted according to what happens in class. (See also 'PRESENTATION – PRACTICE – PRODUCTION' SEQUENCE.)

BIBLIOGRAPHY
Rivers, W. M. (1981). *Teaching Foreign-Language Skills*. Chicago: University of Chicago Press, 483–8.
Scrivener, J. (1994). *Learning Teaching*. Oxford: Heinemann. [Chapter 5.]
Ur, P. (1996). *A Course in Language Teaching*. Cambridge: Cambridge University Press, 213–26.
CLF

**lexical syllabus**  The use of word counts as a basis for language teaching has a long pedigree (West, 1953). This term, however, is a more recent coinage. It is particularly associated with the large computerized database known as COBUILD ('Collins-Birmingham University International Language Database'), which has generated a dictionary and subsequently a set of teaching materials based on lexical frequency. The lexical syllabus is not designed as a mere word list, but in principle links the learning of vocabulary thematically to real-world communicative contexts. It is roughly co-terminous with research into the processing strategies whereby vocabulary is acquired.

BIBLIOGRAPHY
Collins (1987). *COBUILD English Language Dictionary*. London and Glasgow: Collins.
Lewis, M. (1993). *The Lexical Approach*. Hove: Language Teaching Publications.
McDonough, J. and Shaw, C. (1993). *Materials and Methods in ELT*. Oxford: Blackwell, 50–2.
Sinclair, J. M. and Renouf, A. (1988). A lexical syllabus for language learning. In R. Carter and M. McCarthy (eds), *Vocabulary and Language Teaching*. London and New York: Longman, 140–60.
West, M. (1953). *A General Service List of English Words*. London: Longman.
Willis, D. (1990). *The Lexical Syllabus*. London and Glasgow: Collins.*
JMCD

**lexis**  The term used in SYSTEMIC GRAMMAR in opposition to GRAMMAR, both being aspects of linguistic form. In GENERATIVE GRAMMAR, the term *lexicon* denotes a dictionary-like component of the speaker's linguistic competence. The lexicon consists of lexical entries for words (lexical items), in which the phonological properties of a given word, its part of speech, its combinatorial properties within a sentence, and its meaning are stated. A distinction between lexical (content) and non-lexical (or 'functional') categories separates major word classes (noun, verb, adjective and adverb) from minor word classes (prepositions, determiners, conjunctions and pronouns). The distinction is supported by language acquisition and language disorder data: lexical categories are acquired before non-lexical categories and in certain language disorders (Broca's aphasia) functional categories are lost while content categories remain. (See also LEXICAL SYLLABUS.)

BIBLIOGRAPHY
Caplan, D. (1992). *Language: Structure, processing and disorders*. Cambridge, MA: MIT Press, 331–43.
McCarthy, M. and Carter, R. (1993). *Language as Discourse: Perspectives for language teaching* (Applied Linguistics and Language Study). London: Longman. [Chapter 3, esp. pp. 104–17.]*
Radford, A. (1988). *Transformational Grammar: A first course* (Cambridge Textbooks in Linguistics). Cambridge: Cambridge University Press. [Chapter 7.]
——(1990). *Syntactic Theory and the Acquisition of English Syntax: The nature of early child grammars of English*. Oxford: Blackwell.
EJ

**linguistics and language teaching**
Linguistics, the study of language and languages, is only one of a number of academic disciplines relevant to language teaching; others include psychology, education and sociology. In the twentieth century, however, it is the influence of linguistics which has been pre-eminent. This is in part due to its high profile as a new and innovative

discipline, and the general belief that it is the nature of language (rather than the mind in general, or education, or society) which is most relevant to language teaching. The scope of linguistics itself has been an issue of contention with some (notably Chomsky) seeking to confine it to the study of the formal system of PHONOLOGY and GRAMMAR and their representation in the mind, and others (notably functional linguists) regarding language as inseparable from its social context. The functional view inevitably incorporates within the scope of linguistics insights from the other disciplines listed above, while the formal approach, by treating language as a mental rather than a social phenomenon, has discounted insights from sociology and education. Though Chomsky declared linguistics to be a branch of cognitive psychology, his belief that its acquisition and representation are separate from other mental processes has in effect kept formal linguistics separate from psychology too. Successive schools and areas of both formal and functional linguistics have exerted a direct and/or indirect influence on language teaching. They include: philology, PHONETICS, Saussurean SEMIOTICS, structural linguistics, CHOMSKYAN LINGUISTICS, FIRST AND SECOND LANGUAGE ACQUISITION studies, SOCIOLINGUISTICS (including theories of COMMUNICATIVE COMPETENCE), PRAGMATICS, DISCOURSE ANALYSIS and COMPUTATIONAL LINGUISTICS (especially CORPUS LINGUISTICS). In writings on language teaching, the reporting and interpretation of these schools and areas has often resulted in considerable distortion of the original ideas and also in some time delay as new theories filter through. The influence has also largely been one way and top down, with linguists sometimes unaware or disdainful of the application of their ideas. Language teaching practitioners on the other hand, swayed by the scientific claims and academic status of linguistics, have often been too readily persuaded to change their approach in line with new theories of language and language acquisition

without taking into account the moderating effect of other factors which, as language teaching is a practical activity, are inevitably also important. For as well as being concerned with the acquisition of a language code, language teaching takes place in social settings and is a part of students' and teachers' lives and personal development; it is often a commercial enterprise and a means of establishing or preserving political influence; it makes use of the available technology for communication and takes place within educational institutions. For these reasons, changes of fashion in language teaching, though frequently justified by appeals to theories of linguistics, are often also determined, in varying proportions, by social, economic, ideological, technological and administrative factors. Since its foundation in the 1950s the intermediary discipline of APPLIED LINGUISTICS has attempted to integrate the influence of linguistics with that of other disciplines and with consideration of practical factors. At its worst applied linguistics has been merely the handing down of ideas from linguistics to language teachers; at its best it has attempted to assess their relevance and to stress the potential for a dynamic relationship in which the experience of language teaching and reflection upon it would both benefit from and contribute to the study of linguistics.

## EARLY INFLUENCES

Two academic influences on language teaching from the end of the nineteenth century onwards, were philology and phonetics (Howatt, 1984: 169–81). In philology, the discovery of the common ancestry and relationship of many European and Asian languages raised doubts about the supposed superiority of Latin and Ancient Greek (Sampson, 1980: 13–33), and this in turn initiated a movement away from the study of the classics, with its inevitable emphasis on written language, as a model for language teaching. At the same time, the new discipline of phonetics provided a systematic basis for the study of spoken language. Scholars of the self-styled Reform Movement attacked GRAMMAR-TRANSLATION teaching in favour of DIRECT METHOD and advocated greater attention to spoken language (Howatt, 1984: 169–81).

## SEMIOTICS AND STRUCTURALISM

Ferdinand de Saussure's *Course in General Linguistics*, first published in French in 1915, profoundly influenced – and for many people defines – the scope of twentieth-century linguistics (Saussure, 1974). Saussure regarded linguistics as a branch of semiotics, the study of signs. His programme asserted the primacy of speech, and relegated writing to the status of a secondary representation (p. 23). This questionable principle has found an echo in twentieth-century approaches to language teaching, most of which, in contrast to their classics-influenced antecedents, have shared an emphasis on developing spoken rather than written skills. (This emphasis echoes popular expressions about language proficiency which make no reference to writing: 'can you speak Hindi?', 'we need an Arabic speaker,' etc. (see TEACHING SPEAKING).)

Saussure argued that the relationship between a linguistic unit (signifier) and its meaning (signified) is usually arbitrary and determined by its place in the synchronic (i.e. present) system rather than by any resemblance between signifier and signified or by their diachronic (i.e. developmental) history (see SYNCHRONIC/DIACHRONIC). Saussure's treatment of communication as primarily an act of encoding and decoding, dependent upon a shared conventional code, has provided a theoretical underpinning to the assumption that the central core of language learning is the acquisition of knowledge of phonology, LEXIS and grammar rather than the development of an ability to use these systems in context. This assumption was shared

by almost all twentieth-century approaches to language teaching before the advent of COMMUNICATIVE METHODOLOGY in the 1970s.

These emphases on speech and the language code were perpetuated by the structural linguistics of Leonard Bloomfield and Charles Fries ascendant from the 1930s to the 1950s. Both men published works on language teaching. Structural linguistics studied the place and distribution of units within a linguistic system, with little reference to meaning or use. This approach, combined with the acceptance of BEHAVIOURISM as a theory of learning, had a profound and long-lasting influence on language teaching. Learning was seen as the acquisition of structural patterns through habit formation, best effected through the spoken drills, repeated dialogues and pattern practices of AUDIOLINGUALISM (see also GI METHOD).

## CHOMSKYAN LINGUISTICS

The revolution in linguistics effected by Noam Chomsky (see CHOMSKYAN LINGUISTICS) and his followers from the late 1950s onwards dethroned behaviourism, encouraging the belief that language learning involves active mental processes and is not simply the formation of habits. Chomsky stated explicitly that he did not believe his ideas should affect language teaching, yet inevitably, in the general change of beliefs about language which he brought about, his work did exert a considerable indirect influence. The results for language teaching, however, were not radical. Chomskyan linguistics shared with structural linguistics an exclusive attention to the formal language system, so the new influence did not result in a movement away from the existing emphasis on phonology and grammar. The shift of attention was a more subtle one, away from surface forms and behaviour, towards underlying mental representations (see COGNITIVE CODE), but was not one which had any major or long-lasting effect upon the actual practice of teaching.

One significant filter for Chomskyan ideas into language teaching (which *has* caused changes in practice) is second language acquisition theory (SLA). Although Chomsky's ideas about language acquisition were explicitly concerned with the acquisition of a first language by children, many SLA theorists have suggested that the same acquisitional processes (the principles of UNIVERSAL GRAMMAR, the setting of parameters) may still be activated in learning a second language in adulthood (Krashen, 1982; Cook, 1991). The emphasis is thus, as in structural approaches to language teaching, still upon a knowledge of grammar, though this time upon a tacit knowledge whose development is natural, unaffected by conscious explicit learning, internally generated, triggered by a favourable environment and following a universal route. Like children acquiring the grammar of a first language, learners are regarded as passing through a number of approximative systems, which are systematic but differ from the adult grammar. As in first language acquisition, these intermediate systems (or INTERLANGUAGES) are not seen as a phenomenon to be discouraged, but as a natural route to the desired end state, and are regarded as primarily determined by universal factors and only in a small part by first language interference (Selinker, 1972). During the 1970s and 1980s these quasi-Chomskyan ideas became extremely fashionable in language teaching (Krashen and Terrell, 1983 – see NATURAL APPROACH). Language learning was equated with the development of a mental representation of the grammar. The reconstruction of aspects of a first language learning environment was favoured. Grammar acquisition was believed to take place naturally when the conscious focus of attention was on meaning rather than on form, when the atmosphere was friendly and relaxed, and when learners were allowed to remain silent in the initial period. In recent years, SLA

theorists have modified this rather simplistic approach, incorporating notions of INDIVIDUAL DIFFERENCES in SLA, variable routes and rates (see RATE/ROUTE IN SLA) and the role of explicit conscious knowledge (see CONSCIOUS/UNCONSCIOUS KNOWLEDGE).

## FUNCTIONAL LINGUISTICS AND COMMUNICATIVE COMPETENCE

The schools and areas of linguistics discussed so far share a belief that language can be idealized and studied without reference to its use and context. In Chomskyan theory (and the SLA theories which derive from it) this premise is reinforced by the belief that the mental representation and acquisition of language is different and separate from that of other types of knowledge, and is determined to a large degree by innate, genetically inherited elements. Other schools of linguistics, however, believe that language should not be separated from its context either as a convenience for the purposes of study or because it is actually separate in the mind. Functional linguistics, which is concerned with the way in which language form is determined by its uses, has a long history dating back to work by the Prague School in the 1920s, the work of J. R. Firth during the 1940s and 1950s, and is continued most prominently today by M. A. K. Halliday and his followers. A functional approach is implicit in sociolinguistics, which studies the relationship between language and society.

Neither functional linguistics nor sociolinguistics, however, exerted more than a marginal influence on language teaching before the publication of Del Hymes's theory of COMMUNICATIVE COMPETENCE in 1970 (Hymes, 1970). Influenced by Hymes, advocates of NOTIONAL/FUNCTIONAL SYLLABUSES (Wilkins, 1976) and of the communicative approach (e.g. Widdowson, 1978), argued that language learning must involve not only mastery of the linguistic code but also knowledge of how to use that code appropriately in social contexts. Language was conceived as social action, and the criterion of success was no longer to be only the production and comprehension of grammatically correct sentences, but also of language which was contextually meaningful and did what the speaker wanted it to do.

Although the seminal writings on communication cited above take care to stress that knowledge of the language code remains an essential component of language use, sadly in practice functional syllabuses and communicative teaching often ignored this caution. In an over-reaction against the earlier preoccupation with correct grammar, they often promoted immediate communicative effectiveness at the expense of the development of accuracy. In this disdain for conscious focus on form, there is a superficial coincidence between the communicative approach and the natural approach influenced by SLA. The natural approach would tolerate student language deviating from the standard as interlanguage; the communicative approach would tolerate it as functional. Neither took adequate heed of the danger of FOSSILIZATION when inaccurate but successful structures are used by adult learners, nor of the fact that accurate use of the code is essential in any complex effective communication. In this and other respects the SLA emphasis on the crucial role of meaningful interaction appears to fit well with the communicative approach. Both were in the ascendant during the 1970s and 1980s; many materials and pedagogic practices from this period are acceptable to both camps. This superficial concord of practice, however, masks a deep theoretical divide, for in mainstream SLA attention to meaning is valuable not in itself but only in so far as it activates the language acquisition device (LAD); the emphasis is still entirely upon the language system as the desired goal of language learning. In some versions of the communicative approach on the other hand, realizing meaning is seen as an end in itself, achieved by deployment of the language code

along with other competences and abilities which are essential for successful language use.

The new attention to language function and meaning opened the way for influence from two disciplines concerned with the systematic study of language in use: pragmatics and discourse analysis. The former has elaborated principles to explain *how* speakers achieve meaning and how hearers interpret it by relating utterances to their non-linguistic context. It has also considered *why* people do not speak directly, explicitly and fully, but allow their interlocutors to infer their meaning from context and shared knowledge. As such, pragmatics has provided language teaching with a basis for consideration of the contextual appropriateness of utterances (which together with possibility, feasibility and attestedness is one of the four parameters of Hymes's communicative competence) rather than only their grammaticality and semanticity. It also illuminates cross-cultural communication by considering the similarities and differences in notions of appropriateness in different societies.

Discourse analysis also offers insight into appropriateness and inference, analysing not only how utterances relate to their non-linguistic context, but also how they relate to each other, and take on meaning in sequence. This too is relevant to language teaching in that it allows learners to consider how text becomes coherent and meaningful, both through its interaction with factors outside the text, and through the deployment of linguistic signals within it. Here too there is insight into cross-cultural similarities and differences, revealed by such areas of discourse analysis as conversation analysis, interaction analysis and the study of GENRE.

## CORPUS LINGUISTICS

Although Hymes had presented the four components of communicative competence as equal, early communicative methodology had focused disproportionately upon appropriateness, often at the expense of the other three parameters. Knowledge of what is possible was felt to have been over-emphasized by structural approaches; feasibility was felt to have little relevance to language learning; as for attestedness (what is actually done), there was in fact little evidence to distinguish this aspect of language knowledge from the other three. From the 1980s onwards, the rapid development of CORPUS LINGUISTICS (in which large collections of occurring language running into millions of words are analysed by computer to demonstrate frequencies and patterns of occurrence) has made possible a principled study of what language is actually performed. The findings of corpus linguistics, however, have done far more than flesh out the fourth of Hymes's parameters; they have changed perceptions of language and language knowledge in general. The evidence that many possible combinations do not in fact occur, while others occur with disproportionate frequency, has engendered a fundamental reassessment of the relation of lexis to grammar, and to the acquisition and representation of 'native-like' language. Corpus linguistics suggests that grammatical rules cannot be stated without reference to particular lexical items, nor word meanings without reference to the particular grammatical constructions into which they may enter (Sinclair, 1991). Knowledge of language is no longer seen as involving only parsimonious rules operating elegantly to generate grammatical utterances but also to involve substantial knowledge of ready-made chunks of language which are often retrieved partly or wholly lexicalized from memory (Pawley and Syder, 1983).

The implications of corpus linguistics for language teaching are immense, and its influence is already substantial. It remains to be seen, however, whether this influence will result in a more balanced view of the knowledge which is needed to use a language successfully, or whether the structuralist over-emphasis on grammar and the communicative over-emphasis on appropriateness will merely be succeeded by an over-emphasis on attestedness. Such a development would be unfortunate, for it is not the case that every learner needs to be native-like, nor that the only effective use of a foreign language is one whose processes and products imitate those of native speakers. As with any other revolution in linguistics, what is needed is an integration of the theoretical and descriptive insights of corpus linguistics with pedagogic criteria and the consideration of learners' needs (Aston, 1995).

One area of language teaching in which corpus linguistics has already had a considerable impact is VOCABULARY TEACHING. Although popular wisdom has always acknowledged the importance of knowing a lot of words, vocabulary teaching has in most methodologies been a haphazard affair, with syllabuses structured around grammar, notions or functions rather than around lexis. Corpus linguistics' insight into lexical frequency and collocation has contributed to the emergence of more principled approaches to vocabulary teaching. In grammar teaching, the analysis of transcribed spoken data will make possible a more systematic description of the grammatical patterns of spoken language which differ in many ways from the grammar of writing on which most language courses are based (Carter and McCarthy, 1995; Yule, 1995).

## NEW INFLUENCES

Recent years have seen a turning away from the influence of linguistics in language teaching, and a reassertion of the relevance of psychological, pedagogic and social factors. A general switch from traditional product-based approaches towards more progressivist process-oriented learner-centred approaches has led to a lessening of interest in idealizations of language and language knowledge (although this may also be conceived as a movement inspired by social and inter-actionist views of language in linguistics). TASK-BASED LANGUAGE TEACHING and PROCESS SYLLABUSES have focused upon the roles and relationships of teachers and learners, and on strategies for learning. At the same time, CRITICAL LINGUISTICS (and its offshoots such as critical discourse analysis, critical language awareness) has propounded a notion of language teaching as a means of political action and social reconstruction which is at odds with the claim of traditional linguistics to scientific objectivity (Fairclough, 1989).

To some extent these movements testify to a reaction against the ascendancy of mainstream linguistic theory as an influence on language teaching, and a reaction against the swings of fashion which have resulted when changes in linguistic theory have been followed without due concern for other relevant factors in pedagogy. Linguists and applied linguists are rightly criticized for having either sought too direct and immediate an influence, or for having remained aloof from debates about pedagogic relevance. Yet linguistics remains a major source of insight into the nature of language and its acquisition (whether spontaneous or instructed), and it is to be hoped that in the years to come a more fruitful integration of its findings with the needs of language teaching will be achieved.

BIBLIOGRAPHY
Aston, G. (1995). Corpora in language pedagogy: matching theory and practice. In G. Cook and B. Seidlhofer (eds), *Principle and Practice in Applied Linguistics*. Oxford: Oxford University Press, 257–71.
Carter, R. A. and McCarthy, M. (1995). Grammar and the spoken language. *Applied Linguistics*, 16/2, 141–59.
Chomsky, N. (1965). *Aspects of the Theory of Syntax*. Cambridge, MA: MIT Press.
Cook, V. (1991). *Second Language Learning and Language Teaching*. London: Edward Arnold.
Fairclough, N. (1989). *Language and Power*. London: Longman.
Howatt, A. P. R. (1984). *A History of English Language Teaching*. Oxford: Oxford University Press.*
Hymes, D. (1970). On communicative competence. In J. J. Gumperz and D. Hymes (eds), *Directions in Sociolinguistics*. New York: Holt, Rinehart and Winston. [Page references are to the 1972 reprint in J. B. Pride and J. Holmes (eds), *Sociolinguistics*. Harmondsworth: Penguin Books, 269–93. Original paper presented at the Research Planning Conference on Language Development in Disadvantaged Children, New York City, June 1966.]
Krashen, S. D. (1982). *Principles and Practice in Second Language Acquisition*. Oxford: Pergamon.
Krashen, S. D. and Terrell, T. D. (1983). *The Natural Approach: Language acquisition in the classroom*. Oxford: Pergamon.
Pawley, A. and Syder, F. (1983). Two puzzles for linguistic theory: nativelike selection and nativelike fluency. In J. Richards and J. Schmidt (eds), *Language and Communication*. London: Longman.
Sampson, G. (1980). *Schools of Linguistics*. London: Longman.
Saussure, F. de (1974). *Course in General Linguistics*, trans. W. Baskin. London: Fontana. [First published in 1915.]
Selinker, L. (1972). Interlanguage. *International Review of Applied Linguistics*, 10, 209–31.
Sinclair, J. M. (1991). *Corpus, Concordance, Collocation*. Oxford: Oxford University Press.
Stern, H. H. (1983). *Fundamental Concepts of Language Teaching*. Oxford: Oxford University Press.* [Part 3.]
Widdowson, H. G. (1978). *Teaching Language as Communication*. Oxford: Oxford University Press.
Wilkins, D. (1976). *Notional Syllabuses*. Oxford: Oxford University Press.
Yule, G. (1995). The paralinguistics of reference: representation in reported discourse. In G. Cook and B. Seidlhofer (eds), *Principle and Practice in Applied Linguistics*. Oxford: Oxford University Press, 185–97.

GC

**literature teaching**   Traditional views of literature as providing the language learner with access to the best language, to high culture, and to profound and accurate observations of life have been challenged in a number of ways this century. New emphases on spoken language and functional communication, together with a broader view of culture, have combined to detract from literature's unquestioned centrality. STYLISTICS has rejected views of literary language as a transparent medium and concentrated on unusual linguistic choices and their relation to meaning. Some recent approaches have been influenced by post-modernist criticism and functionalist linguistics which have tended towards a view of literariness as contextual: a way of reading rather than a type of text. In addition, in English language teaching, concern has been expressed about the cultural imperialism of literature syllabuses which continue to give prominence to British and American literature. Nevertheless, despite changes of approach, misgivings about pedagogic validity and even doubts about its distinct existence as a discourse type, literature continues to be popular with students, and an unrivalled resource for the language teacher.

Traditionally, literature has long occupied a central position in the teaching of both the classics and modern foreign languages, including English. Implicit in its centrality are beliefs in its general civilizing value, in the window it provides into a foreign culture and in its role as a model of the 'best' language. In the classical humanist educational tradition, the study of literature is not only a means of language learning, but its goal: a major reason for learning a language, in other words, is to read its literature. This presupposes that literature is untranslatable, and can only be fully appreciated in the original.

Language learning in which literature is central inevitably focuses more upon the written than the spoken language, and tends to make the learner's experience of the language passive rather than active. With the coming of a more functional orientation in ELT, greater emphasis upon spoken

language and a growing demand for courses with an immediate SURRENDER VALUE, this emphasis on the passive appreciation of literature inevitably weakened. Nevertheless the intrinsic value of literature, and the fact that it does provide interesting and authentic use of the language, has guaranteed it continued prominence. The twentieth century has witnessed a number of radically different theories of the nature of literature (see Eagleton, 1983; Jefferson and Robey, 1986; Cook, 1994: 125–77). Some movements have seen it as a means of social documentation and action, others as psychological observation; others still have focused upon its formal aspects, including its use of language and larger textual structures. Postmodernist movements have emphasized the role of the reader and society in constructing literariness in certain texts, rather than regarding it as a quality of the language, text structure, or observation of the world. Approaches to literature teaching have been influenced to varying degrees by these changing theories.

Not surprisingly, the literary theories most influential in applied linguistics have been those which concentrate upon linguistic and textual features, and this focus has been passed on to ELT. Particularly influential has been the functional theory of Roman Jakobson, who suggested that there is a 'poetic function' of language in which attention is focused upon the language code itself, producing messages in which linguistic choices are paramount and paraphrase impossible (Jakobson, 1960). Particularly important in literary discourse, in this view, are patterns of formal features and deviations from normal use. Literary stylistics, evolving from this approach, has closely scrutinized the linguistic idiosyncrasies of particular texts, and speculated upon the connection between linguistic choices and effects upon the reader. A number of highly influential works in this tradition were published from the 1960s onwards (Leech, 1969; Widdowson, 1975; Carter, 1982).

Stylistics, however, poses a number of problems as an inspiration for language teaching. By drawing attention to the ways in which literary language often departs from normal usage, it has raised doubts about the validity of literary language as a model for all but the most advanced language learners. Writers on stylistics have been at pains to counter these doubts, and convincing arguments for the relevance and usefulness of stylistics in literature teaching have been advanced, notably by Widdowson (1975, 1992). At its inception, stylistics was also a radical departure from earlier approaches. Not only did it run counter to the literary critical tradition with its emphasis upon the meaning rather than the form of literature, but it was also at odds with a neo-Romantic emphasis upon literature as a stimulus for self-expression and development in English mother-tongue teaching of the 1960s and 1970s.

Theoretical and descriptive doubts about defining literariness as a particular use of language, coupled with the growing popularity of the view that orders of discourse are socially constructed (see DISCOURSE ANALYSIS), have led to some adjustment of the original stylistics stance. Recent approaches have tended to stress the similarities between literary and non-literary texts. Considerable attention has been paid to literary uses of language in non-literary texts (Carter, 1991– ). Exercises often draw attention to similarities and encourage students to rewrite one genre as another (Carter and McCarthy, 1995).

In ELT there has also been concern about the role of literature as a promoter of cultural imperialism. The English language curricula in many post-colonial societies continue to expose students to British and American literature at the expense of their own cultures. A number of factors make this a more complex issue than it appears at first. Much of the best recent literature in English has come from the post-colonial English-speaking countries, written by authors with an unquestionable commitment to their countries' political and cultural independence. In addition, as literature often subverts rather than asserts the values of the society from which it comes, much British and American literature is far from uncritical of Western values.

Despite changing fashions, cultural differences, and disputes over its nature and its teaching, literature continues as an internationally recognizable discourse. Like language learning itself, it allows people to step beyond the constraints of their own social environments and gain insights into other cultures while also appreciating the universality of human concerns, and to enjoy a universal pleasure in language art. It is these factors which have ensured that literature teaching has survived the many changing approaches to it, and even the doubts expressed about its validity, and continues strengthened rather than weakened by the dynamic debate with which it is constantly surrounded.

BIBLIOGRAPHY

Brumfit, C. J. (1985). *Language and Literature Teaching: From practice to principle*. Oxford: Pergamon.

Brumfit, C. J. and Carter, R. (1986). *Literature and Language Teaching*. Oxford: Oxford University Press.*

Carter, R. A. (1982). *Language and Literature*. London: Allen and Unwin.

——(1991– ). Books in the Interface series. London: Routledge.

Carter, R. A. and Long, M. N. (1991). *Teaching Literature*. London: Longman.*

Carter, R. A. and McCarthy, M. (1995). Discourse and creativity: bridging the gap between language and literature. In G. Cook, and B. Seidlhofer (eds), *Principle and Practice in Applied Linguistics*. Oxford: Oxford University Press.

Cook, G. (1994). *Discourse and Literature*. Oxford: Oxford University Press.

Eagleton, T. (1983). *Literary Theory*. Oxford: Blackwell.

Jakobson, R. (1960). Closing statement: linguistics and poetics. In T. A. Sebeok (ed.),

*Style in Language*. Cambridge, MA: MIT Press, 350–77.

Jefferson, A. and Robey, D. (1986). *Modern Literary Theory: A comparative introduction*. London: Batsford.

Leech, G. N. (1969). *A Linguistic Guide to English Poetry*. London: Longman.

Widdowson, H. G. (1975). *Stylistics and the Teaching of Literature*. London: Longman.

——(1992). *Practical Stylistics*. Oxford: Oxford University Press.

GC

# M

**macro/microlinguistics** These are broad terms which refer to two major types of linguistics. Microlinguistics refers to PHONETICS, PHONOLOGY, GRAMMAR and SEMANTICS, whereas macrolinguistics covers SOCIOLINGUISTICS, DISCOURSE ANALYSIS and other related disciplines. In sociolinguistics, the micro level is often equated with variation and face-to-face communication, whereas macrosociolinguistics involves LANGUAGE PLANNING and sociology of language.

BIBLIOGRAPHY
Bell, R. T. (1976). *Sociolinguistics: Goals, approaches and problems*. London: Batsford.

AJ

**management in language teaching** It is self-evident that matters of organization and administration are of central importance in the overall planning of any language programme. However, it is only in the last few years that management issues have been explicitly studied in their own right, particular attention being given to the lessons to be learned from much more developed management training outside ELT, most obviously in the world of business. Key areas of interest are the structure of organizations, staff selection and development, resource management, marketing, budgeting and finance, alongside the more conventional focus of project/curriculum planning and innovation.

BIBLIOGRAPHY
Everard, K. B. and Morris, G. (1985). *Effective School Management*. London: Paul Chapman.
Kennedy, C. (1987). Innovation for change: teacher development and innovation. *ELT Journal*, 41/3, 163–71.
White, R., Martin, M., Stimson, M. and Hodge, R. (1991). *Management in English Language Teaching*. Cambridge: Cambridge University Press.

JMCD

**markedness** This concept has been typically applied to cases where a group of languages displays grammatical property p, and a smaller group of languages displays not only p but also a related property q. Because property q is rarer and additional to p, it is said to be 'marked', whereas p is unmarked. For example, French and English can both form questions on direct objects: *Who did she see?/Qui a-t-elle vu?*, but only English can form questions on the object of prepositions: *Who did she speak to?/ *Qui a-t-elle parlé à?* Question formation on the objects of prepositions would be held to be more 'marked' than question formation on direct objects.

BIBLIOGRAPHY
Eckman, F. (1977). Markedness and the contrastive analysis hypothesis. *Language Learning*, 27, 315–30.
Eckman, F., Moravcsik, E. and Wirth, J. (eds) (1986). Markedness. New York: Plenum Press.*
Rutherford, W. (1982). Markedness in second language acquisition. *Language Learning*, 32, 85–108.
White, L. (1987). Markedness and second language acquisition: the question of transfer. *Studies in Second Language Acquisition*, 9, 261–86.

RH

**meaning potential**  This term was coined by M. A. K. Halliday as part of his conceptualization of language within systemic-functional grammar (see SYSTEMIC GRAMMAR). Halliday views language as social behaviour. In social terms the speaker has the potential to act; he or she 'can do'. In linguistic, functional-semantic terms, this behavioural potential is realized as 'can mean'. In turn, this meaning potential is realized in language as lexico-grammatical potential, i.e. what the speaker 'can say'. All these levels can be represented as options or sets of choices. For example, depending on the choice of the type of clause, the potential meaning expressed in an utterance can be indicative or imperative, declarative or interrogative, yes/no or 'wh-', and so on.

BIBLIOGRAPHY
Halliday, M. A. K. (1973). *Explorations in the Functions of Language.* London: Edward Arnold.
——(1978). *Language as Social Semiotic: The social interpretation of language and meaning.* London: Edward Arnold.

AJ

**mean length of utterance** (MLU)  A measure of complexity in L1 children's speech taken by calculating the average number of morphemes per utterance, using standardized rules; the purpose is to compare children at the same level of language knowledge, thus establishing stages of acquisition independent of chronological age. MLU deals best with early stages of acquisition. (See also MEASUREMENTS OF SECOND LANGUAGE PROFICIENCY.)

BIBLIOGRAPHY
Brown, R. (1973). *A First Language: The early stages.* London: Allen and Unwin.
Fletcher, P. (1985). *A Child's Learning of English.* Oxford: Blackwell.

VJC

**measurements of second language proficiency**  There are two broad areas of ability in SLA: on the one hand, knowledge of the structural properties of the L2 and the conditions under which the L2 is used, and on the other, the capacity to access that knowledge for real-time use, often termed *language processing*. In the case of the former, a learner has to construct mental representations for L2 sounds, lexical items, syntactic structure, representations for when to use forms appropriate to the social setting and so on. In the case of the latter, a learner has to develop the ability to access these representations at speed and accurately in order to make successful telephone calls, sell a product, engage in a debate and so on.

Researchers wishing to measure second language *proficiency* have therefore tended to devise testing instruments which focus on the levels of success achieved by learners in one of these domains. Tests which aim to measure proficiency in knowledge of the linguistic *system* have come to be known as *system-referenced tests*; tests which aim to measure proficiency in language processing have come to be known as *performance-referenced tests*. See Baker (1989: 7–28) for discussion of these broad domains within which measurement takes place.

One of the earliest examples of a system-referenced testing procedure is outlined in Lado (1961). Lado starts from the assumption that proficiency at the level of the system is not unitary, but can be broken down into dimensions created by the intersection of strictly linguistic knowledge (PHONOLOGY, LEXIS, SYNTAX, discourse) with the four perceptual channels of aural and visual comprehension (listening and reading) and oral and visual production (speaking and writing). For example, Lado would suggest that the ability to *perceive* L2 phonemes is different from the ability to *produce* distinct L2 sounds, which is itself different from the ability to use appropriate vocabulary items in writing and so on. Any system-referenced tests of proficiency should therefore measure each of these dimensions separately.

Typical examples of the kinds of tests used from this perspective are:

- testing to see whether subjects are able to distinguish MINIMAL PAIRS of phonemes by presenting them aurally with words like: *bit/beat*, *bit/bid*, *pit/bit* and asking them to identify them;
- testing subjects' syntactic knowledge in production by asking them to transform one sentence into another sentence which 'means the same thing', for example:

*An architect bought the barn.*
*The barn* _____.

- testing subjects' syntactic knowledge in comprehension by giving them a multiple choice test in which they have to choose the sentence which 'sounds most natural', for example:

When I am in France I
  *drink always wine in the evenings.*
  *drink wine in the evenings always.*
  *always drink wine in the evenings.*

Tests like these are known as *closed-response* tests or *discrete-point* tests, because they attempt to measure proficiency in specific areas of competence in the L2 by forcing the learner to respond on carefully selected types of L2 knowledge. Once responses are recorded, they are then measured either against the responses of other L2 learners or against the responses of native speakers on the same test. Proficiency can be described for an individual either in terms of whether she or he is the same as, worse than or better than comparable peer L2 speakers, or in terms of the degree to which she or he approximates to native-speaker norms.

The general enterprise of using discrete-point/closed-response tests to measure the various dimensions of proficiency is known as *psychometric testing*. While it was popular in the 1960s and 1970s, it came under attack for two reasons. First, the kinds of test used (phoneme discrimination, sentence transformation, multiple-choice grammaticality judgement, etc.) are a long way from most everyday types of language use, and there was a feeling that the tests may be tapping aspects of knowledge not really involved with L2 competence. Second, the way in which the reliability of discrete-point/closed-response tests was determined was on the basis of CORRELATION statistics: learners' performance on one test was correlated with their performance on others: e.g. performance on a phoneme discrimination task might be correlated with performance on, say, a multiple-choice morphological task focusing on agreement. If such knowledge develops independently, one would expect to find low correlations between the two performances. Similarly, one would not expect there to be significant correlations between performance on discrete-point/closed-response tests and tests which appear to tap global L2 ability. However, work by Oller (1979) in the 1970s, correlating learners' performance on such tasks with their performance on dictation and CLOZE tests (cloze tests require learners to restore every n-th word which has been deleted from a passage), which are supposedly *holistic* and not discrete-point/closed-response tasks, found very high correlations between them indeed. Oller claimed that this undermined the notion that proficiency is modular (develops along a number of dimensions), and offered instead the UNITARY COMPETENCE HYPOTHESIS, which could be measured by holistic tests like cloze and DICTATION.

Unfortunately, the statistics on which Oller based his claims have subsequently been shown to be suspect (see Baker, 1989: 70–1), and this has created a situation in which at present 'there is no generally accepted credible model of second language proficiency' (Baker, 1989: 72). Many researchers interested in measuring proficiency in the linguistic system these days tend to use a battery of tests consisting of both discrete-point/closed-response and holistic tests.

*Performance-referenced tests* are those which aim to measure a learner's ability to access linguistic knowledge in real time to perform specific tasks. Testers often distinguish between *direct* tests and *indirect* tests. In direct tests the testee is asked to perform a simulation, and the performance is then taken as an indicator of the testee's ability to repeat such a task in a non-test situation (e.g. using the phone, requesting information, selling a product, persuading someone to do something and so on). In indirect tests an attempt is made to isolate the characteristics of performance in general and to test learners' proficiency on those general characteristics, on the assumption that this will be indicative of a learner's performance in real-life situations. For example, if the proficiency to be measured is the ability to read for academic purposes, this might be broken down into the characteristics of successful reading (ability to follow cohesive devices, ability to detect synonymy, antithesis, etc.) and a learner's proficiency in following cohesive devices (see COHESION), detecting synonymy might be tested.

Finally, one should be aware that the measurement of second language proficiency can have at least two quite separate functions. One function is vocational or instrumental: L2 learners are tested in order to *grade* them for the purpose of awarding certificates, placement in higher-level language classes, etc. The other function is to gain access to the nature of L2 learners' competence. In this function, measuring proficiency is an adjunct to theoretical studies of the nature of second language knowledge and the process of second language acquisition. (See also LANGUAGE TESTING.)

BIBLIOGRAPHY
Bachman, L. (1990). *Fundamental Considerations in Language Testing*. Oxford: Oxford University Press.*
Baker, D. (1989). *Language Testing: A critical survey and practical guide*. London: Edward Arnold.*

Lado, R. (1961). *Language Testing*. London: Longman.
Oller, J. (1979). *Language Tests at School*. London: Longman.

RH

**media resources** include all the technology, ranging from tape-recorders to PC labs, which is involved in the aiding of learning. They encompass the resources (both software and hardware) outlined in figure 1 (see p. 212).

A multimedia approach gives the learner access to text, video and audio recording. It provides the possibility of being interactive and having a degree of STUDENT AUTONOMY. (See also COMPUTER–ASSISTED LANGUAGE LEARNING, VIDEO IN LANGUAGE TEACHING.)

CLF

**mentalism** is the belief that mental states and processes are prior to and exist independently of behaviour. As such, it is the opposite of BEHAVIOURISM. The mentalist notions of CHOMSKYAN LINGUISTICS, such as the COMPETENCE/PERFORMANCE distinction and UNIVERSAL GRAMMAR, have had a profound influence on APPLIED LINGUISTICS.

BIBLIOGRAPHY
Chomsky, N. (1988). *Language and the Problems of Knowledge*. Cambridge, MA: MIT Press.
Cook, V. and Newson, M. (1995). *Chomsky's Universal Grammar*. Oxford: Blackwell.
Ellis, R. (1985). *Understanding Second Language Acquisition*. Oxford: Oxford University Press. [Chapters 3 and 8.]

GC

**message-focus**   A task has message-, as opposed to FORM-FOCUS, if the learner is encouraged to concentrate on the content of the message being conveyed rather than on its form. The form/message-focus distinction plays an important role in VARIABILITY IN SLA studies, where less accuracy is sometimes associated with less formal 'styles' in

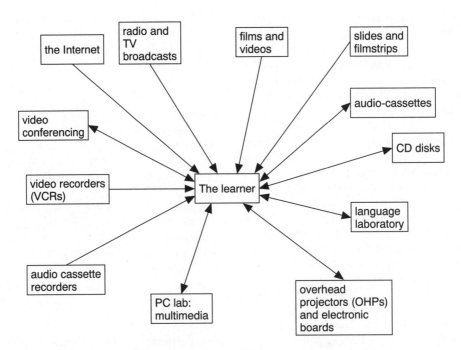

**Figure 1**   The variety of media resources (see p. 211).

which less form-focus might be thought to occur; see Tarone (1988). A major objective of COMMUNICATIVE METHODOLOGY is to achieve message-focus in classroom tasks, often by means of INFORMATION/OPINION GAP activities where emphasis is placed on 'getting a message across' rather than on formal correctness.

BIBLIOGRAPHY
Johnson, K. and Morrow, K. (1981). *Communication in the Classroom*. Harlow: Longman.
Tarone, E. (1988). *Variation in Interlanguage*. London: Edward Arnold.

KJ

**metalanguage** is language about language. Grammars, dictionaries, linguistics and applied linguistics are all metalinguistic; so are mundane remarks such as 'what does this word mean?', 'he mumbles' etc. This reflexiveness allows language to be both the means and the object of description.

Metalanguage is essential to any conscious consideration of a language being learned.

BIBLIOGRAPHY
Lyons, J. (1977). *Semantics*. 2 vols. Cambridge: Cambridge University Press. [Chapter 1.]

GC

**method comparisons**   Historical accounts (for example, Kelly, 1969) show that debates about methods as sets of techniques used by teachers to transmit a foreign language to learners go back over many centuries. Sometimes the debates have occurred between those supporting the same method but disagreeing about details of application, while others have been conducted, often with open hostility, between those ascribing to completely different methods. The latter type of debate assumes that methods may indeed be meaningfully compared with regard to efficacy. The debate between, for example, the rival camps in favour of the DIRECT

METHOD and GRAMMAR-TRANSLATION respectively continued for some seventy years, and was only finally halted by the Second World War and the birth of AUDIOLINGUALISM. It was not only that audiolingualism occupied the limelight, but that its founders introduced a new formalism for discussing language teaching and a new paradigm for method comparisons. Whereas exchanges over methods had previously rested on common-sense arguments, and no doubt much prejudice, the imperative now was to compare methods experimentally and measure their effects quantitatively, i.e. to turn away from attempts to *persuade* language teachers that a given method was more effective than others, and instead to furnish *proof* of its greater effectiveness. Simultaneously, the idea that there must be 'one best method' for learners anywhere, and that empirical research would reveal it, became an overriding obsession. In practice, the experiments designed to compare methods foundered and the 'one best method' concept was largely abandoned, especially as individual learner differences began to receive more attention and individualization of language instruction was advocated by many. However, the intensive preoccupation with method comparisons in the postwar years did at least focus attention on the difficulties involved.

Small-scale empirical investigations of language teaching began in about 1944 with Paul Delattre's experiment at the University of Oklahoma, in which he tried to compare 'traditional' with audiolingal teaching of French. For an outline of his and others' work, see Scherer and Wertheimer (1964). Dissatisfaction with the results of small-scale studies led to three major investigations. The first, conducted by Scherer and Wertheimer themselves between 1960 and 1962 at the University of Colorado, aimed to compare the 'traditional' and audiolingual methods of teaching German. In the autumn 1960 semester 289 subjects participated in the project. The second, run by Keating in New York, with 5000 subjects, set out to compare

language laboratory drilling with classroom teaching in French (Keating, 1963). The third and most complex was Smith's 'Pennsylvania Project', running from 1965 to 1969 and seeking to compare the 'traditional' (grammar-translation) method, the functional skills (i.e. audiolingual) method and the functional skills method plus a component of grammatical explanation (Smith, 1970). Almost all the experiments, small and large in scale, were motivated by the desire to *prove* the superiority of audiolingualism over other methods.

For the furnishing of empirical *proof* that one method was superior to others, the design of the psychology experiment was adopted. The subjects constituting the sample had to be divided into two groups (more if more than two methods were being compared), one group being exposed to method X and the other to method Y, and the results measured by testing the subjects at various points in, and on conclusion of, the experiment. Adherence to the 'rules of science' was also required. These are explained clearly in Anderson (1966), but of particular relevance here is 'the principle of controlled observation'. To quote Anderson: 'One can make the descriptive statement that a change in variable A produces a change in variable B only if all variables other than A can be discounted as causes of the change in B.'

In method comparison experiments this meant that one could not claim that method X was superior to method Y without certainty that the *only* variable affecting the groups differently was the method applied. If, for example, one group received more hours of instruction than the other or some subjects in one group came from bilingual backgrounds, then the results of the experiment were invalid. It was above all the difficulties in keeping to 'the principle of controlled observation' that defeated the experimenters. The large-scale studies arose partly because defects in this respect had been revealed in the small-scale experiments, but, despite careful planning, the former magnified the faults of the latter. In the end, the absence of clear data from the large-scale investigations only (further) eroded teachers' confidence in audiolingualism, demonstrated that the variables germane to method comparisons – including learners, teachers, materials, resources and constraints – seem to defy control and discouraged further empirical work on comparing methods globally.

In retrospect, the empirical work executed between the mid-forties and the mid-sixties was perhaps ill-conceived, since it did not consider the *aims* of different methods. GRAMMAR-TRANSLATION, for example, does not *aim* to make learners fluent *speakers* of a foreign language, whereas audiolingualism does. It is therefore unsurprising that one of the indications (rather than conclusive results) of many experiments was that learners taught by grammar-translation read and write the language better than those taught audiolingually, and that those taught audiolingually are by contrast better in listening and speaking. Another complicating factor is that some methods are inspired by psychological or even 'political' stances, or proceed from broad educational aims whose fulfilment may not be measurable quantitatively. It is also questionable whether *method* is the most significant factor in language learning, as opposed to others such as relationships with teachers and personal motivation. Method comparisons continue to be made, and to some extent there has been a reversion to debates revolving around *persuasion* rather than *proof*.

Despite the problem of controlling the variables, quantifiable data regarding the relative efficacy of methods would still be useful to support qualitative judgements, but though it is unlikely that the results of empirical research alone will ever be the determining factor in method comparisons and attitudes towards methods, there is at the present time a resurgence of interest in conducting empirical research into aspects of language teaching and learning.

For discussion of the issues in the contemporary context, see Richards and Rodgers (1986). For detailed information on research methods, see Nunan (1992). See also CLASSROOM STUDIES IN SLA.

BIBLIOGRAPHY
Anderson, B. F. (1966). *The Psychology Experiment*. Belmont, CA: Wadsworth.
Keating, R. F. (1963). *A Study of the Effectiveness of Language Laboratories*. New York: Columbia University, Institute of Administrative Research.
Kelly, L. G. (1969). *25 Centuries of Language Teaching*. Rowley, MA: Newbury House.
Nunan, D. (1992). *Research Methods in Language Learning*. Cambridge: Cambridge University Press.
Richards, J. C. and Rodgers T. S. (1986). *Approaches and Methods in Language Teaching*. Cambridge: Cambridge University Press.
Scherer, G. A. C. and Wertheimer, M. (1964). *A Psycholinguistic Experiment in Foreign Language Teaching*. New York: McGraw-Hill.*
Smith, P. D. (1970). *A Comparison of the Cognitive and Audiolingual Approaches to Foreign Language Instruction: The Pennsylvania foreign language project*. Philadelphia: Center for Curriculum Development.*

JTR

**methodics**    As conceived by Halliday, McIntosh and Strevens (1964: 201), this is 'a framework of organization for language teaching which relates linguistic theory to pedagogical principles and techniques'. It entails for each teaching situation decisions regarding *limitation* (restriction, selection), grading (staging, sequencing), *presentation* (initial and repeated teaching, reinforcement, remedial teaching) and *testing*. See also GRADING/SEQUENCING and STAGING.

BIBLIOGRAPHY
Halliday, M. A. K., McIntosh, A. and Strevens, P. (1964). *The Linguistic Sciences and Language Teaching*. London: Longman, 200–22.
Stern, H. H. (1983). *Fundamental Concepts of Language Teaching*. Oxford: Oxford University Press, 482–6.

JTR

**micro-teaching** A form of teaching practice devised in the USA in the 1960s to enable pre-service teachers (of any subject) to practise particular teaching skills in isolation and in highly controlled circumstances. Micro-teaching formed part of a general movement towards the analysis of teaching into specific, separately observable, and therefore separately trainable, classroom skills. In a typical micro-teaching arrangement pre-service teachers would be asked to prepare for five or fewer minutes of teaching, involving just one teaching skill and one teaching point, with a small group of learners who might be simply the other pre-service trainees role-playing the target learners.

Micro-teaching feeds into the later notion of competency-based TEACHER EDUCATION.

BIBLIOGRAPHY
Allen, D. W. and Ryan, K. A. (1969). *Micro-teaching*. Palo Alto, CA: Addison-Wesley.

RLA

**minimal pairs** refers to any pair of sounds that differ in a single aspect such that two words containing them differ in meaning. In English this may consist of a distinction between vowels (bit/beat), or consonants (shop/chop). Much of the teaching of pronunciation is based on these distinctions. See PHONOLOGY and PRONUNCIATION TEACHING.

JMCD

**miscue analysis** This research technique (see Goodman, 1973) focuses on errors (miscues) in oral reading as indicators of the reader's strategies in using various cues (graphophonic, syntactic, semantic) present in the text. Central to the analysis is the nature of the reader's reaction to a miscue (i.e. correction or non-correction). (See TEACHING READING.)

BIBLIOGRAPHY
Goodman, K. S. (1973). Analysis of oral reading miscues: applied psycholinguistics. In F. Smith (ed.), *Psycholinguistics and Reading*. New York: Holt, Rinehart and Winston.

KSM

**Monitor Model** The Monitor Model was proposed by Stephen Krashen in the 1970s (Krashen, 1979) to combine a theory of learning (that acquisition and learning are separate processes) with a theory of production (that learnt knowledge acts only as a control on language originating from acquired knowledge). The Monitor Model became part of the much wider model proposed by Krashen in the 1980s (e.g. Krashen, 1981, 1982, 1985a), mostly known for its concepts of COMPREHENSIBLE INPUT and the INPUT HYPOTHESIS, which were directly applied to teaching (Krashen and Terrell, 1983). While originally widely acclaimed, it received a number of hostile attacks (e.g. Gregg, 1984; McLaughlin, 1987) and is now chiefly of interest to language teachers rather than to Second Language Acquisition researchers.

The fundamental distinction is between *acquisition* and *learning*. *Acquisition* is essentially the same process as the acquisition of the first language. It is not conscious; it does not occur in formal situations or through formal grammatical rules; it reveals itself in a fixed order of acquisition; it is unrelated to the learner's age; acquired knowledge is accessible by 'feel'; L2 success goes with the learner's attitude to the second language. *Learning* differs by being conscious learning of information about the language spelled out by teachers in formal classrooms; it varies in order; it can only be used by learners when they are old enough to handle it, say, in the early teens when they can understand grammatical explanation; learners vary in their propensity to use 'learning'; the product is verbalizable knowledge of 'rules'. The distinction between acquisition and learning is far-reaching and has persisted through Krashen's different formulations.

The relationship between acquisition and learning in speech production is spelled out by Krashen in an oft-repeated figure.

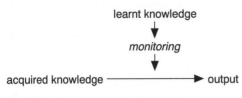

learnt knowledge

↓

*monitoring*

↓

acquired knowledge —————————→ output

**Figure 1** The Monitor Model of L2 production.

Anything learners want to say originates in their acquired knowledge, and is turned into spoken output by the process of speech production. Learnt knowledge, if available, may monitor the learner's production either before or after the actual sounds are produced. Such monitoring is highly variable and depends on whether the task is concerned with language form or message, on whether the learner has a certain personality type, age, etc. and on whether the task allows the learner sufficient time to monitor, though the latter requirement has latterly been dropped. Crucially, learnt knowledge is *never* transformed into acquired knowledge – the source of all production – but remains potentially available as a monitor.

The mid-eighties version of the model adds further elaboration through five so-called hypotheses (Krashen, 1985a). The *Acquisition/Learning Hypothesis* asserts the separation of acquisition from learning. The *Monitor Hypothesis* claims that learnt knowledge is used only for monitoring. The *Input Hypothesis* itself maintains that acquisition depends solely on comprehensible input – language that is always slightly ahead of the learner's current stage of progress but which contains messages that the learner can comprehend through means such as situational clues (see I + 1). Hence any teaching method is said to succeed to the extent that it provides comprehensible input. The NATURAL ORDER HYPOTHESIS claims that acquisition takes place in a predictable order. The AFFECTIVE FILTER *Hypothesis* provides a reason for learners' varying success: a negative attitude to L2 learning raises a mental block

that prevents comprehensible input being used by the learner.

A variety of evidence is cited in favour of these hypotheses. Comprehensible input is demonstrated by adaptations of speech to language learners, by the initial Silent Period (see SILENCE) during which L2 learners prefer not to speak, by the success of teaching that employs comprehensible input, such as immersion and bilingual classrooms. Monitoring is supported by case studies of L2 learners using or not using monitoring. Natural order depends upon such evidence as the grammatical morphemes research and other 1970s research that demonstrated orders of L2 acquisition of syntax (see MORPHEME ACQUISITION STUDIES). Much evidence thus consists of the reinterpretation of research carried out with other ends in mind rather than testing the Monitor Model itself, not only the order of acquisition but also research into ATTITUDES and APTITUDE.

From their first appearance the Monitor Model and the Input Hypothesis have provoked violent reactions. Criticism has focused on the inherent circularity of the interlocking hypotheses and on the lack of substantial evidence for *any* of them in isolation. In particular, few apart from Krashen have seen the necessity for an absolute separation of acquisition and learning. Personal experiences and successful teaching methods suggest that, at least for some learners in some situations, some aspects of learnt knowledge are converted into acquired knowledge, despite Krashen's claims. Conferences and journals in the mid-eighties were often marred by contributions that attempted to disembowel Krashen's theory in public, an activity that received its own name of 'Krashen-bashing' and sometimes extended even to Krashen's punctuation.

One reason for this reaction was the tremendous impact that Krashen's ideas had upon language teachers in North America, particularly through the book by Krashen and Terrell (1983). The concepts of acquisition/learning, monitoring and comprehensible input seemed to ring true of teachers' own experiences in ways not reflected in contemporary teaching methods. On the one hand, the dangers of monitoring undermined the tenets of formal traditional language teaching by showing that at best they would work only for certain minor aspects of language (rules of thumb) and at worst actually hindered the learner's progress; on the other the overriding importance of comprehension supported the teacher's common belief that literally anything goes in the classroom provided it makes the students try to understand. In American-influenced areas of language teaching, the impact of Krashen's ideas and of the NATURAL APPROACH promulgated by him and Tracey Terrell was considerable. In British-influenced areas, the actual teaching consequences have seemed a thin variation on the COMMUNICATIVE LANGUAGE TEACHING then at the height of its influence. But despite his critics, Krashen's ideas continue to have a popular appeal to language teachers, still figuring prominently in SLA books aimed at this market and still good for a lively argument whenever they are mentioned.

BIBLIOGRAPHY

Gregg, K. (1984). Krashen's Monitor and Occam's Razor. *Applied Linguistics*, 5/2, 79–100.
Hulstijn, J. and Hulstijn, W. (1984). Grammatical errors as a function of processing constraints and explicit knowledge. *Language Learning*, 34, 23–43.
Krashen, S. (1979). The Monitor Model for second language acquisition. In R. Gingras (ed.), *Second Language Acquisition and Foreign Language Teaching*. Washington, DC: Center for Applied Linguistics.
——(1981). *Second Language Acquisition and Second Language Learning*. Oxford: Pergamon.
——(1982). *Principles and Practice in Second Language Acquisition*. Oxford: Pergamon.*
——(1985a). *The Input Hypothesis: Issues and implications*. Harlow: Longman.
——(1985b). *Language Acquisition and Language Education*. Englewood Cliffs, NJ: Prentice-Hall.
Krashen, S. and Terrell, T. D. (1983). *The Natural Approach*. Oxford: Pergamon.
Lightbown, P. M. (1987). Classroom language as input to second language acquisition. In C. W. Pfaff (ed.), *First and Second Language Acquisition Processes*. Rowley, MA: Newbury House.
McLaughlin, B. (1987). *Theories of Second-Language Learning*. London: Edward Arnold.*

VJC

**morpheme** The smallest linguistic unit that has meaning. In English, the word *cats* is composed of two morphemes, {cat} (referring to the animal – note the use of curly brackets to indicate morphemes) and {-s}, signifying plurality. As this example indicates, some morphemes like {cat} can stand alone, while others like the plural {-s} must be attached to another morpheme. Different realizations of morphemes are called allomorphs. For example, the English plural {-s} morpheme may be pronounced /s/ (as in the word *cats*) or /z/ (as in the word *cars*). /s/ and /z/ are therefore allomorphs of the plural {-s} morpheme. (See MORPHOLOGY; also Atkinson et al., 1982, and MORPHEME ACQUISITION STUDIES.)

BIBLIOGRAPHY

Atkinson, M., Kilby, D. and Roca, I. (1982). *Foundations of General Linguistics*. London: Unwin Hyman.

KJ

**morpheme acquisition studies** were a branch of Second Language Acquisition research that tried to elaborate the order of acquisition of so-called 'grammatical morphemes' such as the article *the* and the 'progressive' *-ing*. Massively influential and numerous in the late 1970s, they dwindled to a trickle in the 1980s mostly because of their limited concept of GRAMMAR and their increasingly suspect methodology.

The *point du départ* was the original L1 work of Roger Brown (1973) with three children learning English as a first language.

Brown collected transcripts of the children's speech every month up to the age of 4. He was struck with the absence from the early stages of their speech of such 'grammatical morphemes' as the free morphemes *the* and the preposition *to* and the bound morphemes *-ing* and *-s* (see MORPHOLOGY). Accordingly he devised a scheme to show how children introduce fourteen of the most common morphemes into their speech over time. Each transcript was examined for obligatory contexts for each morpheme. An obligatory context is when a morpheme is required to make an equivalent grammatical sentence in adult speech, whether for linguistic or contextual reasons. *Man run* might then be an obligatory context for the article *a*, the auxiliary *be* and the progressive *-ing*. The percentage of correct items supplied for each morpheme is calculated in each transcript. If a morpheme is supplied in over 90% of its obligatory contexts in three consecutive transcripts, the child is regarded as having acquired it. Then the dates on which each morpheme was acquired can be put in sequence to arrive at the acquisition order. Brown's order for nine of the morphemes was then:

*-ing* > plural *-s* > irregular *-ed* past > possessive *-s* > copula *be* > articles *the/a* > regular past *-ed* > 3rd person *-s* > auxiliary *be*.

This true longitudinal study was largely corroborated by cross-sectional work by de Villiers and de Villiers (1973).

The first L2 research was carried out by Dulay and Burt in a series of studies. In 1973 they administered picture description tasks to Spanish-speaking children learning English, scored the success-rate for eight grammatical morphemes in obligatory contexts and ranked the scores from easiest to most difficult. This yielded a sequence:

plural *-s* > *-ing* > copula *be* > auxiliary *be* > articles *the/a* > irregular *-ed* past > 3rd person *-s* > possessive *-s*.

This was claimed to represent a common order for morpheme acquisition in an L2, similar to the L1 acquisition order but not identical.

The research paradigm was rapidly expanded by Dulay and Burt and several others such as Hakuta (1977) to show consistent orders for children with L1 Chinese, Japanese and French; for adults from mixed backgrounds; for different types of test and scoring systems; and for learners inside and outside classrooms. For the most part, similar orders to the Dulay and Burt study were found, with certain exceptions, for example, one Japanese child learnt plural *-s* last rather than first. Some argued that the morphemes should be seen as groups, i.e. NP morphemes grouped together, etc. and the stages of acquisition measured within each group rather than individually. Others grouped the morphemes into groups that tended to occur at the same time, even if the order within the groups varied, for example, Group 1 usually occurs first and consists of *-ing*, plural *-s* and copula *be*.

The research was gradually seen to have a number of flaws. First there was scant syntactic rationale for the choice of these morphemes: some were bound (*-s*), some free (*the*); some were allomorphs of the same morpheme (irregular and regular *-ed*); some were inflections of the noun, some of the verb. This heterogeneity prevented any clear linguistic analysis. A proper application of linguists' views on morphology to Second Language Acquisition research has still to be tried.

Second, the logic seemed odd in that a sequence of acquisition over time, as studied by Brown, is not necessarily the same as an order of difficulty at a single moment of time, as studied by the Second Language Acquisition researchers, even if these in fact turned out to be similar.

Third, the results have not been replicated with languages other than English, with rare exceptions. Some hints from other languages suggest that inability to produce grammatical morphemes may be an oddity of English rather than of all languages; Icelandic 2-year-olds already use forty inflectional endings.

Finally the underlying reason for the sequence was not clear; it was presented as a 'natural order' almost as if the actual morphemes of English were programmed to appear in the mind in a definite sequence, rather than reflecting some general principle of language exemplified by the English sequence.

The research contributed to the 1980s INPUT HYPOTHESIS model and still figures as an established dogma in much Second Language Acquisition research. It liked to make strong claims about the natural order of acquisition, again treated as an explanation rather than as something to be explained. Consequently, though it was clear that second language acquisition took place in a definite order, it was unclear whether the implications for language teaching were either to use no order of presentation (since the learner's mind will automatically impose one) or to follow the 'natural' order (since learners will be unable to absorb things that are too far distant from their current point of acquisition) or indeed to use the reverse order (since learners need to pay most attention to the things they will find difficult rather than those that are easy). (See also GRAMMAR TEACHING, MONITOR MODEL, NATURAL ORDER HYPOTHESIS, TEACHABILITY HYPOTHESIS.)

BIBLIOGRAPHY
Brown, R. (1973). *A First Language: The early stages*. London: Allen and Unwin.
Cook, V. J. (1993). *Linguistics and Second Language Acquisition*. Basingstoke: Macmillan.
De Villiers, J. and de Villiers, P. (1973). A cross-sectional study of the acquisition of grammatical morphemes in child speech. *Journal of Psycholinguistic Research*, 2/3, 235–52.
Dulay, H. C. and Burt, M. K. (1973). Should we teach children syntax? *Language Learning*, 23/2, 245–58.*
Dulay, H. C., Burt, M. and Krashen, S. (1982). *Language Two*. Rowley, MA: Newbury House.*
Hakuta, K. (1976). A case study of a Japanese child learning English as a second language. *Language Learning*, 26/2, 321–51.
Zwicky, A. M. (1975). Settling an underlying form: the English inflectional endings. In D. Cohen and J. R. Wirth (eds), *Testing Linguistic Hypotheses*. Now York: John Wiley, 129–86.

VJC

**morphology** This branch of linguistics investigates word structure and word formation. Every word consists of one or more morphemes – the smallest grammatical units carrying meaning. The word *danger*, for example, has one free-standing (*free*) morpheme. Words may include inflectional and derivational (lexical) morphemes, usually as affixes. *Dangers* contains the inflectional suffix -*s*, which means that the noun is in the plural form. *Endanger* contains the derivational prefix *en*-, where the addition to the stem creates a new word. Inflectional forms are a matter of inflectional morphology. This is often regarded as a component of GRAMMAR, alongside SYNTAX and LEXIS. Morphological relations between lexical forms are the domain of lexical (or derivational) morphology. (See MORPHEME ACQUISITION STUDIES.)

BIBLIOGRAPHY
Bauer, L. (1983). *English Word-formation* (Cambridge Textbooks in Linguistics). Cambridge: Cambridge University Press.*
Fromkin, V. and R. Rodman (1993). *An Introduction to Language*. 5th edn. Fort Worth, TX: Harcourt Brace Jovanovich. [Chapter 2.]
Spencer, A. (1989). *Morphological Theory: An introduction to word structure in generative grammar*. Oxford: Blackwell.

EJ

**motivation** is usually defined as a psychological trait which leads people to achieve some goal. In language learning, that goal may be mastery of the language or achievement of some lesser aim. In language learning research, attempts have been made to explain:

- what people who are motivated do to achieve their goals;
- how they view the task;
- how they are distinguished from people not so motivated;
- what external agencies like a teacher, course materials, instructional organization can do to promote motivation;
- whether motivation can be analysed into different kinds.

## MOTIVATION AND ACHIEVEMENT – A COMPLEX RELATIONSHIP

*A researcher's or a teacher's concern?* The research literature is quite full of references to motivation in language learning, mainly using correlational methods: that is, measuring strength of motivation on some criterion, often by questionnaire, and correlating that strength with measures of achievement. By contrast, the teaching literature seems remarkably silent on this question, at least in recent years. A quick trawl through the pages of the *English Language Teaching Journal* back to 1981, surprisingly produced only one article with motivation in the title. This might reflect a lack of interest in the topic, or perhaps a feeling among the kind of practising teachers who contribute to *ELTJ* that although motivation is the stuff of achievement in language classes it is not a topic on which to write articles. In the research literature the topic of motivation is often linked to that of ATTITUDES, so it is sensible to consider the present entry in parallel with that on attitudes for a fuller picture.

*INTRINSIC/EXTRINSIC MOTIVATION* An important distinction within motivation can be drawn between intrinsic and extrinsic motivation. Intrinsic motivation is thought of as being within the task itself: a sense of achievement, self-esteem, pride in solving the problem, enjoyment of the class, being able to use the language as desired. Extrinsic motivation is therefore external to the task itself, usually other consequences of success on the task: prizes for doing well, getting the job of one's choice, a higher position, gaining some certificate on a test score.

The question of whether intrinsic or extrinsic motivation is the more powerful leads to consideration of another very important component of motivation: the learner's scale of values. It is not possible to generalize about intrinsic or extrinsic motivation without considering what the learner regards as important. To some learners, the extrinsic benefits of success may be sufficient to keep them working at the (often distant) goal of mastery; to others, the supposed benefits of ultimate success may mean little but the sense of achievement all. Thus, motivation depends on the learner's evaluation of the motivating forces.

*Feedback in action* Since motivation is goal-directed, it is also partly dependent on information about success or failure. Thus many learners need immediate feedback on how well they are performing or how they compare with others; many learners, however, only act on their own perceptions of success. Thus, the learner's estimate of the probability of success on a particular task will interact with their evaluation of the worth of that success to affect the strength of their motivation to complete the task.

*Goals and sub-goals* Motivation is goal-directed, but there may be many kinds of goals and sub-goals. Typically, motivation has been related to five different aspects of the goal of mastering a language. Each of these aspects is approached by learners in different ways.

The first is *volitional undertaking*: actually starting to learn a language. People begin with remarkably different views of language and the learning process, and although these are discussed more often under the heading of attitudes, they are closely related to motivation.

The second is *perseverance*, or continuing with the task. Learning a language is a time-consuming activity, and the arguments, benefits or other motivating factors which started the process are often not the same as those required to continue for the months and years which learning a second language normally requires.

The third is *tolerance of frustration*. A strongly motivated person is likely to persevere through the ordinary and some extraordinary frustrations in learning a language better than one with low motivation. Such frustrations may arise from access to resources, exposure to the language, time pressure, disputes with the teacher, or the pace of other learners.

The fourth is *risk preference*. Highly motivated people may be more willing to risk cognitive and social stability than others. Cognitive risk-taking refers to information overload, forgetting, incomprehension, faulty identification and categorization. Social risk-taking refers to loss of face, nerves about performing in front of peers, fear of communication failure.

Lastly, motivation may have a role to play in *anxiety management*. Highly motivated people may be able to cope with anxiety about the learning experience better than others.

## THEORIES OF MOTIVATION

There have been a number of theories of motivation proposed during this century but they fall essentially into two kinds: mechanistic and cognitive. The early mechanistic theories centred around the notion of need reduction: learning occurred with the purpose of gaining benefits that reduced a need (whether primary, like getting food to satisfy hunger, or secondary, like information to satisfy curiosity). Human needs identified

ranged from subsistence needs through concepts like affiliation, curiosity, achievement, power, acquisitiveness, status defence, to Maslow's hierarchy of safety > love > self-esteem > self-actualization.

It is also clear that need reduction cannot be an explanation for much higher-level human motivation, since as needs are reduced by satisfaction, the motivation for learning is reduced. This is untypical of complex human learning. More recent cognitive analyses of motivation have emphasized the subjective evaluation of the probability of success, particularly with regard to level of aspiration and the attributions of causality of success. Attribution theory argues that attributions of responsibility determine future action on at least three dimensions:

| | |
|---|---|
| locus of control | self vs others |
| intentionality | ability vs effort |
| stability | stable vs unstable |

A person may believe that his or her present level of success is mainly due to the teacher's skill but that is unstable because that teacher is not always available; such a person is likely to approach the next task in a different frame of mind to another person who attributes his or her level of success to themselves, believing that they are not very talented but put in a lot of effort. If given a choice of level difficulty of task, the first person might go for a difficult task if the same teacher was around; the second might go for a medium level of difficulty because of the instability of effort. Such decisions will also be affected by the value of the task itself to the person.

## THE WORK OF GARDNER

Research on motivation in language learning is reviewed in detail in Skehan (1989). The dominant work in the field is that of R. C. Gardner, beginning in collaboration with W. E. Lambert and continuing to the present. It is therefore appropriate to begin this section with an appraisal of his output, and other approaches will be reviewed subsequently. The majority of Gardner's work has been with one method of research, using many questionnaires and analysing the resulting correlation matrices with multivariate statistics such as factor analysis and complex regression like Linear Structural Relations (LISREL).

Gardner has consistently found that his scales of motivational intensity, desire to learn the language and attitudes to learning the language have been strongly related to achievement. Gardner and MacIntyre (1993) showed, however, that a different variable, language anxiety, was more strongly and consistently related to achievement even than motivation. In the present context one can only speculate whether anxiety acts as a kind of negative motivation, perhaps as fear of failure.

*Attitude Motivation Index*   Gardner has constructed this index, consisting of 11 variables, to measure motivation. He considered motivation to be a composite construct involving intensity of the desire to achieve a goal and various specific attitudes. The three main terms in his view of motivation are therefore effort, desire to achieve a goal, and attitudes.

The AMI is an additive mixture of:

(1)  Attitudes to French-speaking Canadians;
(2)  Attitudes to European French people;
(3)  Interest in foreign languages;
(4)  Integrative orientation;
(5)  Motivational intensity;
(6)  Desire to learn French;
(7)  Attitudes towards learning French;
(8)  French teaching – evaluative;
(9)  French course – evaluative;
(10) Instrumental orientation;
(11) French class anxiety.
      (No. 11 is subtracted from the total of the other 10.)

Gardner's consistent use of questionnaires and scales for estimating the strength of his variables among large numbers of learners

(usually but not exclusively of French in English-speaking Canada) has allowed extensive testing of the measures themselves, but has rather removed the discussion of motivation in this area from mainstream developments in theorizing.

*Orientation Index*   The contribution toward understanding language learning motivation which is most famously associated with Gardner and his associates of these years is, however, the concept of orientation to language learning. Originally orientation was assessed by a questionnaire designed to elicit preferred reasons for learning a language, grouped into a bipolar contrast between INTEGRATIVE MOTIVATION and INSTRUMENTAL MOTIVATION. Integrative orientation concerned the learner's perceptions of himself or herself in the second language community – making more and different kinds of friends, having a share in the culture, being a member of another culture, even actually changing cultural allegiance. Instrumental orientation concerned the individual's place in his or her own culture: being regarded as an educated person, having access to better jobs. Early results in Canada appeared to show that an integrative orientation was more strongly associated with achievement than instrumental (Gardner and Lambert, 1972). However, in other cultural situations the results were diverse. Lukmani (1972) found a preference for instrumental orientation for English as a Foreign Language in Bombay; Gardner himself found an even distribution in the Philippines; Burstall (using a different questionnaire) found instrumental preferences for French as a foreign language in Britain.

The concept of integrative motivation changed over the years as it was found that it was also associated with a generalized interest in foreign languages and parental encouragement. Still, in Canada, it was found to be associated with difference in language attrition, and with benefits from school outings to the L2 speech community's territory. However, Gardner and MacIntyre (1993) found, in a study mainly devoted to demonstrating the VALIDITY of the AMI, that orientation was not strongly related to achievement in their sample. Whether that was due to the refined quality of the developed measuring instruments, or perhaps reflected a mood change in the Canadian population is impossible to say.

Gardner's methods increased in statistical sophistication and in 1985 he produced his 'Socio-educational Model' which attempted to specify causal chains among the many variables using a computer program based on multiple regression called LISREL (LInear Structural RELations).

*Criticisms of Gardner* The validity of Gardner's whole approach was challenged by Au (1988) on the grounds that it had not been demonstrated that the questionnaires and scales used in the AMI were themselves valid. Gardner and MacIntyre (1993) responded with a study which compared three different ways of estimating each of the variables and the achievement criteria, using a complex technique called a multi-trait multi-method matrix. Put simply, this technique compares the degree to which measures of different traits and measures of the same trait by different means (questionnaires, SEMANTIC DIFFERENTIAL, one-word methods) are associated together or converge, or are independent or diverge. In the present context, a measurement would be considered to have a high degree of validity if it was strongly associated with different ways of measuring the same trait, and weakly, or not at all, associated with measures of other traits. Gardner and MacIntyre found that, by and large, this was true of their main traits and their measurements – though, for example, the Orientation Index was not associated equally strongly with either other measures of the integrative motive or the instrumental motive, or with any tests of achievement in learning French. Thus, after thirty years of research, it is not at all clear what traits the orientation to language learning really measures, nor how it is related to actual learning outcomes.

## PROBLEMS

*Motivation research and the classroom* Several problems have appeared in the development of our understanding of motivation, apart from the validity of measurement. The first is the relationship of theory and research to the classroom situation. Motivation is clearly regarded as important by teachers and course writers and is firmly included in a number of methodological and syllabus design proposals. It is, however, difficult to demonstrate that particular constructs measured in the ways described above have identifiable effects on types of classroom behaviour. Studies have shown that integrative orientation may be related to frequency of volunteering in class, receiving more positive reinforcement, being asked more questions by the teacher. There is a suggestion that integrative orientation might be more associated with hypothesis formation and a restructuring of the linguistic system for learning. However, it is rather surprising that there appear to be no studies of mainstream language teaching classrooms which have combined use of correlational type measures like the AMI and qualitative techniques developed for classroom observation studies, to see if the theoretical constructs can be given identifiable form in actual classroom behaviour.

*Cause or result* A second problem is the notion of motivation as cause. The assumption of most of this work is that learning follows from motivation: but clearly motivation might be the result of successful learning. The level of aspiration idea neatly encapsulates both, because it sees motivation influencing future performance and performance influencing future motivation. Burstall's (1974) famous dictum 'nothing succeeds like success' was grounded on extensive research; however, Skehan (1989) concludes that the extant research in general on balance favours the motivation as cause argument.

## MOTIVATION IN THE CLASSROOM AND IN MATERIALS

In relation to classroom language teaching and learning, there has been a consistent move towards motivation-enhancing learning activities. Crookes and Schmidt (1989) describe many ways in which teachers try to influence their students' motivation, particularly appealing to effects intrinsic to the classroom situation, and suggest new avenues for classroom-based empirical research in the area. Many years ago, Stevick (1971), in a discussion of evaluating and adapting old materials for less commonly taught languages, suggested there were five types of reward that could be built into materials and would encourage students to persevere and succeed. They were:

(1) Relevance – of the content to the students' own language needs;
(2) Completeness – inclusion of all the language necessary for the stated aims of the course;
(3) AUTHENTICITY – both linguistic and cultural;
(4) Satisfaction – the student should leave each lesson feeling he has benefited more than simply progressed;
(5) Immediacy – the student should be able to use the material straight away.

*Some examples*   Two very important areas of development in modern language teaching are more or less explicitly based on these ideas. The first is the Language for Specific Purposes (see ENGLISH FOR SPECIFIC PURPOSES) movement. Within this, the notion of language NEEDS ANALYSIS (or target situation analysis) has been crucial, and the intention of such an analysis is to provide the means of selecting language items, interactional functions, vocabulary, skills, etc. that are

relevant and authentic for the situations of language use in which the student is intending to work. The motivational argument is that perceiving relevance and authenticity will increase the learner's intensity of motivation and so increase the effort. Of course, the degree to which relevance and authenticity can be perceived is a function of how much the student actually knows about the target situation (see the discussion in McDonough, 1984).

A second area of development, closely related in fact to ESP and the communicative approach as well, has been NOTIONAL-FUNCTIONAL SYLLABUSES. An explicit principle leading to a preference for notional/functional selection and grouping of language was, again, relevance and immediacy (termed SURRENDER VALUE). It was considered important, because attractive to the learner, to group syntactic forms to be learned around interactional meanings that learners would want to communicate, and to do so in a way that would allow learners to use the language learned immediately, rather than only conditionally upon learning some further complications later in the course. Stevick's other two principles, completeness and satisfaction, have been less conspicuous in methodological discussions, but not absent. His suggestion that language lessons should give more benefits than mere progress links up with the serious debate about what language lessons should actually be about, and the practical suggestions for content-based language teaching, LANGUAGE ACROSS THE CURRICULUM and teaching by immersion (see IMMERSION PROGRAMMES).

The principle of completeness has had less active consideration, perhaps because it is not obvious that a language course or course book can ever in fact be complete in a sense beyond that of simply fulfilling its own objectives. Rather, it has an enabling function, enabling its takers to become independent learners who can continue to acquire the language they need even after the course is over.

*Client-centred teaching* The last methodological developmental area in which motivation of the learners is explicitly acknowledged is that of client- or learner-centred teaching. Nunan (1988) details the research into the clients and teachers of the Australian Migrant English Programme (AMEP) and the development of materials based on what the learners preferred to learn and how they preferred to learn it. Such an approach may be actually uncomfortable for the teachers – student and teacher evaluations of techniques such as student error discovery and pair work in the class differed wildly – but motivation in such a difficult and volatile client population was too important to put at risk.

## SUMMARY

This overview has given a brief account of motivational theory, of research work on motivation in language learning and the complex link with attitudes, and of methodological developments which appear to emphasize motivation in different ways. Despite the great amount of work on these topics, it is clear that there are many issues remaining, and a personal view of these leads to the following questions, which will perhaps form part of the research agenda into the next century:

(a) How may motivation be best described?
(b) How do views of motivation derived from quantitative measures compare with those derived from socio-psychological and ethnographic views of learners in classrooms?
(c) What is the optimum relationship between motivation and the design of syllabuses and materials?
(d) How do motivation and STRATEGIC COMPETENCE interact?
(e) How do strength of motivation and anxiety interact?

In the future one would hope for studies which allow for more individual contributions in what is, after all, an individual difference construct, through interviews, participant observation, protocol analysis, diary studies, against the background of the valuable development of large-scale correlational studies.

BIBLIOGRAPHY
Au, S. Y. (1988). A critical appraisal of Gardner's social-psychological theory of second language learning. *Language Learning*, 38, 75–100.
Burstall, C., Jamieson, M., Cohen, S. and Hargreaves, M. (1974). *Primary French in the Balance*, Windsor: NFER.
Crookes, G. and Schmidt, R. (1989). Motivation: reopening the research agenda. *University of Hawaii Working Papers in ESL*, 8, 217–56.
Gardner, R. C. (1985). *Social Psychology and Second Language Learning: The role of attitudes and motivation*. London: Edward Arnold.*
Gardner R. C. and Lambert, W. E. (1972). *Attitudes and Motivation in Second Language Learning*. Rowley, MA: Newbury House.
Gardner R. C. and MacIntyre, P. (1993). On the measurement of affective variables in second language learning. *Language Learning*, 43/2, 157–94.
Lukmani, Y. (1972). Motivation to learn and language proficiency. *Language Learning*, 22, 261–73.
McDonough, J. E. (1984). *ESP in Perspective*. London and Glasgow: Collins.
Nunan, D. (1988). *The Learner-centred Curriculum*. Cambridge: Cambridge University Press.
Skehan, P. (1989). *Individual Differences in Second Language Learning*. London: Edward Arnold.*
Stevick, E. (1971). Evaluating and adapting language materials. In H. Allen and R. Campbell (eds), *Teaching English as a Second Language*. 2nd edn. New York: McGraw-Hill, 102–7.

SMCD

**move** is a functional-linguistic unit used in DISCOURSE ANALYSIS. In their work on classroom discourse, Bellack and others (1966; quoted in Coulthard, 1974) described interaction in terms of four moves: *structuring, soliciting, responding, reacting*. Structuring moves organize interaction, e.g. summonses. Soliciting moves elicit verbal and physical responses, and cognitive attention, e.g. questions, commands, requests. Responding moves occur in response to the soliciting moves, e.g. answers to questions. Reacting moves are occasioned by any of the other three types of move but need not be directly elicited by them (see TURN-TAKING).

BIBLIOGRAPHY
Bellack, A. A., Kliebard, H. M., Hyman, R. T. and Smith, F. L. (1966). *The Language of the Classroom*. New York: Teachers College Press.
Coulthard, M. (1974). *An Introduction to Discourse Analysis*. London: Longman.

AJ

**multidimensional syllabuses**   Johnson (1982) uses the term for a syllabus which changes orientation at different points in a programme. Sometimes the focus might be on structures, sometimes on functions, sometimes on settings (for example), according to changing learner needs, Morrow and Johnson (1979) exemplifies. Others use similar terms ('multi-syllabus' for example) to refer to an organization where more than one orientation operates at the same time; hence each teaching unit might be constructed following structural, functional and setting-based specifications. Swan (1981) advocates these syllabus types.

BIBLIOGRAPHY
Johnson, K. (1982). *Communicative Syllabus Design and Methodology* Oxford: Pergamon Institute of English.
Morrow, K. and Johnson, K. (1979). *Communicate 1 and 2*. Cambridge: Cambridge University Press.
Swan, M. (1981). False beginners. In K. Johnson and K. Morrow (eds), *Communication in the Classroom*. London: Longman, 38–44.

KJ

**multiple-choice testing** involves the selection of one correct or most appropriate response to a given stem (e.g. question, gapped sentence) from a number of distractors. Scoring is reliable and economical. The technique, however, does not measure productive abilities; there are difficulties in producing plausible distractors, and candidates may use guesswork. (See LANGUAGE TESTING.)

BIBLIOGRAPHY
Hughes, A. (1989). *Testing for Language Teachers*. Cambridge: Cambridge University Press.

KSM

# N

**native speaker** A native speaker is traditionally considered to be a person who, having acquired a language in infancy, has expertise and intuitions about its grammaticality, uses it automatically, accurately and creatively, and identifies with a community in which it is spoken. This view, however, combines criteria which do not necessarily occur together: language history, expertise and loyalty. Some argue that it is not a satisfactory linguistic notion, but one used to declare or deny group membership. This is disturbing to entrenched opinion both in linguistics, where 'native-speaker intuition' has been a source of evidence, and in language teaching, where native-speaker teachers are often considered the best.

BIBLIOGRAPHY
Coulmas, F. (ed.) (1981). *A Festschrift for the Native Speaker*. The Hague: Mouton.
Davies, A. (1991). *The Native Speaker in Applied Linguistics*. Edinburgh: Edinburgh University Press.*
——(1996). Proficiency or the native speaker: what are we trying to achieve in ELT? In G. Cook and B. Seidlhofer (eds), *Principle and Practice in Applied Linguistics*. Oxford: Oxford University Press.
Rampton, M. B. H. (1990). The 'native speaker': expertise, affiliation and inheritance. *English Language Teaching Journal*, 44/2, 97–101.

GC

**natural approach** A language teaching initiative elaborated by Krashen and Terrell. Though reminiscent of the DIRECT METHOD, it allegedly respects 'natural' principles of acquisition. The theoretical bases, deriving from Krashen's interpretations of second language acquisition research, reside in five premises: the ACQUISITION/LEARNING, the natural order, the monitor, the input and the AFFECTIVE FILTER hypotheses. The methodological crux flows from the INPUT HYPOTHESIS: progress is made if teacher-input is 'roughly tuned' to the learner's present level of competence ('i') *plus* elements representing the next stage of competence (+1), following 'natural order'. The proposals have attracted controversy; McLaughlin's critique is particularly mordant. (See MONITOR MODEL.)

BIBLIOGRAPHY
Krashen, S. and Terrell, T. D. (1983). *The Natural Approach: Language acquisition in the classroom*. Oxford: Pergamon.
McLaughlin, B. (1987). *Theories of Second-language Learning*. London: Edward Arnold. [Especially pp. 55–8.]

JTR

**natural order hypothesis** One of the five hypotheses which make up Krashen's (1985) INPUT HYPOTHESIS model of SLA. It holds that language learners acquire properties of an L2 in a predictable order, going through a series of common transitional stages in moving towards target language forms. Krashen also suggests that the natural order is unaffected by instruction. (See INTERFACE/NON-INTERFACE POSITIONS IN SLA, MONITOR MODEL, MORPHEME ACQUISITION STUDIES.)

BIBLIOGRAPHY
Krashen, S. (1985). *The Input Hypothesis: Issues and implications*. London: Longman.

SMCD

**need achievement theory**   This – nAch – was one of H. Murray's secondary human needs, explaining MOTIVATION. Atkinson considered the strength of nAch to be the net result of two tendencies, motivation towards success and motivation to avoid failure. These could give different outcomes. Different societies value striving for achievement differently. See McDonough (1986).

BIBLIOGRAPHY
McDonough, S. H. (1986). *Psychology in Foreign Language Teaching*. London: Allen and Unwin, 152–3.

SMCD

**needs analysis** is a term which gained prominence during the 1970s. Although not coterminous with it, the concept of needs analysis developed alongside the formulation of a COMMUNICATIVE APPROACH to language teaching. It has been particularly associated with the field of ESP, where it has been extensively discussed and modified from the perspectives of both principle and practice.

Expressed in general terms, the identification of language needs 'consists primarily in compiling information both on the individuals or groups of individuals who are to learn a language and on the use which they are expected to make of it when they have learnt it' (Richterich, 1983: 2). In other words, the procedures associated with the analysis of needs offer the course designer a framework for the selection of language content according to the goals of particular learners (see INDIVIDUALIZATION) and therefore the possibility of creating tailor-made programmes, rather than starting with a ready-made syllabus that does not of itself discriminate between differing objectives. Behind these straightforward observations, however, are a number of different approaches and a certain degree of controversy.

ANALYSING THE TARGET SITUATION

One of the cornerstones of ESP has been the assumption that it is necessary to analyse the study or professional context in which the learner will be using the target language. This assumption is, of course, not exclusive to ESP, and can be extended to any situation where it is possible to specify clearly the eventual goals of a language programme. (See Richterich, 1983, for a variety of examples, including school-level ones.) A postgraduate student, for instance, will require English to listen to lectures, write assignments, take examinations, participate in seminars and to read widely; a secretary will need to deal with correspondence and use the telephone extensively; a technical adviser will need skills of discussion and report-writing. In other words, this kind of specification is concerned with ends rather than means, with the external reference points fundamental to ESP course planning, and is usually referred to as *target situation analysis* (TSA).

A key exponent of this approach is Munby (1978), who proposes a processing model for the analysis of communication needs that is intended to provide an explicit and comprehensive profile for any learner(s). At the heart of the model is the Communication Needs Processor (CNP), which takes in information on the target context in eight different categories, the eventual output being a detailed list of syllabus content in terms of skills and language items. Thus data are gathered on reasons for learning, place and time of anticipated target use, others with whom the user will interact, content areas and skills required. A comparable procedure for assessing language needs in a business environment is discussed by Pilbeam (1979) under the heading of an 'audit', which examines the language requirements of specific jobs in a company measured against the current proficiency of relevant staff.

There is a range of possible methods for collecting data on target needs. The most frequent are the questionnaire and the interview (for instance, Mackay, 1978), carried out variously with sponsors, receiving institutions, people already in the target situation, or possibly intending course participants. Other methods include observation, informal discussion, or the collecting of linguistic data.

## ISSUES IN NEEDS ANALYSIS

Systematic TSA procedural models such as that offered by Munby and Chambers (1980) have sharpened our understanding of a crucial element in programme design as well as providing a comprehensive checklist of questions for carrying out a needs analysis. There are, however, a number of areas which are not taken into account in a TSA. They have been extensively discussed in the literature on needs analysis and just three of the most central are set out here.

First of all, it is clear that language learners (unlike Munby's 'participant', with its stereotype implication (1978: 52)) are not merely a package of identified target needs. Learners have expectations, demands and wishes which may sit uncomfortably in a programme that is focused on final objectives. They will also have perceptions of their own needs, which will probably change over time as learning goals are reset and as they become clearer about their own developing proficiency. A postgraduate arriving in Britain, for example, may initially be more concerned with social interaction and establishing a personal living framework than with his future academic needs; a professional person may be preoccupied with novel aspects of the methodology of the language classroom in relation to previous learning experiences.

Second, there are a number of others who will have their own perceptions of needs in a particular context. These include sponsors such as companies or government agencies, the future workplace or receiving academic department, the institution in which the language programme takes place and the language teachers themselves. Richterich and Chancerel (1980), working in the context of a large-scale European language learning scheme for adults (COUNCIL OF EUROPE), offer a very different kind of model from Munby's TSA. It allows for the identification of needs along several parameters by the learner, the teaching establishment and the user institution. It also builds in a consideration of resources and other environmental factors, which in Munby's view are simply 'constraints' that are to be attended to at the syllabus implementation stage and after establishing the needs profile.

Finally, it is improbable that a language course can consist only of a series of replications derived from the target situation. Such teaching by objectives ignores the reality of the learning situation itself and of the process of acquiring language. Hutchinson and Waters (1987) offer a checklist of learning needs in parallel to the TSA which take such factors into account: they include motivation and attitudes, interests, personal reasons for learning, learning styles, and resources and time available.

Needs analysis, then, is a complex process which, using data from a variety of sources, potentially takes into account a wide range of variables both in the target context and the learning environment.

BIBLIOGRAPHY
Chambers, F. (1980). A re-evaluation of needs analysis in ESP. *ESP Journal*, 1/1, 25–33.
Coleman, H. (1988). Analysing language needs in large organisations. *English for Specific Purposes*, 7/3, 155–69.
Hawkey, R. (1983). Programme development for learners of English. In R. Richterich (ed.), *Case Studies in Identifying Language Needs*. Oxford: Pergamon, 79–87.

Hutchinson, T. and Waters, A. (1987). *English for Specific Purposes*. Cambridge: Cambridge University Press.

Mackay, R. (1978). Identifying the nature of the learner's needs. In R. Mackay and A. Mountford (eds), *English for Specific Purposes*. London: Longman, 21–37.

Markee, N. (1986). Towards an appropriate technology model of communicative course design: issues and definitions. In *English for Specific Purposes*, 5/2, 161–72.

Munby, J. (1978). *Communicative Syllabus Design*. Cambridge: Cambridge University Press.*

Pilbeam, A. (1979). The language audit. *Language Training*, 1/2, 593.

Richterich, R. (ed.) (1983). *Case Studies in Identifying Language Needs*. Oxford: Pergamon.*

Richterich, R. and Chancerel, J.-L. (1980). *Identifying the Needs of Adults Learning a Foreign Language*. Oxford: Pergamon.

JMCD

**negotiation of meaning**    In human interaction, meanings are not simply transferred from one person to another but 'negotiated'. That is to say, my success (or otherwise) in conveying my intentions (my meanings) is dependent upon a process of negotiation between us. I may initially try to adjust the way I express myself to fit better what I think to be your preferred ways of looking at things – to make it easier for you to see what I am getting at. If you are not convinced you know what I am trying to say to you, you may then try out your understanding on me to see if it is 'correct'. At that point I may decide that what you think I meant is near enough to let it pass, or I may decide further negotiating work is necessary.

The negotiation of meaning has been proposed as the key to second (and/or foreign) language development (see also INTERACTION HYPOTHESIS, PROCESS SYLLABUSES.)

BIBLIOGRAPHY
Breen, M. P. (1984). Contemporary paradigms in syllabus design, Parts 1 and 2. *Language Teaching*, 20, 80–92 and 157–74.

Breen, M. P. and Candlin, C. N. (1980). The essentials of a communicative curriculum in language teaching. *Applied Linguistics*, 1, 89–112.

RLA

**norm vs criterion referencing**    In a norm-referenced test, a candidate's score is compared with those of a large group of broadly similar people. The score is interpreted in terms of how far above or below the mean of the reference group it lies, or in terms of the percentage of candidates scoring worse. An example is TOEFL. A criterion-referenced test has a set of descriptions of criterial performance, for example, the English Speaking Union Framework. An example of a large-scale criterion-referenced test is the IELTS. In practice, however, most proficiency tests rely on both concepts. See also TESTS IN ENGLISH LANGUAGE TEACHING.

BIBLIOGRAPHY
Hughes, A. (1989). *Testing for Language Teachers*. Cambridge: Cambridge University Press, 17–19.

SMCD

**noticing**    Schmidt (1990) distinguishes various forms of 'consciousness' relevant to language learning. One of these is 'noticing', which occurs when something is attended to to the extent that it is 'available for verbal report'. Using a diary study, Schmidt and Frota (1986) explore the role of noticing for one learner, plotting what aspects of received input are noticed by the learner. They then relate these noticed features to the learner's speech production, and find that new features occurring in the learner's speech are often those that have first been noticed. This leads Schmidt and Frota to suggest that noticing plays an important role in language acquisition. See also CONSCIOUSNESS RAISING.

BIBLIOGRAPHY
Schmidt, R. (1990). The role of consciousness in second language learning. *Applied Linguistics*, 11, 129–58.
Schmidt, R. and Frota, S. (1986). Developing basic conversational ability in a second language: a case-study of an adult learner. In R. Day (ed.), *Talking to Learn: Conversation in second language acquisition*. Rowley, MA: Newbury House.*

KJ

**notional/functional syllabuses** In this type of syllabus (called N/F for short) teaching items are arranged according to the notions (concepts) and/or functions (uses) thought to be required by the learner. Developed partly as a reaction to overemphasis on structural teaching, N/F is associated with the COUNCIL OF EUROPE team, particularly David Wilkins. N/F syllabuses were predominant in many parts of the world during the latter part of the 1970s, and found particular application in short-term intensive programmes, ESP courses and situations where learners needed to have their grammatical knowledge activated. N/F has come to be criticized for providing learners with 'useful phrases' but no generative knowledge of how the language works. For a general description of N/F see Wilkins (1976); for applications of this syllabus type see Johnson (1982); for criticisms, Wilkins and others (1981).

In a paper which may be regarded as the genesis of N/F, Wilkins (1973) proposes the use of two types of category in syllabus design: the SEMANTICO-GRAMMATICAL CATEGORIES and the CATEGORIES OF COMMUNICATIVE FUNCTION. Examples of the first type of category (from Wilkins, 1973) are frequency, duration, quantity. They are semantic because they are categories of meaning; but the word 'grammatical' is used since, in most European languages at least, they 'interact significantly with grammatical categories'. For example, the expression of duration in English is closely associated with particular tenses and certain prepositions. Examples of Wilkins's 'communicative functions' are inviting, requesting services and apologizing. Unlike the semantico-grammatical categories, these do not interact significantly with grammatical categories; hence there is no one structure associated with (for example) the function of inviting. In his 1976 book Wilkins added a third category which he called *modal meaning*.

Wilkins's proposal is that the N/F syllabus should introduce language to be taught under semantico-grammatical and/or functional headings. He himself uses the term *notional syllabus* to describe this syllabus type. But it has become common practice (followed here) to use the term *notion* to refer to semantico-grammatical categories alone, implying that a *notional syllabus* would be one listing semantico-grammatical categories only. Nowadays the term *notional/functional syllabus* is more common as the umbrella term, though the labels *semantic syllabus* and COMMUNICATIVE SYLLABUS are also used in this sense.

In the Council's model, syllabus content would generally be arrived at by a process of NEEDS ANALYSIS, which identified notions and functions to be taught. These would provide the basis for teaching materials teaching learners lesson by lesson how to invite, request services, apologize, for example. Of the two category types – the notional and the functional – it is the latter which caught the imagination of textbook writers, and at least one generation of language teaching materials came to be organized on functional lines (see, for example, White, 1979; Morrow and Johnson, 1979). For an attempt to organize materials notionally, see Jones (1979).

To understand the impact of N/F it is necessary to view its development within a broader context than that of the Council of Europe's work. In the 1960s discontent was increasingly being expressed with an overemphasis on grammar teaching, the result often being grammatically competent learners unable to use their knowledge to perform communicative acts. This particular discontent reflects the more general one in linguistics with the importance given to syntax, which led to Hymes's work on COMMUNICATIVE COMPETENCE. N/F responded to the discontent in language teaching by providing a framework whereby the learner can be taught to perform communicative acts.

There are certain sorts of courses with which N/F has become particularly associated. Partly because it provides a principled way of selecting and rejecting items (through needs analysis), it is suitable for much ENGLISH FOR SPECIFIC PURPOSES teaching; indeed, though ESP predated N/F, the two have flourished together. A further application is on short-duration intensive courses (e.g. the PRE-SESSIONAL COURSE) where again selection through needs analysis is an important benefit. A more general situation where N/F has an obvious application is with learners who already have a grasp of grammar but need to have this 'activated'. Many N/F textbooks are based on this activation principle; for an example, see Johnson and Morrow (1980). It may further be argued that because N/F introduces structures through their uses it is almost central to communicative language teaching in programmes for all students, including those without any prior grammar. There are certain problems, however, with using the functional syllabus with beginner students (see Johnson, 1977). For one claimed advantage of N/F over structural syllabuses, see SURRENDER VALUE.

Particularly during the 1980s, N/F has been the subject of many criticisms. According to Paulston (in Wilkins et al., 1981: 93), Wilkins's approach 'is quite atheoretical; it says nothing about how languages are learned' (this in spite of the fact that Wilkins (1976) spends considerable time associating N/F with what he calls an 'analytic', as opposed to a synthetic, mode of learning – see ANALYTIC/SYNTHETIC TEACHING STRATEGIES).

A second area of criticism concerns the so-called lack of generativity of N/F. There is the danger that N/F will simply provide a kind of elaborate phrasebook, without any real generative capacity for communication. For discussion of these issues, see Wilkins and others (1981).

It is now rare to find textbooks which are organized exclusively along N/F lines, and the problem of generativity has led some to return to a predominantly structural syllabus, where generativity is not in question. But even in such cases it has become commonplace for materials to include an N/F dimension (see MULTIDIMENSIONAL SYLLABUSES). Others have responded with more drastic measures to the issues raised by the criticisms of N/F; the PROCEDURAL SYLLABUS may be seen as one such response.

BIBLIOGRAPHY
Finocchiaro, M. and Brumfit, C. J. (1983). *The Functional-Notional Approach: From theory to practice.* Oxford: Oxford University Press.*
Johnson, K. (1977). Adult beginners: a functional or a communicative structural approach? In K. Johnson (1982), *Communicative Syllabus Design*, 106–14.
——(1982). *Communicative Syllabus Design and Methodology.* Oxford: Pergamon Institute of English.*
Johnson, K. and Morrow, K. (1980). *Approaches.* Cambridge: Cambridge University Press.
Jones, L. (1979). *Notions in English.* Cambridge: Cambridge University Press.
Morrow, K. and Johnson, K. (1979). *Communicate.* Cambridge: Cambridge University Press.
White, R. V. (1979). *Functional English.* Sunbury-on-Thames: Nelson.
Wilkins, D. A. (1973). The linguistic and situational content of the common core in a unit/credit system. In *Systems Development in Adult Language Learning.* Strasbourg: Council of Europe.
——(1976). *Notional Syllabuses.* Oxford: Oxford University Press.*
Wilkins, D. A., Brumfit, C. J. and Paulston, C. B. (1981). Discussion on notional syllabuses. *Applied Linguistics*, 2/1, 83–100.*

KJ

# Nuffield primary French project

The 1960s saw many curriculum and text-book revision projects, and in Britain one of the most ambitious was associated with the Nuffield Foundation. Their aim was to make foreign languages available in schools on a non-selective basis, and they produced a French course for British primary schools. *En Avant* uses a SITUATIONAL SYLLABUS together with aspects of AUDIOVISUALISM. Courses for other languages followed, and overall the project brought a greater degree of professionalism to British foreign language teaching. Associated with this work is the experiment on primary French teaching reported by Burstall and others (1974). (See TEACHING YOUNG LEARNERS.)

BIBLIOGRAPHY
Burstall, C., Jamieson, M., Cohen, S. and Hargreaves, M. (1974). *Primary French in the Balance*. Slough: National Foundation for Educational Research.*
Howatt, A. P. R. (1984). *A History of English Language Teaching*. Oxford: Oxford University Press.
Spicer, A. (1969). The Nuffield foreign languages teaching materials project. In H. H. Stern (ed.), *Languages and the Young School Child*. Oxford: Oxford University Press, 148–61.

KJ

# O

**organizations for applied linguists**
There is one unitary organization worldwide
specifically for the profession of 'APPLIED
LINGUISTICS', the International Association
of Applied Linguistics (AILA is the acro-
nym, from the original French version of
the name: l'Association Internationale de la
Linguistique Appliquée). AILA was founded
in the mid-1960s as an association of
national associations for individual applied
linguists. It held its first meeting as an
international colloquium in Nancy, France,
in 1964, and its first international congress
in 1969, in Cambridge, England. Since 1969
it has held an international congress every
three years, most often in greater Europe,
but the congress has also been held in
Canada (1978) and in Australia (1987). As
an association of national associations it has
no individual members. Its affairs are managed by an international committee, and its
intellectual work is mainly conducted by a
number of international 'Commissions', each
with a responsibility for a different academic
area of the field. AILA is associated with a
major academic journal, *Applied Linguistics*,
which is sponsored by AAAL (the American Association for Applied Linguistics) and
BAAL (the British Association for Applied
Linguistics), and published quarterly by
Oxford University Press. AILA also publishes its own *Newsletters*, *Bulletins* and
occasional *Reviews*.

The national associations that belong to
AILA are individual membership associations each with their own structure and
rules. It is therefore difficult to say much that
would be universally true about them. But
typically they have their own national congresses (or 'conferences'), their own publications and a restriction on membership in
that it is expected that people applying for
membership will have a formal qualification
(or the equivalent in terms of respected professional experience) in applied linguistics
as a branch of academic study.

AILA and the associated national associations are the obvious 'home' for applied
linguists, but there are many other associations around the world that would be of
interest to applied linguists, especially to
those with a particular interest in language
teaching. There is, for example, another
major international association of associations: the FIPLV (Fédération Internationale
des Professeurs de Langues Vivantes) or
'world federation of associations of teachers
of living languages'. FIPLV, founded in 1931,
has as its members principally national associations for modern language teachers and
unilingual international associations. FIPLV
has its own system of triennial international
congresses, typically in greater Europe.
FIPLV is developing a worldwide regional
structure, although again the European area
seems most active in this respect. FIPLV
also produces a newsletter, *FIPLV World
News*, and other occasional publications.

The unilingual international associations
for language teachers referred to above
represent a further associational 'home' for
applied linguists (again, at least for those
especially concerned with language teaching). The biggest of these is TESOL (the
international association of Teachers of English to Speakers of Other Languages), with

approximately 20,000 individual members worldwide, with many more thousands of members represented by more than seventy national and subnational associations affiliated to TESOL. TESOL's stated mission is 'to strengthen the effective teaching and learning of English around the world while respecting individuals' language rights'. TESOL was established just after the mid-1960s, as was the other international association for English language teachers, IATEFL (the International Association of Teachers of English as a Foreign Language). IATEFL also has a mix of individual and affiliate membership, though a much smaller individual membership than TESOL. TESOL was founded in the United States of America, has its headquarters there (in the Washington area) and most of its individual members live in the USA. IATEFL was founded in England, has its headquarters there, and most of its individual members live in Europe. Both associations are independent of the governments of the countries in which they are based, although IATEFL does have a special relationship with the British Council. As might be expected, TESOL's annual international congresses take place principally within the USA's borders, though occasionally they go outside, for example, to Mexico or Canada, while IATEFL's annual conferences are typically located in the United Kingdom, though occasionally they take place elsewhere in Europe. TESOL publishes the *TESOL Quarterly*, a scholarly journal, and the *TESOL Journal*, aimed at a more strictly professional readership, as well as an in-house newsletter, *TESOL Matters*. IATEFL publishes a newsletter and, in association with the British Council and Oxford University Press, the quarterly *ELT Journal*.

The main issues facing such major international associations are typically focused around how best to serve an international individual membership. It is difficult for them to provide much in the way of membership services to members who are too far from the places where their major conferences are held to be able to attend them, and yet the conferences are seen as the major professional events in the annual calendar. It is similarly difficult to foster a spirit of international cooperation in a widely dispersed membership, although some progress has been made in recent years, principally through the notion of affiliate twinning, whereby two affiliates from different parts of the world (typically a relatively 'rich' affiliate pairs with a relatively 'poor' one) develop a special relationship to exchange professional information and make mutual visits. A third difficulty for associations like TESOL and IATEFL, linked historically as they are with the countries in which they have their headquarters, is how best to represent the concerns of the profession within their own national boundaries, without losing sight of the international dimensions of their overall aims. It is an irony of history that there is no integrated USA national affiliate of TESOL and no integrated UK national affiliate of IATEFL (although both in the USA and the UK there are a number of sub-national affiliates) to represent the professions nationally in those two countries.

National associations can, of course, work more comfortably to a more 'national' agenda. Some may focus on actively cooperating with their national governments in the provision of, say, in-service teacher education work, while others may have a role more as a professional lobby, seeking primarily to influence policy decisions wherever these impinge upon the profession. As an illustration of the importance accorded to relations with national governments by associations of language teachers it is interesting to note that the workshop mounted by the Council of Europe in 1995 to bring together more than twenty representatives of language teacher associations on the topic of 'Starting and Running a Teachers' Association' produced, as its 'most important results' (*FIPLV World News*, August 1995: 9), the following Recommendations to Ministries of Education:

We, the undersigned, participants of the workshop on Teachers' Associations, ask Ministries of Education to consider and act upon the following recommendations:

(1)   that Teachers' Associations be considered as professional bodies to be consulted in matters of curriculum development, textbooks, national education reforms, examination procedures and other related areas;

(2)   that Teachers' Associations be informed about decisions to be made by governmental and/or educational bodies. (One way to ensure this is to have a representative of TA's on respective committees);

(3)   that the channelling of information (regarding summer courses, grants, conferences, study trips, Council of Europe workshops, EU programmes, etc.) between Ministries and TA's be mutual and free-flowing;

(4)   that Ministries, while respecting the independence of TA's, be prepared to recognize and finance work done by TA's, especially considering the share TA's take in in-service training.

It is easy to give the impression that the only associations worthy of mention are the major national or international ones. However, it is at least arguable that the most valuable work that teachers can do in association with each other can be done at the local level, by teachers who get together quite informally, for mutual support and self-development. At the same time, it is also understandable if their work goes largely unheeded, precisely because it is so highly localized. An important example of a local, and relatively informal, association that has become quite widely known and respected for its professional self-development work is the Bangalore English Language Teaching Community, in India (see Naidu et al., 1992).

The above discussion has limited itself to what we may call 'professional' associations, but it is important to distinguish between such associations, which exist principally for the sake of the profession as a whole, and associations that act more as 'trade unions',

principally for the sake of their members as individuals and especially as employees, rather than for the sake of the profession as a whole. This is sometimes a very delicate distinction to make in practice, but it can be an extremely important one, especially when a group of people is attempting to obtain official governmental permission to set up a national association. It can also be important when people are deciding which association or associations to belong to. Do they want primarily a pressure group that will represent them as employees, for example, or a networking system that will assist them to develop as professionals? Some associations can clearly take on both functions, but in some countries it may be politically necessary to follow a policy of strict separation between the two notions of what an association primarily exists for.

There does not appear to be a great quantity of material published to help people interested in starting up an association, but the major associations such as TESOL and IATEFL are always willing to assist with advice, especially if there is a prospect of affiliation, as this is where they have accrued very considerable experience over the years, and of course it is a way in which they can extend their own influence. A brief handbook on how to set up and run either a formal or informal association has been published by the Centre for Research in Language Education at Lancaster University.

BIBLIOGRAPHY

Centre for Research in Language Education (1995). *Developing an Association for Language Teachers: An introductory handbook*. 2nd edn. Lancaster University, Department of Linguistics and Modern English Language.

Naidu, B., Neeraja, K., Ramani, E., Shivakumar, J. and Viswanatha, A. (1992). Researching heterogeneity: an account of teacher-initiated research into large classes. *ELT Journal*, 46/3, 252–63.

RLA

**output hypothesis** Swain (1985) develops the idea that for full grammatical competence to be developed, learners need to be pushed into the production of comprehensible output. Though comprehensible input may lead to understanding, it does not involve the development of syntactic plans which PRO-DUCTION PROCESSES require. Schmidt (1983) shows that opportunities for production alone will not necessarily lead to improvement; it is important that the learner be 'pushed' to produce accurate output, in the face of communicative failure. Johnson (1992) discusses one proposal for achieving this in the classroom.

BIBLIOGRAPHY
Johnson, H. (1992). Defossilizing. *ELT Journal*, 46/2, 180–9.
Schmidt, R. (1983). Interaction, acculturation and the acquisition of communicative competence. In N. Wolfson and E. Judd (eds), *Sociolinguistics and Second Language Acquisition*. Rowley, MA: Newbury House.
Swain, M. (1985). Communicative competence: some roles of comprehensible input and comprehensible output in its development. In S. Gass and D. Madden (eds), *Input in Second Language Acquisition*. Rowley, MA: Newbury House.*

KJ

# P

paralinguistic features    Paralinguistic features are a suprasegmental (see PHONO-LOGY) aspect of language. The term is applied to the various tones of voice which can be used by speakers to affect the meaning of utterances, though, as the word suggests, in ways which are less important communicatively than features, such as INTONATION and STRESS. Examples are whispering, breathiness, huskiness and nasality. Such effects tend not to have universal meaning. The term is sometimes also applied to non-verbal behaviour such as the use of gesture.

BIBLIOGRAPHY
Abercrombie, D. (1972). Paralanguage. In J. Laver and S. Hutcheson (eds), *Communication in Face to Face Interaction*. Harmondsworth: Penguin Books, 64–70. [First published in 1968 in the *British Journal of Disorders of Communication*, 3, 55–9.]

AJ

peer teaching is an activity carried out principally in teacher training. The term is used in the context of the simulation of teaching practice where other trainees (the peers) pretend to be the learners. The creation of this artificial environment is common in the very focused training technique of MICROTEACHING.

BIBLIOGRAPHY
Wallace, M. J. (1991). *Training Foreign Language Teachers: A reflective approach*. Cambridge: Cambridge University Press. [Chapter 6.]

JMCD

personality variables    The role of personality in language learning has been the subject of much speculation and some research. The research has usually adopted the strategy of correlating (see CORRELATION) personality assessment techniques brought over from academic and clinical psychology with measures of various aspects of language learning – either achievement measures or process observations. This entry will briefly outline the success and shortcomings of this strategy by looking first at traditional concepts of personality, and at the logic of the suggestion that personality and language learning might be linked, then outlining the major areas of research on relevant aspects of personality, concluding with an evaluation of the utility of what has been learned and the prospects for future research.

*Concepts of personality*    Personality typically refers to traits of an individual which are relatively independent of language and social context, although that does not deny the formative influence of early socialization, nor the fact that many aspects of personality are most obvious in social interaction, in work, leisure, education and domestic situations. Conceptions of personality have been in terms of typology, collections of traits and self-views. There are measures, usually but not exclusively based on questionnaires, to assess such types as the Extrovert and the Introvert (the Eysenck Personality Inventory), traits as in the large-scale Minnesota Multiphasic Personality Inventory and self-views such as personal constructs. These and many others are used for research purposes and clinical diagnosis of personality disorders and psychosocial maladjustment and are also increasingly used in personnel selection in the world of business.

*The interaction of personality and language learning* The suggestion that language learning varies with personality takes several forms. It may be that certain personality traits are good for language learning success; thus possessing those traits might make language learning easier and therefore more successful for the possessors, and conversely more difficult for those lacking them. Alternatively, those positively related traits may make it more likely for the possessors to choose to learn a language in the first place. Another possibility is that certain personality types might be better predisposed to learning languages than others. A third possibility is that differences in personality are associated with different preferred modes of language learning: thus persons of type x might learn best through methods using one set of techniques, and those of type y through another set.

It is evident, therefore, that significant evidence of an interaction between personality measures and language learning, either with process or product, is potentially serious. The interaction would mean that people, by virtue of the kind of people they were, and not because of resources, the skill of the teachers, motivation, aptitude or any qualities of cognitive processing, or any other manipulable factor, could find language learning either restricted by the non-availability of appropriate instructional methods, or difficult – at worst impossible – because language learning is closed off to their personality types. This situation would be to say the least in conflict with the principle that human languages are learnable by any human, and could lead to bizarre policies of channelling language teaching resources only to those who were the 'right kind of people' or to advising individuals not to undertake language learning because they were the 'wrong

kind of people' – on the basis of 'scientific research'. As we shall see, the evidence that personality has any great influence on language learning is actually rather weak and certainly not strong enough to be used to support any such discrimination.

## MAJOR CONTROVERSIES

Before reviewing the major controversies in the area it is important to point out that the category boundaries between personality, ATTITUDES and MOTIVATION are blurred, and certain concepts, such as anxiety, might be equally well discussed under any or all of these categories.

*EXTROVERSION/INTROVERSION* Eysenck's famous distinction between these two personality types appears to involve a number of dimensions: sociability, gregariousness, adventuresomeness, risk-taking, impulsiveness and liking change, which may boil down to sociability and impulsivity. Skehan (1989: 101) points out that while, in general learning research, the evidence points to a superiority among the introverted learners, in language learning the expectation has been that extroverts would be superior because they tend to dominate in obtaining talk opportunities. Actual research results have been somewhat conflicting. Naiman and others (1978), in the Good Language Learner project, found no relationship between the Eysenck Personality Inventory and language learning achievement (see GOOD LANGUAGE LEARNER STUDIES). However, on a combined measure of class activity, using the foreign language and demanding attention, they did find a positive relationship with higher scores on their measures of listening comprehension and sentence repetition.

Other researchers have found positive correlations between extroversion and other measures, like oral fluency and pronunciation, but these are not consistent and vary with the learners (as between children and adults), with the nature of the language learning experience (whether naturalistic or classroom-bound) and particularly with the kind of achievement being measured.

There is also the possibility, suggested by general educational research, that being extroverted is an asset younger than puberty, but after puberty introverted learners do better in scholastic environments. This last point reminds us that, at least in discussing school-based language learning, the nature of personality is changing as the learner develops socially and intellectually. Strong (1983) studied sociability and language learning among kindergarten children, and found a number of positive correlations, in particular with talkativeness and responsiveness – so very young language learners seem to benefit if they are likely to engage in conversations. This result is interesting but difficult to generalize to others of the same age group, let alone school-age children or adults.

In short, the evidence for a general correlation of sociability and language learning is positive but weak and highly context-dependent. Whether this constitutes grounds for supporting or revising the use of language teaching methods which favour active participation and public performance in social interaction in class is something for language teaching theorists to decide. Observational classroom research has suggested that in certain contexts, learners who mainly observe other learners engaged in interaction remember more of the lessons than those participating (Slimani, 1989).

The other main plank of extroversion–introversion, impulsivity or a craving for excitement, has not received much attention in studies with language learners. It is difficult to see why this aspect should be any more relevant to language learning than to any other kind of learning.

The fate of studies of extroversion–introversion in language learning may be taken to illustrate a central problem in this kind of research. In adopting categories from a background discipline, here psychology, language learning may be blurring distinctions and traits which, separately, are important in many different contexts of language learning, rather than designing studies which can discover the determinants of language learning achievement, and are using measurements which mask these traits. Another difficulty that these kinds of studies encounter arises from the use of correlational research designs: personality tests, usually using questionnaires, are correlated against product measures. More valuable insights may come from studies using process measures such as CLASSROOM OBSERVATION, reflection, or protocol analysis, and individual 'clinical' methods.

*Risk-taking* Another element in the extroversion–introversion cluster is risk-taking. Communicative approaches to language teaching have set something of a premium on the learners' willingness to take risks with the chances of more or less public failure on the grounds that formulating a learner's own meanings in sentences of their own construction in the foreign language is beneficial, and that in situations of looming communicative failure, the learner's use of communicative strategies helps to reduce the risk. Thus, a learner who prefers high-risk situations should perform better in the classroom than a more conservative learner who prefers low-risk situations, and would be able to draw more lasting benefit from the opportunities afforded by this approach. Risk-taking might also be seen as preferable in terms of cognition as well as in a social sense: language learners who are willing to try out their own conclusions before they have sufficient evidence from the language input may have an advantage. Beebe's (1983) review lays out the parameters clearly. However, theories of risk-taking by language learners are generally based on psychological laboratory work which does not involve important elements of the language-learning context, like public performance in the language via pronunciation, nomination and volunteering of turns in a class, etc.

There are not many direct studies of risk-taking by language learners. One is the small-scale classroom-based study by Ely (1986). On the basis of six items in a questionnaire which were relevant to the risk-taking construct, he found that there was a correlation between high risk-taking and classroom participation. As for the correlations between class participation and achievement itself, only one comparison achieved significance, between the lower group of students and oral retelling of a story. Therefore, the modest results, and the other design features of this interesting, detailed, but small-scale classroom study, must make us conclude that the evidence for a definite advantage for language learners in being happy in high-risk situations is very weak. One should, however, be wary of concluding that because the research has failed by and large to confirm an assumption, it has refuted it.

*Self-confidence* Gardner and MacIntyre (1993) point out that self-confidence is related to language learning in an inverse way to anxiety, and that both traits play a part in motivation and are related to stable personality characteristics. Work in Canada has shown that self-confidence may, however, be more than just the opposite of anxiety. In work in multicultural settings, self-confidence may be a mixture of lack of anxiety, good opinions of one's own proficiency and using the second language outside the classroom. Contacts with the other language-speaking group therefore go with self-confidence in the language, in multi-cultural and multilingual societies. Self-confidence is also obviously related to self-esteem or a high positive self-evaluation, which in turn affects MOTIVATION.

*Empathy* The Good Language Learner study hypothesized that such people possessed a trait known as empathy – the ability to imagine oneself in someone else's position, to see the world with their eyes, to be sympathetic with their goals and ways of thinking. This construct was taken up by Guiora and a series of colleagues (1975) and investigated in a series of experiments. They suggested that empathy required the boundaries of a person's ego to be permeable, so that a person could reach beyond their normal representation of self to that of others. They introduced the concept of *language ego*, and thus made a connection between language and personality, namely that learning another language means interacting with others whose views of themselves as language users are different. They also suggested that of all the aspects of language skill, pronunciation accuracy was the most vulnerable to variations in empathy, because pronunciation is a public statement of all kinds of attitudes to one's own culture and that of the other language. Accurate pronunciation of another language in short requires some entrance into the language ego of speakers of the other language. (See also EGO PERMEABILITY.)

Evidence quoted for these ideas involved a test of ability to spot small differences in facial expressions, but this Micro-Momentary Expression test failed to correlate with pronunciation accuracy; more successful was a test involving removing inhibitions via alcohol. A study with ambiguous results concerned pronunciation by more or less hypnotized students. A general problem with all of these studies has been construct VALIDITY: (a) to what extent are the little tests involved truly representative of empathy? (which is difficult to answer because empathy is difficult to define satisfactorily) and (b) to what extent is pronunciation accuracy (by which is meant, presumably, closeness to native pronunciation, as the words were rated by native speakers) a reasonable measure of language mastery?

*Other traits* A group of somewhat minor traits have all been associated with language learning at various times, and although the research evidence on each of them is scanty, they are mentioned here for comprehensiveness. TOLERANCE OF AMBIGUITY was investigated in the Good Language Learner study on the grounds that language learners are often faced with various kinds of ambiguity, linguistic and conceptual – from the interpretation of polysemous words which can only be disambiguated by context (like 'ear') to structural opacity as in Chomsky's famous example 'Visiting relatives can be a bore.' Learners who can tolerate this feature of languages might fare better than those who cannot. Here, the evidence is very thin: Naiman and others used a pencil and paper test of tolerance of ambiguity and did obtain a correlation with listening. In any case, the concept is closely related to risk-taking: a person who can take risks can cope with ambiguity.

*Ethnocentricity* was investigated in a number of pieces of research, using a questionnaire, by Gardner and Lambert (1972). They found a negative correlation – success in language learning was related to lack of ethnocentricity – as did the Good Language Learner study. Later research by Gardner in his 'socio-educational model' has not used the ethnocentricism scale, and it does not feature in the Attitude Motivation Index.

A classical personality dichotomy is referred to as *locus of control*. According to this, people tend to be either self-directed or other-directed: in other words, they are either more likely to do what they find is in accordance with their own central beliefs, or are likely to follow someone else's agenda. This has not been tested directly in language learning studies, but it underlies other more familiar distinctions: field-independent and -dependent COGNITIVE STYLES, perhaps extroversion/introversion, and certainly the version of motivational theory known as attribution theory, in respect of attributions of the value of self and others.

An aspect of personality which has received a rather different form of attention in language teaching is that of personality development and the counselling of disturbed personalities. One whole method of language teaching, Curran's Counselling-Learning or COMMUNITY LANGUAGE LEARNING (1976), was based on the analogy between the teacher/pupil relationship and the client/therapist relationship. These ideas were based on notions of personality development and change and the role of the therapist as an agent for such change which originated in individual psychology, Curran's own psychological counselling experience and Carl Rogers's idea of *non-directive client-centred therapy*. In client-centred therapy, the therapist acts as a facilitator who re-expresses or translates what his client says, with all its perhaps disturbed variability and apparent self-contradictions, into simple and meaningful language as a way of helping the client to understand him- or herself. (It is important to remember that there are many other models of professional therapy.)

Curran developed his language teaching method on the analogy between this situation and a teacher translating what a student wants to say, but doesn't know how to express, in the foreign language. Curran specifically argued that learning a foreign language required the engagement of the learner's whole personality – called 'investment' – because learning a language was analogous to developing a new aspect to the personality. This kind of proposal treats the relationship between personality and language learning in a quite different way to most of the correlational research referred to earlier. Thus some (Brown, 1977) have criticized counselling learning precisely on the grounds that it is not sufficiently flexible to cater for individual differences: it may work for some but not for others.

## CLASSICAL PERSONALITY CATEGORIES AND LANGUAGE-BASED CATEGORIES

Personality is an elusive concept, about which there is a long history of study outside language learning, in terms of description, assessment and clinical practice. As we have seen, it may be that the most important aspects of personality study for language learning are not the classical categories, but rather more specific traits which can be shown to have an involvement in particular aspects of the learning situation, such as strategic preference, teaching mode preference, independence from teacher direction, level of aspiration and possibly choice of material, sensory mode of learning or classroom participation.

Two examples of linguistic differences that are relevant in this connection but do not obviously coincide with classical notions of personality are Seliger's (1977) notion of HIGH/LOW INPUT GENERATORS and Krashen's conception of monitor under- and over-users (see MONITOR MODEL). Seliger described high and low input generators as differing in the amount of language they caused, solicited, invited or demanded to be addressed to them and to the class by the teacher and the other students: not therefore in terms of their own talkativeness, but in terms of the linguistic yield of their behaviour. The suggestion was, naturally, that increases in proficiency were associated with gaining more input to process. It is tempting to look for an explanation of such behaviour from within the study of personality in this language learning context. Krashen's distinction (1981) between monitor over- and under-users relates to accuracy vs fluency (see ACCURACY/FLUENCY). People are described as overusers if their speech is characterized by excessive concern for accuracy, and Krashen suggested this is because they check what they wish to say very carefully for grammatical, phonological and lexical accuracy before they say it. Again, a personality difference of some kind might underlie this performance difference.

## SUMMARY

In this entry, the relationship between personality and language learning has been reviewed from several aspects. First, doubts were raised about what can be expected in terms of both research and application from this particular area. Second, a number of classical concepts in the field of personality were reviewed and investigations of their relationship with aspects of language learning reported. Third, a number of individual traits within personality were described, about which there have been relevant enquiries. Fourth, some examples of language teaching which claim to be based on personality development theories were discussed. Lastly, some speculations were indulged in about what avenues of future research might develop.

BIBLIOGRAPHY

Beebe, L. (1983). Risk-taking and the language learner. In H. Seliger and M. Long (eds), *Classroom Oriented Research in Second Language Acquisition*. Rowley, MA: Newbury House.

Curran, C. (1976). *Counselling-Learning in Second Languages*. Apple River, IL: Apple River Press.

Ely, C. M. (1986). An analysis of discomfort, risktaking, sociability, and motivation in the L2 classroom. *Language Learning*, 36/1, 1–25.

Gardner, R. C. (1985). *Social Psychology and Second Language Learning: The role of attitudes and motivation*. London: Edward Arnold.

Gardner R. C. and Lambert W. E. (1972). *Attitudes and Motivation in Second Language Learning*. Rowley, MA: Newbury House.

Gardner R. C. and MacIntyre, P. (1993). On the measurement of affective variables in second language learning. *Language Learning*, 43/2, 157–94.

Guiora, A. Z., Paluszny, M., Beit-Hallahmi, B., Catford, J. C., Cooley, R. E. and Yoder Dull, C. (1975). Language and person – studies in language behaviour. *Language Learning*, 25, 43–61.

Krashen, S. D. (1981). *Second Language Acquisition and Second Language Learning*. Oxford: Pergamon.

Naiman, N., Fröhlich, M., Stern, H. H. and Todesco, A. (1978). *The Good Language Learner*. Research in Education Series 7. Toronto: Ontario Institute for Studies in Education.*

Seliger, H. (1977). Does practice make perfect? A study of interaction patterns and L2 competence. *Language Learning*, 27, 263–78.

Skehan, P. (1989). *Individual Differences in Second Language Learning*. London: Edward Arnold.*

Slimani, A. (1989). The role of topicalization in classroom language learning. *System*, 17/2, 223–34.

Strong, M. H. (1983). Social styles and second language acquisition of Spanish-speaking kindergartners. *TESOL Quarterly*, 17/2, 241–58.

SMCD

**phatic communion**   A term for the use of language to create social bonds and to avoid uncomfortable silence, as opposed to the use of language for expressing thoughts, exemplified by greetings, weather-talk or football-talk. It was invented by Malinowski (1923) and was a formative part in the British sociologically influenced functionalist tradition of linguistics.

BIBLIOGRAPHY

Firth, J. R. (1957). *Papers in Linguistics*. Oxford: Oxford University Press.

Malinowski, B. (1923). The problem of meaning in primitive languages. In C. K. Ogden and I. A. Richards, *The Meaning of Meaning*. London: Routledge and Kegan Paul.

VJC

**phoneme**   The smallest sound segment which can differentiate meanings in a language. Hence in English /p/ and /b/ are phonemes because it is these sounds that differentiate the words *pat* and *bat*, which have separate meanings. Different realizations of phonemes are called allophones. These may vary one from the other, but not in ways which distinguish meaning. For example, the /p/ in *pat* is produced with a burst of air which does not occur in the /p/ of *hop*. But the presence or absence of this burst of air is never used in English to distinguish the meaning of one word from another. See PHONOLOGY; also Gimson (1980).

BIBLIOGRAPHY

Gimson, A. C. (1980). *An Introduction to the Pronunciation of English*. London: Edward Arnold.

KJ

**phonetics** is the linguistic science which describes and classifies the sounds of human languages. The articulatory processes involved in sound production are the subject of *articulatory phonetics*. *Acoustic phonetics* investigates the sounds' physical properties. Commonly, sounds are divided into vowels and consonants, and further classified according to features like voicing, aspiration, nasality, roundedness, etc., taking into account the place and the manner of articulation. The specialized International Phonetic Alphabet (figure 1, p. 245) provides an accurate orthography for transcribing speech. Phonetic descriptions constitute essential background to much language research and practice, including PHONOLOGY, historical linguistics, social variation in pronunciation and foreign language learning.

BIBLIOGRAPHY

Fromkin, V. and Rodman, R. (1993). *An Introduction to Language*. 5th edn. Fort Worth, TX: Harcourt Brace Jovanovich. [Chapter 5.]

Gimson, A. C. (1994). *An Introduction to the Pronunciation of English*. 5th edn. Oxford: Oxford University Press.*

Roach, P. (1991). *English Phonetics and Phonology: A practical course*. 2nd edn. Cambridge: Cambridge University Press.

EJ

**phonology** is a branch of linguistics investigating the sound systems of human languages. Segmental phonology traditionally takes PHONEMES as the central units of analysis; they are abstractions from the sets of sounds related by articulatory properties and capable of changing the meaning of a word given the MINIMAL PAIRS test (figure 1, p. 246). For example, /r/ and /l/ are

## CONSONANTS (PULMONIC)

| | Bilabial | Labiodental | Dental | Alveolar | Postalveolar | Retroflex | Palatal | Velar | Uvular | Pharyngeal | Glottal |
|---|---|---|---|---|---|---|---|---|---|---|---|
| Plosive | p b | | | t d | | ʈ ɖ | c ɟ | k ɡ | q ɢ | | ʔ |
| Nasal | m | ɱ | | n | | ɳ | ɲ | ŋ | N | | |
| Trill | ʙ | | | r | | | | | R | | |
| Tap or Flap | | | | ɾ | | ɽ | | | | | |
| Fricative | ɸ β | f v | θ ð | s z | ʃ ʒ | ʂ ʐ | ç ʝ | x ɣ | χ ʁ | ħ ʕ | h ɦ |
| Lateral fricative | | | | ɬ ɮ | | | | | | | |
| Approximant | | ʋ | | ɹ | | ɻ | j | ɰ | | | |
| Lateral approximant | | | | l | | ɭ | ʎ | ʟ | | | |

Where symbols appear in pairs, the one to the right represents a voiced consonant. Shaded areas denote articulations judged impossible.

## CONSONANTS (NON-PULMONIC)

| Clicks | | Voiced implosives | | Ejectives | |
|---|---|---|---|---|---|
| ⊙ | Bilabial | ɓ | Bilabial | ʼ | Examples: |
| ǀ | Dental | ɗ | Dental/alveolar | pʼ | Bilabial |
| ǃ | (Post)alveolar | ʄ | Palatal | tʼ | Dental/alveolar |
| ǂ | Palatoalveolar | ɠ | Velar | kʼ | Velar |
| ǁ | Alveolar lateral | ʛ | Uvular | sʼ | Alveolar fricative |

## VOWELS

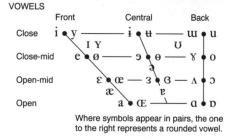

Where symbols appear in pairs, the one to the right represents a rounded vowel.

## OTHER SYMBOLS

ʍ Voiceless labial-velar fricative

w Voiced labial-velar approximant

ɥ Voiced labial-palatal approximant

H Voiceless epiglottal fricative

ʢ Voiced epiglottal fricative

ʡ Epiglottal plosive

ɕ ʑ Alveolo-palatal fricatives

ɺ Alveolar lateral flap

ɧ Simultaneous ʃ and x

Affricates and double articulations can be represented by two symbols joined by a tie bar if necessary.

k͡p t͡s

## DIACRITICS   Diacritics may be placed above a symbol with a descender, e.g. ŋ̊

| | | | | | | | |
|---|---|---|---|---|---|---|---|
| ̥ | Voiceless | n̥ d̥ | ̤ | Breathy voiced | b̤ a̤ | ̪ | Dental | t̪ d̪ |
| ̬ | Voiced | s̬ t̬ | ̰ | Creaky voiced | b̰ a̰ | ̺ | Apical | t̺ d̺ |
| ʰ | Aspirated | tʰ dʰ | ̼ | Linguolabial | t̼ d̼ | ̻ | Laminal | t̻ d̻ |
| ̹ | More rounded | ɔ̹ | ʷ | Labialized | tʷ dʷ | ̃ | Nasalized | ẽ |
| ̜ | Less rounded | ɔ̜ | ʲ | Palatalized | tʲ dʲ | ⁿ | Nasal release | dⁿ |
| ̟ | Advanced | u̟ | ˠ | Velarized | tˠ dˠ | ˡ | Lateral release | dˡ |
| ̠ | Retracted | e̠ | ˤ | Pharyngealized | tˤ dˤ | ̚ | No audible release | d̚ |
| ̈ | Centralized | ë | ̴ | Velarized or pharyngealized | ɫ | | | |
| ̽ | Mid-centralized | e̽ | ̝ | Raised | e̝ | (ɹ̝ = voiced alveolar fricative) | |
| ̩ | Syllabic | n̩ | ̞ | Lowered | e̞ | (β̞ = voiced bilabial approximant) | |
| ̯ | Non-syllabic | e̯ | ̘ | Advanced Tongue Root | e̘ | | | |
| ˞ | Rhoticity | ɚ a˞ | ̙ | Retracted Tongue Root | e̙ | | | |

## SUPRASEGMENTALS

ˈ  Primary stress

ˌ  Secondary stress

ˌfoʊnəˈtɪʃən

ː  Long  eː

ˈ  Half-long  eˈ

˘  Extra-short  ĕ

|  Minor (foot) group

‖  Major (intonation) group

.  Syllable break  ɹi.ækt

‿  Linking (absence of a break)

## TONES AND WORD ACCENTS

| LEVEL | | CONTOUR | |
|---|---|---|---|
| e̋ or ˥ | Extra high | ě or ꟷ | Rising |
| é  ˦ | High | ê | Falling |
| ē  ˧ | Mid | e̋ | High rising |
| è  ˨ | Low | e̖ | Low rising |
| ȅ  ˩ | Extra low | e᷈ | Rising-falling |
| ↓ | Downstep | ↗ | Global rise |
| ↑ | Upstep | ↘ | Global fall |

From the *Journal of the International Phonetic Association*, 25/1 (June 1995)

**Figure 1**   The International Phonetic Alphabet (revised to 1993).

**Vowels**

| | |
|---|---|
| /iː/ – /ɪ/ | seat – sit |
| /ɪ/ – /e/ | sit –set |
| /e/ – /a/ | set – sat |
| /a/ – /ʌ/ | cat – cut |
| /ʌ/ – /ɑː/ | cut – cart |
| /ɑː/ – /ɒ/ | cart – cot |
| /ɒ/ – /ɔː/ | cot – caught |
| /ɔː/ – /ʊ/ | cord – could |
| /ʊ/ – /uː/ | pull – pool |
| /uː/ – /ɜː/ | pool – pearl |
| /ɜː/ – /eɪ/ | pearl – pale |
| /eɪ/ – /aɪ/ | day – die |
| /aɪ/ – /ɔɪ/ | buy – boy |
| /ɔɪ/ – /əʊ/ | toy – toe |
| /əʊ/ – /aʊ/ | hoe – how |
| /aʊ/ – /ɪə/ | now – near |
| /ɪə/ – /ɛə/ | tear (noun) – tear (verb) |
| /ɛə/ – /ʊə/ | tear – tour |
| /ʊə/ – /iː/ | sure – she |
| /ə/ – zero | waiter – wait |

**Consonants**

| | |
|---|---|
| /p/ – /b/ | pig – big |
| /b/ – /t/ | bee – tea |
| /t/ – /d/ | tin – din |
| /d/ – /k/ | din – kin |
| /k/ –/g/ | cap – gap |
| /g/ – /h/ | gag – hag |
| /h/ – /m/ | hen – men |
| /m/ – /n/ | map – nap |
| /n/ – /ŋ/ | sin – sing |
| /ŋ/ – /l/ | sink – silk |
| /l/ – /r/ | lid – rid |
| /r/ – /w/ | red – wed |
| /w/ – /j/ | well – yell |
| /j/ – /tʃ/ | you – chew |
| /tʃ/ – /dʒ/ | chin – gin |
| /dʒ/ – /f/ | large – laugh |
| /f/ – /v/ | fat – vat |
| /v/ – /θ/ | heave – heath |
| /θ/ – /ð/ | wreath – wreathe |
| /ð/ – /s/ | though – so |
| /s/ – /z/ | bus – buzz |
| /z/ – /ʃ/ | zoo – shoe |
| /ʃ/ – /ʒ/ | Confucian – confusion |
| /ʒ/ – /t/ | beige – bait |

**Figure 1**   Some minimal pairs for English phonemes (southern British; from David Crystal, *The Cambridge Encyclopedia of Language and Linguistics* (Cambridge University Press, 1984), p. 160).

phonemes in English because they contrast in pairs like *rate–late*. Phonemes are analysed in terms of distinctive features (figure 2, p. 247). For example, /b/, /d/ and /g/ are [+plosive] and [+voiced], and distinguished by [+labial], [+dental] and [+velar] respectively. Possible combinations of phonemes are analysed with reference to the *syllable*. For example, the word *phoneme* [fəʊniːm] has two syllables of the form CV-CVC. Syllables and larger units also play a role in suprasegmental phonology, which deals with STRESS, RHYTHM and INTONATION. Within CHOMSKYAN LINGUISTICS, generative phonology characterizes the NATIVE SPEAKER's phonological COMPETENCE. (See also PHONETICS.)

BIBLIOGRAPHY
Clark, P. (1993). *Phonology*. London: Macmillan.*
Coates, R. (1987). Phonology. In J. Lyons, R. Coates, M. Deuchar and G. Gazdar (eds), *New Horizons in Linguistics 2: An introduction to contemporary linguistic research*. London: Penguin Books, 30–58.
Fromkin, V. and Rodman, R. (1993). *An Introduction to Language*. 5th edn. Fort Worth, TX: Harcourt Brace Jovanovich. [Chapter 6.]
Hawkins, P. (1984). *Introducing Phonology*. London: Hutchinson.*
Spencer, A. (1996). *Phonology: Theory and description*. Oxford: Blackwell.

EJ

**Piagetian developmental stages**   The Swiss psychologist Jean Piaget distinguished four stages in the development of a child's thinking from birth to around the age of 15: the *sensorimotor stage* (birth to about 2 years) during which representational thought develops; the *pre-operational stage* (about 2 to 7 years) during which the child is an 'egocentric' thinker; a stage of *conrete operational thinking* (about 7 to 11 years) during which the child can 'think through' concrete problems; finally the stage of *formal operational thinking* (about 11 to 15 years) during which the child develops abstract reflective thinking. Only the onset of formal operational thinking appears to have had a major impact on SLA research. A number of researchers have suggested that AGE LEARNING DIFFERENCES result from the change in general cognitive ability which occurs at this stage (Krashen, 1982).

The features are listed on the left of each matrix, and the segments are listed along the top. Each segment is analysed in terms of all features. The terminology used in these particular matrices relates to the traditional articulatory terms ( V = vowel, C = consonant):

| | |
|---|---|
| + compact | low V |
| – compact | high and mid V |
| + consonantal | obstruction in vocal tract |
| – consonantal | no vocal tract obstruction |
| + continuant | fricative/approximant C |
| – continuant | stop/affricate C |
| + diffuse | high V; labial/dental/alveolar C |
| – diffuse | low V; palatal/velar/back C |
| + flat | rounded V |
| – flat | unrounded V |
| + grave | back V; labial/velar/back C |
| – grave | front V; dental/alveolar/palatal C |
| + nasal | nasal C |
| – nasal | oral C |
| + strident | fricative/affricate C with high-frequency noise |
| – strident | C with low-frequency noise |
| + vocalic | glottal vibration with free passage of air through vocal tract |
| – vocalic | no glottal vibration or free passage of air |
| + voice | voiced C |
| – voice | voiceless C |

English consonant matrix

```
                p b f v m t d θ ð s z n tʃ dʒ ʃ ʒ k g l r w j h ŋ

consonantal     + + + + + + + + + + + + +  +  + + + + + - - - +
vocalic         - - - - - - - - - - - - -  -  - - - - - + + - - -
diffuse         + + + + + + + + + + + +  -  - - - - + + - - - -
compact         - - - - - - - - - - - - -  -  - - - - - - - - - -
grave           + + + + + - - - - - - -  -  - - + + - - + - + +
flat            - - - - - - - - - - - -  -  - - - - - + - - -
voice           - + - + + - + - + - + +  -  + - + - + + + + - +
continuant      - - + + - - - + + + + -  -  + + - - + + + + + -
strident        - - + + - - - - - + + -  +  + + + - - - - - - -
nasal           - - - - + - - - - - - +  -  - - - - - - - - - +
```

Matrix for a seven-vowel system

```
                i e a u o ɔ ɑ

consonantal     - - - - - - -
vocalic         + + + + + + +
diffuse         + - - + - - -
compact         - - + - - + +
grave           - - - + + + +
flat            - - - + + + -
voice           + + + + + + +
continuant      + + + + + + +
strident        - - - - - - -
nasal           - - - - - - -
```

**Figure 2** Distinctive–feature matrices (from David Crystal, *The Cambridge Encyclopedia of Language and Linguistics* (Cambridge University Press, 1984), p. 162).

BIBLIOGRAPHY
Donaldson, M. (1978). *Children's Minds*. Harmondsworth: Penguin Books.*
Dulay, H., Burt, M. and Krashen, S. (1982). *Language Two*. Oxford: Oxford University Press.
Inhelder, B. and Piaget, J. (1958). *The Growth of Logical Thinking from Childhood to Adolescence*. New York: Basic Books.
Krashen, S. (1982). Accounting for child-adult differences in second language rate and attainment. In S. Krashen, R. Scarcella and M. Long (eds), *Child-Adult Differences in Second Language Acquisition*. Rowley, MA: Newbury House.

RH

**pidgins and creoles** Communication between groups of people without a common language gives rise to simplification of one of the contact languages, e.g. the colonial language. Such languages, which are known as pidgins, have limited LEXIS, MORPHOLOGY, SYNTAX and a narrow range of use (e.g. trade). They are not 'corrupt' versions of the source languages but highly regularized varieties. When a pidgin acquires NATIVE SPEAKERS it becomes a creole. The lexicon, GRAMMAR and functions of a creole expand rapidly and equal any other natural language. However, with few exceptions such as the English-based creole Tok Pisin (Neomelanesian) in New Guinea, creoles rarely enjoy the status of official languages. (See SIMPLIFIED CODES.)

BIBLIOGRAPHY
Mühlhäusler, P. (1986). *Pidgin and Creole Linguistics*. Oxford: Blackwell.
Romaine, S. (1988). *Pidgin and Creole Languages*. London: Longman.
Todd, L. (1974). *Pidgins and Creoles*. London: Routledge and Kegan Paul.

AJ

**placement tests** provide information about students' ability which will assist their placement at suitable levels in a teaching programme, i.e. in classes appropriate to their language ability. Such tests are usually constructed 'in house' to reflect the characteristics of the teaching programme, although externally (commercially) produced tests are also available. (See LANGUAGE TESTING.)

BIBLIOGRAPHY
Hughes, A. (1989). *Testing for Language Teachers*. Cambridge: Cambridge University Press.

KSM

**politeness** In PRAGMATICS, the politeness principle (PP) explains aspects of how people interpret each other's meanings. To be polite, speakers attempt to give options, avoid intrusion and make their interlocutor feel good (Lakoff, 1973; Leech, 1983). Departure from the PP signals urgency, intimacy, aggression or unfriendliness (Wolfson, 1988). Following the PP may sometimes lead speakers to be untruthful (e.g. praising a hairstyle they do not like). Although the PP is universal, its realization varies between cultures (Brown and Levinson, 1987; Tannen, 1989). Effective operation (enabling speakers to be polite or not polite as required) is an important interpersonal aspect of discourse, and is thus important in language teaching. (See SOCIOLINGUISTICS IN LANGUAGE TEACHING.)

BIBLIOGRAPHY
Brown, P. and Levinson, S. (1987). *Politeness: Some universals in language usage*. Cambridge: Cambridge University Press.*
Lakoff, R. (1973). The logic of politeness: on minding your p's and q's. *Papers from the 9th Regional Meeting, Chicago Linguistic Society*, 292–305.
Leech, G. N. (1983). *Principles of Pragmatics*. London: Longman.
Tannen, D. (1989). *Talking Voices: Repetition, dialogue, and imagery in conversational discourse*. Cambridge: Cambridge University Press.
Wolfson, N. (1988). The bulge: a theory of speech behaviour and social distance. In J. Fine (ed.), *Second Language Discourse: A textbook of current research*. Norwood, NJ: Ablex.

GC

**pragmatic competence** is an aspect of COMMUNICATIVE COMPETENCE and refers to the ability to communicate appropriately in particular contexts of use. It contrasts with linguistic competence (see COMPETENCE/ PERFORMANCE), which refers to the mastery of the general rules of language abstracted from its use. (See PRAGMATICS.)

BIBLIOGRAPHY
Thomas, J. (1988). *Speaker Meaning*. London: Longman.

AJ

**pragmatics** is the study of how language is interpreted by its users in its linguistic and non-linguistic context. The non-linguistic context considered may include relationships between participants, their attitudes and emotions, their inferencing procedures, their cultural and world knowledge, their perception of the situation and their paralanguage (see PARALINGUISTIC FEATURES). The linguistic context may include other parts of the same text (sometimes referred to as co-text) and participants' knowledge of other texts (intertext). Pragmatic meanings which are contextually variable are often contrasted with semantic meanings which are more fixed. (See also DISCOURSE ANALYSIS, PRAGMATIC COMPETENCE, SEMANTICS, SPEECH ACT THEORY.)

BIBLIOGRAPHY
Leech, G. N. (1983). *Principles of Pragmatics*. London: Longman.
Levinson, S. C. (1983). *Pragmatics*. Cambridge: Cambridge University Press.
Mey, J. (1993). *Pragmatics: An introduction*. Oxford: Blackwell.
Yule, G. (1996). *Pragmatics*. Oxford: Oxford University Press.

GC

**presentation of new language** The presentation stage is the first in the traditional 'PRESENTATION – PRACTICE – PRODUCTION' SEQUENCE. It is the stage at which a new language point is introduced to the learners; the 'point' may be a grammatical one, a notional/functional one, or indeed one related to any linguistic level.

Central to the question of how language items are best presented is the induction/ deduction issue. In *induction*, particular examples of an item will be given, with any generalization left until the end (the formula EGRUL – 'example → rule' – expresses this); in *deduction*, rules are followed by examples (RULEG). The induction/deduction issue has long aroused strong passions in language teaching. For a full discussion, see Rivers (1964), whose terms are *analogy* (learning by generalization from example) and *analysis* (learning by understanding a rule). Rivers discusses arguments for and against both positions. AUDIOLINGUALISM favours induction, and she cites the words of Politzer, a staunch advocate of that method, who claims (1961: 5) that 'rules ought to be summaries of behaviour.' Rivers identifies over-generalization as the inherent danger of induction. This example of over-generalization is based on her own (1964: 118): the learner who practises converting 'to + place' into 'there' ('I'm going to the university' → 'I'm going there') may, if no explanation is provided, mistakenly assume that any 'to + noun phrase' sequence converts into 'there'. The learner would then produce 'I'm speaking there' believing it to mean 'I'm speaking to my friend'.

The gestalt psychologist Wertheimer's defence of deduction is that 'to live in a fog . . . is for many people an unbearable state of affairs. There is a tendency [to want] structural clearness, surveyability' (1945: 199). A danger of deduction is that the teacher may falsely believe that *teaching about* is the same as *teaching how to* – that the learner who knows the rules will automatically be able to perform the associated behaviour. See DECLARATIVE/PROCEDURAL.

One might be tempted to claim relationships between the level of intelligence and a preference for induction or deduction. But

Rivers (1964: 120) warns thus against simplistic associations: 'students of low intelligence are, of course, much happier just repeating what is given to them, and do not feel a strong compulsion to understand what they are doing, but the same low intelligence also makes it hard for them to see analogies.'

It may be argued that the two central characteristics of a good presentation are *clarity* and *memorability*; the teaching point must be made clear to the learner in as memorable a way as possible. Unfortunately these characteristics may lead in different directions. Clear presentation may, for example, suggest the provision of a few clear key sentences, containing just examples of the teaching point, baldly laid before the learner. Memorability may on the other hand point to the need for rich contextualization of the teaching point. The characteristics will be discussed below in relation to some common presentation modes.

*Explanation* was a common presentational mode in the GRAMMAR-TRANSLATION method. In it, both memorability and clarity are often absent. There is some evidence that explanation of an elaborate nature (which the teacher may feel necessary to do justice to the complexity of the teaching point) can severely affect performance; see Johnson (1996) for discussion.

Much audiolingual teaching presents through *key sentences*, in which a few short sentences, possibly accompanied by visuals, capture the essence of the teaching point. The mode may certainly offer clarity, but memorability often suffers – it is difficult to create memorable text in the space of a few sentences.

*Dialogues* are used in various teaching methods, and widely differing types of dialogue can be found. At the 'clarity' end are dialogues which contain little more than exemplars of the item being taught, and are in effect just sequences of key sentences. Clarity may be achieved, but unnaturalness and lack of memorability are unfortunate

side-effects. At the other end of the spectrum are dialogues where efforts are made to create an authentic tone and to include interesting (and hence memorable) content. Such dialogues will tend to be long and to contain few examples of the teaching point. *Written passages* occur at times when (or situations where) the written word is given predominance; as with dialogues, a wide spectrum of types of passage is to be found.

*Teacher action* is particularly suited to certain language items. Hence it is easy to present the contiguous action sense of the present continuous tense by using it to describe an action the teacher is actually doing (e.g. 'I am walking to the door,' 'I am opening it'). Such presentations may be both clear and memorable.

The precise nature of the teaching point introduced will depend partly on the teaching method being followed. In grammar-oriented teaching the focus is commonly on a STRUCTURE exemplified by specific SENTENCE PATTERNS; the teaching points often deal with both form (how the structure is formed) and meaning (teaching, for example, that 'contiguous action' is one meaning of the present continuous). Widdowson (1972) convincingly illustrates how focus on some levels (e.g. form and meaning) may fail to provide information about others (e.g. functional use). His example is of the present continuous where 'commentary on one's own actions' is often used to clarify the contiguous action meaning (see the description of *teacher action* above), but which is in itself a rare, unnatural, functional use for the structure. Johnson (1977) argues that grammar teaching should seek at the very least to avoid what he calls 'functional dishonesty'.

In teaching associated with NOTIONAL/ FUNCTIONAL SYLLABUSES the 'teaching point' will nearly always be related to how to expound a particular speech act. In such teaching 'appropriateness of use' is almost certain to play a central part. For example, when teaching greetings like 'Hi' and 'Good morning,' it will be necessary to develop awareness of the context in which each will be appropriate. Contextualization of exponents will therefore be more central to the presentation than it will be in some grammar teaching. For further discussion of practical issues, see Spratt (1985).

BIBLIOGRAPHY
Johnson, K. (1977). Adult beginners: a functional or a communicative structural approach? Paper delivered at the Annual Meeting of the British Association for Applied Linguistics, Colchester. [Reprinted in 1982 in K. Johnson, *Communicative Syllabus Design and Methodology*. Oxford: Pergamon Institute of English, 106–14.]
——(1996). *Language Teaching and Skill Learning*. Oxford: Blackwell.
Politzer, R. L. (1961). *Teaching French: An introduction to applied linguistics*. Boston: Ginn.
Rivers, W. M. (1964). *The Psychologist and the Foreign Language Teacher*. Chicago: University of Chicago Press.*
Spratt, M. (1985). The presentation stage. In A. Matthews, M. Spratt and L. Dangerfield (eds), *At the Chalkface*. London: Edward Arnold, 5–7.*
Wertheimer, M. (1945). *Productive Thinking*. New York: Harper and Row.
Widdowson, H. G. (1972). The teaching of English as communication. *English Language Teaching Journal*, 27/1, 15–19.

KJ

## 'presentation – practice – production' sequence

It is common to divide what van Els and others (1984: 264) describe as the 'cycle of teaching/learning activities' in a lesson into the three stages of presentation, practice and production (PPP). At stage 1 new language material is presented to the learner. At stage 2 this is practised in a controlled way by means of drill-like activities, and at the final stage it is utilized in more natural interactions, where the learner has greater freedom for creative language use. *Presentation* is widely accepted as the term for the first stage, but *practice* is sometimes called *manipulation* or *repetition*, and *production* may be referred to as *transfer, free practice* or *comprehension and development*. For descriptions of the PPP model and each of its stages, see van Els and others (1984) and Byrne (1976).

The three-stage model is clearly applicable to many types of learning, not just of language, and Spratt (1985) illustrates it in relation to learning to drive a car, where the instructor first demonstrates and describes an action, then allows the learner to practise it as far as possible in isolation, finally requiring it to be performed in integration with other skills already learned.

Various sequences underlie the PPP model. One is show → do (stage 1 → stages 2 and 3), with this in itself implying a reception → production sequence – listen (or read) → speak (or write). Control → free (stages 1 and 2 → stage 3) is also present. The DECLARATIVE/PROCEDURAL distinction is also involved, with stage 1 often (though not always) being associated with the provision of declarative knowledge, the other two stages with proceduralizing this knowledge.

Although most learning models will have something equivalent to these three stages, there are clear associations with learning theories which espouse habit formation, and the historical roots of the sequence in language teaching reflect this. Frisby (1957, cited in Richards and Rodgers, 1986) uses Palmer as the authority that 'there are three processes in learning a language – receiving the knowledge or materials, fixing it in the memory by repetition, and using it in actual practice until it becomes a personal skill.' This view is clearly reflected in the teaching procedures propounded by such individuals as Palmer, Hornby and Pittman. Richards and Rodgers give Pittman's (1963) example of a typical lesson plan, in which the presentation and practice stages are clearly represented. There is, however, no 'production stage'. Although the oral approach and situational teaching (associated with these individuals) may have disappeared as separate and discrete movements, there are strong echoes of them in language teaching today around the world – one reason why the PPP sequence remains ubiquitous.

De-emphasis of the production stage (or its omission, as noted above) is commonplace, and can be related to two other influential teaching models – those of Mackey (1965) and Halliday and others (1964). Both these have something akin to presentation and practice, but no specific reference is made to free production. The omission is presumably partly based on behaviourist attitudes towards errors. Because errors repeated are errors learned, they are to be avoided at all costs; and it is particularly at the free production stage that errors may occur. Perhaps there is also the belief that once material has been automated through drilling, no further practice is required.

In more recent times, both these beliefs have been strongly challenged, particularly within COMMUNICATIVE LANGUAGE TEACHING. Errors are no longer regarded as so undesirable, and it is recognized that for material to become part of a learner's active repertoire, a good deal of activation in free practice is required. It is further recognized that for important risk-taking skills to be developed, learners need to be put in the position of having to use material that they may not have mastered completely – something which may occur at the free practice stage. This realization of the importance of free practice has led to a proliferation of new FREE PRACTICE TECHNIQUES in recent years. If the importance of any of the three stages is nowadays questioned, it is of the practice stage (stage 2).

The change of stage described above has led to proposals to modify the traditional PPP model. The most influential of these is the DEEP-END STRATEGY associated with communicative language teaching. Stage 1 is production, with stages 2 (presentation) and 3 (practice) following if shown to be necessary by what occurs at stage 1. Two assumed advantages of the strategy are that risk-taking skills are brought into play (at stage 1), and the fact that learner performance at that stage controls what is presented and practised at stages 2 and 3. Another variant is found in Walmsley (1979), who has presentation → production → practice, the advantage again being that with free practice occurring before controlled drilling a kind of 'discovery learning' may occur. Less drastic modifications to the basic PPP model are also found. Byrne (1976), for example, introduces a 'from practice to production' stage, signalling that some gradual transition from controlled to free will be required.

The central role which the traditional PPP sequence plays in an influential text like Byrne (1976) indicates how commonly the sequence is used in methodology and teacher-training books as a framework for discussing teaching procedures. Byrne associates specific teacher roles with each P. At the presentation stage the teacher has the role of informant; at the practice stage that of conductor: 'he becomes ... the skilful conductor of an orchestra, drawing the music out of the performers, giving each a chance to participate' (1976: 2). Others also mention the role of error corrector at this stage. At the production stage the teacher acts as a guide and adviser.

In a chart which summarizes well the differences between the three Ps, Read (1985) lists (among other things) activity types, types of interaction and types of correction in relation to each P.

BIBLIOGRAPHY

Byrne, D. (1976). *Teaching Oral English*. Harlow: Longman.*

Frisby, A. W. (1957). *Teaching English: Notes and comments on teaching English overseas*. Harlow: Longman.

Halliday, M. A. K., McIntosh, A. and Strevens, P. (1964). *The Linguistic Sciences and Language Teaching*. Harlow: Longman.

Mackey, W. F. (1965). *Language Teaching Analysis*. Harlow: Longman.

Pittman, G. (1963). *Teaching Structural English*. Brisbane: Jacaranda.

Read, C. (1985). Presentation, practice and production at a glance. In A. Matthews, M. Spratt and L. Dangerfield (eds), *At the Chalkface*. London: Edward Arnold, 17.

Richards, J. C. and Rodgers, T. S. (1986). *Approaches and Methods in Language Teaching* Cambridge: Cambridge University Press.

Spratt, M. (1985). The presentation stage. In A. Matthews, M. Spratt and L. Dangerfield (eds), *At the Chalkface*. London: Edward Arnold, 5–7.

Van Els, T., Bongaerts, T., Extra, G., van Os, C. and Janssen-van Dieten, A.-M. (1984). *Applied Linguistics and the Learning and Teaching of Foreign Languages*. London: Edward Arnold.*

Walmsley, J. (1979). Phase and phase-sequence. *Modern Language Journal*, 63, 106–16.

KJ

**probability**   In statistics, tests should be performed on results to discover how the figures obtained compare with what might have been expected from chance. If the prediction from chance is very different to the actual results, a real effect can be recognized. In practice, if the difference obtained between the mean scores of two groups receiving different treatment could have occurred by chance only one in a hundred times of performing the experiment, the result is deemed 'significant', sometimes written $p \leq .01$ (probability of the result by chance is equal to or less than one hundredth). If the probability is only one in twenty times, it is termed 'probably significant' ($p \leq .05$). (See also STATISTICS IN APPLIED LINGUISTICS RESEARCH.)

BIBLIOGRAPHY
Woods, A., Fletcher, P. and Hughes, A. (1986). *Statistics in Language Studies*. Cambridge: Cambridge University Press, 59–75.

SMCD

**procedural syllabus**   This type of syllabus is associated with the name of Prabhu and with a teaching experiment which took place in South India in the late 1970s and early 1980s. The experiment's central hypothesis is that 'structure can best be learned when attention is focused on meaning.' For Prabhu, two consequences follow. The first involves the abolition of any linguistic syllabus. If we truly wish, he argues, for 'natural' classroom communication, then we cannot impose on the teaching any syllabus which preselects what language items will be focused on. Or, put another way, if we structure teaching around a linguistic syllabus, then we shall not achieve natural communication in the classroom. Prabhu therefore replaces the linguistic syllabus by a procedural syllabus, or a syllabus of tasks. The content of lessons is planned in terms of what tasks or activities will occur, but no preselection of linguistic content occurs.

The second consequence of the central hypothesis is largely to eschew formal teaching procedures, like drilling and error correction, where the result would be FORM-FOCUS rather than MESSAGE-FOCUS. The circumstances under which these procedures would be permitted are where they occur naturally and incidentally, for example, if a learner actively seeks explanation of a language point. In the general avoidance of these procedures the teacher is expected to behave like the parent of an L1 child (parents neither drill nor, in general, correct linguistic errors). Other parallels to the L1 situation are exploited in the experiment; for example, learners are not forced to produce language before they are ready – they are permitted to 'incubate' in the same way that the L1 child incubates.

The following three examples illustrate the kinds of tasks used in the experiment. They appear under the heading of 'School timetables' in Appendix 5 of Prabhu (1987):

(a)   Constructing class timetables from instructions/descriptions.

(b)   Comparing such timetables to identify the frequencies of lessons in different subjects (or possibilities for different students to exchange shared materials, etc.).

(c) Constructing timetables for teachers of particular subjects from given class timetables, and vice versa.

Each lesson normally focuses on one task. This involves 'a sustained period (say 15 minutes) of self-reliant effort by learners to achieve a clearly-perceived goal ... The effort involved should be an effort of the mind, and it should offer to learners a "reasonable challenge"' (RIE, 1980). The remaining class time would be taken up by pre- and post-task activities. The former might well entail the introduction of linguistic items, but would not involve form-focused linguistic preparation.

The initial experiment involved intermediate students in Bangalore; beginners were later included and other locations added. Classes were large and the number of teaching hours restricted, with no real exposure to English available outside class. For the first few months students and teachers alike struggled with the unfamiliar approach, and the results were discouraging. But over time a degree of success was achieved. The experiment was formally evaluated by Beretta and Davies (1985), and the suggestion is that experimental groups fared better on certain types of test than control groups; it is suggested that the experimental groups were more able to deploy language items than those taught by more conventional means. For full description of the procedural syllabus experiment, see Prabhu (1987).

Prabhu's experiment falls firmly within a tradition of 'acquisition-based' language teaching; teaching, that is, founded on the view that learners will acquire language if exposed to it and where there is (in the words of Krashen, 1977) 'participation in natural communication situations'. Such approaches enjoy a degree of popularity at the present time, Krashen and Terrell's NATURAL APPROACH being another example. For background to 'acquisition-based' approaches, and to possible parallels between L1 and L2

learning, see FIRST AND SECOND LANGUAGE ACQUISITION: also Newmark (1966) and Newmark and Reibel (1968). Prabhu's procedural syllabus shares one characteristic with the PROCESS SYLLABUS, which distinguishes both from conventional syllabuses: both are (in Breen's 1983 term) 'means-focused'. A conventional 'ends-focused' syllabus aims to teach the items listed (be they structures, notions or functions). But the aim of the procedural syllabus is not to teach the learner how to undertake the listed tasks. These are 'means' towards the 'end' of teaching language. See also TASK-BASED SYLLABUSES.

Prabhu's approach takes pains to distance itself from other approaches enjoying popularity at the time the experiment was conceived – particularly NOTIONAL/FUNCTIONAL SYLLABUSES and COMMUNICATIVE METHODOLOGY. Prabhu viewed notional/functional as an attempt to add a sociolinguistic dimension to teaching, while for him the problem in India was how to achieve better structural teaching, rather than add any new dimension. He sees communicative methodology essentially as a covert way of practising grammar; techniques like the information gap may appear to involve message-focus, but they are in fact disguised form-focus, resulting not in free language production, but in the 'reproduction' of language items the teacher intends to have practised. Prabhu uses the term 'communicational' to distinguish his approach from the 'communicative'. A further way in which the approach distinguishes itself from other recent approaches is in its lack of interest in GROUP WORK/PAIR WORK. Much (though not necessarily all) of the interaction in the approach is teacher to student(s), and student(s) to task.

For critiques of the procedural syllabus, see Brumfit (1984) and Johnson (1982). One persistent criticism is that such teaching will lead to a kind of classroom pidgin, comparable to pidgins or creoles which occur naturally in communities where an L2 is required for communication. Although it might be argued that erroneous, pidgin-like forms will disappear over time, much as the L1 child eventually discards non-standard developmental forms, the experiment (whose length was naturally restricted) provides no evidence. Another problem often voiced is how the approach might fit within institutional constraints. The concept of incubation illustrates this; institutional assessment procedures usually require some overt display of knowledge, and sit very uncomfortably with a notion of incubation which implies some state of knowledge which cannot easily be demonstrated or measured. But despite these and other problems, the procedural syllabus experiment constitutes a bold, fascinating and rare attempt to put a view of language learning and teaching into practice.

BIBLIOGRAPHY

Beretta, A. and Davies, A. (1985). Evaluation of the Bangalore project. *ELT Journal*, 39/2, 121–7.

Breen, M. P. (1983). Prepared comments to K. Johnson, Syllabus design: possible future trends. In K. Johnson and D. Porter (eds), *Perspectives in Communicative Language Teaching*. London: Academic Press, 58–66.

Brumfit, C. J. (1984). The Bangalore procedural syllabus. *ELT Journal*, 38/4, 233–41.

Johnson, K. (1982). The procedural syllabus. In K. Johnson, *Communicative Syllabus Design and Methodology*. Oxford: Pergamon Institute of English, 135–44.

Krashen, S. D. (1977). The monitor model for adult second language performance. In M. K. Burt, H. C. Dulay and M. Finocchiaro (eds), *Viewpoints on English as a Second Language*. New York: Regents, 152–61.

Newmark, L. (1966). How not to interfere with language learning. *International Journal of American Linguistics*, 32/1, 77–83.

Newmark, L. and Reibel, D. A. (1968). Necessity and sufficiency in language learning. *International Review of Applied Linguistics*, 6/2, 145–64.

Prabhu, N. S. (1987). *Second Language Pedagogy: A perspective*. Oxford: Oxford University Press.*

RIE (1980). *Newsletter 4 (special series)*. Bangalore: Regional Institute of English. South India (mimeograph).

KJ

**process syllabus** The PROCESS VS PRODUCT distinction has been taken into language teaching from general educational studies, where it dates back to at least the 1960s; Mitzel (1960), for example, utilizes it. White (1988) traces back the concept of the 'process curriculum', noting (p. 34) a course produced by Bruner (1960) which is described in terms which would be familiar to today's language teaching syllabus designers: 'the ... aims ... centre around the processes of learning rather than the products.' In applied linguistics the term *process* has come to be used primarily in relation to PROCESS WRITING as well as to syllabus design, though it may be argued that the use of the term in these two areas is not identical.

White's survey of syllabus design (1988) is founded on a distinction between what he calls Type A and Type B syllabuses. The former are *product syllabuses*, 'based on the pre-specification of content' (p. 94), whether this be stated in structural, notional-functional or other terms (see STRUCTURAL SYLLABUS and NOTIONAL-FUNCTIONAL SYLLABUSES). The *process syllabus* – Type B – in contradistinction, focuses on the 'processes of learning and procedures of teaching – in other words [on] methodology' (p. 94).

Proposals for a language teaching process syllabus are particularly associated with Breen, whose 1984 paper provides useful discussion. He acknowledges a role for the 'syllabus as plan', because learners 'need plans in order to have a sense of direction and continuity in their work' (p. 51). But, he continues, the plan's value may not reside in what it actually shows or represents (its content), so much as on how it is used in the classroom. Different uses are possible; for example, rather than standing as a prescription of content and its order of presentation, the syllabus might provide a checklist by which learner progress can be measured.

Breen characterizes the product syllabus as one in which a 'repertoire *of* communication' is specified, whereas the process syllabus deals with a 'capacity *for* communication'

(p. 51). In the latter, the emphasis is 'upon the capabilities of applying, reinterpreting, and adapting the knowledge of rules and conventions during communication by means of underlying skills and abilities' (p. 52). The view that (in the words of Breen and Candlin (1980: 91) this time) communication involves 'convention-creating as well as convention-following' might be said to lead naturally towards a syllabus giving predominance to the creative reinterpretation of conventions in communicative acts rather than to mastery of a discrete repertoire of rules. Another related though rather different claim for the process model is that it concerns the process of *learning*. As part of his extended comparison between syllabuses and maps, Breen makes the point that in a product syllabus the syllabus 'map' designer 'draws the map beginning at the destination'. The process syllabus on the other hand would 'prioritize the route itself' (p. 52), and would hence presumably take due account of present learner position as much as of final destination. A further useful distinction, found in Breen (1983), related to the process/product one is between a syllabus of 'ends' and of 'means'.

For Breen the process syllabus is seen as 'interrelating with a syllabus of subject-matter [product]' (1984: 59). An initial point in his discussion is that product syllabuses are in fact reinterpreted by learners and teachers alike once actual classroom teaching begins. Utilizing a process syllabus in the classroom would create the circumstances in which a product syllabus would be generated as teaching proceeded. In this sense the process syllabus does not supplant the product version, but instead creates a framework for it.

Breen (1984) provides some indication of what a process syllabus would contain. Four levels or elements are recognized. The first, *decisions for classroom language learning*, concerns matters of participation, procedure and subject-matter, and provides answers to the questions: 'who does what with whom, on what subject-matter, and with what resources, when, how, and for what learning purpose(s)?' The alternatives chosen at this level would become the second level of *alternative procedures*, which would be adopted by a particular set of learners and perhaps stated in a 'working contract' drawn up between them and their teacher. At the third level *alternative activities* are specified, and these break down into actual *tasks* (level 4). Breen's examples of tasks include 'agreeing a definition of a problem' and 'organizing data'. The model also has a place for ongoing evaluation and 'thereby, a cyclic process through the levels from level 1 to 4 and from level 4 to level 1 again' (p. 57).

White (1988) classifies the process and the PROCEDURAL SYLLABUS together as 'Type B syllabuses'. But Breen (1984: 60) sees these two as 'different in function and nature'. One difference is that the procedural syllabus is a pre-designed one (though, one might point out, this is true only in relation to activities to be undertaken, and not at all in terms of language content). Secondly, Breen's process syllabus will generate 'language subject-matter'; but while Prabhu's procedural framework will in certain circumstances permit the possibility of form-focused work, this would certainly be the exception rather than the rule, and the two syllabus types do therefore differ in this respect.

White (1988) indicates that in the general educational literature process approaches are not without their critics, and the problems which writers like Taylor and Richards (1979) note with the process curriculum in general are likely to hold for language teaching process syllabuses in particular. These problems include the heavy demands process teaching is likely to make on teacher competence, as well as the issue of how objective assessment may be made in the absence of predetermined outcomes. Further, Hirst (1975) argues that the process syllabus is still, like its product counterpart, concerned with ends rather than means even if these are not specified in a behavioural manner; the sentiment is echoed by Johnson (1983), who suggests that processes, once listed, in fact become products.

BIBLIOGRAPHY
Breen, M. P. (1983). Prepared comments to K. Johnson, Syllabus design: possible future trends. In K. Johnson and D. Porter (eds), *Perspectives in Communicative Language Teaching*. London: Academic Press, 58–66.
——(1984). Process syllabuses for the language classroom. In C. J. Brumfit (ed.), *General English Syllabus Design*. ELT Documents 118. Oxford: Modern English Publications with the British Council, 47–60.*
Breen, M. P. and Candlin, C. N. (1980). The essentials of a communicative curriculum in language teaching. *Applied Linguistics*, 1/2, 89–112.
Bruner, J. S. (1960). *The Process of Education*. Cambridge, MA: Harvard University Press.
Hirst, P. (1975). The curriculum and its objectives: a defence of piecemeal curriculum planning. In *The Curriculum*. Studies in Education 2. Windsor: National Foundation for Educational Research.
Johnson, K. (1993). Review of R. V. White and V. Arndt, *Process Writing*. *English Language Teaching Journal*, 47/1, 89–91.
Mitzel, H. E. (1960). Teacher effectiveness. In C. W. Harris (ed.), *Encyclopedia of Educational Research*. New York: Macmillan, 1481–6.
Taylor, P. H. and Richards, C. (1979). *An Introduction to Curriculum Studies*. Windsor: National Foundation for Educational Research.
White, R. V. (1988). *The ELT Curriculum*. Oxford: Blackwell.

KJ

**process vs product**  As with many polarizations, it is more helpful to see these concepts as complementary rather than opposites. The terms are used in a number of spheres in language teaching. A common distinction is between text as a finished product – the 'what' – and the reader/listener as language processor – the 'how' – methodology thus being concerned with both the features of language data and the strategies used to comprehend and produce it. The literature also discusses the notion of the 'PROCESS SYLLABUS' as an evolving phenomenon based on learning stages, rather than as predetermined. (See also NEEDS ANALYSIS, PROCEDURAL SYLLABUS.)

BIBLIOGRAPHY
Breen, M. (1987). Contemporary paradigms in syllabus design. *Language Teaching*, 20/2, 81–92 and 20/3, 157–74.
McDonough, S. H. (1995). *Strategy, Process and Skill in Language Learning*. London: Edward Arnold.

JMcD

**process writing**  represents a shift in emphasis in TEACHING WRITING from the product of writing activities (the finished text) to ways in which text can be developed: from concern with questions such as 'what have you written?', 'what grade is it worth?' to 'how will you write it?', 'how can it be improved?'

This major paradigm shift has entered L2 teaching, under the influence of exponents such as Raimes, Spack and Zamel, from L1 teaching and research in America since the 1960s. Grabe and Kaplan (1996) describe the following four-stage division in the history of process writing approaches in this context.

The *expressive stage* focused on the need for the writer to express himself freely in his own 'voice'. Exponents based the approach on insights into good practice; there were no theoretical underpinnings but it resulted in influential innovations in teaching writing.

The *cognitive approach*, seeing writing as thinking, came in the 1970s, especially from the pioneering work of psychologists Flower and Hayes (figure 1).

Their theory of writing suggests that it is a highly complex, goal-directed, recursive activity. It develops over time as writers move from the production of egocentric, writer-based texts (typically, writing everything

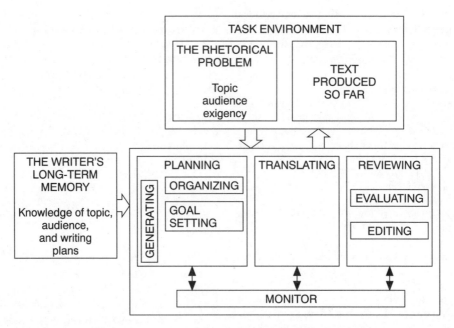

**Figure 1**   A cognitive process theory of writing (Flower and Hayes, 1981).

they know on a topic without thinking of what the reader wants or needs to know) to reader-based texts, which are written with the reader in mind. This model has been criticized for being too vague (with no reference to how text is actually produced) or too generalized (the model suggests a uniform process for all writers). Criticism has been made of the basic research tool, protocol analysis, on the grounds that thinking aloud while writing interferes with the process. However, this model has had enormous influence on subsequent research and writing pedagogy in L1 and L2.

Other cognitive models followed, the most significant being Bereiter and Scardamalia's (1987). They propose a developmental view of writing, with two models: less skilled writers operate at the level of 'knowledge telling' (as in simple narrative), while more skilled writers are involved in 'knowledge transforming' (as in expository writing). Problems arise in explaining how or when writers move from one stage to the other, or if all do.

The *social stage* appeared in the 1980s when studies in SOCIOLINGUISTICS, Halliday's functional linguistics and educational ethnography led to criticism that the above approaches to the writing process omitted the crucial dimension of social context. Educational movements in America such as writing across the curriculum (with writing being taught in content, not language, classes) and the British primary level National Writing Project have emphasized that writers do not operate as solitary individuals, but as members of a social/cultural group. This influences what and how they write and how their writing is perceived.

The *discourse community* stage developed from the above view of writing as a social activity. The notions of audience and genre are fundamental here and attention has focused on tertiary-level writing, with its demand that students produce writing acceptable to the academic community. Debate centres on two main areas: defining a discourse community and whether it is necessary, or even desirable, to oblige students to adopt the norms of a different community from their own.

The central question for language teaching is: how similar is L2 writing to L1 writing? L2 writing research is still in its infancy, but initial findings suggest that, while L1 general composing skills – both good and bad – transfer from L1 to L2 (see Arndt, 1987), 'L2 composing is more constrained, more difficult and less effective' (Silva, 1993: 668). Most L2 writers bring with them knowledge and experience of writing in their L1 and this resource should not be ignored. However, they also bring the limitations of their knowledge of L2 language and rhetorical organization.

Although we are far from a theoretically proven model of L2 writing, the developments in thinking about writing outlined above have led to enormous changes in the way writing is taught. The initial ELT cognitive process bandwagon was criticized by the English for Academic Purposes movement (see Horowitz, 1986) for failing to meet the needs of EAP students. Most experts would now agree that writing is a socio-cognitive, problem-solving process affected by cultural and rhetorical norms. Writing teachers need to encourage learners to think about and develop their writing process, and to consider their audience and the rhetorical norms of L2 text.

Although there is not, as is sometimes thought, one 'process approach' there are many useful process writing techniques which feed in to a variety of approaches. White and Arndt's diagram (1991: 4; see figure 2 below) offers teachers a framework which tries to capture the recursive, not linear, nature of writing. Activities to generate ideas (e.g. brainstorming) help writers tap their long-term memory and answer the question, 'What can I say on this topic?' Focusing (e.g. fast writing) deals with 'What is my overall purpose in writing this?' Structuring is organizing and reorganizing text to answer the question: 'How can I present these ideas in a way that is acceptable to my reader?' Activities include experimenting with different types of text, having read examples. Drafting is the transition from writer-based thought into reader-based text. Multiple drafts are produced, each influenced by feedback from teacher and/or peers. Activities such as REFORMULATION and the use of checklists in guiding feedback develop essential evaluating skills. Feedback focuses initially on content and organization. When these are satisfactory, comment on language is given on penultimate drafts for final amendment. Re-viewing is standing back from the text and looking at it with fresh eyes, asking 'Is it right?' The overall aim is to create meaningful, purposeful

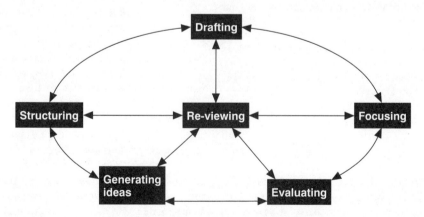

**Figure 2** White and Arndt's (1991) diagram of process writing (arrows added).

writing tasks that develop the writer's skills over several drafts. Collaboration between learners and with teachers is essential. This results in changes in teacher and learner roles (see Leki, 1990) and has implications for teacher and LEARNER TRAINING.

BIBLIOGRAPHY
Arndt, V. (1987). Six writers in search of texts: a protocol-based study of L1 and L2 writing. *ELT Journal*, 41, 257–67.
Bereiter, C. and Scardamalia, M. (1987). *The Psychology of Written Composition*. Hillsdale, NJ: Erlbaum.
Flower, L. and Hayes, J. R. (1981). A cognitive process theory of writing. *College English*, 44, 765–77.
Grabe, W. and Kaplan, R. B. (1996). *Theory and Practice of Writing*. London: Longman.*
Hedge, T. (1988). *Writing*. Oxford: Oxford University Press.
Horowitz, D. (1986). Process, not product: less than meets the eye. *TESOL Quarterly*, 20, 141–4.
Leki, I. (1990). Coaching from the margins: issues in written reponse. In B. Kroll (ed.), *Second Language Writing*. Cambridge: Cambridge University Press, 57–68.
Raimes, A. (1983). *Techniques in Teaching Writing*. Oxford: Oxford University Press.
Silva, T. (1993). Towards an understanding of the distinct nature of L2 writing: the ESL research and its implications. *Journal of Second Language Writing*, 27, 657–77.
Spack, R. (1988). Initiating ESL students into the academic discourse community: how far should we go? *TESOL Quarterly*, 22, 29–51.
Susser, B. (1994). Process approaches in ESL/EFL writing instruction. *Journal of Second Language Writing*, 3, 31–47.
White, R. and Arndt, V. (1991). *Process Writing*. London: Longman.*
Zamel, V. (1985). Responding to student writing. *TESOL Quarterly*, 19, 79–101.

CLF

**production processes**   There has been much less research done on processes of production than on comprehension processes, doubtless because of the methodological difficulties involved in researching the former. Models of speech production have, however, been formulated, using evidence from a variety of sources. Hesitation phenomena, slips of the tongue and 'tip of the tongue' (TOT) experiences provide much of the evidence, with errors in other media (slips of the hand in sign language and slips of the pen in writing) also contributing information. Abnormal speech production in aphasia and schizophrenia also adds to the picture. For accessible general discussions of production processes see Clark and Clark (1977), Carroll (1994) and Harley (1995).

As with the study of many areas of language processing, it is examples of malfunction which provide clues as to what is involved. In the case of language production, hesitation phenomena and slips of the tongue suggest levels at which processing occurs, and sometimes also information about the ordering of processing stages. Clark and Clark (1977: 263) list the main types of speech error. They distinguish between *silent pauses* (in which nothing is uttered) and *filled pauses* in which words like 'uh' may be inserted, or words repeated, or false starts occur. Under the heading of slips of the tongue Clark and Clark (following Fromkin, 1973) include: *anticipations*, where a sound is brought forward from a later occurring one ('bake my bike' for 'take my bike'); *perseverations*, where an earlier occurring sound is attached to a later occurring word ('pulled a pantrum' for 'pulled a tantrum'); *reversals* (spoonerisms), where two segments are reversed ('fats and kodor' for 'Katz and Fodor') and *blends*, where two words are joined together to form a nonexistent word ('grizzly' + 'ghastly' to form 'grastly').

Levelt (1989) provides a four-stage model of speech production which serves as a framework for consideration of the issues. At the *conceptualization* stage the message to be conveyed is planned. *Formulation* into a linguistic plan then follows, including the processes of lexicalization and syntactic planning. *Articulation* is the third stage, at which the plan is executed by the use of physiological organs. Finally comes *self-monitoring*, where the speaker assesses the success of what has been said in terms of initial intention, and may make repairs.

The first of these stages (conceptualization) is the least open to empirical investigation, and very little has been written about it. Carroll (1994: 195) identifies two issues associated with this stage: 'where do ideas come from?' and 'in what form do ideas exist before they are put into words?' These are clearly questions which will be extremely difficult to research.

Much more has been written about the formulation stage. Clark and Clark (1977) list the levels of planning that occur in the production of an utterance. Some (but not all) of these levels are now considered. At the discourse level, a language user (engaged in a conversation) must coordinate behaviour with that of the interactant. This involves adherence to TURN-TAKING rules and, among other things, to conventions regarding the opening and closing of conversations. At the sentence level are the planning categories of propositional content, illocutionary content and thematic structure. The first of these involves 'experiential chunking', which relates to what a speaker chooses to focus on and how it is structured propositionally. Speakers attend particularly to such matters as conceptual salience and pertinence. Illocutionary content planning concerns adherence to felicity conditions associated with the relevant speech acts (see SPEECH ACT THEORY). Thematic structure planning involves issues such as the distribution of old and new information. For discussion of this, see Halliday (1970), whose own theory of language production conceptualizes the processes made at his various levels as a series of choices (or 'potentials'). This theory is developed in Halliday (1973).

Lexicalization is the process of turning thoughts into words (and ultimately into sounds), and much has been written about this level of formulation. Evidence from speech errors suggests that the process occurs in two stages. Fay and Cutler (1977) note that whole-word substitution in speech may take two forms. Semantic substitutions may occur, as when the word 'toe' may erroneously be used for 'finger'. Substitution of the word 'historical' by 'hysterical' would be an example of the second form, known as phonological word substitutions (malapropisms). The first of these two stages is referred to as *lemma selection*. At this stage words are represented in an abstract form, and it is here that semantic substitutions would occur. The second stage of *lexeme selection* specifies the actual phonological form of the word, and errors at this processing stage would take the form of phonological word substitutions.

Evidence for two stages also comes from TOT experiences, where a speaker 'knows' a word but cannot produce it. Brown and McNeill (1966) provided subjects with descriptions of rare words, and studied those cases where the subjects claimed TOT knowledge of them. The researchers found that in many cases subjects had information about a word (e.g. the letter it started with) without being able to recall it. Such experiences may be associated with correct lemma selection, but failure at the lexeme selection stage.

Among models which deal with syntactic planning, those of Fromkin (1971, 1973) and Garrett (1975) are predominant. Both exemplify in some degree what Clark and Clark (1977) call the 'skeleton + constituent' paradigm. Once decisions regarding intended message have been made, the utterance 'outline' is planned, and the constituent items are then 'filled in'. Figure 1 illustrates the Garrett model, exemplified for production of the sentence 'the mother wiped the plates'. The 'outline' is represented at level C, with some 'filling in' occurring at level D.

At level A the decision is made what to say. This is converted at level B into an abstract semantic representation with relationships specified. An abstract syntactic

(A)   Message-level – intention to convey particular meaning activates appropriate propositions

(B)   SUBJECT = 'mother concept',
VERB = 'wipe concept', OBJECT = 'plate concept'
TIME = past
NUMBER OF OBJECTS = MANY

(C)   (DETERMINER) $N_1 V$ [+ PAST]
(DETERMINER) $N_2$ [+ PLURAL]

(D)   /mother/ /wipe/ /plate/

(E)   (DETERMINER) /mother/ /wipe/ + [PAST]
(DETERMINER) /plate/ + [PLURAL]

(F)   /the/ /mother/ /wiped/ /the/ /plates/

(G)   Low-level phonological processing and articulation

**Figure 1**   The Garrett (1975, 1976) model of speech production (from Harley, 1995: 262).

frame is formed at level C, with phonological representations of concept words retrieved at D. Words are inserted into the syntactic plan at E. Level F gives sound-level representations, which are translated into phonological features at G. Note that the model distinguishes between content ('concept') words and function words, with Garrett (1975) noting that slips of the tongue never confuse the two (an utterance like 'the of pot gold' never replaces 'the pot of gold').

Evidence for the stages of the model and their sequence is provided again by speech errors. Fromkin's (1973) often cited example of 'a maniac for *weekends*' for 'a weekend for *maniacs*' illustrates the kind of argument used. The italicized words are where primary stress occurs. The syntactic outline of this example (the result of stage C) would be *Det + N + prep + N(PLURAL + 1st STRESS)*. It is important to note that this whole plan, including the plural and STRESS items, remains in place, unaffected by the slip of the tongue. The error occurs at stage D where lexical items are inserted. These facts suggest that the two stages are indeed different, with the syntactic outline generated independently of the lexical items

involved. They suggest in addition that level D does indeed occur after C. It is also significant that the realization of the plural morpheme is phonetically appropriate for the word to which it is attached, as opposed to the word it was originally intended for. That is, it is /z/, appropriate to 'weekend' (following the final voiced /d/) and not /s/ as it would be to 'maniac' (following the final unvoiced /k/). This indicates that the plural item is specified in the plan before it is phonologically realized.

Harley (1995) lists further evidence for the Garrett model from the study of aphasia. The two main types of aphasia are Broca's type and Wernicke's type, according to the brain area affected. One characteristic of the former type is agrammatism, where sentence construction and grammatical elements are affected, but content words remain intact. In Wernicke's type of aphasia the opposite occurs, and there may be major content word-finding difficulties. As Harley notes, this supports the Garrett model's separation of syntactic planning and grammatical element retrieval on the one hand (affected in Broca's but not Wernicke's type aphasia), and content word retrieval on the other (affected in Wernicke's but not Broca's type aphasia). Harley also cites evidence from aphasia studies for the lemma/lexeme selection distinction and separation in processing.

Slips of the tongue also provide much information about the processes of articulation, particularly as regards the identification of the levels at which they operate. The general argument is that levels where slips of the tongue occur are levels at which processing occurs. Following Fromkin (1973), Clark and Clark (1977) identify three levels below the word: distinctive features, phonetic segments and syllables. Slips like 'Derry and Chulia' for 'Terry and Julia' indicate that a single phonetic feature like voicing can become switched, leaving other aspects of the relevant sound segments intact – in this example the initial voiceless sound of

'Terry' becomes voiced and the initial voiced sound of 'Julia' becomes unvoiced. There are plenty of examples of tongue slips where whole phonetic segments become reversed. Often the reversals are with initial word segments, but this need not be the case: in 'David food the peach' for 'David, feed the pooch' it is the medial vowels that become reversed. Slips like 'carp-si-hord' for 'harp-si-chord' indicate that reversal can occur within a word at the syllable level. All the above examples are from Fromkin (1973).

Three sets of muscles are involved in the articulatory process for speech. The *respiratory* muscles control air flow from the lungs. The *laryngeal* muscles are the vocal cords which may be made to vibrate (for voicing) or otherwise. The *supralaryngeal* muscles work within the vocal tract above the vocal cords, where the size and shape of the oral and nasal cavities are altered by movements of the tongue, lips, teeth, jaw and velum. In articulation, the brain sends messages to the muscles specifying the 'target locations' required to produce particular sounds. But, as Carroll (1994) points out, it is an oversimplification to see articulation as the production of discrete sounds. It is rather a continuum of sound production in which much accommodation has to be made to surrounding sounds. The result is often 'undershooting', where only approximations of target locations are achieved (MacNeilage, 1970). This is particularly likely to occur where the distance the articulators must travel from one sound to the next is great. 'Distant targets' might simply be left out; an example would be the /t/ in 'wanta', giving 'wanna'.

The final stage in Levelt's model is self-monitoring. Levelt (1983) studied the structure of self-repairs and distinguished three stages. At the first we interrupt ourselves; at the second we may use an editing expression like 'uh' or 'oh'; at the third we repair the utterance. Nooteboom (1980) indicates how common a process repair is; he examined 648 speech errors and found that 64%

were corrected. For a summary of findings relevant to each of these stages, see Carroll (1994: 207).

It will be clear from the above discussion that most of the work on production processes relates to speech production, with much evidence coming from slips of the tongue. But slips of the pen in writing and slips of the hand in sign language also provide evidence, which is of interest precisely because different modalities are involved. Carroll (1994) discusses sign language at some length. The study of slips of the hand suggests that the same processes occur for sign language as for speech, with errors identifying similar processing levels. What differences there are relate to physiology. Speakers pause more than signers, because of the need to breathe; but signers sometimes take longer to produce signs, because of the physical movements involved.

There is no reason to believe that, in broad outline, writing processes are substantially different from those of speech. But because writing is emphatically not 'speech written down', the production of written language will involve rules, conventions and procedures which differ from those found in speech.

As in other skill areas, it is now the case that language teaching is taking heed of psycholinguistic descriptions of processes, and attempting to reflect what is known of such processes in teaching practice. Johnson (1979) considers what conditions should be simulated in classroom speaking practice, and gives prominence to the provision of an information gap (see INFORMATION/OPINION GAP). His argument is made in terms of the processes of production which need to be simulated in the classroom. More recent examples of pedagogic attention paid to speech production processes are Bygate (1987) and Littlewood (1992). The former in particular makes reference to research findings related to speaking processes, and considers their classroom implications.

It is also the case that language teaching has become receptive to the general notion of processing conditions. It is recognized that different speaking or writing activities will entail variable processing loads, and it is acknowledged that the language user needs practice at handling such variable loads. TASK-BASED LANGUAGE TEACHING is particularly associated with this area, and work such as Skehan and Foster (1995), Bygate (1996) and Johnson (1996) reflects attempts to study the processing characteristics of tasks as a step towards providing a framework for teaching in which processing ability is developed.

Recent work in the PROCESS SYLLABUS and in PROCESS WRITING are further indications of interest in the process dimension of language teaching. Though the processes typically dealt with in process writing approaches are often principally concerned with the discourse level, time will doubtless provide more detailed and sophisticated considerations of processes which may form the basis for classroom process practice.

BIBLIOGRAPHY
Brown, R. and McNeill, D. (1966). The 'tip of the tongue' phenomenon. *Journal of Verbal Learning and Verbal Behaviour*, 5, 325–37.
Bygate, M. (1987). *Speaking*. Oxford: Oxford University Press.*
——(1996). Effects of task repetition: apprising the developing language of learners. In D. Willis and J. Willis (eds), *Challenge and Change in Language Teaching*. London: Heinemann, 136–46.
Carroll, D. W. (1994). *Psychology of Language*. Pacific Grove, CA: Brooks/Cole.
Clark, H. H. and Clark, E. V. (1977). *The Psychology of Language*. New York: Harcourt Brace Jovanovich.
Fay, D. and Cutler, A. (1977). Malapropisms and the structure of the mental lexicon. *Linguistic Inquiry*, 8, 505–20.
Fromkin, V. A. (1971). The non-anomalous nature of anomalous utterances. *Language*, 51, 696–719.
——(1973). *Speech Errors as Linguistic Evidence*. The Hague: Mouton.
Garrett, M. F. (1975). The analysis of sentence production. In G. Bower (ed.), *The Psychology of Learning and Motivation*, Vol. 9. New York: Academic Press, 133–77.
——(1976). Syntactic processes in sentence production. In R. J. Wales and E. C. T. Walker (eds), *New Approaches to Language Mechanisms*. Amsterdam: North Holland, 231–55.
Halliday, M. A. K. (1970). Language structure and language function. In J. Lyons (ed.), *New Horizons in Linguistics*. Harmondsworth: Penguin Books, 140–65.
——(1973). *Explorations in the Functions of Language*. London: Edward Arnold.
Harley, T. A. (1995). *The Psychology of Language*. Hove: Erlbaum.
Johnson, K. (1979). Communicative approaches and communicative processes. In C. J. Brumfit and K. Johnson (eds), *The Communicative Approach to Language Teaching*. Oxford: Oxford University Press, 192–205.
——(1996). *Language Teaching and Skill Learning*. Oxford: Blackwell.
Levelt, W. J. M. (1983). Monitoring and self-repair in speech. *Cognition*, 14, 41–104.
——(1989). *Speaking: From intention to articulation*. Cambridge, MA: MIT Press.*
Littlewood, W. (1992). *Teaching Oral Communication*. Oxford: Blackwell.
MacNeilage, P. F. (1970). Motor control of serial ordering of speech. *Psychological Review*, 77, 182–96.
Nooteboom, S. (1980). Speaking and unspeaking: detection and correction of phonological and lexical errors in spontaneous speech. In V. A. Fromkin (ed.), *Errors in Linguistic Performance*. New York: Academic Press, 87–95.
Skehan, P. and Foster, P. (1995). Task type and task processing conditions as influences on foreign language performance. In P. Skehan (ed.), *Thames Valley University Working Papers in English Language Teaching*. London: Thames Valley University, 139–88.

KJ

**proficiency tests** measure proficiency, either in terms of ability to use language for a given purpose (e.g. entry into university) or in more general terms (as in the case of tests such as the Cambridge First Certificate and Proficiency). Test content is independent of the content and objectives of courses followed. (See LANGUAGE TESTING.)

BIBLIOGRAPHY

Hughes, A. (1989). *Testing for Language Teachers.* Cambridge: Cambridge University Press.

KSM

**programmed instruction**, a technique dating from Sidney Pressey in the 1920s, assumes that: learning tasks can be broken down into 'bit learnings' to be assembled step by step into a whole; that error should be avoided; that reinforcement should follow rapidly. Two main variants emerged: *linear* (B. F. Skinner) and *intrinsic* or *branching* (Norman A. Crowder).

BIBLIOGRAPHY

Rivers, W. M. (1981). *Teaching Foreign-Language Skills.* 2nd edn. Chicago: University of Chicago Press. [*Passim*, but especially pp. 111–23.]

JTR

**pronunciation teaching** Consideration of the teaching of pronunciation involves questions of both content and coverage, and a range of pedagogical issues including appropriate models of dialect and accent, intelligibility criteria in relation to context of use, TRANSFER errors and the relevance of learners' mother tongues, and the optimum classroom format for dealing with pronunciation skills. There is also a direct relationship with other language skills, most obviously speaking and listening. More generally, the learning of a target language pronunciation impinges on communicative ability and therefore on perceptions of personal and group identity (see Kenworthy, 1987, for example).

ELEMENTS OF THE SOUND SYSTEM OF ENGLISH

In principle – in other words, independent of considerations of context and learning goals – the sound system of English comprises a set of phonological features which form the basis of choice for specific pedagogical frameworks (see PHONOLOGY). Within these features a standard distinction is usually made between 'segmental' and 'supra-segmental' phonology (a distinction which has been carried over into the teaching of pronunciation). 'Segmental' aspects of the sound system are particularly concerned with individual vowels and consonants and their combinations, 'supra-segmental' with ways in which these can be varied in communication, as in sentence rhythm or INTONATION (Crystal, 1971). The key features under both headings are the following:

(1) Individual sounds: vowels and consonants where there are phonemic distinctions, such as between the English words *bit* and *bet*, or *shop* and *chop*, or *meat* and *neat*, for example. (This is in contrast to allophonic distinctions which make no difference to meaning, but where the pronunciation of an individual sound varies according to phonetic context.)

(2) (a) Diphthongs: vowels in combination, as in *near* or *boy*.
    (b) Consonant clusters, as in *school* /sk/, *train*, or *empty*.

(3) Linkage of sounds, an important phenomenon in English and a frequent source of difficulty for learner-listeners. For example, the phrase 'Put it on' will not be heard as three separate words.

(4) STRESS patterns in polysyllabic words, which themselves are related to word grammar (as in 'responsible' and 'responsibility', for example).

(5) Sentence stress and rhythm, and the related phenomenon of weak forms, whereby unstressed syllables are most frequently reduced to *schwa* /ə/. Regular stress in English tends to fall on nouns, adjectives, adverbs and main verbs (as in 'I've been líving hére for over a yéar,' for instance. Contractions (as in 'won't' or 'would've') are also to be included here.

(6) INTONATION, and the use of varying pitch to formulate meaning and intention.

Ancillary features to be considered include

(7) The complex relationship between the orthography and the sound system of English.

(8) The phonetic alphabet and the use of phonetic transcription to represent features of pronunciation (see PHONETICS).

## METHODOLOGY AND MATERIALS

The longest-established approach to the teaching of pronunciation has principally been concerned with contrastive practice based on individual sounds and using patterns of minimal pairs, i.e. single-syllable words with just one phonemic distinction within each pair (cup–cub; hat–hate; bit–pit; ship–shop). Furthermore, originally within the CONTRASTIVE ANALYSIS paradigm, practice is commonly focused on sounds which are different as between English and the learner's mother tongue (Baker, 1982; Bright and McGregor, 1970: 179ff.; Swan and Smith, 1987). Practice of this kind at the segmental level is clearly important, and continues to be incorporated in virtually all pronunciation teaching materials. It may also be combined with diagrams of the organs of speech as a visual assistance for the accurate articulation of these individual sounds.

An approach to teaching based on minimal-pair aspects of segmental phonology alone is, however, necessary but not sufficient. It is essentially an imitative 'laboratory' activity concerned with the formation of sounds, and both the lexical items and mini-dialogues used in practice are often a long way removed from a concern with meaning and communicative purpose. It is also not clear that sounds practised and apparently improved in isolation are then transferred to the learner's speech in real-world situations of language use. Moreover, incorrectly pronounced sounds are frequently unambiguous in context and therefore – all other things being equal – less significant than supra-segmental features of rhythm and intonation. For instance, 'I came

from Belgium by /ʃiːp/ (heard as 'sheep' rather than 'ship') is not likely to be misunderstood in the flow of conversation. Over-emphasis on sounds may therefore be misleading, just as a teaching style that uses full forms instead of weak forms presents learners with a distorted model of natural spoken English.

Thornbury (1993), making a conventional but useful distinction between 'atomistic' (or 'bottom-up') and 'holistic' (or 'top-down') approaches to language learning, argues that, whereas the latter have become dominant in the teaching of lexis, grammar, skills and so on, they have strangely not been so prevalent in the area of pronunciation. Thornbury points out that, in some current materials, even supra-segmental phenomena may be handled segmentally (although the converse is also possible). That said, most published coursebooks now do cover the whole range of features outlined in (1)–(6) in the preceding section (O'Connor and Fletcher, 1989). Several also deal with the close relationship between pronunciation and listening skills (Rogerson and Gilbert, 1990, for example; see also TEACHING LISTENING), and the use of phonetic transcription in dictionaries to show pronunciation is a commonly taught reference skill (see also STUDY SKILLS).

A broader view of pronunciation teaching is clearly grounded within a communicative paradigm, and with its associated criterion of variability in context. Harmer (1993) makes the point that it is unrealistic for teachers and learners to aim for native-sounding speech, the number of variables – place of learning, age, possibilities for interaction, availability of models and so on – making it an improbable target. Rather, he prefers to think in terms of 'communicative efficiency', which simply supposes that a student can say, and be understood to say, what he wishes to communicate. Kenworthy (1987: 13ff.) glosses this as 'intelligibility', as 'close enough' to be understood in any given context, which of course will vary from any other in its demands and expectations.

BIBLIOGRAPHY
Baker, A. (1982). *Introducing English Pronunciation*. Cambridge: Cambridge University Press.
Bright, J. A. and McGregor, G. P. (1970). *Teaching English as a Second Language*. London: Longman.
Crystal, D. (1971). *Linguistics*. Harmondsworth: Penguin Books.
Harmer, J. (1993). *The Practice of English Language Teaching*. London and New York: Longman.
Kenworthy, J. (1987). *Teaching English Pronunciation*. London and New York: Longman.*
O'Connor, J. D. and Fletcher, C. (1989). *Sounds English*. Harlow: Longman.
Rogerson, P. and Gilbert, J. B. (1990). *Speaking Clearly*. Cambridge: Cambridge University Press.
Swan, M. and Smith, B. (1987). *Learner English*. Cambridge: Cambridge University Press.
Thornbury, S. (1993). Having a good jaw: voice-setting phonology. *ELT Journal*, 47/2, 126–31.

JMCD

**proportional syllabus** In Yalden's proportional syllabus the focus shifts from linguistic form to communicative function as the programme progresses. There is an initial 'structural phase' which concentrates on formal and ideational meaning. 'Communicative phases' follow, in which functional, discourse and rhetorical components are added. There is a final 'specialized phase'.

BIBLIOGRAPHY
Yalden, J. (1983). *The Communicative Syllabus: Evolution, design and implementation*. Oxford: Pergamon Institute of English.

KJ

**psycholinguistics** is concerned broadly with how linguistic knowledge is acquired (developmental psycholinguistics), how it is put to use in comprehending and producing utterances (language processing) and how it can be impaired by brain injury (aphasia). Key issues in the field are: how language is stored in the mind/brain, the relation between language and articulatory/perceptual mechanisms, and the relation between language and other cognitive systems (e.g. vision, propositional thought, memory). Psycholinguistic research is typically experimentally interventionist (rather than observational), using techniques like reaction timing, measurement of brain activation, measurement of levels of recall, etc. (See COMPREHENSION PROCESSES, PRODUCTION PROCESSES.)

BIBLIOGRAPHY
Clark, E. and Clark, H. (1977). *Psychology and Language: An introduction to psycholinguistics*. New York: Harcourt Brace Jovanovich.*
Garman, M. (1990). *Psycholinguistics*. Cambridge: Cambridge University Press.
Harris, M. and Coltheart, M. (1986). *Language Processing in Children and Adults: An introduction*. London: Routledge.
Taylor, I. (1990). *Psycholinguistics: Learning and using language*. Englewood Cliffs, NJ: Prentice-Hall.*

RH

# Q

**qualifications in English language teaching** Qualifications accepted by employers for teaching posts in ELT are rather varied in the UK. They are available at several levels and in a number of areas, both general and specialist. Since EFL is not a fundamental subject in the national curriculum, there are no courses with ELT as a main subject which are approved for the award of Qualified Teacher Status for employment in the British state education system. In the UK, the 'English in Britain' accreditation scheme run by the British Council for private language schools and state-sector colleges determines the level and spread of qualifications appropriate for staff in recognized institutions. At the time of writing (1997), the British Association of TESOL Qualifying Institutions is developing a framework for the new concept of 'TESOL Qualified Status' (TQS).

Five levels of training course can be distinguished. These are (a) introductory, (b) initial, (c) qualified, (d) advanced diploma, (e) higher. The levels are distinguished by the mandatory length of the course, the entry requirements in terms of general level of education and experience, the amount of supervised teaching practice specified, and the nature of the posts for which they prepare the candidate. The courses are offered in many institutions both in the UK and abroad, but the qualifications are currently awarded by only two organizations for EFL: the University of Cambridge Local Examinations Syndicate and Trinity College, London, and by one for ESOL: the City and Guilds, London. The Cambridge schemes were introduced by the Royal Society of Arts, then run jointly by UCLES and the RSA, and the connection remains for some of their schemes; UCLES has spent four years developing their 'Cambridge Integrated Language Teaching Schemes (CILTS)' with new syllabuses, new topics, and a decoupling of methodology and language proficiency for non-native speaker candidates. These organizations set the standards, monitor the delivery of the course and the assessment of the students, but leave considerable flexibility for the training institution to interpret the guidelines and organize the actual course, frequency of sessions, whether part- or full-time, arrangements for assessment and for observation and practice in actual classrooms with real learners. Therefore, the opportunity to choose a method and a location for the course to suit a candidate does not prejudice the quality standards, which are monitored across all modes of delivery.

The very restricted, *introductory* level of qualification is usually either a short course offered by a language teaching organization with the purpose of preparing teachers for employment within that organization, or a short course acting as a 'taster' for people who are unsure of their commitment to a higher level.

The *Initial Certificate* is the basic level required of teachers in the private sector in institutions seeking recognition by the English in Britain, and abroad in posts recruited for by the British Council and other UK-based agencies. Certificates require a certain level of general education (generally sufficient for entry to higher education), but no previous teaching experience.

The RSA/Cambridge *Certificate in Teaching English Language to Adults* (CELTA) specifies 100 hours' contact time with 6 hours' supervised teaching practice and 8 hours' supervised observation of live classes; there is continuous assessment of written work and monitoring of practical classroom teaching.

The Trinity College *Certificate in TESOL* stipulates 130 hours' contact time with 6 hours of supervised teaching experience; again, there is assessment of written work and observation of practical classroom teaching.

For the teacher of English as a Second Language, the City and Guilds *Initial Certificate in Basic Skills* (ESOL) (9284), run by the Adult Literacy and Basic Skills Unit (ALBSU), provides a parallel level of initial training. This Certificate specifies a minimum of 30 hours' training, but requires other teaching experience and is also concerned with practical work with individual students.

Some initial qualifications are taken early in service instead. UCLES *Certificate for Overseas Teachers of English* (COTE) (in which teaching practice has to be conducted locally, outside the UK) has a language component and also requires some 300 hours of teaching experience. Specialist training for primary EFL is provided by the Trinity *Certificate in Teaching English to Young Learners*; this is for serving, experienced teachers wishing to add this expertise to their professional competence. CILTS has introduced a Certificate in Teaching English for Young Learners for a similar purpose and clientele.

The normal full qualification accepted in the profession for career posts leading to responsible positions is the diploma. A graduate level of education and two years' experience is usually required. Cambridge offers a *Diploma in Teaching English as a Foreign Language to Adults* (DTEFLA) and one for Overseas Teachers of English (DOTE), which are in process of being merged into a single new qualification within CILTS. Approved courses have a minimum of 100 hours' contact time, including 10 hours' classroom teaching practice and 10 of observation. There is both written and practical assessment. Courses for the Trinity Licentiate Diploma (LTCL) in TESOL normally take 100–140 hours, and the examination is in four parts: two written papers, an oral interview and observation of classroom teaching. The post-experience parallel qualification in ESOL is the City and Guilds In-service Certificate in Basic Skills (ESOL) (9285). CILTS is also developing a diploma for teaching young learners.

An advanced *Diploma in Language Teaching Management*, to be approximately one-third the workload of an MA degree, is being piloted by CILTS and will soon be offered regularly.

Qualifications in higher education of relevance to English language teachers are offered by more than fifty universities at academic levels of certificate, diploma and Master's degree. Certificates usually take one term full-time, diplomas usually one year and Master's one year but at a more intense pace or requiring the addition of a thesis to course work. Part-time options also exist. Topics range from general English language teaching, applied linguistics or linguistics, to specific ESP, research, materials development. The British Council has a comprehensive list and the *EFL Guide* publishes one. Since most Master's schemes do not include supervised teaching practice, they do not usually attract recognition for employment purposes in sectors accredited by 'English in Britain', but they are required for many posts of higher responsibility and for many overseas contract posts, and normally for teaching EAP in university departments accredited by the British Association of Lecturers in English for Academic Purposes.

The situation regarding qualifications, their topics, currency and recognition for employment purposes is thus in a period of intense re-evaluation and development. (See also TEACHER EDUCATION.)

SMCD

**question types** can be grouped in different ways. Questions can, for instance, be:

(1)  'closed', with only one acceptable answer ('What's 2 plus 2?') or 'open-ended', with various possible answers (most 'Why?' questions);
(2)  'echoic', confirming/checking comprehension ('Pardon?') or 'epistemic', leading to knowledge acquisition (as in 3 below);
(3)  'display' ('How do you spell "film"?') or 'referential' ('Why are you late?');
(4)  FORM-FOCUSed or MESSAGE-FOCUSed.

The questions asked are important in COMMUNICATIVE LANGUAGE TEACHING as they affect student production and motivation. Research suggests (see Ellis, 1994) that EFL teachers use more closed, display questions than are asked in 'real-life' contexts.

BIBLIOGRAPHY
Chaudron, C. (1988). *Second Language Classrooms.* Cambridge: Cambridge University Press.
Ellis, R. (1994). *The Study of Second Language Acquisition.* Oxford: Oxford University Press, 586–92.*
Long, M. and Sato, C. J. (1983). Classroom foreigner talk discourse: forms and functions of teachers' questions. In H. W. Seliger and M. H. Long (eds), *Classroom Oriented Research in Second Language Acquisition.* Rowley, MA: Newbury House, 268–86.

CLF

# R

**rate/route in SLA** This distinction is probably due to Ellis (1985). Route refers to the transitional stages that L2 learners go through in acquiring properties of the L2 (see NATURAL ORDER HYPOTHESIS). Rate refers to the time it takes to pass through them. While all learners go through the same stages in acquiring some L2 phenomena, certain individuals are faster at doing so than others. Learners who consciously 'know the rules' seem to be faster than those who do not (see TEACHABILITY HYPOTHESIS and CLASSROOM STUDIES IN SLA). Adolescent and young adults appear to be faster than young children in the early stages of SLA (see AGE LEARNING DIFFERENCES). (See also CONSCIOUSNESS RAISING, TEACHING GRAMMAR.)

BIBLIOGRAPHY
Ellis, R. (1985). *Understanding Second Language Acquisition*. Oxford: Oxford University Press.
RH

**realia** are a type of visual aid; they are objects from the real world, ranging from coins to food items, and used in language teaching. First advocated by DIRECT METHOD teachers, they clarify the meaning of concrete nouns and can be used in role plays.

CLF

**received pronunciation (RP)** This ACCENT, spoken natively by approximately 3–5% of the population in the UK, is the norm of pronunciation among upper middle-class speakers and most foreign language teachers of British English. It is also known as 'Queen's English', 'Oxford English' and 'BBC English', although BBC announcers today use a wider range of accents.

BIBLIOGRAPHY
Abercrombie, D. (1990). RP today: its position and prospects. In D. Abercrombie (ed.), *Fifty Years in Phonetics*. Edinburgh: Edinburgh University Press.
Gimson, A. C. (1962). *An Introduction to the Pronunciation of English*. London: Edward Arnold.
AJ

**reduction strategies** Following a similar distinction in Corder (1983), Faerch and Kasper (1983) classify COMMUNICATION STRATEGIES into reduction and ACHIEVEMENT STRATEGIES. In the former, the learner uses reduced linguistic means, or simplifies the communicative goal ('formal' and 'functional' reduction strategies respectively). The purpose may be error avoidance or increased fluency.

BIBLIOGRAPHY
Bialystok, E. (1990). *Communication Strategies: A psychological analysis of second-language use*. Oxford: Blackwell.
Corder, S. P. (1983). Strategies of communication. In C. Faerch and G. Kasper (eds), *Strategies in Interlanguage Communication*. Harlow: Longman, 15–19.
Faerch, C. and Kasper, G. (1983). Plans and strategies in foreign language communication. In C. Faerch and G. Kasper (eds), *Strategies in Interlanguage Communication*. Harlow: Longman, 20–60.
KJ

**Reform School**   This movement started in 1882 with Wilhelm Viëtor's pamphlet *Der Sprachunterricht muß umkehren!* (Language teaching must change direction!), which demanded a break with slavish language teaching based on formal grammar and disconnected written sentences in favour of an oral, inductive, 'natural' approach using the foreign language as the medium of instruction. The principal figures, all phoneticians, were, besides Wilhelm Viëtor, Paul Passy, Otto Jespersen and Henry Sweet. Reform or phonetic and other 'natural' methods emerged, often considered variants of the DIRECT METHOD. The immediate impetus of the school lasted about twenty years and led to some adventurous teaching, but failed to reform mainstream education significantly.

BIBLIOGRAPHY
Howatt, A. P. R. (1984). *A History of English Language Teaching*. Oxford: Oxford University Press. [Chapter 13.]
Mackey, W. F. (1965). *Language Teaching Analysis*. London: Longmans, Green. [Chapter 5.]
                                                                            JTR

**reformulation** is a PROCESS WRITING activity introduced to language teachers by Cohen (1983) and then Allwright (1988). It helps writers develop awareness of native-speaker norms. The teacher selects one draft text from a group of students' work. He asks a native speaker (ideally not a language teacher – they tend to over-emphasize language) to rewrite the text, correcting the language and restructuring the discourse to make it acceptable, but not changing any of the content. This reformulated text is taken into class for the students to compare with the original. They then redraft their texts in the light of the discussion.

BIBLIOGRAPHY
Allwright, J. (1988). Don't correct – Reformulate! In P. C. Robinson (ed.), *Academic Writing: Process and product*. Oxford: Modern English Publications and the British Council, 109–16.
Cohen, A. (1983). Reformulating compositions. *TESOL Newsletter*, 17/6, 1–5.
White, R. and Arndt, V. (1991). *Process Writing*. London: Longman, 128–31.
                                                                            CLF

**register**   Linguistic variation across ACCENTS and DIALECTS is described as variation 'according to the user', whereas different registers reflect variation 'according to the use' (Halliday, 1978). Many situational factors such as degree of formality, domain or professional setting determine the speaker's choice of a given register or style (Joos, 1962), e.g. formal speech, prayer, legalese, baby-talk or SIMPLIFIED CODES. Register variation is closely related to style shifting, which is described in SOCIOLINGUISTICS as a result of changes in an individual's awareness as to what and how to speak in different contexts (Labov, 1972), or as the speakers' accommodation (adjustments) of their speech to that of their audiences (Bell, 1984).

BIBLIOGRAPHY
Bell, A. (1984). Language style as audience design. *Language in Society*, 13, 145–204.
Finegan, E. and Besnier, N. (1989). *Language: Its structure and use*. San Diego: Harcourt Brace Jovanovich. [A good textbook introduction to registers, especially chapter 13.]
Halliday, M. A. K. 1978. *Language as Social Semiotic*. London: Edward Arnold, 31–5.
Joos, M. (1962). *The Five Clocks*. New York: Harcourt Brace Jovanovich. [A readable introduction to the concept of 'style'.]
Labov, W. (1972). The isolation of contextual styles. In W. Labov, *Sociolinguistics Patterns*. Philadelphia: University of Pennsylvania Press, and Oxford: Blackwell (1978), 70–109. [First published in 1966 in W. Labov, *The Social Stratification of English in New York City*. Washington, DC: Center for Applied Linguistics.]
                                                                            AJ

**regression analysis** Regression is a numerical expression of the relationship between two or more VARIABLES; it may be linear or multiple. Multiple regression may be used in LANGUAGE TESTING research to determine the relative contributions of each test in a battery to the discriminatory power of the whole test.

BIBLIOGRAPHY
Woods, A., Fletcher, P. and Hughes, A. (1986). *Statistics in Language Studies.* Cambridge: Cambridge University Press, 224–48.
SMCD

**reinforcement** in Skinnerian BEHAVIOURISM referred to the consequences of behaviour. It may be negative, lowering the frequency, or positive, raising the frequency. In audiolingual language teaching the term often referred to reward by the teacher and to the third phase (giving the correct answer) of a four-phase laboratory drill. (See AUDIOLINGUALISM.)

BIBLIOGRAPHY
McDonough, S. H. (1986). *Psychology in Foreign Language Teaching.* London: Allen and Unwin, 96–7.
SMCD

**relational syllabus** The term is associated with Crombie, who wishes her syllabus to take account of language as coherent discourse, and notes that 'discourse value' is a relational concept, largely being determined by how sentences relate to their context. She lists discourse relationships through a series of 'relational frames'.

BIBLIOGRAPHY
Crombie, W. (1985). *Discourse and Language Learning: A relational approach to syllabus design.* Oxford: Oxford University Press.
KJ

**relevance theory** According to this cognitive, pragmatic theory (see PRAGMATICS) all communication is ostensive-inferential and not code-based. The communicator's aim is to minimize the information-processing effort and maximize the contextual effects of an utterance. Inferential comprehension of the communicator's ostensive behaviour relies on deductive processing of new information presented in the context of old information. This derivation of new information gives rise to certain contextual effects in the cognitive environment of the audience. Thus, the relevance of an utterance (phenomenon) increases when its contextual effects are large, and when the effort required to process it optimally is small.

BIBLIOGRAPHY
Blakemore, D. (1992). *Understanding Utterances.* Oxford: Blackwell. [A useful introduction to pragmatics from a relevance perspective.]
Sperber, D. and Wilson, D. (1986). *Relevance: Communication and cognition.* Oxford: Blackwell. [The original formulation of relevance theory.]
AJ

**reliability** A test, a data-coding system, or an attitude measurement (*inter alia*) can be called 'reliable' if it can be trusted to 'work' (e.g. give similar outcomes) under varying conditions (with different administrators, for example). 'Reliability' is often linked to, and confused with, 'VALIDITY'. A clock may be highly reliable, in that it can be trusted to gain three minutes every day, but necessarily the time it 'tells' will be incorrect, not 'valid'.

BIBLIOGRAPHY
Brown, J. D. (1988). *Understanding Research in Second Language Learning.* Cambridge: Cambridge University Press.
Nunan, D. (1992). *Research Methods in Language Learning.* Cambridge: Cambridge University Press.
RLA

**repair** is a feature of spoken discourse (see SPOKEN AND WRITTEN DISCOURSE) in which a speaker retrospectively changes some preceding item. For example: 'That'll be forty – no, fifty – dollars.' It is the spoken equivalent of crossing out or redrafting in writing. Repair may focus on either meaning or form, and operate at any level: PHONEME, MORPHEME, word, phrase, clause, sentence or discourse. Techniques for self-repair (correction of the speaker's own utterances) differ from those of other-repair (correction of the interlocutor). Although techniques of repair are language-specific and an important part of STRATEGIC COMPETENCE, they have received little attention in language teaching.

BIBLIOGRAPHY
Levinson, S. C. (1983). *Pragmatics*. Cambridge: Cambridge University Press.
Widdowson, H. G. (1984). *Explorations in Applied Linguistics*. Oxford: Oxford University Press, 114–17.

GC


**research methodology for language learning**   The most obvious thing that needs to be said as a prelude to any discussion of method, in any field, is that how to do something must surely always depend, first and foremost, on what it is we want to do and why we want to do it. It is therefore very difficult to discuss methodology sensibly except in the context of a particular research issue. Only after a research issue has been chosen can decisions be made as to what data would be relevant to its investigation and how such data will best be obtained. This remains true whatever position is adopted with regard to the choice to be made between a theory-first or a data-first approach to research in general (see THEORY-THEN-RESEARCH/RESEARCH-THEN-THEORY). For example, if we are interested in investigating the use beginning language learners make of dictionaries, then one starting-point

would be to formulate a theoretical position on the matter – a hypothesis – which would subsequently be tested by observing actual dictionary use. (Perhaps, for example, following the work on INDIVIDUAL DIFFERENCES, we might hypothesize that different personality types could be expected to exhibit different patterns of dictionary use.) Alternatively, actual dictionary use may be observed first, with the observation itself leading to the formulation of thoughts about what might account for the different patterns of dictionary use. In either case data will be required, and the more thinking we do about the issue itself the clearer we will become about what data we are going to need. Note also that, even if the approach known generally as ACTION RESEARCH is adopted, for which a practical classroom problem is identified and tackled by trying out a possible solution in class, a decision will still have to be made as to which data are necessary to establish whether the solution has worked. For example, if an 'action research' perspective were adopted on beginners' dictionary use, the problem might be thought to be that the learners did not make good use of their dictionaries because they did not know how to; if we then chose to try out some dictionary use training materials, we would still need to decide what data would count as evidence that the training had or had not been effective.

Throughout what follows we shall use the above example of beginners' dictionary use as a possible research issue, using it to illustrate the methodological choices that have to be made.


'SAMPLING'

This introduction suggests that the issue of collecting the relevant data is the central methodological question for any research investigation. The techniques of data collection are certainly the subject of endless discussion in the field, but they can be decided in any particular case only after a prior consideration of which data are needed and where they are to come from. The question of location is at least two questions in itself. First there is the issue of the most appropriate setting for the investigation, and second the issue of precisely who will provide the data. Both of these are issues that have often been discussed under the heading of 'sampling procedures'. 'Sampling' implies an acknowledgement that it is not possible to investigate absolutely everything of interest at the same time, and therefore we have to choose a 'sample'. If we are interested in finding out how beginning language learners use dictionaries, then we have to work with a particular set of beginners, not all the beginners in the world, and with just a few dictionaries, not all the dictionaries currently available. Then a choice has to be made of the type of dictionary – monolingual or bilingual or both – and the type of learner – those who have been given specific training in dictionary use or beginners who have not been trained at all. All these choices are issues in 'sampling', and in principle they are all amenable to rational discussion. For example, most investigators would probably want to look at dictionary use involving widely available dictionaries that could be considered in some rational sense 'representative' of the total range of dictionaries currently available (e.g. selling at least as well and as widely as the others, and based on similar principles) rather than obscure and bizarre ones, because they would want to feel able to generalize their results. But such investigations have to be conducted in the 'real world', if we are interested in what learners are actually doing with their dictionaries, rather than what they might be capable of doing, and we may not be able to find learners using the dictionaries we would think most 'representative'. The investigation can then be abandoned, or we can do what most researchers interested in actual learner behaviour would probably do now and choose what is called an 'opportunistic'

sample – a sample chosen not because it is most representative but simply because it is available. However, even teachers investigating their own learners in their own classrooms, and perhaps not interested in generalizing to other people's classes, still have the problem of selecting exactly what to investigate, exactly which learners, precisely when and for how long. All of these are problems of research method, and all revolve around the issue of representation.

On the face of it, it may seem that maximum representation is the only possible respectable overall aim, however much circumstances may force us to behave opportunistically at times, and however much we may feel able to justify limiting ourselves to investigating only our own situation. But there is another point of view possible. It is at least arguable that studying unrepresentative cases can be especially illuminating. For example, to pursue again the issue of dictionary use, it is perfectly possible to imagine that it might be extremely interesting to study just one learner, if it happened to be a learner whose dictionary use behaviour was outstanding in some way. And if you were studying just one learner you might be able to go into much greater depth than if you were trying to study a 'representative' number of learners. Indeed 'depth' may be so much more important than 'breadth' for a particular study that it is more appropriate to adopt a 'case study' approach anyway, just looking at one 'case' (just one learner perhaps), whether or not there is a particularly remarkable case to investigate.

The issue of sampling thus comes down to two separate issues. First there is the issue of 'representation' versus 'illuminating uniqueness', and second there is the issue of 'breadth' versus 'depth'. Over recent years it seems to have become much more usual in our field, as we move away from experimental psychology as the source discipline to take our ideas more from general educational research, to place greater emphasis on 'illuminating uniqueness' and on 'depth'.

## ACCESS AND CONSENT

However the sample is chosen, and on whatever basis, we still face the issue of 'access' – the issue of obtaining permission from all relevant parties to conduct the investigation we have in mind. In educational settings the notion of the 'relevant parties' may extend to school authorities and to parents, not forgetting the learners themselves, whose permission cannot be taken for granted. This raises ethical problems of at least two sorts. The first of these is the intrusiveness of the research investigation itself. Some investigations may be conducted without any time being lost from useful pedagogic activities, but typically at least some time will be taken away from normal concerns. We need to be sure that this potential waste of time, for the learners, will not be so damaging that the project overall becomes unethical. The second ethical consideration concerns the notion of 'informed consent'. It is generally unethical to ask people to agree to something being done to them unless they can fully understand what is being proposed. But if learners are alerted to exactly what aspect of their behaviour is being studied, then it may be almost impossible for them to continue to behave 'normally'. In such circumstances either we can ask their permission to withhold the full 'story' until afterwards, with the consequent risk that their curiosity will still cause them to behave abnormally but in unpredictable ways, or we can play a different game altogether and call openly for their co-operation in the investigation. For example, to return to the example of dictionary use, we might ask them to keep a detailed daily diary record of their dictionary use for a week or more. This would be something quite novel for them, no doubt, and potentially very distorting (they may use their dictionaries a lot more, if they think that is what we want them to do), but it could also be very illuminating, not as direct evidence of what

they normally do (the 'observer's paradox' – the notion that being observed necessarily changes the behaviour of whatever or whoever is being observed – probably makes that an unavailable option anyway), but of what they are capable of doing, and perhaps even more important, what they are capable of saying about what they are doing, if their diary records are treated as food for thought and discussion.

## DATA SELECTION AND COLLECTION

We have at last moved on to the issue that is usually considered central to discussions of research method – the various options for the collection of data. But we still need to delay a while to consider the question of what data, the issue of the variety of types of data that anyone might wish to collect. Here it is normal to distinguish basically between data recording 'performance' of some kind (often 'behavioural' data) and data recording 'thought' rather than performance. For example, the daily diary of instances of dictionary use would be some sort of performance data, while the ensuing class discussion, if recorded for later analysis, would provide access to learners' thoughts about their use of dictionaries. Alternatively, from the beginning, the daily diary idea could also be used to ask learners to reflect daily in writing on their experiences of using dictionaries, as a way of collecting their thoughts as well as their performance.

The second basic distinction within the collection of performance data is whether or not the performance to be recorded is spontaneous (naturally occurring, which would have occurred even if no investigation was going on) or contrived in some way (occurring only because the investigation is going on). In the dictionary use study, for example, a prior decision would have to be taken as to whether to study learners' current behaviour or to try to influence them in some way (perhaps by giving them specific dictionary use training, as with a classical experimental or an action research approach, or setting aside a particular time in class for them to do tasks for which a dictionary would be available). If we do try to influence them in some way then we face the serious problem of trying to decide if we also need simultaneously to study a group of learners (a classical 'control' group, as opposed to the original 'experimental' group) who will not be subject to that influence, so that by making a direct comparison between the outcomes for the two groups we can be sure that any differences are necessarily due to whatever we did to influence the behaviour of the 'experimental' group. However obvious it must be that such comparisons between 'control' and 'experimental' groups are crucial to a rational and convincing interpretation of any sort of research study involving deliberate intervention, it is also clear that meaningful comparisons can only be made when the two groups are adequately similar in all other relevant respects except that of the experimental intervention. Unfortunately it has proved extremely difficult in practice to set up such groups in normal educational settings without simultaneously distorting the situation itself. For example, the 'control' group is most unlikely to remain entirely unaware that another group is getting some special treatment that they are not getting, and this may well cause resentment (or some other potentially distorting reaction). In addition, the need to study two groups instead of just one inevitably increases the overall research workload and that in turn risks reducing the amount of 'depth' that can be reached in the study. In consequence of such problems, it is increasingly common to see research studies that do not embark upon an intervention in the first place and look for 'illuminating insights' rather than causal relationships. Alternatively some researchers (for example, teachers doing 'action research' projects in their own classrooms) do include an intervention but omit a control group, and thus have to accept, if they are concerned to establish the value of their chosen intervention, that it may be quite impossible to determine satisfactorily if the intervention has in fact been the cause of whatever outcomes arise.

The next distinction, also within the category of performance data, is that between behaviour that is directly observed in some way (so that we can say we know it has occurred, for example, when we have a video record of a language lesson) and behaviour that is reported to have occurred. We may be interested in trying out a particular dictionary use training package and decide to record ourselves using it. We could then go back to the recording to see just what we had done with the training package. This might mean making a full transcription from the recording, so that it can be intensively studied. Twenty or so years ago recording the lesson would probably have involved an observer present in the classroom who would have kept a systematic observational record in the form of tallying the occurrence of particular teaching behaviours expected to be relevant and effective (perhaps using Flanders' (1960) list of such behaviours or the special one produced for language teaching by Moskovitz (1967)), but in recent years it has become more common for recordings to be fully transcribed and analysed in terms either of categories especially designed for the purpose of investigating a particular aspect of language teaching (for example, the COLT system (Allen et al., 1984), designed for the purpose of determining the extent to which a given example of language teaching can be said to be 'communicative') or in terms of categories derived from the data itself. Even more recently the tendency is for investigators to be interested in indepth analyses of particular episodes, with no attempt being made to reduce the data to a set of categories.

If instead of being interested in teacher behaviour we are seriously interested in how language learners use their dictionaries at home, it is unlikely that we will be able to observe them doing so, so we will need to ask them to produce something like the daily diary already discussed, as a record (in this case a 'self-report') of their behaviour. We may then worry that the picture we obtain of their behaviour is not entirely valid, and is probably somewhat distorted in the direction of 'self-flattery' (i.e. angled to help them 'feel good' in their own eyes and 'look good' in the eyes of the researcher). An alternative that is less open to such distortion would be to ask learners to report not by diary entries but by actually making a tape-recording of their thinking (producing a so-called 'think-aloud protocol'; see Cohen and Hosenfeld, 1981) while they are doing a task involving dictionary use. Perhaps they could do this in class if it is too much to ask of them at home, or in a special session at school. If we are interested in how useful their dictionary use is practically, we may wish to extend the study further by obtaining data from the learners that will help us decide if they have learned anything. Now we are in the realm of performance data that constitute a measure of learning. We might be able to devise some sort of test that will give us an idea of how well they understand the abbreviations that a dictionary uses, for example. If the test itself was good enough (see VALIDITY) then it could be very useful in helping us interpret any other data we get from the learners. Quite recently, increased interest has been shown among testing researchers in how learners take tests. This sort of research could obviously help people who wish to train learners to be more efficient test-takers, but typically researchers who study test-taking are interested in the area because of the light it could shed on issues of test design and interpretation.

When we turn to the other sort of data, data consisting of 'thoughts', once again we need to take account of some fundamental distinctions. First there is the distinction between thoughts directly related to a particular performance and thoughts not so related. For example, in their daily diaries of their use of dictionaries learners could be asked to make specific comments (their evaluations of usefulness, perhaps) on specific diary-using events they have just experienced, or they could be asked to reflect in general terms on their use of resource materials, what they find good about the dictionaries, what they find unhelpful and so on.

The second major distinction in this area concerns timing. If we are trying to get people's reactions to particular events in their lives, are we concerned to get their thoughts immediately after the events themselves, before anything else has happened to cloud the picture, or can we afford to wait for what may become a mature, considered opinion? A related issue is whether or not we feel a need to stimulate their recall of events in their lives. If we have video-recorded a lesson and want to know what the learners think of it, then it might be useful to play at least part of the lesson back to them, as a way of reminding them of what happened, especially if they have lived through several more lessons since the one that was recorded. Of course, it may be useful to play back a recording just to stimulate general discussion. A third distinction is to be made between data obtained privately and data obtained publicly. Taking the diary study of dictionary use again, the diary itself would be produced in private, presumably, and could therefore be held to represent each learner's private opinions, while a class discussion of the learners' thoughts would be a public occasion, and the learners would then be potentially influenced by what they heard each other say.

A fourth distinction concerns whether 'thought' data are obtained orally or on paper. Apart from the class discussion possibility already mentioned, an investigator might choose to interview learners to find out what they can say about their experiences of using dictionaries. The interview could be based on just a few open-ended questions, perhaps leading to quite general discussion, or it could follow a very strict schedule of previously worked-out questions, with the interviewer recording each answer on spaces provided on the sheet of questions. In such a case the data collection procedure would constitute an orally administered questionnaire. In the former case it might be necessary to record the interview on audio tape, for later analysis, while in the latter case the written record might suffice as the data to be analysed. The reason for administering a questionnaire orally might be that the learners might need help in understanding the questions, especially if the questions are presented in the target language rather than in a language they already know well and can handle confidently. The investigator could try to make sure not only that the questions are fully understood but also that they are understood in the same way by all the respondents. By contrast, a written questionnaire answered in respondents' own time, though much cheaper to administer (in terms of the investigator's time) has to aim at being entirely self-explanatory. Since this is asking too much of even the most accomplished questionnaire designer, it is becoming increasingly normal for investigators to follow up such written questionnaires by interviewing at least a few of the respondents, to find out first if and second how they have understood the questions.

An alternative approach to sets of previously devised questions for oral data collection is the 'repertory grid' technique. This is a procedure that is increasingly used in our field for working with teachers as well as with learners. Space prohibits all but the briefest description here (see Bannister and Fransella, 1986), but the technique typically involves the interviewee in making comparisons. For example, if our 'dictionary use' learners had three different dictionaries available to them the interviewee might ask them to pick any one and say how it differs from the other two. The sort of response the

learner gives would be a guide to the way the learner thinks about such things. A whole succession of such comparisons could then provide a wealth of information about the learners' criteria for evaluating the dictionaries in question.

## ANALYSING AND INTERPRETING THE DATA

Once we have the data we have to find a way of analysing and then interpreting them. To a large extent that will depend upon the nature of the data, of course, as well as upon the questions we wish the data to answer (or at least to throw light on). If our questions amount to an attempt to establish proof of a hypothetical cause for something (for example, if we wish to prove that using a dictionary in one way will cause greater success than using it in some other way) we will need a very different sort of analysis from what would be appropriate for other purposes. It is probably true to say that relatively few people in our field still believe that it makes sense to attempt to try to establish definitive causes in educational research work in the classroom, if only because it is so very difficult to conduct the research project in such a watertight way that a causal interpretation is legitimate. A watertight research design would require control of all the relevant factors, but educational settings are notoriously complex in terms of the number of factors likely to influence outcomes, and there are not many factors amenable to control in a way that leaves the project 'lifelike'. For example, some methodological comparison experiments in the 1960s (see Clark, 1969, and METHOD COMPARISONS) were held to be uninterpretable because of the potential influence of the teachers involved, so some experimenters in Sweden (see Lindblad, 1969) put all the teaching materials on audio tape to avoid the possible influence of different teachers. But then, of course, all they could discover was what happened when you eliminated the teacher in this way, so relatively little could be learned about teaching and learning under 'normal' circumstances (i.e. with a teacher doing his or her best to help learners).

## RESEARCH ON TEACHING AND LEARNING

The discussion above has not made any real attempt to distinguish between research on language learning and research on language teaching. That has been deliberate, given that the same principles apply in the two cases, but there are of course significant differences between the two enterprises. First of all, research on language learning does not necessarily have to concern itself with educational matters. There is much that we do not know about how learners learn languages when they are not being explicitly taught them. It is imaginable that research on such learners, uncomplicated by the efforts of teachers to help them, could throw important light on underlying principles of language learning that could be of use to people trying to understand and promote classroom language learning. In any case, it could be of interest in its own right, regardless of its educational implications. Similarly, research on language teaching could be of interest, quite independently of the effect of teaching on learning. In recent years, in fact, research on language teaching has increasingly moved away from the idea of trying to find out what teaching behaviours make teaching successful towards trying to find out what it is that teachers know, and can tell us, about what it means to be a language teacher. Research on teacher thinking has largely taken over from research on teacher effectiveness. Research on learner thinking is still relatively rare, but it does seem increasingly unlikely that we are going to understand very much about teaching if we fail to try to understand learning at the same time. Finally, both research on teaching and research on learning have become accepted in recent years as an integral part of work on teacher development (see TEACHER EDUCATION), with the implication that such research can most appropriately be conduced by teachers in their own classrooms. 'Action research' has been generally accepted as the most appropriate model for this, but it is at least arguable (see Allwright and Lenzuen, 1997) that action research's use of standard academic research methodological procedures is not optimal (if only because these are so demanding that they risk early 'burn-out'), and that teacher-based research will need to develop its own methodological practices and ultimately its own position on what constitutes an appropriate notion of research itself. (See also CLASSROOM OBSERVATION, CLASSROOM STUDIES IN SLA, STATISTICS IN APPLIED LINGUISTICS RESEARCH.)

BIBLIOGRAPHY
Allen, J. P. B., Fröhich, M. and Spada, N. (1984). The communicative orientation of language teaching. In J. Handscombe, R. A. Orem and B. P. Taylor (eds), *On TESOL '83. The Question of Control*. Washington, DC: TESOL, 231–52.
Allwright, D. and Lenzuen, R. (1997). Exploratory practice: work at the Cultura Inglesa, Rio de Janeiro, Brazil. *Language Teaching Research*, 1/1, 73–9.
Bannister, D. and Fransella, F. (1986). *Inquiring Man: The psychology of personal constructs*. 3rd edn. London: Routledge.
Clark, J. L. D. (1969). The Pennsylvania Project and the 'Audio-Lingual vs Traditional' question. *Modern Language Journal*, 53, 388–96.
Cohen, A. D. and Hosenfeld, C. (1981). Some uses of mentalistic data in second language research. *Language Learning*, 31, 285–313.
Flanders, N. A. (1960). *Interaction Analysis in the Classroom: A manual for observers*. Ann Arbor: University of Michigan Press.
Lindblad, T. (1969). *Implicit and Explicit: An experiment in applied psycholinguistics*. GUME Project 1, Report 11. Gothenburg.
Moskovitz, G. (1967). The Flint system: an observational tool for the foreign language classroom. In A. Simon and E. G. Boyer (1967). *Mirrors for Behavior: An anthology of*

*classroom observation instruments*. Philadelphia: Research for Better Schools and Center for the Study of Teaching, Temple University.

RLA

**role play and simulation** are DRAMA activities that range from guided conversations, with participants playing themselves in specified situations, to simulated scenarios, with adopted roles as part of a complex task. Role plays can be relatively simple and short (e.g. 'You are in a restaurant. Order a drink from the waiter.'). A simulation (e.g. the production of a plan for a new town) requires the creation of a complete world, with background information and more detailed role cards. These activities promote communicative GROUP WORK/PAIR WORK, providing learners with a broad range of linguistic and social experiences.

BIBLIOGRAPHY
Jones, K. (1982). *Simulations in Language Teaching*. Cambridge: Cambridge University Press.
Ladousse, G. P. (1987). *Role Play*. Oxford: Oxford University Press.
Sturtridge, G. (1981). Role-play and simulations. In K. Johnson and K. Morrow (eds), *Communication in the Classroom*. Harlow: Longman, 126–30.

CLF

**RP**   see RECEIVED PRONUNCIATION.

# S

**St-Cloud** *La méthode audio-visuelle structuro-globale de Saint-Cloud* was developed in the 1950s principally by Petar Guberina and Paul Rivenc. From it arose the courses *Voix et Images de France* and *Bonjour Line*. The principles were: speech is prime; meaning is conveyed through pictures. Lessons consisted of sketches, grammatical exercises and phonetic exercises. See AUDIOVISUALISM.

BIBLIOGRAPHY
Guberina, P. (1964). The audio-visual global and structural method. In B. Libbish (ed.), *Advances in the Teaching of Modern Languages*. Vol. 1. Oxford: Pergamon, 1–17.

JTR

**Sapir–Whorf hypothesis** The work of the American anthropological linguists Edward Sapir and Benjamin Lee Whorf on the relation between language, thought and culture is commonly compressed into the Sapir–Whorf hypothesis. It consists of two interrelated parts: 'linguistic relativity' which claims that languages which differ radically in their vocabulary and structure express different cultural meanings, and 'linguistic determinism' which, in its 'strong' version, assumes that patterns of thought and perceptions of reality are determined by one's native language. The basis for the hypothesis had been laid by Franz Boas, who observed that languages classify experience differently and beyond the speakers' awareness. His widely misquoted example concerns the four Eskimo words related to 'snow'.

BIBLIOGRAPHY
Carroll, J. B. (ed.) (1956). *Language, Thought, and Reality: Selected writings of Benjamin Lee Whorf*. Cambridge, MA: MIT Press.
Lucy, J. A. (1992). *Language Diversity and Thought: A reformulation of the linguistic relativity hypothesis*. Cambridge: Cambridge University Press. [An excellent presentation of the work by Boas, Sapir and Whorf.]

AJ

**scanning** A specialized type of reading which involves rapidly searching a text either 'for a specific piece of information or to get an impression of whether the text is suitable for a given purpose' (Nuttall, 1982: 34). One of Nuttall's examples of a scanning question is 'Look at page 00 and find out when Shakespeare died.' She emphasizes the speed element in scanning exercises, suggesting they may sometimes be conducted as races. Williams (1984) shows how scanning text (e.g. a travel agent's brochure) can lead to INFORMATION TRANSFER and role play (see ROLE PLAY AND SIMULATION). See also SKIMMING.

BIBLIOGRAPHY
Nuttall, C. (1982). *Teaching Reading Skills in a Foreign Language*. London: Heinemann.
Williams, E. (1984). *Reading in the Language Classroom*. Basingstoke: Macmillan.

KJ

**schema theory** A schema (plural, schemata) is a mental framework based on past experience developed as a means of accommodating new facts, and hence making sense of them. Schiffrin (1994: 103–4) describes one version of schema theory (Erving Goffman's frame analysis) as 'a view of the means by which ... presuppositions are externally constructed and impose external constraints on the ways in which we understand messages'.

Schema theory was first developed by Bartlett (1932), following the work of the neurologist Henry Head. As well as developing the concept in relation to the description of skilled actions (like strokes in tennis), Bartlett also applied the theory to story recall. He noted that when an American Indian story was told to British subjects, they changed many of the details (when retelling it) to fit in with their mental framework, omitting unfamiliar details and adding familiar ones. Bartlett's work remained largely forgotten under BEHAVIOURISM, but was revived in the 1970s within the field of artificial intelligence by those who sought to develop systems whereby computers might represent the kinds of knowledge humans brought with them to newly encountered situations, as a step towards enabling computers to comprehend in the same way that humans do.

Various models of schema theory have been developed, each bringing its own terminology. Minsky (1975) uses the term *frame* to describe schemata dealing particularly with stereotypical situations; the use of the term in relation to linguistics is essentially the same – see PRODUCTION PROCESSES for an example of the term 'syntactic frame'. Schank and Abelson (1977) use the term *script* in a similar way, to describe event sequences, while Sandford and Garrod's (1981) preferred term is *scenario*. Schema theory has played a central part in the development of story grammars (in, for example, Mandler, 1984).

Schank and Abelson's (1977) celebrated and often quoted example of a script relates to the restaurant setting. We all have knowledge – a script – of the events that occur (in our own culture) in a restaurant, of the order in which they occur, and of how we are expected to behave as these events unfold. Our script might have us entering the restaurant, depositing our coats, sitting down, being brought the menu, summoning the waiter when we are ready to order and so on.

Schemata (scripts, frames, scenarios) play an important role in comprehension. When a restaurant scene is mentioned in a reading text, for example, the reader's restaurant script will be activated in memory as a natural part of the comprehension process (see TOP-DOWN PROCESSING). This essential role for schemata in comprehension is in itself important. Learners of a second language need practice in activating schemata in comprehension, otherwise they are likely to engage in BOTTOM-UP PROCESSING only, which will mar their ability to comprehend speedily and naturally. Further, it is natural that many of the restaurant script details will not be explicitly stated in the text, but will form part of the presuppositions the reader is expected to bring to that text. If the reader does not possess the appropriate presuppositions, then parts of the text are likely to be incomprehensible; a sentence like 'I caught the waiter's eye and finally got the menu,' for example; just the sort of sentence that a computer would have difficulty interpreting unless it was provided with relevant schemata. There is experimental evidence to show that comprehension and recall are poor if the reader or listener cannot bring appropriate schemata to bear to aid understanding (Bartlett's British subjects, for example, had poor recall of the Indian stories). Restaurant scripts will of course differ in details from culture to culture; the implication is that learners of a second language need to be equipped with appropriate schemata if they are to comprehend properly. Cultural knowledge of this sort may need to be taught.

For accessible general discussion of schema theory, see Hampson and Morris (1996); for discussion within the field of discourse analysis, see Brown and Yule (1983).

BIBLIOGRAPHY
Bartlett, F. C. (1932). *Remembering*. Cambridge: Cambridge University Press.
Brown, G. and Yule, G. (1983). *Discourse Analysis*. Cambridge: Cambridge University Press.
Hampson, P. J. and Morris, P. E. (1996). *Understanding Cognition*. Oxford: Blackwell.
Mandler, J. M. (1984). *Stories, Scripts, and Scenes: Aspects of schema theory*. Hillsdale, NJ: Erlbaum.
Minsky, M. (1975). A framework for representing knowledge. In P. H. Winston (ed.), *The Psychology of Computer Vision*. New York: McGraw-Hill.
Sandford, A. J. and Garrod, S. C. (1981). *Understanding Written Language*. Chichester: John Wiley.
Schank, R. C. and Abelson, R. (1977). *Scripts, Plans, Goals and Understanding*. Hillsdale, NJ: Erlbaum.
Schiffrin, D. (1994). *Approaches to Discourse*. Oxford: Blackwell.

KJ

**selection of units of organization in syllabus design**   The selection of a unit of organization is determined by a number of different variables, including contextual considerations, learner characteristics, the specification of instructional goals, the types of syllabus available in principle and the syllabus designer's views on language and learning. Dubin and Olshtain (1986: 46) express it thus: 'Decisions relating to the organization of course content, the presentation of new topics, and their sequence and scope of treatment, all depend on the underlying educational and linguistic assumptions as well as on our concurrent understanding of the learning process.' Stern's (1983) model covers views of (a) the nature of language, (b) learners and learning, (c) the teacher and (d) the whole environment in which learning takes place.

SYLLABUS PLANNING

Before a syllabus can be designed in detail, there needs to be a clear specification of overall aims and objectives of the language programme, whether in terms of nation-wide educational planning or, at the other end of the spectrum, a short intensive course. The specification itself, and the possibilities for implementation, will be related to the educational setting and to the characteristics of the target learners (McDonough and Shaw, 1993: ch. 1). The former includes such factors as the role of English in the local environment, teachers' status and training, resources and time available, and the numbers to be taught. The latter covers age, proficiency, motivation, needs, L1 and so on. Clearly, the appropriate choice of any particular syllabus type will need to be a dependent one, filtered through these kinds of variables, which Dubin and Olshtain (1986) refer to globally as the 'societal setting'.

APPROACHES TO SYLLABUS DESIGN

Once goals have been set and factors of implementation taken into consideration, it is then in principle possible to establish relevant organizational criteria for syllabus design. In other words, operational decisions about syllabus type will ideally match context and objectives. Taking 'syllabus' to refer simply to the organizing principle(s) for the arrangement of learning content, then there are a number of possibilities from which a choice may be made for any specific situation: suitable criteria will clearly differ as well according to whether the language programme is designed (for example) for general school use, adults learning for academic purposes, professional people, tourist and social purposes, immediate 'survival' use and so on.

Richards and Rodgers (1986) make a well-known and useful hierarchical distinction for course planning between 'APPROACH', 'design' and 'procedure'. Briefly, 'approach' is concerned with underlying attitudes to language and learning that form the basis for materials and methodological design and hence for classroom techniques and procedures. For current purposes we are particularly interested in the 'approach', which will initially be operationalized into the overall organizing principle for a particular syllabus. Thus, to take an obvious example, a view of language as a set of discrete grammatical items will be converted into the familiar structural syllabus. There is space here to list only the main organizational criteria for syllabus design, and a fuller discussion will be found in entries under the headwords indicated here.

(1) *Language structure*: traditionally an ordered list of units of learning arranged according to grammatical items (see STRUCTURAL SYLLABUS).

(2) *Functions* and *notions* (see NOTIONAL/FUNCTIONAL SYLLABUSES and COMMUNICATIVE METHODOLOGY). These refer to two rather different parameters, *functions* to interpersonal and communicative use and *notions* to more general and abstract semantic categories, but they are usually grouped together. Such 'communicative' principles have an important implication for the possibility of learning language at a level beyond that of the sentence (see also DISCOURSE ANALYSIS and COHESION).

(3) *Situations*, using everyday settings (e.g. at a hotel, at the airport, shopping and so on) as a context for language practice (see SITUATIONAL SYLLABUS).

(4) *Skills*, concerned with the processes used by language learners as readers, listeners, speakers and writers (see FOUR SKILLS, and separate entries for individual skills).

(5) *Topics*, simply themes on which to hang language and skills practice.

(See Dubin and Olshtain, 1986; McDonough and Shaw, 1993; Richards and Rodgers, 1986.)

Over the last three decades or so, three of these organizational criteria – structures, functions and notions, and skills – have had primacy, and have developed chronologically from language analysis based on sentence structure, then to a communicative perspective, with a focus on the learner as language processor gaining particular prominence during the 1980s. Situations and topics are less likely to be defining features in themselves and tend to be vehicles for language content, whether structurally or functionally organized. There have also been a number of attempts to classify the main criteria, most notably by Wilkins (1976), into synthetic (discrete-item) and analytic syllabuses (oriented to language behaviour and overall communicative purpose) (see ANALYTIC/SYNTHETIC). A number of other organizing principles are discussed elsewhere (see LEXICAL SYLLABUS, PROCEDURAL SYLLABUS, TASK–BASED SYLLABUS).

## IMPLEMENTING APPROACHES TO SYLLABUS DESIGN

Assuming that a decision has been made as to the most appropriate organizational criteria for a particular educational context, there still remain a number of other important factors affecting implementation. The main ones are, first, the different possibilities for linking one or more syllabus design principles. Few syllabuses are, in Johnson's (1982) terms, *uni-dimensional*: they are much more likely to have at least two units of organization (structure and topic, say, or skill and function), and probably more, in which case we are concerned with a multidimensional syllabus (see MULTI-DIMENSIONAL SYLLABUSES). The latter is increasingly finding expression in current published materials under the heading of the 'multi-syllabus'. Second, a list of items to be included in a syllabus is not synonymous with the syllabus *per se*: a set of structures, or topics, or functions, is in itself merely a SYLLABUS INVENTORY which cannot be used directly in the classroom. Third, implementation must be concerned with decisions about sequencing and grading (linear, cyclical or modular, for instance) (see GRADING/SEQUENCING), selection of learning content, STAGING, and methods of presentation and practice, in other words, with the organization of inventory items into teachable and learnable units.

BIBLIOGRAPHY
Dubin, F. and Olshtain, E. (1986). *Course Design*. Cambridge: Cambridge University Press.
Johnson, K. (1982). Selecting units of organization for a semantic syllabus. In K. Johnson, *Communicative Syllabus Design and Methodology*. Oxford and New York: Pergamon, 55–69.*
McDonough, J. and Shaw, C. (1993). *Materials and Methods in ELT*. Oxford: Blackwell.
Richards, J. C. and Rodgers, T. S. (1986). *Approaches and Methods in Language Teaching*. Cambridge: Cambridge University Press.
Stern, H. H. (1983). *Fundamental Concepts of Language Teaching*. Oxford: Oxford University Press.
Wilkins, D. (1976). *Notional Syllabuses*. London: Oxford University Press.

JMCD

**semantic differential**   A technique for measuring attitudes, emotional reactions to words or concepts. The item to be rated is given, together with a 'bi-polar adjective scale' – a series of (say, twenty) pairs of adjectives with opposite meanings. Subjects state how they rate the item in relation to the adjectives. For example:

countryside

exciting:___ : :___ : :___ : :___ : :___ : :___:boring

The technique was developed by Osgood and others (1957) as a means of quantifying representations of meaning. A common use in applied linguistics is for the measurement of attitudes towards (for example) a particular second language, or its speakers.

BIBLIOGRAPHY
Osgood, C. E., Suci, G. J. and Tannenbaum, P. H. (1957). *The Measurement of Meaning*. Urbana: University of Illinois Press.

KJ

**semantico-grammatical categories**
One of three category types in Wilkins's notional syllabus. Commonly called 'notions' (though not by Wilkins), these categories express concepts. Examples from Wilkins (1976) are *duration* and *frequency*. The concepts are semantic, but are called 'grammatical' because in many languages they are closely associated with grammatical categories. (See also NOTIONAL/FUNCTIONAL SYLLABUSES.)

BIBLIOGRAPHY
Wilkins, D. A. (1973). An investigation into the linguistic and situational common core in a unit/credit system. In J. L. M. Trim, R. Richterich, J. A. van Ek and D. A. Wilkins, *Systems Development in Adult Language Learning*. Oxford: Pergamon Institute of English, 129–46.
——(1976). *Notional syllabuses*. Oxford: Oxford University Press.

KJ

**semantics** is the study of meaning in language. Although it can be conceived as concerned with meaning in general, it is often confined to those aspects which are relatively stable and context-free, in contrast to PRAGMATICS, which is concerned with meaning variation with context. Semantics is sometimes described as concerned with the relation of linguistic forms to states of the world; more sensibly, it may be seen as concerned with the relation of linguistic forms to non-linguistic concepts and mental representations, as well as with relationships of meaning between linguistic forms, such as synonymy, antonymy and hyponymy. Semantic theories have influenced approaches to describing word meaning, and are thus particularly relevant to lexicography and VOCABULARY TEACHING. See also LEXICAL SYLLABUS, LEXIS.

BIBLIOGRAPHY
Cruse, D. A. (1986). *Lexical Semantics*. Cambridge: Cambridge University Press.

Leech, G. N. (1981). *Semantics.* 2nd edn. Harmondsworth: Penguin Books.*

Lyons, J. (1977). *Semantics.* 2 vols. Cambridge: Cambridge University Press.

McCarthy, M. (1990). *Vocabulary.* Oxford: Oxford University Press.

GC

**semilingualism** The limited linguistic and/or cognitive competence of minority children from low socio-economic backgrounds in majority educational systems. In view of current studies on BILINGUALISM and CODE-SWITCHING, Martin-Jones and Romaine (1986) criticize this concept and the arguments behind it as unsound and promoting the deficit view of minority children's language.

BIBLIOGRAPHY
Martin-Jones, M. and Romaine, S. (1986). Semi-lingualism: a half-baked theory of communicative competence. *Applied Linguistics,* 7/1, 26–38.

Skutnab-Kangas, T. (1984). *Bilingualism or not: The education of minorities.* Clevedon: Multilingual Matters.

AJ

**semiotics** (or semiology) is the theory and study of signs. Language is the most important and complex sign system; others are traffic signals, clothing (in its social rather than functional aspect), myths. Saussure suggested that linguistic signs are composed of a sound image (the signifier) and a concept (the signified) and that the relationship between the two is usually arbitrary and conventional. Linguistic signs are discrete rather than graded; they mean by virtue of their difference from other signs; and they combine with other signs according to the rules of SYNTAX to create complex meanings.

BIBLIOGRAPHY
Cook, G. (1992). *The Discourse of Advertising.* London: Routledge. [Chapter 4.]

Lyons, J. (1977). *Semantics.* 2 vols. Cambridge: Cambridge University Press. [Chapter 3.]

Saussure, F. de (1974). *Course in General Linguistics,* trans W. Baskin. London: Fontana. [Original work first published in 1915.]

GC

**sentence pattern** The term typically used in a grammatical analysis of sentence STRUCTURE highlighting the linear arrangement of the elements S(ubject), V(erb) (= Predicator), O(bject), C(omplement) and A(dverbial). Languages are classified according to their basic sentence pattern or word order. For example, English is an SVO language, Welsh is VSO, Turkish is SOV and Malagasy is VOS. (See also TYPOLOGY.)

BIBLIOGRAPHY
Fromkin, V. and Rodman, R. (1993). *An Introduction to Language.* 5th edn. Fort Worth, TX: Harcourt Brace Jovanovich. [Particularly chapter 3.]

Huddleston, R. (1988). *English Grammar: An outline.* Cambridge: Cambridge University Press. [Particularly chapter 4.]

EJ

**shaping** A behaviourist concept, associated with B. F. Skinner. Complex behaviours are divided up into smaller parts, each of which is practised thoroughly. Skinner 'shaped' complex action sequences, like teaching pigeons to play table tennis. AUDIO-LINGUALISM, through the structural syllabus, shaped language by dividing it into structural patterns and drilling each thoroughly.

BIBLIOGRAPHY
McDonough, S. H. (1981). *Psychology in Foreign Language Teaching* London: Allen and Unwin.

KJ

**silence** The use of silence in communication is, as in the case of speech, rule-governed, and it is also variable and culture-specific. Apart from its common function to signal lack of communication, silence is used to express or maintain certain types of inter-personal relations (e.g. respect, submission, defiance), manifest emotions (e.g. anger, sympathy) and express propositional meanings (e.g. to refuse an invitation). The facilitative role of silence in the learning/teaching process is associated with allowing students time to reflect on the newly learned material (the silent period) and with giving them an 'in' into classroom interaction (wait-time). (See MONITOR MODEL, SILENT WAY.)

BIBLIOGRAPHY
Jaworski, A. (1993). *The Power of Silence: Social and pragmatic perspectives*. Newbury Park, CA: Sage.
Jaworski, A. (ed.) (1997). *Silence: Interdisciplinary perspectives*. Berlin: Mouton, de Gruyter.
Tannen, D. and Saville-Troike, M. (eds) (1985). *Perspectives on Silence*, Norwood, NJ: Ablex.

AJ

**silent way**   This is a cognitive method pioneered by Gattegno, originally for teaching mathematics, but later adapted for foreign languages to impart mastery over basic structures. It incorporates an element of 'If others can do it, so can I.' Learners sit in a circle, and lessons commence with the teacher uttering a phrase once only. The teacher locates a perfect mimic, who is then used as a model. Errors are indicated silently, often using a signalling system with the fingers. 'Fidels' are used to show sound-spelling, and Cuisenaire rods to illustrate syntactic relationships. Though silent, the teacher directs and controls strictly. (See also SILENCE and HUMANISTIC APPROACHES.)

BIBLIOGRAPHY
Gattegno, C. (1963). *Teaching Foreign Languages in Schools the Silent Way*. New York: Educational Solutions.

JTR

**simplified codes**   All speech communities have in their repertoires special REGISTERS used to address small children, foreigners, mentally handicapped people, hard of hearing people and anyone else who is believed to have problems with processing 'normal' speech. Such simplified codes as 'baby talk' (BT), 'foreigner talk' (FT) and so on share many structural affinities with pidgin (see PIDGINS AND CREOLES) languages. Simplified codes have been studied in SLA due to their similarities with INTERLANGUAGE (IL). Applied linguists have also debated whether simplification of learner input facilitates L2 acquisition.

PIDGINS, BABY TALK AND
FOREIGNER TALK

There are three basic processes which occur in simplified registers: structural simplification (see below), clarification of presentation (e.g. slow, loud, clear articulation, avoidance of vowel reduction, frequent repetition of words and so on), and expression of affect (e.g. the use of diminutives in speech to children, sound symbolism, mimicking a foreign accent and so on). The formal properties of pidgins, BT and FT (and other simplified codes which will not be dealt with here, except IL) show striking similarities.

*Pidgins*   The grammar of pidgin languages is 'shallow', for example, with no syntactic marking of subordination (Romaine, 1994: 174). Pidgin MORPHOLOGY is greatly simplified or regularized in that pidgins discard grammatical redundancy. The typical features of grammars of pidgin languages are:

(1) Lack of the copula (verb 'to be'), e.g. *De pikni sik* (Jamaican Creole English) 'The child is sick.'
(2) Use of the same verb to indicate possession and existence, e.g. *Get wan uman we get gyal pikni* (Guyanese Creole English) 'There is a woman who has a daughter.'
(3) Pre-verbal negation by particle 'no', e.g. *Hongri man no de set dan won ples* (Kru Pidgin English) 'A hungry man doesn't sit down in one place' (adapted from Romaine, 1994: 173–4).

(4)  Loss of subject–verb agreement marking.
(5)  Simplification of verbal inflection, e.g. loss of the third person singular -s.
(6)  Simplification of plurality marking, e.g.:

| English: | the two big newspapers |
| | one man/person |
| | ten men/people |
| | lots of men have no wives |
| Neomelanesian: | tupela bikpela pepa |
| | wanpela man |
| | tenpela man |
| | plenti man i no get meri |
| Cameroon pidgin: | di tu big pepa |
| | wan man |
| | ten man |
| | plenti man no get woman |

Simplification of pidgins extends to their lexicons. For example, speakers of ordinary languages have approximately 25–30,000 words. Speakers of Neomelanesian use approximately 1500 lexical items. Many lexical processes which occur in pidgin languages 'make up' for this loss of vocabulary. Here are some examples:

(1)  Expansion of meaning: words are combined into phrases and circumlocutions, e.g. *singsing long taim maus i pas* (to sing when the mouth is closed) 'to hum'.
(2)  Extension of meaning to cover larger semantic domains, e.g.:

| | Standard Fijian | Pidgin Fijian |
|---|---|---|
| case, box, basket | kato | kato |
| fishing basket | noke | kato |
| coconut leaf basket | su | kato |
| woven leaf tray | i lalakai | kato |

(3)  Reduplication: *ile* 'hilly', *ileile* 'choppy sea'; *drai* 'dry', *draidrai* 'unpalatable' (food) (Pitcairnese).
(4)  Reduction of homophony: *san* 'sun', *sansan* 'sand'; *was* 'wash', *waswas* 'wasp' (Krio, Sierra Leone).
(5)  Intensification, continuity, repetition: *smal* 'small', *smalsmal* 'very small'; Neomelanesian *tok* 'talk', *toktok* 'chatter' (Jamaican Creole).
(6)  Diagrammatic iconic relations:

| Tok Pisin | English |
|---|---|
| gras | grass |
| mausgras | moustache |
| gras bilong fes | beard |
| gras bilong hed | hair |
| gras bilong pisin | feather |
| gras antap long ai | eyebrow |
| gras nogut | weed |
| han | hand/arm |
| han bilong diwai | branch of a tree |
| han bilong pisin | wing of a bird |

(Unless otherwise stated, all the above examples have been adapted from Romaine, 1977.)

*Baby talk*  Baby talk displays similar formal properties across different languages, involving simplification and regularization of the more complex forms used in adult grammar and pronunciation. For example, at the phonological level, the structure of words is reduced to a few limited favourite shapes ('canonical forms'), e.g. *rabbit* → *wabbit*. Common simplifications of BT grammar include:

(1)  reduction of inflections, e.g. *Daddy go*.
(2)  omission of the copula, e.g. *the baby is hungry* → *baby hungry*.
(3)  use of all purpose auxiliaries like 'go' and 'make', e.g. *go sleepy-bye, make peepee*.
(4)  replacement of first and second person pronouns by other personal forms, e.g. *Baby is finished? Mummy is coming*.

The greatest simplification of BT is in the lexicon, especially with reference to terms for members of the immediate and extended family, the body, qualities of events and the immediate environment of the child (e.g. fire = hot = burn), animals (e.g. widespread reference to animals through onomatopoeia) and games (particularly identification of games played by infants in the pre-verbal stage) (Ferguson, 1977).

*Foreigner talk*  FT is characterized by exaggerated, slow and loud pronunciation, as well as frequent pauses and repetition. At the structural level, the characteristic features of FT include omissions, expansions, replacements and rearrangements (Ferguson, 1975):

(1)  omission, e.g.:
● the definite article 'the'.
● copula (the verb 'to be').

- coordinating and subordinating conjunctions.
- all inflectional suffixes (plural markers, possessive markers, third person singular '-s', etc.), internal stem changes and auxiliaries which signal case, person, tense and number in nouns and verbs, e.g. *Do you understand?* → *You understand?*
- subject pronoun.

(2) expansion, e.g.:
- reduplication, e.g. *He's working with me. He with me. He work with me.*
- addition of subject 'you' to imperatives, e.g. *You come and see me tomorrow.*
- use of tags, e.g. *yes? ok? see? no? is it right?*

(3) replacements and rearrangements, e.g.:
- replace all negative constructions by a 'no' preceding the negated item.
- replacement of negated items by non-negative equivalents e.g. *don't forget* → *remember, ok?*
- analytic paraphrase: *my/your brother* → *brother (to) me/you.*
- when not omitted (see above), the nominative subject pronoun 'I,' 'he,' 'she,' etc. replaced by 'me,' 'him,' 'that woman,' etc.

Apart from these grammatical properties, FT is also characterized by frequent lexical substitution. Some typically replaced words and their substitutes are:

> understand → savvy
> tomorrow → next day
> always → all (the) time
> father → papa
> gun → bang-bang

## SIMPLIFICATION AND PIDGINIZATION OF LEARNER TALK

Simplification and TRANSFER are the main features of learner talk described by Nemser (1974 [1971]) as *approximative system*. For example, the learner may omit the plural marker in numeral phrases such as *three boy*, which is also typical of the pidginization

processes, BT and FT. In this example, simplification of the target language is a learner strategy employed to make the learning and speaking of the target language easier. Other instances of simplification, e.g. copula deletion as in *they in bed* can even become *fossilized* 'errors', i.e. appear in the learner stable approximative system (or *IL*) (Richards, 1974 [1972]).

Structural simplification of IL and pidgin languages in both cases results from the situation of language contact. Richards (1974 [1972]) draws a close analogy between pidgin languages and second language acquisition. He states that each code can be described 'as an IL arising as a medium of communication between speakers of different languages, characterized by grammatical structure and lexical content originating in differing sources, by unintelligibility to speakers of the source languages and by stability' (Richards, 1974: 77; see also Schumann, 1982).

A comparative study of pidgin languages and the IL of a Spanish learner of English (Alberto) led Schumann (1978) to the conclusion that Alberto's speech was in fact a pidginized version of English. The simplified, pidgin-like features of Alberto's English included:

(1) General pre-verbal negators: 'no' and 'don't'.
(2) Lack of question inversion (rigid word order).
(3) Lack of auxiliaries.
(4) No inflection for the possessive case.
(5) Unmarked (uninflected) forms of the verb.

(Schumann, 1978, quoted in McLaughlin, 1987: 12).

Based on Schumann's work on Alberto's English IL, and on Bickerton's (1977) research on Hawaiian Pidgin English, Andersen (1981) arrived at the following similarities between both types of linguistic codes (although it is worth mentioning that Bickerton did not conceptualize pidginization as 'simplification' but more as 'regularization' of linguistic structure):

(1) Reliance on word order rather than inflections for expressing grammatical relations.

(2) Native-language transfer in word order as well as use of English word order.

(3) Sporadic merging of pre-verbal markers which come from lexical verbs promoted to auxiliary status.

(4) A basic pidgin negation.

(5) Lack of inversion in questions.

(6) Preponderance of uninflected verb forms.

(Andersen, 1981, quoted in McLaughlin, 1987: 117).

As has been stated above, IL simplifications may become fossilized. Their occurrence and persistence are linked to the L2 speaker's limited acculturation, i.e. maintenance of a great social and/or psychological distance towards the target language speakers and culture (see ACCULTURATION HYPOTHESIS).

## SIMPLIFIED CODES AS INPUT IN L2 ACQUISITION

Much research on simplified codes, especially on FT, has been carried out in connection with input/interaction features of teacher talk in the classroom. Bingham Wesche (1994) offers a detailed review of this work, referring to different forms of classroom talk as 'modified' rather than 'simplified' input.

One of the main proponents of the use of simplified codes in language teaching is Krashen (1982, 1985). For him, the use of simple codes, such as BT, can be useful and encouraging to the learner in acquiring the target language. Krashen argued that simple codes are used as tools for communication, not instruction, and therefore provide comprehensible input (see INPUT HYPOTHESIS, I + 1). Simple codes are also said to be congruent with the level of the learner's proficiency in L2, and they are perceived by the learner as pertaining to his or her local concerns.

However, the idea that simple codes facilitate language (L1 or L2) acquisition is not uniformly accepted. For example, Heath (1983) studied a black, working-class community in the USA, in which children were largely ignored in conversation until they became information-givers. Family members, including parents and siblings, and friends simply did not address speech to these children, who learned to speak by 'picking up' and imitating sounds which they heard around them. None of this talk was simplified and it always exceeded the children's own level of competence. Similar evidence is cited by Ochs (1982) from her research in Western Samoa, where parents do not use BT to their children.

Furthermore, modification of teacher talk to non-native speakers does not follow the same structural principles as FT in other contexts. Although teacher talk *is* modified, it is characterized by standard norms of the target language, whereas other types of FT appear to be a non-standard, reduced code. Bingham Wesche (1994) quotes Long's (1983) research in which he supports the difference between classroom and non-classroom FT, and states that the use of ungrammatical FT occurs in other (non-educational) situations:

(1) with non-native speakers with zero or low proficiency;

(2) native speaker perception of own higher social status;

(3) prior native speaker experience with non-native speakers but only those at low proficiency levels;

(4) spontaneous occurrence of native speaker–non-native speaker conversation (in task-oriented conversations, e.g. on a factory floor);

(adapted from Bingham Wesche, 1994: 223–4).

The actual form and scope of native speaker modifications to learners depends on a wide range of factors such as speech style, type of discourse, social and cultural context, and the personal characteristics of the speaker. As has been mentioned, native speaker language to L2 learners is predominantly grammatical and well-formed. Its formal characteristics in comparison to normal native speaker talk include:

*Morphology and syntax*
(1) shorter utterances
(2) syntax less complicated
(3) semantic transparency
(4) canonical word order
(5) overt marking of optional grammatical relations
(6) greater use of present tense and adverbials of time
(7) avoidance of certain tenses and conditionals
(8) overt, formulaic framing of certain types of utterances (e.g. definitions)

*Vocabulary*
(1) frequent use of neutral and concrete vocabulary
(2) avoidance of idioms and slang
(3) higher percentage of copulas to other verbs

*Discourse* Several discourse strategies identified in native–non-native classroom talk are aimed at giving learners a better understanding of teacher talk (repetition, pausing), an easier way of participating in classroom interaction (preponderance of *yes–no* questions, use of topics relevant to the immediate situation, expansion by native speakers of learner statements) and so on. Although the exact effect of the use of modified/simplified code on L2 acquisition is not easy to pinpoint, its function is believed to ease the learning task of the learner by accommodating to his or her communicative level (Bingham Wesche, 1994).

## CONCLUSION

Simplified codes and simplification are closely related to L2 acquisition. Learner IL shares a number of formal properties with other simplified codes (pidgins, BT, FT) and simplified/modified language is used in the teaching process to ease the

students' efforts to participate in classroom interaction and to facilitate their language acquisition.

BIBLIOGRAPHY
Andersen, R. (1981). Two perspectives on pidginization as second language acquisition. In R. W. Andersen (ed.), *New Dimensions in Second Language Acquisition Research*. Rowley, MA: Newbury House.
Bickerton, D. (1977). Pidginization and creolization: language acquisition and language universals. In A. Valdman (ed.), *Pidgin and Creole Linguistics*. Bloomington: Indiana University Press.
Bingham Wesche, M. (1994). Input and interaction in second language acquisition. In C. Gallaway and B. J. Richards (eds), *Input and Interaction in Language Acquisition*. Cambridge: Cambridge University Press, 219–49.
Ferguson, C. (1975). Toward a characterization of English foreigner talk. *Anthropological Linguistics*, 17/1, 1–14.
——(1977). Baby talk as simplified register. In C. E. Snow and C. Ferguson (eds), *Talking to Children: Language input and acquisition*. Cambridge: Cambridge University Press, 209–35.
Heath, S. B. (1983). *Ways with Words: Language, life and work in communities and classrooms*. Cambridge: Cambridge University Press.
Krashen, S. (1982). *Principles and Practices of Second Language Acquisition*. Oxford: Pergamon.*
——(1985). *The Input Hypothesis: Issues and implications*. London: Longman.
McLaughlin, B. (1987). *Theories of Second-Language Learning*. London: Edward Arnold.
Nemser, W. (1974). Approximative systems of foreign language learners. In J. C. Richards (ed.), *Error Analysis: Perspectives on second language acquisition*. London: Longman, 55–63. [Originally published in 1971 in *International Review of Applied Linguistics*, 9/2, 115–23.]
Ochs, E. (1982). Talking to children in Western Samoa. *Language in Society*, 11, 77–104.
Richards, J. C. (1974). Social factors, interlanguage, and language learning. In J. C. Richards (ed.), *Error Analysis: Perspectives on second language acquisition*. London: Longman, 64–91. [Originally published in 1972 in *Language Learning*, 22/2, 159–88.]
Romaine, S. (1988). *Pidgin and Creole Languages*. London: Longman.

——(1994). *Language in Society: An introduction to sociolinguistics*. Oxford: Oxford University Press. [Particularly chapter 6.]

Schumann, J. (1978). *The Pidginization Process: A model for second language acquisition*. Rowley, MA: Newbury House.*

——(1982). Simplification, transfer and relexification as aspects of pidginization and early second language acquisition research. *Language Learning*, 33, 49–76.

AJ

**situational syllabus** This is a syllabus aiming, by contrast notably with the GRAMMATICAL SYLLABUS, to prepare learners to cope in a foreign language with concrete situations of the world such as 'going through customs' or 'booking into the hotel'. Ideally, it is planned in accordance with the specific needs of certain learners, such as tourists, especially where time for teaching is short. Problems with it are that: situations have to be defined simple-mindedly; it depends upon predictability, and neither all the language arising in nor all the emergent properties of situations are predictable; it may obscure linguistic generalities cutting across various situations.

BIBLIOGRAPHY
Ockenden, M. (1972). *Situational Dialogues*. London: Longman.
Wilkins, D. A. (1976). *Notional Syllabuses*. Oxford: Oxford University Press, 15–18.

JTR

**skill-getting/skill-using** Rivers and Temperley (1978) distinguish between two sets of processes involved in learning to communicate. The first, skill-getting, focuses on cognition and production rather than on real communication (interaction). Here learners gain familiarity with isolated elements of the linguistic system (typically through structure-manipulation activities and exercises to help internalize rules) and practise

message formulation through pseudo-communication activities, in which content is still structured. Genuine, autonomous communication, in which learners meet their own communicative demands through content selection and management of interaction in real time, is referred to as skill-using. (See TEACHING SPEAKING.)

BIBLIOGRAPHY
Rivers, W. and Temperley, R. S. (1978). *A Practical Guide to the Teaching of English*. New York: Oxford University Press.

KSM

**skimming** involves 'glancing rapidly through a text to determine its gist' (Nuttall, 1982: 34). More than SCANNING, it can involve high-level processing, as information is sifted and collated. One of Nuttall's examples of a skimming question is 'what methods of plant propagation are dealt with in this article?' Williams (1984) notes the importance of skimming as a study skill, and associates it with the first stage of the traditional SQ3R sequence of 'survey, question, read, rewrite and revise'. For discussion of this sequence in an L2 context, see Yorkey (1982).

BIBLIOGRAPHY
Nuttall, C. (1982). *Teaching Reading Skills in a Foreign Language*. London: Heinemann.
Williams, E. (1984). *Reading in the Language Classroom*. Basingstoke: Macmillan.
Yorkey, R. C. (1982). *Study Skills for Students of English*. New York: McGraw-Hill.

KJ

**SLOPE** The Second Language Oral Production Test (Fathman, 1975) has twenty sections (each involving three items) testing grammatical phenomena (article, negation, wh-questions, etc.). Test items are usually two pictures and a question. For example, to elicit plurals, an interviewer points to a picture of one man and says 'Here is a man', then to a picture of two men and asks: 'Here are two ____ ?' The SLOPE test, like the BILINGUAL SYNTAX MEASURE, was designed to elicit spontaneous production data bearing on the L2 acquisition of grammatical knowledge.

BIBLIOGRAPHY
Fathman, A. (1975). Language background, age and the order of acquisition of English structures. In M. Burt and H. Dulay (eds), *On TESOL 75: New directions in second language learning, teaching and bilingual education*. Washington, DC: TESOL.

RH

## socio-educational model

**socio-educational model**   One model of language learning encompassing INTEGRATIVE MOTIVATION, APTITUDE, ATTITUDES to the classroom situation and attitudes to language study has been proposed by Gardner (1985). His model is dynamic and shows the strengths and direction of influence of the variables using LISREL, a computerized statistical programme. (See MOTIVATION.)

BIBLIOGRAPHY
Gardner, R. C. (1985). *Social Psychology and Second Language Learning: The role of attitudes and motivation*. London: Edward Arnold.

SMCD

**sociolinguistics**   Variationist work on regional and social ACCENTS and DIALECTS correlates linguistic variables with speakers' socio-economic status, sex, age and so on. Interactional sociolinguistics is interested in the discursive projection and identification of interlocutors' identities and relations (see DISCOURSE ANALYSIS). A related field of the ETHNOGRAPHY OF COMMUNICATION is concerned with MICROLINGUISTIC choices in performing speech acts, uses of forms of address, linguistic routines, etc. in different functions of speech. MACROLINGUISTIC studies of languages in communities deal, among other questions, with the spread and use of PIDGINS AND CREOLES, BILINGUALISM, CODE-SWITCHING and DIGLOSSIA (see SOCIOLINGUISTICS IN LANGUAGE TEACHING).

BIBLIOGRAPHY
Fasold, R. (1984). *The Sociolinguistics of Society*. Oxford: Blackwell.
——(1990). *The Sociolinguistics of Language*. Oxford: Blackwell.
Holmes, J. (1992). *An Introduction to Sociolinguistics*. London: Longman.*
Hudson, R. A. (1980). *Sociolinguistics*. Cambridge: Cambridge University Press.
Romaine, S. (1994). *Language in Society: An introduction to sociolinguistics*. Oxford: Oxford University Press.

AJ

**sociolinguistics in language teaching**   Different branches of SOCIOLINGUISTICS have had considerable impact on second and foreign language teaching. This entry will discuss the pedagogical applications of variation studies (dialectology), ETHNOGRAPHY OF COMMUNICATION, PRAGMATICS and DISCOURSE ANALYSIS (for a recent, comprehensive treatment of these issues see McKay and Hornberger, 1996).

Since the late 1960s sociolinguists have focused their attention on naturally occurring language use and the description of the COMMUNICATIVE COMPETENCE of speakers from various speech communities (see also PRAGMATIC COMPETENCE, DISCOURSE COMPETENCE). This prompted foreign and second language specialists to look to sociolinguistic research for clues in designing syllabuses (see NOTIONAL/FUNCTIONAL SYLLABUSES) for language teaching, and developing teaching methodologies suitable for the teaching of this material (see COMMUNICATIVE METHODOLOGY).

### VARIATION STUDIES

This branch of sociolinguistics, also known as *urban dialectology*, has been concerned with linguistic variation as a function of many interlocking factors. It has studied how ACCENTS and DIALECTS (or simply *linguistic varieties*) change from region to region, across social and economic classes, ethnic groups, age groups, different situations and so on.

Variation occurs at all levels of linguistic analysis: PHONOLOGY, MORPHOLOGY, LEXIS, SYNTAX and DISCOURSE. Everything we say can be said in more than one way. In other words, each time we speak we have to make a choice of how to express what we want to say. One important aspect of this fact is that from the *descriptive* (as opposed to the *prescriptive*) point of view, all the choices made by speakers are equally acceptable. For example, whether the speaker says *looking* or *lookin'*, *I go* or *I goes*, *Nobody knows anything*, *Nobody knows nothing*, or *Nobody don't know nothing* is equally 'good'. Value judgements labelling some of these forms as acceptable or non-acceptable, right or wrong, are not linguistic but social. Linguists do recognize that some of these forms belong to what is known as STANDARD ENGLISH and the others to non-standard varieties of the language, but they stress that what makes a form standard or non-standard varies from place to place, from one time to another, or across speech communities. For example, the audible *r* sound in words like *car* and *barn* is standard in American English and non-standard in British English (RP).

The patterning of variation also depends on the linguistic environment of a feature. A much simplified example from the study of /t/ and /d/ deletion in one variety of American English can be used for illustration. It was discovered that, other things being equal, /t/ and /d/ were least likely to be deleted when they represented a distinct morpheme attached to the root of a verb, e.g. the *-ed* suffix. Thus, given the pair of homonyms such as *missed in* and *mist in*, the word final /t/ will be more prone to deletion in the latter word (*mist*) than in the former (*missed*). Word final /t/ and /d/ also tend to be deleted less frequently when they are followed by a vowel than a non-vowel (e.g. *missed in* vs *missed by*) (summarized in Preston, 1989).

The well-established position of variation studies is that linguistic and non-linguistic factors are responsible for variation and language change, which are universal processes. One basic lesson from these studies which language teaching research has learnt is that it is inevitable for the learners to show variable behaviour in their INTERLANGUAGE too. Empirical evidence suggests that this is indeed the case (see Preston, 1989) and VARIABILITY IN SLA has become an important area of research (Tarone, 1988).

The recognition of universal variation in L1 and L2 has also led language teaching experts to recognize the fact that the existence of only one L2 pedagogical 'standard' is not viable. With regard to English, several regional standards already exist and learners in different parts of the world will identify with or follow the influences of different norms. For example, European learners of English may increasingly adopt American English as their dominant standard, whereas Malaysian learners of English may show more influences of Australian English in their interlanguage.

With regard to non-standard varieties of L2, it is obviously not very desirable to encourage the learners to master and use any specific (non-standard) regional or social variety. These dialects or sociolects often carry connotations of strong group identity, and foreigners (outsiders) attempting to speak these varieties may be perceived as intruders violating the integrity of a group. Besides, adopting non-standard linguistic forms in the target language (including slang and other colloquialisms, as well as regional accentual and dialectal features) without near-native fluency in L2 can sound awkward and inappropriate. However, in developing the learner's listening skills it is essential that he or she be exposed to as many varieties of L2 as possible.

## ETHNOGRAPHY OF COMMUNICATION AND DISCOURSE ANALYSIS

Teaching language as use rather than GRAMMAR, emphasis on function rather than form and related issues of pragmatic transfer and failure became central to language teaching with the developments in the ethnography of communication and discourse analysis. A large volume of comparative, sociolinguistic research has been amassed in an attempt to aid language learners and teachers in understanding and mastering different 'ways of speaking' or 'conversational styles' across languages, differences in realization of speech acts, and adoption of politeness strategies in communication (see ATTITUDES for discussion of some relevant social psychological research in relation to language teaching and learning).

*Conversational style in cross-cultural communication*   Following the work of anthropological linguists and sociolinguists, Tannen (1985) and Scollon and Scollon (1995) identified several areas of linguistic and discoursal behaviour which assure (or, when lacking, prevent) conversational synchrony (COHESION) between members of different speech communities (native speakers of different languages or dialects). Conversational synchrony depends on many factors, of which two will be discussed here in relation to cross-cultural communication: *cohesive devices* and *cognitive schemata*.

Cohesive devices help organize, present and understand information in an utterance and include: reference, verbal forms, conjunction and information structure (Scollon and Scollon, 1995). The authors quote a hypothetical example illustrating how American English speakers and Chinese speakers of English might construe their utterances differently with respect to the last category. In suggesting a new idea in a business meeting, a Chinese speaker might say:

*Because most of our production is done in China now, and uh, it's not really certain how the government will react in the run-up to 1997, and since I think a certain amount of caution in committing to TV advertisement is necessary because of the expense. So, I suggest that we delay making our decision until after Legco makes its decision.*

On the other hand, an American businessman is more likely to say:

*I suggest that we delay making our decision until after Legco makes its decision. That's because I think a certain amount of caution in committing to TV advertisement is necessary because of the expense. In addition to that, most of our production is done in China now, and it's not really certain how the government will react in the run-up to 1997.*

In the first example, the speaker presents his reasons and background for his suggestion first, and then goes on to reveal the new idea. In the second example this order is reversed. The idea comes first and its rationale follows. Such differences in the organization of discourse may lead to mutual, negative valuations and stereotyping of speakers. Thus, Americans may picture East Asians as 'inscrutable', and Asians will think about Americans as 'frank and rude westerner[s]' (Scollon and Scollon, 1985: 2).

Cognitive schemata (scripts or frames) give speakers the certainty of predictability of different communicative situations. Thanks to these schemata, interactants know how to interpret each other's linguistic and non-linguistic behaviour and they can be sure about what to do in a given situation.

It is not uncommon for miscommunication in intercultural settings to arise due to clashes between the interactants' schemata (see SCHEMA THEORY). For example, if an American businessman comes to Mexico and in a series of brief meetings suggests to his Mexican partners: 'Just have your purchasing agent call our guy when you've decided what you want,' he is not likely to succeed in his trade mission because such an aggressive and direct conversational style is not part of the Mexican frame 'doing business' (Agar, 1994: 228).

Likewise, Scollon and Scollon (1985: 57) suggest that the scripts for the expected sequences of activities in the US and Japanese coffee shops may vary slightly, the typical script in a US coffee shop being as follows:

(1)  You find a seat.
(2)  You detemine your order.
(3)  You place your order with the waiter or waitress.
(4)  You receive your food.
(5)  When you finish eating, you pay your bill at the cashier's.

Whereas in a Japanese coffee shop one would follow this pattern of behaviour:

(1)  You determine your order.
(2)  You pay for your order at the cashier's.
(3)  You find a seat.
(4)  You place your order with the waiter or waitress.
(5)  You receive your food.
(6)  You eat, and leave when you have finished.

One can imagine the grave consequences of mixing up these scripts in the relevant contexts.

*Rules of speaking and strategies of communication*  Languages differ with respect to their rules of speaking (Wolfson, 1983) and strategies of communication. Many cross-linguistic, sociolinguistic studies which have dealt with those differences have also been applied to language teaching, either to raise students' communicative awareness of L2 or as specific points of instruction. Topics of such research include: the amount of talk required and/or permitted in a given situation, differences in permissible topics, different repertoires of formulaic expressions and realizations of speech acts, and different uses of POLITENESS strategies. These will be discussed below.

The relative amount of talk and silence in different speech communities is not fixed. For example, white Anglos in the USA will tend to use more talk in greetings than their Indian counterparts. When members of the latter group use more silence than they are expected to by the Anglos, negative stereotyping ensues: the 'silent' Indians are described by Anglos as stupid, obstinate or unfriendly. On the other hand, the Indians stereotype the Anglos as pushy and excessively voluble (Scollon and Scollon, 1995).

The decision what to say, i.e. the choice of topic in conversation, is as important as when to talk (Tannen, 1985). For example, enquiries about prices of different personal possessions are commonly exchanged between relatively distant acquaintances in Polish, whereas in the UK such questions are perceived as too personal and rude. Possible reasons for different taboo topics in Poland and the UK may be linked to various historical, economic and cultural factors. The cultural explanation possible here is that mutual asking of personal questions in Poland corresponds to showing involvement between individuals and their avoidance in the UK signals respect for the privacy of another person (see politeness strategies discussed below).

Formulaic expressions are useful in L2 production because they offer easy scripts in many situations when the non-native speaker's fluency is still rather underdeveloped. However, the repertoires of formulaic expressions (e.g. greetings and leave-takings, birthday wishes, proverbs and so on) differ across languages. Moreover, speakers attach great importance to the way they use linguistic formulae, seeing them as one of the important aspects of marking their group affiliation, and are unwilling to give up their use in L2. Thus, negative attitudes towards L2 formulaic expressions are frequently cited as 'insincere' greetings, invitations, etc. Many Polish learners of English, for example, avoid the use of the English greeting *How are you?* dismissing it as 'not genuine'. Misunderstanding may also occur if a non-native speaker misinterprets or misuses an L2 formula. For example, when a Canadian speaker of English wanted to terminate politely her telephone conversation with a Polish friend, she said *I've got to go now*. She became very confused when her formula was followed by a question: *Where are you going?* (Jaworski, 1990; see also Coulmas, 1980).

Extensive research into the use of speech acts (apologies, requests, compliments and so on) indicates that their linguistic and pragmatic aspects across linguistic and cultural boundaries vary and are subject to TRANSFER (Blum-Kulka et al., 1989; Wolfson and Judd, 1983).

An example of speech act research oriented towards language teaching is presented by Holmes and Brown (1987). The authors demonstrate some differences in the use of compliments in New Zealand English by Pakehas (white New Zealanders of European descent) and members of other ethnic groups (pp. 526–7).

One form of misunderstanding concerns the interpretation of the force of the compliment. In the following example, speaker A intends it as an expression of praise and speaker B interprets it as a request:

A:  *What an unusual necklace. It's beautiful.*
B:  *Please take it.*
A – female Pakeha (New Zealander of European descent).
B – Samoan friend of A.

Cultures may also vary with respect to what is the expected topic of a compliment. In the example below, speaker A initially expresses concern over B's loss of weight, believing it to be disadvantageous to her health. In the first instance, however, speaker B interprets A's remark as a compliment:

A:  *You've lost a lot of weight. What have you been doing?*
B:  *Thank you. I've started jogging regularly and it seems to work.*

A:  *You shouldn't overdo it. You are looking quite thin.*
A – female Pakeha.
B – female Tokelau.

Much of the research reported above has been incorporated into a relatively wide-ranging study of politeness strategies. In the framework proposed by Brown and Levinson (1987), politeness is a notion understood as a regulative procedure in communicative behaviour between individuals. Societies differ in their preferred ways of organizing the interpersonal relations of their members. The two dominant patterns are based on (1) maintaining involvement, in-groupness and the desire of self to be liked by others (*positive politeness*), and (2) maintaining deference and the desire of self to have his or her actions unimpeded (*negative politeness*). Although all societies will manifest both positive and negative politeness strategies in communication, they will differ in the frequency or concentration of one type of strategy over others.

Greece and England are examples of countries (cultures) with different dominant politeness strategies and orientations (Sifianou, 1992). Greece is a predominantly positive politeness culture, where interpersonal ties with in-group members are strong, manifestation of solidarity tends to override freedom from imposition and the appropriate behaviours within in-groups are characterized by cooperation, protection and help. Relations with members of the out-group are essentially competitive. In England privacy and intimacy are likely to be valued more than in Greece. Even intimates may employ many strategies indicating tentativeness, lack of imposition and respect for the other.

Observation of non-verbal communication in Greece suggests that the use of physical space and touching between participants corroborates the view of this culture as predominantly solidarity oriented. When two persons meet or part, in Greece they signal access to each other and mutual solidarity by hand-shaking. This may be accompanied by kissing, embracing or patting on the shoulder. In a comparable situation in England, hand-shaking is not preferred and is reserved for more formal (congratulations) or unique (meeting someone for the first time) situations. The avoidance of hand-shaking and other forms of touching in England between casual acquaintances expresses the desire of participants not to impose on each other rather than a lack of solidarity.

Likewise, other things being equal, the speech act of requesting, for example, is perceived as less of an imposition in Greece than in England. In the former context, requesting a favour from another person is likely to be interpreted as a sign of intimacy and in-groupness. In England, requests tend to be perceived more in terms of the violation of another person's right to remain free to do what he or she wants. Therefore, one will find more examples of mitigatory strategies (negative politeness strategies) such as *interrogative mood, modal verbs, hedging* and so on in English requests than in their Greek equivalents, which tend to be more direct and use the *imperative mood* to a greater extent. For example, an English husband may ask his wife for a small favour in the following way: *Would you mind making me a cup of coffee?* This is an indirect request, realized in the interrogative mood with an extra degree of tentativeness marked by the modal verb *would*. The Greek, unmarked version of such a request will be realized as: *ftiakse mu ena kafeðak ʃi* 'make me a little cup of coffee.' Here the imperative mood is used, and the only overt politeness strategy present is a positive politeness-oriented use of the diminutive *kafeðak ʃi* 'little cup of coffee', which signals to the listener affection and familiarity. (See Sifianou, 1992, for a more detailed discussion of these examples.)

An important implication of cross-cultural politeness research is that different speech communities will display preferences for different politeness orientations and L2 speakers ought to realize that what may seem rude and imposing in one language may be a display of positive politeness of involvement, whereas what may seem to be snooty and aloof behaviour in another culture may be an expression of concern for the well-being of another person by mitigating imposition.

## CONCLUSION

Does it matter how L2 learners use conversational style, how they perform linguistic rituals and speech acts, how they express affect or independence in inter-ethnic and cross-cultural communication? Certainly, miscommunication and communication breakdown of varying degrees of severity do result from mismatched communicative systems between different speakers (see research in Coupland et al., 1991). A degree of cross-cultural awareness and the approximation of target cultural norms facilitated in language teaching by the existence of relevant sociolinguistic research may help alleviate these problems.

In addition, with the secure place of English as a world language (see WORLD ENGLISH), it is important to bear in mind the fact that many L2 learners will use English for self-presentation in contexts where their future social, educational and economic well-being is dependent on the culture-dependent *style* and *content* of their job application, job interview or lecture. Conforming to the cultural norms of the target community does matter, as the lack of success of the following (authentic) letter of application to a British university seems to suggest:

To (address)

Dear Sir,
 I am fine and prey to God, that my these words may please find you in the best of you health and all beautiful colours of life.

Sir,
I am (nationality), and keen in English studies but the big huddle in my studies is my financial position. Will you please send me, complete information regarding my studies, along with information will you please guide me, how can I get a Job there. So that I can get my education and support myself too. I hope you kindness do me a favour. An early reply is requested please

Truly yours.
First Name Surname

A detailed analysis of the style and cultural norms underlying this letter fall outside the scope of this entry. One can safely argue, however, that the fact that its author was rejected from the considerations for acceptance to a course he had applied for was largely due to its non-native-like style. The role of sociolinguistics in language teaching is to provide the learners with the appropriate rules of speaking (and writing) as well as to raise their awareness of the socio-cultural differences across languages.

BIBLIOGRAPHY
Agar, M. (1994). The intercultural frame. *Journal of Intercultural Relations*, 18/2, 221–37.
Blum-Kulka, S., House, J. and Kasper, G. (eds) (1989). *Cross-cultural Pragmatics: Requests and apologies*. Norwood, NJ: Ablex.
Brown, P. and Levinson, S. (1987 [1978]). *Politeness: Some universals in language usage*. Cambridge: Cambridge University Press.
Coulmas, F. (ed.) (1981). *Conversational Routine: Explorations in standardized communication situations and prepatterned speech*. The Hague: Mouton.
Coupland, N., Wiemann, J. M. and Giles, H. (eds) (1991). *'Miscommunication' and Problematic Talk*. Newbury Park, CA: Sage.
Gumperz, J. J. (1982). *Discourse Strategies*. Cambridge: Cambridge University Press.
Herbert, R. K. (1991). The sociology of compliment work: an ethnocontrastive study of Polish and English compliments. *Multilingua*, 10/4, 381–402.
Holmes, J. and Brown, D. F. (1987). Teachers and students learning about compliments. *TESOL Quarterly*, 21/3, 523–46.

Jaworski, A. (1990). The acquisition and perception of formulaic language and foreign language teaching. *Multilingua*, 9/4, 397–411.
McCarthy, M. and Carter, R. (eds) (1995). *Language as Discourse: Perspectives for language teaching*. London: Longman.*
McKay, S. and Hornberger, N. H. (eds) (1996). *Sociolinguistics and Language Teaching*. Cambridge: Cambridge University Press.
Preston, D. (1989). *Sociolinguistics and Second Language Acquisition*. Oxford: Blackwell.
Scollon, R. and Scollon, S. Wong (1995). *Intercultural Communication*. Oxford: Blackwell.*
Sifianou, M. (1992). *Politeness Phenomena in England and Greece: A cross-cultural perspective*. Oxford: Clarendon Press.
Tannen, D. (1985). Cross-cultural communication. In T. van Dijk (ed.), *Handbook of Discourse Analysis*. Vol. 4. London: Academic Press, 203–15.
Tarone, E. (1988). *Variation in Interlanguage*. London: Edward Arnold.
Watts, R. J., Ide, S. and Ehlich, K. (eds) (1992). *Politeness in Language: Studies in its history, theory and practice*. Berlin and New York: Mouton, de Gruyter.
Wolfson, N. (1983). Rules of speaking. In J. C. Richards and R. W. Schmidt (eds), *Language and Communication*. London: Longman, 61–87.
Wolfson, N. and Judd, E. (eds) (1983). *Sociolinguistics and Language Acquisition*. Rowley, MA: Newbury House.

AJ

**special purpose testing**    Testing language required for specific purposes is an aspect of ESP (see ENGLISH FOR SPECIFIC PURPOSES). Where individuals or small groups are concerned, there may be no need for a standardized test. Cases of large-scale use are the fields of academic English, business English and medical English. In these fields there has been considerable test development, aimed at accurately assessing appropriate language skills for relevant activities. Features of this development are the use of authentic tasks, authentic materials from appropriate situations, communicative activities and group tasks for assessing spoken

language as if in the real situation. See LAN-
GUAGE TESTING and TESTS IN ENGLISH LAN-
GUAGE TEACHING.

SMCD

**speech act theory** is a part of PRAG-
MATICS explaining how utterances affect
social action, and how people realize and
infer the intended function of an utterance
when it is not explicitly stated. The theory
posits necessary conditions for particular
acts. In an order, for example, the speaker
must refer to a possible future action by the
addressee and must have the right to give
orders; the addressee must have the obliga-
tion and ability to do the action. Reference
to any one condition (e.g. 'you ought to tidy
up') will then suffice to achieve the act
of ordering. 'Families' of speech acts sharing conditions have been suggested. (See
CATEGORIES OF COMMUNICATIVE FUNCTION,
NOTIONAL/FUNCTIONAL SYLLABUSES.)

BIBLIOGRAPHY
Austin, J. K. (1962). *How to do Things with Words*.
Oxford: Clarendon Press.
Cook, G. (1989). *Discourse*. Oxford: Oxford Uni-
versity Press. [Chapter 3.]*
Searle, J. (1975). Indirect speech acts. In P. Cole
and J. L. Morgan (eds), *Syntax and Semant-
ics*. Vol. 3. *Speech Acts*. New York: Academic
Press, 59–82.
Widdowson, H. G. (1979). Approaches to dis-
course. In H. G. Widdowson, *Explorations in
Applied Linguistics*. Oxford: Oxford Univer-
sity Press.

GC

**spoken and written discourse** In DIS-
COURSE ANALYSIS a distinction is often made
between spoken and written discourse.
Although there are typical differences between the two, there is also a considerable
overlap and a frequent mixture, which has
been accelerated by new technology. Analysis of both modes encounters the problem
of representing relevant context, but this
problem is especially acute in the analysis
and transcription of spoken discourse. At
present, opinion on the differences between
written and spoken discourse is often speculative. Systematic analysis of corpora is
beginning to reveal actual differences, as well
as those among the various written and spoken GENRES, and some of this information
will be useful for the design of courses for
language learners which wish to focus upon
one mode or the other.

When the distinction between spoken and
written discourse refers simply to a difference of mode, in that spoken discourse utilizes sound and written discourse is visual,
it is both self-evident and unremarkable.
When, more interestingly, an attempt is
made to distinguish linguistic or discoursal
features peculiar to one mode or the other,
the distinction becomes more complex.
(That differences are not merely determined
by the channel of communication is demonstrated by the use of deaf sign languages in
conversation.) Spoken communication is
widely regarded as typically time-bound,
ephemeral, informal and produced in a particular situation for particular participants;
writing is regarded as typically spatial, static,
permanent, displaced in time and frequently
aimed at a wide and unknown audience. A
number of discoursal and linguistic features
are believed to arise from these differences.
There are lexical differences between the
two, with some words being more likely to
occur in speech than in writing or vice versa.
Deixis (language which refers to the immediate situation) is more prominent in speech.
Clausal structure is more complex in writing. Spoken discourse is considered to be
typically less formal, more loosely and col-
laboratively organized, with frequent repetition and repair. Written discourse, which
both demands and permits reprocessing and
reflection, is considered to be typically more
concentrated, organized and dense. (For
further discussion see Biber, 1988; Chafe

and Tannen, 1987; Crystal, 1987: 178–82; Halliday, 1989.) It would seem from these characterizations that the language learner needs both different linguistic knowledge and different discourse strategies to be effective in both modes.

There are, however, a number of problems in any clear-cut division and too many exceptions for the typical characteristics listed above to be regarded as defining features. There is at present a lack of information, and there is ambiguity about whether the many discourses which involve reading aloud or which mix speech and writing should be regarded as spoken or written. The distinction between speech and writing has been complicated by the impact of a succession of new technologies on the modes of communication. Sound recording, the telephone, radio, television and video have fundamentally altered the nature of the distinction, making spoken discourse recoverable, repeatable and transmissible over long distances. In the case of radio and television, it is also often monologue allowing no response from the receiver. In the mirror image of this process, more recent technologies, such as electronic mail, have given some written discourse an informality and interactivity more usually associated with speech. At the same time, the wider availability of printing has made some written discourse far less prestigious and permanent, and many written texts are now highly ephemeral (Cook, 1992: 24–59). In addition, there are many interactions in which there is a mixture of speech and writing, either because one is used as a prompt for the other (note-reading and note-taking, for example) or because the two are used together (books and handouts are used during a lecture or lesson, for example). Many spoken discourse events (such as news bulletins and legal judgements) are formal and carefully planned monologues, wholly or partly read aloud.

Twentieth-century technology has thus blurred the clear differences between spoken and written discourse which existed before sound recording. In the contemporary world it is preferable to think of a continuum between two prototypes of discourse: ephemeral situation-bound discourse (typically spoken) and permanent displaced discourse (typically written). Discourse analysts have tended to concentrate on discourse at the extremes of this continuum (e.g. casual conversation and written narrative) rather than on more problematic cases in between. There is surprisingly little work on the relation between speech and writing in many communications which make use of both together.

To a large extent, the degree to which speech and writing do actually differ is unknown, and speculation has been used instead of evidence. The collection of large corpora, such as the British National Corpus, in which speech and writing can be distinguished and compared will provide more rigorous evidence of the degree to which the mode of communication does actually influence linguistic and discoursal choices (Crowdy, 1995). It may be, for example, that the grammar of spoken discourse is substantially different from that of writing. If so, grammatical descriptions aimed at language learners, which have in the past drawn only on grammatical structures occurring in writing, should be adjusted accordingly (Carter and McCarthy, 1995). (See CORPUS LINGUISTICS.)

TEXT ANALYSIS AND TRANSCRIPTION ANALYSIS

While the analysis of written discourse allows direct access to the object of study, the analysis of spoken interaction is very often an analysis of a transcript (ironically a piece of writing) rather than of the interaction itself. As spoken interaction involves many essential non-linguistic features such as the paralinguistic use of voice, eyes, face and body, as well as the mutual perception of the physical situation, a number of theoretical and practical problems arise concerning how these features may best be represented in the transcription (Cook, 1995). Any inclusion of non-linguistic features will involve considerable selection and interpretation by the transcriber, and it is by no means clear what principles should govern this. On the other hand, these non-linguistic features cannot be overlooked, as they are often crucial to an understanding of the interaction. Sadly, but inevitably, most analyses of spoken discourse have until recently simply ignored these problems, treating a written transcription of the words as if it were the spoken discourse itself. However, new possibilities brought by advances in technology, and a growing awareness of the inseparable nature of spoken discourse, paralanguage and non-linguistic context, suggest that this area is one in which substantial advances can be expected.

BIBLIOGRAPHY
Biber, D. (1988). *Variation across Speech and Writing*. Cambridge: Cambridge University Press.*
Carter, R. and McCarthy, M. (1995). Grammar and the spoken language. *Applied Linguistics*, 16/2, 141–59.
Chafe, W. and Tannen, D. (1987). The relation between written and spoken language. *Annual Review of Anthropology*, 16, 383–407.
Cook, G. (1992). *The Discourse of Advertising*. London: Routledge.
——(1995). Theoretical issues: transcribing the untranscribable. In G. Leech, G. Myers and J. Thomas (eds), *Spoken English on Computer: Transcription, mark-up and applications*. London: Longman, 35–54.
Coulthard, M. (ed.) (1992). *Advances in Spoken Discourse Analysis*. London: Routledge.
——(1994). *Advances in Written Text Analysis*. London: Routledge.
Crowdy, S. (1995). The BNC spoken corpus. In G. Leech, G. Myers and J. Thomas (eds), *Spoken English on Computer: Transcription, mark-up and applications*. London: Longman, 224–34.
Crystal, D. (1987). *The Cambridge Encyclopaedia of Language*. Cambridge: Cambridge University Press.
Halliday, M. A. K. (1989). *Spoken and Written Language*. 2nd edn. Oxford: Oxford University Press.

GC

**staging** Halliday, McIntosh and Strevens (1964) subdivide the syllabus grading process (see GRADING/SEQUENCING) into *sequencing* and *staging*. The latter involves dividing a course into time segments and allocating items to each segment to achieve a reasonable learning load, given factors like the time available for learning and the difficulty of the items concerned.

BIBLIOGRAPHY
Halliday, M. A. K., McIntosh, A. and Strevens, P. (1964) *The Linguistic Sciences and Language Teaching*. Harlow: Longman.
White, R. V. (1988). *The ELT Curriculum* Oxford: Blackwell.

KJ

**standard deviation** (or s) is a statistical indication of the variability or dispersion of values around the mean. It is calculated as the square root of the variance, and provides a sort of average of all differences from the mean. As a measure of the relative homogeneity of a group, it is useful in comparing behaviour of different groups. (See STATISTICS IN APPLIED LINGUISTICS RESEARCH.)

KSM

**Standard English** is a DIALECT with the most prestige and/or influence within the English-speaking community, used to perform various official and ceremonial functions in spoken and written forms. It is the most widespread variety in education, though the extent to which children should be obliged to adhere to it at the expense of their own dialects is a much debated issue. Due to its association with the upper and middle classes, it is considered to be the 'correct' version of English. With the spread of English around the world (see WORLD ENGLISH), English has acquired many different standards (see LANGUAGE PLANNING).

BIBLIOGRAPHY
Andersson, L. and Trudgill, P. (1990). *Bad Language*. Oxford: Blackwell.
Milroy, J. and Milroy, L. (1985). *Authority in Language*. London: Routledge and Kegan Paul.
AJ

**statistics in applied linguistics research**   Statistics play a relatively small part in linguistics research, but many applied linguistics research projects require numerical analysis. This may appear contradictory, but it is evidence that the two disciplines differ considerably. The crucial areas in which statistical analysis is required are those in which there is variability, both in the sense that large numbers of people are involved, and in the sense that many measurements are taken, sometimes on only one person. For example, both experimental phonetics and experimental psycholinguistics are disciplines in which linguistic descriptions and rule systems can be put to empirical test as models of human linguistic functioning.

Within applied linguistics, statistics of one kind or another are required as soon as measurements are taken from a number of people to see how some linguistic trait is distributed. A large number of measurements – e.g. of vocabulary size, test scores, intelligibility ratings, etc. – may be incomprehensible unless reduced to a typical figure or average, and an indication of the average spread around that typical figure (or how typical it is). These two basic descriptors are usually the *mean* and the STANDARD DEVIATION, though different kinds of measurements produce different figures that do the same job. Another problem concerns the way two sets of scores vary together. Some people may have completed a strength of motivation questionnaire and taken an achievement test in a language: perhaps in general, those with high motivation also scored high on the achievement test, and those with low motivation also scored low. Other outcomes are just as likely. Looking at a large number of pairs of scores is not going to tell anybody anything: the data need to be reduced to a figure summarizing the size and direction of the co-variance – loosely, the agreement between the two sets of figures. This is a CORRELATION.

Statistical description normally involves reducing a large number of figures to one or two powerful figures which reveal the story behind the original scores. There are many more complicated techniques for situations in which there are more than two measurements per person: *multivariate analysis* methods include regression, cluster analysis and factor analysis.

However, statistics offer more than powerful descriptions. Take the situation where two groups of otherwise similar people have different attitudes to learning. The question might arise, does attitude affect learning outcome? There is likely to be a difference between the average scores of the two groups on a language test anyway, simply because it would be unreasonable to expect every occasion of measurement to give exactly the same answer. After all, measuring a pound of sugar several times on a sensitive scale gives a slightly different answer each time. The question then turns on whether the size of any difference you observe between the groups' scores is big enough to support the statement: 'The difference between the groups is not due to chance.' Statistics may be used to infer that the observed difference is so unlikely on a chance basis that there must be some positive factor influencing the results, and you hope that your original hunch of attitude is that factor. Notice that statistics by themselves cannot answer the original question: the design of the research itself has to exclude all other possible confounding factors (like different initial proficiency, access to the language, aptitude, teachers and resources, etc. – see VARIABLE) before you can be confident that the observed non-chance difference is actually due to the factor hypothesized. *Inferential* statistics essentially test observed results from experiments, comparisons, correlations, time series, etc. against predictions from chance, and researchers conventionally accept low levels of PROBABILITY as *significant* – namely 5%, 1% or 0.1%. Significance levels, sometimes more comfortably called confidence levels, give an indication of the likelihood of the results from chance, and therefore of the strength of confidence the researcher can place in the conclusions. The choice of descriptive and inferential statistics to be used and the specification of significance level to be accepted are part of the research design, which also includes the method of measurement, the way the groups are matched, the checks and counterbalances in the design which enable other possible explanations to be eliminated.

Numerical analysis plays a large part in applied linguistics research, but not an exclusive one. There are many situations in which statistics are not the appropriate method of analysis. For example, statistical analyses of classroom processes have not proved fruitful; interpretative methods such as participant observation, stimulated recall and even ethnographic methods of description have produced more valuable insights than counting coding tallies. Another example is the widespread use of DIARY STUDIES and other introspective methods such as protocol analysis; statistical analysis of these is relatively crude compared to methods of content analysis. Statistics are used to measure inter-coder and inter-rater agreement, and as such contribute to the establishment of reliability in these more subjective areas. It may be argued that descriptions of language learning behaviour in educational settings in particular are better analysed qualitatively than quantitatively. Usually researchers in these fields are more interested in the behaviour, strategies or language use of individuals than in a general trend described by reduction from a mass of data; statistical analysis can say little about particular individuals and the way individuals contribute to patterns of classroom interaction, for example.

On the other hand, statistical analysis is very important in the analysis and evaluation of tests. Many aspects of VALIDITY, such as comparison with other tests and comparison with other kinds of performance, and of RELIABILITY, such as internal consistency, agreement between raters, estimates of internal error, and of *item analysis*, such as discrimination and facility values, require statistical analyses of test performance by relatively large numbers of people. Mostly, such operations use relatively simple computations such as correlations; more powerful statistics can be used to answer more difficult questions. (See also RESEARCH METHODOLOGY FOR LANGUAGE LEARNING.)

BIBLIOGRAPHY
Woods, A., Fletcher, P. and Hughes, A. (1986). *Statistics in Language Studies*. Cambridge: Cambridge University Press.

SMCD

**strategic competence**   A subdivision of COMMUNICATIVE COMPETENCE which enables the second and native language users to cope with problematic communicative situations and to keep the channel of communication open. Speakers realize strategic competence through their knowledge of COMMUNICATION STRATEGIES or psycholinguistic plans designed to solve production problems.

BIBLIOGRAPHY
Canale, M. and Swain, M. (1980). Theoretical bases of communicative approaches to second language teaching and testing. *Applied Linguistics*, 1, 1–47.

AJ

**stress**   A supra-segmental feature of the spoken language, associated with increased pitch, duration and intensity allocated to a syllable. In '*photograph*, the first syllable has the primary stress (accent), in *pho'tography*, the second. In English unstressed syllables the vowels are often reduced to 'schwa', the term applied to the sound /ə/ as it appears, for example, in the word *sugar* /ʃʊgə/. Some English words and compounds bear distinguishing stress patterns, compare '*export* (noun) and *ex'port* (verb); '*blackbird* (compound) and '*black* '*bird* (phrase). Such manifestations of *lexical* stress contrast with *sentence* stress, which contributes to the meaning of a sentence/utterance: *John came* '*yesterday* conveys information different to '*John came yesterday*, with *yesterday* and *John* stressed in the respective examples.

See also INFORMATION STRUCTURE, PHONETICS, PHONOLOGY.

BIBLIOGRAPHY
Scott, D. R. (1987). Prosody. In J. Lyons, R. Coates, M. Deuchar and G. Gazdar (eds), *New Horizons in Linguistics 2: An introduction to contemporary linguistic research*. London: Penguin Books, 82–102.

EJ

**structural syllabus**   Though some people use this term as synonymous with GRAMMATICAL SYLLABUS, it is also used to refer to a syllabus type associated with methods like AUDIOLINGUALISM. Structural syllabuses in this sense often use the SENTENCE PATTERN as the unit of analysis, and may be said to adhere, albeit somewhat loosely, to the principles of STRUCTURALISM, particularly the notion of minimally contrasting units. For discussion of the structural syllabus within a historical context, see White (1988); also Halliday and others (1964).

BIBLIOGRAPHY
Halliday, M. A. K., McIntosh, A. and Strevens, P. (1964). *The Linguistic Sciences and Language Teaching*. Harlow: Longman.
White, R. V. (1988). *The ELT Curriculum*. Oxford: Blackwell.*

KJ

**structuralism**   An approach developed in various disciplines, including literary criticism, and associated with the procedures of the French anthropologist Claude Lévi-Strauss, who analysed behaviour in terms of contrastive units. Structural linguistics is associated with Bloomfield (1933) and is so called because of the techniques it employs, involving the use of contrastive units like the phoneme and morpheme. The name is also appropriate because the approach studied language as formal structural patterning rather than as a social construct. The term STRUCTURAL SYLLABUS is used to identify syllabuses which state teaching content in terms of language structures (see STRUCTURE).

BIBLIOGRAPHY
Bloomfield, L. (1933). *Language*. New York: Holt, Rinehart and Winston.

KJ

**structure**   Linguistic units such as texts, sentences, phrases, words and speech sounds are structured, i.e. they consist of smaller units typically arranged in a linear and a hierarchical order. Structural units enter into syntagmatic and paradigmatic relations (see SYNTAGMATIC/PARADIGMATIC). This assumption lies at the heart of STRUCTURALISM, including contemporary theoretical linguistics.

BIBLIOGRAPHY
Fromkin, V. and Rodman, R. (1993). *An Introduction to Language*. 5th edn. Fort Worth, TX: Harcourt Brace Jovanovich. [Particularly Part 2.]

EJ

**student autonomy** is one of a number of closely related concepts within the general paradigm of learner-centred education. It underpins the INDIVIDUALIZATION of instruction, the development of patterns of self-directed learning and of the methodology of self-access, as well as implying some degree of LEARNER TRAINING. It has particular relevance for adults, who are deemed to be able to take responsibility for their own learning, and has been particularly explored in the area of ENGLISH FOR SPECIFIC PURPOSES.

## DEFINITIONS

Although some of the above terms tend to be used interchangeably, it is more helpful to distinguish between them and to see 'autonomy' as an educational position statement which then has operational and behavioural outcomes in terms of learning patterns and the management of classrooms. The term, then, refers to a learner's capacity to take charge of both the strategy and content of learning, and is obviously predicated on an assumption that the educational environment will provide the freedom for him or her to do so. Initially the statement is a philosophical and ideological one, whereby 'the individual has the right to be free to exercise his or her own choices, in learning as in other areas, and not become a victim . . . of choices made by social institutions' (Crabbe, 1993: 443): reality is self-constructed, not imposed. Decisions taken as a consequence of adopting this point of view tend to be strategic and long-term rather than tactical and immediately applicable (Houghton et al., 1988).

From the perspective of individual learners themselves, Crabbe (1993) usefully identifies a 'psychological' argument in favour of autonomy, and suggests that learning is more efficient and motivating to the degree that it matches a learner's own style and strategies. Some learners will be able to be more autonomous than others, and the extent to which the characteristics of autonomy are trainable rather than innate remains unclear (see LEARNER TRAINING and the GOOD LANGUAGE LEARNER STUDIES). Dickinson (1993) identifies five features associated with the autonomous learner: (a) they can identify what has been taught; (b) they are able to

formulate their own learning objectives; (c) they select and implement appropriate strategies; (d) they can monitor these for themselves; and (e) they know how to give up on strategies that are not working for them (see also Wenden, 1991).

## PEDAGOGICAL IMPLICATIONS

The goal of autonomous learning may be realized through the various procedures designed to address the INDIVIDUALIZATION of instruction (see also NEEDS ANALYSIS). However, this latter notion also opens up quite different avenues, including the possibility of very directive and externally imposed pedagogic frameworks. For this reason, autonomy is more commonly associated with practical outlets for self-directed learning (SDL), where learning pathways are self-selected along a number of possible parameters, including time, frequency, pacing, skill(s), content.

A classic and very well-known example of an autonomous learning environment in practice is CRAPEL (Centre de Recherches et d'Applications Pédagogiques en Langues) at the University of Nancy, France. Their commitment to SDL is based on both the philosophical arguments already outlined above and on the very practical rationale that SDL frameworks are more suited to the requirements of professional people embarking on a programme of language study (Henner-Stanchina and Riley, 1978). These authors describe the CRAPEL autonomous learning scheme in detail, with 'case study' examples of individuals proceeding through it.

The Brookes and Grundy collection of papers (1988) is illustrative specifically of the exploration of the autonomous learning paradigm in the area of EAP (see ENGLISH FOR SPECIFIC PURPOSES). There is discussion of – among other issues – syllabus negotiation, the role of autonomy in whole-class instruction, one-to-one tuition and institutional responsibility. Dickinson (1988: chapter 3) offers a broad spectrum of examples of self-instructional systems based on the autonomy principle, both for adult learners and at school level. Henner-Stanchina and Riley's (1978: 94–5) 'recapitulative chart' sets out in diagrammatic form the respective roles of learner, helper and institution in which the programmes are offered.

An obvious corollary of such an arrangement is that a teacher in the normally understood sense is superfluous: instead, an experienced 'helper' assists in establishing goals, working out a schedule within the learner's constraints of time and so on, and introducing the range of materials and methods available. A further corollary is the fact that learners have to assume a degree of responsibility over the assessment of the progress of their own learning, externally imposed and broad-based testing procedures being inappropriate. A seminal work in this regard is Oskarsson (1978) (see also COUNCIL OF EUROPE), which explores several different and practical forms of self-evaluation that address the needs and objectives of adult learners and also train the learners in the means to make such assessments.

Given that the main thrust of development in autonomy and SDL has been outside the conventional classroom format, with learners selecting their own individual pathways, it is clear that the resource implications for institutions providing such facilities are quite considerable. A popular manifestation is in the provision of some kind of self-access resource or centre where learners may go in their own time and select the material they wish, often with some way of keeping a record of work covered. The CRAPEL version is large-scale, including a wide range of print material, hardware, tapes and so on; many institutions operate small-scale self-access facilities in the framework of a standard teaching programme, thus allowing for a limited kind of guided SDL and a modicum of autonomy (see Sheerin, 1989).

There are several complications that arise both from the principle of student autonomy and its implementation. One is the resource base and the expertise of teachers-cum-helpers; another is the trainability of autonomous learning skills. Finally, autonomy may well not be universally applicable: the roles of teachers and learners differ widely in different contexts and, as Riley (1988) argues, the whole concept and its associated attitudes to the acquisition of knowledge may be an ethnocentric one acceptable only in certain cultures.

BIBLIOGRAPHY
Brookes, A. and Grundy, P. (eds) (1988). *Individualization and Autonomy in Language Learning*. Oxford: Modern English Publications with the British Council.
Crabbe, D. (1993). Fostering autonomy within the classroom: the teacher's responsibility. *System*, 21/4, 443–53.
Dickinson, L. (1988). *Self-Instruction in Language Learning*. Cambridge: Cambridge University Press.*
——(1993). Aspects of autonomous learning. *ELT Journal*, 47/4, 330–6.
Henner-Stanchina, C. and Riley, P. (1978). *Aspects of Autonomous Learning*. ELT Documents 103. London: British Council, 75–97.
Houghton, D., Long, C. and Fanning, P. (1988). Autonomy and individualization in language learning: the role and responsibilities of the EAP tutor. In A. Brookes and P. Grundy (eds), *Individualization and Autonomy in Language Learning*. Oxford: Modern English Publications, 75–87.
Oskarsson, M. (1978). *Approaches to Self-Assessment in Foreign Language Learning*. Oxford and New York: Pergamon.
Riley, P. (1988). The ethnography of autonomy. In A. Brookes and P. Grundy (eds), *Individualization and Autonomy in Language Learning*. Oxford: Modern English Publications, 12–34.
Sheerin, S. (1989). *Self-access*. Oxford: Oxford University Press.*
Wenden, A. (1991). *Learner Strategies for Learner Autonomy*. Englewood Cliffs, NJ: Prentice-Hall.

JMCD

**study skills** This term and its associated activities are most widely applied first in the field of teaching English for academic purposes to non-native speakers (see ENGLISH FOR SPECIFIC PURPOSES), and secondly in educational contexts where the language of study is the student's mother tongue. In both cases the framework is usually that of higher and further education. In the former area in particular it has become quite a major industry, with many courses, conferences, teaching materials and academic papers devoted to it. Furthermore, it is receiving increasing attention in so-called 'GENERAL PURPOSE ENGLISH' programmes and course books.

DEFINITION AND COVERAGE

The concept of study skills is a very wide-ranging one, and the following list shows a selection of the individual skills that typically recur in the literature and in practice, whether in ESL/EFL or in the L1:

- listening and note-taking;
- using the library;
- research skills;
- note-making from reading;
- planning your time and getting organized;
- seminar strategies;
- writing in examinations;
- outlining;
- reading faster;
- preparing bibliographies.

It is clear from this small sample that at one end of the spectrum we are concerned with relatively 'mechanical' skills or techniques (libraries; referencing), and at the other end with study processes and strategies that are virtually synonymous with the skills and sub-skills of language use (reading; listening). Others are defined according to the study situations themselves (seminars; examinations) and yet others are concerned with personal aspects of efficiency and time management quite unrelated to linguistic competence. The language focus will of course

differ according to whether the students are learning in their mother tongue or in a foreign language.

The treatment of these multifarious perspectives in handbooks and teaching materials varies correspondingly. Many are concerned with a global view, with straightforward titles such as *The Good Study Guide* (Northedge, 1990) or *Study Skills in English* (Wallace, 1980), and covering most of the spectrum outlined above. Others deal with a specific area, such as *Developing Reference Skills* (O'Brien and Jordan, 1985), with chapters on efficient dictionary skills, using indexes and contents pages, and finding one's way round an academic library. To a certain extent this is in the 'how to . . .' tradition, of which Rowntree's (1970) programmed learning handbook is a classic example. Particularly in EFL, many materials examine in detail one language skill in relation to a study context, sometimes in general terms (for example, *Study Listening* (Lynch, 1983)) or by linking it to a specific academic subject. The language skills perspective has been usefully explored by Candlin and others (1978), who suggest that a 'macro-skill' such as listening or reading can be defined quite precisely as a study skill if filtered through an academic study activity or 'mode'. This enables the sub-skills of listening and of note-taking, for example, to be integrated in a realistic and authentic way (see also FOUR SKILLS and TEACHING INTEGRATED SKILLS). Finally, in general course books, 'study skills', although more restricted in scope, nevertheless cover comparable techniques to those used in EAP or L1 study. Frequently practised skills are the use of monolingual dictionaries, and efficient ways of recording and learning new vocabulary items.

The philosophy underpinning all materials and background papers that are concerned with the development of study techniques and strategies is expressed in the following words by Rowntree (1970: 8): 'Study involves you in deciding goals and

choosing methods, solving problems ...
collecting information, separating facts from
opinions, comparing facts and weighing up
opinions, and looking for proof or truth.'
The objective, in other words, is to offer a
model – often prescriptive – of 'good' study
habits in order to encourage increased personal autonomy and responsibility for one's
own learning (see AUTONOMOUS LEARNING).

## ISSUES IN STUDY SKILLS

In an area as diverse as this, with a broad
range of applications and often a prescriptive stance, there will inevitably be some
unanswered questions and the possibility of
controversy. One area of debate, then, is
the extent to which particular study skills
may be considered as universal or conversely
discipline-specific. This point is picked up
by C. Johns (1978) in relation to the skills
required to take part in academic seminars:
her argument is that the 'seminar skills' typically taught in the framework of EAP and
pre-sessional courses are in fact derived from
the humanities and social science perspective of the 'inward-facing circle', whereas
science students may well have to adapt to
an entirely different format not based on
free discussion. A. M. Johns pursues this
line of argument, claiming that there is
insufficient empirical research, both qualitative and quantitative, on transferable vs
non-transferable skills. Her own enquiries
indicate, for example, that summarizing and
note-taking techniques may be discipline-
specific, as may turn-taking and question-
posing skills, so that it is inappropriate to
suppose a list of skills in advance of a firmer
research base.

A second problem area in EAP in particular concerns the extent to which skills
are already familiar and simply in need of
activating in another language. For many
learners this may indeed be the case, but
there are many others who either come

from very different academic cultures, with
different learning traditions and expectations, or who are just starting out in higher
education and to whom study skills are
therefore not familiar.

Finally, Waters and Waters (1992) offer
a re-orientation in established thinking about
the nature and pedagogy of study skills.
Claiming that conventional approaches in
EAP/EFL (less so in L1 contexts) often fail
because they only try to impart a repertoire
of learnable techniques, the authors propose a distinction between study *skills* and
study *competence*. The latter perspective, they
argue, allows for a non-atomistic, holistic
view of studying, based on core characteristics and abilities typically identified with
the 'successful student'. These include being
good at critical questioning; a high degree
of self-awareness; being able to think clearly
and logically; and imposing their own framework on study data (p. 263). Their paper
puts forward a procedure for using these
cognitive and affective features as a basis
for study skills materials design.

BIBLIOGRAPHY
Candlin, C. N., Kirkwood, J. M. and Moore,
  H. M. (1978). Study skills in English: theoret-
  ical issues and practical problems. In R. Mackay
  and A. Mountford (eds), *English for Specific
  Purposes*. London: Longman, 172–216.
Johns, A. M. (1988). The discourse commun-
  ities dilemma: identifying transferable skills
  for the academic milieu. *English for Specific
  Purposes*, 7/1, 55–9.
Johns, C. (1978). Seminar discussion strategies.
  In *Pre-sessional Courses for Overseas Students*.
  ETIC Occasional Paper. London: British
  Council, 60–3.
Lynch, T. (1983). *Study Listening*. Cambridge:
  Cambridge University Press.*
Northedge, A. (1990). *The Good Study Guide*.
  Milton Keynes: Open University.*
O'Brien, T. and Jordan, R. R. (1985). *Developing
  Reference Skills*. London: Collins.
Rowntree, D. (1970). *Learn How to Study*. Lon-
  don: Macdonald.

Wallace, M. (1980). *Study Skills in English.* Cambridge: Cambridge University Press.*

Waters, M. and Waters, A. (1992). Study skills and study competence: getting the priorities right. *ELT Journal,* 46/3, 264–73.*

JMCD

**stylistics** In general terms, stylistics is the study of factors governing the linguistic choices made by individuals or social groups. More particularly, the term refers to literary stylistics, and the way linguistic form amplifies meaning in literary texts. Initially inspired by Roman Jakobson's identification of a 'poetic function' in which the message form is all-important (Jakobson, 1960), stylistics has often been concerned with deviation from normal usage, and linguistic patterning, particularly in poetry. In recent years stylistics has moved away from this formal approach, and adopted a view of literariness as a quality relative to context. (See also LITERATURE TEACHING.)

BIBLIOGRAPHY
Jakobson, R. (1960). Closing statement: linguistics and poetics. In T. A. Sebeok (ed.), *Style in Language.* Cambridge, MA: MIT Press, 350–77.

Wales, K. (1989). *A Dictionary of Stylistics.* London: Longman.

Widdowson, H. G. (1975). *Stylistics and the Teaching of Literature.* London: Longman.

——(1992). *Practical Stylistics.* Oxford: Oxford University Press.

GC

**subset principle** A principle of learning theory (rather than UNIVERSAL GRAMMAR itself) that learners always make the minimal assumptions about the language they are acquiring which they extend, instead of the maximal assumptions which they restrict; the main example is the governing category parameter setting for pronominals and anaphors in the Binding Theory.

BIBLIOGRAPHY
Atkinson, M. (1992). *Children's Syntax.* Oxford: Blackwell.

Cook, V. J. (1990). Timed comprehension of binding in advanced learners of English. *Language Learning,* 40/4, 557–99.

Wexler, K. and Manzini, M. R. (1987). Parameters and learnability. In T. Roeper and E. Williams (eds), *Parameters and Linguistic Theory,* Dordrecht: Reidel.

VJC

**suggestopaedia** Elaborated by Lozanov, this language teaching method rests upon twelve psychological and pedagogical (but not linguistic) premises whose thrust is that if learning blocks and psychic tension are de-suggested, learning can be accelerated. Long tracts of material organized into *acts* are provided. Baroque music and comfortable surroundings are used to induce relaxation. Familiarization with each *act* includes a whispered *concert reading* to music. Vast claims have been made for the method, e.g. that 1000 target-language words per day can be retained. Detractors (e.g. Scovel) assert that suggestopaedia is a 'pseudo-science' and any success it has is explained by its 'placebo' effect. (See also HUMANISTIC APPROACHES.)

BIBLIOGRAPHY
Lozanov, G. (1978). *Suggestology and Outlines of Suggestopedy.* New York: Gordon and Breach.

Scovel, T. (1979). Review of *Suggestology and Outlines of Suggestopedy. TESOL Quarterly,* 13, 255–66.

JTR

**surrender value** This concept is taken from the world of insurance. A policy with high surrender value yields a quick return on investment. Wilkins (1974) observes that in some situations (e.g. on PRE-SESSIONAL COURSES) the learner requires a swift 're-turn' on 'investment' made, in terms of ability to communicate. Wilkins argues that the NOTIONAL/FUNCTIONAL SYLLABUS provides this since the learner is soon able to use language to communicative ends. The STRUCTURAL SYLLABUS, in contrast, has low surrender value because it may take a considerable time before the learner has enough grammar to attempt communication.

BIBLIOGRAPHY
Wilkins, D. A. (1974). Notional syllabuses and the concept of a minimum adequate grammar. In S. P. Corder and E. Roulet (eds), *Linguistic Insights in Applied Linguistics*. Brussels: AIMAV, 119–28.*
——(1976). *Notional Syllabuses*. Oxford: Oxford University Press.* [Particularly chapter 3.]
                                                    KJ

**syllabus**   The term is used in many different ways, but the central concept is of a statement of a programme's aims and content (and for some methodology and evaluation also). See PROCESS SYLLABUS for proposals that procedures rather than content are what should be specified. Many syllabuses organize content for teaching purposes. This usually involves selecting one item type to act as the unit of organization, and names like STRUCTURAL SYLLABUS, SITUATIONAL SYLLABUS, NOTIONAL/FUNCTIONAL SYLLABUSES identify these item types; see SYLLABUS INVENTORY and SELECTION OF UNITS OF ORGANIZATION IN SYLLABUS DESIGN for further discussion. Organization of content also often involves ordering items for pedagogic presentation. (See White, 1988; also APPROACH and A PRIORI/POSTERIORI SYLLABUS.)

BIBLIOGRAPHY
White, R. V. (1988). *The ELT Curriculum* Oxford: Blackwell.
                                                    KJ

**syllabus inventory**   Some writers distinguish between syllabus and syllabus inventory. This latter is a set of lists, usually of the THRESHOLD LEVEL sort, of topics, roles, settings, notions, functions, structures. The syllabus designer may take any one of these as his 'unit of organization'. For example, he might choose to create a TOPIC SYLLABUS, organizing the programme around the topic list. This syllabus would utilize the other inventory lists in the construction of materials, but the topic list would provide the programme with its focus and organization. A syllabus is thus a syllabus inventory with a 'unit of organization' identified. (See SELECTION OF UNITS OF ORGANIZATION IN SYLLABUS DESIGN.)

BIBLIOGRAPHY
Johnson, K. (1982). *Communicative Syllabus Design and Methodology*. Oxford: Pergamon Institute of English.
                                                    KJ

**synchronic/diachronic**   The linguist Ferdinand de Saussure is associated with the distinction between diachronic linguistics, which studies language change over time, and synchronic linguistics, which focuses on one particular point in time. In Saussure's age (the first decades of the twentieth century), linguistic studies had been predominantly diachronic (concerned with language evolution) and he advocated a shift towards synchrony.

BIBLIOGRAPHY
Saussure, F. de (1974). *Course in General Linguistics*, trans. W. Baskin. London: Fontana/Collins. [Originally published in 1916.]
                                                    KJ

**syntagmatic/paradigmatic**   The linguist Ferdinand de Saussure considered two relationships between linguistic items. When viewed as a linear sequence, an item holds syntagmatic relations with those preceding and following it. For example, in *they will eat*, the modal *will* is syntagmatically related to *they* and *eat*. Paradigmatic relations hold between an item and similar ones that can appear in the same position in a sequence. The above example indicates that other modals like *can*, *should*, *must* would be paradigmatically related to *will*. Both these types of relationship are useful at various levels of linguistic study. For example, in establishing what a modal verb is, it is useful to consider where in a sentence one may occur (syntagmatic relations), and what other items have the same occurrence (paradigmatic relations). See STRUCTURE, and Lyons (1968).

BIBLIOGRAPHY
Lyons, J. (1968). *Introduction to Theoretical Linguistics*. Cambridge: Cambridge University Press.
Saussure, F. de (1974). *Course in General Linguistics*, trans. W. Baskin. London: Fontana/Collins. [Originally published in 1916.]

KJ

**syntax**   Traditionally, a component of GRAMMAR, alongside the lexicon (LEXIS) and inflectional MORPHOLOGY, which determines how words combine to form sentences. In CHOMSKYAN LINGUISTICS, syntax is central to linguistic theory, alongside PHONOLOGY, MORPHOLOGY and SEMANTICS, in characterizing the NATIVE SPEAKER's linguistic COMPETENCE. Modern syntactic theories adopt either a dependency (see DEPENDENCY GRAMMAR) or a phrase structure view of sentence STRUCTURE. Within the latter, words form phrases and phrases combine into sentences. In recent approaches, the sentence is just another type of phrase. For Chomskyan linguistics the syntax of languages varies within quite narrow limits, the range of possibilities being given by a small set of parameters.

An example is the head parameter, which allows heads to be phrase-initial, as in English, or phrase-final, as in Japanese. See also GENERATIVE GRAMMAR, NON-GENERATIVE GRAMMAR, SENTENCE PATTERN.

BIBLIOGRAPHY
Haegeman, L. (1994). *Introduction to Government and Binding Theory*. 2nd edn. Oxford: Blackwell.
Roberts, I. (1996). *Comparative Syntax*. London: Edward Arnold.

EJ

**systemic grammar**   A model for analysing linguistic STRUCTURES as interrelated systems of choices of formal categories (classes) for the expression of meaning in social context, developed by the British linguist M. A. K. Halliday and his associates. Systemic functional grammar, particularly prominent in British EDUCATIONAL LINGUISTICS, is descended from systemic grammar.

BIBLIOGRAPHY
Berry, H. M. (1977). *An Introduction to Systemic Linguistics*. London: Batsford.
Halliday, M. A. K. (1995). *An Introduction to Functional Grammar*. 2nd edn. London: Edward Arnold. [The first edition of this book (1985) was reviewed by one of Halliday's early collaborators, R. Huddleston, in 1988. See Constituency, multi-functionality and grammaticalization in Halliday's *Functional Grammar*. *Journal of Linguistics*, 24/1, 137–74.]*
Hudson, R. A. (1986). Systemic grammar. [Review of Berry (1977).] *Linguistics*, 24, 791–815. [A critique of the theory by one of its founders.]*

EJ

# T

**task-based syllabuses** A syllabus is said to be 'task-based' when the organizing principle involved is not the presentation and practice of the language to be learned but the specification of activities designed to engage learners in language-using work, usually without regard to the precise linguistic features such activities are likely to involve. (See also PROCEDURAL SYLLABUS, TASK-BASED TEACHING.)

BIBLIOGRAPHY
Candlin, G. N. and Murphy, D. (eds) (1987). *Language Learning Tasks*. Englewood Cliffs, NJ: Prentice-Hall.
Nunan, D. (1989). *Designing Tasks for the Communicative Classroom*. Cambridge: Cambridge University Press.
Prabhu, N. S. (1987). *Second Language Pedagogy*. Oxford: Oxford University Press.

RLA

**task-based teaching** Much current interest is focused on the nature of classroom activities (tasks) learners are asked to undertake, and on the possibility of using these tasks as the basis for syllabus design. Prabhu's work (1987) on the PROCEDURAL SYLLABUS is a major attempt at task-based teaching, one of his motivations for the approach being to achieve true MESSAGE-FOCUS in the classroom. Others like Skehan (1992) are led in a similar direction through belief in the importance of interaction to language learning. There is a growing literature classifying task types (for details see Nunan, 1989) and also on identifying criteria for grading task difficulty (see Skehan and Foster, 1995; also PRODUCTION PROCESSES). Criteria for deciding on task content for a teaching programme differ: Long (1985) uses needs analysis, a procedure which is entirely contrary to the spirit of Prabhu's work. For general discussion on tasks, see Crookes and Gass (1993a, b).

BIBLIOGRAPHY
Crookes, G. and Gass, S. M. (1993a). *Tasks and Language Learning: Integrating theory and practice*. Clevedon: Multilingual Matters.*
——(1993b). *Tasks in a Pedagogical Context: Integrating theory and practice*. Clevedon: Multilingual Matters.*
Long, M. H. (1985). A role for instruction in second language acquisition: task-based language training. In K. Hyltenstam and M. Pienemann (eds), *Modelling and Assessing Second Language Acquisition*. Clevedon: Multilingual Matters, 77–100.
Nunan, D. (1989). *Designing Tasks for the Communicative Classroom*. Cambridge: Cambridge University Press.
Prabhu, N. S. (1987). *Second Language Pedagogy: A perspective*. Oxford: Oxford University Press.*
Skehan, P. (1992). Second language acquisition strategies and task-based learning. In P. Skehan and C. Wallace (eds), *Thames Valley University Working Papers in English Language Teaching*. London: Thames Valley University, 178–208.
Skehan, P. and Foster, P. (1995). Task type and task processing conditions as influences on foreign language performance. In P. Skehan (ed.), *Thames Valley University Working Papers in English Language Teaching*. London: Thames Valley University, 139–88.

KJ

**teachability hypothesis** This notion is associated with the work of Pienemann (1988, 1989), who claims to have shown that instruction can speed up the rate of development in SLA (see RATE/ROUTE IN SLA), providing that learners are instructed on one stage beyond their current proficiency level (see also CLASSROOM STUDIES IN SLA). Pienemann (1989) reports, for example, that teaching the German verb-second phenomenon (*Heute bin ich ins Kino gegangen* 'Today have I to the cinema gone') to a group of Italian-speaking adolescents who were at the stage just prior to verb-second (in fact, the verb-separation stage: *Heute ich bin ins Kino gegangen* 'Today I have to the cinema gone') led to their acquiring verb-second productively. Subjects who were at earlier stages of development did not acquire productive use of verb-second, however. (See also CONSCIOUSNESS RAISING, TEACHING GRAMMAR.)

BIBLIOGRAPHY
Pienemann, M. (1988). Determining the influence of instruction on L2 speech processing. *AILA Review*, 5, 40–72.
——(1989). Is language teachable? Psycholinguistic experiments and hypotheses. *Applied Linguistics*, 10, 52–79.

RH

**teacher education** The first issue is to decide whether or not to opt for a broad definition or a narrow one. Under a broad definition 'teacher education' would refer to all planned interventions intended to help teachers, directly or indirectly, to become better at, or at least better informed about, their job. Across the range that such a definition could cover, several considerations would be crucial to productive discussion:

(a)   the *stage* of a teacher's career at which the intervention comes, whether it is initial (pre-service) or after the teacher has accrued some experience (in-service);

(b)   the *setting* for the intervention, whether it comes in the teacher's workplace or whether the teacher has to go elsewhere for it, perhaps for a substantial amount of time;

(c)   the *source* of the intervention, whether it comes from someone in the role of an 'expert' (the hierarchical model) or from a peer (the non-hierarchical model) or from the teacher him- or herself;

(d)   whether the intervention is relatively *formal*, for example, a one-year course in a training institution, or *informal*, for example, a regular gathering of teachers on a voluntary basis;

(e)   whether the intervention is primarily aimed at directly helping a teacher become better, in some obviously practical sense, at the job ('knowing how', e.g. *training*), or at helping him or her become better informed ('knowing that', e.g. *education*).

A broad definition would therefore cover the provision of professional courses for initial (or pre-service) training, and for teachers already working (in-service), as well as academic courses such as MA programmes for pre-service or for serving teachers. It would also extend to any non-course provision of relatively informal opportunities for teachers to learn more about their work. Most broadly, it could also extend to what is typically called 'teacher development', where 'development' is distinguished both from 'education' and from 'training' by being seen as essentially something you do for yourself (though not necessarily alone), rather than something someone else does to you.

Under a narrow definition 'teacher education' would exclude both 'training' and 'development' altogether, and would confine itself to the provision of formal opportunities for becoming better informed about the job of being a teacher, itself probably broadly conceived.

The second issue, if we opt for a broad definition of the overall topic of 'teacher education', is: what sorts of intervention are most helpful to teachers? Here the major issue that has dogged formal teacher training, at least over recent decades, is probably how best to strike a satisfactory balance between a transmission and an experiential approach to any intervention, or, put more crudely, how to solve the problem that trainers need to 'practise what they preach' in order to be credible to their trainees, who will otherwise complain that they are 'lectured' to about practical matters of which they have insufficient practical experience, and by people whose own practical classroom experience seems at best remote.

An obvious extra question then arises from our preliminary list of considerations: can the same sorts of intervention be appropriate at any time in a teacher's career, or do interventions need to be designed to respect the stages we can expect any teacher to go through as experience accrues, and do interventions need to be designed differently for teacher training, teacher education and teacher development?

A further question is then prompted in respect of all pre-service work: even if initial teacher education is effective in helping teachers survive their first difficult years, will it not simply succeed in producing teachers who for the rest of their careers will teach in the way that was perhaps appropriate to them as absolute beginners, but not to them as experienced professionals? This is particularly problematic in circumstances quite commonly encountered around the world, where resources are unlikely to make it possible for teachers to have much in the way of follow-up work to anything they get at the initial, pre-service stage of their careers. This suggests that teachers in such circumstances may need to be trained initially in a way of teaching that will be appropriate only later in their careers, and which may therefore represent an extremely difficult challenge for beginners. This certainly does seem to be the preferred pattern around the world, and clearly it carries the considerable risk that teachers will have a somewhat traumatic start to their careers, a start that will encourage them to resist innovations later, if they have already had

to struggle so hard just to teach in the way that they have at last become accustomed to using.

The dilemma, then, is that it seems right to want teachers to get off to a good, confident start to their careers, and so we need to help them with a way of teaching that is suitable for beginners, and yet at the same time we want them to develop in a way that leaves them open to changing their teaching as their career progresses. The obvious answer, wherever circumstances permit, is to offer regular opportunities for teachers to follow up their initial training. But where circumstances are not so favourable, teachers perhaps need to be trained at the beginning of their careers in a way that will not only make their initial survival in the classroom relatively painless for them, but also in a way that will simultaneously help them to understand, even at that early stage, that that is all that is being done for them. They can be offered an extremely practical classroom skills development course, for example, to make sure that they can at least write legibly on the blackboard and be heard at the back of the room (to give two very basic examples of crucial classroom skills). They can also be offered a very substantial amount of supported teaching practice, with the degree of support gradually being reduced so that by the time they leave the training situation they are reasonably well used to managing a class by themselves. But they will also need to understand very clearly that all they are being 'given' is survival skills, and that they will have to gradually develop their own 'sense of plausibility' (Prabhu, 1987: 103–4) about how best to teach as their experience grows, and hopefully their professional competence and confidence along with it. To this end their initial training could help them by exploring ways in which even beginning teachers can be fruitfully reflective about their work. For example, if in our support for teaching practice we focus exclusively on simply asking them to consider whether or not their own performance was satisfactory, we cannot expect to be very successful at stimulating their curiosity about classroom language learning (and therefore teaching). They will probably be too anxious about their own performance. Perhaps by using such methods as team-teaching and peer observation, however, we might be able to help them articulate their puzzles about what happens in the classroom, taking them far beyond their immediate and highly practical concern for their own classroom performance towards a preliminary degree of reflectiveness.

This notion of reflectiveness has become a key one in recent discussions of all forms of teacher education (broadly defined). It is commonly held that being 'reflective' is a major part of being a modern professional language teacher, and an essential element in teacher development. Being 'reflective' is an aspect of 'teacher thinking', which itself has become the object of considerable study. Becoming 'reflective' is also often seen as a likely outcome of encouraging teachers to become researchers in their own classrooms, and therefore, in all aspects of teacher education, as broadly conceived here, the notion of the 'teacher as researcher' is also current. Student teachers in initial training are encouraged to undertake small-scale research projects (usually along the lines of ACTION RESEARCH), students in teacher education, for example on MA courses, are required to produce research-based dissertations, and adopting a 'research perspective' is seen as a crucial element in development work. In such matters, language teacher work is slowly catching up with work in education in general. It is intriguing to speculate what the reasons for language teaching coming so late to these ideas might be. One possibility is that language teaching is very unusual, though not entirely unique, among school subjects in having a tradition behind it of academic research on the way in which the subject is learned. This might have diverted people from looking at what was happening in research on education in general,

since it might have been expected that it would be much more useful to look at research specific to the field. This perception might have been reinforced by the name given to that academic research field – APPLIED LINGUISTICS – since it implied that answers to teachers' questions could be expected from applications of the highly developed, and highly esoteric, field of linguistics. The second, and equally if not more ironic, possibility is that the field of language teaching has also had a quite vigorous tradition of classroom research behind it, but that tradition has had its base more among academics in universities than among teachers in schools. This may have given the impression that the field was already well catered for in research terms. It also seems to have given the impression that the field already had a well-worked-out methodology for doing research in the classroom, which seems in turn to have meant that when 'action research' began to be advocated for teachers, it was readily assumed that the already developed procedures of academic classroom research on language teaching would provide an appropriate model for teachers to follow in their own professional development through research in their own classrooms. In the 1990s Allwright began drawing attention to the possible inappropriateness of the accepted procedures of academic classroom research by proposing an alternative – 'exploratory practice' – based first on the articulation of classroom 'puzzles' and then on the exploitation of familiar language classroom activities as tools to investigate them with.

A further irony in the field of teacher education in general, and potentially a much more problematic one, stems from the observation that all this work is based on the idea that teachers of all subjects (not just of languages) need, right from the very beginning of their careers, to develop their own understanding of their work from their own intellectual enquiry. This idea, however, runs counter to the prevailing ideology among many governments in the 1990s that teachers are to be judged primarily in terms of their ability to act as relatively efficient 'delivery systems' for national curricula. It is not at all clear how such current 'best practice' in teacher education can be reconciled with such a conception of the teacher's role. Indeed, teacher education in the 1990s could be said to be working directly against that conception, towards a conception of the 'reflective practitioner' as someone who will be well placed to challenge it. (See also QUALIFICATIONS IN ENGLISH LANGUAGE TEACHING.)

BIBLIOGRAPHY

Allwright, D. (1993). Integrating 'research' and 'pedagogy': appropriate criteria and practical possibilities. In J. Edge and K. Richards (eds), *Teachers Develop Teachers Research*. Oxford: Heinemann, 125–35.

Allwright, D. and Lenzuen, R. (1997). Exploratory practice: work at the Cultural Inglesa, Rio de Janeiro, Brazil. *Language Teaching Research*, 1/1, 73–9.

Nunan, D. (1989). *Understanding Language Classrooms*. New York: Prentice-Hall.

Prabhu, N. S. (1987). *Second Language Pedagogy*. Oxford: Oxford University Press.

Richards, J. C. and Lockhart, C. (1994). *Reflective Teaching in Second Language Classrooms*. Cambridge: Cambridge University Press.

Richards, J. C. and Nunan, D. (eds) (1990). *Second Language Teacher Education*. Cambridge: Cambridge University Press.

Roberts, J. (1993). Review of J. C. Richards and D. Nunan (eds), *Second Language Teacher Education*. *ELT Journal*, 47/2, 177–80.

Wallace, M. (1991). *Training Foreign Language Teachers: A reflective approach*. Cambridge: Cambridge University Press.

Widdowson, H. G. (1990). Pedagogic research and teacher education. In H. G. Widdowson, *Aspects of Language Teaching*. Oxford: Oxford University Press. [Chapter 4.]

Woodward, T. (1991). *Models and Metaphors in Language Teacher Training*. Cambridge: Cambridge University Press.

RLA

## teacher research and development

(TR and TD)   These terms, both of which are in frequent current use, stand in a close relationship to each other. They are, however, most usefully regarded as overlapping yet distinct, with somewhat different terms of reference. Teacher development subsumes teacher research, which itself derives from a clearly defined orientation to research and the nature of knowledge, albeit one based on a wide range of possible research techniques. The TD/TR relationship is explored in detail in a recently published collection of conference papers with the intentionally ambiguous title of *Teachers Develop Teachers Research* (Edge and Richards, 1993). Neither term is restricted to language teaching: both have roots in general education, but also draw on a multiplicity of other sources.

## TEACHER DEVELOPMENT

TD is very broad in scope, and potentially takes in many aspects of a teacher's personal development alongside more mainstream professional areas. The term is frequently contrasted with 'teacher training' and 'TEACHER EDUCATION'. Wallace (1991: 3) puts it straightforwardly: 'The distinction is that training or education is something that can be presented or managed by *others*; whereas development is something that can be done only by and for *oneself*.' Lange explains this in the context of a model – or 'blueprint' – for a whole programme of teacher development, and offers the following definition: 'a term used . . . to describe a process of continual intellectual, experiential and attitudinal growth of teachers . . . the intent here is to suggest that teachers continue to evolve in the use, adaptation, and application of their art and craft' (1990: 250). TD, then, is to be seen as an ongoing process and an integral characteristic of a fully professional teacher.

From a general educational perspective, Hopkins (1993) is one of several authorities to formulate a direct connection between

TD and school development as a whole, particularly in a climate such as the one currently prevailing in the UK in which individual schools are increasingly under pressure to implement change themselves. Teacher research in classrooms – as a major element of TD – clearly has a key role to play. The underlying philosophy is one of 'empowerment' of teachers to take their own decisions and some control of their own professional pathways.

In the field of ELT, a large segment of which takes place outside the framework of mainstream educational systems, the focus has been somewhat different, even if the underlying ethos of TD has been similar. The most accessible manifestations of TD activity are found in the work of the Teacher Development Special Interest Group (TD SIG for short) of IATEFL. The TD SIG was established in 1986, 'with the aim of enabling and encouraging teachers to explore the opportunities for personal and professional evolution throughout their careers' (*Newsletter* no. 25, 1994: 15). The kind of work that it has spawned is multi-faceted, as a survey of its regular *Newsletter* or IATEFL conference proceedings shows, and covers the whole of the professional-personal spectrum. Teachers are concerned, for example, with the nature of 'bottom-up' change and innovation and with facets of their own classroom or school environment; they often choose to further their understanding of their own learners by themselves learning a new language; or they may wish to explore more personal notions of 'self-esteem' or 'failure', sometimes tapping directly into the writings of clinical psychologists or psychotherapists such as Abraham Maslow or Carl Rogers.

## TEACHER RESEARCH

It is important to note that TR has had a long and established tradition in education, at least since the 1960s, more recent developments in ELT drawing very closely on those traditions (see also ACTION RESEARCH). A key figure in promoting TR in both principle and practice was Stenhouse (1975), who questioned traditional approaches to curriculum development and educational research. In essence, he challenged authority for its own sake and encouraged autonomy, preferring to see teachers as critical professionals and active researchers rather than as merely on the receiving end of decisions taken elsewhere. In terms of TR specifically, this led to the development of an alternative view to the traditional experimental research paradigm based on sampling in controlled circumstances, measurement, generalization and prediction. Research is instead done *by*, not just *on*, teachers in classrooms, in other words, in natural rather than experimental settings and allowing for subjectivity, multiple perspectives and what Stenhouse refers to as 'the immediate and local meanings of action'. The paradigm, then, is interpretive and qualitative rather than numerical, although – at least at the level of research techniques – these terms should not be regarded as mutually exclusive.

In the context of teacher education in ELT, Wallace (1991) explores the implications of three current models. The first is the 'craft' model, in which trainees essentially learn the techniques or tools of the trade from an expert. The second is the very prevalent 'applied science' model where, put simply, there is a one-way transmission and application of the established knowledge base of a discipline: in ELT this might be, for instance, work in behavioural or cognitive psychology, or linguistic theory. With both of these models in operation, it is argued, 'practice' and 'theory' are largely separated. To overcome this, Wallace then proposes a third possibility, the 'reflective' model, which has the potential to formalize and systematize teachers' *experiential* knowledge. By reflecting on their practice, teachers will be able to formulate hypotheses and clarify issues of importance to their own working environment, and then to investigate them. (The notion of the 'reflective practitioner' is borrowed from Schön's work (1983) on the professions in general.)

There are, of course, a vast number of possible areas for teachers to investigate: they may be to do with whole classes or with individual case studies, with methodology, language development, school or classroom management, teacher attitudes, evaluation and many more. (An illustrative list from one context is set out in Nunan, 1990.) The range of available research techniques is in principle likewise very wide. Techniques of data collection include various kinds of observation, field notes and diaries (see DIARY STUDIES), interviews and questionnaires, audio and video recording, and documentary evidence. Clearly a teacher-researcher would need to match the method to the type of issue under investigation. (See also RESEARCH METHODOLOGY.)

BIBLIOGRAPHY
Edge, J. and Richards, K. (eds) (1993). *Teachers Develop Teachers Research*. Oxford: Heinemann.*
Hopkins, D. (1993). *A Teacher's Guide to Classroom Research*. 2nd edn. Buckingham and Philadelphia: Open University Press.
Lange, D. L. (1990). A blueprint for a teacher development program. In J. C. Richards and D. Nunan (eds), *Second Language Teacher Education*. Cambridge: Cambridge University Press.
Nunan, D. (1990). The teacher as researcher. In C. Brumfit and R. Mitchell (eds), *Research in the Language Classroom*. Oxford: Modern English Publications with the British Council, 16–32.
Schön, D. (1983). *The Reflective Practitioner*. London: Temple-Smith.
Stenhouse, L. (1975). *An Introduction to Curriculum Research and Development*. London: Heinemann.
Wallace, M. J. (1991). *Training Foreign Language Teachers*. Cambridge: Cambridge University Press.*

JMCD

**teacher talk** is the term used to describe the register which teachers use in class with learners. It is natural that in the language learning context the language used is often the target language, of which the teacher is a NATIVE SPEAKER (NS) and the learners non-native speakers (NNS). In this case the teacher talk will also be FOREIGNER TALK (NS to NNS interaction), and indeed many teacher talk studies compare and contrast teachers' classroom talk to NNSs and to NSs. Many studies deal with language classrooms, but there are those which look at other subject lessons where NNS students are present. For accessible summaries of the applied linguistics teacher talk literature, see Chaudron (1988) and Ellis (1985).

Some studies attempt to measure the quantity of teacher and learner class talk, often with the pedagogic aim of alerting trainee teachers to the risk of dominating classes. Research shows that in L1 classes teachers take up about 60% of classroom talk, and although various L2 class studies cite different figures, the consensus is that about two-thirds of L2 class talk comes from the teacher. A number of studies use CLASSROOM OBSERVATION systems such as that of Bellack and others (1966) to analyse teacher talk functions. Bellack has a four-part framework for analysing classroom interaction: structure → solicit → respond → react, and the other systems all have comparable categories. The unsurprising finding of various studies is that teacher talk is largely associated with Bellack's structuring, soliciting and reacting moves (see MOVE), with learners typically confining themselves to responding. There have been various other ways of analysing teacher talk functions and behaviour. Mitchell and others (1981), for example, analyse in terms of activities (e.g. presentation, drill/exercise, etc.) rather than of moves. One aspect of teacher behaviour that has been particularly well studied is ERROR CORRECTION.

Teacher talk is one of the SIMPLIFIED CODES, like PIDGINS AND CREOLES, motherese and foreigner talk. Central characteristics of these, which teacher talk shares, are simplification and reduction. A number of detailed studies look at the differences on various linguistic levels between teachers' speech to L1 and to L2 learners. Speech to L2 learners is found to have a slower rate of delivery, with more frequent and longer pauses, more exaggerated intonation and greater volume. Vocabulary use is more basic, more stylistically neutral, less idiomatic, less diverse. For phonological and lexical characteristics of teacher talk, see Henzl (1979). Much attention has been given to the issue of how to measure syntactic complexity. The most common means are by T-UNIT (e.g. Gaies, 1977) and MEAN UTTERANCE LENGTH, though other measures like degree of MARK-EDNESS have also been used (e.g. Long and Sato, 1983). Whatever the preferred measure, a common finding is that teachers use syntactically simpler language with NNSs, and are also sensitive to learner level. Gaies (1977), for example, shows regular incremental increases in the syntactic complexity of teacher talk according to learner level. There have been some detailed examinations of teacher discourse, for example, how rules and explanations are given in class (Faerch, 1986). Gaies (1977) notes similarities between teacher discourse modifications – like repetition, prodding, prompting and modelling – and those of motherese. Indeed, a major characteristic of both registers is that they are rough- (but not fine-) tuned to interactant level. Ellis (1985) notes that it is a matter for speculation how the teacher determines what adjustments are felt to be appropriate.

The similarities between motherese and teacher talk play an important role in theorizing associated with 'acquisition-based' approaches to language teaching. In the 1960s, applied linguists like Newmark and Reibel argued that the mother's (care-taker's) input to the L1 child results in successful acquisition, and suggested that a similar type of input from the teacher would result in successful L2 acquisition. In Krashen's model, COMPREHENSIBLE INPUT (see also I + I) is seen as a characteristic of motherese which may also play a central role in L2 acquisition. There has been at least one pedagogically oriented study (Willis, 1981) which seeks to advise NNS teachers on how to modify their speech for language teaching purposes.

Some of the views expressed concerning the role of teacher talk in L2 acquisition are statements of belief rather than empirically verified facts, but there have been studies attempting to link characteristics of teacher talk to learner outcomes. On the sound level, there is some evidence that a slower rate of speech has a positive influence on comprehensibility. For syntax, Long (1985) found that learners given a syntactically simplified version of a lecture were significantly better at a comprehension task than a control group, although Chaudron (1988: 156) cites some counter-evidence.

Despite such studies, there are in general few which show direct beneficial consequences of teacher talk, and indeed some point up the relative imperviousness of interlanguage development to external influences such as teacher input. One example of this is the apparent lack of influence which frequency of input (e.g. a teacher's repeated use of a chosen structure) has on learner acquisition. There is evidence, for example, that instructional procedures have little effect on morpheme acquisition orders. Such conclusions are generally in line with L1 acquisition studies in the Chomskyan tradition, which place importance on processes of creative construction (see CREATIVE CONSTRUCTION THEORY).

Another somewhat negative finding relates to how different teacher talk is from natural out-of-class interaction. Although it is true that teacher talk simplifications do not in general result in ungrammatical speech, they can create very unnatural discourse. Long and Sato (1983) compared instances of teacher talk to out-of-class talk and found striking differences; for example, teachers use more display than referential questions, more imperatives, more comprehension checks. From this it might be argued that in important respects teacher talk fails to simulate aspects of natural discourse – the very discourse which teachers want their learners to perform.

BIBLIOGRAPHY

Bellack, A., Kliebard, H., Hyman, R. T. and Smith, F. L. (1966). *The Language of the Classroom*. New York: Teachers' College Press.

Chaudron, C. (1988). *Second language classrooms*. Cambridge: Cambridge University Press.\*

Ellis, R. (1985). *Understanding Second Language Acquisition*. Oxford: Oxford University Press.

Faerch, C. (1986). Rules of thumb and other teacher-formulated rules in the foreign language classroom. In G. Kasper (ed.), *Language, Teaching and Communication in the Foreign Language Classroom*. Aarhus: Aarhus University Press, 125–43.

Gaies, S. J. (1977). The nature of linguistic input in formal second language learning: linguistic and communicative strategies in ESL teachers' classroom language. In H. D. Brown, C. A. Yorio and R. H. Crymes (eds), *On TESOL '77: Teaching and Learning English as a Second Language: Trends in research and practice*. Washington, DC: TESOL, 201–12.

Henzl, V. M. (1979). Foreigner talk in the classroom. *International Review of Applied Linguistics*, 17, 159–67.

Long, M. H. (1985). Input and second language acquisition theory. In S. M. Gass and C. G. Madden (eds), *Input in Second Language Acquisition*. Rowley, MA: Newbury House, 377–93.

Long, M. H. and Sato, C. J. (1983). Classroom foreigner talk discourse: forms and functions of teachers' questions. In H. W. Seliger and M. H. Long (eds), *Classroom-Oriented Research in Second Language Acquisition*. Rowley, MA: Newbury House, 268–85.\*

Mitchell, R., Parkinson, B. and Johnstone, R. (1981). *The Foreign Language Classroom: An observational study*. Stirling Educational Monographs, no. 9. Stirling: University of Stirling, Department of Education.

Willis, J. (1981). *Teaching English through English*. London: Longman.

KJ

**teaching integrated skills**    One of the major features of the traditional language teaching paradigm has been the separating out of the so-called FOUR SKILLS of listening, speaking, reading and writing into pedagogically convenient units of learning. This compartmentalized view of the nature of a language skill has by and large been superseded as a foundation for course design by one that is closer to real-world usage, where skills are not normally activated in isolation from each other. The main thrust of this argument clearly derives from the development of COMMUNICATIVE METHODOLOGY, and it has also been an important element in ESP (see ENGLISH FOR SPECIFIC PURPOSES).

DEVELOPMENT AND PRINCIPLES

In the traditional model of language teaching, the four skills are often linked sequentially within a unit of learning: thus, for example, a reading passage may precede a listening task, or written homework may be set that recapitulates the grammar points taught in a lesson. Byrne (1981: 108) refers to this as 'reinforcement', and makes the important point that in this case 'the process of integrating language skills involves linking them together in such a way that what has been learnt . . . through the exercise of one skill is reinforced and perhaps extended through further . . . activities which bring one or more of the other skills into use.'

With the development of the principles of communicative methodology (for an overview see McDonough and Shaw, 1993), a quite different perspective on the integration of skills came to the fore, namely one which was more concerned with the replication of reality in the language classroom.

The starting-point is therefore to examine relevant contexts of language use in order to establish the natural occurrence and sequencing of language skills as appropriate to situations. It is, of course, by no means always the case that all skills will be activated every time: for a simple example, we might consider the noting down of a telephone message (short conversation and brief writing down) or a letter responding to a written advertisement. A more complex instance (though not necessarily more difficult in learning or practice terms) would be where a written response is followed through by further correspondence and by face-to-face interaction. The sequence of skills may then be reading → writing → reading → speaking → writing; note that individual skills may recur in a single context. Byrne (1981: 114) refers to this as a 'nexus of activities which bring different skills into play as and when they are appropriate'. Nunan (1989: 130) explains a similar principle in a different way by proposing such communicative design criteria as AUTHENTICITY, *task continuity* and *real-world focus*.

In the field of ESP, there is a natural link between the principle of integrated skills teaching and the notion of the 'target situation' (see NEEDS ANALYSIS), for the obvious reason that a learner's eventual goal is a real-world professional or academic context. The business person learning English may be doing so in order to engage in sales negotiations, involving all language skills in authentic combinations and proportions. The postgraduate student will be involved in many different study activities – lectures, examinations, seminars, private study – each of which will require a different range of effective skills use.

## INTEGRATED SKILLS IN THE CLASSROOM

Following developments in communicative methodology, and the pedagogical applications of a growing understanding of the components of skills and learning processes, practitioners have incorporated an integrated skills perspective directly into teaching materials and classroom tasks. A recent and explicit example is a series of course books simply entitled *Integrated Skills* (Milne, 1991, for instance). All four skills are practised in the context of topic-focused units (such as sport, jobs, holidays) and are also broken down into a wide range of component sub-skills within the overall goal of providing realistic learning frameworks. Thus writing covers letters, notes, instructions, descriptions, reports and so on. Further examples of a methodology based on skills integration are role plays, simulations and project work, though much smaller-scale classroom activities, such as INFORMATION-GAP tasks, clearly incorporate the same basic principle. From an ESP angle, listening and note-taking is just one example of the approach among many.

It is difficult to argue, however, that the language classroom can or should be merely a replication of reality exclusively fulfilling the demands of authenticity and 'naturalness' of use. The classroom is clearly also a pedagogic construct, with its own objectives and reality, by no means to be entirely equated with the outside world. First of all, specific skills may need to be 'weighted', perhaps because of their difficulty for learners or the need for remediation and reinforcement, or alternatively because of the frequency with which they will be required. Secondly, like points of grammar, skills can legitimately be broken down into smaller units or sub-skills to serve as enabling steps in the process of learning. Nunan's (1989) criteria for the integrated language lesson, in addition to the three principles listed earlier, also contain an explicit pedagogic focus, allowing for the itemization of language and learning factors in order to facilitate acquisition. Byrne too (1981) is aware that an integration of skills on communicative principles necessarily entails some degree of contrivance to match the classroom environment. Finally, the social organization of the classroom and its concomitant role relationships are themselves significant: tasks may also be devised with the purpose of establishing a cooperative principle within a group of learners working together (see Jacobs, 1988).

The points made here are readily illustrated in many current teaching materials, where communicative practice is balanced by practice in specific areas, by group and pair tasks, or by reinforcement. (See also JIGSAW PRINCIPLE; and for suggestions revolving around writing skills, Hedge, 1988.) The teaching of integrated skills, then, is best seen as a natural development of communicative methodology tempered by the specific requirements of learning in classrooms. See also TEACHING LISTENING, TEACHING READING, TEACHING SPEAKING, TEACHING WRITING.

BIBLIOGRAPHY
Byrne, D. (1981). Integrating skills. In K. Johnson and K. Morrow (eds), *Communication in the Classroom*. Harlow: Longman, 108–14.*
Hedge, T. (1988). *Writing*. Oxford: Oxford University Press.
Jacobs, G. (1988). Co-operative goal structure: a way to improve group activities. *ELT Journal*, 42/2, 97–101.
McDonough, J. and Shaw, C. (1993). *Materials and Methods in ELT*. Oxford: Blackwell.
Milne, B. (1991). *Integrated Skills: Intermediate*. Oxford: Heinemann.
Nunan, D. (1989). *Designing Tasks for the Communicative Classroom*. Cambridge: Cambridge University Press.

JMCD

**teaching listening** The traditional, classical view of skills entailed a simple classification into 'active' (speaking and writing) and 'passive' skills (listening and reading) (see also FOUR SKILLS). Furthermore, 'text' – whether written or spoken – was typically a vehicle for the acquisition and practice of grammar and lexis. This dual perspective on the comprehension skill itself and the nature of the linguistic input has undergone very considerable changes, which have had a direct impact on the ways in which listening skills are taught and on the type of listening materials available. Listening comprehension is now treated as an active process, paralleled by a finer discrimination between the written and spoken language, and between different styles of spoken material (see also TEACHING READING). As Richards (1985: 189) points out, 'current understanding of the nature of listening comprehension draws on research in psycholinguistics, semantics, pragmatics, discourse analysis, and cognitive science.'

PRINCIPLES

Consequently, it is useful to consider listening in terms of, first, the nature of the input – the text – and secondly the mechanisms of comprehension – the process. The subsequent main section then examines the implications of these principles for second/ foreign language learners and for the design of instructional materials.

*The spoken language* Although listening and reading are both comprehension skills and therefore self-evidently have much in common, it is equally obvious that the difference of medium will generate a range of input styles that differ from material intended to be read (with some exceptions such as the reading aloud of a formal speech or a news bulletin, for instance). The key distinctions are these (Brown and Yule, 1983; McDonough and Shaw, 1993; McKeating, 1981; Richards, 1985):

- The medium itself is sound, not print, and it therefore has a transience that the written medium does not. Moreover, the listener has little if any control over the speed of input.
- Information presented in spoken form tends to be less 'dense' and more redundant than

in written form. It may be more repetitive, too. There is also evidence to show that its grammatical and discourse structure tends to be less complex, for example, in its clausal basis and types of cohesive devices used (see COHESION).

- At least at the more informal end of the spectrum, speech is typically characterized by such phenomena as hesitation, pauses, false starts, half-completed sentences and changes of direction and even topic. It is also frequently ungrammatical.
- Speech is usually accompanied by a number of supra-segmental (see PHONOLOGY), non-linguistic and PARALINGUISTIC FEATURES such as INTONATION, tone of voice, gesture and the like which may act as aids to comprehension and which are anyway integral to the formulation of speech acts. However, there may also be different kinds of extraneous noise that interfere with message uptake.
- Conversational speech is cooperative; it is also constructed jointly between speaker and listener as roles shift and meaning develops interactively (Rost, 1990).

(See also SPOKEN AND WRITTEN DISCOURSE.)

From the summary above it should be clear that the features of speech are largely determined by the efforts made by the producer of language to plan and organize utterances in ongoing time, 'ideational COHERENCE' being more relevant than strict formal accuracy (Richards, 1985: 194). Some features facilitate comprehension; others make it a more complex process. Particularly in interactional speech (distinguished by Brown and Yule (1985) from 'transactional'), the product itself is not a fixed entity, but is constantly being developed and modified.

## PROCESSING THE SPOKEN LANGUAGE

It has already been noted that the listener should not be seen merely as a passive recipient of input, but instead as an active processor who actually interprets and creates meaning as utterances unfold. Listeners can activate a range of perceptual and cognitive strategies which, taken together, constitute the sub-skills that make up the concept of comprehension (see COMPREHENSION PROCESSES). Conventionally these sub-skills are divided into 'lower-order' and 'higher-order' ones, although they are interdependent, and the distinction is not to be regarded as one of mutually exclusive categories. The first are broadly concerned with skills involving perception and recognition; the second with the processing of meaning. These are discussed in turn in this section, and the discussion will then be followed by a comment on the role of real-world knowledge in relation to comprehension strategies.

At the most basic level, a listener needs to be able to segment the incoming stream of sound into recognizable component units such that word and phrase boundaries are identified. With a language like English, this is complicated by the phenomenon of linking sounds, where a word may be perceived as running into the next and thus misidentified ('he's in'; 'an egg'; 'some onions' are simple examples). It is also necessary to be able to recognize a number of other localized features of the spoken language, particularly clause and sentence boundaries, contracted forms (such as 'I'd've done it if I'd had time'), patterns of stress at both word and sentence level, including so-called 'marked' stress, and supra-segmental aspects such as INTONATION.

These lower-order skills are clearly necessary but not sufficient to account for the ability to comprehend speech. Furthermore, research evidence has shown that surface features are very rapidly lost to memory, even in a matter of seconds; longer-term comprehension and retention, in other words, work with propositions, not with the linear structure of sentences. The stages involved in recognizing raw speech, and holding it in short-term memory before transferring it to longer-term store, are detailed in Clarke and Clarke (1977), as quoted in Richards (1985: 190). At the higher level of semantic

**Table 1**   Processing sound and meaning (from McDonough and Shaw, 1993: 135).

| *Processing sound* | *Processing meaning* |
| --- | --- |
| Phonological | Semantic |
| Lower-order/automatic skills | Higher-order skills of organizing and interpreting |
| Recognition of sounds, words | Comprehension |
| Localized: the immediate text | Global: the meaning of the whole |
| Decoding what was said | Reconstruction after processing meaning |
| Perception | Cognition |

processing, the listener therefore needs to be able to organize speech into meaningful segments, including the use of linguistic clues to identify discourse boundaries; recognize redundancy and use the processing time gained by doing so; anticipate and think ahead; guess and make inferences; adapt to different kinds of spoken material. Richards (1985: 198–9) offers a comprehensive taxonomy of micro-skills for both conversational and formal speech. Table 1 (McDonough and Shaw, 1993: 135) is a simple list of the two sets of sub-skills enumerated here.

Comprehension also takes place along the further parameters of context and knowledge. Strategies are not activated in a cognitive vacuum, but also depend on the number of speakers, their role relationships, the setting and the overall purpose of the discourse, all of which contribute to the ways in which meaning is interpreted. Comprehension of the spoken language therefore has a pragmatic (see PRAGMATICS) as well as a semantic and syntactic dimension: 'The semantic structure of a sentence specifies what that sentence means as a structure in a given language, in abstraction from speaker and addressee; whereas pragmatics deals with that meaning as it is interpreted interactionally in a given situation' (Leech, 1977, quoted in Richards, 1985: 191; see also Rost, 1990). Finally, listeners have knowledge and experience which they will bring to bear in the process of comprehension. This may be straightforward knowledge of facts:

involvement in a discussion of European politics, for instance, will be facilitated if participants are already informed about the topic. It is common to bring such knowledge frameworks to bear, whether they are directly to do with a specific topic, or at the level of more general anticipation and expectation when a theme is announced: most listeners will have a frame of reference for, say, holidays or weddings or families, although cultural backgrounds may mean that such frames are quite divergent (see SCHEMA THEORY and TOP-DOWN PROCESSING).

TEACHING LISTENING COMPREHENSION

The principles underpinning the skill of listening described in the previous section have had a direct pedagogical impact on both the understanding of ways in which learners process the spoken language and the design and use of teaching materials. Listening comprehension skills have now come to be fully developed in their own right, in a way which is much less likely to approximate the traditional teaching model whereby a written text was read aloud in class, the task then being to answer generally factual comprehension questions.

*Learner characteristics*   However proficient as listeners in their mother tongue, clearly learners of a second or foreign language will be unlikely to be able to activate the full range of strategies available to a native speaker. Depending on current levels of proficiency (as well as a number of other individual variables such as motivation, age, aptitude and the like), learners will be at various stages of approximation to full competence. In terms of listening comprehension skills, this shortfall may have a variety of manifestations. A learner may, for instance, have insufficient grammatical knowledge, so that there is a reluctance to engage higher-order skills of guessing at meanings and anticipating subsequent utterances, the focus instead remaining at a very localized sentence or clause level of immediate decoding. If this process is itself unsuccessful, then very little of the utterance will be understood; and even if grammatical parsing does work, the constraints on memory retention of verbatim text will mean that the wider elements of the message – propositions – are not grasped. Secondly, and particularly where there is a lack of lexical knowledge, there is evidence that learners, at least at intermediate levels, tend to 'guess' and think they have heard even a nonsense word, instead of using all the discourse clues (topic, their own knowledge, the 'co-text') to try to make sense of what they have heard. The focus, in other words, is only on phonological features. Overall, these problems point to a tendency to play safe by overusing lower-order strategies rather than risking the apparent insecurity of attempting to listen for gist and process meaning. Richards (1985) quotes Brindley's (1982) formulation of a set of points relating to these issues in terms of a rating scale to evaluate competence in listening, and suggests that such a scale, juxtaposed with a taxonomy of listening skills, can be a basis for the setting of instructional objectives. Underwood (1989) offers a number of plausible reasons for these kinds of obstacles to efficient listening comprehension:

(1) The learner-listener cannot control the speed of delivery.

(2) He/she cannot always get things repeated.
(3) He/she has a limited vocabulary.
(4) He/she may fail to recognize 'signals'.
(5) He/she may lack contextual knowledge.
(6) It can be difficult to concentrate in a foreign language.
(7) The learner may have established certain learning habits, such as a wish to understand every word.

The question then arises as to the techniques available for teaching listening comprehension in a way that addresses learners' current competence at the same time as taking into account what is known about listening as a skill.

*Classroom applications: materials for teaching listening comprehension* The kinds of teaching materials now generally available (whether supplementary skills courses or the listening sections of main course books) reflect quite directly the two main aspects of listening comprehension set out in the first section, namely (a) the nature of the spoken language and (b) the micro-skills identified as components of efficient listening. Activities and exercises typically consider such factors as the various possible goals of listening, listener roles, the transactional-interactional spectrum, setting and context, as well as learners' proficiency levels measured against processing criteria.

Richards (1985: 202–3) converts these features into a set of criteria for evaluating listening activities. In particular, he highlights the following aspects.

*Content validity*: whether the tasks are representative of the micro-skills involved in listening (as opposed, for example, to being closer to activities that require reading skills, or perhaps external knowledge not dealt with in the text.

*Comprehension vs memory*: whether the tasks activate learners' processing mechanisms, or merely require them to retrieve information from memory store. This is closely related to the testing–teaching dichotomy, where exercise material may require evidence of understanding without a concern for the steps by which that understanding might be achieved.

*Purposefulness and transferability*: whether the tasks at least approximate real-world listening goals, so that skills learnt are then transferable to comparable situations.

*Authenticity*: whether input at least resembles natural discourse (although, as Rixon (1986) reminds us, the features of natural spoken language, such as sentence stress patterns, strong and weak forms and so on, can be retained without necessarily using fully authentic material with its associated and sometimes unhelpfully distracting complexities). (See AUTHENTICITY.)

In the broadest terms, teaching materials most typically incorporate the process features discussed by following a now fairly conventional sequence of tasks classified as (i) pre-listening, (ii) while-listening and (iii) post-listening activities, with each stage representative of a subset of the whole range of listening skills and strategies. The text – the choice of input – depends on such factors as level, purpose and so on. Listening tasks may also be integrated with other skills, particularly but not only speaking, either to be representative of authentic real-world use or for more narrowly focused instructional purposes such as reinforcement of lexical, grammatical or functional items (see also TEACHING INTEGRATED SKILLS). A brief overview is offered in what follows: much more extensive lists of tasks and their underlying rationale are provided in Anderson and Lynch (1988), Underwood (1989) and Ur (1987).

*Pre-listening activities* The principal function of tasks and exercises at this stage is to provide orientation to the input topic and to activate learners' own knowledge and frames of reference (see SCHEMA THEORY).

This may be done in a variety of ways: with pictures, open discussion, a reading text on the same theme, prediction of content, or with more specific language practice such as the identification of relevant lexis or a set of pre-listening comprehension questions.

*While-listening* The spectrum of microskills, classified above into lower- and higher-order ones, is loosely paralleled by a distinction between intensive and extensive listening, though the parallel should not be pushed too far, because intensive listening may require semantic processing as much as identification and perception of discrete items. Richards (1985, quoting a number of different authorities) in fact makes a useful two-way distinction between 'global' and 'partial' comprehension (listening for gist as opposed to picking up on specific points); and between 'mechanical', 'meaningful' and 'communicative' responses, in other words ranging from, say, sound discrimination to overtly expressed personal response. Depending on proficiency levels, listening tasks may also be placed on a scale of 'closed' to 'open' (e.g. Rost, 1990), where the degree of control and support ranges from providing a detailed framework for listening through to the point where learners are expected to construct such frameworks for themselves, by organizing the incoming data, making inferences, interpreting attitudes and assessing relevance.

*Post-listening* These are difficult to systematize because they often relate only to listening comprehension tasks in a very indirect way, and are sometimes intended more as language remediation or reinforcement rather than as skills development. Post-listening activities comprise a range of follow-up possibilities, including lexical and grammatical development, role play, writing practice, various homework tasks and so on. Particularly in the area of EAP (see ENGLISH FOR SPECIFIC PURPOSES), students may have taken notes in a transactional lecture-style context while listening, and may go on to use those notes to construct a written assignment.

An increasing number of listening comprehension materials exploit the skill from the angles outlined here. *Soundtracks* (Axbey, 1989) is just one typical example. Most units begin with a small amount of written input alongside pre-listening activities that refer to the written material and invite learners to guess at further information. The while-listening tasks comprise extensive, gist listening and intensive listening for specific information, sometimes with the completion of a note-taking framework. Follow-up exercises are open-ended, involving discussion in pairs; functional, grammatical and morphological practice; and a more extended written task. Such materials address the now accepted principle of the authentic replication of listening comprehension in 'natural' use, at the same time as serving more obviously pedagogic functions of language practice and development.

## SUMMARY

There remain a number of grey areas in the practice of teaching listening that impinge in varying degrees on matters of principle. One, already touched on, concerns the extent to which authentic spoken discourse can appropriately be used in the classroom, and conversely, whether specially scripted material contains sufficient features of natural language without misrepresentation to learners. A further problematic factor in many educational contexts, albeit not necessarily criterial, may be the question of the language model when, for example, no native speakers are available either actually or in the form of voices on audio tape. Moreover, it could be argued that video material (see VIDEO IN LANGUAGE TEACHING) is preferable to audio recordings because of the para-and non-linguistic detail that the former is able to capture; indeed, the desirability or otherwise

of electronic aids is open to question, as well as their simple availability. Finally, real-world listeners can be participants (in a conversation), addressees (in a transactional framework, for example) and occasionally overhearers of other people's interactions. It is at least arguable that the majority of learners most often find themselves in an overhearer role, listening vicariously to strangers talking on a tape and being insufficiently involved themselves.

The current methodology of teaching listening comprehension has evolved gradually as a broader range of models for describing language has become available, as research into human language processing has allowed for the identification of areas that are applicable to language learning pedagogy, and as the key arguments in favour of COMMUNICATIVE METHODOLOGY have come to be regarded as broadly persuasive. As a consequence of these various influences, the elements of listening as a skill have become decoupled from a reliance on written material and too close an association with structural methodology and comprehension viewed only as the testing of usage (see USE/USAGE).

BIBLIOGRAPHY
Anderson, A. and Lynch, T. (1988). *Listening*. Oxford: Oxford University Press.*
Axbey, S. (1989). *Soundtracks*. Harlow: Longman.
Brown, G. and Yule, G. (1983). *Teaching the Spoken Language*. Cambridge: Cambridge University Press.
McDonough, J. and Shaw, C. (1993). *Materials and Methods in ELT*. Oxford: Blackwell.
McKeating, D. (1981). Comprehension and listening. In G. Abbott and P. Wingard (eds), *The Teaching of English as an International Language: A practical guide*. Glasgow and London: Collins, 57–80.
Richards, J. C. (1985). Listening comprehension: approach, design and procedure. In J. C. Richards, *The Context of Language Teaching*. Cambridge: Cambridge University Press, 189–207.
Rixon, S. (1986). *Developing Listening Skills*. London and Basingstoke: Macmillan/Modern English Publications.

Rost, M. (1990). *Listening in Language Learning.* London and New York: Longman.*

Underwood, M. (1990). *Teaching Listening.* London: Longman.

Ur, P. (1987). *Teaching Listening Comprehension.* Cambridge: Cambridge University Press.

JMCD

**teaching reading** is an ambiguous phrase in second language pedagogy. On one hand, it can refer to the teaching of initial reading skills in a second language to those who cannot read in either L1 or L2. On the other hand, it can refer to teaching aimed at enhancing the reading skills in L2 of those who can already read in that language. Both areas will be reviewed in this article, although it should be acknowledged that most effort in terms of research and material production has been directed to the latter.

THE TEACHING OF INITIAL READING IN A SECOND LANGUAGE

It is generally agreed that people are more likely to learn to read in a language that they already know, preferably their first language. None the less a large number of children, especially in Third World countries, are taught a foreign language and taught to read in that language at the same time. In countries where English is used as a medium of instruction, initial reading methods usually involve one or more of the following: phonic, syllabic, whole word/whole sentence or 'language experience'.

The phonic approach is based on the 'conventional sound values' of letters – the letter *t* being given the value 'tuh' /tə/ for example and the word *den* being sounded out as /duh/, /eh/, /nuh/ and then synthesized or blended to /den/. This approach enables learners to 'build up' words that they know from spoken English but have not previously met in printed form, and then to try to identify them. Disadvantages of the phonic method include the fact that there is a lack of a consistent letter–sound relationship in English, such that pronunciation cannot regularly be predicted from spelling. Although the phonic approach or *phonics* has fallen out of favour in some English L1 educational circles, *phonological awareness* (cf. Bryant and Bradley, 1985) is widely recognized as an important enabling factor in initial reading.

The syllabic method, a variation on the phonic, is commonly used for teaching L1 reading in the Middle East, Africa and Asia. In this method learners are drilled in the pronunciation of written syllables such as *ka, ke, ki, ko, ku,* or *la, le, li, lo, lu,* etc. They then move to reading whole words, and making up words based on given syllables. However, English is not ideally suited to this approach since its syllabic structure is not restricted to a consonant plus a vowel.

In the whole word and whole sentence methods, learners are presented with whole words, phrases or sentences, often through flash cards. The teacher reads the card aloud and learners are expected to memorize words through repetition and recognize them as whole units. The claimed advantage of this is that it facilitates rapid recognition of whole units and thus is closer to the automatic recognition of fluent readers than is the letter by letter phonic approach. The disadvantage is that it does not help learners to identify for themselves words which they have not previously been taught. The method is sometimes called the *look and say* method. A particular danger of this method for L2 learners is that they may learn to vocalize in response to recognized written patterns, thus producing 'reading-like' behaviour, but with no understanding of what they are saying.

Methods that explicitly draw on the knowledge that learners have of their first or second language may be treated together as *language experience methods.* Observing initial readers shows that they use their knowledge of syntactic structure and vocabulary to help them decode. For example, L1 English readers (or fluent bilinguals) may be able to recognize *about* in the sentence *This rabbit is fussy about his food* since they know that *fussy* is often followed by that preposition. However, the same reader may not be able to read *about* in isolation. It is clearly a method to be used with caution in EFL, where learners have a restricted knowledge of English.

In order to promote a positive attitude towards reading, any approach may be supplemented by learners regularly listening to motivating stories read aloud by the teacher. An effective addition to this is the *shared book approach* where learners have their own copy of the book, and are able to listen and follow the teacher reading aloud. In addition, some publishers provide specially enlarged 'big books' for the teachers, so that the latter can point out relevant features of the text or pictures as they proceed.

In cases where learners are already literate in their own language, then there may be some transfer of skills from first to second language reading, in terms of an awareness that writing is 'language in another form', or that spaces between written words correspond to word boundaries. Furthermore, there will be, in the case of languages that use the Roman alphabet, many letter–sound correspondences, which, although they may be only approximate, will obviate the need to begin from the very first principles. Thus learners who are already literate in French learn to read in English with little overt attention to initial reading skills, although there may be some ad hoc attention to the pronunciation of letters, e.g. that the letters *th* are pronounced as /d/ or /ð/. On the other hand, if learners are literate, but in a non-Roman script, then explicit initial literacy training in Roman script may be provided.

The practice of requiring learners to read aloud is contentious. In L1 reading it is used as a means of assessing whether, or how well, learners can read. In L2 teaching, however, even where learners are known to be proficient readers, they may be required to read aloud as a means of practising pronunciation, although it is a questionable method of doing so because of the interference effect of written forms.

## IMPROVING SECOND LANGUAGE READING SKILLS

The most widely accepted view of reading in both first and second language learning is that it is an 'interactive' process whereby 'bottom-up' operations involving the physical text on the page, such as letter and word recognition, interact with 'top-down' processes such as prior knowledge of the text type or topic (cf. Carrell et al., 1988). According to this model, deficiencies at one level may to some extent be compensated for by proficiencies at another. This model of reading has led to interest in readers, in texts, and especially in the interaction between the two, and has had a clear influence on materials for L2 reading. (See BOTTOM-UP PROCESSING, COMPREHENSION PROCESSES, TOP-DOWN PROCESSING.)

## THE READER

Important factors relating to the reader include:

*Language*   Readers should have a knowledge of language adequate to deal with the text they are reading.

*Relevant knowledge*   The term *schema* (see SCHEMA THEORY) is now well established to describe what a learner knows about a topic (a mathematics schema, a football schema, a marriage schema, etc.). The view that prior knowledge of the text topic can enhance comprehension has led to a great deal of pre-reading activity where learners carry out various tasks, for example, listing questions, discussing facts, brainstorming on titles or illustrations (e.g. Tomlinson and Ellis, 1988). These are intended to activate readers' knowledge of the topic and of the relevant language. Another approach to building up learners' topic knowledge is to group together reading comprehension texts on a common theme.

*Interest*  As might be expected, research supports the view that interest in the text topic enhances comprehension; however, interest is not independent of text, and if the text does not meet the readers' expectations (for example, if it is too difficult) then interest will diminish. Conversely, a text may increasingly engage the readers' interest as they proceed.

## THE TEXT

Foreign language learners who are general purpose learners are now encouraged to read a wide range of types of text (or GENRES), from short texts such as birthday greetings to stories or novels. Texts in reading comprehension collections usually cover a variety of functions and language levels. Underwood (1994) has a particularly wide range of text types, aimed at general purpose EFL secondary school students. Pedagogic treatment of these texts generally attempts to be sympathetic to the text's apparent 'real-life' function in terms of activities and exercises. Thus in reading a dictionary entry the focus may be on extracting precise relevant information, while in reading a narrative the focus may be on the sequence of events. Language difficulties in text may be approached in three ways: first, the teacher may attempt to teach 'more language'; second, the teacher may select more linguistically accessible text; third, the teacher can attempt to teach strategies to cope with unknown language.

Teaching sufficient language for authentic texts may be an impractical objective for the classroom, especially for vocabulary. In English, for example, approximately 80% of the words in most 'general' texts are drawn from the most common 2000 words.

However, the other 20% of the text comes from the remaining several hundreds of thousands of words, and since this 20% consists of those words that contribute to the differences between texts, they are important. While guessing at the meaning of unknown words can be a valid and occasionally necessary recourse, it has limitations. Research indicates that good readers typically do not guess, but have large vocabularies and automatic word recognition (Eskey and Grabe, 1988). However, it should be borne in mind that the L2 activity of guessing at the meaning of words is not the same as the initial L1 reading activity of guessing at the identity of words that are already known. An awareness of the importance of language competence in reading is reflected in the grammar and vocabulary work in a number of books, e.g. Haines (1988) and Eckstut and Lubelska (1989).

The second approach to language difficulty is to select texts that are linguistically controlled in terms of syntax (from simple to complex structures) and lexis (from frequent to less frequent words). Many publishers have produced series of 'readers' based on these principles. The problems with the linguistically controlled approach are that the language presented may not correspond to the learner's 'internal' language development, and also that spoon-feeding readers may not prepare them to cope with authentic texts. The 1980s insistence upon the superiority of authentic text as a model of communicative use has waned in recent years, and many intermediate level reading course books now contain adapted or specially written texts.

The third approach to language difficulties consists of teaching 'coping strategies'. For vocabulary this includes attempting to guess the meaning from the form of the word (known cognates or affixes) or from its context, or even ignoring the word and carrying on. Use of a dictionary is also a possibility. However, it is clear that a very high proportion of unknown lexis is likely to result in a breakdown of communication. Unfamiliar syntax poses considerable difficulties for readers and 'coping strategies' here are rarely suggested (a partial approach being Greenall and Swan's (1986) suggestion that readers carry out simple 'chunking' of long and complicated sentences).

## INTERACTION OF READER AND TEXT

The term *reading skills* is used rather loosely to refer to different types of interaction between reader and text. A number of different taxonomies of reading skills have been drawn up, no two of which are identical. Many lists include reading 'styles' along with reading 'skills'. Reading styles are behavioural responses to text, instigated by the reader's purpose, and affected by the reader's language competence. The styles most commonly referred to are SKIMMING (rapid perusal of text to get a 'general idea'), SCANNING (rapid reading to locate a specific piece of information), intensive reading (slow and careful reading to 'absorb' the text) and extensive reading (fairly rapid reading, typically for pleasure or interest). Skimming is rapid reading to establish what the text is about, while scanning is rapid reading to find a specific piece of information. Scanning of text which is structured (e.g. a dictionary or a table of contents) would appear to be an easier task than scanning continuous prose. It may be, in fact, that both skimming and scanning are developmental reading styles that require readiness on the part of the reader.

Reading strategies can be defined as deliberate and conscious processes by which the reader attempts to overcome a problem. They might involve the word attack strategies mentioned above, using text titles, examining visuals or reflecting on existing relevant knowledge. In the research literature, reading strategies are typically identified by asking readers to consider their own work and report on their reading.

Reading skills, as apart from styles and strategies, result from an attempt to break down the monolith 'reading comprehension' into smaller components (or sub-skills as they are sometimes called) that are more teachable, and possibly more testable. Activating skills in fluent reading may be less 'conscious' than activating reading strategies, although it must be admitted that the terms 'skill' and 'strategy' are often used without distinction. Typical skills lists include:

- understanding word meaning;
- understanding words in context;
- literal comprehension;
- inferencing;
- understanding the gist of a text;
- identifying main ideas;
- separating principles from examples;
- following the development of an argument;
- following the sequence of a narrative.

The skills approach has had considerable influence in research and materials design, despite the fact that research aimed at identifying individual skills has found no evidence for their psycholinguistic validity. Moreover, the currently accepted view of reading is that it is an interactive process with a number of processes, drawing on a number of skills, going on simultaneously. If this is the case, then it may well not be possible for specific skills to be taught or tested in complete isolation. Furthermore, the skill of inferencing, which appears in most lists, is perhaps too powerful a notion, since it refers to the fundamental capacity of reasoning in the construction of meaning, and arguably enters into all other skills. In reading skill activities, inferencing is often divided into three types:

(1) Identifying pronoun reference: this is not merely mechanical recovery of the nearest noun phrase, as the following example shows: *The police chased the criminals but they managed to slip away* and *The police chased the criminals but they failed to catch them.*

(2) Establishing relationships between sections of text, especially cause and effect as in the

following: *The rain came down harder. Jane put up her umbrella.* Here we infer that Jane put up her umbrella because the rain came down harder, although the text does not explicitly tell us so.

(3)    Pragmatic inferencing where the reader draws on knowledge outside the text to construct meaning. Thus in the sentence *The man pulled down the stocking and walked into the bank* most readers familiar with bank robberies would infer that the man pulled the stocking down over his face, and that he did so in order not to be recognized. (See PRAGMATIC COMPETENCE.)

Despite the problems of trying to establish the existence of separate skills, they feature prominently in EFL/ESL reading materials, where they have provided authors with a wealth of ideas for exercises (good examples include Barr, Clegg and Wallace, 1981, and Nolan-Woods and Foll, 1986). However, the approach can sometimes be rather confusing, with authors listing skills that are vague, overlapping, and do not seem to form a coherent cognitive category. Underwood (1994), for example, has *recognizing adjectives, comparing data between two texts* and *recognizing the language of crossword clues* in her list of over thirty sub-skills.

The skills approach often relies on close and careful reading, referred to as 'intensive reading'. There is a widespread view that such reading should be complemented by 'extensive reading'. Intensive reading generally takes place in the classroom under the teacher's control, using relatively short texts, with a high proportion of task to text. The classroom approach focuses on practising or checking language, skills, and strategies. Very often an intensive reading lesson may be carried out in three phases: a pre-reading phase where the teacher attempts to activate the learners' knowledge of the topic; a reading phase where the learners read the text and carry out comprehension, strategy or skill-focused work; and finally a post-reading phase where learners reflect on or develop in some way what they have read.

Extensive reading, by contrast, is typically the kind of reading which occurs in self-access class library schemes. It usually involves the reading of longer texts, which are selected by the reader and usually read out of class; there is very little outside intervention: indeed, a reader may be free to stop reading if interest wanes (as occurs in real life). Extensive reading is also consistent with the view of reading as a holistic process (rather than one based on discrete skills), where readers 'learn reading' through practising reading rather than 'being taught reading' through practising separate reading skills or strategies. Extensive reading is also claimed to improve writing and enhance language proficiency, especially vocabulary. Finally, proponents of extensive reading claim that learners are more likely to adopt a positive attitude to reading if they have been free to choose the texts themselves, and furthermore read them undisturbed by the threat of external checking and assessment. The disadvantage of extensive reading programmes is that a class library may present problems of logistics and management. Obviously, the books should be accessible linguistically, otherwise readers will struggle and extensive reading will simply not be possible, because readers are forced into close and laborious reading. Finally, learners who do not come from backgrounds where reading for pleasure or interest is practised may resist the idea of reading except in response to INSTRUMENTAL MOTIVATION.

In recent years (at least as far as ESL/EFL is concerned) two further perspectives on reading, which would appear to be relevant to intensive reading work, have attracted attention: metacognition in reading and critical reading. Metacognition in reading is concerned with helping readers to be aware of how they monitor their own comprehension, i.e. whether, and to what extent they understand what they are reading. It also encourages readers to be aware of where their comprehension is coming from, i.e. from the text or from their own personal knowledge. Bernhardt (1991) provides a brief account of metacognition in ESL reading.

Critical reading, on the other hand, introduces a social dimension in that it raises the issue of a text as the product of a given sociocultural group, and focuses not on the reader's comprehension of text content but on critiquing the ideological assumptions underpinning the text (Wallace, 1992). It is an approach which requires readers to have adequate language competence and, in addition, a degree of ideological awareness. Although in theory applicable to any text type, it is perhaps most fruitful when applied to texts that have a clear social or political stance. (See also CRITICAL LINGUISTICS.)

Classroom observation suggests that much of the time in 'reading lessons' is not actually devoted to reading, but to activities such as brainstorming, answering questions, writing notes, etc. Extensive reading is an antidote to such lessons, and there is a widespread view that an effective reading programme should include both intensive and extensive components. There is, in brief, no short cut to effective reading, and as yet no challenge to the view that one only becomes a good reader through reading.

BIBLIOGRAPHY

Alderson, J. C. and Urquhart, A. H. (eds) (1984). *Reading in a Foreign Language.* London: Longman.

Barr, P., Clegg, J. and Wallace, C. (1981). *Advanced Reading Skills.* London: Longman.

Bernhardt, B. (1991). *Reading Development in a Second Language.* Norwood, NJ: Ablex.

Bryant, P. and Bradley, L. (1985). *Children's Reading Problems.* Oxford: Blackwell.

Carrell, P. L., Devine, J. and Eskey, D. E. (eds) (1988). *Interactive Approaches to Second Language Reading.* Cambridge: Cambridge University Press.

Eckstut, S. and Lubelska, D. (1989). *Widely Read.* London: Longman.

Eskey, D. and Grabe, W. (1988). Interactive models for second language reading: perspectives on instruction. In P. L. Carrell, J. Devine and D. E. Eskey (eds), *Interactive Approaches to Second Language Reading.* Cambridge: Cambridge University Press.

Greenall, S. and Swan, M. (1986). *Effective Reading.* Cambridge: Cambridge University Press.

Haines, S. (1988). *Reading 4.* London: Cassell.

Nolan-Woods, E. and Foll, D. (1986). *Penguin Advanced Reading Skills.* Harmondsworth: Penguin Books.

Nuttall, C. (1996). *Teaching Reading Skills in a Foreign Language.* London: Heinemann.\*

Tomlinson, B. and Ellis, R. (1988). *Reading: Advanced.* Oxford: Oxford University Press.

Underwood, M. (1994). *Reading Plus, Book 4.* Basingstoke: Macmillan.

Wallace, C. (1992). *Reading.* Oxford: Oxford University Press.\*

Williams, E. (1984). *Reading in the Language Classroom.* Basingstoke: Macmillan.\*

EW

**teaching speaking** Whether or not speech is viewed as the primary medium of communication, its centrality to language use is undeniable. In language teaching, this centrality is reflected in the wide range of approaches which involve the active production of language. Over the decades, and under the influence of different teaching approaches, the role of oral production has varied from that of a means to an end, the end being mastery of the target language items of product syllabuses, to that of an end in itself, a skill to be developed in its own right. In the sections below, these different perspectives on oral production are briefly reviewed, focusing on a fundamental tension in language teaching between structural and communicative approaches. Within an orthodox communicative teaching context, the nature of the learner's experience of oral production in the light of various factors, such as choice of task and type of interaction, will be examined.

FROM STRUCTURAL PRACTICE TO
COMMUNICATIVE USE

Focus on form (see FORM-FOCUS), based on the view that language is a system to be mastered, has a long tradition in language teaching. In structural, system-based approaches such as those popular from the mid-point of this century, the content of teaching is seen as a set of structures or patterns, which through repetition and practice are to be internalized by the learner. Materials such as Hornby's (1954) pedagogical grammar *Guide to Patterns and Usage in English* and Fries's (1952) *The Structure of English* are based on such structural principles. Building on these basic tenets of language teaching, developments were made in France (AUDIOVISUALISM), in Britain (for example, through materials such as Alexander's (1967) *New Concept English*, Broughton's (1968) *Success with English*) and in America in the form of AUDIOLINGUALISM, which flourished under the support of behaviourist theories of language learning (stimulus–response–reinforcement, conditioned learning, shaping, habit formation) (see BEHAVIOURISM). The audiolingual preoccupation with the drill, while giving primacy to speech, restricted its role to the imitation and repetition of patterns, the controlled practice of correct forms.

With the attack on the principles underlying audiolingualism from arguments put forward by Chomsky at the end of the 1950s, and the extension of the notion of language competence to embrace appropriate use of language according to context and purpose, following Hymes's definition of COMMUNICATIVE COMPETENCE, language teaching had a strong theoretical basis for a transition towards a meaning-based approach. This signalled an important step towards the development, particularly in Britain and the rest of Europe, of COMMUNICATIVE LANGUAGE TEACHING. Situated against an established background in Britain of interest in the context of language use (Firth, Halliday), and coinciding with attention to meaning through the work in the philosophy and sociology of language by Austin and Searle (see SPEECH ACT THEORY), the time was right for a shift in pedagogy towards a more functional perspective.

By the 1970s, practical concerns for a language teaching solution to the demands across Europe of foreign language learners wishing to learn useful everyday discourse led to the work of the COUNCIL OF EUROPE Modern Languages Project and the development of NOTIONAL/FUNCTIONAL SYLLABUSES (Wilkins, 1976). This involved the specification of language as notions and functions (such as agreeing, requesting, persuading, time, etc.) rather than as structures, offering teachers a framework for the design of courses geared to the communicative needs and demands of learners. The impact on teaching materials has been considerable. Since the 1970s, such (notional/functional) categories of language use have become a common unit of organization in materials (for example, Jones's (1977) *Functions of English*), and although the structural syllabus has not been abandoned, the concept of function is of great importance in the specification of language content in many mainstream language courses (see, for example, the *Strategies* series (Abbs and Freebairn, 1977), Morrow and Johnson's (1979) *Communicate 1*, and Swan and Walter's (1984) *Cambridge English Course*).

Although alternative, stronger interpretations of communicative language teaching have found support through so-called PROCESS and PROCEDURAL SYLLABUSES, in which a genuine preoccupation with meaning is fostered through task- rather than language-driven activity (see the discussion of COMMUNICATIVE LANGUAGE TEACHING, and Howatt, 1988), what has been described above is a standard (weaker) version of communicative language teaching. Here, the shift to include (or substitute) function (for structure) has led to little change in terms of the syllabus type, which remains product-oriented and synthetic (see ANALYTIC/SYNTHETIC) with the linguistic content divided into discrete units and learning involving the accumulation and internalization of these units. What has changed, however, is the scope at the level of methodology for a focus on a wider range of practice activities than the limited controlled practice of the drill. Spoken production within this mainstream communicative approach can therefore be seen as broadening the types of experience for real or simulated communication within the classroom.

## SPOKEN COMMUNICATION WITHIN THE CLASSROOM

Principles of communicative language teaching, now taken as orthodoxy in many teaching contexts, have led to significant changes in materials and procedures (see COMMUNICATIVE METHODOLOGY), with an impact on the role and nature of oral production within the classroom. With a considerable extension of the aims of language teaching beyond attention only to the correct, accurate production of language, to the use of appropriate language in real (or pseudo-real) contexts of use, stress is now placed on active, meaningful production by the learner, and on engagement in message-focused activity (see MESSAGE-FOCUS) which simulates the contexts and conditions of genuine communication.

Such goals are translatable into a number of typical features of communicative classroom activity. These have been outlined by Johnson (1982), Nation (1989) and others, and include the following:

(1) *Roles*: learners take on a variety of roles, simulating a wide range of experiences. This develops awareness of appropriateness (see ROLE PLAY AND SIMULATION) and responsibility/accountability of the learners' contribution; this reflects a concern for AUTHENTICITY;

(2) *Outcomes*: communication is purposeful and outcomes are clearly identifiable; the message-focus of activities such as giving directions to a partner, problem-solving through negotiation, identifying differences in information establishes a clear set of goals for the interactants;

(3) *Split information*: the establishment of an INFORMATION/OPINION GAP guarantees a purpose for the activity, motivates and involves the learners in communicating; INFORMATION TRANSFER is another technique based on the principle of message-focus.

A key feature of natural communication, which is seen as a characteristic of communicative activity is that it involves the production of a message in *real time*. Handling the demands of spontaneous production (and processing by the receiver) under what Bygate (1987) calls 'processing conditions' accounts for performance features of speech, such as pauses, hesitations, repetitions, the use of formulaic expressions to relieve the processing load, the use of repairs, repetitions, clarifications. The fact that oral communication typically also involves *reciprocity* or interaction between participants adds another set of demands on the speaker ('reciprocity conditions') to manage the interaction, to negotiate meaning with fellow interlocutors, and to adjust the message to the demands of the communicative context. Reciprocity involves the use of TURN-TAKING skills, strategies to interrupt and to control the topic, as well as to react to and perform confirmation and clarification appeals necessary to maintain meaningful interaction between interlocutors (for a fuller discussion of characteristic features of speech, see SPOKEN AND WRITTEN DISCOURSE). Communicative activities would, then, by definition to some degree build in features of real-time processing and reciprocity.

Oral production, then, involves the construction and execution of a message under these constraints of processing and reciprocity conditions. A view of language as skill leads us to recognize a combination of cognitive and behavioural aspects of oral skill (see Littlewood, 1992). A hierarchy of cognitive plans underlies the performance of the skill. At the highest level of the hierarchy is the communicative goal to be achieved; from the construction of a general meaning representation, the selection of broad syntactic and semantic frames is made; at a lower level, plans allow the determination of specific syntactic, morphological, phonological and lexical forms; finally, at the level of motor skills, articulatory plans are created for the actual production of speech.

General models of oral language production (Faerch and Kasper, 1983; Levelt, 1989) tend to agree on two main phases in the process of speaking: planning and execution. The first of these involves the development of plans at various levels according to a communicative goal. Levelt's model (1989) specifies a component called the 'conceptualizer' which retrieves information from stored knowledge appropriate for the elaboration of the communicative goal (and sub-goals) into a pre-verbal message. This is then converted through the selection and application of grammatical and phonological rules by the 'formulator' into a message which has linguistic form (a 'phonetic plan'). The 'articulator' then converts this plan into actual speech. This output is monitored and subjected to repair where necessary (see PRODUCTION PROCESSES).

Skilled oral behaviour involves the adaptive and automatic operation of these plans. The automatization of lower-level plans releases attention which may be put to forming effective higher-level plans. This means that the skilled speaker is able to cope with higher-level changes of ideas, meanings, intent, for example (that is, is flexible or adaptive to changing circumstances), since lower-level skills operate automatically. The less skilled speaker may have to devote conscious attention to lower-level plans, and as a result may have less attentive capacity available for higher-level concerns. If attention must be given to higher levels, the result for the less skilled user may be a loss of FLUENCY and/or of ACCURACY.

For the second language speaker operating within the context of the classroom, the question arises as to the nature of oral language production promoted in this setting. Among the potential variables here are the type of interaction opportunities (e.g. GROUP WORK/PAIR WORK, etc.), the nature of the learner's contribution and the design of the tasks themselves. Drills, mingling activities,

information gap exercises, simulations, problem-solving tasks, for example, may differ in terms of such features as the presence or absence of collaboration towards a common goal, of one- or two-way information exchange, in the degree of linguistic control and so on. Other matters such as the familiarity of the participants with the task and with each other, and the different roles required by the task cut across concerns with both learners and task design. So what kinds of opportunity are available for learners to produce language in the classroom? Different factors in the learning and teaching process may influence the type of experience of oral production a learner may receive. We will deal with these under three main points: (i) the task type, (ii) the learner's contribution and (iii) patterns of interaction, including teachers' behaviour.

## TASK TYPES

Tasks (or activities) may be classified according to the extent to which they are focused on language or communication. In an early framework, Littlewood (1981) proposes a distinction between 'pre-communicative' and 'communicative' activities. The former category consists of part-skill 'structural' and 'quasi-communicative' activities, which concentrate on aspects of the target system and their meaning, in a way which is clearly language-focused. Within this category one would expect to find activities such as drills, which typically provide practice in manipulating discrete elements of the language, rather than engaging in the genuine communication of a message. 'Communicative' activities are those which include the features of communication described above (information gap 'functional communication' activities, or 'social interaction' activities within a (simulated) social context). Rivers and Temperley (1978) use the labels 'SKILL-GETTING' and 'SKILL-USING' to refer to roughly the same distinction between 'pre-' and 'communicative' activities. (For examples of a range of such activities, see Klippel, 1985.)

Rather than a strict separation of part-skill and whole-task focus, Littlewood (1992) suggests a continuum, with maximum control at one end and free communication at the other. Tasks may be more or less controlled, and involve the speaker in more or less freedom to negotiate meaning, control the topic agenda, draw on stored knowledge of discourse routines and world knowledge. For example, a language-focused activity may incorporate elements of pseudo-communication (as in the case of an information-gap drill or a mingling activity 'Find someone who . . .'). Role plays may be scripted (and therefore controlled) or freer, involving little predetermination of the topic agenda, turn-taking routine, content selection and so on.

Current research on the effect of the selection of certain task types on acquisition opportunities focuses on both the quantity and linguistic form of language produced under different task conditions (the total number of words, range of lexicon, certain features of syntax) and also in terms of the different opportunities for negotiation work (see the collections of papers in Crookes and Gass, 1993a, b).

Research has pointed to fairly predict-able differences in the quantity of speech and certain grammatical features in different tasks (discussion, picture description and storytelling), although it is not clear what the effect of the topic might be on output. Tasks may also differ in terms of the goal of the task (convergent/collaborative or divergent/independent), the distribution of information to be exchanged (one-way or two-way exchange), the requirement or optionality of information exchange and the closed or open-ended outcome of the task.

Of these features, some studies (see Crookes and Gass, 1993a, b) investigate differences in opportunities for negotiation between jigsaw, information gap, problem-solving, decision-making and opinion-exchange tasks. Other research points to the

benefits for negotiation work of two-way tasks. Problem-solving (convergent) tasks are reported to lead to more negotiation than debates (divergent). Another area of investigation is that of the level of challenge or difficulty offered by the task. The related issue of task complexity is also the subject of current research (Crookes and Gass, 1993a, b), which suggests that a greater number of confirmation and clarification checks occur on more complex tasks. The concept of task complexity, however, is far from straightforward to define, and may involve such issues as the familiarity of the interlocutor with the task, and the presence of 'critical episodes' or points of conceptual or perceptual difficulty built into the task, which stimulate negotiation between interlocutors. In subtle ways, therefore, similar tasks may generate quite different language outcomes. (See TASK-BASED TEACHING and NEGOTIATION OF MEANING.)

## THE LEARNER'S ORAL CONTRIBUTION

Theoretical support for a focus on productive oral practice comes from the INTER-ACTION HYPOTHESIS, which promotes the idea that learners acquire through active use. This extends the claim that a necessary condition for SLA is the availability of roughly tuned linguistic input. The language available to a learner may be made into useful comprehensible input through a process of modification by the interlocutors: in other words, interaction between speakers may lead to the clarification or confirmation of the meaning of a message. The argument, therefore, is that it is through opportunities for interaction or productive use of language that the non-native speaker acquires language.

Given that greater opportunities for productivity may be associated with increased opportunities for acquisition, one interesting question might be what factors to do with the individual learner help to determine his or her participation patterns. One obvious factor may be the willingness, motivation (and also ability) to contribute to oral practice. It is possible that those learners who initiate more are better able to turn input into 'intake'. Such a claim may be circular, however, since the degree of participation by a learner may be related to, and even determined by, his or her proficiency ranking in the first place. In other words, the language proficiency of the learner may determine the extent to which she or he exploits the learning opportunities available. A further question arises about this claim, namely that participation may not in fact be providing benefit for the contributor him- or herself, but for *other* learners. Although an individual may generate a large amount of input, it is not necessarily the case that that input becomes intake for that learner.

Initiating behaviour may vary according to other factors, including age, personality, gender and cultural background. Research into the behaviour of learners from Asian and non-Asian backgrounds, for example, has suggested different interaction patterns (and hence different opportunities to manipulate input). Other studies report differences in turn-taking styles according to the gender composition of dyads. Familiarity of the interlocutors with each other may also affect the nature of interaction on a task.

CLASSROOM INTERACTION

Learners' interaction is heavily influenced by the organization of interaction in the classroom, that is, the groupings of interactants and the roles assigned to them. One major source of comparison is between teacher-fronted and small-group interactions (Long, 1985). In general, research findings suggest greater scope for negotiation-for-meaning, including a significantly greater quantity of student talk over a larger range of functions, in group work than in lock-step teacher-fronted sessions. The quality of group-work production was found not to suffer in terms of accuracy and contained significantly more opportunities for conversational adjustment.

The teacher's role in providing input and supporting the learners' language development has been investigated in terms of speech rate, pauses, phonological features such as loudness, intonation and articulation, vocabulary choice, syntax and discourse function (see Chaudron, 1988). QUESTION TYPES (closed/open; display/referential; degree of modification; wait-time) and feedback procedures also throw light on the nature of the interaction between teacher and learner in different classroom contexts. Studies suggest, for example, that student contributions vary following certain question types: display questions elicit a greater number of student turns; referential questions lead to fewer students producing longer turns; open referential questions elicit more (and more complex) responses than closed questions.

Current research regarding the nature of spoken language production under different task and interaction conditions suggests that pedagogic decisions about task selection and procedure carry with them clear consequences for the treatment of oral skill. Becoming aware of the possible impact of such choices on the kind of oral practice experienced by our learners may be a step towards promoting more systematic, comprehensive or carefully planned coverage of this centrally important skill. The development of the complex skill of oral production may then be viewed as too important to be left to chance, or as a hostage to the fortunes of changing trends in approaches to language teaching.

BIBLIOGRAPHY

Abbs, B. and Freebairn, I. (1977). *Starting Strategies*. London: Longman.

Alexander, L. G. (1967). *New Concept English: First things first*. London: Longman.

Broughton, G. (1968). *Success with English*. Harmondsworth: Penguin Books.

Bygate, M. (1987). *Speaking*. Oxford: Oxford University Press.*

Chaudron, C. (1988). *Second Language Classrooms*. Cambridge: Cambridge University Press.*

Crookes, G. and Gass, S. M. (eds) (1993a). *Tasks and Language Learning: Integrating theory and practice*. Clevedon: Multilingual Matters.*

——(1993b). *Tasks in a Pedagogical Context: Integrating theory and practice*. Clevedon Multilingual Matters.*

Faerch, C. and Kasper, G. (eds) (1983). *Strategies in Interlanguage Communication*. London: Longman.*

Fries, C. C. (1952). *The Structure of English: An introduction to the structure of English sentences*. New York: Harcourt Brace.

Hornby, A. S. (1954). *Guide to Patterns and Usage in English*. London: Oxford University Press.

Howatt, A. P. R. (1988). From structural to communicative. *Annual Review of Applied Linguistics*, 8, 14–29.

Johnson, K. (1982). *Communicative Syllabus Design and Methodology*. Oxford: Pergamon.

Jones, L. (1977). *Functions of English*. Cambridge: Cambridge University Press.

Klippel, F. (1985). *Keep Talking*. Cambridge: Cambridge University Press.

Levelt, W. (1989). *Speaking*. Cambridge, MA: MIT Press.

Littlewood, W. T. (1981). *Communicative Language Teaching: An introduction*. Cambridge: Cambridge University Press.

——(1992). *Teaching Oral Communication: A methodological framework*. Oxford: Blackwell.*

Long, M. H. (1985). Input and second language acquisition theory. In S. M. Gass and C. G. Madden (eds), *Input in Second Language Acquisition*. Rowley, MA: Newbury House.

McDonough, J. and Shaw, C. (1993). *Materials and Methods in ELT*. Oxford: Blackwell.

Morrow, K. and Johnson, K. (1979). *Communicate 1: English for social interaction*. Cambridge: Cambridge University Press.

Nation, P. (1989). Speaking activities: five features. *English Language Teaching Journal*, 43/1, 24–9.

Pica, T. (1987). Second language acquisition, social interaction and the classroom. *Applied Linguistics*, 8/1, 3–20.

Rivers, W. and Temperley, R. S. (1978). *A Practical Guide to the Teaching of English*. New York: Oxford University Press.

Swan, M. and Walter, C. (1984). *The Cambridge English Course*. Cambridge: Cambridge University Press.

Wilkins, D. A. (1976). *Notional Syllabuses*. London: Oxford University Press.

KSM

**teaching writing** In recent decades, the teaching of writing has been the focus of considerable interest within both first and second language contexts. This has come in reaction to the scant attention it received for many years and the current growing concern for tackling problems experienced in communicating within educational and wider social contexts. Writing, while for many painfully difficult, is often of crucial importance as a gate-keeping activity: judgements on the performance of an individual may have consequences for the writer, such as exclusion from or successful entry into a specific discourse community. As well as being the means through which testing and assessment of learning regularly take place, for the learner writing is an important skill in supporting other learning experiences, as a means of recording, assimilating and reformulating knowledge, and of developing and working through his or her own ideas. It may be a means of personal discovery, of creativity and of self-expression.

Different emphases have been given in language teaching to aspects of the production of written text. This discussion of pedagogic approaches to writing will begin by considering current theories of writing and their research bases with particular reference to second language writing. The main trends in second language instruction over recent decades will be outlined, together with the main principles of classroom methodology.

## MODELS OF WRITING

Current theoretical approaches to writing take a number of diverse perspectives, linguistic, cognitive and social, through which particular emphasis is given to the text, the writer or the context (audience or community). These different angles on the same complex phenomenon of writing have fed into quite different pedagogic approaches. The discussion here will concentrate on the first two of these perspectives on writing, since this leads to one of the principal oppositions, both theoretical and methodological, in language teaching: that of PROCESS VS PRODUCT.

## WRITING AS PRODUCT

One meaning of 'writing' is, of course, the output or end-product of the activity of writing ('Show me your writing,' 'I find X's writing rather flowery'). This product view is one of more or less static text, visible on paper or screen, and more or less separable in time and place from the producer and the act of production.

Research into written products reflects concerns at both grammatical and discoursal levels. In comparisons of first and second language texts (see Silva, 1993, for a survey of research), various aspects of written text have been considered: length (fluency), accuracy of form (error), effectiveness (quality) and structure. This latter category draws on the wide range of tools and frameworks for the analysis of written text which have developed in the field of DISCOURSE ANALYSIS.

One particular influence in the discourse analysis of second language written text stems from the pioneering work of Kaplan (1966), who opened up the question of cultural variation in textual patterning derived from preferences in L1 'thought patterns'. Since his early work, the field of contrastive rhetoric has generated interesting research into L2 text structure, including work at a number of levels (from the distribution of information, inter-clause relations to macro-patterning at the whole-text level) in different languages (German, Japanese, Korean, Mandarin, Hindi, among others) usually compared with English. Kaplan's original

study of ESL essays led to the characterization of text structure preferences of languages in contrast to the assumed linearity of English text. Although the empirical basis of these claims has been seriously questioned, other contrastive work has confirmed many of Kaplan's general intuitions (for references, see Silva, 1993).

Other discourse-level comparisons of L1 and L2 texts have suggested differences in the way clauses are sequenced to build up argument structure, in the organization and elaboration of narratives, and in the extent to which readers' requirements are appropriately met through topic-signalling and attention-getting devices. Stylistic features of L2 writing have been characterized in terms of relative inconsistency, inappropriateness or limitations in variety of style and tone, as well as by a wide range of specific morphosyntactic and lexicosemantic features. The nature and frequency of clause connection, types of modification, occurrence of passives, frequency of cohesive ties (see COHESION) and use of COLLOCATION are examples of features studied.

## WRITING AS PROCESS

In addition to a product-based approach to writing, other research focuses on the process of producing text, the activity of transforming ideas to written text, rather than on the outcome of that activity.

The starting-point for modelling the writing process is the notion of writing as a complex cognitive activity involving the use of a range of problem-solving strategies and composing processes. Research into identifying these hidden mental processes has required the development of tools such as the verbal protocol (borrowed from cognitive psychology, involving the subjects in thinking aloud as they are composing; verbalizations are audio-recorded for future codification and analysis to reveal the frequency, distribution and sequencing of processes), as well as the use of more familiar observation and post-event interviewing techniques. One of the earliest studies by Emig (1971), which had significant impact on composition process research in both L1 and L2 domains, uses a combination of these research methods in a case study of L1 student writers.

Based on similar process data, Flower and Hayes (1981) developed a model of composing which is still cited as one of the most powerful. The model identifies three main components of writing: the writer's long-term memory (knowledge of the topic, audience and stored writing plans), the task environment (the assignment topic, audience and exigency, and the text produced so far) and the processes themselves. These processes comprise planning (generating ideas, goal setting and organizing), translating or expressing ideas in verbal form and reviewing, which involves reading and editing. Evidence from protocol analyses suggests the non-linearity of the composing process. Rather than an orderly progression from plan to draft to revision, writers may move between drafting, planning, revising, planning and so on, in a complex, recursive manner. The potential for transition between processes is represented in the model by a monitor component. Both writers' internal resources and external context interact with the composing processes, making the whole an interactive, responsive model.

Research into writers' composing processes opens up the possibility of the comparison of skilled and novice writers, and of L1 and L2 writers. In general, L2 process research is closely informed by the design and findings of L1 research (see Krapels, 1990, for a useful overview of L2 studies). Zamel (1983), for example, compared her L2 writers with the reported tendencies of L1 writers, and suggests that both types of unskilled writer spend less time on essays, tend not to exhibit recursiveness and edit early. Raimes's (1985) case study of eight L2 writers composing aloud, however, presents less categorical evidence of similarities between unskilled L1 and unskilled L2 writers. Like other studies, this points to variety among L2 subjects, and the possibility of differences between L2 and L1 composing.

Some contradictions clearly arise in the literature concerning the nature of L2 composing. Process research suffers from the limitations of small case-study work and from uncertainties about the validity and reliability of the protocol research tool. Kowal and O'Connell (1987: 125) have criticized the method as providing 'a great deal of data about something other than the process of writing'. Thinking aloud while composing may interfere with the process of writing by involving a second medium, speech; it may slow down or disrupt the activity, or provide data only about conscious (rather than automatic) processes. It may lead to a rarefication of the actual process, and a representation of what the writer thinks he or she is thinking about (or thinks the researcher would like to hear!).

Alternatives to protocol analyses tend to involve high levels of inference on the part of the researcher. Pause analysis, for example (see Matsuhashi, 1987), works on direct evidence of time on and off writing, but relating this observable behaviour to internal cognitive processes such as planning is potentially risky. Retrospective reporting using video-recording of writing sessions also offers an alternative, but the time-lag between writing and discussion brings with it clear disadvantages. Other research techniques using a combination of while-writing and post-event discussion appear to offer the best set of options for opening up the hidden cognitive processes underlying the activity of writing. (See also RESEARCH METHODOLOGY FOR LANGUAGE LEARNING, PROCESS WRITING, PRODUCTION PROCESSES.)

## WRITING AS SOCIAL ACTIVITY

Writing is an act of communication between writer and reader within an external context.

This type of approach to writing looks at the interaction between producer and receptor in terms of shared knowledge and situational context. Beyond the reader as an individual is the concept of the discourse community, the social construction of knowledge, the community's norms and expectations.

### TEACHING APPROACHES

The main focus of interest for each of these different writing research approaches, which draw on linguistic, cognitive and social theories of writing, is reflected in the diagram presented by Raimes (1983; figure 1), in which components of writing are represented as spokes of a wheel.

Since writing pedagogy over recent decades has given different emphases to aspects of writing, Raimes's diagram also provides us with a useful summary of major concerns underlying different teaching approaches. These main trends in teaching writing are discussed below.

### TEXT-BASED APPROACHES

Emphasis on language form, both grammatical and discoursal, has long been the principal concern of language teaching (see Silva, 1990; Raimes, 1991). We will first consider the dominance in writing pedagogy of grammatical form practice, before discussing more rhetoric-based approaches.

Following the strong audiolingual tradition in language teaching (see AUDIOLINGUALISM), involving practice of isolatable linguistic patterns (usually syntactic and morphological), one view of writing is as a means to an end (the reinforcement of linguistic habits) rather than as an end in itself. The controlled practice of predetermined language structures through writing would typically follow practice through the other skills (listening, speaking, reading), and would relegate writing, therefore, to the position of 'handmaid of the other skills' (Rivers, 1968: 241) at the end of the course unit, for homework and for testing. Consolidation of target structures would take

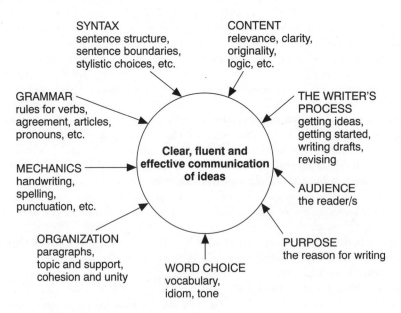

**Figure 1**   Components of writing.

place through sentence completion and combining tasks, gap-filling, or manipulation and imitation activities using model passages embodying the selected structures. The aim is formal linguistic accuracy, not appropriateness to context and self-expression, and the output is checked and corrected by the teacher/reader.

As interest grew in the late 1960s in discourse analysis and the organization of extended text, the limitations of a sentence-bound approach to writing instruction became more apparent. The scope of the form to be consolidated through writing might now move to paragraph patterns and sequences of units of meaning over longer stretches of discourse, but the aims remain structural. Silva (1990) refers to this approach as 'current-traditional rhetoric'. Building on the classification of discourse into rhetorical categories (e.g. description, narration) and functions (e.g. contrast/comparison), it places emphasis on the writer constructing and manipulating discourse forms through controlled completion-type tasks (e.g. topic sentence and paragraph development exercises). The model text is made use of in parallel writing activities, through which students work with a predetermined discourse template, slotting in either their own or given content in an attempt to consolidate these discourse structures (for examples of materials see Pincas, 1982; Cullup, 1981). Such approaches continue to have a strong influence on writing pedagogy, and much current writing material gives a central place to practice of grammatical and discoursal features (see, for example, Byrne, 1988: 49–60; Hedge, 1983). A focus on these aspects of writing, however, may limit the development in the writer of an ability to use the language of real or simulated communication. Such concerns, widely voiced within a framework of COMMUNICATIVE METHODOLOGY in language teaching (see COMMUNICATIVE LANGUAGE TEACHING), will be briefly explored below with reference to writing pedagogy.

## COMMUNICATION-BASED APPROACHES

The emphasis on MESSAGE- (rather than FORM-)FOCUS, and the goals of purposeful interaction within the classroom lead to the development of tasks and activities which incorporate principles of real or simulated communication. These include a concern with appropriateness to the context (i.e. according to the purpose of the communication, the content and audience), the establishment of a need to communicate (most obviously set up through INFORMATION/OPINION GAP and INFORMATION TRANSFER exercises), and an emphasis on real-time, holistic practice, encouraging risk-taking strategies, often through free practice/production activities. Written communication activities which develop a sense of audience and purpose abound within mainstream teaching materials (see, for example, Byrne, 1988: 40–2, 60–8; Raimes, 1983; Hedge, 1983, 1988; Burbidge et al., 1996; Lynch, 1996). These include pair- and group-based writing such as letter- and report-writing tasks based on exchange of information/opinion, transfer of information from visual to text, story-writing and writing as part of roleplay scenarios. Here, then, the main focus is on conveying a message appropriately, of language use rather than form practice.

## WRITER-BASED APPROACHES

A further shift of focus onto the writer rather than the text, coinciding with the growth in the 1970s in research into first-language composing, has had a significant impact on writing pedagogy. Following on from the work on modelling the cognitive processes of writing which revealed a 'non-linear, exploratory, and generative process' (Zamel, 1983: 165), certain tenets emerged for a pedagogy which reflected aspects of this process. The means rather than the end now become crucial. The focus moves to the writer's efforts to formulate and communicate ideas. Writing is viewed as a problem-solving cognitive activity, involving strategies of goal-setting, idea generation, organization, drafting, revising and editing. Meaning focus, exploration, multiple drafts became buzz-words of a new 'process revolution'.

The translation into methodology of these principles through the classroom-based support of components of the writing process is seen to flourish in second language circles during the 1980s. We might summarize the following features of current process approaches as:

(1) *Draft-based* Text is gradually shaped, worked and reworked through a number of draft versions (although this of course depends on what is being written, and in what circumstances). At points both before onset of writing and during drafting, the writer is involved in generating (and evaluating) ideas against goals. New directions may be taken in response to the generation of new plans. Pedagogic implications of this include supporting the generating of ideas, integrating reading and discussion, focusing on whole-text writing (rather than part-practice), developing a flexible attitude to text, as a series of versions potentially infinitely improvable.

(2) *Peer-influenced* Writing becomes a collaborative activity to be shared within the classroom. Reader response is developed through peer feedback, and a focus is put on real audience requirements and expectations.

(3) *Writer-centred* Students' evaluative abilities are developed with a consequent shift towards the teacher as adviser rather than assessor. The writers (and peers) act as critics and the generators of ideas.

The implementation of such principles in the classroom (see, for example, White and Arndt, 1991; Hedge, 1988) has not been without problems. Johnson's review (1993) of White and Arndt (1991) points to questions about the identification for teaching purposes of processes which (a) might not

be generalizable, given the wide individual variation of writers' procedures, (b) might be incomplete as a set of processes, and (c) by their very sequencing into a teaching order might be seen as discrete rather than integrated components of one complex phenomenon.

Questions have been raised concerning the appropriateness of such activities for beginner levels, in particular, the demands on linguistic resources of conferencing (feedback discussion with teacher and peers), and whether the need for maturity and a predisposition to engage in this type of collaborative learning might limit the applicability of such an approach.

Strong comments have also been made about the implementation of process methodology in academic (and ESP – see ENG-LISH FOR SPECIFIC PURPOSES) writing circles (Belcher and Braine, 1995; Horowitz, 1986). These arguments are reviewed in the following section, which concerns the reader/writer within context.

## CONTEXT-BASED APPROACHES

Doubts have been raised, in particular from the domain of English for academic purposes, concerning much of the emphasis in process-based methodology on the personal, the writer in his or her 'internal world': the writer's journey of self-discovery, the writer as generator of content and the apparent freedom from content- and time-constraints of exam-led syllabuses. One question which is raised, for example, is the centrality of process in academic writing by suggesting that the discovery of meaning should not deflect from issues of audience and rhetoric which are at the heart of university writing demands. In an early attack, Horowitz (1986) presents several arguments against process methodology in an academic context, including the specific (exam-led) goals, the reality of the context for producing text and the importance of the product in this context, the frequently non-involved, display type of writing, and the constraints of narrowly defined expectations about text format and content.

Attention away from the internal to the external world of the writer led in the 1980s on one hand to a movement towards content-based instruction, through content-linked or field-specific instruction, and on the other to an interest in writing as situated within a specific discourse community. Instruction aimed at socializing writers within this community by developing sensitivity to the needs and expectations of the audience focuses on the range and nature of academic GENRES in that context. Appropriate, effective communication is often associated with adherence to discourse conventions, although other current thinking promotes the challenging of such conventions (see CRITICAL LINGUISTICS).

The shifting influences of text (particularly grammatical and rhetorical form), writer and context, generated over recent decades by quite different research agendas, have led to quite separate trends in writing pedagogy. As differences between approaches are accentuated, the wholeness of the construct of writing is lost to sight. There is no process without product, and no product which has not arisen out of a process; this is a false dichotomy. Recognition of the necessary integration of all components in the production of text, as Raimes's simple diagram sets out, allows us to keep sight of the scope of our claims about any one approach to teaching writing.

BIBLIOGRAPHY

Belcher, D. and Braine, G. (1995). *Academic Writing in a Second Language: Essays on research and pedagogy*. Norwood, NJ: Ablex.

Burbidge, N., Gray, P., Levy, S. and Rinvolucri, M. (1996). *Letters*. Oxford: Oxford University Press.

Byrne, D. (1988). *Teaching Writing Skills*. London: Longman.

Cullup, M. (1981). *Write it in English*. Walton-on-Thames: Nelson.

Emig, J. (1971). *The Composing Processes of Twelfth Graders*. Urbana, IL: National Council of Teachers of English.

Flower, L. and Hayes, J. R. (1981). A cognitive process theory of writing. *College English*, 44, 765–77.

Hedge, T. (1983). *Pen to Paper, in a Word*. Walton-on-Thames: Nelson.

——(1988). *Writing: Resource books for teachers*. Oxford: Oxford University Press.*

Horowitz, D. (1986). Process, not product: less than meets the eye. *TESOL Quarterly*, 20, 141–4.

Johnson, K. (1993). Review of *Process Writing*. *English Language Teaching Journal*. 47/1, 89–91.

Kaplan, R. B. (1966). Cultural thought patterns in intercultural education. *Language Learning*, 16, 1–20.

Kowal, S. and O'Connell, D. C. (1987). Writing as language behaviour: myths, models, methods. In A. Matsuhashi (ed.), *Writing in Real Time: Modelling production processes*. Norwood, NJ: Ablex.

Krapels, A. (1990). An overview of second language writing process research. In B. Kroll, (ed.), *Second Language Writing*. Cambridge: Cambridge University Press.

Lynch, T. (1996). *Communication in the Language Classroom*. Oxford: Oxford University Press.

Matsuhashi, A. (ed.) (1987). *Writing in Real Time: Modelling production processes*. Norwood, NJ: Ablex.

Pincas, A. (1982). *Teaching English Writing*. Basingstoke: Macmillan.

Raimes, A. (1983). *Techniques in Teaching Writing*. Oxford: Oxford University Press.*

——(1985). What unskilled ESL writers do as they write: a classroom study of composing. *TESOL Quarterly*, 19, 229–58.

——(1991). Out of the woods: emerging traditions in the teaching of writing. *TESOL Quarterly*, 25, 407–30.

Rivers, W. (1968). *Teaching Foreign Language Skills*. Chicago: University of Chicago Press.

Rivers, W. and Temperley, R. S. (1978). *A Practical Guide to the Teaching of English*. New York: Oxford University Press.

Silva, T. (1990). Second language composition instruction: developments, issues, and directions in ESL. In B. Kroll (ed.), *Second Language Writing*. Cambridge: Cambridge University Press.

——(1993). Toward an understanding of the distinct nature of L2 writing: the ESL research and its implications. *TESOL Quarterly*, 27, 657–77.

White, R. and Arndt, V. (1991). *Process Writing*. London: Longman.*

Zamel, V. (1983). The composing process of six advanced ESL students: six case studies. *TESOL Quarterly*, 17, 165–87.

KSM

**teaching young learners**    Teaching foreign languages to young learners (aged 8 or younger) is becoming widespread throughout the world, with many countries having started the practice in recent years. Howatt (1991) provides a historical perspective. In the second half of this century, the FLES (Foreign Languages in the Elementary School) movement was developed in America from the 1950s with Andersson's (1953) book being a particularly eloquent plea for an early start to language learning. But research undertaken in the 1960s questioned the practice, and was influential in delaying primary level foreign language teaching in many places. This research (Burstall et al., 1974) involved teaching French in Britain at the primary level, to a total of approximately 17,000 8-year-old pupils (spread over a number of years). The tuition continued into the secondary school, so that all pupils learned the language for an uninterrupted five years. Evaluation of the scheme took place over a period of ten years (1964–74).

The aims of this research were various, and included investigation of the effect of pupil variables such as age and socio-economic status. Burstall (1980) provides a useful summary of the project and its findings. In relation to the early start issue she observes that: 'the older children tended to learn French more efficiently than the younger ones did. Pupils taught French from the age of eight did not show any substantial gains in achievement, compared with those who had been taught French from the age of eleven. By the age of 16, the only area in which the pupils taught French from the age of eight consistently showed any superiority was that of listening comprehension' and even in that area the gains were not substantial. The situation was different where attitude as opposed to achievement was measured.

This investigation (and others that followed it) needs to be seen within the context of the view, associated with Penfield (1953) and Lenneberg (1967), that there is an optimum age for learning languages. See CRITICAL PERIOD HYPOTHESIS, also AGE LEARNING DIFFERENCES. It is this view that gave a theoretical dimension (alongside the obvious practical one) to the study of the young learner issue at this historical moment.

Other later research does little to refute these findings. Snow and Hoefnagel-Höhle (1978), for example, report on English speakers of various ages learning Dutch in the target language environment. The 12- to 15-year-olds made the best progress, with the 3- to 5-year-olds performing consistently worse than older age groups.

Various commentators (Vilke, 1979, for example) have questioned the interpretation that may be placed on findings such as those of Burstall and others – that an early start is not cost-effective. Snow and Hoefnagel-Höhle themselves suggest that the better performance of the 12- to 15-year-olds in their study may be explained in terms of environmental factors, while others (e.g. Carroll, 1975) consider length of instruction time a crucial factor. A major further issue relates to the teaching methods used in such experiments and their suitability for the age group. The question arises whether some different teaching approach might have led to greater success with young learners.

It is indeed the case that one particular teaching approach – early immersion – has had particular success with early foreign language learning. Early IMMERSION PROGRAMMES were pioneered in Canada in the 1960s; the first French immersion kindergarten class took place in Saint Lambert (a suburb of Montreal) in 1965, and a plethora of similar programmes followed. There is much evidence to suggest the advantages of immersion programmes, but it has also been shown that the sociocultural and even political context of the teaching will play an important part in whether or not it will be successful.

A central characteristic of early immersion is that emphasis is placed on MESSAGE-FOCUS as opposed to FORM-FOCUS. This is also a central characteristic of many versions of COMMUNICATIVE LANGUAGE TEACHING (CLT), and indeed many textbooks for young learners (e.g. Wright et al., 1976; Johnson, 1982; Nolasco, 1990; Abbs et al., 1993) make clear attempts to apply the principles of CLT to the teaching of young learners. Techniques commonly associated with COMMUNICATIVE METHODOLOGY (particularly those involving an INFORMATION/OPINION GAP and INFORMATION TRANSFER) have made their way *en masse* into materials for young learners. It is natural that games should play an important part in teaching this age group, and it may be argued that an information gap naturally occurs in many children's games. A number of traditional children's games, for example, involve a blindfolded child attempting to discover something or undertake some task. Blindfolding may be seen as a physical means of creating an information gap. Other games use other forms of concealment (e.g. hiding objects, drawing a picture and concealing it from one's partner) and children's language materials have not been slow to adapt these to language learning purposes.

There have also been attempts to utilize the procedures of COMMUNICATIVE SYLLABUS design, like NEEDS ANALYSIS, with young learners. It is difficult to identify a discrete set of needs for the general learner, a category into which the young learner falls. An interesting approach to this problem was undertaken in Canada in the late 1970s. Malenfant-Loiselle and Munro Jones (1979) report on a large-scale study involving teaching English to French-speaking children in Quebec Province. The study analyses the interests of the L1 age group as part of the process of developing materials which would appeal to those same pupils learning the L2.

BIBLIOGRAPHY

Abbs, B., Worrall, A. and Ward, A. (1993). *Splash*. London: Longman.

Andersson, T. (1953). *The Teaching of Foreign Languages in the Elementary School*. Boston: Heath.

Burstall, C. (1980). Primary French in the balance. In S. Holden (ed.), *Teaching Children*. London: Modern English Publications.*

Burstall, C., Jamieson, M., Cohen, S. and Hargreaves, M. (1974). *Primary French in the Balance*. Windsor: NFER.

Carroll, J. B. (1975). *The Teaching of French as a Foreign Language in Eight Countries*. New York: John Wiley.

Howatt, A. P. R. (1991). Teaching languages to young learners: patterns of history. In C. J. Brumfit, J. Moon and R. Tongue (eds), *Teaching English to Children*. London: Collins ELT, 289–301.*

Johnson, K. (1982). *Now for English*. Walton-on-Thames: Nelson.

Lenneberg, E. H. (1967). *Biological Foundations of Language*. New York: John Wiley.

Malenfant-Loiselle, L. and Munro Jones, J. (1979). *Recherche des Centres d'Intérêts et des besoins langagiers des élèves de 9 à 11 ans en vue de l'élaboration du programme d'anglais, langue seconde, niveau primaire*. Document de Travail. Québec: Ministry of Education.

Nolasco, R. (1990). *Wow*. Oxford: Oxford University Press.

Penfield, W. G. (1953). A consideration of neurophysiological mechanisms of speech and some educational consequences. *Proceedings of the American Academy of Arts and Sciences*, 82, 199–214.

Snow, C. E. and Hoefnagel-Höhle, M. (1978). Age differences in second language acquisition. In E. M. Hatch (ed.), *Second Language Acquisition: A book of readings*. Rowley, MA: Newbury House, 333–44.

Vilke, M. (1979). Why start early? In R. Freudenstein (ed.), *Teaching Foreign Languages to the Very Young*. Oxford: Pergamon Institute of English.

Wright, A., Betteridge, D. and Hawkes, N. (1976). *Kaleidoscope*. Basingstoke: University of York and Macmillan Education.

KJ

## tests in English language teaching

Tests and examinations of proficiency are produced by many organizations in the UK, North America, Australia and other countries. Tests tend to be open and on demand; examinations tend to be closed and restricted to particular educational systems. Tests are available at all levels of proficiency, and with emphasis on a number of different areas of language use. Some tests are restricted to particular proficiency levels, others claim to measure across the range of levels. Some tests concentrate on particular skill areas, like oral skills; others test all the FOUR SKILLS.

In the UK, proficiency levels are conventionally specified by reference either to the UCLES range of general English tests:

Diploma in English Studies (DES);
Certificate of Proficiency in English (CPE);
First Certificate in English (FCE);
Preliminary English Test (PET);
Key English Test (KET);

because the FCE is possibly the most frequently taken language test in the world; alternatively, reference is made to the English Speaking Union Framework's nine-point scale, which is approximately equivalent to the nine-band descriptors used by the International English Language Testing System (IELTS):

9 Expert user;
8 Very good user;
7 Good user;
6 Competent user;
5 Modest user;
4 Limited user;
3 Extremely limited user;
2 Intermittent user;
1 Non-user.

In the USA, a set of levels of speaking proficiency has been developed in a collaboration including the Council on the Teaching of Foreign Languages, the Educational Testing Service and the Federal Inter-Agency Language Roundtable. They are known as the ACTFL Proficiency Guidelines and exist in parallel forms for a number of languages including English. There are four levels:

Novice;
Intermediate;
Advanced;
Superior.

In addition, if a candidate has most of the attributes of one of the levels but not all, he or she is labelled more finely as the next lower level with 'High': thus Novice High, Intermediate High, Advanced High. In a sense, therefore, there are really seven levels.

Tests are available at some or all of these levels for a range of uses.

*General English:* the Cambridge range already mentioned; the Certificate in Communicative Skills in English (Cambridge CCSE); the Association of Recognized English Language Schools (ARELS) and the Oxford Delegacy of Local Examinations (ODLE); the English Speaking Board; the Institute of Linguists; Pitman's Examinations Institute; Trinity College.

*Placement:* Nelson Quickcheck; Oxford Placement Test.

*Study English:* IELTS; TOEFL; CENTRA; Northern Examinations and Assessment Board; Pitman; Cambridge CPE and Certificate in Advanced English (CAE); Michigan English Language Battery; University of London.

*Business English:* London Chamber of Commerce and Industry (LCCI); Oxford International Business English Certificate; Pitman's English for Business; Cambridge's

Certificate in English for International Business and Trade; Educational Testing Service's (USA) Test of English for International Communication (TOEIC).

*Tourism:* Oxford's Tourism Proficiency; LCCI.

*Teaching English:* Cambridge Examination in English for Language Teachers (CEELT).

*Young learners:* ARELS/ODLE: 'Junior Counterpart' (ages 12–17); Associated Examinations Board: English as an acquired language (ages 7–12); Pitman (ages 9–13).

Addresses from which to obtain further information about the UK based tests can be obtained from the English Speaking Union, Dartmouth House, 37 Charles St, London W1X 8AB (telephone: 0171 493 3328; fax 0171 495 6108) or from the British Council.

## COMPARABILITY

It is rather confusing for test consumers – both those who want to take a test and those who need to interpret the results of applicants – to have such an array of tests at different levels, with very different methodologies, designed for different purposes. There have been several moves to establish comparability procedures. The English Speaking Union Framework (Carroll and West, 1989) is one, using a specially chosen set of samples of learners' performance in spoken and written English which has been marked by the various test producers using the marking scales used for their own tests. Thus the interpretation of a particular test's result on the ESU general nine-band scale (very similar to the IELTS scale above) can be 'verified' by reference to a common set of language performance samples which range across the proficiency levels. A large-scale, cross-national research project has been undertaken to compare TOEFL and

FCE tests (Davidson and Bachman, 1990). UCLES is currently researching methods of comparison to establish levels of proficiency across tests for the European languages represented by the Association of Language Testers in Europe (English, French, Catalan, Spanish, Italian, Irish, Danish, German, Dutch).

The issue of comparability is likely to remain important. It is not restricted to tests with low currency being compared with large-scale tests; there are large-scale tests, for instance, the English Proficiency Test produced by the Beijing Ministry of Education, which have huge numbers of takers and can be interpreted within their countries on internal, local criteria, but which are very difficult to interpret outside the educational system which produced them. For this reason applicants from such countries wishing to gain access to study in English-speaking countries often have to take another 'international' test: usually the TOEFL or IELTS, simply because they are more easily interpretable by the receiving authorities.

This entry should be read in conjunction with the entry on LANGUAGE TESTING, in which a more theoretical discussion of background issues in language testing will be found. These isues of principle are of course relevant to testing language proficiency for any language, without the restriction to English only. However, the range of tests described here for English illustrates many of the problems of practicality and theoretical principle which are currently being discussed in the literature. Two recent books which give a flavour of such discussions are Bachman (1990) and Davies (1992).

BIBLIOGRAPHY
Bachman, L. (1990). *Fundamental Considerations in Language Testing.* Oxford: Oxford University Press.*
Carroll, B. J. and West, R. (1989). *ESU Framework.* Harlow: Longman.
Davidson, F. and Bachman, L. (1990). The Cambridge-TOEFL comparability study: an

example of the cross-national comparison of language tests. *AILA Review 7: Standardization in Language Testing*, 24–45.

Davies, A. (1992). *Principles of Language Testing*. Oxford: Oxford University Press.

SMCD

**text grammar**   A text grammar attempts to state formal linguistic or semantic rules governing the succession of sentences in a given text type, and as such is an activity of text linguistics. Notable work was done on simple narratives, especially in ARTIFICIAL INTELLIGENCE. The growing realization that the development and COHERENCE of a text cannot be predicted or explained in purely formal terms but must make reference to context and PRAGMATICS has led to a decline. Text linguistics has been replaced by DISCOURSE ANALYSIS and text grammars by GENRE analysis, although these approaches often make use of earlier insights gained from text grammars.

BIBLIOGRAPHY

Krzeszowski, R. P. (1973). Is it possible and necessary to write text grammars? In S. P. Corder and E. Roulet (eds), *Theoretical Linguistic Models in Applied Linguistics*. Brussels: Aimav, and Paris: Didier.

Van Dijk, T. A. (1972). *Some Aspects of Text Grammars*. The Hague: Mouton.

Werlich, E. (1976). *A Text Grammar of English*. Heidelberg: Quelle and Meyer.

Widdowson, H. G. (1979). Approaches to discourse. In H. G. Widdowson, *Explorations in Applied Linguistics*. Oxford: Oxford University Press.

GC

**theory-then-research/research-then-theory**   The first position holds that meaningful practical experimentation depends upon first formulating a theory which will make predictions (see HYPOTHESIS) which you can then test by empirical investigation, for the further refinement (if not immediate endorsement or complete abandonment) of the original theory. The second position holds that it is helpful to conduct empirical investigations before formulating an explicit theory (that would permit precise prediction and hypothesis testing), on the grounds that empirical investigation motivated by informed speculation may itself be productive for theory-building. In practice a cyclical relationship is typically found. (See RESEARCH METHODOLOGY.)

BIBLIOGRAPHY

Larsen-Freeman, D. and Long, M. H. (1991). *An Introduction to Second Language Acquisition Research*. London: Longman.

Snow, R. E. (1973). Theory construction for research on teaching. In R. M. W. Travers (ed.), *Second Handbook of Research on Teaching*. Chicago: Rand McNally, 77–112.

RLA

**threshold hypothesis**   The claim that, below one threshold of bilingual development, children suffer cognitively as they are not able to interact effectively with their environment; above another threshold, children gain cognitively in terms of mental flexibility, etc.; in between they know only one language adequately and neither lose nor gain. See BILINGUALISM.

BIBLIOGRAPHY

Cummins, J. (1979). Linguistic interdependence and the educational development of bilingual children. *Review of Educational Research*, 49, 222–51.

Skutnabb-Kangas, T. (1981). *Bilingualism or Not: The education of minorities*. Clevedon: Multilingual Matters.

VJC

**threshold level**   In the COUNCIL OF EUROPE's unit/credit system, the T-Level is the 'lowest level of foreign-language ability to be recognised' (van Ek, 1975: 8). For the COMMON CORE of this level, van Ek produced a syllabus inventory which has come to stand as a model for inventories associated with NOTIONAL/FUNCTIONAL SYLLABUSES. It lists situations, activities, functions, topics, notions (general and specific), forms and degrees of skill. As a common core inventory most of the areas covered relate to social and interpersonal language uses. T-Levels for other European languages have since been produced.

BIBLIOGRAPHY
Trim, J. L. M. (1973). Draft outline of a European unit/credit system for modern language learning by adults. In J. L. M. Trim, R. Richterich, J. A. van Ek and D. A. Wilkins, *Systems Development in Adult Language Learning*. Strasbourg: Council of Europe.
Van Ek, J. A. (1973). The 'Threshold Level' in a unit/credit system. In J. L. M. Trim, R. Richterich, J. A. van Ek and D. A. Wilkins, *Systems Development in Adult Language Learning*. Strasbourg: Council of Europe.
——(1975). *The Threshold Level*. Strasbourg: Council of Europe.

KJ

**tolerance of ambiguity** is a trait thought to be good for language learning. A person with high tolerance should be able to cope with the confusing spectacle of apparent anomalies in the language data encountered. Its exact relationship with language learning has not been determined. (See PERSONALITY VARIABLES.)

BIBLIOGRAPHY
Naiman, N., Fröhlich, M. and Stern, H. H. (1975). *The Good Language Learner*. Ontario: Modern Language Centre, Department of Curriculum, Ontario Institute for Studies in Education.

SMCD

**top-down processing** A term from cognitive psychology often applied to language comprehension (listening and reading). Unlike the method in BOTTOM-UP PROCESSING, we 'bring to' a text background knowledge which we utilize in the interpretation of its meaning. See SCHEMA THEORY.

BIBLIOGRAPHY
Brown, G. and Yule, G. (1983). *Discourse Analysis*. Cambridge: Cambridge University Press.

KJ

**total physical response** Developed by Asher (though perhaps inspired by Palmer and Palmer), this method for beginners, emphasizing meaning and aural/oral skills, rests on the assumptions that first language acquisition involves physical (before verbal) responses to commands; second language acquisition should mirror this process; motor activity strengthens recall; listening and responding physically to acquire the language profile should precede production; language acquisition can be stress-free if there is no compulsion to 'produce' early on. Learners execute teacher commands for about 120 hours before conversation is encouraged. The commands are simple initially, but become increasingly sophisticated, involving hypotactic as well as paratactic constructions.

BIBLIOGRAPHY
Asher, J. (1965). The strategy of the total physical response: an application to learning Russian. *International Review of Applied Linguistics*, 3, 291–300.
——(1969). The total physical response approach to second language learning. *Modern Language Journal*, 53, 3–17.
Palmer, H. and Palmer, D. (1959). *English through Actions*. London: Longmans, Green. [First published in 1925.]

JTR

**transfer** Language transfer is one of the important factors shaping the learner's INTERLANGUAGE. The origins of the term go back to BEHAVIOURISM and its view that the first/native language (L1) habits influence the acquisition of the second/foreign language (L2) habits. Although it was later discredited, the notion of transfer has been revived again and remains one of the most fundamental in L2 acquisition research (see also CROSS-LINGUISTIC STUDIES, CONTRASTIVE ANALYSIS and ERROR ANALYSIS).

## EARLY VIEWS ON TRANSFER

According to Lado (1957), the productive and receptive skills of L2 speakers are influenced by their own L1 patterns and meanings, at both the linguistic and the cultural levels. Lado's idea was based on the behaviourist view of language use as a 'habit'. Linguistic patterns of the L1 which have become so habitual as to be below the level of an individual's awareness are liable to be transferred into an L2.

At the core of Lado's conception of transfer were the notions of similarity and difference between L1 and L2 as the predictors of ease and difficulty in the learning of L2. In general, those structures which were similar in the two languages were thought to be the source of ease in learning L2, and those which were different were thought to result in the learning difficulties. CONTRASTIVE ANALYSIS was then conceived of as the discipline which would identify the similarities and differences between languages so that its findings would predict the areas of difficulty in L2 learning and errors in L2 production (and reception).

An elaboration of this view of transfer, based on a statistical analysis of the occurrence of L1 structural forms in the learners' L2, or INTERLANGUAGE (IL), distinguishes two major types of transfer: *positive* and *negative* transfer (Selinker, 1983). Positive transfer occurs when a native form is used in the production of an L2 utterance, and it is also a part of the L2 norm. Here the role of transfer is facilitative. Negative transfer occurs when the L1 form used in L2 production is not a part of the L2 norm, and

the resultant utterance is erroneous. Negative transfer (or *interference*) is inhibitive.

## OPPOSITION TO TRANSFER

L2 acquisition research, inspired by CHOMSKYAN LINGUISTICS, voiced strong opposition to the somewhat simplistic, early views on language transfer (Corder, 1993; Dulay, Burt and Krashen, 1982). Structural differences between two languages have not always been shown to result in learning difficulties, and errors were more readily attributed to the learner's COMMUNICATION STRATEGIES than to the transfer of ill-chosen structures from L1.

Moreover, the developmental research in the universalist tradition has shown that certain L2 errors were shared by all learners regardless of their native language, and that many of these errors resembled those made by children acquiring their L1 (Dulay, Burt and Krashen, 1982). Likewise, Corder (1993) argued for a limited importance of transfer in L2 acquisition. He claimed that there was no empirical corroboration of the existence of negative transfer (interference), perhaps, as he admitted, with the exception of phonology. According to Corder, the mother tongue plays a role in L2 acquisition but it is closer to *borrowing*, and therefore has a facilitative role in L2 learning and production. Furthermore, when a grammatical structure of L2 appears to the learner to be particularly different from L1, the learner is more liable to resort to AVOIDANCE STRATEGIES rather than to the transfer of the native construction.

## FURTHER DEVELOPMENTS IN TRANSFER THEORY

Despite these criticisms, further refinements of language transfer theory have firmly put cross-linguistic influence on the map of L2 language research. Reconciliatory solutions between the traditional behaviourist and the cognitive, universalist approaches have been suggested (Odlin, 1989). The two volumes on language transfer by Gass and Selinker (1983, 1993), the collections by Kellerman and Sharwood Smith (1986), Dechert and Raupach (1989), Kellerman and Perdue (1992) and numerous other publications (e.g. Faerch and Kasper, 1987; Ringbom, 1987; Gass, 1996) have been among the most influential in the field.

In their revised position on transfer, Gass and Selinker (1993) state that it is not incompatible to think of L2 acquisition as being affected by two interrelated processes: first, the learner's build-up of a body of knowledge in which he or she tests hypotheses formed on the basis of the available L2 data (the view advocated by Dulay, Burt and Krashen) and second, the learner's utilization of the knowledge of L1 and other languages known to him or her (the view echoing Lado's early ideas).

## TRANSFER IN COMMUNICATION AND LEARNING

In their cognitive approach to transfer, Faerch and Kasper (1987) postulate the idea of transfer as a single *process* which should be studied separately from its effects on L2 utterances. Therefore, the distinction between *positive* and *negative* transfer should be abandoned as it is too product-related. Instead, the learner is said to transfer his or her prior knowledge of L1 which results in IL forms, and only through the comparison of these forms with the L2 norms can the *results* of transfer processes be termed 'positive', 'negative' or 'neutral' (see also Gass and Selinker, 1993). (Interestingly, Kasper (1992) adheres to the 'positive–negative' transfer distinction in her overview of *pragmatic transfer*.)

IL speakers resort to transfer in communication: L2 *production* and *reception*, as well as in L2 *learning*. Transfer in production

is a procedure of activating L1 (or indeed prior L2) knowledge to accomplish a communicative goal. In reception, this procedure leads to the reliance on L1 patterns in interpreting the incoming utterances. The processing of utterances in this way is also known as 'interlingual inferencing'. Similarly, inferencing processes are central to transfer as a learning procedure, whereby the learner uses the knowledge of his or her L1 in order to form hypotheses about the rules of L2 (see Schachter, 1993 [1983]).

## TRANSFERABILITY

Transfer processes have been documented to occur at all the levels of linguistic analysis: PHONOLOGY, MORPHOLOGY, SYNTAX, LEXIS and SEMANTICS (e.g. see Odlin, 1989; on pragmatic transfer see below). The degree to which transfer is present in the speakers' IL will vary greatly. Phonological transfer is probably the most common of all in nonnative speech, and the least controversial in the literature. There is no question that most IL speakers can be recognized on the basis of their 'foreign' accents. However, some IL speakers will manifest a more noticeable or 'heavier' accent than others, as they will not be able to reprogram their speech organs to the native-like production of the new sounds.

Likewise, grammatical (morphological and syntactic) transfer may range from the most extreme reproduction of L1 word order in L2 (*relexification*) to a loose adaptation of L1 grammatical features in L2 utterances. Thus, one of the central issues in the literature on transfer has dealt with the factors favouring and disfavouring the occurrence of transfer. This question is discussed under the heading of *transferability* and researchers (e.g. Faerch and Kasper, 1987) have identified its three major criteria as *linguistic*, *psycholinguistic* and *socio-psychological*.

*Linguistic criteria* An important influence on the transferability of a grammatical form (such as word order, relative-clause formation and negation) is related to the question of universality and typological characterization of the feature. The surface realization of a form is more likely to be transferred if it is marked, that is, more basic than an alternative one. Markedness of a feature may result in its greater prominence, perceptual saliency, semantic transparency, which will lead to its greater susceptibility to transfer. By the same token, the surface realization of a structure is more likely to be transferred the more universal rather than (L1) language-specific it is (see Gass and Selinker, 1983, 1993).

*Psycholinguistic criteria*    In production, speakers are more likely to transfer elements of their L1 to L2 if they *perceive* L1 and L2 as sufficiently close, despite the actual genetic distance between the two languages. For example, Dutch speakers are more likely to transfer Dutch-like features to their German IL than to their English IL (Kellerman, 1983). Likewise, Swedish-speaking Finns transfer linguistic elements from Swedish to English, but not from Finnish, and Finnish monolingual speakers rely on native language transfer to a lesser degree than their bilingual counterparts (Ringbom, 1987).

Another important psycholinguistic criterion for transferability is the speaker's perception of the linguistic form as *language-specific* and therefore not easily transferable, or *language-neutral* and easily transferable. It is important to bear in mind that the markedness and semantic transparency of linguistic forms mentioned above, and the speaker's perceptions of forms as more or less transferable will overlap greatly, but not fully. What may be linguistically marked need not be perceptually so for the IL speaker (and vice versa).

*Socio-psychological criteria*    A complex web of social and psychological factors may be responsible for the occurrence of transfer. The processes of *convergence* and *divergence* described by accommodation theory (e.g.

Giles and Powesland, 1975), as well as the speaker's need for *identity marking*, may influence a speaker's recourse to L1 features in L2, or to their avoidance. Age, style of learning, proficiency in L2 and knowledge of other second languages can also play a role in the likelihood of the speaker's reliance on transfer. Thus, it has been hypothesized that, other things being equal:

- adult learners rely on their prior experience in concept and language learning more than children, and consequently the former will use transfer in their learning and production of L2 more often than the latter;
- there is more transfer in foreign- than second-language learning situations as teachers are often encouraged to overstate the similarities between L1 and L2 (but see below for an opposite effect of instruction on transfer in language teaching);
- there is more transfer in elicited than spontaneous IL utterances as the IL speaker has more time to plan what to say and therefore is more likely to 'borrow' L1 forms;
- early stages of language learning are more likely to lead to transfer as the L2 data available to the IL speaker are not fully accessible to form hypotheses about L2 rules;
- 'item-learning' (especially with respect to LEXIS) is more likely to facilitate transfer than 'system-learning'.

These and other social and psychological criteria (see Ringbom, 1987, for discussion), together with linguistic and psycholinguistic factors, are responsible for facilitating or inhibiting the role of language transfer in L2 acquisition. Ongoing research will doubtless explain the mechanism of language transfer in greater detail. Other work, to be discussed in the next section, has focused on why learners resort to transfer from the communicative point of view.

## TRANSFER AS A COMMUNICATION STRATEGY

Transfer has been identified as an element of LEARNER STRATEGIES, and more specifically, communicative strategies. As has already been mentioned, in L2 communication transfer can occur in reception and production. The reliance on transfer as a receptive communication strategy is especially clear in the case of genetically closely related languages (e.g. Norwegian and Danish, Polish and Slovak), when communicators process utterances in the 'other' language without any prior formal instruction, relying solely on interlingual inferencing.

In communicative production strategies, transfer can take the form of 'literal' translation: *He invite other person to drink* for the target language 'they toasted each other'; 'language switch': *balon* for the target language 'balloon'; and 'phonological adaptation': *cuffer* for 'hairdresser' (from French 'coiffeur') (examples based on Poulisse, 1994). These strategies are largely conscious and form part of the learner's STRATEGIC COMPETENCE.

## AUTOMATIC TRANSFER

However, many instances of transfer occur below the level of the speaker's awareness in a highly automatized fashion. Examples of such automatic transfer are quoted by Faerch and Kasper (1987: 128), for example, Danish learner of English: *I think I better like to maybe (laughs) I really don't know* men *maybe I better like to live here*, where *men* is a Danish word for 'but'. Such transfer 'slips' are common even among advanced speakers of L2.

Strategic transfer and automatic transfer are not meant to be discrete and disjunctive concepts. Many instances of transfer are less clear-cut with regard to attention and automatization. One general term suggested to cover such fuzzy cases is *subsidiary transfer*, which occurs in L2 utterances as part of the speaker's plan in IL where momentarily the focus of attention shifts back to L1, for example (Danish learner of English demonstrates strategic transfer of Danish wordorder in conditional clauses in English IL): *can I understand English can I – understand*

*[lidt amerikænsk] well* (Danish 'kan jeg forstå engelsk kan jeg også forstå lidt amerikånsk' = 'if I understand English, then I also understand a little American') (Faerch and Kasper, 1987: 130).

## PRAGMATIC TRANSFER

Similarly to IL studies, interlanguage PRAGMATICS is interested in how many of the pragmatic strategies of L1 are transferred to the learner's L2. Kasper (1992) defines pragmatic transfer as 'the influence exerted by learners' pragmatic knowledge of languages and cultures other than L2 on their comprehension, production and learning of L2 pragmatic information' (1992: 207).

Following other researchers' work in pragmatics, Kasper distinguishes between *pragmalinguistic* and *sociopragmatic* transfer. Pragmalinguistic transfer occurs when the speaker uses L2 equivalents of syntactic and semantic L1 forms to express the intended illocutionary force or type of politeness. For example, Japanese speakers of English have been found to use refusal expressions not normally used in English but showing influences from Japanese, such as 'statements of philosophy': *to err is human, I never yield to temptations*, and 'suggestions for alternative action': *why don't you ask someone else* (Beebe et al., 1990, quoted in Kasper, 1992: 215).

Sociopragmatic transfer takes place when the speaker copies from L1 to L2 his or her perceptions of social distance, power, speaker's rights and obligations, degrees of imposition involved in different linguistic acts, and other contextual factors affecting relationships between interlocutors. For example, Japanese speakers of English vary their choices of refusal strategies reflecting their native preferences, which are different from those of American native speakers. The latter choose a refusal strategy depending on whether they are speaking to a status equal or non-equal, regardless of the direction (high to low or low to high). Japanese speakers, on the other hand, vary their refusal strategies depending on whether they are speaking to status superiors or status inferiors.

The question of *transferability* in pragmatic transfer is as important as in generic transfer. In fact, it may be quite difficult to establish when the speaker is transferring his or her pragmatic and cultural knowledge of L1 to L2, and when he or she is over-generalizing L2 rules, or when he or she is relying on universal pragmatic knowledge when adopting specific pragmatic strategies in L2 IL. But, similarly to generic transfer, there are factors which will increase the probability of the occurrence of pragmatic transfer. For example, the speaker's perception of linguistic and cultural L1 features as more language- and culture-specific, rather than universal, will make them less prone to transfer. Formal instruction and overt mention of such forms to the learners may also, rightly or wrongly, diminish their chance of being transferred to L2 IL. For example, Kasper notes that a group of German speakers of English consistently avoided the cajoler *I mean*, equivalent to the German *ich meine*, because they had been told that its use was a 'Germanism'.

Other factors increasing the likelihood of pragmatic transfer are the speaker's advance in linguistic proficiency in L2, and the lack of knowledge of the cultural schemata of L2. The possible explanation behind the former claim is that having improved his or her proficiency in L2, the speaker is more able to render L1 pragmatic strategies in L2 form. The latter claim is almost self-explanatory: if the speaker does not know when or whether to apologize, complain, express gratitude or perform another type of speech act in L2, the resulting behaviour may reflect his or her L1 usage deemed appropriate for a given social occasion.

In the concluding parts of her overview of pragmatic transfer, Kasper rightly emphasizes that negative pragmatic transfer need not be equated with miscommunication.

Sometimes, L1 speakers living among L2 speakers may adhere to L1 cultural patterns of speaking in L2 in order to preserve or mark their identity. They may also be expected to follow slightly different norms of behaviour by members of the host culture as complete communicative integration with the host culture might be perceived as a threat to its members. According to this view, pragmatic transfer, like generic transfer above, can be viewed as a communicative strategy or a meta-pragmatic strategy of IL speakers.

## SUBSTRATE TRANSFER

Apart from the rich literature on transfer in L2 acquisition, there is also evidence of cross-linguistic influence in situations of language contact. Known as *substrate* transfer, this type of cross-linguistic influence is effected by a language once spoken in a community on a new language adopted by a community which has undergone language shift and/or has become bilingual. For example, Hiberno-English (the 'superstrate') in Ireland shows influences of Irish Gaelic (the 'substrate') (Odlin, 1992), and Sridhar and Sridhar (1992) argue that various *indigenized varieties of English* (e.g. Indian English) have acquired their distinctiveness partly due to the processes of substrate transfer through the influence of the indigenous languages on English.

BIBLIOGRAPHY
Beebe, L. M., Takahashi, T. and Uliss-Weltz, R. (1990). Pragmatic transfer in ESL refusals. In R. C. Scarcella, E. Andersen and S. C. Krashen (eds), *Developing Communicative Competence in a Second Language*. Rowley, MA: Newbury House, 55–73.
Blum-Kulka, S., House, J. and Kasper, G. (eds) (1989). *Cross-Cultural Pragmatics: Requests and apologies*. Norwood, NJ: Ablex.
Corder, S. P. (1993). A role for the mother tongue. In S. Gass and L. Selinker (eds), *Language Transfer in Language Learning*. Rev. edn.

Amsterdam and Philadelphia: John Benjamins, 18–31. [Originally published in the 1983 edition of Gass and Selinker.]

Dechert, H. W. and Raupach, M. (eds) (1989). *Transfer in Production*. Norwood, NJ: Ablex.

Dulay, H., Burt, M. and Krashen, S. (1982). *Language Two*. New York: Oxford University Press.

Faerch, C. and Kasper, G. (1987). Perspectives on language transfer. *Applied Linguistics*, 8/2, 111–36.

Gass, S. (1996). Transference and interference. In H. Goebl, P. H. Nelde and Z. Starý (eds), *Contact Linguistics: An international handbook of contemporary research*. Vol. 1. Berlin: Walter de Gruyter, 558–67.

Gass, S. M. and Selinker, L. (eds) (1983). *Language Transfer in Language Learning*. Rowley, MA: Newbury House.

—— (1993). *Language Transfer in Language Learning*. Rev. edn. Amsterdam and Philadelphia: John Benjamins.

Giles, H. and Powesland, P. F. (1975). *Speech Style and Social Evaluation*. London: Academic Press.

Kasper, G. (1992). Pragmatic transfer. *Second Language Research*, 8/3, 201–31.

Kellerman, E. (1983). Now you see it, now you don't. In S. Gass and L. Selinker (eds), *Language Transfer in Language Learning*. Rowley, MA: Newbury House, 112–34.

Kellerman, E. and Perdue, C. (eds) (1992). *Second Language Research*, 8/3, Special Issue on Cross-Linguistic Influence.

Kellerman, E. and Sharwood Smith, M. (eds) (1986). *Crosslinguistic Influence in Second Language Acquisition*. Oxford: Pergamon.

Lado, R. (1957). *Linguistics across Cultures*. Ann Arbor: University of Michigan Press.

Odlin, T. (1989). *Language Transfer: Cross-linguistic influence in language learning*. Cambridge: Cambridge University Press.*

—— (1992). Transferability and linguistic substrates. *Second Language Research*, 8/3, 171–202.

Poulisse, N. (1994). Communication strategies in a second language. In R. E. Asher (ed.), *The Encyclopedia of Language and Linguistics*. Vol. 2. Oxford: Pergamon, 620–4.

Ringbom, H. (1987). *The Role of the First Language in Foreign Language Learning*. Clevedon: Multilingual Matters.

Schachter, J. (1993). A new account of language transfer. In S. Gass and L. Selinker (eds), *Language Transfer in Language Learning*. Rev. edn. Amsterdam and Philadelphia: John Benjamins, 31–46. [Originally published in the 1983 edition of Gass and Selinker.]

Sridhar, K. K. and Sridhar, S. N. (1992). Bridging the paradigm gap: second-language acquisition theory and indigenized varieties of English. In B. B. Kachru (ed.), *The Other Tongue: English across cultures*. Urbana: University of Illinois Press, 91–107.

Thomas, J. (1983). Cross-cultural pragmatic failure. *Applied Linguistics*, 4, 91–112.

AJ

## transformational generative grammar

has been developed by Noam Chomsky and others since 1957. The surface structure of sentences is derived from the deep structure by ordered transformations such as movement, copying, substitution and deletion. Since the 1980s, a single general transformation – move α – is assumed, which interacts with various conditions on rules and representations. (See also CHOMSKYAN LINGUISTICS and GENERATIVE GRAMMAR.)

BIBLIOGRAPHY

Fromkin, V. and Rodman, R. (1993). *An Introduction to Language*. 5th edn. Fort Worth, TX: Harcourt Brace Jovanovich. [Particularly chapter 3.]

Haegeman, L. (1994). *Introduction to Government and Binding Theory*. 2nd edn. Oxford: Blackwell.

Radford, A. (1988). *Transformational Grammar: A first course*. Cambridge: Cambridge University Press.*

EJ

## translation in language teaching

Although continuously in use, translation in language teaching has been dismissed by almost all twentieth-century theories and methodologies. Reasons include: a reaction against GRAMMAR TRANSLATION; a change of emphasis from writing to speech; a belief in 'natural' second language acquisition; a belief that translation promotes false equivalence. In ELT the rejection has served the interests of the English-speaking countries by supporting the view that the NATIVE SPEAKER teacher is best, irrespective of his or her knowledge of the students' L1. There are now signs of revival, and recognition that translation is an aid to language learning, a useful testing device and an invaluable skill in itself.

BIBLIOGRAPHY

Duff, A. (1989). *Translation*. Resource Books for Teachers. Oxford: Oxford University Press.

Howatt, A. P. R. (1984). *A History of English Language Teaching*. Oxford: Oxford University Press. [Chapters 11 and 13.]

Stern, H. H. (1992). *Issues and Options in Language Teaching*, edited by P. Allen and B. Harley. Oxford: Oxford University Press.* [Chapter 10.]

GC

**t-unit** is a text unit originally designed to measure syntactic complexity. It is defined (Hunt, 1966) as a single independent clause plus any subordinate clauses attached to it or embedded in it. The c-unit is similar to the t-unit, but also includes non-clausal structures which have communicative value.

BIBLIOGRAPHY

Crookes, G. (1990). The utterance, and other basic units for second language discourse analysis. *Applied Linguistics*, 11, 183–99.

Hunt, K. W. (1966). Recent measures in syntactic development. *Elementary English*, 43, 732–9.

KSM

**turn-taking** Speakers' PRAGMATIC COMPETENCE includes the knowledge of who speaks when. Other things being equal, English shows a preference for avoidance of pauses and overlapping speech between turns. Turn-taking is highly structured and

speakers signal when they are prepared to give up the floor, often 'nominate' the next speaker (verbally or non-verbally) and the next speaker can nominate him- or herself simply by starting to speak. Some linguistic sequences are not complete without the participants taking turns (*adjacency pairs*), e.g. greetings, sequences of compliments–compliment responses. In problematic talk, an extra turn (*repair*) may occur, e.g. A: *I want ice-cream*. B: *What?* A: *I said that I want ice-cream*.

BIBLIOGRAPHY

Graddol, D., Cheshire, J. and Swann, J. (1987). *Describing Language*. Milton Keynes: Open University Press. [Chapter 6.]

Sacks, H., Schegloff, E. A. and Jefferson, G. (1974). A simplest systematics for the organization of turn-taking in conversation. *Language*, 50, 696–735.

AJ

**type-token** Tokens are actually occurring instances of some phenomenon, p, in a corpus of data. A type is the class p itself to which the tokens belong. For example, in *Max wrote to Sharon, and she wrote to him*, *she* and *him* are both tokens of the type 'pronoun'.

RH

**typology** The classification of languages into groups. A long linguistic tradition has been concerned with this in terms of historical roots, seeking common origins between languages. Today, typologists are more concerned with formal similarities and differences. For example, it is possible to characterize world languages according to where in the sentence the verb is typically placed; there are verb-initial languages (Welsh, Hebrew), verb-medial ones (English, French) and verb-final ones (Japanese, Turkish). Typologists study a broad spectrum of languages to establish similarities and differences at all linguistic levels.

Though there may be strong theoretical and methodological differences between typologists and those interested in UNIVERSAL GRAMMAR, there is clear common ground in the two pursuits.

BIBLIOGRAPHY
Nichols, J. (1992). *Linguistic Diversity in Space and Time*. Chicago: University of Chicago Press.

KJ

# U

**unitary competence hypothesis** The (controversial) view, associated particularly with Oller (e.g. 1979), that an individual possesses one underlying linguistic competence that can be measured by one single test. The alternative view (the 'divisible competence hypothesis') is that the individual will have different degrees of proficiency in different skill areas. An integrative test (see INTEGRATIVE TESTING) like the CLOZE test would, it was thought, measure unitary competence – an attractive alternative to the multiple tests which the opposing hypothesis requires.

BIBLIOGRAPHY
Oller, J. (1979). *Language Tests at School: A pragmatic approach*. London: Longman.

KJ

**universal grammar** (UG) One meaning of universal grammar concerns aspects of language found in many languages, called statistical, typological (see TYPOLOGY) or 'Greenbergian' universals, for instance, word-order correlations and the accessibility hierarchy for relative clauses. The meaning of universal grammar (UG) within Chomskyan theories is the language faculty – the aspects of language built in to the mind that become knowledge of a particular grammar when exposed to language input. UG theory explores the nature of language knowledge and of acquisition in both L1 and L2. Since the mid-eighties UG has been identified with the principles and parameters theory. See CHOMSKYAN LINGUISTICS.

BIBLIOGRAPHY
Chomsky, N. (1986). *Knowledge of Language: Its nature, origin and use*. New York: Praeger.
Cook, V. J. and Newson, M. (1995). *Chomsky's Universal Grammar*. 2nd edn. Oxford: Blackwell.
Hawkins, J. A. (1983). *Word Order Universals*. New York: Academic Press.
Lightfoot, D. (1982). *The Language Lottery: Toward a biology of grammars*. Cambridge, MA: MIT Press.
Tomlin, R. S. (1986). *Basic Word Order: Functional principles*. London: Croom Helm.

VJC

**use/usage** The distinction is Widdowson's (1978). *Usage* refers to the function of a linguistic item as an element of the linguistic system, while *use* refers to how it functions in communication, as a speech act (see SPEECH ACT THEORY). Language teaching had, Widdowson argued, concentrated on usage and ignored use, and an aim of COMMUNICATIVE LANGUAGE TEACHING was to redress the balance.

BIBLIOGRAPHY
Widdowson, H. G. (1978). *Teaching Language as Communication*. Oxford: Oxford University Press.

KJ

# V

**validity** The validity of language tests, and in general of any measuring instrument like a performance sample, a questionnaire or an interview, is the extent to which the result truly represents the quality being measured. Traditionally, validity of language tests is estimated by internal criteria or content validity; comparison with other language tests or concurrent validity; comparison with other kinds of performance (such as occupation or subject examination), or predictive validity, or comparison with a theory of the performance in question (i.e. reading or listening comprehension, oral skills, or writing skill), or construct validity. (Contrast with RELIABILITY; see LANGUAGE TESTING.)

BIBLIOGRAPHY
Hughes, A. (1989). *Testing for Language Teachers.* Cambridge: Cambridge University Press, 22–8.

SMCD

**variability in SLA** refers to cases where an L2 learner uses two or more linguistic variants to express a phenomenon which has only one realization in the target language. For example, Ellis (1985) reports a learner of L2 English who uses two variants for expressing negation in contiguous chunks of speech: *No look my card/ Don't look my card.* In trying to explain the sources of such variability in SLA, researchers have generally worked from an assumption, first elaborated in work by Labov (1972) on native speakers of English, that variability is a systematic function of factors like the degree of formality of the context of utterance and the nature of the surrounding linguistic context.

There have been a number of proposed explanations of L2 variability: learners have a set of L2 grammars, each appropriate to different contexts of use (Tarone, 1983); learners go through a developmental phase of variability (Ellis, 1985); variability is the result of using two types of knowledge, one subconsciously acquired, the other consciously learned (Krashen, 1981); variability results from differences in processing loads associated with different types of task (Hulstijn and Hulstijn, 1984).

## THE LABOVIAN BACKGROUND

Labov (1972) showed that in native (American) English there is systematic variability which correlates both with the social group membership of the speaker, and the communicative purpose for which she or he is speaking. Taking 'postvocalic' /r/ in phrases like 'fourth floor' as a potential linguistic variable, his investigators found that shop assistants in three New York department stores (roughly classified as 'working-class', 'lower middle-class' and 'upper middle-class') realized postvocalic /r/ in different proportions. In response to a question which required them to produce the phrase 'fourth floor' (for example, 'Where are women's shoes?'), it was found that the assistants in the working-class store produced fewer postvocalic /r/s than shop assistants in the lower middle-class store, who produced fewer postvocalic /r/s than assistants in the upper middle-class store. Assuming that the shop assistants who worked in the three stores are representative of the socio-economic groups who shop there, it is clear from these results that a linguistic variable – presence versus absence of postvocalic /r/ – correlates with social group membership.

When Labov's investigators pretended to be hard of hearing, saying 'Excuse me?' after the assistants first uttered 'fourth floor', thereby forcing them to repeat the phrase, it was found that the proportion of postvocalic /r/s increased for all three groups. If the two types of responses elicited from the shop assistants are examples of different speech styles — the first casual or informal speech, and the second an example of a more careful 'citation' style – the results suggest that the speech of individual native speakers may vary as a function of the context in which they are speaking: in this case more postvocalic /r/s are found in the speech of all speakers when they adopt a careful style of speech than when they are speaking casually.

## Studies of L2 variability

Studies of L2 variability have typically focused on phenomena in which second language learners, but not native speakers, vary. As mentioned above, Ellis (1985) cites the case of a Portuguese-speaking boy learning English who, while playing a game, produced the following utterances within the same stretch of speech: *No look my card* and *Don't look my card*. Here the learner is varying between *no* and *don't* as negators in a way which native speakers would not.

Another example of L2 learner variability where the native speaker would not vary is provided in a study by Dickerson (1974), who looked at a number of features of the English pronunciation of ten Japanese speakers on three tasks: reading a list of words, reading a dialogue and free speech. Taking just one of the phonological phenomena studied by Dickerson – prevocalic /r/, as in *run* – it was found that the accuracy of subjects' pronunciation varied as a function of two factors: the nature of the task and the nature of the vowel sound following the /r/. Subjects were most native-like in reading the list of words, less native-like in reading the dialogue and least native-like in free speech. Furthermore, the pronunciation of /r/ was more native-like before mid vowels, as in *run*, than before high vowels as in *read*.

These two examples illustrate two kinds of variability which have been signalled in the SLA literature: *systematic variability* (Dickerson's example) and *non-systematic variability* (Ellis's example).

## Explanations for variability

Tarone (1983) has attempted to explain systematic variability by suggesting that L2 learners have a series of overlapping mental grammars which correspond to different contexts in which the L2 is used. At one extreme learners have a grammar for informal or *vernacular* L2 use (e.g. in spontaneous casual conversation). At the other extreme learners have a grammar for formal or careful use of the L2 (e.g. in writing or classroom use of the L2). In between these extremes there are mental grammars for different levels of formality of use. Tarone refers to this set of overlapping styles as the INTERLANGUAGE *capability continuum*. Learners acquire grammars on the continuum through exposure to the L2 in contexts of different levels of formality.

An important element in Tarone's (1983) account is the idea that degrees of 'attention to form' are what determine the particular grammar on the continuum which an L2 learner accesses. The grammar for formal or careful speech requires the learner to pay a high degree of attention to form, whereas the grammar for producing casual or vernacular speech requires no attention to form. If this theory is correct, then asking L2 speakers to perform different tasks in the L2 which require different degrees of attention to form should produce variability.

For example, Tarone (1985) examined the accuracy of four linguistic variables in the advanced L2 English of ten Arabic and ten Japanese speakers. They were the 3rd person singular verb inflection -*s* (as in *she sing -s*), the articles *the/a*, the plural -*s* (as in *cake -s*), and 3rd person singular direct object pronouns (like *it* in *John saw it*). Tarone asked her subjects to undertake three tasks: a written grammar test, an oral interview and an oral narrative. It was assumed that the written grammar test would induce most attention to form, the oral interview less attention and the oral narrative least attention. Subjects should therefore be most target-like on the written grammar test, less target-like in the interview and least target-like in the oral narrative.

In fact, Tarone did not quite find this. While the 3rd person singular -*s* did decrease in accuracy from one task to another, as predicted, plural -*s* changed little over the three tasks, and accuracy on the article and direct object pronouns actually increased, so that subjects were more target-like in the oral narrative than on the grammar test.

This led Tarone to modify her hypothesis to suggest that 'style-shifting' is not the effect of global levels of attention to form (i.e. the more a speaker attends to form, the more accurate will he or she be), but the result of attention to particular linguistic phenomena required by the task. Tarone suggests that articles and pronouns are particularly important for discourse cohesion in narratives, and these are attended to by subjects when they are engaged in narratives. Agreement marking on the verb is less important in narratives than in grammar tests, where learners are judged on the accuracy of phenomena like agreement marking, and so in grammar tests learners

pay more attention to 3rd person singular verb inflections than they do in narratives.

Ellis (1992: 121–2) attempts to account both for systematic and non-systematic variability. He suggests that there are three stages involved in the development of variability in SLA. In an initial stage L2 learner productions are not variable (for example, in the early acquisition of negation learners will have just one negator: 'I *no* like it'). In a second stage a new form enters the learner's grammar and coexists in free variation with the earlier form (for example, *don't* enters the learner's grammar and is in free variation with *no*: 'I *no* like "it/I *don't* like it'). This is where non-systematic variability arises. In a third stage each form is restricted to an independent set of functions; *don't* might become the form used exclusively in careful styles, while *no* becomes restricted to the most vernacular style. This is where systematic variability arises. On this view, non-systematic variability is an important precursor to interlanguage development, because it signals that target-like forms have entered the L2 learner's grammar.

Krashen (1981) attributes variability in L2 learner productions to the interaction of two types of L2 knowledge: subconsciously acquired linguistic knowledge and consciously learned linguistic knowledge. Learned knowledge cannot initiate output, but it can check the accuracy of output initiated by the acquired system, if the task conditions are right. Typically these are where the L2 learner 'knows the rule' in question, and is 'focusing on the form' of what she or he is saying. Tasks which promote focusing on form, according to Krashen, are typically those used in classroom testing, for example, translation, grammar exercises, guided written compositions, etc. The prediction is that on these tasks learners will be more target-like than under conditions where they use the language spontaneously. Krashen (1985: 21) estimates that L2 learners can increase their accuracy by between 7% and 50%

when they are focusing on form. (See MON-ITOR MODEL.)

Beebe (1980) has suggested that L1 prestige norms may be transferred into careful styles in the L2, thereby producing less target-like performance in careful styles than in vernacular styles. For example, Beebe studied the pronunciation of /r/ in the L2 American English of native speakers of Thai in two linguistic environments: prevocalically (e.g. '*r*ob') and postvocalically (e.g. 'ca*r*'). She asked her subjects to read word lists and also recorded them using English in free speech. She found that whereas postvocalic /r/ was more target-like in the reading of the word list than in free speech, prevocalic /r/ was less target-like when subjects read the word list than when they were speaking freely. Assuming that the reading of a list of words induces more attention to form than free speech, Beebe attributes the lower accuracy of the subjects on prevocalic /r/ in the word list to the fact that the [r] they used in this case was a prestige pronunciation in Thai. Learners had transferred a prestige form from their native language when they were trying to use a careful form of the L2.

Finally, some researchers have attributed L2 variability to a distinction between controlled and automatic knowledge (Hulstijn and Hulstijn, 1984). According to these researchers, when L2 knowledge is first acquired it is not present in an automatic form. The accessing of it is 'costly' in processing terms. As it is used by a speaker for comprehension and production it becomes more automatic and less costly. If L2 learners use the L2 in contexts where there are other demands on their processing capacity, for example, when their attention is taken up by the content of what they are saying, they will only be able to access automatic linguistic knowledge. Where L2 learners are able to attend to linguistic form, they may be able to access both controlled and automatic knowledge.

This account predicts not only that earlier acquired forms will be more likely to appear in 'processing costly' environments than later acquired knowledge (because they are more automatic), but also that the context of utterance is less important than the L2 learner's perception of the nature of the processing involved. To test this, Hulstijn and Hulstijn (1984) manipulated the L2 performance of learners of Dutch by asking them to retell short stories which had been read aloud to them. Subjects were told either to be as accurate as they could in recalling the information contained in the stories, or to be as accurate as they could in recalling the form of the stories. On one of the phenomena investigated (the placement of tensed verbs in final position in subordinate clauses, as in *Deze dame zegt dat er een inbraak was* 'This lady says that there a burglary was') they found that the accuracy of their subjects improved considerably when they were asked to be as accurate as possible on the form, rather than on the information. This finding suggests that it is not the task *per se* which influences the linguistic forms which an L2 speaker produces, but the speaker's perception of the nature of the task.

## SUMMARY AND FUTURE TRENDS

It will be clear from the preceding discussion that a variety of perspectives have been taken on the nature of variability in SLA. Tarone (1985, 1988) assumes that task differences are what gives rise to variability. Ellis (1992) assumes that it is acquisition itself which gives rise to variability: the acquisition of competing forms for the same function which are at first in free variation (non-systematic variability) and then become restricted to separate domains of use (systematic variability). Krashen (1981, 1985) suggests that variability arises as the result of learned knowledge monitoring the output of acquired knowledge. Beebe (1980) suggests that L1 transfer of sociolinguistic prestige norms in careful styles produces variability. Finally, Hulstijn and Hulstijn (1984) suggest that it is the nature of second language processing which causes variability.

Any future theory of variability in SLA will need to determine explicitly the weight to be given to the various factors that these researchers have isolated: the context of utterance, linguistic context, metalinguistic knowledge, L1 sociolinguistic prestige norms and processing abilities. Moreover, such a theory will need to explicate how these factors relate to strictly linguistic knowledge in order to produce the patterns of variability that are observed in L2 development.

BIBLIOGRAPHY

Beebe, L. (1980). Sociolinguistic variation and style-shifting in second language acquisition. *Language Learning*, 30, 433–47.

Dickerson, L. (1974). Internal and external patterning of phonological variability in the speech of Japanese learners of English: toward a theory of second-language acquisition. Unpublished doctoral dissertation, University of Illinois.

Ellis, R. (1985). Sources of variability in interlanguage. *Applied Linguistics*, 6, 118–31.

——(1992). *Second Language Acquisition and Second Language Pedagogy*. Clevedon: Multilingual Matters.

Hulstijn, J. and Hulstijn, W. (1984). Grammatical errors as a function of processing constraints and explicit knowledge. *Language Learning*, 34, 23–43.

Krashen, S. (1981). *Second Language Acquisition and Second Language Learning*. Oxford: Pergamon.

——(1985). *The Input Hypothesis*. London: Longman.

Labov, W. (1972). *Sociolinguistic patterns*. Philadelphia: University of Pennsylvania Press.

Tarone, E. (1983). On the variability of interlanguage systems. *Applied Linguistics*, 4, 143–63.

——(1985). Variability in interlanguage use: a study of style-shifting in morphology and syntax. *Language Learning*, 35, 373–404.

——(1988). *Variation in Interlanguage*. London: Edward Arnold.*

RH

**variable** is a term used in research to refer to something which may vary (e.g. across time or among individuals) and which can be observed or measured. Independent variables are selected and manipulated to determine the effect on the dependent variable (e.g. scores). Variables not under consideration may be controlled. Extraneous variables threaten validity and need to be minimized. (See STATISTICS IN APPLIED LINGUISTICS RESEARCH.)

KSM

**video in language teaching** came into use for ESP (see ENGLISH FOR SPECIFIC PURPOSES) and teacher training in the early 1970s with reel-to-reel equipment. The advent of cassettes (1980s) extended its use to other areas, with videos produced to: (i) supplement specific coursebooks, (ii) be free-standing input and (iii) show life and culture in target-language communities. Teacher resource books (see bibliography) suggest ways to exploit this rich medium. All emphasize the necessity of promoting active viewing with classroom exploitation of short extracts, not the usual passive viewing of television as entertainment. In addition, access to camera equipment enables language learners to produce their own videos as part of their learning.

BIBLIOGRAPHY

Allan, M. (1985). *Teaching English with Video*. Harlow: Longman.

Cooper, R., Lavery, M. and Rinvolucri, M. (1991). *Video*. Oxford: Oxford University Press.*

Lonergan, J. (1984). *Video in Language Teaching*. Cambridge: Cambridge University Press.*

Stempleski, S. and Tomalin, B. (1990). *Video in Action: Recipes for using video in language teaching*. Hemel Hempstead: Prentice-Hall.

Strange, J. and Strange, D. (1991). Survey: video materials. *ELT Journal*, 45, 335–59.

CLF

**vocabulary teaching** is concerned with the selection and presentation of words (LEXIS) for learners. Neglected for much of the twentieth century in favour of pronunciation and grammar, it has re-emerged since the 1980s as a central factor in language teaching.

Vocabulary played a central role in GRAMMAR-TRANSLATION and early DIRECT METHOD approaches but AUDIOLINGUALISM and the STRUCTURAL SYLLABUS subordinated vocabulary to the requirements of pattern practice. NOTIONAL/FUNCTIONAL SYLLABUSES and COMMUNICATIVE METHODOLOGY gave no special emphasis to vocabulary. In the 1980s, research into lexis and DISCOURSE ANALYSIS combined with arguments from PSYCHO-LINGUISTICS and L1 literacy research to reassert the importance of vocabulary in language learning. Computerized databases (such as COBUILD – the Birmingham University research project in lexical development with a corpus of over 20 million words of spoken and written English) gave researchers and materials writers access to powerful tools for vocabulary analysis. Proposals were made for a lexical syllabus (Willis, 1990) and approach (Lewis, 1993), assuming that 'Language consists of grammaticalised lexis, not lexicalised grammar' (Lewis, 1993: p. iv). In practice, a lexical syllabus is hard to develop: grammatical structures are easier to select and sequence for teaching than vocabulary. Furthermore, while it is obvious that vocabulary is of more use than grammar at the early stages of second language learning, supporters of grammar point out that successful processing and production of language will always rely heavily on grammatical knowledge.

It is estimated that the educated native English speaker has a vocabulary of about 50,000 words. Attempts have been made to determine a common core vocabulary for non-native learners. The 1930s Vocabulary Control Movement was concerned with delineating a minimum adequate vocabulary, primarily based on frequency counts. Ogden and Richard's Basic English project (1930) listed 850 basic words which would allow learners to express complex ideas. West's more influential General Service List (1953) consisted of the 2000 words that comprised 80% of the words in any written text.

Such word lists and frequency counts avoid the issue of multiple meanings: it has been calculated that the 850 words of Basic English have 12,425 meanings and that each of West's 2000 words has, on average, 21 meanings. Which meaning(s) should be taught and in what order? High frequency of use may be less important than coverage (the contexts in which the word is used). LEARNABILITY is also a consideration: factors like spelling, syntactic or phonological difficulties can make a word difficult to learn. 'Familiarity' is another important issue, bringing together the concepts of frequency, concreteness and meaningfulness. In addition, low-frequency words are precisely those which demarcate topic and therefore carry essential meaning. It is clear that trying to identify a common core vocabulary for all learners is almost impossible; while students of general English may benefit from learning such a core, students with specific needs will have different vocabulary requirements. Decisions will be affected by whether students need access to spoken and/or written language and by whether lexical items need to be in the active/productive vocabulary, which is always smaller than the receptive/passive one.

Learners cannot be taught all the vocabulary they will need and therefore must develop inferential strategies for dealing with unfamiliar vocabulary: e.g. by means of CLOZE and words-in-context exercises. (See Nunan, 1991, for suggestions for inferring meaning in context in written discourse.) Research reported by Carter (1987) suggests more proficient learners benefit most from these techniques. For all learners, the issue of how much unknown vocabulary impedes comprehension is an important one; Nation and Coady (in Carter and McCarthy, 1988) recommend West's guideline of a maximum of 2% unknown words in a written text.

Exploitation of what linguists identify as the crucial area of lexical relations in teaching

**Table 1** Recall and conceptual mapping (Rudzka et al., 1981: 28).

| | tea | influence | leader | weapon |
|---|---|---|---|---|
| strong | + | + | + | |
| powerful | | + | + | + |

vocabulary is another issue, including consideration of COHESION and COHERENCE. Meaningful and appropriate context is vital, helping learners to develop an awareness of lexical patterns such as COLLOCATION and sense relations (e.g. synonymy). Componential analysis can help by grouping vocabulary into lexical fields according to common features or attributes. Word sets and grids have been developed for advanced learners, based on research that recall of words is often according to conceptual mapping of categories or semantic fields (table 1). Lower-level students may find lexical relations confusing; research, for example, argues against teaching pairs of opposites together, as only one item tends to be retained. However, creating associations within the language (e.g. by organizing vocabulary according to topic and studying word formation) can promote learnability. Interlanguage associations are also useful, particularly in the early stages. Traditionally, students learned paired L1–L2 word lists; recall of these can be improved by association of target words with native words plus graphic or mnemonic representation. The more words are analysed or enriched by association, the greater the possibility they will be remembered. Recycling vocabulary taught in similar and different contexts is, of course, also crucial to learning.

Analysis of words can be enhanced by efficient dictionary use. Developments in lexicography mean there is a range of dictionaries for non-native learners of English. Bilingual dictionaries are useful in the beginning stages and should then be used to check insufficiently understood explanations from monolingual dictionaries. The latter give considerably more information about entries and learners must be taught how to exploit these features.

Concordancing texts on computers also develops analytical skills. A concordance shows all the occurrences in context of a given word-form in a particular corpus and therefore allows learners to discover the range and frequency of uses of that word in the corpus. (See CONCORDANCE, CORPUS LINGUISTICS, LINGUISTICS IN LANGUAGE TEACHING.)

Increased attention to vocabulary teaching has resulted in several books devoted to the topic (see bibliography). It is likely that this interest will continue.

BIBLIOGRAPHY

Carter, R. (1987). Vocabulary and second/foreign language teaching. *Language Teaching*, 20/1, 3–16.

Carter, R. and McCarthy, M. (eds) (1988). *Vocabulary and Language Teaching*. Harlow: Longman.*

Gairns, R. and Redman, S. (1986). *Working with Words*. Cambridge: Cambridge University Press.

Lewis, M. (1993). *The Lexical Approach*. Hove: Language Teaching Publications.

McCarthy, M. (1990). *Vocabulary*. Oxford: Oxford University Press.*

Nation, I. S. P. (1990). *Teaching and Learning Vocabulary*. New York: Newbury House.*

Nation, P. (ed.) (1994). *New Ways in Teaching Vocabulary*. Alexandria, VA: TESOL.

Nation, P. and Coady, J. (1988). Vocabulary and reading. In R. Carter and M. McCarthy (eds), *Vocabulary and Language Teaching*. Harlow: Longman, 97–110.

Nunan, D. (1991). *Language Teaching Methodology*. Hemel Hempstead: Prentice-Hall.

Ogden, C. K. (1930). *Basic English: A general introduction*. London: Kegan Paul.

Rudzka, B., Channell, J., Putseys, Y. and Ostyn, D. (1981). *The Words you Need*. London: Macmillan.

West, M. (1953). *A General Service List of English Words*. London: Longman.

Willis, D. (1990). *The Lexical Syllabus*. London: Collins.

CLF

# W

**washback effect**  Also known as backwash, this is the effect (positive or negative) of testing on teaching. Influence may be beneficial, for example, when a test leads to improvement of syllabus and teaching. Negative backwash may occur when the test inadequately reflects course objectives, but exerts an influence on what is taught. (See LANGUAGE TESTING.)

BIBLIOGRAPHY
Alderson, C. and Wall, D. (1993). Does washback exist? *Applied Linguistics*, 14/2, 115–29.
Promodou, L. (1995). The backwash effect: from testing to teaching. *English Language Teaching Journal*, 49/1, 13–25.

KSM

**waystage**  Following production of its THRESHOLD LEVEL, the COUNCIL OF EUROPE developed an intermediary level halfway between zero and T-Level. This 'Waystage' syllabus inventory appears in van Ek and Alexander (1977). It follows the same pattern as the T-Level, and contains a selection from its contents.

BIBLIOGRAPHY
Van Ek, J. A. and Alexander, L. G. (1977). *Waystage: An intermediary objective below threshold-level in a European unit/credit system for modern language learning by adults*. Strasbourg: Council for Cultural Co-Operation of the Council of Europe.

KJ

**world English**  English is spoken by at least 1 billion people. Approximately 300 million are NATIVE SPEAKERS, 300 million speak English as a second language and 100 million as fluent foreign-language speakers. The spread of English has led to the adoption of several versions of STANDARD ENGLISH (British, American, Australian, New Zealand, etc.) and in some regions (e.g. India) it has also undergone the process of nativization.

BIBLIOGRAPHY
Crystal, D. (1987). *The Cambridge Encyclopedia of Language*. Cambridge: Cambridge University Press.
Kachru, B. B. (ed.) (1992). *The Other Tongue: English across cultures*. 2nd edn. Urbana: University of Illinois Press.

AJ

# Index

Note: Page numbers in bold type refer to main dictionary entries.

# ALSO FROM
# BLACKWELL PUBLISHERS